The Sixties in America

The Sixties in America

Volume I
Abernathy, Ralph — Ginsberg, Allen

Editor

Carl Singleton
Fort Hays State University

Project Editor

Rowena Wildin

SALEM PRESS, INC.
PASADENA, CALIFORNIA
HACKENSACK, NEW JERSEY

Managing Editor: Christina J. Moose
Project Editor: Rowena Wildin   *Production Editor:* Janet Long
Research Supervisor: Jeffry Jensen   *Research Assistant:* Jun Ohunki
Acquisitions Editor: Mark Rehn   *Graphics and Design:* James Hutson
Photograph Editor: Karrie Hyatt   *Layout:* William Zimmerman

Title page photo: AP/Wide World Photos

Library of Congress Cataloging-in-Publication Data

The Sixties in America / editor, Carl Singleton ; project editor, Rowena Wildin.
    p. cm.
    Includes bibliographical references and index.
    ISBN 0-89356-982-8 (set : alk. paper). — ISBN 0-89356-983-6 (v. 1 : alk. paper). — ISBN 0-89356-984-4 (v. 2 : alk. paper). — ISBN 0-89356-985-2 (v. 3 : alk. paper)
    1. United States — History — 1961-1969 — Encyclopedias.
  I. Singleton, Carl. II. Wildin, Rowena, 1956-   .

E841.S55   1999
973.92—dc21

98-49255
CIP

Fifth Printing

PRINTED IN THE UNITED STATES OF AMERICA

■ Contents

■ Publisher's Note

Salem Press's three-volume set *The Sixties in America* surveys the events and people of the 1960's, a turbulent decade that had a profound and lasting effect on the life and culture of the United States. The set not only provides in-depth coverage of all aspects of the three major events of the 1960's that give the decade its distinctive character—the Civil Rights movement, the social revolution, and the Vietnam War—but also surveys important developments in the arts, science and technology, business and the economy, government and politics, and gender issues. In addition, to impart a sense of what people were doing and thinking during the decade, the set looks at the most important people and events in the arts, media, music, and sports and covers the headline-grabbing news items of the period.

The encyclopedia's 554 articles range from 250-word, focused articles on subjects such as Olympic track star Billy Mills to 3,000-word surveys of broad, far-reaching topics such as the Cold War. Given the focus of this work on a significant, tumultuous period of time, many articles are associated with the three events that shaped the decade: 68 articles concentrate on civil rights, 21 on the Vietnam War, 74 on government and politics (roughly divided between the Vietnam War and the Cold War), and 80 on the social revolution. The 61 articles on the arts, the 39 on the media, and the 43 on music demonstrate how the dramatic happenings of the decade were both reflected in and inspired by artistic efforts. The impact of the Civil Rights movement and social revolution are evident in the 25 articles on gender issues, which include essays on the developing women's movement and fledgling gay liberation movement. The space race, the triumphant lunar landing, and major scientific developments including heart and kidney transplants and lasers are covered in the 44 articles on science and technology. The 14 articles on demographics and the environment look at the interplay between what humankind has produced and the forces of nature—a consciousness that was first raised during the decade by such clarions as Rachel Carson—and the 19 articles on business and the economy examine the industries and institutions that people have created and how they affect and are affected by each other and the world around them. The 41 articles on sports show, among other things, how television helped turn fun and games into major sporting events and eventually big business, and the 25 articles on crimes and scandals reveal the violence and corruption that sometimes accompanied the social experimentation of the decade.

Written with the needs of students and general readers in mind, the articles present clear discussions of the topics, explaining any terms and references that may be unfamiliar. The articles in the encyclopedia are arranged in alphabetical order, with clear, concise titles followed by brief descriptions or definitions of the topic. The essays are divided into six easy-to-use formats: 199 overviews, 153 biographical pieces, 82 events, 73 artistic works, 38 organizations, and 10 Supreme Court cases. Important dates and selected facts are highlighted in ready-reference top matter at the beginning of the biographical pieces, events, and artistic works. Boldfaced subheads such as "Impact" or "Subsequent Events" make finding information within each article quick and easy. The cross-references at the end of each article will guide readers to additional entries on the topic or related subjects, and the "Additional Information" section will direct them to other publications on the subject.

No encyclopedia on the first full "television decade" would be complete without photographs and other visual elements. This set contains nearly 300 photographs of the decade's events and more than 40 graphs, charts, and sidebars highlighting interesting facts and trends.

The encyclopedia contains a number of useful tools to help readers find the entries of interest. An alphabetical list of all entries appears at the beginning of each volume. A list of entries by thirty-one subject categories appears at the end of each volume, and the third volume contains a comprehensive index and personages index. Also in the third volume are fourteen appendices that provide additional information about selected aspects of the decade in easily and quickly accessible formats. The three drama appendices list the major films, major Broadway plays and theatrical awards, and most-watched television shows of the 1960's. The literature appendix lists the U.S. best-selling books and Pulitzer Prize winners, and the two music appendices list the decade's top-selling recordings and its popular musicians and their hits. A sports index provides a quick look at the winners of the major sporting events of the 1960's. The two legislative appendices look at the U.S. Supreme Court and its major decisions and major legislation passed by Congress during the decade. A statistical appendix provides a snapshot of major demographic trends in the United States through a series of graphs and charts. Among the appendices are two time lines, one listing the major developments in science and technology and the other providing a view of the decade's major events in civil rights, the Vietnam War, and numerous other areas as they unfolded. Rounding out the appendices is a bibliography and mediagraphy listing sources to which readers can turn for additional study. The annotated bibliography is divided into twelve categories so that readers interested in a particular aspect of the 1960's can find additional resources more easily. The mediagraphy lists electronic materials (including CD-ROMs), videocassettes, and Web sites that involve the decade.

Creating an encyclopedia on the 1960's requires the expertise of many people in a broad range of fields. Salem Press would like to thank the nearly four hundred scholars who have contributed to this encyclopedia. Their names and affiliations follow the introduction. We would also like to thank the editor for the set, Carl Singleton, who, in addition to graciously providing the introduction, time line, and bibliography and mediagraphy, has spent many hours shaping this reference work and ensuring that it accurately and interestingly reflects the decade.

■ Introduction

Second only to the decade that saw the Civil War, the 1960's were the most cataclysmic, exhilarating, controversial, action-packed, and divisive ten-year period in the nation's history. It was a time full of contradictions working toward resolutions that were always dramatically and painfully accomplished; extremes manifested themselves in every identifiable facet of life. Dormant tensions, both historical and contemporaneous, repeatedly surfaced only to become worse, much worse, before stabilizing. And when, at some point in the 1970's, there was a vague return to calmness, the nation knew that it had been transformed: What it meant to be an American had changed; the nation's people were living their lives in a different way—the underpinning complexities of their basic myths had been altered if not redefined.

The 1950's as Prelude After World War II, the United States experienced an unprecedented period of peace and prosperity. The upper classes commandeered more wealth and became more numerous as the economy maintained a healthy, progressive growth. Similarly, the middle classes were earning significantly more income, living in better houses, and becoming better educated; they, too, were growing in numbers. As for the lower classes, it cannot be put forth that their plight was improving, but their problems (poverty, disease, hunger, housing) were kept at least functionally invisible to mainstream society. America successfully pretended to itself that the victims of poverty and racism were not there; or, that it was their own fault; or, that they could all improve their lot if they would only try. Troubles presented themselves, of course, but these were dealt with efficaciously as they occurred; they did not go away, but they did not linger, expand, and escalate into even more serious, irresolute situations as so relentlessly happened in the 1960's.

Primarily because of this relative peace and prosperity, the 1950's are stereotypically and correctly characterized as a decade in which only positive things were happening in the nation. Seemingly, everyone's personal circumstances in life were getting better as the country moved to fulfill its destiny to lead the free world, to serve as the world's police, and to fulfill an Edenic version of the American Dream. Before leaving the presidency in 1961, Dwight D. Eisenhower pointed out that the production of manufactured goods had increased 15 percent and wages had grown 20 percent during his two terms and that 25 percent of the country's housing had been built in the preceding ten years.

There were, of course, troubles and problems. The Korean War and the Cold War dominated international politics. The Soviets launched Sputnik to lead the Americans in the space race. Closer to home, Fidel Castro was rearing his head in Cuba. Domestically, Senator Joseph McCarthy successfully staged a manufactured communist witch-hunt for years, Elvis Presley was performing with suggestive hip thrusts, the Clutter family was murdered in Kansas, and African American seamstress Rosa Parks refused to sit in the colored section at the back of the bus. There was a national sense, however, that such matters could be dealt with, and once they were "over," they would recede into the past without any real and definable consequences. Certainly, these events and others like them were not seen by most people as things that would precipitate and actualize changes in American society, character, and identity. When applied to the 1950's, perhaps, such thinking may be correct. But this was all to prove a matter of delayed reality. Such events were mere preludes to the subsequent decade: They were introductions, they were prequels, they were warnings, and they were ominous and imminent.

Civil Rights Foremost among all changes were those brought about by the Civil Rights movement. The nation had struggled for a century with the hypocrisy and injustice of the "separate but equal" idea, which the Supreme Court had in fact ruled against in a 1954 decision that made segregation by color illegal in public schools. In many parts of the country, but particularly in the South, life was entirely segregated. Education, housing, business, religion, and public transportation all maintained two "separate" systems. Also, though not often pointed out, there had been protests, demonstrations, riots, and legal campaigns all along against this way of doing things, so why is it that nothing really changed until the 1960's?

First of all, previous decades, for whatever reasons, had produced a paucity of leaders and organizations. In the 1960's, African Americans saw a marked increase in both of these; there were dozens of well-known leaders and nearly as many organizations that were devoted to civil rights. Also, in the 1960's, "leadership" came to mean something very different. Previously, leaders of African American communities were typically people who served as liaisons with whites in maintaining peace to prevent bloodshed. They worked for "slow change" and generally viewed an end to segregation as a rather impossible goal; hence, they tried to improve the conditions of African Americans within the separate-but-equal frame. Suddenly, all that changed; Martin Luther King, Jr., and others were demanding an end to the separate-but-equal rule in every aspect of life in what amounted to a starting point for other changes, and they demanded that it happen immediately.

A second reason that the 1960's became a decade of change is that mainstream white Americans involved themselves in civil rights issues in noteworthy, visible numbers. Of these, perhaps the most prominent were the northern white college students who went to the South to demonstrate (by the tens of thousands) hand-in-hand with black students and black local residents. Unfortunately, no real changes occurred in the nation's civil rights practices until white blood was spilled. Blacks had been killed, lynched, and burned for decades, but it was the deaths of white civil rights activists that made an incalculable contribution to effectiveness.

A third important reason behind the impact of the 1960's is the role of the media. For the first time, large numbers of people throughout the country could on a daily basis learn about events by witnessing them on evening television news broadcasts in their living rooms. Such broadcasts not only reported on events but also inadvertently worked to promote the civil rights cause. Televised footage of church bombings that resulted in dead children, Ku Klux Klan crosses aflame in people's yards, and fire hoses and police dogs turned on protesters peacefully walking down streets not only recorded but also changed outcomes of events.

In 1954, the Supreme Court's decision in *Brown v. Board of Education of Topeka, Kansas,* reversed a century of legally sanctioned "separate but equal" segregation. Between 1954 and 1970, segregation in its various forms was eliminated to a significant degree. In the 1960's, the federal government passed and enacted three major civil rights bills, and it was actually enforcing the acts' provisions. Problems were not over, of course; many schools throughout the

nation, for example, were still segregated or nearly so; laws against discrimination in housing were proving both hard and slow to enforce; public restaurants and other businesses initially succeeded in finding ways to prevent black patronage; blacks could legally register to vote but actually did so in disappointingly small numbers; and churches remained mostly segregated because both races evidently wanted it that way. Sit-ins, freedom rides, marches, demonstrations, protests, or riots occurred nearly every day of the decade.

Vietnam As the war in Southeast Asia unfolded and escalated, efforts to continue the fighting were met with the greatest, most numerous, and most violent antiwar protests in the nation's history. Political leaders cited Eisenhower's "domino theory" to assert that communism must be stopped in one country so that it would not spread to others and eventually consume the world. American businesses and industries tended to support the war for their own aggrandizement. Self-proclaimed patriots, mostly veterans from World Wars I and II and the Korean War, were seen by the nation's young people as having adopted a "my country, right or wrong" attitude for supporting the idea of staying in Vietnam until victory was achieved. Pervading it all was a belief that the nation would be permanently shattered if it suffered its first defeat in war.

Those against the war argued that it was another country's civil war, and the United States simply should not interfere. Monetary profits to some businesses and to the nation's collective economy were not worth the price being expended in blood. True patriots wanted peace, not war. Finally, they asserted, Americans should not continue to fight a war that could not possibly be won.

Americans were not only divided but also hopelessly and uncompromisingly polarized. Following the example set by civil rights leaders, antiwar protesters organized several marches on Washington, D.C. College campuses were shut down and Reserve Officers' Training Corps (ROTC) buildings were burned. Selective Service Centers were occupied by protesters who destroyed records; others publicly burned their draft cards. The 1968 Democratic National Convention in Chicago became a rallying point for protesters; it was only secondarily a meeting to nominate a presidential candidate.

Vietnam also became rightfully known as the first

"television war." During the second half of the decade, nearly every nightly news broadcast contained reports from Vietnam—many were lead stories with pictures of dead or dying Americans. News anchors started to give running counts of the number of American casualties, which reached nearly 60,000 by 1972. Also, pictures such as those of the My Lai massacre, Buddhist monks burning themselves in protest, and summary executions all abetted the cause of antiwar crusaders.

In 1968, Richard M. Nixon, who had promised "peace with honor" and to end the war during his first term, was elected president. Initiating what he called "Vietnamization" and "pacification" programs, he began to bring soldiers home while otherwise increasing military support for the continued war, mostly through funding. By 1972, all American combat personnel were officially out of Vietnam. The country fell to the communists in 1975.

Social Revolution The staid orderliness and ordinariness of the 1950's had a short shelf life in the next decade. Seemingly, the society was not merely changing but actually disintegrating as "radicals" and members of the New Left saw triumphs. Not only did they succeed in bringing about changes in race relations and in winding down the war in Vietnam, but also they achieved victories in sundry and largely symbolic skirmishes over long hair, rock music, and miniskirts as well as in more far-reaching battles over sexual relations outside marriage, drug use, women's rights, and liberalization of divorce laws. Supreme Court decisions of the late 1960's and early 1970's reflected these radically altered attitudes. The nation was not merely changing itself; it was abolishing important aspects of its previous way of life. And all of this was accomplished at an incredibly fast pace. The counterculture, youth rebellion, generation gap, and sexual revolution were never refined, organized movements (as were the Civil Rights and antiwar movements) so much as they were nebulous, undefined causes. Nevertheless, change America they did. It was a time when presidents staged prayer breakfasts and priests burned draft cards.

Among the most far-reaching of these changes were those that occurred in women's rights. Birth control pills went on sale in 1960 and were instantly in great demand. Readers of Betty Friedan's *The Feminine Mystique* (1963) not only identified with women's problems as she described them but also started living their lives in new ways. Sexual equality with men was often cited as the foremost goal; others included the right to an abortion, equal pay for equal work, passage of the Equal Rights Amendment (ERA), and the ability to pursue a career and be elected to political office. Women succeeded in redefining themselves: They might very well choose to continue their roles as wives and mothers, but they would also pursue careers and interests outside the home with the same sense of freedom to do so as men possessed.

During the 1960's, the nation's sexual behaviors and attitudes also changed. Couples lived together without marrying and did so in open defiance of many state laws. Silicone injections and sex-change operations were introduced in the country and publicized. Homosexuals fought back at police who raided gay bars. Pregnancies of unmarried women skyrocketed. Sex became common and acceptable in movies and plays, if not on television. Nudity at the 1969 Woodstock Festival shocked many Americans but served as an example for others to emulate. University professors conducted "sensitivity sessions" wherein participants sat naked in circles. Whatever expression the new sexuality took, it was clear that society itself would no longer maintain as the only convention the accepted practice of sex only within marriage. Nor would sex continue to be a topic closed to public discussion.

For many segments of society, particularly hippies and intellectuals, drug use became common. Rock music lyrics extolled the virtues of marijuana and LSD, billing these hallucinogens as tickets to pleasure, enlightenment, and fulfillment. Timothy Leary, Allen Ginsberg, Ken Kesey, and others successfully set forth the idea that smoking pot (marijuana) and dropping acid (LSD) were not only acceptable but also desirable. The result of all this was that the nation quickly became what could rightfully be called a "drug culture."

Changes brought by the social revolution also manifested themselves in other ways, particularly in fashion. Long hair, hip boots, bell-bottom pants, loud colors, tie-dyed shirts, and, most important of all, blue jeans served to demonstrate that many Americans were changing not only the way they lived and thought but also the way they looked. Hippies slept on mattresses without sheets; they painted their cars and vans psychedelic colors; they wore peace symbols and ribbons. More important than what "real" hippies were doing was the fact that they were being imitated by hundreds of thousands of others who never actually quit school or work to join a commune but who wanted, at least, to look like those who had. The social revolution, though not organized, did occur by design.

Science and Technology The 1960's also evidenced a wealth of advances in every field of science, and, concurrently, in their application to daily life. Most items, such as color televisions, air conditioners, and microwave ovens, had been available for decades, but their cost prevented their use by the middle class. In the 1960's, though, engineers developed newer, cheaper ways to manufacture such products, which found their way into the homes of many Americans. As the economy grew, personal income increased, and housewives became "homemakers" and eventually working mothers; any product that made life's daily routines quicker and easier and more comfortable achieved quick acceptance on the market. By the end of the decade, many if not most Americans could come home from work or school, sit down in an air-conditioned living room in front of a television set, and eat a TV dinner. This had not been the case ten years earlier.

New discoveries in medicine were also momentous. Although transplanting hearts and unraveling the genetic code received the lion's share of media attention, less spectacular developments included many advances taken for granted today: cryosurgery, limb reattachment, kidney dialysis, artificial insemination and fertility drugs, new birth control methods and devices, new drugs for treating hundreds of medical problems, and new ways of treating cancer and heart disease. Among these, the Pill had a cataclysmic effect, not only on the sexual revolution but also on women's ability to establish economic independence. Americans were becoming healthier because of drug therapies and medical technology, and they began to live longer and more healthful lives.

Also an issue during the decade were concerns about the environment. Scientific discoveries and applications often meant the mass production of new industrial products—hence, industrial waste and pollution. More than anything else, Rachel Carson's book *Silent Spring* (1962) awakened Americans to the fact that air and water pollution were destroying (or could destroy) the planet. The nation's largest cities had smog, not clouds; the Great Lakes and many rivers were cesspools; radioactive fallout was everywhere, and it was killing anything green and causing cancer among humans. The nation smoldered as it suddenly realized that government would have to make and enforce controls. The irony was lost to no one: The problems caused by technology would have to be contained by even newer technologies.

The most visible achievements in science, however, did not take place in the home but in space. During the decade, the United States placed artificial satellites in orbit, sent animals and humans into space, achieved the first spacewalks, and, finally, landed people on the Moon. Along the way, the federal government-funded research produced hundreds of products that affected the lives of Americans and changed them forever—computers, VCRs, and devices that allowed for instant, global communication. The race to the Moon did not occur in a vacuum; going to the Moon in and of itself was never important enough for the nation actually to commit itself to doing so. It was the geopolitics of the 1960's that made such an achievement possible: The United States did not go to the Moon to get there—Americans went to the Moon in order to beat the Soviets there. The National Aeronautics and Space Administration (NASA) was a product of the Cold War, not of John F. Kennedy's desire to advance scientific knowledge.

The Cold War Any significant event dealing with international politics during the decade can be interpreted only within the context of the Cold War. At seemingly irreconcilable odds were the United States and the Soviet Union, capitalism and communism, the free world and the Iron Curtain, East and West, human rights and inhumane oppression. Waged on every front except an actual battlefield pitting Americans against Soviets, the conflict between the two superpowers was evident in the media, in propaganda, in the United Nations, in the space race, but most of all, in the nuclear arms race. Both nations were convinced that to be "ahead" in the nuclear arsenal count was to be "ahead" on all fronts—at least in those that would finally matter. Accordingly, both sides maintained extensive programs to test nuclear weapons, both sides developed new technologies and produced newer, faster and deadlier weapons, and both sides became increasingly aware that "mutually assured destruction" was the only possible outcome of actual nuclear warfare. Treaties were signed that attempted to slow the promulgation of such weapons, but they achieved only a modicum of success.

The Cold War manifested itself in the Berlin Wall and in Cuba more pronouncedly than in other places. The Soviet invasion of Czechoslovakia in 1968 proved to the world that the communists really did maintain one singular purpose: to take over the world. The American public believed that Lyndon B. Johnson's invasion of the Dominican Republic, in contrast, had been to protect freedom, not capitalism. Both countries played tit for tat in most respects, especially in the space race and in Cuba (where the two nations agreed that the Soviets would remove all nuclear weapons and that the United States would not invade the island to overthrow Fidel Castro). At home, the Cold War was always present: Americans built fallout shelters by the thousands, children at school and employees at work practiced bomb drills, and radio and television stations went through test alerts. More important than any particular event, however, was the pervasive fear that the planet could be destroyed at any time within a few minutes. All humanity found itself walking through the valley of the shadow of death.

The Arts All forms of art thrived during the decade. Set loose by the social revolution and no longer bound by conventions and traditions, artists and writers began to express themselves not only with new works but also with different kinds of works. They found fresh subject matter in the common, the unusual, the bizarre, the trivial, and the absurd. If reality was disjointed, incongruent, and inconsequential, then so was the expression of that reality. Artists photographed soup cans; sculptors made turning screws; dramatists concocted lines as their plays unfolded in front of audiences; and writers indulged in metafictional diatribes with the soul.

More significant, however, than any of these identifiable trends was the outrage produced by many of the individual works and productions. The film version of *Who's Afraid of Virginia Woolf?* (1962) was the first mainstream, popular film to make use of endless vulgarities in the dialogue. The Broadway musical *Hair* (1968) gave Americans public nudity on stage. William S. Burroughs's novel *Naked Lunch* (1962) demonstrated that anything that could be thought could be written and published. The outrage felt by

many was never truly about the content of any specific work so much as it was about the public expression of such content. Americans never really cared if George and Martha (the two main characters of *Who's Afraid of Virginia Woolf?*, who are at least symbolic references to George and Martha Washington) talked with endless vulgarities and obscenities, but they did care if the characters' talk were publicly permitted and thereby evidently condoned.

Most visible of all artists were the musicians, whose most memorable accomplishments were in rock and roll. A product of black music from the American South first nationally popularized by Elvis Presley in the 1950's, rock had been exported worldwide to return from England during the British Invasion of the early 1960's. Leading this invasion were the Beatles, who successfully blended American rock with their own talents to become the most successful and popular rock group of all time. In their shadow were dozens of other groups, eventually hundreds, on both sides of the Atlantic. Music became a way not only to identify with the counterculture but also, more important, to change the world. Lyrics pushed drug use, free sex, peace and love, and rebellion. Born were discos, rock operas, festivals, folk and protest songs, rock concerts, surf music, and the twist (along with dozens of other dances that flouted conventions of previous generations). Music was a surreal and psychedelic bedrock to things politic.

Media During the decade, communication became instant, massive, and global. For the first time in history, events could be reported to millions as they happened; moreover, they could be seen rather than read about or listened to, which made them not only more immediate but also somehow more real. Televised debates could help determine the winners of presidential elections; film footage from Vietnam could increase resistance to the war; a live telecast of Americans walking on the Moon could make the nation—and the world—proud of its accomplishments in space and could simultaneously embarrass the Soviets as losers in the space race and, by extension, in the ideological race. It is true that most events would have happened anyway, but slowly a realization occurred that the actual reporting and witnessing of events by the population were in and of themselves affecting those events. Perhaps John F. Kennedy would still have defeated Richard M. Nixon in the 1960 election if their debates had not been televised. Perhaps resistance to the war in Vietnam would still have escalated without the ceaseless television coverage. Clearly, astronauts would have walked on the Moon with or without television cameras to record their doing so, and Jack Ruby would have murdered Lee Harvey Oswald had no cameras been present. What happened, though, is that the significance of events themselves escalated and multiplied because of the media's ability to show them endlessly at will.

The media affected all aspects of life. It abetted the Civil Rights movement, the antiwar protests, the Cold War, the space race, the youth rebellion, the women's movement, politics, entertainment, drug use, fashions, and fads. The nation had always known that blacks were being lynched in the South and that war is bloody, but newscasts showing these activities in motion and in color provoked much more dramatic reactions from viewers. After all, so it seemed, such things were now unfolding in one's living room; they were no longer solely occurring in Selma, Alabama, a place most people had never heard of and that few would want to know about. It worked both ways, of course: Viewers often found material and evidence for existing beliefs. When radical feminists, for example, crowned a sheep Miss America, many saw the act as a clear and effective statement about the role of women in society; others saw only laughable fools revealing their own breed of fanaticism. Whatever the interpretation, no one could deny the importance of the media as it took its place in our society as an institution with influence to rival that of education, government, and religion.

The 1970's as Aftermath When the 1970's were ushered in, Nixon was still president and the Watergate break-in had not occurred, hundreds of thousands of troops were in Vietnam, busing to achieve school desegregation was in hot contest, racial riots were still occurring, NASA was still sending spacecraft to the Moon, women were working for passage of the Equal Rights Amendment, the nuclear arms race was at its zenith, and the Cold War was as hot as ever. Few of these issues and developments were fully resolved in the 1960's. The nation not only changed but also continued to change in subsequent decades. Usually, however, it did so in accord with principles that had firmly taken root during the previous decade.

Perhaps it surprised no one that the legacy of the tumultuous decade was both good and bad. On the positive side, the nation had achieved great success in eliminating "separate-but-equal" practices and making strides for equality under the law for all citizens. The many lessons of Vietnam were known by many and were being learned quickly by others, especially political leaders. Advances in science, technology, medicine, and industry had given most people a noticeably higher standard of living and a more comfortable lifestyle. The arts flourished, producing high-quality works of lasting importance. Federal programs such as Job Corps, Work Corps, food stamps, Medicare, and Medicaid were providing resources to persons who genuinely needed them and who could benefit from them. Individuals gained additional freedom and protection under the legal system. All in all, any number of improvements could be counted during the ten-year period.

Less familiar—but becoming more so with increasing chronological distance from the decade—is the dark underside to the 1960's. In some sense, the violence that had often characterized the Civil Rights movement (a main offshoot of which was race riots in dozens of the country's major cities) embedded itself in other ways within the society. Veterans returned from the Vietnam War to find themselves out of place or even unwanted in their own communities. Drug use became an epidemic that killed thousands of people and ruined many more thousands of lives (not one person was enlightened by drugs—that reality, at least, became clear). Any product of science and technology could be put to evil uses as well as benevolent ones. Art productions could be violent, obscene, even scatological, and could serve to traumatize viewers needlessly—especially the young. The War on Poverty not only was costly and inflationary but also created a class of people endlessly dependent upon the system who were passing that dependency on to their own children. Women were relatively free to pursue careers, but the burden of domestic responsibilities remained primarily on women. The divorce rate skyrocketed. Civil rights came to mean affirmative action or quotas, items that thinkers on either side of the issue usually felt uncomfortable defending. Crimes, scandals, and assassinations took something of a toll on the national psyche, leaving Americans numbed and therefore, if not more accepting of such things, at least less shocked than most people believed they should have been. The nation paid a high price for the 1960's.

Carl Singleton

■ Contributors

Christopher M. Aanstoos
State University of West Georgia

Michael Adams
Graduate School,
City University of New York

Richard Adler
University of Michigan—Dearborn

Cherri N. Allison
Independent scholar

William Allison
University of Saint Francis

Emily Alward
Independent scholar

Carolyn Anderson
University of Massachusetts at Amherst

Earl R. Andresen
University of Texas at Arlington

Gerald S. Argetsinger
Rochester Institute of Technology

Charles Avinger
Washtenaw Community College

Sue Bailey
Tennessee Technological University

Peter Bakewell
Emory University

Susan Benforado Bakewell
Kennesaw State College

Mary Pat Balkus
Independent scholar

Carl L. Bankston III
University of Southwestern Louisiana

Linda Kearns Bannister
Loyola Marymount University

Susan Green Barger
Idaho State University

Carole Barrett
University of Mary

Amanda Smith Barusch
University of Utah

Garlena A. Bauer
Otterbein College

Joseph E. Bauer
State University of New York,
College at Buffalo

Jonathan J. Bean
Southern Illinois University

Patricia A. Behlar
Pittsburg State University

Alvin K. Benson
Brigham Young University

Christopher Berkeley
Independent scholar

Milton Berman
University of Rochester

Karan A. Berryman
Andrew College

Terry D. Bilhartz
Sam Houston State University

Cynthia A. Bily
Adrian College

Margaret Boe Birns
New York University

Nicholas Birns
The New School for Social Research

Joe Blankenbaker
Georgia Southern University

Steve D. Boilard
Western Kentucky University

Bernadette Lynn Bosky
Independent scholar

Nila M. Bowden
Morgan State University

Michael W. Bowers
University of Nevada, Las Vegas

J. Quinn Brisben
Independent scholar

Wesley Britton
Grayson County College

Daniel A. Brown
California State University, Fullerton

Kenneth H. Brown
Northwestern Oklahoma State University

Susan Love Brown
Florida Atlantic University

Valerie Brown
Fort Hays State University

Robert D. Bryant
Georgetown College

Faith Hickman Brynie
Independent scholar

Thomas W. Buchanan
Ancilla College

Fred Buchstein
Dix and Eaton/John Carroll University

David Buck
West Virginia University

Mary Louise Buley-Meissner
University of Wisconsin—Milwaukee

Ryan A. Burrows
Fort Hays State University

Charles J. Bussey
Western Kentucky University

Donna Bussey
Independent scholar

Joseph P. Byrne
Belmont University

Douglas Campbell
Texas Technical University

Edmund J. Campion
University of Tennessee

Phillip A. Cantrell II
West Virginia University

Richard K. Caputo
Barry University

Kathleen Carroll
John A. Logan College

Thomas P. Carroll
John A. Logan College

Jack Carter
University of New Orleans

Beau David Case
Ohio State University

Ranès C. Chakravorty
University of Virginia

Cheris Shun-ching Chan
City University of Hong Kong

Richard N. Chapman
Francis Marion University

Paul J. Chara, Jr.
Loras College

Nan K. Chase
Appalachian State University

Ron Chepesiuk
Winthrop University

Lawrence Clark
Independent scholar

Thomas Clarkin
University of Texas at Austin

Tom Cook
Wayne State College

David A. Crain
South Dakota State University

Richard D. Cronk
Augusta State University

Daniel E. Crowe
University of Kentucky

Edward R. Crowther
Adams State College

Alice A. Dailey
Loyola Marymount University

Eddith A. Dashiell
Ohio University

Mary Virginia Davis
Independent scholar

Robert C. Davis
Pikeville College

Jennifer Davis-Kay
Education Development Center, Inc.

Bill Delaney
Independent scholar

Andy DeRoche
Community College of Aurora

Tom Dewey II
University of Mississippi—Oxford

Corey Ditslear
Ohio State University

Stephen B. Dobrow
Fairleigh Dickinson University

Margaret A. Dodson
Boise Public Schools

Theresa R. Doggart
University of Tennessee at Chattanooga

Andrea Donovan
Western Michigan University

Paul E. Doutrich
York College of Pennsylvania

John D. H. Downing
University of Texas

Kegan Doyle
University of British Columbia

Michael Wm. Doyle
Ball State University

David Allen Duncan
Tennessee Wesleyan College

Adolph Dupree
Independent scholar

H. J. Eisenman
University of Missouri—Rolla

Mark R. Ellis
University of Nebraska—Lincoln

Robert P. Ellis
Independent scholar

Charles H. Evans
LaGrange College

Thomas H. Falk
Michigan State University

L. Fleming Fallon, Jr.
Bowling Green State University

Susan A. Farrell
Kingsborough Community College

John W. Fiero
University of Southwestern Louisiana

David G. Fisher
Lycoming College

Cheri Vail Fisk
Independent scholar

Dale L. Flesher
University of Mississippi

George J. Flynn
State University of New York—Plattsburgh

Carol Franks
Portland State University

Tim Frazer
Western Illinois University

Raymond Frey
Centenary College

C. George Fry
Lutheran College

Ben Furnish
University of Kansas

Cecilia M. Garcia
Independent scholar

Janet E. Gardner
University of Massachusetts, Dartmouth

Keith Garebian
Independent scholar

R. Brooks Garner
Oklahoma State University

Karen L. Gennari
Independent scholar

Phyllis B. Gerstenfeld
California State University, Stanislaus

Patricia Leigh Gibbs
University of Hawaii at Manoa

K. Fred Gillum
Colby College

Priscilla June Glanville
University of South Florida

John L. Godwin
University of North Carolina at Wilmington

Marc Goldstein
Independent scholar

Nancy M. Gordon
Independent scholar

Robert F. Gorman
Southwest Texas State University

Ignacio L. Götz
Hostra University

Karen K. Gould
Independent scholar

Lewis L. Gould
University of Texas at Austin

Daniel G. Graetzer
University of Washington

Hans G. Graetzer
South Dakota State University

J. Justin Gustainis
State University of New York—Plattsburgh

Larry Haapanen
Lewis-Clark State College

Michael Haas
University of Hawaii at Manoa

Marian Wynne Haber
Texas Wesleyan University

Frank E. Hagan
Mercyhurst College

Irwin Halfond
McKendree College

Patricia Wong Hall
Northern Arizona University

Jacob Darwin Hamblin
University of California, Santa Barbara

Paul Hansom
Independent scholar

Richard P. Harmond
St. John's University

Dennis A. Harp
Texas Tech University

Fran Hassencahl
Old Dominion University

P. Graham Hatcher
Georgetown College

James Heaney
Hall Psychiatric Hospital

Kim Heikkila
University of Minnesota

Peter B. Heller
Manhattan College

Terry Heller
Coe College

Martha M. Henze
Independent scholar

Mark L. Higgins
Wayne State College

Richard A. Hill
Concordia University

Myrna Hillburn-Clifford
Independent scholar

Randall W. Hines
East Tennessee State University

Joseph W. Hinton
Independent scholar

Arthur D. Hlavaty
Independent scholar

John R. Holmes
Franciscan University of Steubenville

Charles C. Howard
Tarleton State University

Tonya Huber
Wichita State University

Ronald K. Huch
University of Papua New Guinea

Sue Hum
University of Akron

E. D. Huntley
Appalachian State University

Caralee Hutchinson
Independent scholar

Raymond Pierre Hylton
Virginia Union University

John Quinn Imholte
University of Minnesota, Morris

Telemate Alioma Jackreece
Mississippi State University

Robert Jacobs
Central Washington University

Ron Jacobs
University of Vermont

Jennifer Raye James
University of Oklahoma

Helen Jaskoski
California State University, Fullerton

Jeffry Jensen
Independent scholar

Patricia Jessup-Woodlin
California State University, Los Angeles

Jeffrey A. Joens
Florida International University

Bruce E. Johansen
University of Nebraska at Omaha

Dale W. Johnson
Southern Wesleyan University

Rebecca Strand Johnson
Independent scholar

Phyllis M. Jones-Shuler
University of Oxford, Somerville College

Gary Juliano
Independent scholar

Mathew J. Kanjirathinkal
Texas A&M University

Cynthia R. Kasee
University of South Florida

Steven G. Kellman
University of Texas at San Antonio

W. P. Kenney
Manhattan College

Nancy D. Kersell
Northern Kentucky University

Kimberley H. Kidd
East Tennessee State University

Joseph C. Kiger
University of Mississippi

William B. King
Coastal Carolina University

Bill Knight
Western Illinois University

Joseph M. Knippenberg
Oglethorpe University

Gayla Koerting
University of Missouri—Rolla

Lillian D. Kozloski
Smithsonian, National Air and Space Museum

Beth Kraig
Pacific Lutheran University

Philip E. Lampe
University of the Incarnate Word

Gary Land
Andrews University

LeeAnn Bishop Lands
Georgia Institute of Technology

Lisa Langenbach
Middle Tennessee State University

Ralph L. Langenheim, Jr.
University of Illinois—Urbana

Abraham D. Lavender
Florida International University

James E. Lawlor
Stevens Point Public Schools

William T. Lawlor
University of Wisconsin—Stevens Point

Jama Lazerow
Wheelock College

J. Wesley Leckrone
Temple University

Daniel Y. Lee
Shippensburg University

Richard M. Leeson
Fort Hays State University

Susan Lehrer
State University of New York, New Paltz

Ronald Lettieri
Mount Ida College

Peter B. Levy
York College

Charles Lewis
Mankato State University

Leon Lewis
Appalachian State University

Roy Liebman
California State University, Los Angeles

Victor Lindsey
East Central University

Paul T. Lockman, Jr.
Eastern New Mexico University

Brad Lookingbill
Columbia College

Dolores Lopez
Independent scholar

Janet E. Lorenz
Independent scholar

Denise Low
Haskell Indian Nations University

Herbert Luft
Pepperdine University

Robert D. Lukens
University of Delaware

David C. Lukowitz
Hamline University

Joanne McCarthy
Tacoma Community College

Robert McClenaghan
Independent scholar

Craig Sean McConnell
University of Wisconsin—Madison

Mark R. McCulloh
Davidson College

Andrew F. Macdonald
Loyola University

Gina Macdonald
Loyola University

Robert E. McFarland
North Georgia College

Roderick McGillis
University of Calgary

Ed McKnight
John A. Logan College

Jean McKnight
Southern Illinois University

Susan McLeland
University of Texas at Austin

David W. Madden
California State University, Sacramento

Paul D. Mageli
Independent scholar

Yale Magrass
University of Massachusetts-Dartmouth

Richard L. Mallery
Intrepid Quill Writing Services

Jo Manning
University of Illinois

Martin J. Manning
United States Information Agency

Joseph R. Marbach
Seton Hall University

Carl Henry Marcoux
University of California, Riverside

Trent Marshall
Southern Illinois University

Grace Maria Marvin
California State University, Chico

Sherri Ward Massey
University of Central Oklahoma

Joseph A. Melusky
Saint Francis College

Beth A. Messner
Ball State University

Gregg L. Michel
University of Virginia

Ken Millen-Penn
Fairmont State College

Tracy E. Miller
Towson University

Akilah Monifa
New College of California

William V. Moore
College of Charleston

Edward P. Morgan
Lehigh University

Brian Morley
The Master's College

Thomas S. Mowle
St. Mary's University

J. Todd Moye
University of Texas at Austin

Megan Mullen
University of New Hampshire

Maureen K. Mulligan
Grand Valley State University

Jeremy Mumford
Yale University

R. David Myers
New Mexico State University

Ronald Nelson
Independent scholar

Robert Niemi
St. Michael's College

Terry Nienhuis
Western Carolina University

Norma Corigliano Noonan
Augsburg College

Holly L. Norton
Tiffin University

Charles H. O'Brien
Western Illinois University

John F. O'Connell
College of the Holy Cross

Gary A. Olson
San Bernardino Valley College

James F. O'Neil
Edison Community College

Max C. E. Orezzoli
Florida International University

Linda Pratt Orr
Transylvania University

Eric W. Osborne
Texas Christian University

William Osborne
Florida International University, Main Campus

David E. Paas
Hillsdale College

Lisa Paddock
Independent scholar

Robert J. Paradowski
Rochester Institute of Technology

Joseph R. Paretta
Hofstra University

Robert L. Patterson
Armstrong Atlantic State University

Darryl Paulson
University of South Florida

Tinaz Pavri
Spelman College

Valentina Peguero
University of Wisconsin-Stevens Point

William E. Pemberton
University of Wisconsin—La Crosse

Nis Petersen
Jersey City State College

Gene D. Phillips
Loyola University

John R. Phillips
Purdue University Calumet

Jerome Picard
Mount Saint Mary College

John C. Pinheiro
University of Tennessee, Knoxville

Julio César Pino
Kent State University

Harry Piotrowski
Towson University

J. P. Piskulich
Oakland University

G. R. Plitnik
Frostburg State University

Marjorie Podolsky
Penn State University at Erie—Behrend College

Michael Polley
Columbia College

Francis Poole
University of Delaware

David L. Porter
William Penn College

John Powell
Pennsylvania State University, Erie

Verbie Lovorn Prevost
University of Tennessee at Chattanooga

Victoria Price
Lamar University

Maureen Puffer
Valdosta State University

Catherine Rainwater
Saint Edward's University

P. S. Ramsey
Independent scholar

Sharon Randolph
Fort Hays State University

Jonah Raskin
Sonoma State University

R. Kent Rasmussen
Independent scholar

Brandon Raulston
University of Tennessee at Chattanooga

Margaret A. Ray
Mary Washington College

Michaela Crawford Reaves
California Lutheran University

E. A. Reed
Saint Mary's College of California

Christl Reges
Western Michigan University

Akim D. Reinhardt
University of Nebraska—Lincoln

Thomas Reins
California State University, Fullerton

William L. Reinshagen
Independent scholar

John S. Reist, Jr.
Hillsdale College

Michael Richards
Sweet Briar College

Vivian L. Richardson
Central Missouri State University

James W. Riddlesperger, Jr.
Texas Christian University

Edward A. Riedinger
Ohio State University

Edward J. Rielly
Saint Joseph's College

Janice Rienerth
Appalachian State University

Ernest Rigney, Jr.
College of Charleston

St. John Robinson
Montana State University at Billings

Richard Allen Roe
Independent scholar

Carl Rollyson
Baruch College, City University of New York

Barbara Roos
Grand Valley State University

Peggy Waltzer Rosefeldt
Independent scholar

John Alan Ross
Eastern Washington University

Joseph R. Rudolph, Jr.
Towson University

Rose M. Russell
Houston Community College

Carol J. Sample
State University of New York College at Brockport

Mark E. Santow
University of Pennsylvania

Bophasy Saukam
Independent scholar

Sean J. Savage
Saint Mary's College

William J. Scheick
University of Texas at Austin

J. Christopher Schnell
Southeast Missouri State University

Larry Schweikart
University of Dayton

Michael F. Scully
University of Texas at Austin

Peter S. Seavor
St. Joseph's College

Rose Secrest
Independent scholar

Susan M. Shaw
Oregon State University

John P. Shields
University of Massachusetts

Carroll Dale Short
Independent scholar

R. Baird Shuman
University of Illinois at Urbana-Champaign

Michael J. Siler
California State University, Los Angeles

Donald C. Simmons, Jr.
Mississippi Humanities Council

Donna Addkison Simmons
Independent scholar

Amy Sisson
Independent scholar

Andrew C. Skinner
Brigham Young University

Roger Smith
Independent scholar

Brett Eric Smithson
Southern Illinois University

Ira Smolensky
Monmouth College

Alan L. Sorkin
University of Maryland—Baltimore County

Bes Stark Spangler
Peace College

Joseph L. Spradley
Wheaton College

Glenn Ellen Starr
Appalachian State University

Leon Stein
Roosevelt University

Barry M. Stentiford
Grambling State University

Roger J. Stilling
Appalachian State University

Lloyd Stires
Indiana University of Pennsylvania

Eric Strauss
Independent scholar

Leslie Stricker
Park College

Pearlie Strother-Adams
Western Illinois University

Susan A. Stussy
Independent scholar

Darlene Mary Suarez
University of California, Riverside

Robert Sullivan
Independent scholar

Roy Arthur Swanson
University of Wisconsin—Milwaukee

Eric G. Swedin
Weber State University

Glenn L. Swygart
Tennessee Temple University

James Tackach
Roger Williams University

Vanessa Tait
University of California, Santa Cruz

G. Thomas Taylor
University of Maine

Gina R. Terinoni
Independent scholar

Terry Theodore
University of North Carolina at Wilmington

Nicholas C. Thomas
Auburn University at Montgomery

Leslie V. Tischauser
Prairie State College

Marilyn Tobias
Independent scholar

Brian G. Tobin
Lassen College

Cathy Travis
Independent scholar

Paul B. Trescott
Southern Illinois University

Mfanya Donald Tryman
Mississippi State University

Spencer C. Tucker
Virginia Military Institute

Tamara M. Valentine
University of South Carolina—Spartanburg

Mary Moore Vandendorpe
Lewis University

Marc E. Waddell
Morris College

Thomas J. Edward Walker
Pennsylvania State University
College of Technology

Annita Marie Ward
Salem-Teikyo University

Robert P. Watson
University of Hawaii at Hilo

William E. Watson
Drexel University

Gregory Weeks
University of Graz

Henry Weisser
Colorado State University

Thomas Whissen
Wright State University

Richard Whitworth
Ball State University

Edwin G. Wiggins
Webb Institute

Rowena Wildin
Independent scholar

Richard L. Wilson
University of Tennessee at Chattanooga

John D. Windhausen
Saint Anselm College

Mike Wise
Independent scholar

C. A. Wolski
Independent scholar

James L. Wood
San Diego State University

Fatima Wu
Loyola Marymount University

Susan J. Wurtzburg
University of Canterbury

Cynthia Gwynne Yaudes
Indiana University

Cynthia Young
Yale University

Kristen L. Zacharias
Albright College

Paul J. Zbiek
King's College

Benjamin Zibit
City University of New York

■ Alphabetical List of Entries

Volume I

Volume II

Volume III

The Sixties in America

A

■ Abernathy, Ralph

Born March 11, 1926, Linden, Alabama
Died April 17, 1990, Atlanta, Georgia

Baptist minister, leader in the Civil Rights movement from the mid-1950's until 1990. Upon Martin Luther King, Jr.'s death in 1968, Abernathy became the head of the Southern Christian Leadership Conference (SCLC).

Early Life Ralph David Abernathy, the grandson of slaves and the tenth of the twelve children of William L. and Louivery Bell Abernathy, was born on March 11, 1926, in Linden, Alabama. After serving in World War II, Abernathy was ordained a Baptist

minister in 1948. In 1950, he received his B.S. from Alabama State College and, in 1951, his M.A. from Atlanta University. From 1951 to 1961, he was pastor of the First Baptist Church, Montgomery, Alabama, and for a while was dean of men and an instructor at Alabama State College. In 1955, he came to national attention when he organized a boycott of the Montgomery bus system after Rosa Parks, an African American seamstress, was arrested for not yielding her seat to a white passenger. Abernathy's home and church were bombed, but the transit system was integrated after a year. "Violence," he said, "is the weapon of the weak," and "nonviolence is the weapon of the strong."

Baptist minister Ralph Abernathy (right), a leader in the struggle for civil rights, was a close friend and adviser to the Reverend Martin Luther King, Jr. (left). After King's death, he became the head of the Southern Christian Leadership Conference. (Library of Congress)

The 1960's Abernathy, like Jesus, Henry David Thoreau, and Mohandas Gandhi, placed his trust in nonviolent resistance to evil. He helped found the Southern Christian Leadership Conference (SCLC) in 1957, becoming its secretary-treasurer. Deferring to Martin Luther King, Jr., its president from 1957 to 1968, Abernathy wrote, "Someone has to *make* leaders," viewing himself as King's "strongest supporter." Hosea Williams said of the Civil Rights movement that King was its Moses and Abernathy its Joshua. In 1961, Abernathy became pastor of the West Hunter Street Baptist Church in Atlanta, which allowed him more time for the SCLC. Segregation was successfully fought by marches, rallies, sit-ins, voter registration drives, and court cases. Seventeen times King and Abernathy were jailed. While middle-class African Americans gained politically with desegregation, masses of African Americans remained trapped in poverty. The SCLC began to address economic issues. In 1968, King went to Memphis, Tennessee, to support a strike by city sanitation workers. While there he was assassinated, with Abernathy, whom he termed his "closest friend," by his side. Abernathy assumed leadership of the SCLC and directed the massive Poor People's March on Washington, D.C., to reveal "the human face of American poverty."

Later Life By the 1970's, Abernathy was widely honored as a civil rights leader, receiving honorary degrees from many universities. In 1971, he addressed the United Nations and received the peace medal from the German Democratic Republic. Abernathy resigned from the presidency of the SCLC in 1977 and ran unsuccessfully for the Georgia Fifth District Congressional seat left vacant by Andrew Young. He then started the Foundation for Economic Enterprises Development to help African Americans obtain better economic opportunities. Abernathy lectured, pastored the West Hunter Street Baptist Church, and, in spite of poor health, enjoyed life with his wife, Juanita Odessa Jones (married, August 31, 1952) and their four children. He died, in Atlanta, on April 17, 1990.

Impact Abernathy, "dearest friend" and "closest adviser" to King, for four decades helped lead a nonviolent campaign for civil rights and for economic justice for African Americans and later for Hispanics, Native Americans, and marginalized poor whites. The Civil Rights movement proved to be one of the greatest social revolutions in U.S. history.

Subsequent Events In 1980, Abernathy was criticized for his endorsement of Ronald Reagan for the presidency and, in 1989, for his critical remarks concerning King's personal life in his 1989 autobiography.

Additional Information Two valuable studies of the man and the movement are Abernathy's own biography, *And the Walls Came Tumbling Down: An Autobiography* (1989), and Ralph E. Luker's *Historical Dictionary of the Civil Rights Movement* (1997).

C. George Fry

See also Civil Rights Movement; King, Martin Luther, Jr.; Poor People's March; Southern Christian Leadership Conference (SCLC).

■ Abortion

The purposeful early termination of a pregnancy. Social changes in the 1960's and advances in medical technology created a cultural climate that became more tolerant of abortion.

Before 1800 in the United States, a fetus was generally not regarded as a human being until the mother experienced "quickening" (movement in the womb). Abortion was not defined as a crime unless performed after quickening. In the mid-nineteenth century, abortion had become a thriving business, with providers—often midwives and herbal healers rather than physicians—advertising for patients. As increasing numbers of women had abortions to delay or prevent childbearing, some people were troubled by the declining birthrates, particularly among white, middle-class families. In addition, physicians, who had just begun performing abortions, were displeased by their lack of control over this medical procedure and the deaths that sometimes occurred at the providers' hands. By the late nineteenth century, these concerns led to the prohibition of abortion, a policy that would remain in effect until the 1960's.

Although the procedure was illegal, many women continued to have abortions. By the 1950's, sex researcher Alfred Kinsey estimated that nine out of ten premarital pregnancies were terminated by abortion and that 22 percent of married women had had an abortion. By the late 1960's, according to a New York State Governor's Commission appointed to study abortion, between 200,000 and 1.2 million illegal abortions were being performed each year in the United States.

Forces for Abortion The move toward legalization of abortion was indicative of major social changes taking place in the 1960's. Fear of global overpopulation, in contrast to nineteenth century worries about declining birthrates, had led policymakers to discuss birth control and contraception. Many viewed abortion as a necessary weapon in the fight against overpopulation. Research on better contraceptive methods, encouraged by the U.S. government, culminated in the development of the birth control pill, which helped separate sexual intercourse from procreation. The Supreme Court, in *Griswold v. Connecticut* (1965), struck down Connecticut's laws against using contraception, nullifying the Comstock Act, which placed restrictions on the sale and use of birth control products.

Other factors favoring abortion were the liberalized attitude toward sexuality that developed during the decade and women's liberation. As women's roles expanded, ideas about sexuality, procreation, contraception, and abortion changed. According to sociologist Barbara Katz Rothman, abortion became "the touchstone for understanding motherhood and womanhood." Legalization of abortion was one of the top priorities for the National Organization for Women (NOW) and was a major focus for many feminists. In order for women to compete equally in the workforce, feminists argued, they needed access to contraception and abortion.

The thalidomide situation was another impetus for changing laws against abortion. Some women who were prescribed thalidomide to control nausea during pregnancy gave birth to infants with various disabling conditions including missing limbs. Mass media depiction of the plight of women who sought abortions because of the likelihood of giving birth to a severely handicapped child contributed to reconsideration of abortion.

A Woman's Health and Freedom Another crucial aspect in the move to legalize abortion was the concern for women's health and safety. Many women continued to obtain abortions, but because they were illegal, many were performed by doctors who had lost their licenses to practice or by people totally uneducated as to safe medical practices and procedures. Although many women were well served, the illegality of the practice cost many women their fertility and others their lives. Wealthy women could get an abortion outside the country or through subterfuges that some doctors were willing to maintain for their paying customers. Some hospitals colluded with physicians to provide such services. Women were admitted for appendectomies or other surgeries and would actually have an abortion. Doctors began to find this ethical sleight of hand distasteful. Their voices added professional weight to the argument for legalizing abortion. Doctors, members of a profession that had led the fight for criminalizing abortion during the nineteenth century, now led the fight for legalization. They

Demonstrators march in front of St. Patrick's Cathedral in New York to protest the Roman Catholic Church's efforts to prevent the state from liberalizing its abortion laws. New York was one of the first states where women—even nonresidents—could legally obtain an abortion. (Library of Congress)

no longer wanted to risk their licenses and careers performing illegal abortions.

Women's well-being and reproductive freedom became bound together as a result of the feminist and health movements. Sexual and reproductive freedoms were seen as basic rights for women. Some feminists began to train other women to perform abortions because not all women could hire a legitimate doctor to perform the procedure and going to a back-street abortionist was dangerous. For example, a feminist collective called Jane or the Service was set up in 1969 to provide women with safe abortions until 1973, when the procedure was legalized throughout the nation.

Change Arrives For nearly the entire 1960's, there were signs that change was coming. The concern about overpopulation was gaining ground, and states and cities with large populations received reports from groups such as the Rockefeller Foundation that abortion was inevitable and unstoppable. Continued prohibition could lead to civil unrest and erosion of the social fabric, especially in light of women's increasing political power at the local and federal levels. The medical profession continued to argue for legalization of abortion based on public health concerns. Continued reports about the unnecessary deaths of women who sought illegal abortions created a groundswell of support for decriminalization. In reaction to these attitudinal and economic changes, legalization began at the state level. Based on reports such as that of the New York State Governor's Commission, several states recognized that abortion—legal or not—was a fact of women's lives.

Impact In 1967, three states—California, Colorado, and North Carolina—relaxed legal restrictions on abortion. In California and Colorado, the decision came after severe German measles epidemics had resulted in large numbers of babies being born with birth defects, and North Carolina legislators were influenced by visits to institutions where abandoned children in near-vegetative states were kept. By 1970, twelve states passed liberalization laws. New York, a traditionally liberal state, took the most radical step, eliminating residency requirements for those wishing to have abortions. In 1970, the American Medical Association (AMA), acknowledging this growing trend toward liberalization, began a state-by-state campaign to repeal abortion laws.

Subsequent Events In the early 1970's, Georgia allowed some abortions while banning others. The case decided by the Supreme Court in 1973, *Roe v. Wade*, involved a challenge of Georgia's restrictions on abortion along with a challenge to a severely restrictive Texas law. The Court ruled that both laws violated a woman's right to privacy and established guidelines for abortion. Justice Harry Blackmun drafted an opinion stating that the woman had essentially an unrestricted right to abortion in the first trimester of pregnancy. If the woman was in the second trimester, the states could regulate abortion to protect her health; in the third trimester, abortion could be restricted but must be permitted to save a woman's life. The tide for the legalization of abortion had already turned in the 1960's, and by the time the Court handed down its decision in *Roe v. Wade*, most states had already overturned their legal bans and restrictions on abortion, reflecting a public demand for these policy changes.

Additional Information James C. Mohr's *Abortion in America: The Origins and Evolution of National Policy* (1978) gives an excellent history of the transformation of abortion politics from the eighteenth century to 1973. Barbara Katz Rothman's *Recreating Motherhood: Ideology and Technology in a Patriarchal Society* (1989) discusses abortion in the context of changing ideas about women and procreation and how they affect social policies in the United States. Other works on abortion in the United States are *A Private Choice: Abortion in America in the Seventies* (1979), by John T. Noonan; *Abortion Wars: A Half Century of Struggle, 1950-2000* (1998), edited by Rickie Solinger; and *Abortion: The Clash of Absolutes* (1990), by Laurence H. Tribe.

Susan A. Farrell

See also Birth Control; Feminist Movement; *Griswold v. Connecticut*; National Organization for Women (NOW); Supreme Court Decisions; Thalidomide.

■ Abzug, Bella

Born July 24, 1920, New York, New York
Died March 31, 1998, New York, New York

Feminist lawyer, politician, and activist. Abzug's career as an outspoken organizer helped draw women of the 1960's into the mainstream political arena.

Early Life Bella Savitzky was born in the east Bronx in New York City to working-class Russian-Jewish immigrants. She attended public schools and a special Hebrew high school after the regular school day. While student body president at Hunter College, she demonstrated against the rise of Nazism and against the fascists in the Spanish Civil War. She married Maurice M. Abzug in 1944 and earned her law degree at Columbia University the following year. During the next fifteen years, she took cases involving abuses of civil and human rights then concentrated on labor law. She also defended writers accused of un-American activities by Senator Joseph McCarthy.

The 1960's During the 1960's, Abzug turned her attention to the antinuclear, peace, and women's movements. In response to nuclear testing by the United States and the Soviet Union, she joined other women in protesting nuclear proliferation. In 1961, she helped establish Women Strike for Peace, which held large demonstrations at the United Nations in New York City, at the White House in Washington, D.C., and in other large U.S. cities. After the Nuclear Test Ban Treaty was signed in 1963, the organization began holding protests against U.S. involvement in Vietnam. Abzug served as the group's national legislative director and political action director from 1961 to 1970. During the late 1960's, she attempted—with only limited success—to build political coalitions of liberals, women, African Americans, and the poor to change the political direction of the country.

Later Life In 1970, Abzug was elected to the U.S. House of Representatives, where she earned the nickname "Bellicose Bella" for her outspoken championing of the environment, welfare, consumer protection, U.S. aid to Israel, and issues affecting the lives of women, minorities, and the poor. While in Congress, she coauthored the Freedom of Information and Privacy Acts. She left Congress in 1976 but continued to write and speak on politics and gender issues. In 1984, she published *Gender Gap: Bella Abzug's Guide to Political Power for Women*. She died in New York at age seventy-seven after heart surgery.

Impact As both an early example and a strong advocate, Abzug paved the way for women interested in serving in political office. She helped organize women into effective groups for achieving social change, including bringing a close to U.S. involve-

New York lawyer Bella Abzug worked tirelessly for the women's, antiwar, and antinuclear movements during the 1960's. In 1970, she won election to the House of Representatives. (Russell Reif/Archive Photos)

ment in Vietnam and reducing the proliferation of nuclear arms.

Subsequent Events In 1971, Abzug was one of the founders of the National Women's Political Caucus, which helped organize women at local, state, and national levels and supported women as political candidates. She was also an early member of the National Organization for Women.

Additional Information Abzug described her first year in Congress in *Bella! Ms. Abzug Goes to Washington* (1972), offering background information interwoven with pages from her diary.

Cynthia A. Bily

See also National Organization for Women (NOW); Nuclear Test Ban Treaties; Vietnam War.

■ Advertising

A means by which people learn about and are encouraged to buy products and services. Advertising, like the society that created it, exploded with self-expression in the 1960's. This era is known for its creative appeal to the independent consumer, its sense of humor, and its superstar admakers.

In the 1960's, the American advertising industry was undergoing a creative revolution largely shaped by the independent thought, self-expression, and human rights movements occurring in the culture that surrounded the industry. The healthy financial status of the United States and other countries combined with the attitudes of the time resulted in some memorable advertising. Suddenly, small agencies and creativity were more important than large agencies and the research-oriented, scientific approach of the past. The phrase "creative revolution" was not actually used until the mid-1960's; however, advertising copywriters were picking up on the trends going on around them, targeting a variety of audiences, and looking for ways to sell the products produced by all the new companies that arose in the healthy economy. They were also producing more entertaining advertisements than those from years past. Some of the new brand names and products were Domino's Pizza, Gatorade sports drink, McDonald's Big Mac, and Nike shoes. The top three advertising agencies of the period were Leo Burnett in Chicago, Ogilvy and Mather in New York, and Doyle, Dane, Bernbach (DDB) in New York.

The advertising campaign considered the most successful and one of the most popular ever belonged to the German import car, the Volkswagen. The admakers at DDB took an unusual and humorous approach to promoting this little buglike automobile. Their print and broadcast advertisements focused on the size of the car and its value for the dollar. They emphasized the ease of getting parts and talked about the small insurance payments and how easy it was to park the car. Their print advertisements featured black-and-white photos—in contrast to the bright colors of other car ads—little text and no technical information. DDB wrote copy such as "Think small" and "It's ugly, but it gets you there." The latter slogan was accompanied by a photo of a lunar landing vehicle rather than the Volkswagen. DDB also led an innovative campaign for Avis, the car rental company. In the early 1960's, Avis found itself falling rapidly behind leader Hertz. DDB proposed a campaign that had never been seen before—one in which Avis admitted being ranked second in the industry. In another bold move, the creative team also focused on comparative advertising: "Avis is only number two in rental cars. So why go with us?" The answer: "We try harder."

The Leo Burnett agency was responsible for the highly successful television and print campaigns for Marlboro cigarettes. The advertisements featured actual cowboys, not models, suggesting that people "Come to where the flavor is. Come to Marlboro Country." The same agency launched a successful campaign for Kellogg's Special K cereal.

David Ogilvy came to prominence with his promotions of the Shell Oil Company and, after merging with Mather and Crowther, as part of one of the world's top ten agencies, Ogilvy and Mather. Ogilvy helped ensure a place in the market for Sears, Hathaway shirts, Schweppes, and Rolls Royce.

Diversity and Advertising The roles of women and minorities in advertising were changing, but the revolution was slow. The housewife of the 1950's was replaced by a woman who was sexy, sophisticated and who, although still primarily a housewife, sometimes chose to work outside the home. More women were being hired by agencies. DDB hired a number of women, including one of the most famous in the business, Mary Wells, who while working at Jack Tinker Partners produced a successful campaign for Alka-Seltzer: "No matter what shape your stomach is in." The television spot featured jiggly stomachs and a hit jingle. Wells was also successful in her work on the Braniff International Airlines' "Flying Colors" campaign. For the Braniff campaign, she employed the sex appeal of female flight attendants in Pucci outfits and airplanes painted in pastel colors. Wells started her own agency, Wells, Rich, and Greene, in 1966. She continued to create for Alka-Seltzer ("I can't believe I ate the whole thing") and for Benson and Hedges 100's cigarettes. For the latter, the campaign focused on the "disadvantages" of smoking the extra-long cigarette: the ripping of a too-small pocket, a fire in a man's beard, and getting caught in an elevator door.

During this time, as African Americans pushed forward with civil rights demonstrations, admakers followed the trend of Afrocentric looks in dress and behavior. Light-skinned African Americans who promoted products for hair straighteners, skin bleaches, and health care products in the 1950's were replaced by darker-skinned African Americans wearing their hair in natural Afro styles and sometimes dressed in traditional African clothing. The newer advertisements, which appeared primarily in magazines that appealed to African Americans readers (such as *Ebony*), featured more traditional self-care products. The roles of African Americans as portrayed in advertisements also changed. Aunt Jemima's "mammy" character took on a more modern look, slimming down and donning earrings. Lena Horne (Sanka coffee) and Bill Cosby (Jell-O gelatin) pitched products to people of all ethnic backgrounds. DDB created a series of advertisements featuring a variety of ethnic groups for Levy's bread. The advertisements included African Americans, Asian Americans, and Native Americans, usually with the words, "You don't have to be Jewish to love Levy's." Agencies also began to recruit more minority employees, including Jews, Greeks, and Italians.

Memorable Campaigns A number of memorable characters first appeared in the 1960's. These included the Pillsbury Doughboy, Star-Kist's Charlie the Tuna, Nine Lives' Morris the Cat, and the Maytag washing machine repairman. Many of the slogans and songs of the 1960's are either still used or at least remembered many years after they first appeared. The slogans include Kentucky Fried Chicken's "finger-lickin' good," "You've come a long way, baby!" for Virginia Slims cigarettes, and "I can't believe I ate the whole thing" for Alka-Seltzer. An entire generation of baby boomers (born 1946-1964) grew up listening to the jingles for Oscar Mayer wieners and Armour hot dogs. The "black is beautiful" slogan of the Civil Rights movement became a common theme in advertisements.

The 1960's also featured one of the most famous and controversial television commercials of all time. In 1964, the Democrats stirred talk with a spot created by DDB that aired only once. The advertisement was written for Lyndon B. Johnson during his presidential campaign. In the commercial, a little girl picked petals from a daisy juxtaposed against a nuclear countdown. The countdown ended in a nuclear explosion with a warning from Johnson that "The stakes are too high for you to stay at home."

Impact The 1960's was a period of maturation for advertising, just as it was for society. The attention to minorities and women was not strong nor was it always accurate or realistic. However, the advertising industry did begin to reflect the interests of a diversified group of people more than it ever had before. The impact on society was that minorities and women responded to the advertising and began to demonstrate, especially in the years to follow, their buying power. They demanded—and got—more attention from advertisers. Advertising, while encouraging more consumption of goods and services, became a kind of icon of consumption itself.

Subsequent Events By the early 1970's, more women and minorities had begun to see themselves as individuals with choices regarding their lives. The advertisements that showed people as independent thinkers were becoming reality. By the mid-1970's, admakers kept checklists to avoid sexist and racist remarks and overt stereotyping in their advertisements. One of the most successful campaigns ever, for Virginia Slims cigarettes, targeted women with its "You've come a long way, baby!" slogan, referring to the heightened acceptance of women smokers produced as a by-product of the women's movement. When new advertising copywriters look for examples of creativity, many still turn to the 1960's. In the 1980's and 1990's, the advertisers found themselves recycling 1960's favorites to appeal to the same (now grown-up) audience of baby boomers. Oscar Mayer brought back the jingle, "My bologna has a first name, it's O-S-C-A-R," and Borden brought back Elsie the Cow for its dairy products. Even Volkswagen evoked the aura of the 1960's in its successful ad campaign for the 1990's version of the now-famous "bug."

Additional Information Most historical studies of advertising connect closely with studies of cultural and societal change. Some good references include *Advertising in America: The First 200 Years* (1990), by Charles Goodrum and Helen Dalrymple; *Advertising in Contemporary Society: Perspectives Toward Understanding* (1996), by Kim B. Rotzoll and James E. Haefner; and *Soap, Sex, and Cigarettes: A Cultural History of American Advertising* (1998), by Juliann Sivulka.

Sherri Ward Massey

See also Feminist Movement; Media; Social Satires.

■ Affirmative Action

A method for dismantling discriminatory policies, practices, and procedures. Affirmative action is a method by which agencies and companies identify and remove artificial barriers to equal opportunity that are often erected against minorities and women.

The term "affirmative action" first appeared in the National Labor Relations Act of 1935, which required employers to engage in affirmative action, that is, to voluntarily rehire those who had been fired because they were union members and, in the future, to hire without regard to union membership rather than awaiting lawsuits to enforce the law.

In 1941 and 1943, after President Franklin D. Roosevelt issued Executive Orders 8802 and 9346, which mandated nondiscrimination by defense contractors, African Americans were hired in record numbers by contracting corporations in a voluntary effort to demonstrate compliance. However, after World War II, these executive orders were abolished, and segregation continued in nondefense contractors despite subsequent executive orders by presidents Harry S Truman and Dwight D. Eisenhower that proclaimed the goal of nondiscrimination but provided no enforcement mechanisms.

Kennedy Takes Action After the election of President John F. Kennedy in 1960, civil rights organizations asked the new president to expand the scope of existing executive orders banning discrimination by federal contractors. Southern contractors, such as firms supplying paper to the Government Printing Office in Washington, D.C., were opposed, preferring to continue the practice of segregating workers by race.

On March 6, 1961, Kennedy issued Executive Order 10925, which required businesses receiving contracts with the federal government not only to refrain from discriminating in employment but also to "take affirmative action to ensure that employees are treated during employment without regard to their race, creed, color, or national origin." This latter requirement was understood at the time to mean that employers should desegregate—putting an end to all-black and all-white work units, departments, or divisions. On June 22, 1963, Kennedy issued Executive Order 11114, which empowered federal agencies to terminate contracts with businesses disobeying Executive Order 10925. Neverthe-

less, southern firms continued to resist compliance, and the enforcement mechanism for the executive orders was weak.

Johnson, Nixon, and Affirmative Action The term "affirmative action" next appeared in Title VII of the Civil Rights Act of 1964, which empowered courts to require employers guilty of discrimination to engage in "such affirmative action as may be appropriate." The statute suggested such affirmative remedies as reinstatement or hiring of employees with or without back pay, but enforcement of the law required complainants to file lawsuits, a lengthy and costly process, so such advocacy groups as the Congress of Racial Equality (CORE) pursued boycotts, demonstrations, and strikes. Accordingly, James Farmer, founder of CORE, urged President Lyndon B. Johnson to require federal contractors to take "affirmative action" in advance of complaints and to set up an administrative agency that would closely monitor compliance.

On September 24, 1965, Johnson issued Executive Order 11246, which extended the scope of affirmative action to the recruitment, screening, and selection of new employees; enforcement was assigned to the Office of Federal Contract Compliance within the U.S. Department of Labor. The Equal Employment Opportunity Commission (EEOC), empowered to enforce Title VII, began to ask errant employers to draw up affirmative action plans, that is, blueprints for changes in policies, practices, and procedures that have been identified as responsible for discrimination. On October 13, 1967, Johnson extended affirmative action to cover sex discrimination in Executive Order 11375. On May 28, 1968, the Department of Labor for the first time required contractors to write affirmative action programs. On August 8, 1969, President Richard M. Nixon issued Executive Order 11478, thereby extending affirmative action requirements to all federal agencies under the jurisdiction of the U.S. Civil Service Commission (now the Office of Personnel Management).

Thus, affirmative action could come about because a corporation is a federal contractor, an agency is a part of the federal civil service, or a court has ordered affirmative action as a remedy for past discrimination. In addition, an agency or corporation could voluntarily adopt an affirmative action plan.

Impact Insofar as affirmative action was understood to mean the inclusion of ethnic groups and women in occupations from which they were formerly excluded, employers were tempted to provide only token responses, such as hiring just one African American or one woman in a particular job. In the years immediately after Executive Order 11246, African Americans vigorously protested tokenism. Urban riots, increasing civil rights militancy, and the promise of the Great Society produced pressures for affirmative action efforts to yield tangible results.

Accordingly, the Department of Labor's Philadelphia office decided in 1968 to require contractors to demonstrate compliance quantitatively. What became known as the Philadelphia Plan was the practice of comparing employees and applicants for employment with certain statistical norms. For example, if 30 percent of all forklift operators in the Philadelphia area were African Americans, as determined by Department of Labor statistics, then all contractors were asked to show that 30 percent of their forklift operators were African Americans; a substantially smaller percentage was equated with continuing segregation of workers into black and white firms. Similarly, employers had to show that rates of promotion, salaries, and other aspects of employment treated both sexes and all ethnic groups equally or state specific reasons why disparities existed. The Philadelphia Plan insisted that where disparities were found, employers must draw up timetables for removing them. By the end of the 1960's, the Philadelphia Plan had become the model for monitoring and implementing compliance with affirmative action requirements that was most acceptable to civil rights groups, but the rest of the country was not required to adopt the new statistical methodology.

The affirmative action requirement forced employers to assess whether patterns of exclusion or underemployment of minorities or women existed; if so, changes were to be made in personnel policies, practices, or procedures that were deemed responsible for the anomalous patterns, including goals and timetables. Failure to make an analysis or to correct deficiencies was then assumed to be operating in bad faith, placing a contract in jeopardy. However, as an increasing number of qualified minorities and women were hired, some men complained that an era of reverse discrimination had arisen, and employers began to complain of the cost of collecting, organizing, and analyzing masses of statistics on employees.

The new statistical methodology of affirmative action caught the attention of many. The ripple effect was that any area of civil rights monitoring was said to be an area for affirmative action. Among the new areas where affirmative action was said to be practiced were broadcast licensing, college admissions, housing project regulations, minority contractor set-asides, school desegregation and busing plans, and voting reapportionment plans; none of these areas has a federal administrative or statutory requirement to engage in affirmative action, though federal nondiscrimination requirements apply in all cases.

Subsequent Events The Philadelphia Plan became a nationwide standard on February 5, 1970, when the Department of Labor issued new guidelines for affirmative action. Nevertheless, affirmative action has not always been implemented in a manner consistent with federal guidelines, and judges have supported affirmative action only when remedies have been narrowly tailored to remedy specific deficiencies in reasonable periods of time. In *University of California v. Bakke*, a divided Supreme Court ruled in 1978 that the practice of considering admissions in segregated pools of applicants violated the equal protection clause of the Fourteenth Amendment, but that the school could consider racial diversity as one among several criteria to use in determining who should be admitted. As a result of this case, the goal of diversity came to replace affirmative action as a civil rights priority. In the late 1980's and 1990's, the Supreme Court struck down some overzealous efforts to promote diversity, as in the cases *City of Richmond v. Croson* (1989) and *Adarand Constructors v. Peña* (1995), both of which involved minority contractor set-asides. After the latter case, President Bill Clinton announced four standards for mending affirmative action: Affirmative action should not establish quotas, preferences for the unqualified, involve reverse discrimination, or continue beyond a point where there was demonstrable need. This was the first time that a president of the United States had declared limits to implementation of affirmative action.

Additional Information For a history of the earliest uses of affirmative action, see Frank W. Andritzky and Joseph G. Andritzky's "Affirmative Action: The Original Meaning," *Lincoln Law Review* (1987), and William B. Gould's *Black Workers in White Unions*

(1977). Criticisms of affirmative action are expressed in Nathan Glazer's *Affirmative Discrimination* (1975) and Stephen L. Carter's *Reflections of an Affirmative Action Baby* (1991). A pro-affirmative action view is presented in Gertrude Ezorsky's *Racism and Justice: The Case for Affirmative Action* (1991) and Susan Sturm and Lani Guinier's "The Future of Affirmative Action: Reclaiming the Innovative Ideal," *California Law Review* (1996).

Michael Haas

See also Civil Rights Act of 1964; Johnson, Lyndon B.; Kennedy, John F.; Nixon, Richard M.; Women in the Workplace.

■ Agent Orange Controversy

A chemical defoliant used throughout the Vietnam War. This potent dioxin has been linked to a variety of illnesses suffered by Vietnamese and veterans of the war and to deformities in their children.

During the Vietnam War, the U.S. Air Force sprayed chemical herbicides such as Agent Orange over cropland and jungles. The first limited use of the chemicals occurred in 1962; they were employed over a widespread area from 1965 to 1971. Although many scientists praised the use of herbicides to destroy food sources and dense forage that hid communist insurgents, they slowly grew concerned about the effects of these herbicides on the Vietnamese villagers and U.S. forces who were exposed to them. Toward the end of the conflict, a controversy arose over whether various ailments suffered by U.S. veterans and birth deformities in their children were linked to the use of chemical defoliants in Vietnam.

In 1962, President John F. Kennedy authorized the Air Force to carry out the extensive defoliation campaign in Vietnam to destroy cropland and jungle cover used by North Vietnamese forces. Kennedy's advisers objected to the campaign, fearing that the United States might be accused of using chemical warfare. Modified Air Force C-123s flew thousands of sorties, ultimately destroying half of South Viet-

A U.S. Air Force C-123 sprays a chemical defoliant on the jungle beside a highway in South Vietnam. Many U.S. veterans and Vietnamese have reported various health problems believed to be the result of exposure to these potent dioxins, including Agent Orange. (Archive Photos)

nam's timberland in a campaign called Operation Ranch Hand. By 1969, questions arose concerning the effects of Agent Orange on humans. Vietnamese women exposed to the herbicide gave birth to an unusually high number of children with birth defects. Soldiers complained of persistent headaches and coughing.

Impact One C-123 airplane could carry eleven thousand pounds of Agent Orange and spray the chemical over three hundred acres in less than four minutes. In a matter of weeks, the treated area would become barren. In all, more than one hundred million pounds of chemical herbicides were applied to the Vietnamese countryside. Much of the exposed territory can never be refoliated and can certainly never be farmed. The human cost is more difficult to measure but is substantial nonetheless. The tactical advantage gained from destroying the enemy's cover and food supply was minimal.

Subsequent Events The defoliation campaign ended in January, 1971. Some three million U.S. veterans subsequently contacted the Veterans Administration about possible Agent Orange-related health problems. Veterans receive compensation for several Agent Orange-related diseases, including sarcoma, lymphoma, chloracne, porphyria, prostate and lung cancer, and Hodgkin's disease. As late as 1985, the Pentagon denied any connection between Agent Orange and the ailments suffered by Vietnam veterans, despite a congressional act in 1981 that ordered the Veterans Administration to compensate veterans exposed to Agent Orange and other herbicides. A class-action lawsuit by veterans against the companies that produced Agent Orange and other dioxins used in Vietnam was settled out of court in 1984. The problem continued decades after the war because of time limitations placed on veterans' claims for Agent Orange-related health problems.

Additional Information Sources of information on Agent Orange and the use of herbicides in Vietnam include Cecil Paul Frederick's *Herbicidal Warfare: The Ranch Hand Project in Vietnam* (1986) and Fred Wilcox's *Waiting for an Army to Die: The Tragedy of Agent Orange* (1983).

William Allison

See also Environmental Movement; Vietnam War.

■ Agnew, Spiro T.

Born November 9, 1918, Baltimore, Maryland
Died September 17, 1996, Berlin, Maryland

Richard M. Nixon's controversial vice president from 1968 to 1973. Agnew resigned from office in shame in 1973 after admitting to tax fraud.

Early Life Spiro Theodore Agnew, born and raised in Baltimore, Maryland, attended The Johns Hopkins University. Upon graduation, Agnew began a legal career at the Baltimore Law School while working at several jobs. His pursuit of a law degree was interrupted by World War II. He served in the United States Army for the duration of the war, marrying Elinor Judefind in 1942. He completed his law degree in 1947 and was admitted to the bar in 1949. He worked at Karl F. Steinmann's law firm until he began his own practice in Towson, Maryland.

The 1960's Agnew's political career began in 1957. He held relatively minor public offices in Baltimore County in the first half of the 1960's. Although he leaned toward the Democratic Party very early in life, he eventually became a Republican. Agnew entered national politics in 1966 when he was elected governor of Maryland. His career as governor brought him to the attention of Richard M. Nixon, who chose Agnew to be his vice presidential running mate in the election of 1968. As governor of Maryland, Agnew had gained a reputation for being an outspoken critic of black radicalism, which led many people to believe that Nixon had chosen him in order to gain votes in the South. Agnew was also known as a supporter of the United States' involvement in the Vietnam War. For these reasons, Agnew's nomination as vice president angered many liberals. Agnew proved to be an effective running mate who launched attacks on the news media and on the Democratic nominee, Hubert Humphrey. Agnew's willingness to be outspoken in his attacks on liberals was pleasing to conservatives, and he continued to serve as vice president after Nixon won reelection in 1972.

Later Life When Nixon and Agnew won reelection in 1972, the Watergate scandal was already unfolding. As Nixon struggled to save his presidency, the administration was further damaged by the news in 1973 that Agnew had accepted bribes as governor of

Spiro T. Agnew, vice president under Richard M. Nixon, was a strong supporter of the Vietnam War. During this 1969 speech in New Orleans, he called antiwar protesters "an effete corps of impudent snobs." (AP/Wide World Photos)

Maryland. To avoid a possible prison sentence, Agnew pleaded no contest to a lesser charge of tax evasion and resigned from office in disgrace in October, 1973. Agnew received three years' probation and a ten-thousand-dollar fine. He spent his remaining years writing and engaging in international business activities.

Impact Agnew's resignation was proof to many people that the Nixon administration had been awash in scandal from the beginning. It also acted as a prelude to Nixon's resignation from office in the face of almost certain impeachment.

Additional Information In 1990, Herbert Parmet published *Richard Nixon and His America*, which covers the Nixon and Agnew period in great detail.

Phillip A. Cantrell II

See also Nixon, Richard M.

■ Agriculture

A relatively impoverished sector of the U.S. economy during the 1960's. The numbers of farmers declined and their incomes fell relative to nonfarm workers.

Although agriculture is frequently viewed as a resource-based industry, the expansion of U.S. agricultural output since the 1920's has borne little relation to the total stock of physical resources used in agriculture. Major changes have taken place, however, in the proportions in which resources are used. For example, while the amount of land in agriculture has remained relatively stable, labor has moved out of agriculture at a rapid rate, reflecting the increasing use of work-saving technology. The use of capital in the form of mechanization has increased as has the use of inputs such as fertilizers, pesticides, and hybrid seeds. Agricultural output has become progressively more dependent on resources produced in the nonfarm sector and less dependent on land and labor. Only during World War II when vast amounts of labor were drawn off the farm did a shortage of labor occur. From 1945 to 1960, agriculture was characterized by excess land and labor and abundant supplies of purchased inputs.

Price Supports United States agricultural policy had its origin in the Agricultural Adjustment Act of 1933. This piece of legislation, enacted during the Depression when farm prices and incomes had collapsed, set the government firmly on a course of regulating markets to support the prices of several major farm commodities. The legislation created price supports to increase farm incomes. Subsequent farm legislation, enacted in 1939 and 1949, continued commodity price supports as the basis of U.S. agricultural policy.

Price-support policies worked fairly well during the Depression, during World War II, and in the immediate postwar period, when world food supplies were tight because of wartime devastation. However, these policies became prohibitively expensive during the late 1940's and 1950's because of the enormous commodity surpluses produced. These surpluses stemmed partly from the production incentives of price-support policies and partly from the revolution in farm technology (hybrid seeds, chemicals, farm equipment) that took place during that era. By 1960, a combination of price supports well above free-market levels, dramatic increases in crop

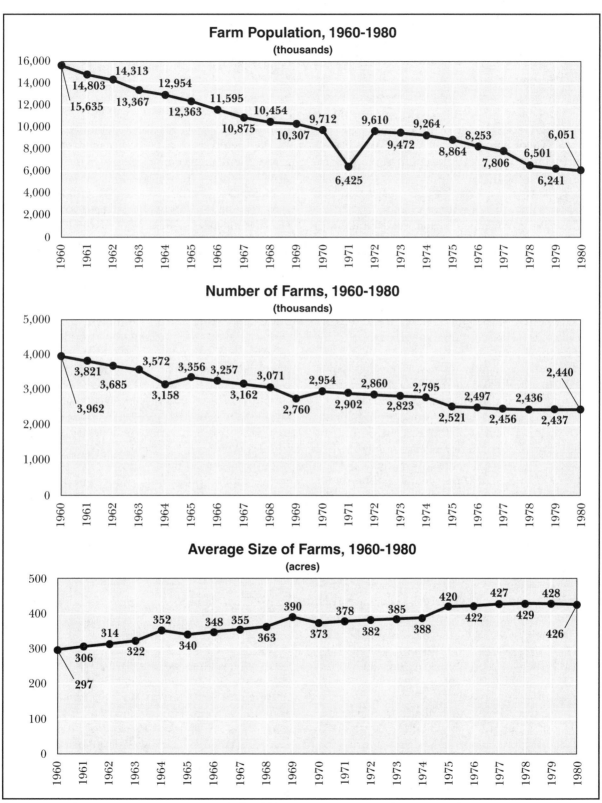

Farm Population, 1960-1980
(thousands)

Number of Farms, 1960-1980
(thousands)

Average Size of Farms, 1960-1980
(acres)

Source: Kurian, George, *Datapedia of the United States, 1790-2000, America Year by Year.* Lanham, Maryland: Bernam Press, 1994.

yields, and the ineffectiveness or obsolescence of acreage limitations had generated record stockpiles of grain, mostly under government ownership.

Labor Changes During the 1960's, the rapid increase in farm productivity compared with other sectors and the slower relative rise in the demand for farm products resulted in a transfer of labor to the nonfarm sector. Farm incomes lagged behind non-farm incomes as this reallocation of human resources continued. Therefore, in 1969, the median income of farm families was thirty-seven hundred dollars less than that of nonfarm families.

The nation's farm population was 16 million in 1960 but fell to 10.2 million in 1969, an average annual decline of 580,000 people. One-third of the decline in farm population was accounted for by African Americans. During the 1960's, the percentage of farms classified as family farms (using less than 1.5 person-years of hired labor) remained constant. Family farms accounted for 70 percent of the land under cultivation.

Although the quantity of labor inputs fell 36 percent during the 1960's, the quality of the labor force improved substantially because of improved education. The major factor behind productivity gains was fertilizer use, which rose 113 percent during the decade. Surprisingly, mechanization, which had increased by 102 percent in the 1940's and 14 percent in the 1950's, rose only 7 percent during the 1960's. By the end of the decade, the amount of labor employed in agriculture was approaching a balance with the normal requirements of food production.

A Growth in Exports A bright spot for agriculture during the 1960's was the growth in agricultural exports. Without exports, farm incomes would have been lower and farm surpluses would have been larger. During this decade, the value of agricultural exports rose 75 percent. The foreign market consumed approximately two-thirds of annual wheat production, nearly two-thirds of rice, one-half of soybeans, one-third of cotton, and nearly one-fourth of tobacco.

During the 1960's, the United States provided nearly half of all grains moving in world trade. In 1969-1970, shipments of soybean meal, a component in animal feeds, were more than three times those in 1959-1961. The large gains in these exports reflected the growing affluence of the developed world and the increased preference for the foods derived from these products—cooking and table fats, poultry, eggs, dairy products, and meats.

Impact By the early 1960's, it was increasingly evident that farm prices and incomes could not be increased with current policies. Although national income was rising steadily, net farm income had fallen below the levels of the early 1950's. During the 1960's, significant progress was made toward less government intervention in and control of farm production. The Agricultural Act of 1965 eliminated mandatory government control programs for major farm commodities and provided a more flexible and effective means of regulating farm output. The 1965 act reduced farm program costs by creating incentives for reduced production and by creating an environment for increased exports.

However, during this decade, about one-sixth of the nation's cropland was withheld from production under government land retirement programs. In addition to withdrawing land from production, farm programs caused sizable stocks of several commodities to be accumulated by the government. Because of the stockpile program, substantial short-term fluctuations in either production or demand were largely offset by the accumulation or release of stocks of farm commodities under the various price-support programs. These policies reduced instability in farm markets in the 1960's.

Agricultural policy underwent considerable evolution during the 1960's. In the early years of the decade, agriculture was characterized by excess productive capacity and burdensome stocks that were primarily the consequence of price-support programs. Agricultural production was brought into better balance with demand by the late 1960's; however, this result was achieved, in part, through land retirement programs and direct payments to producers that reached nearly four billion dollars per year.

Additional Information For further details on agriculture during the 1960's, see *Food Policy and Politics: A Perspective on Agriculture and Development* (1989), edited by George Howich and Gerald Lynch, and *Agricultural Policy Reform: Politics and Process in the EC and USA* (1990), by H. Wayne Moyer and Timothy E. Josling.

Alan L. Sorkin

See also Demographics of the United States; Farm Subsidies.

■ Aid to Families with Dependent Children (AFDC)

Government program, known as "welfare," that assists indigent single-parent families. It became a source of controversy as increasing numbers of poor women with children received aid and was attacked by conservatives for promoting dependency.

Aid to Dependent Children (ADC) was established as part of the first federally sponsored system of social benefits, the Social Security Act of 1935, which created many social insurance programs. It was expanded to cover the parent in 1962, becoming Aid to Families with Dependent Children (AFDC). Its purpose was to provide income support for dependent children and to enable single mothers to stay home and care for their children. Although federally established and funded, it was administered by the states, and discriminatory policies were the norm, especially in the South. States selectively applied moral fitness criteria, such as whether the child's home was a "suitable home" or whether a "substitute father" (a man presumed to be living with the child's mother but not legally responsible for the child) was present, to disqualify otherwise needy children. Welfare caseloads were kept low and restricted to white widows and abandoned mothers.

During the 1960's, the relief rolls more than doubled and changed composition, gradually shifting to single, often unwed, mothers. Although welfare spending increased dramatically, payments to families remained well below the official poverty level in all states. This, coupled with arbitrary administration of the program and humiliating procedures such as midnight searches, led mothers in Los Angeles to organize the first welfare rights group in 1963. The grassroots National Welfare Rights Organization was formed in 1966.

Under President Lyndon B. Johnson's War on Poverty, the Office of Economic Opportunity set up neighborhood legal services for the poor. The lawyers in these offices actively advocated for welfare recipients and brought class action suits as far as the Supreme Court. They argued that welfare recipients must be accorded the same constitutional rights of due process and equal treatment as all other Americans. Lawyers successfully challenged residency requirements that had prevented otherwise eligible people from receiving welfare; the Supreme Court held that freedom to travel was a basic right of all citizens, including the poor. A 1967 case established that welfare recipients had a constitutional right to a fair hearing before, not after, benefits were terminated.

Impact As the political climate shifted, welfare recipients became the target of increasing hostility. By 1967, husbandless women made up three-quarters of AFDC cases. Conservative policy analysts attacked welfare for causing dependency and promoting illegitimacy. Emphasis shifted from providing maintenance for mothers in the home to enforcing work norms. In 1967, amendments to the Social Security Act instituted the Work Incentive program, which required welfare recipients deemed employable to either participate in work training, accept work, or be penalized by up to three months of grant denial. To provide incentive, the program allowed recipients to keep the first thirty dollars and one-third of their earnings before the grant was taxed.

Subsequent Events Economic stagnation and low wages during the 1970's accompanied welfare cutbacks. The Omnibus Budget Reconciliation Act of 1981 cut the "thirty dollars and a third" work incentive while adding more stringent work requirements. In 1996, President Bill Clinton signed a welfare-reform bill that replaced AFDC with federal grants to fund state welfare programs.

Additional Information Guida West's *The National Welfare Rights Movement: The Social Protest of Poor Women* (1981) provides a comprehensive study of the National Welfare Rights Organization. Frances Fox Piven and Richard Cloward's *Regulating the Poor: The Functions of Public Welfare* (1993) is a more general look at welfare.

Susan Lehrer

See also Food Stamp Program; Great Society Programs; Medicare; Prosperity and Poverty; War on Poverty; Welfare State.

■ Air-Conditioning

Air-conditioning became widely used in the 1960's, considerably altering social relations and helping to industrialize the South.

The earliest recorded use of air-conditioning was in 1881 when engineers attempted to cool the room where President James Garfield lay dying for two months. In 1902, drawing on related developing technologies of refrigeration and electricity, engineer Willis Carrier used chilled coils to cool the air and remove excess moisture. He devised his first "apparatus for treating air" and patented it in 1906. Originally used in industrial settings, at the New York Stock Exchange, and in the homes of wealthy Americans, air-conditioning was brought into more residential settings in the 1950's by companies such as General Electric and Westinghouse.

In the 1960's, air-conditioning became widely used and turned Sun Belt cities, once believed by northerners to be uninhabitable in the summers because of the severe heat, into desirable locations. As a result, an extensive population shift occurred from northern to southern cities such as Houston, Texas, and Atlanta, Georgia, and life became increasingly privatized when fewer people congregated in the streets and visited on outside stoops in the evenings to escape the heat that lingered in their homes.

Impact Air-conditioning did not simply affect comfort levels; it had a profound effect on American society by causing employment and population shifts, industrialization of the South, and decreased social interaction among neighbors.

Subsequent Events The use of air-conditioning has grown steadily. Most accounts are positive, and very few take a negative view of the social, economic, and environmental effects of air-conditioning.

Additional Information *Air Conditioning America* (1998), by Gail Cooper, provides a look at the effects of air-conditioning on U.S. society.

Patricia Leigh Gibbs

See also Demographics in the United States.

■ Air Force Academy Cheating Scandal

Date 1965

Revelations of widespread cheating on exams in the nation's newest military academy. The scandal raised questions about academic ethics versus the pitfalls of overly high standards.

Origins and History The Air Force Academy, created in 1954 in Colorado Springs, Colorado, hoped to surpass the older academies' prestige by setting very rigorous academic, athletic, and military standards.

Its Honor Code reflected this aim in that cadets could not lie, cheat, or steal—and had to report any cadet who did. Rapid turnover of and misunderstandings between academy instructors created inconsistent and often silly military requirements. These bred resentment and resistance among cadets already under pressure to meet the academy's regimen.

The Scandal In January, 1965, some cadets reported that before the 1964 fall semester's final exams, a cadet cheating ring had stolen tests and sold them to other cadets. Because of the problem's scale and reported threats against the informers, academy authorities conducted an official service investigation. By March, 1965, 109 cadets had resigned. A later investigation revealed that overzealous military instructors drove cadets, especially cadet athletes, to identify more with their peers than with the academy. It recommended greater longevity in academy officers' tours, less emphasis on intercollegiate athletic success, and sensible enforcement of military rules.

Impact Press reports and public opinion either viewed the scandal as a sign of declining national morals or sympathized with the cadets given their unusual circumstances. Another scandal in 1967 generated less interest, probably because more turbulent national events overshadowed it.

Additional Information The scandal is covered in Vance Mitchell's *Air Force Officers* (1996) and John Lovell's *Neither Athens nor Sparta?* (1979).

Douglas Campbell

See also Crimes and Scandals; Education.

■ Air Pollution

Substances added directly or indirectly to the atmosphere by humankind in such amounts as to affect humans, animals, vegetation, or materials adversely. In the 1960's, health problems related to air pollution produced national action.

At the national level, air pollution initially became a topic of widespread concern when President Dwight D. Eisenhower signed the 1955 Air Pollution Control Act. The act did little actually to control pollution but did set up a framework through which local and state groups could fund research efforts and begin to collect the data on which other legislation was based.

At the start of the 1960's, skies were black, gray, or yellowish brown over much of the urban United States. Factory smokestacks trailed long plumes of sooty smoke and emitted chemicals that stained the neighborhoods near the plants. This visible air pollution was accompanied by invisible but even more hazardous substances. New York City, Detroit, Michigan, and Buffalo, New York, experienced episodes of air pollution during which hundreds of people became seriously ill and dozens died because of the high level of pollutants. The major sources of air pollution in the 1960's were combustion of coal or garbage and the refining of ores, although the operating of motor vehicles also soiled the air. Burning coal, which contains a high percentage of sulfur, produces sulfur dioxide and particulate matter, the first contaminants to raise considerable concern, and the processing of sulfur-containing ores also releases large amounts of sulfur dioxide. Driving automobiles and trucks contributes nitrogen oxides to the pollution load. All of these, as well as open burning in dumps, are activities concentrated in urban areas.

Removing some of the particles from industrial waste gases was the easiest and earliest control step taken. Factory smoke was first passed through filters to lower the amount of particulates, then delivered into the atmosphere from the top of very high smokestacks. Although high stacks do not remove anything, they allow better dilution before the emissions come into contact with the earth's surface. These processes greatly decreased the smoke's density, and visually, the pollution appeared to be gone. However, the smaller particles, which are the most detrimental to respiratory health, were not captured by these treatments and were still emitted. Their continued presence made itself felt another way, in the production of photochemical smog.

Smog Photochemical smog particularly affected Los Angeles, where the geography and large population provide the right conditions for producing it. Smog is produced during temperature inversions, when the temperature of the air rises rather than falls with increasing altitude. The inversion creates a cap under which the pollutants—the unburned

Smog blankets downtown Los Angeles. In the 1960's, California led the fight against air pollution by taking steps to reduce the emissions produced by automobiles. (Archive Photos)

hydrocarbon fuels, the sulfur and nitrogen oxides—and the sunlight react and form a complicated mixture of chemicals, including ozone, called photochemical smog. Particulate materials act as catalysts for these reactions and greatly enhance the rate of production of the smog. Photochemical smog is irritating and damaging to the eyes and lungs and is harmful to construction materials and to synthetic fibers. At high levels, smog has been known to melt nylon stockings.

In a second kind of smog, sulfur dioxide and water vapor combine to form very small droplets of sulfuric acid. Sulfurous smog can penetrate deep into the lungs and cause respiratory distress, is harmful to plant leaves, and dissolves some metal and stone structures. Because of the difference in pollutants and sunlight intensity, sulfurous smog is usually found in eastern and central cities and photochemical smog on the West Coast.

Invisible Pollutants During the 1960's, the amount of invisible pollutants—sulfur dioxide, nitrogen oxides, and unburned fuel—was lowered through a number of methods. Factories switched to coal with a lower sulfur content and to very low-sulfur-content natural gas although both of these alternate fuels were more expensive. More efficient combustion processes were developed so that less fuel was left unburned, and a process that captured sulfur dioxide as solid calcium sulfate, a marketable by-product, was used to remove sulfur dioxide from some exhaust gases. By the late 1960's, a number of plants employing nuclear power, an energy-generating method that did not produce gaseous pollutants, had been built. In California, the problem of smog was attacked by adding catalytic converters to auto exhaust systems. All of these efforts were made at local, regional, or state levels.

National Action At the start of the decade, the responsibility for air pollution control resided mainly with municipalities; only a few states had taken action. Air pollution control took on a federal aspect with the passage of the Clean Air Act of 1963, which directed that scientific information be gathered and analyzed and that criteria be published describing the concentration and dosages of pollutants having adverse health effects. Based on this information, states and cities created control legislation or strengthened existing laws. These laws, for the most part, placed limits on smoke density and prohibited

the open burning of trash in dumps and the burning of some fuels with very high sulfur content. The National Motor Vehicle Emissions Standards Act of 1965 took many of California's emissions regulations and made them apply nationally. This resulted in the widespread introduction of nonleaded gasoline to be compatible with the catalytic converters. In the same year, Congress passed the Clean Air Act Amendments, which tightened control regulations. The federal Air Quality Act, passed in 1967, took further steps to provide uniform national air quality standards.

During the 1960's, Americans learned to be more vocal and active in stating their views. One of the issues that attracted attention was the environment, including air pollution problems. Sit-ins, teach-ins, marches, folk songs, and underground publications were all used to create awareness of humankind's impact on the environment. At the start of the environmental effort, air quality was not as great a concern as water quality; however, the highly visible black plumes over several cities changed that. Citizen groups learned to be effective in creating change locally, and their successes drew others into broadening the effort. Citizen concern and involvement were at the base of the positive changes that were made. Industries began to recognize that for both public relations reasons and their economic well-being, they needed to include environmental concerns in their planning.

Impact During the 1960's, air pollution changed from an acute to a chronic problem. Fatal air pollution incidents ceased, but adverse health effects, erosion of building materials, and climatological effects related to air pollution remained. Pollution control efforts resulted in more governmental regulation of businesses and individuals and had economic consequences for industries. At the close of the 1960's, Americans were living in a much cleaner atmosphere that was much less damaging to respiratory health. The most recognizable legacy of the country's battle against air pollution in the 1960's is the catalytic converter, which lowers harmful emissions from motor vehicles. Other efforts to reduce air-polluting vehicle emissions include the production of lighter cars to improve gasoline efficiency and the promotion of car pooling in urban areas.

Subsequent Events Air pollution remained a problem and topic of interest in subsequent decades.

Congress passed the Clean Air Act in 1969 (signed into law on January 1, 1970, and amended in 1977), authorizing the federal government to abate any material introduced into the air that endangered the health or welfare of any person. From this act came federal air quality standards and, in 1971, the Environmental Protection Agency. In addition, the United States, realizing that air pollution does not recognize national boundaries, began to form pacts with its neighbors to help control the problem over a wider area. Amendments to the Clean Air Act have continued to be made as time passes and more information becomes available.

Additional Information *Fundamentals of Air Pollution* (1973), by Samuel J. Williamson, provides a very good overview of pollution during the decade. The American Chemical Society's *Cleaning Our Environment: The Chemical Basis for Action* (1969) looks at methods of controlling pollution. *Air Pollution* (1968), by R. S. Scorer, looks at the subject from a meteorological viewpoint. *Our Chemical Environment* (1972), edited by J. Calvin Giddings and Manus B. Monroe, and *The Environment: A National Mission for the Seventies* (1970), by the editors of *Fortune* magazine, contain useful chapters on air pollution.

Kenneth H. Brown

See also Automobiles and Auto Manufacturing; Environmental Movement; Motor Vehicle Air Pollution Act of 1965; Science and Technology; Water Pollution.

■ Alaska Earthquake

Date March 27, 1964

One of the most powerful earthquakes ever recorded, registering 8.5 on the Richter scale. Because of the region's sparse population, the number of dead and missing was relatively low, about one hundred people.

Origins and History A shift in the Aleutian Trench, one of the fault lines that run from Chile along the eastern rim of the Americas all the way to Siberia, caused the earthquake, which hit at about 5:30 P.M. local time (10:30 P.M. Eastern standard time). The largest previously recorded earthquake on this fault, also an 8.5, had occurred in Chile on May 22, 1960.

The Quake The earthquake's epicenter was the northern edge of Prince William Sound, thirty to sixty miles below the surface, ten to thirty miles in extent, about one hundred and thirty miles from Anchorage, the state's largest city. It was in Anchorage that the greatest loss of life and property occurred. Other Alaska cities suffering major damage were Seward, Valdez, Cordova, and Kodiak.

Metropolitan Anchorage, home to nearly one hundred thousand people, suffered spectacular destruction, much of it the result of landslides. Roads and airfields, including Elmendorf Air Base, were torn up and became impassable. For a time, the city was cut off from the rest of the world. The one-hundred-twenty-mile stretch of the Alaskan Railroad between Seward and Anchorage was virtually destroyed.

The earthquake spawned massive tidal waves, or tsunamis, that rolled through the northern Pacific at five hundred miles per hour. A deadly twelve-foot wave came ashore at night in Crescent City, California, more than two thousand miles to the south, claiming twenty-seven lives. Waves also killed campers at a beach near Depoe Bay, Oregon.

Impact The day after the temblor hit, President Lyndon B. Johnson declared Alaska a disaster area, making it eligible for assistance from federal agencies such as the Office of Emergency Planning. Army troops began to patrol the streets of Anchorage as a precaution against looting.

As damage estimates in Alaska rose to five hundred million dollars, Governor William A. Egan asked for massive federal aid to allow the state to rebuild. Bankers in the Anchorage region, home to nearly half of the state's population, declared that prospects for recovery were hopeless unless Washington intervened since 60 percent of the state's total developed worth had been affected by the earthquake. The state was unable to dig out from under the ruins on its own since it produced relatively little wealth. About half of Alaska's small income of seven hundred million dollars in 1963 came from employment by state, local, and federal authorities. Federal expenditures in Alaska were twice the national per-capita average. Inevitably, it was Washington, D.C., that paid the lion's share for the rebuilding of Alaska's infrastructure.

Subsequent Events Aftershocks continued to shake the area for some time. In the three months following the earthquake, more than twelve thousand aftershocks, the strongest measured at 6.2, were recorded.

Streets sunk and buildings collapsed in downtown Anchorage, Alaska, during this March, 1964, earthquake. The temblor, registering 8.5 on the Richter scale, sent deadly tidal waves crashing into the Pacific coastline. (Archive Photos)

Additional Information For scientific analyses of the earthquake, see *The Prince William Sound, Alaska, Earthquake of 1964 and Aftershocks* (1969), edited by Louis E. Leipold, and *The Great Alaska Earthquake of 1964* (1970-1972), by the Committee on the Alaska Earthquake of the Division of Earth Sciences National Research Council.

Harry Piotrowski

See also Hurricane Betsy; Hurricane Camille.

■ Albee, Edward

Born March 12, 1928, Virginia

One of the most significant and productive American playwrights of the 1960's. Albee, writing with a sure hand and balanced sense of the dramatic, forged new ground with his tightly constructed absurdist plays, often surrealistic in their execution.

Early Life Edward Franklin Albee was adopted when he was two weeks old by the prosperous Reed Albee, an active partner in the Keith-Albee chain of vaude-

ville houses, and Frances Albee, a former fashion model. Albee, something of a problem child, attended a procession of private schools, finally being graduated from Choate in 1946. He enrolled in Trinity College in Hartford, Connecticut, and attended it for three semesters. He became a Western Union messenger in New York, where Thornton Wilder, whom he had met while a student at the Lawrenceville School where Wilder taught, encouraged him in his writing career. During this period, he came to know W. H. Auden, who also supported his writing efforts.

The 1960's Albee published and produced his absurdist play, *The Zoo Story*, in 1959. *The Death of Bessie Smith*, *The Sandbox*, and *Fam and Yam* were all produced in 1960, followed in 1961 by *The American Dream* and Albee and James Hinton, Jr.'s libretto for *Bartleby*, based on Herman Melville's "Bartleby the Scrivener."

Albee's greatest triumph in the 1960's, however, was the production in 1962 of *Who's Afraid of Virginia*

Woolf?, a dazzling play that questions many of America's most cherished values and traditions, such as beliefs about the family and the child-parent relationship. The play received the Drama Critics Circle Award and the Tony Award for best play of the year. The drama jury awarded it the Pulitzer Prize, but its vote was overturned by the advisory board of Columbia University, which administers the Pulitzer Prize, because of the play's strong language and general iconoclasm. This decision caused John Mason Brown and John Gassner to resign from the drama jury.

Ironically, Albee subsequently won a Pulitzer Prize for *A Delicate Balance* (produced 1966, published 1967), although the play was not equal to the standard Albee had set in *Who's Afraid of Virginia Woolf?*, one of the most thought-provoking and insightful plays of the twentieth century.

In one decade, Albee saw eleven of his plays produced professionally, including, besides those already mentioned, *The Ballad of the Sad Café* (pr., pb. 1963), based on Carson McCuller's novel; *Tiny Alice* (pr. 1964, pb. 1965), a play in which a church barters a soul for a donation; *Malcolm* (pr., pb. 1966), adapted from James Purdy's novel; *Everything in the Garden* (pr. 1967, pb. 1968), based on Giles Cooper's play; and *Box and Quotations from Chairman Mao Tse-Tung* (pr. 1968; pb. 1969).

Later Life Although his productivity peaked in the 1960's, Albee continued to write plays in the years that followed. His *Seascape* (pr., pb. 1975) and *Three Tall Women* (pr. 1990, pb. 1991), a play of considerable substance, both received Pulitzer Prizes.

Impact Albee, with plays such as *The Sandbox*, *The Zoo Story*, and *Who's Afraid of Virginia Woolf?*, altered the course of American theater by applying elements of absurdist theater, such as brutal, almost sadistic dialog and frequent non sequiturs, to plays that had broad public appeal. Albee also contributed significantly to the training of future playwrights through his teaching, his work with aspiring playwrights and actors in Houston's Alley Theater, and his service as president of the Edward F. Albee Foundation, through which he has run summer workshops for writers.

Subsequent Events In the 1990's, Albee spent part of each year in Texas, where he lectured at the University of Houston and was affiliated with the experimental Alley Theater. He also ran a center for aspiring playwrights every summer at Montauk on Long Island, New York, under the auspices of the foundation he created and headed. In 1980, he received the gold medal in drama from the American Academy and Institute of Arts and Letters and in 1985 was inducted into the Theater Hall of Fame. In 1994, he received the Lifetime Achievement Award from the William Inge Festival.

Additional Information The best sources on Albee in the 1960's are Michael E. Rutenberg's *Edward Albee: Playwright in Protest* (1969) and C. W. E. Bigsby's *Albee* (1969).

R. Baird Shuman

See also Literature; Theater; Theater of the Absurd; *Who's Afraid of Virginia Woolf?*

■ Alcatraz Island Occupation

Date November 20, 1969-June 11, 1971

A nonviolent nineteen-month occupation of the deserted federal prison on Alcatraz Island by the Indians of All Tribes.

The federal penitentiary on Alcatraz Island in San Francisco Bay closed in 1963. Four Sioux invoked the 1868 Treaty of Fort Laramie, which stipulated that any abandoned federal properties would be turned over to the Indians, and staged a symbolic occupation of the prison on March 9, 1964. On November 9, 1969, fourteen members of the coalition known as Indians of All Tribes staged a second symbolic takeover, determined to bring about change in federal policy regarding the basic rights of Native Americans, particularly their health, educational, and cultural needs. They were expulsed after nineteen hours.

On November 20, 1969, eighty-nine Native Americans occupied and claimed Alcatraz Island on various legal and moral grounds with a plan for the island that involved establishing an Indian museum, educational center, and memorial. The "Isla de Alcatraces," as it had been named two centuries earlier, was claimed "from the fact of previous possession or ownership" under Title 25, U.S. Code 194. Up to three hundred Native Americans occupied the island, but their numbers diminished as negotiations between the Indians and federal authorities failed to produce a plan that allowed the Indians to achieve their goal of self-determination. On June 11, 1971, armed federal marshals removed the last fifteen

Indians from the island, although during negotiations U.S. Attorney J. L. Browning had promised no action would be taken against the inhabitants.

Impact The Native American unity movement of the twentieth century focused national attention on civil and judicial arenas. Issues faced by Native Americans following European invasion and settlement include termination, assimilation, relocation, and impoverishment. Occupation of the island once again focused attention on these issues.

Additional Information Peter Blue Cloud edited *Alcatraz Is Not an Island* (1972), a collection of perspectives on the occupation written by members of Indians of All Tribes.

Tonya Huber

See also American Indian Movement (AIM); National Indian Youth Council (NIYC).

■ Alcindor, Lew (Kareem Abdul-Jabbar)

Born April 16, 1947, New York, New York

One of history's greatest basketball players. Alcindor emerged in the late 1960's as an African American civil rights leader.

Lewis Ferdinand Alcindor, Jr., began playing basketball at age nine. When he enrolled in high school in 1961, he stood six feet, eight inches tall. During his years at Power Memorial High School, Alcindor led the basketball team to two New York City championships. In 1965, he entered the University of California at Los Angeles (UCLA). In each of his three years of varsity competition, he led UCLA to national championships and earned All-American honors. Though he stood seven feet two inches tall, he was quick and graceful; he also developed a trademark shot, the "sky hook," that was virtually unstoppable, and he poured in more than two thousand points in his college career.

During his last year at UCLA, Alcindor emerged as an activist. To protest racial injustice, he boycotted the 1968 Olympics. He also revealed a strong religious side that year, leaving Catholicism to become a Muslim and taking the name Kareem Abdul-Jabbar. He was drafted by the Milwaukee Bucks of the National Basketball Association (NBA), and in 1969, he won the league's Rookie of the Year Award.

After six years with the Bucks, Abdul-Jabbar was

Lew Alcindor, who would become Kareem Abdul-Jabbar, makes it seem easy as he scores two points for the UCLA Bruins. As a pro, he played first for the Milwaukee Bucks, then the Los Angeles Lakers. (Library of Congress)

traded to the Los Angeles Lakers and helped make them a powerhouse. He retired in 1989, having won six Most Valuable Player trophies and six NBA championships; he also held the league's all-time scoring record. In 1995, he was elected to the Naismith Memorial Basketball Hall of Fame.

Impact During his basketball career, Abdul-Jabbar dominated with finesse rather than power. Moreover, as a devout and scholarly activist, he showed that an athlete could be a serious role model.

Additional Information In 1983, Abdul-Jabbar published an autobiography, *Giant Steps*.

Andy DeRoche

See also Basketball; Chamberlain, Wilt; Nation of Islam; Russell, Bill; Sports.

■ Ali, Muhammad (Cassius Clay)

Born January 17, 1942, Louisville, Kentucky

Three-time world heavyweight boxing champion, international humanitarian, and social activist. Although a controversial figure for much of his career, Ali later won wide acclaim for his courageous battles against racism and his opposition to the Vietnam War.

Early Life Cassius Marcellus Clay, Jr., was the eldest son in the middle-class family of Odessa and Cassius Clay, Sr. He spent his formative years in Louisville surrounded by the last vestiges of de jure segregation in the South. At the age of twelve, he turned to boxing to avenge the theft of his bicycle. Clay first rose to national prominence as an amateur boxer in the late 1950's by winning two National Golden Gloves championships, two National Amateur Athletic Union titles, and the light-heavyweight gold medal at the 1960 Olympics.

The 1960's Clay became a professional boxer at the age of eighteen. During the 1960's, with his flamboyant style both inside and outside the ring, Clay transformed boxing from a minor event on the periphery of the American cultural landscape into a mainstream sport. As a boxer, Clay was best known for quickness, accurate punching, and tactical brilliance. He added to his fame with each of his matches through such self-promotional devices as predicting the round of his opponent's defeat or reciting light poetry pertaining to the match. On February 24, 1964, he shocked the sports world by defeating the heavily favored Sonny Liston to become heavyweight champion of the world at age twenty-two. Two days later, he announced publicly his conversion to the religion of the Nation of Islam and his new name, Muhammad Ali. At the time, the Nation of Islam was a small movement that promoted a racial theology that equated white people with the devil and advocated black separatism. Al-

Former heavyweight champion Muhammad Ali (Cassius Clay) addresses fellow members of the Nation of Islam in 1968. One year earlier, he was stripped of his boxing title and exiled from the ring for refusing to be inducted into the military. The Supreme Court overturned his draft evasion conviction in 1971. (AP/Wide World Photos)

though the media became increasingly hostile because of his outspoken opposition to racism, Ali successfully defended his crown until 1967. In that year, Ali was stripped of his title by boxing's ruling powers after he refused induction into the armed services on religious grounds; on June 20, he was found guilty of draft evasion. He appealed, but he was exiled from boxing for three and a half years during his athletic prime. During his exile from boxing, he traversed the country as a public lecturer. Ali was vindicated in 1971 when the U.S. Supreme Court unanimously overturned his conviction in *Clay v. United States.*

Later Life In the 1970's, Ali's boxing career took on epic proportions, as he became the first heavyweight to capture the title three times. In 1974, he regained the title by defeating heavily favored George Foreman in Zaire; that fight, familiarly known as the "Rumble in the Jungle," was the subject of the award-winning 1996 documentary film *When We Were Kings.* In February, 1978, he lost a decision to Leon Spinks, but he regained the title by beating Spinks in a September rematch. His career is perhaps best remembered for his three memorable battles with Joe Frazier. The first, in 1970, was won by Frazier, but Ali won hard-fought rematches in 1974 and 1975.

Ali attempted unsuccessful comebacks in 1980 and 1981. Despite these defeats and his imposed exile at the peak of his career, Ali compiled an amazing professional boxing record of fifty-six wins and five defeats. According to most boxing historians, Ali was the greatest heavyweight champion of all time. Although he served as heavyweight champion for seven years, his persona pervaded American culture and dominated prizefighting for more than two decades. After his final retirement in 1981, Ali devoted his life to his Muslim faith, world peace, educational opportunity, and social justice.

Although he developed Parkinson's syndrome, Ali continued to traverse the globe with his wife, Lonnie, and longtime companion Howard Bingham on goodwill missions to end hunger, promote religious tolerance, and establish universal brotherhood. Such efforts have made Ali one of the most recognized and beloved people worldwide, a status afffirmed by his countless awards, honors, and medals. In 1996, he was chosen to light the torch during the opening ceremonies of the Atlanta Olympic Games.

Impact Ali, more than simply a great boxer, took principled stands against racism and the Vietnam War that placed him in the forefront of American culture.

Additional Information In addition to Ali's 1975 autobiography *The Greatest,* Thomas Hauser's *Muhammad Ali* (1991) and Howard Bingham's *Muhammad Ali* (1990) provide excellent portraits of Ali and his times.

Ronald Lettieri

See also Civil Rights Movement; Draft Resisters; Frazier, Joe; Liston, Sonny; Nation of Islam; Olympic Games of 1960; Patterson, Floyd; Sports.

■ *Alice's Restaurant*

Released 1969
Director Arthur Penn (1922-   )

The classic cinematic statement of the counterculture of the 1960's. It explores an alienated generation's rejection of mainstream culture and its search for meaningful alternatives, especially a new model of community.

The Work Symbolizing the rejection of accepted societal values and icons, *Alice's Restaurant* opens with the deconsecrating of a church so that it can become a home to young people estranged from their families. Alice and her husband, Ray, (Pat Quinn and James Broderick), though they are older, identify with the troubled youths and operate a restaurant to provide money to keep their quasi-commune afloat. Arlo Guthrie eerily plays himself, maintaining a beatific smile of innocence as he encounters various people and situations. *Alice in Wonderland* is suggested both in the title and also in a scene where Alice serves a cake topped by frosting that spells "Eat Me." When Arlo is ordered to report for his draft physical, buffoonish military authorities tell him that his criminal record for illegally dumping trash makes him morally unfit to serve in the U.S. Army. Endearing moments occur when the diverse group of people comes together as a community. In the former church, a kind of communion takes place, with marijuana replacing bread and wine. After the death of a disturbed youth, a touching funeral again suggests community, enhanced by Joni Mitchell's "Songs to Aging Children Come." There are conflicts in this utopia, especially between Alice and Ray, and a very affecting scene brings Arlo to the death-

Arlo Guthrie (wearing hat) waits his turn to be examined during his draft physical in Alice's Restaurant, *a 1969 film exploring the counterculture.* (Museum of Modern Art/Film Stills Archive)

bed of his father, Woody Guthrie. Guest appearances highlight Woody's old folksinger companions, Pete Seeger and Lee Hays.

Impact Released the same year as the Woodstock concert, *Alice's Restaurant* appeared at the height of the counterculture and hippie movements. Even in the soft, almost romantic colors in which it was filmed, it idealized the vision of adolescents and young adults. It suggested a new, purer, nonmaterialistic approach to society, characterized by Arlo and his friends. Recreational drugs and sex, forbidden in conventional society, were accepted. Appropriate ways of making a living were creating craft items, playing music, or (like Alice) running a people-oriented service business. The small-town setting was also important. Stockbridge, Massachusetts, was director Arthur Penn's hometown, and his landscape views of rural New England suggest that the small-town environment is better than that of the city. In a corrupt system, the film says, dropping out may be

the only sane thing to do. This is, above all, a rosy view of the counterculture, and it shows an awareness that this utopia might be illusory. Other films of this period showed a less optimistic view.

Related Works Dennis Hopper's *Easy Rider* (1969) explores a more violent juxtaposition of the mainstream and counterculture, and Bob Rafelson's *Five Easy Pieces* (1970) also highlights intergenerational disharmony. Mike Nichols's *The Graduate* (1967) uses a church and religion to deflate pretensions.

Additional Information An interesting discussion of the films of the 1960's can be found in Frank E. Beaver's *On Film: A History of the Motion Picture* (1983), especially chapters 13 and 19.

Thomas P. Carroll

See also Communes; Counterculture; Draft Resisters; Drug Culture; *Easy Rider*; Film; *Graduate, The*.

■ Allen, Woody

Born December 1, 1935, Brooklyn, New York

Performer, humorist, and playwright. By the end of the 1960's, Allen was emerging as a filmmaker of international stature.

Early Life After brief sojourns at New York University and the City College of New York, Woody Allen (born Allen Stuart Konigsberg), a gagwriter since his midteens, went to Hollywood in 1955, participating in the National Broadcasting Company's Writers' Development Program. He worked as a television writer until 1958, when he began his association with Jack Rollins and Charles H. Joffe, the future managers and producers of his films. They encouraged him to try stand-up comedy.

The 1960's In his stand-up act, Allen developed his persona, a college dropout whose intellectual pretensions often expose his confusions, a sometime idealist comically incapable of living up to his ideals, and a sexual predator whose neurotic insecurities render him terminally dependent on therapy. The heterodoxy and irreverence of the persona's religious attitudes take on an additional comic edge because he has never gotten over being a nice Jewish boy.

In addition to contributing stories and sketches to *The New Yorker* and writing two successful Broadway plays—*Don't Drink the Water* (1966) and *Play It Again, Sam* (1968)—Allen was increasingly involved in films in the latter half of the 1960's. His work as actor and writer on *What's New, Pussycat?* (1965) and *Casino Royale* (1967) provided little in the way of artistic satisfaction, but *What's New, Pussycat?* did well commercially, enhancing Allen's emerging star quality.

What's Up, Tiger Lily? (1966) remains an amusing footnote to Allen's career, but the emergence of Allen as filmmaker may more properly be dated from 1969, the year *Take the Money and Run* was released. Allen was the star, writer, and director, but the film editor, Ralph Rosenblum, imposed on the material a form and pace that had escaped its crea-

Comedian Woody Allen (far left, holding gun) wrote, directed, and starred in this 1969 film, Take the Money and Run. *(Museum of Modern Art/Film Stills Archive)*

tor. Allen was still serving his apprenticeship as a filmmaker, but he would eventually establish himself as a major film artist.

Later Life Allen, who received an Academy Award for direction for *Annie Hall* in 1977, became a filmmaker of international stature. Although many of his films have had limited appeal outside New York City and a few other major urban centers, his critical reputation has grown steadily, and by the middle of the 1990's, he had won a growing and enthusiastic audience in Europe.

Allen's personal life caused a stir in the 1990's when he acknowledged dating Soon-Yi Farrow, the adopted daughter of actress Mia Farrow with whom he had had a long-term relationship and a son. Allen married the young woman in 1998.

Impact No comedian of the 1960's spoke more effectively to the young audience, even if Allen's effect was rather insidious than overt. The scrawny little man—confessing his sexual obsessions and humiliations; affirming his physical cowardice; avowing his neurotic insecurities; articulating his irreverence toward and continuing fascination with traditional moral and religious beliefs and values; and exposing his intellectual aspirations and inadequacies—told young Americans that the old idea of "manly" could be laughed away.

Additional Information The best biography of the actor, writer, and director is *Woody Allen* (1991), by Eric Lax.

W. P. Kenney

See also Farrow, Mia; Film; Social Satires; Television.

■ Altamont Music Festival

Date December 6, 1969

A rock concert, marred by violence, featuring the Rolling Stones and several other bands. Members of the Hell's Angels motorcycle gang, which provided security for the stage, fatally stabbed and beat an eighteen-year-old spectator.

Origins and History The Rolling Stones planned to end their 1969 United States tour with a free concert in San Francisco's Golden Gate Park. The facility at the park was not large enough to hold the one hundred thousand people expected, so Sears Point Raceway was chosen. However, negotiations with Sears Point broke down over distribution rights to a film documenting the tour that the Rolling Stones planned to make. A contract with Altamont Speedway was signed only twenty-four hours before the event was scheduled to begin.

The Festival On Friday, December 5, supplies and equipment were brought from Sears Point Raceway to Altamont Speedway, and workers rushed to prepare the stage. By nightfall, five thousand spectators had already arrived at the concert site, and by 7:30 A.M. Saturday, December 6, it was clear that the estimate of one hundred thousand attendees was too low (actual attendance was estimated at three hundred thousand). Unfortunately, twenty-four hours was not long enough for event planners to make adequate arrangements. Only one-sixtieth of required toilet facilities was provided, and although medical personnel were on site, no arrangements were made for emergency vehicles to get in or out of the grounds. The sound system was not powerful enough, which meant that the music was barely audible to those any distance from the stage, and the stage itself was only four feet high, with no space between it and the audience. Rolling Stones manager Sam Cutler hired the Hell's Angels to provide stage security for five hundred dollars worth of beer.

The Hell's Angels took their job seriously. As a band began to play, the crowd would move toward the stage, and the Hell's Angels, some wielding sawed-off and weighted pool cues, would beat them back. When the Jefferson Airplane began its set, the violence began to spill onto the stage. Guitarist Marty Balin tried to intervene between a Hell's Angels member and a spectator and was punched by the motorcycle gang member. Balin lay unconscious on the stage for a brief period of time.

The Rolling Stones' set was interrupted by violence several times, and both singer Mick Jagger and guitarist Keith Richard threatened to leave the stage if the violence did not stop. One of these interruptions was a scuffle between a Hell's Angels biker and an audience member, Meredith Hunter, in front of the stage. During this incident, Hunter pulled a revolver and was attacked by an unknown number of Hell's Angels. He was stabbed in the back, neck, and head.

Impact Hunter died as a result of his stab wounds, but no one was ever convicted of the crime. Three other audience members also died at Altamont. Mark Feiger and Richard Savloy, both twenty-two

A young woman expresses her joy at being at the Altamont Music Festival, a rock concert featuring the Rolling Stones. During the Stones' performance, members of the Hell's Angels, hired as security guards, fatally stabbed and beat an audience member. (AP/Wide World Photos)

years old, were killed when a car drove through their campsite at the side of the road. The fourth casualty was an unidentified man who slid into an irrigation canal and drowned. The violence at the Altamont Music Festival, which took place only a few months after the peaceful Woodstock Music and Art Fair, proved to many Americans that the peace and love movement, because it was part of youth culture and rebellion, would ultimately fail.

Additional Information The Rolling Stones produced a film documenting their U.S. tour and the Altamont Music Festival entitled *Gimme Shelter* (1970).

Peter S. Seavor

See also Hell's Angels; Jefferson Airplane; Rolling Stones; Woodstock Festival.

■ *American Bandstand*

Produced 1957-
Host Dick Clark (1929-   )

The longest-running variety show in television history. With disc jockey Dick Clark as its emissary, the show became an anthem for American teenagers throughout the 1950's and 1960's.

The Work Originally hosted by Bob Horn, *Bandstand* began in 1952 as a local teenage dance program on WFIL-TV in Philadelphia. Following Horn's dismissal in 1956, clean-cut, charismatic disc jockey Dick Clark took over and within a year had convinced the American Broadcasting Company (ABC) to produce his popular show nationally. Debuting on August 5, 1957, the newly christened *American Bandstand* catapulted to instant celebrity. Thousands of devoted teenagers across the country rushed home from school every weekday afternoon to watch their favorite teenage couples perform the latest dance fads and to see the latest recording stars lip-synch their hit rock-and-roll songs.

Designed to resemble a record shop, *American Bandstand*'s set consisted of a small dance floor, bleacher seating, Clark's podium, and a weekly top ten board. In addition to the regular teenage dancers, the show featured dance contests, spotlight dances, and record review, a segment in which designated teenage guests numerically rated new songs.

Countless hit records originated on *American Bandstand*, and a parade of stars emerged, from teen idol Frankie Avalon to dance king Chubby Checker to pioneering rock-and-roll artists Chuck Berry, the Everly Brothers, Buddy Holly, and Jerry Lee Lewis. In the 1960's, such diverse recording artists as the Beach Boys, Aretha Franklin, Jefferson Airplane, Pink Floyd, and the Temptations made their network television debuts on the show.

In 1963, *American Bandstand* was reduced from weekdays to Saturday afternoons, and soon after, Clark moved it to Hollywood, where he began prerecording in lieu of making live broadcasts. Although diminished in status, the show, with Clark at its helm, endured for more than thirty years. In 1989, Clark retired and the show moved to cable television with David Hirsch as its host.

Impact In an era of common disregard for teenage culture, *American Bandstand* took the lead in forging the nation's growing teenage population as a powerful constituency that could no longer be ignored. The ordinary teenagers who danced on the show became celebrities, igniting the latest dance crazes and launching the latest fashion trends. Albeit slowly, *American Bandstand* also helped to break new ground in race relations, televising white and black teenagers together in a social setting for the first time and giving African American musicians a national stage on which to perform as mainstream entertainers. Using television as a vehicle to promote the upstart rock-and-roll music, *American Bandstand* afforded the genre unprecedented national exposure and a mainstream respectability that had been heretofore outside its grasp. Clark's ability to transform aspiring young singers into stars became legendary, making his show a premier venue in establishing rock and roll as the most popular music in the United States.

Succumbing to the social upheavals of the late 1960's, the rise of alternative FM radio, and the arrival of MTV (Music TeleVision) in the 1980's, *American Bandstand* eventually relinquished its role as trendsetter of the pop music industry in the United States.

Additional Information For a comprehensive history

and divergent commentaries on *American Bandstand*, refer to *Dick Clark's American Bandstand* (1997), by Dick Clark and Fred Bronson, and to *American Bandstand: Dick Clark and the Making of a Rock and Roll Empire* (1997), by John A. Jackson.

Karen L. Gennari

See also Beach Boys, The; Jefferson Airplane; Motown; Music; Television.

■ American Indian Civil Rights Act of 1968

Controversial legislation designed to guarantee that individual American Indians living under tribal governments receive civil rights protections similar to those granted other citizens by the United States Constitution.

In 1961, numerous Native Americans testified before the Senate about infringements of individual rights by tribal governments. Consequently, Congress proposed special titles to the Civil Rights Act of 1964 that sought to protect individual freedoms while respecting tribal sovereignty.

In 1968, when civil rights legislation was proposed to guarantee equal protection for all groups in the United States, Senator Sam Ervin of North Carolina sought to bring tribal governments under the U.S. Constitution. The proposed act extended the federal Bill of Rights and previously passed civil rights legislation to American Indians who lived on reservations. Many tribal representatives opposed the legislation because it threatened self-rule.

After considerable maneuvering by Congressmen Ben Reifel, a Rosebud Sioux representing South Dakota, and Emmanuel Celler of New York, Public Law 90-284, often called the American Indian Civil Rights Act of 1968, or Indian Bill of Rights, was signed into law on April 11, 1968.

Impact The act prohibits tribal governments from interfering with freedoms of speech, religion, assembly, and petition, although tribes may establish an official religion. It specifically requires a writ of habeas corpus and forbids unlawful search and seizure. Free counsel in criminal proceedings is not guaranteed. To ensure tribal autonomy, states cannot extend civil or criminal jurisdiction over reservations. However, this act continues to be viewed as a violation of tribal sovereignty because it imposes non-Indian values on tribal societies.

Subsequent Events A series of federal court cases have upheld the act, consequently limiting tribal sovereignty.

Additional Information *American Indians, American Justice* (1983), by Clifford M. Lytle and Deloria Vine, Jr., places the act within its context in the U.S. legal system.

Carole Barrett

See also American Indian Movement (AIM); Civil Rights Act of 1960; Civil Rights Act of 1964; Civil Rights Act of 1968; Civil Rights Movement; National Indian Youth Council (NIYC).

■ American Indian Movement (AIM)

An organization of Native Americans responding to perceived oppression by the Bureau of Indian Affairs. The group succeeded in bringing to public attention issues involving treaty violations and sovereignty.

A group of Native Americans stand before an altered dock sign that states their claim to Alcatraz Island near San Francisco. Members of the American Indian Movement and other groups occupied the island for about nineteen months. (AP/Wide World Photos)

Origins and History From 1948 to 1957, American Indians lost approximately 3.3 million acres because of the termination and allotment policies of the Bureau of Indian Affairs (BIA). The resulting sense of deprivation and neglect became more pronounced during the 1960's because of a continuing degeneration in Native American health, education, and welfare. Conditions were worsened by the appalling on-reservation social and housing conditions and inadequate representation by the BIA against non-Indian exploitation of reservation resources. As most Americans expressed their concern about problems raised by the Civil Rights movement and the war in Vietnam, Native Americans voiced their dissatisfaction with national decision making by the "old guard" tribal leaders, lack of protection for Indian land and water rights, legal prohibitions against religious and spiritual practices, and desecration of Indian graves by archaeologists.

In an attempt to encourage cultural revitalism, a group of nearly five hundred Indians representing more than sixty-five tribes held a symposium on the University of Chicago campus in the summer of 1960 and drafted the Declaration of Indian Purpose. Elsewhere, Indians mocked Columbus Day and Thanksgiving, staged sit-ins against museums that housed Indian osteological materials and sacred regalia, and protested against injustices and the flooding of sacred and ancestral lands. Demonstrations for Indian rights were a new type of leadership, and many older and more traditional Indian leaders were opposed to violence against the government; they sensed a loss of their position and authority, particularly to off-reservation Indians.

The American Indian Movement (AIM) was established in 1968 in Minneapolis, Minnesota, as a nonprofit organization. Originally the members called themselves Concerned Indian Americans (CIA), but because of potential conflict with the government, they changed the name to American Indian Movement. The organization sought greater self-determination for Native Americans and to have treaty rights upheld.

Activities Under the leadership of Dennis Banks, Clyde and Vernon Bellecourt, and Russell Means, AIM employed the tactics of the black militants. The organization became concerned with police-community relations and problems such as alcoholism, school truancy, and Indian sovereignty. It also provided bondsmen and attorneys. In addition, the group sought to bring about socioeconomic changes through education and increase needed legal-services programs on reservations.

In 1964, some Native Americans had briefly taken over the defunct prison on Alcatraz Island in San Francisco Bay, based on a Sioux Indian treaty that stipulated that unused federal lands would revert to Indian control. In late 1969, the American Indian Movement executed its most dramatic and sustained protest. Several dozen members of the organization, who were accompanied by several non-Indians concerned about their plight, again occupied Alcatraz Island. They retained control of the island for about nineteen months before dispersing or being removed by officials.

Impact Many colleges and universities incorporated Native American studies programs that attempted to achieve reculturation through the teaching of native languages and traditional lifestyles. On-reservation cultural awareness programs were encouraged in order to reawaken spiritual beliefs and practices, restore Indian leadership, teach native languages, and combat alcoholism and disintegration of the extended family. Native American revitalization also brought a greater awareness by the general public of the American Indian's plight, which resulted in federal and private scholarships, more equitable legal representation, and in some instances, a restatement of Anglo-Indian history.

Additional Information Native American militancy and policy were dramatically documented in Stan Steiner's *The New Indians* (1968) and Vine Deloria, Jr.'s popular *Custer Died for Your Sins* (1969).

John Alan Ross

See also American Indian Civil Rights Act of 1968; Alcatraz Island Occupation; National Indian Youth Council (NIYC).

■ American Nazi Party

A white supremacist organization primarily attacking Jewish Americans. The American Nazi Party achieved notoriety through extreme pronouncements on an international "Jewish-Communist conspiracy," displays of Nazi regalia, and street violence.

Origins and History After being introduced to racist writings while in the Navy in San Diego, George

Lincoln Rockwell (born in 1918, the son of a vaudeville comedian) read Adolf Hitler's *Mein Kampf* (1925) and was riveted by Hitler's ideas. In 1958, after moving to Arlington, Virginia, he founded the American Nazi Party. Rockwell, influenced by people such as the anticommunist crusader Senator Joseph McCarthy and the fundamentalist preacher Gerald L. K. Smith, believed that the source of all political evil was an international Jewish-Communist conspiracy (which he referred to as "the Hebes in Moscow") that was itself responsible for such things as the Arab-Israeli War, the American Civil Rights movement, and the "mongrelization" of white people. Rockwell predicted that after a depression in 1969, he would be elected president by a United States grateful for the economic, political, social, racial, and spiritual programs of the National Socialists. He advocated killing Jews and sending American blacks to Africa as methods for "saving" the white race. Rockwell considered other radical right organizations, such as the John Birch Society, too liberal. In 1967, the organization adopted the name National Socialist's White People's Party—an act intended to broaden its appeal.

Activities Underfunded, though well publicized, Rockwell and his followers—dressed as storm troopers complete with swastikas—took part in street brawls and counter-demonstrations, primarily against civil rights. They followed and harassed Freedom Riders through the south in a "hate bus," disturbed the peace outside civil rights meetings, marched against Martin Luther King, Jr.'s fair-housing drive in Chicago, attacked antiwar demonstrators protesting in Washington, D.C., picketed the White House, and staged various racist rallies. Enough attempts on Rockwell's life failed that he considered himself bulletproof. Finally, on August 25, 1967, John Patler, a former member of the American Nazi Party who had been minister of propaganda and editor of *The Stormtrooper Magazine*, shot and killed Rockwell in a laundry's parking lot. His last words were said to be, "I forgot the bleach." Party secretary Matt Koehl succeeded Rockwell as commander.

Impact With a membership usually estimated to be between twenty and one hundred, the American Nazi Party still made its presence known through the antics of Rockwell, dubbed the "Halfpenny Hitler." The American Nazi Party's greatest impact was the

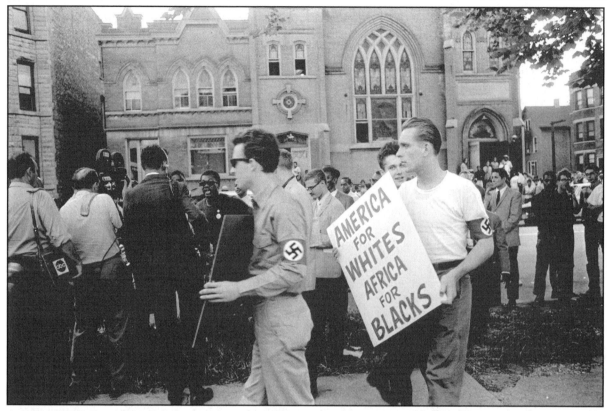

American Nazi Party members protest across the street from a Chicago church in August, 1966. Inside the church, Martin Luther King, Jr., and civil rights activists were planning marches into white neighborhoods. (AP/Wide World Photos)

galvanization of its opposition; few people viewed their presence and activities with anything except revulsion. After Rockwell's death, the organization faded, although offspring organizations continued to exist for several decades.

Subsequent Events In 1977, Frank Collin, a former member of the American Nazi Party and member of a group calling itself the National Socialist Party of America, fought for and received a permit to hold a rally in Skokie, Illinois (a Chicago suburb with a large population of American Jews). The American Civil Liberties Union, viewing the request as an issue of free speech, helped defend Collin's right to secure the permit. The march, however, was never staged.

Additional Information In 1995, Frederick J. Simonelli published *American Fuehrer: George Lincoln Rockwell and the American Nazi Party*; the book provides a thorough discussion as well as bibliographical references.

Sharon Randolph

See also Civil Rights Movement; Decency Rallies; Freedom Rides.

■ Apollo 1 Disaster

Date January 27, 1967

The worst disaster in the nation's race to the Moon. Three astronauts died while performing routine duties in a simulated space flight.

Origins and History The Apollo flights to the Moon followed the Mercury and Gemini programs. Six successful Mercury missions proved that humans could endure the space environment. Gemini astronauts completed five successful missions, one lasting two weeks. These astronauts practiced walks in space and spacecraft rendezvous and docking procedures. The Apollo program would culminate decades of investigations and applications of aerodynamics, rocket propulsion, aerospace medicine, and electronics.

The Disaster The Apollo 1 mission, manned by Virgil I. "Gus" Grissom, Edward H. White, and Roger B. Chaffee, was to verify spacecraft and crew operations and the command service module subsystem's performance for an Earth-orbit mission of up to fourteen days' duration.

Many problems dogged the Apollo program. The spacecraft was held up by problems associated with the water glycol pump for the command module environmental control unit, necessitating a couple of replacement units. When the spacecraft arrived at Cape Kennedy, program managers complained that much of the remaining engineering work should have been completed before the spacecraft left the factory. Training activities did not seem to run more smoothly. Technicians found it nearly impossible to keep up with the multiple modifications needed to keep the training simulator current with changes made to the spacecraft. Grissom finally hung a lemon on the trainer.

By fall of 1966, the Design Certification Review Board met and agreed the spacecraft conformed to design requirements and was flightworthy. On January 27, 1967, an army of technicians ran through the routine checklists. Round-the-clock shifts replaced each other after finishing their checklists and reporting readiness.

Suddenly, during a simulation in the clean room at Launch Complex 34, at 6:31 P.M., technicians heard a cry over the radio circuit from inside the spacecraft, "There is a fire in here." Choking and gasping in dense smoke, technicians finally removed the spacecraft's hatches. By the time firefighters arrived, smoke had cleared enough to attempt to pull the astronauts' bodies out. Just fourteen minutes after the first alarm, the firefighters had great difficulty removing the bodies of Grissom, White, and Chaffee because the molten nylon of the spacesuits had fused from the extreme heat produced by a pure oxygen fire.

Impact Autopsies revealed the astronauts died from asphyxiation brought on by inhalation of toxic gases. It would not be until mid-1969—more than two years later—that acceptable solutions for the many problems evolving from the Apollo 1 investigation could be resolved. The greatest difficulty involved replacing combustible materials with nonflammables in clothing, towels, food bags, and all personal gear. The disaster delayed the mission of reaching the

In January, 1967, a flash fire scorched the Apollo 1 command module and killed the three astronauts inside it. This disaster eroded Americans' confidence in the United States' ability to win the space race. (Archive Photos)

Moon and eroded people's confidence in U.S. space capabilities.

Additional Information Two books that provide further information on the disaster and the Apollo program are *Chariots for Apollo* (1979), NASA History Series, and *Carrying the Fire* (1974), by Michael Collins.

Lillian D. Kozloski

See also Apollo Space Program; Gemini Space Program; Mercury Space Program; Space Race.

■ Apollo Space Program

The space program that put a man on the Moon. On July 20, 1969, the world watched on television as astronauts Neil A. Armstrong and Edwin E. "Buzz" Aldrin walked the Moon's surface, conducted scientific experiments, and collected samples.

In January, 1961, when John F. Kennedy was inaugurated president of the United States, the Cold War, a period of confrontation between the United States and the Soviet Union, was at its peak. During his campaign, Kennedy had charged that the Soviet Union was establishing an image of world leadership and a preeminence in science as U.S. prestige throughout the world was declining.

Nowhere was this decline more evident than in the race to explore space. The Soviet Union had launched the world's first artificial satellite on October 4, 1957. The first U.S. attempt, in December, 1957, was a widely publicized failure: The Vanguard rocket exploded after rising only a few feet. The Soviet Union launched the first spacecraft to orbit the sun in January, 1959, and the first spacecraft to orbit the Moon and return photographs of its unseen far side in October, 1959. Four U.S. efforts to reach the Moon during 1958 all failed.

The Soviet Union launched the world's first space explorer, cosmonaut Yuri Gagarin, on April 12, 1961,

less than three months after Kennedy's inauguration. Kennedy was seeking a dramatic project that would enhance U.S. prestige and demonstrate the nation's leadership in the space race. On May 25, 1961, in an address to Congress, Kennedy announced his objective to land a man on the Moon and return him safely to Earth before the end of the decade.

The Program To accomplish Kennedy's goal, the National Aeronautics and Space Administration (NASA) established the Apollo lunar landing program. This program put twenty-five billion dollars into the economy during the next ten years. Corporations throughout the United States were awarded contracts to develop two new rockets, the Saturn 1B and the Saturn 5, and three new spacecraft, the command, service, and lunar modules.

NASA's plan called for three astronauts to ride into orbit in the command module, a pressurized 11.4-foot-tall cone weighing 5.5 tons, which would sit

In July, 1969, with the Apollo 11, the United States achieved its goal of landing a man on the Moon by the end of the decade. Apollo astronauts planted a U.S. flag on the lunar surface to mark the event. (National Aeronautics and Space Administration)

atop the 363-foot-tall Saturn 5 rocket. The service module, a 15.4-foot-long cylinder weighing 23 tons, was attached to the rear of the command module. The service module carried fuel cells to generate electricity, supplies of oxygen and water, and a large rocket engine to slow the spacecraft for capture into lunar orbit. The lunar module, housed below the service module, was linked to the front end of the command module by a rendezvous and docking maneuver after the spacecraft left Earth orbit. Two astronauts would ride the lunar module to the surface of the Moon, abandon its lower half on the Moon, and ride the upper half back into lunar orbit. There they would rendezvous with the orbiting command module for the trip back to Earth.

Testing In the early 1960's, when these plans were developed, no one had ever attempted the difficult maneuvers for rendezvous and docking of two spacecraft. The Gemini program in the mid-1960's served as a bridge between the United States' "first man-in-space" program, Project Mercury, and Apollo. Gemini spacecraft, each carrying a crew of two astronauts, provided the opportunity to practice docking techniques. At the same time, unmanned Surveyor spacecraft were landing on the Moon, performing engineering tests vital to Apollo, and Lunar Orbiter spacecraft mapped potential landing sites.

The first tests of the Apollo spacecraft were conducted in Earth orbit, to permit a quick return if something went wrong. Tragedy struck the Apollo program on January 27, 1967, a few days before the first manned Apollo launch was scheduled. Three astronauts, Virgil I. "Gus" Grissom, Edward H. White, and Roger B. Chaffee, were killed by a fire in their Apollo 1 capsule during a flight simulation on the ground. A review panel recommended redesigning the Apollo spacecraft to make it more fire resistant. These changes delayed the first manned flight until October 11, 1968, when Apollo 7 was launched into Earth orbit by a Saturn 1B. It carried Walter M. Schirra, Donn F. Eisele, and Walter Cunningham on an eleven-day mission to test the systems of the command and service modules.

On December 21, 1968, a Saturn 5 rocket carried three astronauts, Frank Borman, James A. Lovell, and William A. Anders, on a trip to the moon on Apollo 8. On Christmas Eve, they fired the rocket in the service module, orbited the Moon for twenty hours, then returned to Earth.

Apollo 9, launched on March 3, 1969, carried astronauts James A. McDivitt, David R. Scott, and Russell L. Schweickart on a mission to test the lunar module. Following the pattern of testing each new spacecraft in Earth orbit, this ten-day, Earth-orbital mission involved a thorough checkout of all the lunar module systems, including repeated docking maneuvers between the command and lunar modules.

Apollo 10 carried astronauts Thomas P. Stafford, Eugene A. Cernan, and John W. Young to the Moon in a rehearsal for the landing mission. On May 22, 1969, Stafford and Cernan separated the lunar module from the command module, fired the engine on the lunar module, and descended to within nine miles of the surface of the Moon. However, their mission was a test of the lunar module, and they were not permitted to make the final engine burn, which would have taken them to the Moon's surface.

The Lunar Landing Apollo 11 lifted off from Cape Kennedy, Florida, on July 16, 1969, carrying astronauts Neil A. Armstrong, Edwin E. "Buzz" Aldrin, and Michael Collins on the first lunar landing mission. Even as Apollo 11 flew toward the Moon, the race was not over. The Soviet Union launched an unmanned spacecraft, Luna 15, to return samples of the Moon, in an attempt to beat the Apollo 11 astronauts in this task. However, Luna 15 crashed onto the lunar surface on July 21, 1969.

The Apollo 11 lunar module, named *Eagle*, separated from the command module *Columbia*, where astronaut Collins remained. As the *Eagle*'s fuel supply neared the critical limit, Armstrong piloted it to a landing in the Sea of Tranquility at 4:17 P.M. eastern standard time on July 20, 1969. Armstrong reported the landing with the words, "Houston, Tranquility Base here. The *Eagle* has landed." At 10:56 P.M., Armstrong stepped onto the lunar surface, becoming the first human to set foot on another celestial body. Aldrin soon followed, and they planted a United States flag on the Moon, performed a series of scientific experiments, and collected almost fifty-four pounds of rock and soil samples. They left the Moon's surface on July 21, and *Eagle* docked with *Columbia*, which had remained in lunar orbit. They landed in the Pacific Ocean, were greeted by President Richard M. Nixon, and placed in quarantine for twenty-one days to protect Earth from any lunar microorganisms.

Apollo 12, carrying astronauts Charles "Pete" Conrad, Alan L. Bean, and Richard F. Gordon, was hit by lightning fifty seconds after its November 14, 1969, liftoff. Despite a momentary power failure, the astronauts continued on, landing in the Ocean of Storms, only six hundred feet from an unmanned Surveyor spacecraft. They performed a series of scientific experiments, then returned to Earth with pieces of the Surveyor and seventy-five pounds of lunar rocks.

Impact The Apollo program accomplished Kennedy's objective of restoring the prestige of the United States. In 1968, the Apollo 8 astronauts broadcast a Christmas message to the world as they orbited the moon. In 1969, footage of astronaut Armstrong taking his first step onto the surface of the Moon was televised live and viewed around the world. Scientific experiments conducted by the Apollo astronauts, as well as research on the lunar rocks and soil returned to Earth, provided information on the geology and history of the Moon.

Technology developed in support of Apollo has affected daily life. Smaller and lighter computers, created to navigate spacecraft, led to the desktop personal computers of the 1980's. Miniature video cameras and monitors devised for Apollo led to handheld video cameras and pocket-sized televisions. Sensors, designed to monitor the astronauts' physical condition, are now used in intensive care units in hospitals.

Subsequent Events The Apollo program continued into the 1970's. The flight of Apollo 13 almost ended in disaster when an oxygen tank in the command module exploded. Apollo 14 and Apollo 15, launched in 1971, and Apollo 16 and Apollo 17, in 1972, brought the total number of astronauts who walked on the moon to twelve. The Saturn launch vehicles and the Apollo spacecraft were used in two additional projects. Skylab, the first U.S. space station, was launched by a Saturn 5 on May 15, 1973. During the next nine months, three crews of three astronauts each were launched to Skylab in Apollo capsules. They conducted scientific and medical experiments in space. The first cooperative space mission between the United States and the Soviet Union, the Apollo-Soyuz Test Project, linked an Apollo spacecraft carrying three astronauts with the Soyuz 19 spacecraft, carrying two cosmonauts, in 1975.

Additional Information Apollo 11 astronaut Collins provides a firsthand account in *Carrying the Fire: An Astronaut's Journeys* (1974). John Wilford documents the Apollo program in *We Reach the Moon* (1969), while John Logston describes the politics behind Apollo in *The Decision to Go to the Moon* (1970). Andrew Chalkin's *A Man on the Moon: The Voyages of the Apollo Astronauts* (1994) places the project in its historical context.

George J. Flynn

See also Apollo 1 Disaster; Gemini Space Program; Kennedy, John F.; Mariner Space Program; Mercury Space Program; Space Race.

■ Arbus, Diane

Born March 14, 1923, New York, New York
Died July 26, 1971, New York, New York

One of the nation's most prominent art photographers of the 1960's. Arbus's photographs helped displace traditional art photography and establish the snapshot aesthetic.

Early Life Diane Nemerov Arbus grew up in affluence as her father, David Nemerov, owned a large, stylish department store in New York City. As a girl, she lived in Central Park West and attended a progressive institution, the Ethical Culture School. At age eighteen, she married Allan Arbus. Her career in photography began when she and her husband started taking advertising photographs for her father's store. The couple continued to collaborate and became successful fashion photographers. In 1959, Arbus's career shifted from fashion to art photography after she studied under Lisette Model at New York City's New School for Social Research. Model, who recognized Arbus's unusual talents, encouraged her to pursue her own personal visions.

The 1960's Guggenheim Fellowships in 1963 and 1966 helped support Arbus's abilities to see and convey the bizarre in the ordinary or the ordinary in the bizarre. Arbus quickly gained the attention of the artistic community through her images of people in parks or homes, the wealthy, the poor, and particularly the "freaks," as she called them: midgets, giants, transvestites, and the insane. Many of Arbus's subjects were sharply lighted by some form of frontal lighting and looked directly at her camera, seemingly confronting the viewer. Arbus had the ability to reassure subjects so that they would willingly reveal themselves to her camera.

Arbus and photographers such as Lee Friedlander and Garry Winogrand explored the changing cultural climate of the United States in the 1960's. Through them, distinctions between art and documentary photography were further blurred. Curators, editors, and critics began to pay close attention to the new art photography, especially after the work of Arbus, Friedlander, and Winogrand was showcased in New Documents, a 1966-1967 exhibition curated by John Szarkowski of the Museum of Modern Art. The exhibition, considered one of the landmark shows of the 1960's, received numerous laudatory reviews.

In 1970, Arbus produced a portfolio of ten of her photographs, the first of what was to be a series of limited editions of her work. However, she committed suicide in July, 1971, before more work was completed. Her images have since been included in the permanent collections of numerous museums in the United States and Europe.

Impact Arbus was a leader of the new generation of art photographers who in the 1960's established the "snapshot aesthetic," through which the photograph became an internal, individual, often irreverent, exploration rather than an objective account of reality. The traditional aesthetics of composition and exposure were abandoned by many of the new photographers, who deliberately highlighted the artifice of photography by presenting images that were harshly lighted, unfocused, or framed in confounding manners.

Additional Information Collections of Arbus's images and writing can be found in *Diane Arbus* (1972), edited by Doon Arbus, and *Diane Arbus Magazine Work* (1984), edited by Doon Arbus and Marvin Israel.

Charles Lewis

See also Photography.

■ Architecture

Structures that reflected the attitudes, concerns, habits, and dreams of American society in a time marked by social, technological, and artistic development. The architecture of the 1960's exhibited use of diverse materials and contemporary technology and variances in function and form.

The Pan Am Building (1963) in New York City was designed by American architect Walter Gropius. (National Archives)

In the 1950's, architecture in the United States was at the center of innovation in the field because of the country's wealth, the increasing need for new business and recreational structures, and the high number of architects who had migrated from Europe. Modern American architecture was epitomized by various talented architects such as Frank Lloyd Wright, Ludwig Mies van der Rohe, Eero Saarinen, Walter Gropius, Le Corbusier (Charles-Édouard Jeanneret), and Richard Neutra. From the late 1940's into the 1960's, these architects designed renowned buildings such as Le Corbusier's United Nations Building in New York (1947), Mies van der Rohe's high-rise apartment block on Lake Shore Drive in Chicago (1951) and the Seagram Building in New York (1958), and Wright's Solomon R. Guggenheim Museum in New York (1956-1959). These architects were masters of a modern movement that heralded the combination of innovation, new materials and technology, and a high regard for functionality; they created buildings with innovative designs and function. They also taught and supported a new generation of architects, including Paul Rudolph and Philip Johnson. These younger architects, inspired by the old masters of architecture, took over the reigns of architectural innovation as the 1960's progressed.

Old and New Masters Wright and Mies van der Rohe produced the greatest effect on the architecture of the 1960's. Wright's influence came largely from his ability to combine rich artistic expression with fundamental laws of design to produce exteriors and interiors that were highly functional aesthetic compositions. Mies van der Rohe affected U.S. architectural development by designing buildings that emphasized industry, technology, and scientific proportions. His teaching position at the Illinois Institute of Technology in Chicago brought his ideas and designs to the forefront of American architectural design. Saarinen and Gropius also left their mark on the 1960's through their students and their many building designs.

Expressive architectural design became increasingly popular in the 1960's. Architectural expressionism manifested itself as more curved lines and organic textures incorporated into a building's appearance. At other times, expressive architecture reflected the use and environment of a building. Saarinen's Washington, D.C., Dulles International Airport (1958-1962) embodies a sense of movement and flight in its large, curved roof. His Trans World Airlines (TWA) Terminal Building at Kennedy International Airport (1961) exhibits the same feeling of movement in its birdlike symbolism and the abstract curved forms that dominate its exterior and interior. These designs reflect the technological developments in architecture and the heightened interest in commercial flight. Architects Kevin Roche and John Dinkeloo managed Saarinen's architectural firm after his death and became known for their own distinctive, expressive designs, such as the Oakland Museum in California (1968).

Rudolph was a new-generation architect who became popular in the 1960's. Gropius, known for his Pan Am Building in New York City (1963), was Rudolph's teacher and an early influence. However, Rudolph's building designs rapidly became renowned on their own merits. Rudolph designed the Art and Architecture Building at Yale University (1963) and the Parking Garage in New Haven (1963). Rudolph was particularly interested in building exteriors, and his were typically more organic and expressive than Gropius's straight-line, functional designs.

Another popular new-generation architect was Johnson. Mies van der Rohe, known for his skyscrapers and urban redevelopment schemes such as Lafayette Park in Detroit (1955-1963), was Johnson's teacher and influence. Johnson translated Mies van der Rohe's massive structures into more intimate family houses, museums, and educational buildings. He also incorporated an element of pop architecture into building designs by using colored plastic materials and open spatial forms. Examples of his work include the Museum for Pre-Columbian Art in Washington, D.C. (1963), which boasts nine intersecting domed glass circles for a roof, and the Kline Science Center Tower at Yale University (1964-1966).

Diversity Architects Richard Neutra and Louis Kahn do not belong in either the old or new generation; instead, they represent the diversity of interests during the 1960's. Kahn's work and teachings emphasize his philosophical considerations regarding a structure's integrity, space as the essence of a structure, respect for the building materials, and the use of light to shape a structure. Much of Kahn's most popular work was built in the 1960's. Examples include the Research Institute of the University of Philadelphia (1960), the Unitarian Church in Rochester, New York (1959-1962), and the Salk Institute in La Jolla, California (1964-1968). Neutra also represented an international style and often spoke on his theories of architectural design. His work was usually rectangular, simple, and sensitive to its environment. His influence was especially relevant in California, where landscape could more easily be incorporated into building design. The Los Angeles County Hall of Records (1962) and the Garden Grove Community Church in California (1962-1966) provide examples of his work.

An important architectural firm in the 1960's was SOM, a collaboration of Louis Skidmore, Nathaniel Owings, and John Merril. This firm dominated the increasing market for office space in cities and perfected the functional, straight-edged, glass-and-steel office building. Major designs include the Chase Manhattan Bank Building (1957-1961), the Marine Midland Bank Building (1967), and the Union Carbide Corporation Building in New York City (1960).

Impact Although architectural design experienced many changes during the 1960's, the general style, function, and process of architecture remained largely the same. The influence of established architects was still great throughout the decade. Most of these masters were either designing their last buildings in the 1960's or watching earlier plans be executed. Their later works, and those of the new generation of architects, tended to depict the changes in society, but architectural design in the 1960's still followed a path that had been laid down in the 1950's.

The 1960's provided the field of architecture with stability in that certain architects and common goals and processes of architectural design became established, but the decade also afforded a liberating influence, notably the use of architectural expressionism. Saarinen's expressive curves and symbolism on the TWA Terminal Building were criticized by some critics as being outrageous, but because of the architect's established name and the way he reflected the style of the decade, the design for the terminal building was accepted. The innovative use of building materials emerging in the 1960's influenced building design and also reflected the times. Rudolph, Roche, and Dinkeloo used new materials and deployed structural forms in exciting new ways. Also, the rising need for office space along with the growth in population made it necessary for architects to design buildings that would provide adequate space, which led to an increase in the number of skyscrapers. Although consistency was evident in the designs of the decade, change and innovation were acceptable and, given the decade's climate, often desirable.

Subsequent Events By the beginning of the 1970's, a loss of confidence in established architectural values had begun to emerge. The social failure of housing projects, the energy crisis, the subtle change in societal and cultural values, and the overconfidence of the new-generation architects led to an ideological return to the architectural solutions of the past. Although many of the architectural trends of the 1960's continued through the next decade, they were moderated to the point that innovation and style adaptations slowed down and became more cautious. Still, many notable buildings demonstrated a continuity with 1960's styles. More successful architects of the 1970's included Johnson,

Roche, Dinkeloo, and the SOM partnership. Johnson's work grew more confident in the 1970's with buildings such as the IDS Center in Minneapolis (1973) and the Pennzoil Place in Houston (1976). Roche and Dinkeloo continued their work with the expressive-style demonstrated in the Administration Building of the College Life Insurance Company (1973). SOM grew in popularity through the 1970's as more skyscrapers such as the Sears Tower in Chicago (1974) were erected.

Additional Information General sources on American architecture in the 1960's include Joseph Thorndike's *Three Centuries of Notable American Architects* (1981); *Master Builders: A Guide to Famous American Architects* (1985), edited by Diane Maddex; and Deborah Nevins and Robert Stern's *The Architect's Eye: American Architectural Drawings from 1799-1978* (1979).

Andrea Donovan

See also Art Movements; Geodesic Domes; Urban Renewal.

■ Arms Race

The competitive acquisition of weapons by the Soviet Union and the United States. The destructive power of the amassed weapons eventually reached a point where the very survival of the human race was threatened.

The United States, the Soviet Union, Germany, and other countries pursued separate programs to develop an atomic bomb during World War II. The precise capabilities and effects of such theoretical weapons were not known, but it was generally assumed that they might spell victory for the country that successfully developed them. The United States won that wartime arms race when it dropped two atomic bombs on Japan in August, 1945. The Japanese surrendered within days.

The Race Is On Shortly after the conclusion of World War II, a Cold War arose between the Soviets and the Americans. One of the Soviets' central military goals was to break the United States' monopoly on the atomic bomb, and the Soviets succeeded in doing just that in 1949. From that point onward, both sides were locked in an arms race not only to build more atomic weapons but also to develop more powerful weapons with more accurate delivery systems (such as bombers and missiles). In the early

1950's, both sides developed thermonuclear bombs, which, by utilizing fusion rather than fission, had enormously greater explosive potential.

Clearly, nuclear weapons posed fundamentally different problems for national security than did nonnuclear, conventional weapons. Most obvious was their exponentially greater destructive power, typically measured in kilotons and megatons. Such weapons of mass destruction, as they were called, certainly could not discriminate between soldiers and noncombatants in a war; vast numbers of civilians would necessarily perish. In addition, by the late 1950's, these nuclear warheads were being fitted to missiles with ever-longer ranges, thus making them increasingly difficult to defend against. Both countries competed to achieve a strategic advantage in the number and quality of nuclear weapons. Presumably the country with the larger nuclear arsenal would destroy more of the enemy's population and infrastructure, and therefore would prevail in a nuclear war.

Containing the Race By the early 1960's, both the Americans and the Soviets had acquired enormous arsenals of increasingly powerful nuclear weapons. The thought of actually engaging in a nuclear war became ever more disturbing as major segments of the world's population, and perhaps the human race itself, became threatened with extinction. The rationale for the arms race had gradually been shifting from the quest for strategic advantage to the aim of deterring the other side from launching a nuclear attack. In other words, by the 1960's, both sides were increasingly focused on acquiring nuclear weapons to be used only in retaliation against an unprovoked nuclear attack. The Cuban Missile Crisis in 1962 drove home the point of the dangers posed by the combination of Cold War hostility and nuclear capability and inspired both countries to seek ways to contain the arms race that had continued unabated for almost two decades.

Several different responses to the arms race were pursued in the 1960's. One was the development of nuclear arms control treaties. The 1963 Nuclear Test Ban Treaty prohibited nuclear testing in outer space, under water, and in the atmosphere (though not underground testing), thus slowing the research that facilitates the development of more powerful weapons. (The treaty also stemmed from growing concerns about the effects of fallout on the environ-

ment and people.) Other treaties, such as the Nuclear Non-Proliferation Treaty of 1968, limited the spread of nuclear weapons beyond the five countries that had acquired them by the 1960's (the United States, the Soviet Union, France, Britain, and China).

A second response to the arms race was the attempt to develop antiballistic missiles (ABMs), which could intercept a nuclear attack before it reached its target. In other words, ABMs would permit defense against nuclear attacks, rather than merely retaliation to avenge (or to deter) an attack. The technology necessary to construct an effective ABM defense was in its infancy during the 1960's.

The third response to the nuclear arms race in the 1960's rejected the logic of ABM defense. This approach, which gained popularity by the end of the decade, recognized that the Soviets and Americans had arrived at a situation of mutual assured destruction (MAD). In other words, both countries had acquired the means to destroy the other, but such destruction could be wrought only at the cost of suffering an equally destructive retaliatory attack. The nuclear arms race had brought the world to a point at which nuclear war was entirely unwinnable and therefore irrational. Paradoxically, however, the neutralization of the nuclear threat through MAD could be purchased only by ensuring the mutual vulnerability of both sides to nuclear attack.

The doctrine of MAD was first promoted by the Americans, who earlier seemed to believe that they could remain ahead of the Soviets in the nuclear arms race. By the mid-1960's, the United States conceded that the Soviets had achieved rough nuclear parity, and that further increases in the level of nuclear arms by both sides would be pointless, wasteful, and dangerous. In 1969, a new nuclear arms control process, the Strategic Arms Limitation Talks (SALT), was begun. SALT not only pursued placing ceilings on the quantity of nuclear weapons that could be deployed by both sides (thus establishing an end to the quantitative arms race) but also sought to ban the deployment of ABMs, thereby ensuring the mutual vulnerability of both countries to nuclear retaliation. Banning ABMs would therefore help to institutionalize MAD.

Impact The arms race had a tremendous impact on American society in the 1960's. Most important, it created a sense of vulnerability and even impending doom for many Americans. Surveys revealed that a majority of high school and college-age students believed that they would eventually die in an almost inevitable nuclear war. Particularly in the wake of the Cuban Missile Crisis, many American families constructed nuclear fallout shelters in an effort to survive a nuclear attack. Other outgrowths of the nuclear arms race include civil defense networks, duck-and-cover exercises in grade schools, and the stockpiling of food and water.

The nuclear arms race absorbed a large share of the nation's federal budget. Significant sums of money were earmarked for nuclear weapons tests and development, weapons construction and deployment, security features, espionage, and other considerations. Some scholars have argued that U.S. military leaders and weapons manufacturers took advantage of the international hostility produced by the Cold War to justify allocation of considerable resources to the arms race.

By the 1960's, the economic and social costs of the arms race had spurred large grassroots movements that advocated arms control and generally opposed the priority placed on defense spending. Those antinuclear and peace movements achieved some notable successes by the late 1960's.

Subsequent Events The SALT process, which began in 1969, resulted in an arms limitation treaty in 1972. SALT I, as it was called, virtually banned all ABM systems. The pace of the arms race slowed temporarily, but developments in the late 1970's brought a new round of arms deployments. During President Ronald Reagan's first term, the United States pursued not only new weapons deployments in Europe but also a Strategic Defense Initiative (SDI) designed to resurrect the notion of defense against a nuclear attack. Some critics charged that SDI escalated the arms race to a new level.

In the midst of these developments, a new leader emerged in the Soviet Union. In 1985, Mikhail Gorbachev succeeded a series of aging hard-line Communist leaders and quickly pursued unprecedented domestic and foreign policy reforms. Significant concessions on the part of Gorbachev's regime over the next seven years facilitated a spate of new arms control agreements. As a result, the nuclear arsenals of both countries were reduced by about a third. The end of the Cold War and the collapse of the Soviet Union in 1991 finally brought an end to the bipolar

arms race. Although Russia, the United States, and a handful of other countries retained nuclear weapons, the arms race was over.

Additional Information Some of the better works on the nuclear arms race are *The Nuclear Arms Race Debated* (1986), edited by David Carlton and Herbert M. Levine; Matthew Evangelista's *Innovation and the Arms Race* (1988); William Gay and Michael Pearson's *The Nuclear Arms Race* (1987); and Sidney Lens's *The Day Before Doomsday: An Anatomy of the Nuclear Arms Race* (1977).

Steve D. Boilard

See also Cold War; Cuban Missile Crisis; Fallout Shelters; Nuclear Test Ban Treaties.

■ Art Movements

Visual art movements marked by their diversity. The 1960's movements spawned a pluralism in art that lasted for at least the next thirty years.

The visual art movements of the 1960's, reflecting a decade of frenetic activity and contradictions, appeared and clashed or coexisted with what may have been the last full decade of mainstream modernism. The movements included pop art, minimalism, and varieties of conceptual art from happenings and performance art to process art, earth art, and site installation art.

Pop Art Pop art was the first art movement to consistently take inspiration, in a backhanded way, from commercial art and mass-market advertising. It ushered in the 1960's in the United States with an uproarious commotion and remains the best remembered among the noteworthy art movements of that decade.

By about 1960, a few American painters and sculptors, working independently of and basically unaware of each other's interests, had begun incorporating in their artwork photographic images from films, television news and other programming, weekly magazines, daily newspapers, and especially advertising. The key artists and their signature imagery or themes were Roy Lichtenstein (comic strips, and past art from mass-produced art history textbooks), James Rosenquist (billboard advertising), Andy Warhol (grocery item packaging, celebrities from films, popular music and front-page news stories), Tom Wesselmann (the convention of the classical nude updated via voyeuristic girlie magazines), and Claes Oldenburg (American fast food and ordinary items from office or home, all greatly enlarged). In a parallel track thematically were Jasper Johns and Robert Rauschenberg, although their works used mass urban culture sources more as a springboard to address existing mainstream modernist concerns of form and surfaces.

In 1961, perceptive New York City gallery owners Richard Bellamy (Green Gallery) and Leo Castelli (Castelli Gallery) began to promote some of these artists. The next year, a major art journal responded to the highly recognizable "nonart" imagery as did the mass-media magazines *Life, Time,* and *Newsweek.* The term "pop art," which may sound like American slang, was actually coined by the English art critic Lawrence Alloway a few years earlier while assessing the paintings and ideas of fellow English artists Richard Hamilton, Peter Blake, and Edouard Paolozzi.

Pop art set off a firestorm of criticism because it seemed to embrace commercial art, something mainstream modernists found despicable. It also

Pop artist Andy Warhol displays his latest creation, "Brillo," at a charity art show in March, 1965. The models wear pop art dresses designed by Crazy Horse. (AP/Wide World Photos)

incurred the modernists' wrath because the images were immediate and realistic, again anathema to modernists. Many viewers, including the nonconnoisseurs of avant-garde contemporary art, welcomed the appearance of subjects from their familiar middle-class environment. They also enjoyed the art's humor despite the banality. All this led to a major misunderstanding of the artists' intentions. Pop artists neither emotionally embraced nor hated the bland commercial imagery they appropriated. They regarded it as interesting, new, and outside the modern art dialogue with earlier modern art.

Minimalism In the 1960's, minimal art embarked upon a reductive approach to modern painting and sculpture whereby artists consciously sought to simplify or eliminate materials, forms, external references, color, emotions, spontaneity, and related elements. That purging attitude was part of the goal of repudiating the assumptions of the dominant art movement of the previous decade, abstract expressionism, and to create art in a purer, more rigorous, more literal state. Abstract expressionism in the late 1940's and through much of the 1950's had stressed spontaneity, ambiguity, complexity, biographical introspection, visceral reactions to subjects and art materials, violent color, and often giant canvases. By contrast, minimal art, so termed by 1965, seemed one hundred and eighty degrees from abstract expressionism in its insistence upon simplicity of painted forms (sometimes just a single color or hue) and an almost total absence of brush strokes, especially bravura. Minimal art emerged from the color field abstraction, also called post-painterly abstraction, of the late 1950's with a goal of less complicated abstract imagery and was represented by artists such as Helen Frankenthaler, Ad Reinhardt, and Morris Louis.

Minimal art is best remembered for its distinctive paintings and sculpture. The painter whose work bore the most emblematic features was Frank Stella. He surfaced in 1959 with immense, dark monochrome paintings of subtle, schematic rectilinear outlines—repetitive, angular, intersections or rectangles within rectangles. Those characteristics are found in Stella's so-called Pinstripe series, which essentially launched the movement. A major motivation for Stella and other minimalists was the radical painting stance voiced by Reinhardt in a 1957 issue of *Art News.* Reinhardt's call for change, known as the Twelve Rules for a New Academy (of artistic thought), included no drawing, no color or light, no texture or brushwork, no design of forms, no sense of movement or time, and no subject except the painting as object itself.

As the 1960's progressed, Stella also appropriated selective practices from Johns's maverick experiments with the U.S. flag and targets of the later 1950's, including the preconception of paintings, the adherence to a preset motif, and the regularized repetition of motifs, brush strokes, or colors as rhythm and interval. Initially, the right-angled intersecting image and black paintings satisfied Stella, but their extreme formal reductiveness was eventually deemed more severe than interesting despite the introduction of shaped canvases. To relieve his stark, black enamel abstractions, Stella began to use copper and aluminum colors. By 1967, his stunning protractor-shaped series appeared with multiple, bright Day-Glo colors applied in a restricted manner to clearly demarcate areas of many intersecting protractor shapes. Despite the complexity of the new compositions, the colorful arching bands were self-referential to the composition's closed system. Additional important minimalist painters noted for chromatic scale and shaped canvases include Brice Marsden, Robert Mangold, and possibly Ellsworth Kelly.

The reductive geometry of minimalist painting spread to sculpture and found an articulate spokesperson in Donald Judd. The artist had abandoned painting for sculpture in 1961, totally disenchanted with pictorial illusionism. By 1963, Judd had produced enclosed boxlike volumes in metal and other constructions in pipe and wood. His delight in tangible objects of mass in actual space may also be indebted to his interest in the eighteenth century empiricist philosopher David Hume of Scotland.

By 1965-1966, Judd's metal boxes were being fabricated by a foundry in galvanized iron and in anodized aluminum. The choice of foundry fabrication instead of personal handicraft was a matter of Judd's conceptual aesthetic. Commercial fabrication (entirely to Judd's specifications) plus automobile lacquer finishes and identical unit arrangement in series meshed easily with his newly adopted artistic theory of detachment, providing something both industrial and commercial. Joining Judd with related sculpture interests were Tony Smith (steel cubic box forms scaled to specific sites in nature and conceived

as holistic images—to be seen all at once as a single form); Carl Andre (arrangements of sawed wood pieces twelve by twelve by thirty-six inches stacked like bales of hay and later similar explorations of industrial materials such as fire bricks followed by flat sheets of steel and magnesium emphasizing their mass and form); and Dan Flavin (white or green fluorescent tubes and fixtures, singly or in groups, investigating light as choreography and sculpture as space instead of form).

Minimal art was initially shocking to many art critics and to untold numbers of viewers. It seemed empty, too reductive, neutral, impersonal, mechanical, chilling in its apparent lack of symbolic quality, monotonous, repetitious but not in a rhythmic sense—in a word, boring. Those reactions were understandable considering minimal art came after the romantic hyperbole and grand manner of abstract expressionism. Furthermore, minimal art was almost exactly contemporary with pop art with its easily recognizable and occasionally witty imagery. For other viewers, minimal art bordered on the sinister, with its overtones of aggression and authoritarianism and because it symbolized the presumed power of white male artists, their dealers, and the rest of the art business world. Perhaps viewer frustration was also rooted in the level of concentration needed when looking at the stripped-down singleness of minimalist paintings and sculpture. Ironically, this art movement, which stood for the reduction, negation, and simplification of so much of the fullness of previous modern art, generated a disproportionate amount of polemic. Minimalist artists may have written the bulk of the commentary about their sometimes complicated motivations for the seemingly simple works.

Conceptual Art Conceptual art sprouted in the United States and Europe during the 1960's as an attempt to re-radicalize avant-garde art by emphasizing the thinking processes involved in creating art instead of the visual and emotional responses to it. At first, the art was often something not to be bought and sold and exhibited in galleries or art museums but placed in remote stretches of the landscape and often not seen except by documenting photographers and not written about by critics and art reviewers but by the artists themselves.

On October 23, 1960, artist Yves Klein leapt out of a second-story window of a Paris building in a soaring position as a demonstration of flying and levitation. Assistants for his art action broke his fall with a tarpaulin, but the tarp and his helpers were cut out of the altered photograph, resulting in a frightening image. Klein's bizarre gesture, rooted in a desire for a brave new future of levitation and the immaterial presence, hinted at the astounding actions, events, and site works that would appear throughout the decade.

Conceptual art also grew out of events in the late 1950's called happenings. In 1958, artist and critic Allan Kaprow combined the need to go beyond Jackson Pollock's use of spontaneity and the arbitrary sculpture of Johns and Rauschenberg in attempts at randomly fusing urban cultural artifacts with sounds emanating from radios and his own unstructured performances. Kaprow's 1959 work *Eighteen Happenings in Six Parts*, held at the Reuben Gallery in New York City, combined untrained actors with the artist's relatively unplanned performance.

Other happenings were organized by various art-world notables, including Henry Geldzaher of the Metropolitan Museum of Art in New York City, and artists Rauschenberg, Oldenburg, and Red Grooms. Collectively, happenings tended to consist of viewer participation, interruptions, layers of stimuli somewhat assaulting participants and viewers alike (though little of it verbal), chaos, and no clear ending. Happenings intrigued audiences as a potentially revolutionary art form.

Concurrently, other artists similarly inclined to de-emphasize art as objects created nonpaintings on large wall panels. These works featured, for example, photo-enlarged typeset dictionary definitions of words such as "art" or "idea," reflecting an interest in communication, linguistics, semiotics, and the construction and deconstruction of information. Involved artists were Joseph Kosuth, John Baldessari, Bruce Nauman, Donald Burgy, Lawrence Weiner, Hans Haacke, and Dan Graham.

Simultaneously, the artists Eva Hesse, Keith Sonnier, Lynda Benglis, Richard Serra, and Nauman explored the physical nature of various materials, some used in contemporary sculpture and some not, and a number of concepts of process in art. Benglis poured amorphous shapes of bright-colored latex and also created blubberlike mounds of colored polyurethane foam shaped by chance. Serra's flung molten metalworks of 1968-1969, documented by menacing photographs of that process, seemed to

parallel the reckless violence of the United States during the 1960's. In those years, Serra melted lead, ladled it out, and assuming a stance similar to that of a hammer-throwing athlete, slung the hot material toward the walls of a New York City warehouse. The Splashings and Castings that resulted, a kind of antiform sculpture, depended on the amount of lead thrown, the number of times it was thrown, force or velocity, and gravity.

Still another outlet for conceptual art was performance art, which was the province of artists such as Nauman, Laurie Anderson, Nam June Paik, Chris Burden, and Joseph Beuys. Artists of this mind-set may have been the most rebellious of all the categories in conceptual art. These artists revolted against perceived restrictions of inherited forms of modern art and even the other subcategories of conceptual art. Performance artists assumed roles as actors, seers, and shamans. Best known among them was Beuys, a German sculptor who lectured and performed internationally and also wore the hat of an activist and shaman from the 1960's until his death in 1986. He ambitiously explored ways to heal artists' grievances with educational and commercial art-world institutions in addition to elemental ways for humans to live and work without destroying the earth. Beuys gave the name of "social sculpture" to his multifaceted performance activities, which were laden with myth, legend, and history.

A final area of conceptual art is earth and site works, also known as artists working in the landscape. By whatever name, the movement within a movement produced some of the largest, most breathtaking, most photogenic, and sometimes, the most exasperating works in all of conceptual art. Artists included Michael Heizer, Robert Smithson, Charles Simmonds, Richard Long, Nancy Holt, Walter De Maria, and Christo Javacheff(known as Christo) and his collaborator wife, Jeanne-Claude. A representative survey must list Robert Smithson's *Spiral Jetty* (1969-1970), wherein rocks and earth were bulldozed from an oil-prospecting despoiled site along the shore of the Great Salt Lake, Utah, out into the lake to form a narrow, shallow road bed in the shape of a spiral fifteen hundred feet in length. *Spiral Jetty* was motivated by Smithson's interest in entropism, that is, the decay and rate of decay of all matter, including *Spiral Jetty*.

However, the stage for earth and site art in the 1960's was dominated by Christo and Jeanne-

Claude. Christo fled communist Bulgaria, his native country, by hiding in the trunk of a vehicle. Never forgetting the experience of being packaged on his way to freedom, he began to wrap items to make the general public more aware of parts of the urban or rural environment that were abused or taken for granted. As his wrapping projects grew larger, he sold drawings, collages, and photomontages of his current and future works to finance his projects. The raising of money was mostly supervised by his indispensable partner Jeanne-Claude. In 1969, Christo wrapped the exterior of the Contemporary Art Museum in Chicago. All Christo's projects were intended to be temporary, so the shroud was removed after two weeks.

Conceptual art, in most of its varieties or subcategories, was generally greeted by both the critical and general press with bafflement. The artworks and art actions, especially those judged as extreme, prompted many critics to wonder if conceptual art might mean the end of painting. Others feared that it might be the end of art, given its antiart provocational overtones. The general public found most of it ridiculous, disappointing, ugly, incomprehensible, and unfulfilling. However, conceptual art was gradually accepted by galleries and museums, many of which seemed to prostrate themselves before it rather than be seen as bourgeois or rear guard.

Impact The heyday of pop art was 1961 to 1964. After 1965, the most original of the circle of pop artists seemed more interested in pursuing individual exploration than group continuity. However, exhibitions of pop art increased and became more inclusive, with artists from Chicago and Los Angeles adding diversity and variety. Publications of pop art increased as did gallery sales, all to meet increased demand. By then, the audacity and novelty of this new art passed into acceptance, a maturing of styles, analyses, and the solidification of careers for its leading artists. By the later 1960's, the blatant urban imagery, especially from photographs, was intriguing a scattering of younger artists. Such artists, primarily painters, were quick to value the flattened surrogate reality of the photograph as information already in usable format for their flat canvases. They collectively launched photo-realism, the dominant painting movement of the 1970's in American art.

Minimalist art, which lacked the easily identifiable and accessible images of pop art, was far less popular. The progression of minimalist painting and sculpture toward a possibly irreducible image or structure, (otherwise known generally in modern art as the emptying out of content), may have contained the seeds of both its own loss of impetus and a generation of newer phenomena.

Conceptual art, like pop art, found greater acceptance as it matured. Most of the conceptual artists continued their explorations and investigations in subsequent decades, and their activities increasingly gained sponsors, patrons, gallery affiliation, and museum recognition. Conceptual art, more than any of the other avant-garde episodes or movements of the 1960's, stimulated an artistic pluralism fraught with even more tendencies, directions, and crosscurrents.

Additional Information Among the first books to document pop art were *Pop Art* (1966), by Lucy Lippard; *Pop Art Redefined* (1969), by John Russell and Suzi Gablik; and *American Pop Art* (1974), by Lawrence Alloway. *Pop Art: A Continuing History* (1990), by Marco Livingstone, follows the primary vein of the pop art phenomena in the United States, England, and parts of Western Europe up to the 1980's. Early works that examined minimalism in 1960's painting and sculpture were Gregory Battcock's *Minimal Art: A Critical Anthology* (1968); Judd's *Donald Judd Complete Writings, 1959-1975* (1975); and *Frank Stella: The Black Paintings* (1976), by Brenda Richardson. In 1995, Sidney Guberman's *Frank Stella: An Illustrated Biography* presented a richly illustrated and informative study of Stella's long career in painting, sculpture, and collaborative experimental prints with Ken Tyler of Tyler Graphics. A book that fit the stances of conceptual art when they seemed radical and raw was *The New Avant-Garde* (1970), by Gregiore Muller. Another important early study was sculptor and writer Ursula Meyer's *Conceptual Art* (1972), a key work that presents thirty-nine statements from and interviews with artists, with numerous illustrations. A noteworthy survey of artists working in the landscape is *Earthworks and Beyond* (1984), by John Beardsly. A later book that focused on site-specific works for museum settings is *Blurring the Boundaries: Installation Art, 1969-1996* (1996), with essays by Hugh M. Davies and Ronald J. Onorato.

Tom Dewey II

See also Happenings; Hesse, Eva; Lichtenstein, Roy; Media; Minimalism; Pop Art; Warhol, Andy.

■ Ashe, Arthur

Born July 10, 1943, Richmond, Virginia
Died February 6, 1993, New York, New York

The first African American man to achieve international prominence in tennis. Ashe used his fame to address a variety of issues dealing with human rights.

Early Life Arthur Robert Ashe, Jr., grew up in Richmond, Virginia, where his father was a public parks supervisor. After his mother died when he was six, Arthur and his brother, Johnnie, spent much time at their neighborhood park, and Arthur soon became one of the best young tennis players in the city. At the age of ten, Ashe, encouraged by various role models, began spending his summers traveling the country playing tournaments sponsored by the American Tennis Association. Despite facing segregation in sports and society, he eventually established himself as the premier high school tennis player in the nation.

Arthur Ashe, the top African American tennis player during the turbulent 1960's, became an outspoken champion of human rights. (Edward Hausner/New York Times Co./Archive Photos)

The 1960's Ashe earned a tennis scholarship to the University of California at Los Angeles, in 1961, where he would ultimately win national collegiate singles and doubles championships. During his college career, he continued to develop the composure for dealing with the many pressures he faced both on and off the tennis court. Ashe remained an amateur until after his landmark victory in the 1968 U.S. Open, a tournament that helped establish tennis as a major sport. That same year, he competed on the victorious U.S. Davis Cup team, for which he would also play in 1969 and 1970. In 1969, he contributed to the formation of the Association of Tennis Professionals; that same year, after being denied a visa to participate in a tournament in South Africa because of his race, he began to work to heighten global awareness of apartheid policies. This represented a turning point for Ashe, as he recognized his visibility and influence and began to devote himself to causes beyond tennis.

Later Life Though Ashe did not dominate tennis during his playing career, he did collect wins over the greatest names in the sport. His 1975 Wimbledon championship was the highlight of his three Grand Slam championships and more than eight hundred career victories. Following his retirement from professional tennis, Ashe became involved in writing, broadcasting, and human rights causes. In 1988, Ashe learned that he had contracted AIDS as a result of a blood transfusion he had been given during an earlier surgery. Although he initially sought to keep the nature of his illness private, in 1992 he announced it publicly in response to media pressure. The remaining ten months of his life witnessed an outpouring of compassion and support in tribute to his courage in raising AIDS awareness for victims and their families to a new height.

Impact Ashe became the leading African American male tennis player during a turbulent time in U.S. history. His accomplishments helped to increase the sport's popularity, and he championed causes that transcended simple athletics. He is remembered as much for how he competed as for what he won. Ashe, who had to overcome many obstacles because of segregation, became an articulate spokesperson for human rights and AIDS awareness.

Subsequent Events In 1997, the United States Tennis Association named its tennis stadium in Flushing Meadows, New York, after Ashe.

Additional Information Arnold Rampersad co-authored a memoir with Ashe entitled *Days of Grace*, published in 1993.

P. Graham Hatcher

See also Hard, Darlene; King, Billie Jean; Sports; Tennis.

■ Assassinations of John and Robert Kennedy and Martin Luther King, Jr.

The assassinations of President John F. Kennedy, his brother Senator Robert F. Kennedy, and the Reverend Martin Luther King, Jr. These three assassinations shocked Americans and profoundly changed the nation's politics and society in the 1960's.

Although three of the first thirty-four U.S. presidents had been assassinated, many Americans in the early 1960's believed that political assassinations such as those of Presidents Abraham Lincoln in 1865, James Garfield in 1881, and William McKinley in 1901 were part of distant history.

During the 1960 presidential election, few Americans expected that either candidate—Senator John F. Kennedy from Massachusetts or Vice President Richard M. Nixon—would significantly change American society. Kennedy won an extremely close election on November 8, 1960. When he was inaugurated on January 20, 1961, he was forty-three years old, making him the youngest person ever elected president. He was also the first Roman Catholic president.

Although Kennedy, his wife, Jacqueline, and their two young children, Caroline and John, Jr., were popular with the public, the new president quickly made enemies because of his efforts to end segregation. He ordered federal troops to enforce the inte-

President John F. Kennedy and his wife, Jacqueline, ride in a motorcade down a Dallas street moments before he was fatally shot on November 23, 1963. (AP/Wide World Photos)

Martin Luther King, Jr., stands on the balcony of the Lorraine Hotel in Memphis, Tennessee, the day before he was killed, flanked by Ralph Abernathy (wearing a tie) and Jesse Jackson. Joining the group is Hosea Williams. (AP/Wide World Photos)

gration of the Universities of Alabama and Mississippi despite strong opposition from the Ku Klux Klan and many white southerners, including Alabama governor George Wallace. Similarly, his brother Robert F. Kennedy, in his position as attorney general, made several enemies through his prosecution of violent southerners opposed to integration, Mafia gangsters, and corrupt union officials, including Jimmy Hoffa, the head of the Teamsters. The Reverend Martin Luther King, Jr., was an eminent and eloquent civil rights leader. In his famous "I Have a Dream" speech, delivered to a crowd of at least 250,000 gathered around the Lincoln Memorial in Washington, D.C., on August 28, 1963, King presented his dream of a unified United States in which citizens would be judged by their character and accomplishments and not by the color of their skin. Later that day, President Kennedy received King at the White House and reaffirmed his commitment to end segregation in the United States. These three leaders, though admired by many, were de-

spised by some of those who opposed their views.

Many Americans were appalled by violent incidents such as the beating of civil rights activists in Birmingham, Alabama, and the bombing of African American churches; however, most people did not believe that violence might take the lives of their most distinguished political and social leaders. During the fall of 1963, most Americans thought that things would work out for the best in the country.

John F. Kennedy In an effort to improve his chances of carrying Texas in the 1964 presidential elections, President John F. Kennedy, along with his wife, Jacqueline, and Vice President Lyndon B. Johnson, flew to Dallas, Texas. A victory in Texas, Johnson's home state, was strategically important for the Democrats. The trip was one of the first public appearances in months for Jacqueline Kennedy, who had been in mourning after the death of her newborn son, Patrick, in August, 1963. On November 22, the Kennedys and Johnson and his wife, Lady Bird, rode in separate open limousines from Love Field toward downtown Dallas, where the president was to speak. At approximately 12:30 P.M. central standard time, the president was shot. He was dead on arrival when his limousine reached Parkland Memorial Hospital. Johnson took the oath of office that afternoon in *Air Force One* at Love Field.

That same afternoon, Lee Harvey Oswald was arrested for the murders of President Kennedy and Dallas police officer J. D. Tippit. Oswald was killed two days later by Jack Ruby as Oswald was being transferred to another jail. The weekend after the assassination was a period of public mourning. With disbelief and sorrow, people watched the transfer of President Kennedy's body to the Capitol Building, where it lay in state, and his burial in Arlington National Cemetery on Monday, November 25, 1963. Although the Warren Commission, chaired by Chief Justice Earl Warren, affirmed that Oswald alone had killed President Kennedy, many Americans rejected this theory.

Martin Luther King, Jr. The Reverend Martin Luther King, Jr., was probably the most eminent civil rights leader of the 1950's and 1960's. His father was a clergyman in Atlanta, Georgia, and King also became a clergyman after he received his doctorate from Boston University. King became involved in leading nonviolent resistance to segregation in the United States. For his peaceful efforts to end racism, King was rewarded with the Nobel Peace Prize in 1964. He began to travel extensively to support minority groups across the United States.

In late March, 1968, he was asked to go to Memphis, Tennessee, where African American sanitation workers had gone on strike to protest the decision of the Memphis government to pay higher wages to white employees. After the murder of an African American teenager, rioting broke out in Memphis. King did his best to restore peace to the racially divided city, and he thought that his efforts had succeeded. On the evening of April 4, while he was speaking with his colleagues, Ralph Abernathy and Jesse Jackson, on the balcony of the Lorraine Hotel in Memphis, King was shot and died almost instantly. Many African Americans believed that this assassination was racially motivated, and rioting broke out in many cities. Calm returned when President Johnson declared April 7, 1968, to be a day of national mourning and ordered flags to be flown at half mast.

Two months later, James Earl Ray was arrested in London for the murder of King. In 1969, upon the advice of his lawyer, Ray pled guilty to King's murder and was sentenced to life in prison. Just three days later, he tried to revoke his plea and spent the next twenty-nine years trying to prove his innocence and obtain a trial. Many people, including King's own children, believed that Ray had not acted alone, that others were involved in King's assassination. Still seeking a trial, Ray died of liver and kidney disease in April, 1998.

In 1986, President Ronald Reagan declared King's birthday, January 15, a national holiday.

Robert F. Kennedy Robert F. "Bobby" Kennedy directed his brother's 1960 presidential campaign and later served as his attorney general. In 1964, Kennedy decided to run against the Republican incumbent, Kenneth Keating, for a Senate seat from New York State. He defeated Keating in November, 1964.

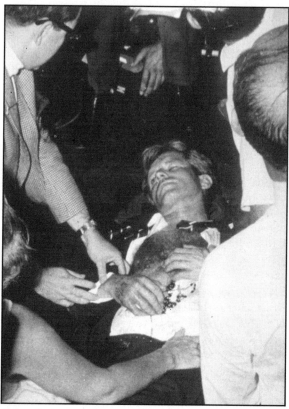

Robert F. Kennedy lies on a kitchen floor in the Ambassador Hotel in Los Angeles, felled by an assassin's bullet just after winning the California Democratic primary in June, 1968. (Popperfoto/Archive Photos)

Kennedy came to oppose U.S. involvement in Vietnam. In early 1968, both he and Senator Eugene McCarthy from Minnesota ran against President Johnson for the Democratic presidential nomination. When Johnson stated on March 31, 1968, that he would not run for reelection, Kennedy became the front-runner.

The decisive primary election took place in California on June 4. With very strong support from Latino and African American communities, Kennedy won this primary, and his nomination at the Chicago Democratic National Convention in August, 1968, seemed all but certain. After Kennedy had given a victory speech in the Ambassador Hotel in Los Angeles, he set off for a press conference. While passing through a kitchen on his way to the exit, he was shot several times at close range by Sirhan Sirhan, a Palestinian opposed to Kennedy's strong support for Israel. Kennedy died early in the morning of June 6.

In 1969, Sirhan was convicted of first-degree murder and was sentenced to death. He avoided execution when the U.S. Supreme Court in 1972 ruled that capital punishment laws were unconstitutional. Sirhan's death sentence was commuted to life in prison. Kennedy was buried in Arlington National Cemetery next to his brother, John.

Impact These three assassinations had significant effects on American society. After John F. Kennedy's death, President Johnson successfully implemented many of Kennedy's domestic policies, including the passage of civil rights legislation, but he also expanded U.S. involvement in Vietnam. King's assassination had an adverse effect on race relations in the United States because many African Americans came to believe that King's policy of nonviolence simply did not work and turned to more militant means of achieving civil rights, alienating many white civil rights activists. The death of Robert F. Kennedy prevented Democrats from remaining united and made it easier for the Republican candidate, Nixon, to win the 1968 presidential election.

The assassinations of three very distinguished political leaders within five years made people understand the reality of violence in U.S. society and also made it too dangerous for leading political figures to have much direct contact with the public. These deaths, coupled with unsuccessful attempts on the lives of Presidents Gerald Ford and Ronald Reagan, have made citizens take very seriously the choice of vice president because they realize that the assassination of the president of the United States is a real possibility.

Subsequent Events Numerous Americans firmly believe that conspiracies were involved in the assassinations of President Kennedy and King. The report of the Warren Commission, which affirmed that Oswald had single-handedly killed President Kennedy, has been viewed by many people as highly questionable. In 1976, the U.S. House of Representatives appointed a select committee on assassinations. In its final report, submitted to the House of Representatives on March 29, 1979, this committee concluded that President Kennedy had probably been killed as the result of a conspiracy. Similar arguments were presented in Oliver Stone's popular 1991 film *JFK*. The sloppiness of the autopsy performed on President Kennedy and the many inconsistencies in the Warren Commission's report have made conspiracies theories seem very plausible.

A similar belief in conspiracies exists concerning the assassination of King. Many people feel that it is inconceivable that a minor criminal such as Ray could have had enough money to travel to England and avoid capture for two months after King's murder. Many people believe that others were involved both before and after the assassination. For years after initially pleading guilty, Ray repeatedly claimed to be innocent and sought a trial. In 1997, ballistic tests performed on the rifle that was supposed to have been used to kill King suggested that the fatal shot may not have come from this rifle.

While he was imprisoned in California, Sirhan spoke of his desire to kill Senator Edward "Ted" Kennedy. Once this information was revealed to the public, it became clear that the California Board of Prison Terms would never release Sirhan on parole. His appeals for parole were repeatedly turned down in the 1980's and 1990's.

Additional Information For more information on these three assassinations, consult *Three Assassinations: The Deaths of John and Robert Kennedy and Martin Luther King* (1971), edited by Janet M. Knight; *King Remembered* (1986), by Flip Schulke and Penelope Ortner McPhee; *Shadow Play: The Murder of Robert F. Kennedy, the Trial of Sirhan Sirhan, and the Failure of American Justice* (1997), by Lester and Irene David, William Klaber, and Philip H. Melanson; and *Presi-*

dent Kennedy: A Profile of Power (1993), by Richard Reeves.

Edmund J. Campion

See also Democratic National Convention of 1968; "I Have a Dream" Speech; Johnson, Lyndon B.; Kennedy, John F.; Kennedy, Robert F.; King, Martin Luther, Jr.; Warren Report.

■ Astrodome, Opening of

Date April 9, 1965

At its opening, the largest domed sports arena in the world. Built as a reflection on the geodesic dome, the Astrodome was the world's first air-conditioned all-purpose domed sports facility.

In 1962, Houston, Texas, was granted a baseball franchise as part of the expansion taking place in the National League. Judge Roy Hofheinz, owner of the Houston club and former mayor, was an acquaintance of R. Buckminster Fuller, designer of the geodesic dome. Hofheinz decided to apply the principle of the dome to a new type of baseball stadium that would replace the open-air stadium then in use.

The Astrodome, used for both baseball and football, was built at a cost of $31.6 million to the citizens of Harris County. Officially named the Harris County Domed Stadium, it was often referred to as the Eighth Wonder of the World. The stadium officially opened on April 9, 1965, hosting an exhibition game between the New York Yankees and the Houston Astros. Governor John Connally threw out the first pitch, and President and Mrs. Lyndon B. Johnson were among the 47,876 fans in attendance.

The dome, at its highest point, reaches 208 feet. The roof originally contained 4,796 panes of glass, and the field consisted of a special strain of Bermuda grass. However, the glare made observing difficult, and the glass was painted over. The grass was replaced with a synthetic variety called Astroturf.

Impact The Astrodome was the first of numerous similar enclosed sports facilities built throughout the United States. Though purists decried the effect that playing indoors had on sports, such arenas minimized the element of weather as a factor in scheduling professional sporting events.

Additional Information Though a book for young readers, *The Houston Astrodome* (1996), by Craig A. Doherty and Katherine M. Doherty, gives much basic information about the construction and history of the Astrodome.

Richard Adler

See also Baseball; Football; Sports.

■ Automobiles and Auto Manufacturing

The product of industry and technology that became central to life in the United States. During the 1960's, automobiles brought much change in the nation's economic and social life as well as in its culture.

Automobiles, a European innovation with no single inventor, are self-propelled vehicles designed to carry people or loads on land. Until about 1910, they were primarily experimental. However, improved roads, better technology, assembly-line production, and World War I stimulated the rapid development and standardization of the vehicles. Steam-driven and battery-operated electric models were soon replaced by vehicles powered by the gasoline-fueled internal combustion engine, which proved to be greatly superior to other power plants.

The majority of automobiles are driven by a water- or air-cooled multicylinder piston-type internal combustion engine mounted in the front or rear of the vehicle. Economical diesel engines are also employed in some automobiles but primarily in trucks and buses.

Detroit Dominates Detroit and southern Michigan became the automotive center of the United States early in the twentieth century and continued to play a pivotal role in the 1960's. By 1913, despite strong challenges from Western European manufacturers, the U.S. automotive industry had come to dominate the world market, producing 485,000 motor vehicles out of an aggregate 606,000. The founders of the "Big Three" automobile manufacturers—William G. "Billy" Durant of the General Motors Corporation, Walter P. Chrysler of the Chrysler Corporation, and especially Henry Ford of the Ford Motor Company—became part of American legend as their industry assumed a leading position in the economic life and culture of the nation. Passage of the 1956 Interstate Highway Act, which greatly increased the national road network, accentuated the country's preference for automobiles over mass transit alternatives.

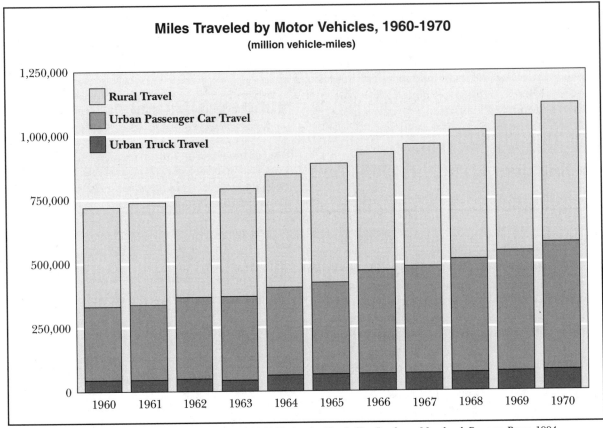

Miles Traveled by Motor Vehicles, 1960-1970
(million vehicle-miles)

Source: Kurian, George, *Datapedia of the United States, 1790-2000, America Year by Year.* Lanham, Maryland: Bernam Press, 1994.

In the 1960's, automobile design initially displayed a reaction against the excesses of the 1950's—flamboyant cars, custom-made vehicles, and hot rods—but soon evolved into a style that reflected both larger disposable incomes and, paradoxically, the various social revolutions of the decade. Under the influence of the increasingly popular German Volkswagen, which was small, spartan, and styleless, U.S. automakers began to build more compact cars such as the Corvair, Valiant, and Lancer.

Overall, this was an ebullient time for U.S. automakers—in hindsight, the calm before the storm. By 1969, more than 80 percent of families in the United States owned at least one automobile. In 1969, the U.S. automotive industry produced more than 8.2 million passenger cars compared with second-ranking West Germany's 2.9 million and third-ranking Japan's 2.6 million. The four major U.S. automakers—General Motors (4.6 million cars), Ford (2.1 million), Chrysler (1.5 million), and the American Motors Corporation (0.26 million)—

grossed nearly $47 billion that year compared with $21.4 billion in 1961. Two-door hardtops were the best-sellers, followed by four-door sedans and four-door hardtops.

The decade also witnessed a number of innovations such as the use of plastics in cars' interiors and exteriors, heralding a time in the 1970's when lightweight metals, synthetics, electronic ignition devices, and sensors would be introduced to lower the overall weight and otherwise help meet government-mandated fuel economy standards. Other 1960's novelties included front-wheel drive with variable-ratio steering, automatic level control, and front disc brakes. The casting of entire engine blocks as single units, drastically reducing the cost, had become commonplace. The use of air-conditioners and bucket seats also increased.

The Mustang and Other Successes In 1961, the first V-6 passenger car engine was introduced by the Buick Division of General Motors. In 1964, Ford unleashed its Mustang, a remarkable success story. One million units sold in just under one year, catapulting the career of the Mustang's creator, Lido A. "Lee" Iacocca, who later was to save Chrysler from bankruptcy. The Ford Mustang contrasted with the Ford Edsel, a marketing and financial disaster. Only 2,846 of the final 1960 model were built, capping total lifetime sales at 110,810 units. Some huge ten-mile-per-gallon gas-guzzlers, such as the 120-inch-wheelbase 1966 Cadillac Eldorado with fully automatic climate-control air-conditioning, were also marketed.

The lavishness of the times was also evident in other ways. For instance, the 1965 Chevrolet was offered in 46 models (out of a total of 348) with a choice of thirty-two different engines, twenty transmissions, thirty colors, and four hundred options— thanks to new, automated, computer-controlled assembly lines.

Though the focus in the 1960's was on the automobile industry's successes, a few problems had appeared. By 1967, the United States had shifted from being a net exporter to a net importer of automobiles and allied products. In addition, traffic fatalities rose from thirty-eight thousand in 1960 to more than fifty-six thousand in 1969.

Impact Americans' love affair with the automobile expanded the trends already present in the 1950's: the exodus of the middle class from the cities to the suburbs, the growth of suburban shopping centers, and the increasing traffic congestion and attendant air pollution. The use of public transportation declined as greater numbers of people bought automobiles. The greater mobility afforded by automobiles led more Americans to drive to vacation spots such as national parks, causing concern among many conservationists and environmentalists. The number of Howard Johnson restaurants and motels and similar businesses along the highways increased to accommodate these travelers. For better or worse, the automobile helped shape the contours of the American Dream.

However, the decade and its excesses also brought the government, at every level, more forcefully into the picture. Despite opposition by the automotive industry, the automobile became subject to regulations regarding emissions (Motor Vehicle Air Pollution Control Act of 1965), safety (National Traffic and Motor Vehicle Safety Act of 1966), and later, fuel economy (Energy Policy and Conservation Act of 1975).

In the 1960's, the question of automobile safety placed the industry on the front burner of the political agenda. Until this decade, safety had been subordinate to style, comfort, and marketing considerations in automotive design. A one-man crusade by consumer advocate and lawyer Ralph Nader focused primarily on the safety of Chevrolet's aluminum, air-cooled, six-cylinder. rear-engine Corvair, which had been involved in a few high-profile accidents because of its tendency to oversteer. Product liability lawsuits followed as did General Motors' harassment of Nader and Nader's final victory and out-of-court settlement. Nader's crusade prompted several congressional and other investigations and the passage of legislation to protect drivers and passengers. Nader's book, *Unsafe at Any Speed: The Designed-in Dangers of the American Automobile* (1965), became a best-seller. As a result of Nader's activities and the withering competition of the Ford Mustang, the Corvair was discontinued after 1969.

Subsequent Events The advent of the first Arab oil embargo in 1973 led to more automobile regulation. The concern in the 1960's about air pollution, traffic congestion, urban sprawl, and environmental degradation, though continuing, became outranked by anxiety about dependence for oil on the foreign-controlled Organization of Petroleum Exporting Countries (OPEC), escalating fuel prices, and the increasing Japanese penetration of U.S. and world automobile markets. Mass transit received renewed assistance from all levels of government, especially from Washington, D.C. In response to the long lines at gasoline stations and higher fuel prices, automobiles were reduced in size and weight, making them more competitive against the surging number of more fuel-efficient foreign imports. Earlier government automobile regulations relating to air pollution and safety were expanded, and gas mileage economy standards were set to cope with the politically sensitive oil shortage. In addition, to save fuel, the speed limit was lowered to fifty-five miles per hour in several states in 1973 and nationally in 1974, a change that also led to lower traffic fatality rates.

Automobile production became more decentralized as the Big Three opened new plants in the South, California, and also outside the United States in order to be more cost-effective. Despite U.S. automakers' efforts to increase competitiveness, by 1972 the German Volkswagen Beetle had become the best-selling car of all time, and by 1980, Japan overtook the United States as the leading world automotive producer. Indeed, by that year, the U.S. share of the world aggregate market had fallen to below one-fifth from more than three-quarters in the 1950's.

Additional Information *The Automobile Age* (1988), by James J. Flink, provides a scholarly, illustrated all-round account of the automotive industry in the 1960's. *The Dream Machine: The Golden Age of American Automobiles, 1946-1965* (1976), by Jerry Flint, is a more entertaining work that intersperses functional with chronological chapters. *Unsafe at Any Speed: The Designed-in Dangers of the American Automobile* (1965), by Ralph Nader, is still one of the most influential though narrowly focused critiques of the industry. *Ward's Automotive Yearbook*, by Ward's Communications, published 1960 through 1970, presents comprehensive statistics and commentary about each year's events and trends.

Peter B. Heller

See also Air Pollution; Business and the Economy; International Trade; Interstate Highway System; Japanese Imports; Motor Vehicle Air Pollution Act of 1965; Nader, Ralph; Route 66; Travel.

B

■ Baby Boomers

Americans born from 1946 through 1964. The baby-boom generation was the largest in U.S. history throughout the twentieth century. The coming of age of its vanguard during the 1960's had a major impact on that decade, resulting in the rise of a new social consciousness, major protest movements, and cultural changes.

Following World War II, women in the United States had babies in unprecedented numbers, beginning in 1946 with 3.4 million births. Although an increase in the birthrate is a normal occurrence following a war, this boom continued unabated for almost twenty years, peaking in 1957 with a record 4.3 million births and ending in 1964. The baby boom constituted the largest generation in the United States up until that time, approximately 76 million people. The boom created a child-centered society at a time when the United States was taking its place as a world power and experiencing a rise in wealth that more than tripled the middle class, making it nearly half of the population. Vanguard baby boomers (those born 1946 through 1951) became idealists, taking for granted that justice and economic security were possible for all. Those coming later (born 1952 through 1964) had less cause for optimism and were more practical.

The size of the baby-boom generation made it a marketing target. Many fads and inventions, including Frisbee flying disks, Barbie dolls, and hula hoops, and the growth of youth organizations such as the Boy Scouts and Girl Scouts had their roots in their appeal to a sizable portion of the population. The baby boomers witnessed the birth of the Civil Rights movement, the Cold War, the space age, and the Vietnam War. Each of these events escalated in importance during the 1960's as boomers reached adolescence and adulthood. In response, baby boomers generated a culture of protest that spilled over to challenge other aspects of American life.

The Effect of Television The 1960's was a decade of trauma and growth for the 46 million members of the baby-boom vanguard who ushered in the decade. Baby boomers varied in gender, race, ethnic origin, and family type and income, and they grew up in urban and rural settings in various regions. However, they shared a wide variety of important experiences. Much of what is considered baby boomer consciousness can be attributed to the enormous integrating effect of television as it sent common images of crisis into most American homes. The number of households with television sets rose from a meager eight thousand the first year of the baby boom to include 90 percent of all households by 1960. Baby boomers all watched the same entertainment shows and advertisements, the same news coverage, and the same dramatic events that characterized the 1960's. Awareness of national and world events was magnified by an unprecedented immediacy, and aggressive advertising created an awareness of new products and trends, resulting in a social and political hyperconsciousness.

Baby boomer political awareness began with the first televised presidential debate, between John F. Kennedy and Richard M. Nixon in 1960, and Kennedy's election when vanguard baby boomers were nine to sixteen years old. In August, 1963, the Reverend Martin Luther King, Jr.'s "I Have a Dream" speech, part of the March on Washington, became a mythical moment in U.S. history. That year was one of extreme national violence, punctuated by televised images of civil rights protesters—mostly young people—beset with police dogs and fire hoses by Birmingham, Alabama, police, the murder of civil rights leader Medgar Evers in Mississippi, and the Sunday bombing of a Birmingham church in which four young girls were killed. However, the assassination of President Kennedy in 1963, when the first boomers were twelve to seventeen years old, was an unprecedented tragedy in their consciousness. The public violence of 1963, brought so graphically into their homes by television, constituted a rude awakening for baby boomers and opened their eyes to much of the hypocrisy in American life. Unfortunately, violence was to characterize the rest of the decade; more civil rights murders, race riots, and protests followed.

The College Years The first members of the baby-boom generation went to college in 1964, swelling freshmen populations. In 1964, the Free Speech movement began at the University of California, Berkeley, setting off the social and political activism that continued throughout the decade and pitted students, in their support of civil rights and their opposition to corruption and war, against the political establishment. Vanguard baby boomers were the best-educated children in U.S. history: About 81 percent of them graduated from high school, and 27 percent of the men and 21 percent of the women born between the years of 1946 and 1951 completed college—a proportion not matched again in the twentieth century. This number reflected the large numbers of men who attended college to obtain an exemption from the military draft.

The Vietnam War focused boomer attention on survival. The military draft affected baby boomer men who were eighteen years old in 1964. The following year, the Selective Service began doubling the number of men it drafted each month, an event that triggered many war protests. When deferments for graduate students ended in June, 1968, hundreds of protests occurred across the country as more baby boomer men became eligible for the draft. Overall, although some 26.8 million baby boomer men were eligible, only about 6.5 million saw military service during the war, and roughly 1 million actually fought in Vietnam. However, the war pointed out the disparity in baby boomer fortunes, for the less-educated men from poorer and minority backgrounds disproportionately bore the brunt of the draft, combat, and death.

Countercultural Views When reality confronted their idealism, many baby boomers reacted strongly. Some of these reactions, however, were decidedly nonpolitical. Many baby boomers chose to express alternative values and lifestyles by dropping out of mainstream American culture and forming a coun-

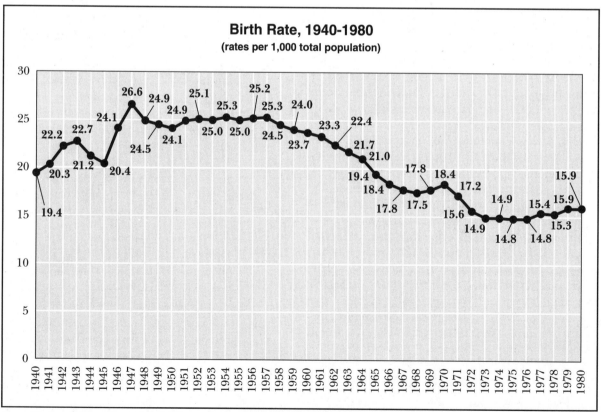

Source: Kurian, George, *Datapedia of the United States, 1790-2000, America Year by Year.* Lanham, Maryland: Bernam Press, 1994.

terculture. They often expressed their cultural dissent at ritual gatherings, such as be-ins and love-ins, and multiday rock festivals such as the Woodstock Music and Art Fair. Rock concerts became a permanent feature in the American cultural landscape, and both folk and rock singers became icons and rallying points for baby boomer interests.

The second half of the 1960's was characterized by the rise of student protests on university campuses and the expansion of these protests into all phases of American life. An emerging sense of peer, or group, consciousness meant that baby boomers related to each other rather than to adults, and this growing awareness of generational differences eventually led to the severing of relationships with establishment figures and the embrace of those who symbolized countercultural views. Therefore, as white baby boomers involved in politics sought out figures such as 1968 presidential peace candidate Senator Eugene McCarthy, African American boomers broke from more conservative racial integrationist views and supported the rise of black power. Toward the end of the decade, the assassinations of civil rights leader King and Senator Robert Kennedy, the escalation of the war in Vietnam, and the evidence of government corruption made it seem to many observers that the United States was in the midst of a revolution and that things were falling apart.

Impact Baby boomers effected a revolution in the nation's cultural values and ushered in fundamental changes in American life during the 1960's by acting as catalysts and carriers of new ideas. The approval of the birth control pill for general use in 1960 allowed baby boomers—particularly women—to experiment with sexual freedom, which led to less conservative ideas about marriage, divorce, and family in the general society. The persistence of student protests, race riots, and the increasing radicalization of political activism eventually forced Americans to confront corruption in their own political institutions and to introduce reforms to address racism, sexism, economic disparities, and the use of communism to justify engaging the nation in foreign wars.

Subsequent Events The 1960's left American society and baby boomers in an institutional turmoil that they would spend the next two decades trying to rectify. Baby boomers forced Americans to reevaluate the institutions of marriage and family, gender relations, racial and ethnic relations, and the rela-

tionship of religious institutions to the rest of society but frequently offered no alternatives to fill the vacuum. Therefore, positive gains were offset by negative ones, and the ultimate impact of the baby boomers was still being assessed at the close of the twentieth century.

Additional Information The most complete account of the baby-boom generation can be found in *Great Expectations: America and the Baby Boom Generation* (1980), by Landon Y. Jones. *A Generation of Seekers* (1993), by Wade Clark Roof, explores baby boomer approaches to religion, and *One Hundred Predictions for the Baby Boom* (1987), by Cheryl Russell, provides demographic projections about the baby boomers' future. Finally, *Generations* (1991), by William Strauss and Neil Howe, puts the baby-boom generation into the context of all American generations.

Susan Love Brown

See also Counterculture; Demographics of the United States; "I Have a Dream" Speech; Sexual Revolution; Woodstock Festival; Youth Culture and the Generation Gap.

■ Baez, Joan

Born January 9, 1941, Staten Island, New York

Folksinger, songwriter, social activist. Baez made headlines during the 1960's for her political activism and her music.

Early Life One of three children born to Albert and Joan Baez, Joan Chandos Baez was no stranger to racial prejudice. Her Hispanic roots, dark skin, and staunchly pacifist beliefs were the fodder for taunts in school. She learned to play guitar at age twelve and distinguished herself musically during high school in Palo Alto, California. After graduation in 1958, she moved with her family to Boston, where she discovered folk music and began to sing professionally. Performances in Chicago and at the Newport Folk Festival in 1959 led to offers from other groups and for recording contracts. Baez declined these and returned to Boston.

The 1960's In 1960, Baez cut her first album, *Joan Baez*, on the Vanguard label. She paid homage to her Hispanic and Celtic roots by including a Scottish ballad and a song sung in Spanish among the album's offerings. She became a very popular singer/songwriter, releasing eleven more albums during the decade. Her expressive voice and three-octave range

Folksinger and songwriter Joan Baez performed many protest songs, some written by Bob Dylan, and participated in many antiwar and antidraft demonstrations. (Peter D. Whitney/Archive Photos)

made her a very appealing performer at festivals, on concert tours, and at political events. Baez gradually expanded her repertoire of traditional folk music to include songs of social awareness, including the civil rights anthem "We Shall Overcome." In the early 1960's, Baez participated in many civil rights demonstrations, lending her voice to protests at southern cities such as Selma, Montgomery, and Birmingham, Alabama, centers of the struggle for racial equality. She also sang beside Martin Luther King, Jr., at the March on Washington in 1963. She recorded protest songs by the still largely unknown songwriter Bob Dylan, became romantically linked with him, and performed in concert with him from 1963 through 1965. When folksinger Pete Seeger, whom Baez admired, was banned from the weekly American Broadcasting Company television show, *Hootenanny,* she refused to appear on the program.

Baez also participated in numerous antiwar protests and refused to pay the portion of her income tax that she calculated went to defense spending. With money from her musical career, Baez founded the Institute for the Study of Nonviolence in Carmel Valley, California, in 1965. Because of Baez's antiwar stance, her albums were banned on U.S. Army bases around the world and the Daughters of the American Revolution (DAR) refused to allow her to perform at Constitution Hall in Washington, D.C. In 1967, she was arrested for taking part in an antidraft protest at the military induction center in Oakland, California. That same year, she traveled around the country with antiwar activist David Harris, singing and speaking out against the Vietnam War. The two married in 1968 and had a son, Gabriel, but were divorced three years later. During the summer of 1969, the year that she released *David's Album,* a tribute to her husband, incarcerated for draft evasion, Baez played to a crowd of more than five hundred thousand people at the Woodstock Music and Art Fair in New York.

Later Life Baez continued to perform and record, producing more than forty albums by the 1990's. She also remained true to her pacifist views and her strong beliefs in equal rights. In 1972, Baez visited Hanoi to further protest the U.S. involvement in Vietnam. She performed at Live Aid to benefit impoverished farmers in 1985; toured the Middle East in 1988; and worked for low-income housing in California in the early 1990's.

Impact Baez personified folk music and the social conscience of the 1960's in the United States. A highly visible activist who was also a national celebrity, Baez effectively worked to help both African Americans and Hispanics obtain their civil rights and helped spread opposition to the U.S. war effort in Vietnam.

Additional Information In 1987, Baez published an autobiography, *And a Voice to Sing With.* She released *Play Me Backwards* in 1992, an album many critics called the best of her career.

Donna Addkison Simmons

See also Civil Rights Movement; Dylan, Bob; Folk Music; Music; Oakland Riot; Vietnam War.

■ Baker Resignation

Date October 7, 1963

The culmination of a scandal involving Bobby Baker, the secretary of the Senate majority, which reflected poorly on Vice President Lyndon B. Johnson, who had hired Baker. When an investigation of Baker's financial dealings revealed strong evidence of impropriety, he was forced to resign.

Origins and History Robert G. "Bobby" Baker came to Washington, D.C., as a Senate page at the age of fourteen in 1943. In 1955, Senate Majority Leader Lyndon B. Johnson appointed Baker to be his secretary. He worked closely with Johnson and then Senator Mike Mansfield until his resignation.

The Resignation On September 9, 1963, a competitor filed a lawsuit in Washington, D.C., alleging that Baker had used his government position to obtain vending machine contracts in defense plants for Serv-U Corporation, an organization in which Baker had invested money. In a subsequent investigation, other irregularities were revealed. Baker was alleged to have been named vice president of an insurance company, to have required that insurance company to buy advertising on the Austin, Texas, station owned by Johnson's family, and to have arranged with the company to insure Johnson's life for two hundred thousand dollars one year after Johnson had had a major heart attack. The investigation indicated Baker's possible involvement in land speculation and questionable stock deals and bank loans. Baker was alleged to have used his position of influence as the basis for all of these financial dealings. Although Baker had been a government employee his entire adult life, he had parlayed his $19,600 salary into a net worth estimated at $1.7 million by 1963. The scandal began in the fall of 1963, just before President John F. Kennedy was assassinated. After becoming president, Johnson began to deny a close affiliation with Baker, a person whom Johnson had once described as the son he had always wanted to have. The Senate responded to these charges against Baker by scheduling hearings to investigate his activities. Rather than answer the charges against him, Baker resigned.

Impact In 1965, the Senate Rules Committee found Baker guilty of "gross improprieties," and in 1966, he was indicted by a federal grand jury on nine counts of tax evasion, fraud, and conspiracy. He was found guilty of some of those charges in 1967, and after his appeals were denied, he began serving a one-to three-year sentence in 1971. He was released from prison in June, 1972. The Baker incident was embarrassing to Johnson and contributed to speculation that Johnson had been involved in shady schemes, charges that were never proven. The scandal contributed to the notion that politics was corrupt and marked the beginning of more careful thinking about congressional ethics.

Additional Information The impact of the Baker affair on the Johnson administration is discussed in Eric F. Goldman's *The Tragedy of Lyndon Johnson* (1969). For a discussion of Baker's legal problems, see Juan M. Vasquez's "Baker, Former Aide of Johnson, Paroled" in the April 28, 1972, edition of *The New York Times.*

James W. Riddlesperger, Jr.

See also Crimes and Scandals; Estes, Billie Sol; Johnson, Lyndon B.

■ Baldwin, James

Born August 2, 1924, New York, New York
Died November 30, 1987, St. Paul de Vence, France

Novelist, essayist, and playwright. Baldwin became a strident voice in the struggle for racial equality during the civil rights conflicts in the United States in the last half of the twentieth century.

Early Life Born in New York City's Harlem, James Arthur Baldwin began to preach when he was fourteen and planned to enter the clergy. Upon graduation from high school in 1942, he became a railroad hand in Belle Meade, New Jersey. Moving to New York City's Greenwich Village in 1944, he met the writer Richard Wright, who encouraged him in his writing. Wright recommended him for the Eugene Saxton Fellowship in 1945. Receiving this fellowship enabled Baldwin to continue work on his novel, *In My Father's House*, which was not published. He used the proceeds from a Rosenwald Fellowship awarded in 1948 to move to Paris, where he worked on his first published novel, *Go Tell It on the Mountain* (1953). From 1948 until his death in 1987, he lived largely in France, although he frequently returned to the United States and retained his United States citizenship.

The 1960's Baldwin was a member of two significant minorities, the racial minority in which his blackness placed him and the sexual minority of homosexuals, about which he wrote in his renowned novel, *Giovanni's Room* (1956), adapted to the stage in 1957. During the 1960's, both groups were clamoring for their civil rights. In 1957, Baldwin returned from France and visited the American South for the first time. The oppression of African Americans living in a segregated society astounded him. He published his impressions in *Harper's* and in *Partisan Review*.

In 1960, Baldwin again returned from France and participated in strategy sessions for student protests and sit-ins organized in Tallahassee, Florida, by the Congress of Racial Equality (CORE) as well as in a civil rights march on Washington, D.C. The following year, his collection of essays, *Nobody Knows My Name*, emphasizing the disenfranchisement of African Americans in the South, caused many people, black and white, to demand that the government protect and enforce the civil rights of those who, because of their race, had second-class citizenship thrust upon them.

During 1962 and into 1963, Baldwin was appalled that John F. Kennedy did not use the power of his presidency to bring about greater equality for oppressed minorities. Baldwin met informally with the president's brother, Attorney General Robert F. Kennedy, on May 23, 1963. Out of that meeting grew another meeting the following day with the attorney general and attended by such luminaries as Rip Torn, Geraldine Page, Lena Horne, and Lorraine Hansberry. Although Baldwin left this meeting feeling that Kennedy was not a strong supporter of civil rights for blacks, in the long term, the meeting greatly influenced the attorney general's activism in the civil rights arena.

The assassinations during a four-year period in the 1960's of Medgar Evers, John F. Kennedy, Martin Luther King, Jr., and Robert F. Kennedy, along with the deaths of four African American girls in the bombing of an Alabama church served to reinforce Baldwin's notion that racial strife, a by-product of segregation and oppression, might very well destroy the nation.

Later Life Baldwin continued to write about social issues related to civil rights for the remainder of his life, during which he lived mostly in France and in Turkey. His play, *Blues for Mr. Charlie* (produced 1964; published 1964) was based largely on the events through which he had lived in the early 1960's. In his later life, his essays received more attention than his novels, with such collections as *No Name in the Street* (1972) and *The Devil Finds Work* (1976) attracting considerable notice.

Impact Baldwin will be remembered for the precision and social impact of his prose. He wrote movingly about matters that concerned him deeply and personally. He led a troubled life, attempting suicide at times when he could bear his pain no longer. A highly successful writer, Baldwin hovered between two worlds, Europe and the United States. Perhaps this hovering became a personal metaphor relating both to his racial background and his sexual proclivities.

Additional Information To date the best biography of Baldwin is David Leeming's *James Baldwin: A Biography* (1994). W. J. Weatherby's *James Baldwin: Artist on Fire* (1989) presents detailed information about the artistry of Baldwin's writing.

R. Baird Shuman

See also Civil Rights Movement; Congress of Racial Equality (CORE); Evers, Medgar; King, Martin Luther, Jr.; Student Nonviolent Coordinating Committee (SNCC).

■ Barbie and Ken Dolls

Probably the best-selling dolls in U.S. history. Mattel's Barbie and Ken dolls first dominated the market for dolls in the 1960's.

After watching her daughter Barbie play dress-up with paper dolls, Mattel cofounder Ruth Handler asked her creative team for a three-dimensional version. Using the German pinup doll Lilli as their model, developers produced the first bathing-suit-clad Barbie in 1959.

Though toy-store buyers were initially reluctant to stock a doll with breasts, Barbie was an immediate hit. Consumers demanded a boyfriend, and the first version of Ken (named for Handler's son) followed in 1961. Feminists decried her unattainable figure, but Mattel blamed her measurements on her wardrobe—the one-sixth-scaled clothes would not hang properly on an anatomically realistic doll.

Impact Before Barbie, little girls played house with their baby dolls and dress-up with their mother's jewelry. "We Girls Can Do Anything," the Barbie doll advertising campaign told them. Barbie got the Dream House, the car, and the camper, and Ken was forever doomed to accessory status. Since her introduction, Barbie has captured the hearts of little girls everywhere, while causing many parents to wonder if her perfect appearance and conspicuous consumption send the wrong message.

Subsequent Events Regular physical modifications and career changes turned Barbie into big business for collectors. By the 1990's, Mattel estimated that two dolls were being sold every minute worldwide.

Additional Information A clever look at Barbie's past can be found in *Forever Barbie: The Unauthorized Biography of a Real Doll* (1994), by M. C. Lord.

P. S. Ramsey

See also Gidget Films; Miniskirts; Woman's Identity.

■ Baseball

A decade of significant changes for major league baseball. During the 1960's, the major leagues expanded from sixteen to twenty-four teams, split the leagues into two divisions, generated large increases in revenue from television contracts, and began to experience labor problems that would profoundly alter the relationship between team owners and players.

After almost a half century of relative stability, major league baseball experienced important changes after World War II. In 1947, major league baseball became racially integrated, and during the next several years, African American and Latino players began to appear on team rosters. During the 1950's, the geographical landscape of major league baseball changed, as the St. Louis Browns, Boston Braves, Kansas City Athletics, New York Giants, and Brooklyn Dodgers relocated.

During the 1960's, major league baseball continued to undergo important changes. The major leagues expanded from sixteen to twenty-four teams. In 1961, the Los Angeles Angels and Washington Senators were added to the American League (the new Senators replacing the former Washington franchise, which had moved to Minnesota after the 1960 season). The following year, the National League added the New York Mets and Houston Colt .45's (later renamed the Astros). In 1969, the American League introduced the Kansas City Royals and Seattle Pilots (who would move to Milwaukee and become the Brewers after a single season), and the National League introduced the Montreal Expos, the first major league team outside the United States, and the San Diego Padres. The expansion of 1969 prompted the decision to split each league into eastern and western divisions, creating a preliminary round of playoffs to precede the World Series.

Expansion reflected baseball's increasing popularity, brought about, in part, by television, which presented the game to fans in cities without major league teams. The team owners reaped the rewards of this popularity by negotiating network television contracts that substantially increased their revenues.

As team revenues increased, the players demanded a larger share of the profits. In 1966, the two top starting pitchers for the world champion Los Angeles Dodgers, Sandy Koufax and Don Drysdale, staged a joint salary holdout, demanding a three-year contract totaling $1.05 million, which they would divide evenly. The two pitchers eventually signed for substantially less money, but the incident helped other players realize their potential to increase salaries markedly by uniting to pressure team owners.

During the Koufax and Drysdale holdout, the Major League Baseball Players' Association, the labor union representing the players, hired as its executive director Marvin Miller, an experienced organizer and negotiator who had previously represented the United Steelworkers. Before the hiring of Miller, the Players' Association, formed in 1954, had achieved only modest gains for its rank and file. In 1968, however, Miller successfully negotiated major league baseball's first Basic Agreement, a contract between the players and team owners covering minimum salaries, the pension fund, and other fringe benefits. During the 1969 season, Miller threatened to call a players' strike if money was not added to the players' pension fund. A strike was averted when the team owners agreed to Miller's demands. In 1968, the major league umpires also unionized.

On the field, baseball also changed in significant ways during the 1960's. The decade opened with the

Sandy Koufax, pitcher for the Los Angeles Dodgers, throws another strike on his way to a no-hitter. In 1966, he, along with Don Drysdale, used his talents to negotiate a better salary. (AP/Wide World Photos)

New York Yankees continuing their dominance of the American League by winning five straight pennants. In 1961, the Yankees' slugging right fielder, Roger Maris, broke Babe Ruth's single-season home run record by hitting 61 homers. In 1965, however, the Yankees' aging stars—Mickey Mantle, Whitey Ford, Maris—began to lose their edge, and the team experienced a sharp decline, tumbling to last place in 1966. No other American League team was able to fill the breach left by the Yankees. From 1965 through 1969, four different American League teams won a pennant, with only one team winning twice—the Baltimore Orioles in 1966 and 1969. In the National League, the Los Angeles Dodgers and St. Louis Cardinals emerged as the decade's dominant teams, each capturing three pennants and two World Series.

The demise of the Yankees, once nicknamed the Bronx Bombers, signaled the end of an era when the teams with the greatest hitters dominated the league. Some of the best teams of the 1960's, such as the Dodgers and the Cardinals, were noted more for outstanding pitching and speed rather than for home-run power. The decade's most successful teams also tended to be those that had most thoroughly integrated their rosters.

The decade ended with one of the great surprises of baseball history. In 1969, the New York Mets, a symbol of ineptitude since their formation in 1962, astonished baseball fans by winning the National League pennant and besting the powerful Orioles in the World Series.

Another significant change that occurred in baseball during the 1960's concerned the diamond itself. In 1965, the Houston Astros opened their new indoor stadium, the Astrodome. Because grass could not grow indoors, the field was covered with a plastic artificial grass, dubbed Astroturf. In subsequent seasons, Astroturf appeared in new stadiums in St. Louis, Cincinnati, Philadelphia, Pittsburgh, and several other major league cities.

Impact The changes that took place in major league baseball during the 1960's had a long-lasting effect on the game. Successful expansion prompted further expansion during the next three decades. The players' union became stronger, enabling players to garner more of baseball's revenue. As players' salary demands increased, tensions between the union and team owners escalated.

Subsequent Events Between 1977 and 1998, major league baseball introduced six new teams, bringing the total to thirty teams. In 1972, baseball fans endured the first players' strike, which lasted almost two weeks and erased 86 games from the schedule. The players struck again for six weeks in 1981 and for two days in 1985. In 1994, a strike that commenced in August wiped out the remainder of the season and the World Series. From 1976 through 1997, the average player's salary increased from $51,000 to more than $1 million.

Additional Information *The Summer Game* (1972), by Roger Angell, collects its author's eloquent *New Yorker* baseball essays from 1962 through 1971. David Halberstam's *October 1964* (1994) recounts a memorable World Series and analyzes the changes occurring in baseball during the mid-1960's. A chapter on the 1960's entitled "A Whole New Ball Game" appears in *Baseball: An Illustrated History* (1994), by Geoffrey C. Ward and Ken Burns.

James Tackach

See also Koufax, Sandy; Mantle, Mickey; Maris, Roger; Mays, Willie; Sports.

■ Basketball

A popular indoor spectator sport. Basketball in the 1960's was one of dynasties at the collegiate, professional, and individual levels.

Basketball was founded in 1891 by James Naismith at the School for Christian Workers, later Springfield College, in Springfield, Massachusetts. The game's popularity grew rapidly as it swept college campuses and club gymnasiums in the early part of the century. By 1936, the game had gone international as it debuted at the Berlin Olympics. In 1946, a group of Eastern-based arena operators, looking for a way to fill their arenas on nights when hockey games were not played, got together to form the National Basketball Association (NBA). The NBA saw steady growth throughout the 1950's and was poised to burst onto the national scene over the next ten years.

Ohio State won the National Collegiate Athletic Association (NCAA) championship in 1960 and returned the next two years to the championship game but was defeated both years by the University of Cincinnati. Cincinnati was defeated in its attempt to win three straight championships by Loyola of Chicago in 1963. Yet as powerful as these teams were early in the decade, they could not compare to those from the University of California at Los Angeles (UCLA), which won the national title in all but one of the remaining years of the decade. The only exception came in 1966, when Texas Western won the national championship.

In the professional game, the Boston Celtics, under the direction of its legendary coach Red Auerbach, won all but one championship in the entire decade. The other team to win a championship was the Philadelphia 76ers in 1967, the year after Auerbach retired from coaching the Celtics. Boston's great center, Bill Russell, had replaced Auerbach as coach and continued playing as well. After losing out to Philadelphia in 1967, Russell led his team, both on the floor and off, to two more championships to close the decade. Yet for all the great play and leadership of Russell, it is Wilt Chamberlain who will always be remembered as the greatest individual player of the 1960's. Although Russell's Celtics routinely defeated Chamberlain's teams, the Philadelphia 76ers and the Los Angeles Lakers, Chamberlain had gaudy statistics that no one else in the league, then or since, came close to matching. In his second season, he grabbed a league-record 55 rebounds in one game and for the season set a record by averaging 27.2 rebounds per game. In the 1961-1962 season, his third, he averaged more than 50 points per game and played 3,882 of a possible 3,890 minutes, and on March 2, 1962, he scored 100 points in a single game. All these records will likely never be broken. Chamberlain led the league in scoring from 1960 to 1966, and, demonstrating his complete set of skills, he led the league in assists in 1968. The team play of the Celtics and the individual feats of Chamberlain created a spectacle that the nation's sports fans could not help but embrace.

With its increased popularity, the NBA began expanding into new cities, and other leagues attempted to form. The American Basketball League was formed in 1961 but lasted only a year. In 1968, the American Basketball Association was formed. Through creative marketing and an emphasis on offensive innovations such as the three-point shot and encouraging the slam dunk, the ABA quickly established itself as a legitimate league and began competing with the NBA for star players. By the end of the decade, the NBA faced a strong threat from the ABA.

Impact Starting the decade well behind baseball, football, and hockey as a popular spectator sport, basketball made a strong impression on sports fans throughout the 1960's. By the end of the decade, it had replaced hockey as North America's third most popular spectator sport. While basketball was still some years away from the incredible increase of popularity it was to have in the 1980's, it had staked its claim as a major sport both in the United States and internationally.

Subsequent Events In the mid-1970's, the ABA folded, with the NBA absorbing the ABA's four strongest franchises and many of its players, including Julius Erving, the ABA's superstar. The collection of stars in one league, the subsequent arrival of charismatic college stars Magic Johnson and Larry Bird in the professional ranks, and a series of exciting collegiate championships helped to broaden the game's appeal enormously. The mid-1980's arrival of a new superstar, Michael Jordan, sealed the universal acceptance of basketball, to such an extent that the game began to challenge soccer as the world's most popular sport.

Additional Information Basketball in the 1960's is covered in more detail in *The Official NBA Basketball Encyclopedia* (1994), edited by Alex Sachare; Peter C. Bjarkman's *The History of the NBA* (1992); Bill Libby's *Goliath: The Wilt Chamberlain Story* (1977); Jeff Greenfield's *The World's Greatest Team: A Portrait of the Boston Celtics, 1957-1969*; and Dwight Chapin's *The Wizard of Westwood: Coach John Wooden and his UCLA Bruins* (1973).

Richard L. Mallery

See also Alcindor, Lew (Kareem Abdul-Jabbar); Chamberlain, Wilt; Russell, Bill; Sports.

■ Bay of Pigs Invasion

Date April 17, 1961

One of the greatest Cold War fiascos of the 1960's. This ill-planned Central Intelligence Agency attempt to overthrow Fidel Castro's regime in Cuba resulted in disaster and major embarrassment for the new administration of John F. Kennedy.

Origins and History The overthrow of Fulgencio Batista y Zaldívar's long and corrupt dictatorship in Cuba in January, 1959, also ended the domination of the Cuban economy by U.S. companies. As Fidel Castro's nationalization of utilities, mines, hotels, oil refineries, and plantations continued during 1959, the new leader's regime came under attack by U.S. congressmen. An ever-increasing number of Cuban exiles in Miami stoked the anti-Castro flames. In addition, Castro's anti-U.S. speeches and public admission that he was a Marxist created a dangerous situation. The Dwight D. Eisenhower administration had already used the Central Intelligence Agency (CIA) to topple the Mohammad Mosaddeq regime in Iran and the Jacobo Arbenz Guzmán regime in Guatemala merely on the suspicion that each leader was Marxist oriented. By April, 1960, Eisenhower gave the CIA permission to secretly arm and train Cuban exiles at bases in Guatemala and Nicaragua in preparation for a clandestine operation to overthrow the Castro regime. Richard Bissell was appointed operations head. Numerous plans were also made for the assassination of Castro, leading to a number of bizarre plots that came to naught.

When John F. Kennedy took office in the spring of 1961, the invasion force was ready to go. Although he had considerable doubts about the venture, Kennedy was ultimately swayed by the self-interested urgings of CIA planners, which were supported by the military joint chiefs of staff who viewed Castro as unpopular and the invasion as a catalyst for a mass anti-Castro uprising. Concern about the increasing number of Soviet advisers and technicians streaming into Cuba and fear of Soviet MiG fighters being delivered to Cuba in the near future—an event that would end further invasion plans—entered into his decision. On March 11, 1961, Kennedy gave his consent for a clandestine invasion. On April 10, the invasion force began moving out of Guatemala to launch an attack at the Bay of Pigs on April 17.

The Fiasco Preliminary activities for the invasion began at dawn on April 15, with a strike by eight B-26 bombers piloted by Cuban exiles. The attack was intended to knock out Castro's airfields; instead, it succeeded in raising international criticism of the United States and alerting Castro that an invasion was imminent. In reaction, United Nations Ambassador Adlai Stevenson succeeded in obtaining a promise from Kennedy to refrain from further air attacks. On April 17, fifteen hundred Cuban exiles, transported by U.S. ships, landed at several sites, with the principal force going ashore on the south central coast at the Bay of Pigs. The invaders' destination

Cuban leader Fidel Castro's militia, pictured at the Laguna del Tosoro, successfully thwarted an invasion of their country by a group of Cuban exiles trained and led by the Central Intelligence Agency. (AP/Wide World Photos)

was the Escambray Mountains about eighty miles away, across a maze of swamps and jungles. According to plan, this force would catalyze a mass uprising against an unpopular Castro regime from its mountain base, leading to the regime's rapid demise. Instead, the Cuban population rallied against the invasion, quickly killing 114 and capturing 1,189 members of the exile force. By April 19, the invasion was over, and the United States was left with a foreign policy disaster of the first magnitude. Everything had gone wrong.

An initial force of paratroopers had landed inland to cut off roads leading to the Bay of Pigs. Unfortunately, it immediately ran into a Cuban patrol and was decimated. Castro was able to use the roads to bring in armored columns to the Bay of Pigs. The ships of the main invading force hit unexpected coral reefs, which were believed to be seaweed. Castro's air force was out to meet the invasion, causing the ships of the invasion armada to return to sea. The invasion force did not receive friendly air support, as many had expected. A ship carrying the bulk

of the invaders' ammunition and communications equipment was sunk. Supply flights from Nicaragua, which were supposed to receive protection from six unmarked U.S. fighter jets, failed to receive this air support because of a timing error.

On April 21, two days after the last resisters surrendered, Kennedy, as chief executive, accepted full blame for the failure of the invasion. However, he fumed at the CIA for feeding him misinformation and causing his administration to begin with a disaster. His embarrassment was compounded by the need to pay ransom for the return of the captured invasion force. Eleanor Roosevelt was put in charge of raising money for a twenty-eight-million-dollar tractor-for-prisoner exchange but was unable to raise the funds. Ultimately, the United States would have to pay twice that amount in food and medical supplies to obtain the return of the survivors of the ill-fated invasion force.

Impact The fiasco caused Kennedy to retire, within a short period of time, the top leadership of the CIA, including Allen Dulles, Bissell, and General Charles Cable. It also caused him to take a strong anti-Castro stand, leading to further assassination conspiracies, support of Cuban exile paramilitary activities, and finally to a strong stand in the Cuban Missile Crisis of October, 1962. It also abetted a strong anticommunist stand in the Berlin crisis of 1961 and in Vietnam, where specially trained Green Beret forces would stand as a symbol of both U.S. commitment and efficiency. In relation to U.S. foreign policy, the invasion for a time upset Kennedy's Alliance for Progress policy in Latin America. The nation's European allies remained uneasy about what seemed to be an increase in the tempo of the Cold War. Meanwhile, Castro won a major victory, ironically making him more popular than ever, not only with Cubans but also with other Third World revolutionary leaders. Castro's insecurity about continued hostile U.S. actions led him to seek Soviet missile protection, in turn causing the Cuban Missile Crisis. Both the CIA and Cuban exiles felt betrayed by Kennedy for not providing more vigorous U.S. military support.

Additional Information A good account of the invasion is contained in Christopher Andrew's *For the President's Eyes Only: Secret Intelligence and the American Presidency from Washington to Bush* (1995). Detailed analyses include Michael Beschloss's *Kennedy v. Khrushchev: The Crisis Years 1960-63* (1991) and Turmbull Higgins's *The Perfect Failure: Kennedy, Eisenhower, and the CIA at the Bay of Pigs* (1989). Peter Wyden's *Bay of Pigs* (1979) remains the most widely used study.

Irwin Halfond

See also Castro, Fidel; Central Intelligence Agency (CIA); Cold War; Cuban Missile Crisis; Kennedy, John F.

■ Be-ins and Love-ins

Free-form festivals of the hippie counterculture. Typically held outdoors in public spaces, these open gatherings blended elements of costumed revelries, theatrical happenings, political demonstrations, and rock concerts.

The term "be-in" originated with the sit-ins of the Civil Rights movement and the teach-ins organized on college campuses by anti-Vietnam War protesters. The era of be-ins, also known as "love-ins," may be said to have begun with San Francisco's Love Pageant Rally on October 6, 1966, when as many as two

thousand hippies converged in Golden Gate Park to observe—and defy—the California law criminalizing the use of LSD (lysergic acid diethylamide), which went into effect on that date. It was followed three months later by the much larger Gathering of the Tribes for a Human Be-in, which took place in mid-January, 1967, also in Golden Gate Park. Haight-Ashbury's underground newspaper, the *San Francisco Oracle*, promoted the latter gathering as a "union of love and activism . . . [for] Berkeley political activists and hip community and San Francisco's spiritual generation and contingents from the emerging revolutionary generation all over California."

Speakers included prominent members of the Beat generation, antiwar activists, and psychedelic drug guru Timothy Leary. Their talks were interspersed with musical performances by local acid rock bands including the Grateful Dead and the Jefferson Airplane. Between ten thousand and thirty-five thousand people, many affecting fanciful costumes and long hairstyles, attended. No admission was charged, no participant received a fee, and volunteers provided all basic services. For example, an anarchist group known as the Diggers distributed free sandwiches, and the Hell's Angels motorcycle club furnished security to the speakers and performers.

Impact The January event served as a prelude to the 1967 Summer of Love and heralded the emergence of the hippie counterculture. It was the first such gathering to garner the attention of the national news media. Shortly thereafter, journalists from around the world flocked to the Haight-Ashbury district to report on the hippies and be-ins. One result of their coverage was that be-ins patterned after San Francisco's were soon being staged in cities throughout the country. New York's Easter Be-in that spring attracted more than ten thousand people to Sheep Meadow in Central Park for a daylong frolic. Its organizers copied many aspects of the Human Be-in, but they also heeded criticism about how the earlier gathering had been too focused on prominent personalities and rock bands. In Central Park, participants entertained each other spontaneously; there was neither a stage nor scheduled events.

Arguably the last be-ins took place in Chicago's Lincoln Park during the Democratic National Convention in August, 1968, and at Berkeley's People's Park the following spring. Both gatherings had a more overtly political purpose and were violently suppressed by law enforcement authorities. After these events, the commercial rock festival supplanted be-ins as the site for countercultural conviviality.

Additional Information The Human Be-in is discussed in Charles Perry's *The Haight-Ashbury: A History* (1984). A contemporary report on New York's Easter Be-in was reprinted in Don McNeill's anthology *Moving Through Here* (1990).

Michael Wm. Doyle

See also Beat Generation; Counterculture; Democratic National Convention of 1968; Flower Children; Grateful Dead; Haight-Ashbury; Happenings; Hippies; Jefferson Airplane; Leary, Timothy; LSD; People's Park, Berkeley; San Francisco as a Cultural Mecca; Summer of Love.

■ Beach Boys, The

A California band that defined—in fact virtually invented—the "California sound." Their songs featured close harmonies; upbeat, sun-drenched lyrics; and simple themes of surfing, hot cars, and young, often unrequited, love.

The Beach Boys embodied the California sound in the early and mid-1960's with their sweet harmonies and songs that spoke of hot cars, surfing, and young love. (AP/Wide World Photos)

The Beach Boys were the brainchild of Brian, Dennis, and Carl Wilson, brothers who lived in Hawthorne, California. Their father, Murry, a sometime songwriter who encouraged his sons' musical experimentation, was a volatile man who abused his sons physically and verbally. Brian Wilson blamed his partial deafness (he has only 6 percent of the hearing in his right ear) to a beating he received from his father in early childhood.

In 1961, the brothers formed a band with their cousin Mike Love and friend Al Jardine and began performing while still in high school. They were known first as Kenny and the Cadets, then as Carl and the Passions, and eventually as the Pendletones (after a popular brand of shirt) before settling on the name the Beach Boys.

Dennis Wilson was an avid surfer who thought the popular California sport would make great song material. His enthusiastic urging led older brother Brian Wilson and cousin Mike Love to write "Surfin'." Like most of the Beach Boys' musical creations, the song featured Chuck Berry-influenced guitar licks and the close, sweet harmonies favored by Brian Wilson, who was a fan of George Gershwin, Stephen Foster, and early 1950's groups such as the Four Freshmen. The song was released on the local label Candix in December, 1961. By early 1962, "Surfin' " was a regional hit, and the Beach Boys were beginning to garner national attention.

The band (with Murry Wilson as manager) signed a contract with Capitol Records in 1962, and a string of hits ensued: "Surfin' Safari" (1962), "Surfin' USA"

(1963, the melody of this song was a virtual duplication of Chuck Berry's "Sweet Little Sixteen"), "Surfer Girl" (1963), and "Fun, Fun, Fun" (1964). Three of their songs—"I Get Around" (1964), "Help Me, Rhonda" (1965), and "Good Vibrations" (1966)— became number-one hits.

Unfortunately, although the Beach Boys' songs painted a carefree world of endless summer, the band's real life was as complex as the decade. By 1965, alcohol and drugs were taking a toll on the group's personal and professional lives. Substance abuse exacerbated the increasingly fragile mental condition of member Brian Wilson, who after a series of nervous breakdowns, informed the band that he would no longer tour.

Although Brian Wilson's retreat hurt the band as a performing entity, during this period of disintegration, the group, with Brian producing as he had since "Surfer Girl," created some of its strongest music, notably *Pet Sounds* (1966)—a complex album with an introspective focus that incorporated amazingly diverse instrumentation: strings and horns, soda cans, and barking dogs. The Beatles cited *Pet Sounds* as the inspiration for their own groundbreaking album, *Sgt. Pepper's Lonely Hearts Club Band*. Three subsequent albums continued the musical experimentation, but Brian Wilson's increasingly erratic behavior (work on the album *Smile* was halted after he destroyed most of the tapes while in the grip of paranoid delusions) dictated that, increasingly, the other group members had to take over writing and production.

Impact Blending the close vocal harmonies of 1950's rock and roll with the dense, eclectic musical layering pioneered by producer Phil Spector, the Beach Boys virtually created the California sound and, in the process, an American icon: the surfer, whose sun-streaked beauty, athleticism, and love of the natural world typified the American ideal of endless summer—and endless youth.

Subsequent Events Dennis Wilson died in an alcohol-related diving accident in 1983. The Beach Boys, in various configurations and mostly without Brian Wilson, continued performing through the 1970's, 1980's, and 1990's. In 1988, the Beach Boys' "Kokomo" became a number-one hit, Brian Wilson released a solo album (*Brian Wilson*), and the Beach Boys were inducted into the Rock and Roll Hall of Fame. Carl Wilson died of lung cancer in 1998.

Additional Information Steven Gaines's biography of the group, *Heroes and Villains* (1986), gives a comprehensive closeup of the Beach Boys' lives and music. Brian Wilson's 1991 autobiography, *Wouldn't It Be Nice: My Own Story*, covers much of the same ground with an inside perspective.

Christl Reges

See also Beach Films; Beatles, The; Music; *Sgt. Pepper's Lonely Hearts Club Band*; Surfing.

■ Beach Films

A short-lived B-film genre that reflected the Southern California surfing culture of the 1960's. These films showcased nubile—though essentially innocent—youngsters whose entire lives seemed to be spent singing and dancing on the beach.

Surfing was as much a lifestyle as a sport, and it came to be identified with the Southern California way of life. The ascendancy of such singing groups as the Beach Boys brought surfing ever more into the public consciousness; it was inevitable that this appealing amalgam of sun, surf, sand, and tanned bodies would find its way into film, as it did with *Gidget* in 1959. The success of this film, starring Sandra Dee, ensured that Hollywood would follow up with similar films—at least until the box office ran dry.

American-International Pictures (AIP) was best known for its sophomoric exploitation films (such as *I Was a Teenage Werewolf*, 1957), the Roger Corman oeuvre, and the so-called sword and sandal epics. It found a winning formula with its series of beach films, beginning with *Beach Party* in 1963. Costarring once popular, but fading Robert Cummings, *Beach Party* was directed by television director William Asher, who also helmed the next two productions. Shot in two weeks, it cost about half a million dollars and earned some six million dollars. Although other studios immediately jumped on the bandwagon, this genre was almost always associated with AIP, which actually produced only seven of the more than forty beach films. Most of AIP's films starred skinny teen idol and singer Frankie Avalon and former Disney Mouseketeer Annette Funicello. Some of the featured actors were television comics such as Morey Amsterdam, Buddy Hackett, Harvey Lembeck, Paul Lynde, and Don Rickles. Other cast members included formerly eminent actors such as Buster Keaton, Elsa Lanchester, Mickey Rooney, and Keenan

Wynn and even the silent film matinee idol Francis X. Bushman. Many of the young people who frequently appeared in the productions (among them Aron Kincaid, Bobbi Shaw, Donna Loren, Ed Garner, Michael Nader, and Susan Hart) were recruited on local beaches. A few, including Tommy Kirk, John Ashley, Jody McCrea, and Dwayne Hickman, had already had some minor career success.

The plots of the beach films, which ranged from encounters with motorcycle gangs to meetings with aliens, were, of course, only thin devices to get a group of young people to cavort on the beach. Though the plots varied from one film to the next, all the films shared certain traits. Despite the 1960's ambience supplied by groups and singers such as the Exciters, Hondells, and Stevie Wonder and contemporary dances such as the frug, pony, and watusi, the films did not really portray the social trends and upheavals of those times. For instance, the story lines only hinted at the sexual revolution. There was plenty of skin, scanty apparel, and even some sugges-

tive talk, but teasing innuendo was generally as far as it went. Because of her Disney connections, Funicello was not allowed to wear a bikini and the characters she played remained militantly pure.

Among the other beach films, some made by more mainstream studios such as Paramount and Columbia were *Ride the Wild Surf* (1964), *Beach Ball* (1965), *Wild on the Beach* (aka *Beach House Party*, 1965), *Bikini Beach* (1964), *Operation Bikini* (1963), *Surf Party* (1964), *How to Stuff a Wild Bikini* (1965), and *Beach Blanket Bingo* (1965). The beach film even met the horror genre in such epics as *The Ghost in the Invisible Bikini* (1965), *The Beach Girls and the Monster* (aka *Monster from the Surf*, 1965), and *The Horror of Party Beach* (1964).

Impact The age of the big motion-picture musical, with some exceptions, essentially died in the mid-1950's. The beach films coincided with the increasing box-office clout of teenage filmgoers, and with their lively, if forgettable, rock-and-roll songs, they

Film stars Annette Funicello and Frankie Avalon enjoy a moment on the beach in Muscle Beach Party *(1964). Motion picture studios turned out a steady stream of fun-in-the-sun beach films aimed at teenagers in the first half of the 1960's.* (Museum of Modern Art/Film Stills Archive)

kept the musical genre alive, however poorly. They, along with the films of rock star Elvis Presley, were among the few musical films to achieve popularity in the 1960's. Replete with surfing lingo such as "cowabunga," "shoot the curl," "woody," and "beach bunny," they reinforced the world's view of Southern California as a sort of sunny, homogeneous paradise. In the beach films, people never really worked, were mainly white and middle class, and seemed unaware of the issues that concerned the rest of the nation, including civil rights and the Vietnam War. Actually, the influence of these films was probably limited because they did not find great popularity outside the United States except in similarly cultured Australia.

Subsequent Events Beach films were popular from 1963 through 1966, and were followed by another short-lived series of films about skiing teenagers, including *Ski Party* (1965). Eventually audiences tired of the supremacy of teen films, and their appetite turned to the more realistic motion pictures of the late 1960's and 1970's. Most of the younger cast members who frolicked on the beach had brief careers and fell into obscurity, but the leads have been somewhat more in evidence. Avalon appeared in numerous films and has maintained his visibility in show business, if not in the cinema. Funicello, one of the few actresses of the genre recognizable by her first name alone, appeared in television commercials and has been in the news because of her valiant struggle against multiple sclerosis. Before she fell seriously ill, she and longtime friend Avalon were reunited in 1986's *Back to the Beach*, an attempt to recapture the nostalgia of the 1960's. The picture did not prove successful.

Additional Information Beach films are described in articles such as "Those Swinging Beach Movies" in the July 31, 1965, issue of the *Saturday Evening Post* and "Peekaboo Sex" in the July 16, 1965, issue of *Life* magazine. A scholarly approach is taken in "Beyond the Beach" in the spring, 1993, issue of the *Journal of Popular Film and Television*. In the summer of 1965, Checkerbooks published two apparently very short-lived fan magazines, *The Beach Boys* and *The Beach Girls*, which dealt solely with beach films and their young players.

Roy Liebman

See also Beach Boys, The; Film; Gidget Films; Surfing.

■ Beat Generation

An artistic movement noted for experimentation and a bohemian lifestyle. The Beats questioned social and artistic values, tested the limits of censorship, innovated in literary techniques and forms, and investigated diverse religions.

In 1944, as the United States concerned itself with atomic weapons, the arms race, fear of communism, and the pursuit of material gain, a friendship formed among Allen Ginsberg, Jack Kerouac, William S. Burroughs, and other writers and artists near Columbia University in New York City. These artists became associated with a movement based on candor, sympathy, joy in life, and tenderness, expressed chiefly in autobiographical literature. The Beat generation, though centered around Ginsberg, Kerouac, and Burroughs, came to include other artists such as Lawrence Ferlinghetti, Gary Snyder, and Gregory Corso, and the movement flowered in San Francisco and spread to various parts of the world, including Mexico, Morocco, India, Japan, and Europe.

Early Beats The Beats' material proved mostly unpublishable for many years, but a successful reading at the Six Gallery in San Francisco on October 7, 1955, inspired Ferlinghetti, director of City Lights Books in San Francisco, to publish Ginsberg's *Howl and Other Poems* (1956) as a slim paperback in the Pocket Poets series. The title poem of the collection begins "I saw the best minds of my generation destroyed by madness, starving hysterical naked" and proceeds through a long catalog of vivid, forceful images and sometimes vulgar language and descriptions. Ginsberg's book precipitated a censorship trial, and widespread media coverage developed. Ferlinghetti was vindicated, and the Beats gained fame as champions of free expression.

In 1957, Kerouac's *On the Road*, after being rejected by various editors, was published by Viking Press. *New York Times* reviewer Gilbert Millstein proclaimed that Kerouac's book was an artistical representation of the author's generation just as Ernest Hemingway's *The Sun Also Rises* had stood for the Lost Generation of the 1920's. The adventures of Sal Paradise and Dean Moriarty captured the imagination of many readers, and *On the Road* became a best-seller. Paradise's description of "all that raw land that rolls in one unbelievable huge bulge over to the West Coast, and all that road going, all the people

dreaming in the immensity of it" made Kerouac the most admired of all Beat writers.

In the 1950's, Burroughs became involved in drug addiction and crime, and to support his habit and avoid the authorities, he traveled to Mexico City and Tangier, Morocco. In 1959, his *The Naked Lunch* was published in Paris. The novel's abandonment of traditional narrative and its inclusion of a circus world of scatological references marked a new direction in experimental prose.

The Beat Lifestyle As the Beats became famous and controversial, the media pursued the idea of what being "beat" involved, and the sensationalized image delivered to the public was that the Beats were wild-eyed men of the road, exploring all possibilities in sex and drugs and seeking out intense experiences in jazz clubs, at parties, and on the highway. Critics and traditional literary scholars attacked the Beats for excessive sentimentality and a lack of artistic

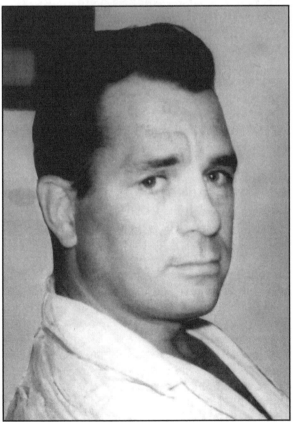

The Beat generation, a group of artists noted for their bohemian lifestyle and literary experimentation, centered around three artists: William S. Burroughs (top left), Jack Kerouac (left), and Allen Ginsberg (right). (Burroughs—Brion Gysin/Archive Photos; Kerouac—Archive Photos; Ginsberg—Camera Press Ltd./Archive Photos)

discipline, but the Beat movement only gained strength from these rejections. Publishers enthusiastically released Kerouac's *The Dharma Bums* (1958), *The Subterraneans* (1958), *Maggie Cassidy* (1959), and *Doctor Sax* (1959). As photo spreads appeared in *Life* and *Look*, producers of television shows, radio programs, and motion pictures hastened to seize upon the interest occasioned by the Beats. On April 2, 1958, *San Francisco Chronicle* columnist Herb Caen coined the word "beatnik" by using it in his column, and soon a caricature of the Beats as lazy, bearded weirdos developed. Maynard G. Krebs exemplified this caricature in the television series *The Many Loves of Dobie Gillis* (1959-1963), and a satire on beatniks appeared in *MAD* magazine (September, 1960), which presented the mock magazine *Beatnik: The Magazine for Hipsters*.

The Beats and the 1960's In December, 1960, Ginsberg, Peter Orlovsky, and Timothy Leary met at Leary's home to experiment with psilocybin, a hallucinogen. Ginsberg had such an intense experience that he wanted all humankind to have the benefits of the drug, and with Leary, he contemplated ways to begin a psychedelic revolution.

Ginsberg's popularity as a writer endured in the 1960's, as his continued publications demonstrate. City Lights Books published *Kaddish and Other Poems* (1961), and the title poem about the poet's mother and her struggle with mental health is often termed Ginsberg's masterpiece because of its extraordinary frankness in dealing with intensely personal information. During the 1960's, Ginsberg also published *Reality Sandwiches* (1963) and later traveled to Cuba and Europe. In Prague, Czechoslovakia, his popularity led the people to proclaim him King of May, but a poetry notebook fell into the hands of the police and provided the Czechoslovakian government with an excuse to expel him from the country.

In 1962, Burroughs's *Naked Lunch* was published in the United States, and a four-year censorship trial ensued in Massachusetts. Efforts to suppress the book failed, and so much attention was directed at the book that Burroughs became well-known despite divided critical opinion. Around the time of the U.S. debut of *Naked Lunch*, Burroughs created works such as *The Soft Machine* (1961), *The Ticket That Exploded* (1962), and *Nova Express* (1964), which serve as didactic and satirical works warning against the forces of control and as experiments in the cut-up

technique, a method of composition influenced by surrealist painters.

Kerouac's prolific writing was evidenced by the publication of *Lonesome Traveler* (1960), *Tristessa* (1960), *Pull My Daisy* (1961), *Big Sur* (1962), *Visions of Gerard* (1963), *Desolation Angels* (1965), *Satori in Paris* (1966), and *Vanity of Duluoz* (1968).

In 1968, Neal Cassady, the personality who inspired Kerouac's creation of Moriarty in *On the Road* and gained notoriety for the activities described in Tom Wolfe's *The Electric Kool-Aid Acid Test* (1968), died of exposure when he slipped into drug-induced unconsciousness while walking along railroad tracks in Mexico.

Ginsberg became active in the antiwar movement, and in *Wichita Vortex Sutra* (1966), he expressed his opposition to the war in Vietnam. In 1967, along with Ferlinghetti, Michael McClure, Leary, Lenore Kandel, and Snyder, Ginsberg participated in the Human Be-in in San Francisco, and in 1968, Ginsberg, along with Burroughs, went to Chicago to observe the Democratic National Convention and the tumultuous events surrounding it. In 1968, Ginsberg published *Planet News*, a book of verse that focused less on confession of personal suffering and more on national and international problems affecting the lives of masses of human beings.

In 1969, Kerouac found himself trying to determine where he stood "between the established politicians and the radicals, between cops and hoods, tax collectors and vandals." After a long struggle with the media's misinterpretation of his artistic accomplishments, Kerouac succumbed to alcoholism in St. Petersburg, Florida, on October 21, 1969.

Impact Because the Beats distrusted conformity, questioned and avoided authority, and were associated with movements for racial tolerance, peace, sexual freedom, and experimentation with drugs, they are often seen as forerunners of the hippies. Kerouac's *On the Road* steadily sold many thousands of copies in the 1960's, and the legendary travels, drug experiences, and sexual and musical pleasures described by Sal Paradise inspired the lives of many flower children. Ken Kesey, Cassady, and the Merry Pranksters' journey in their psychedelic bus, described in the 1968 work *The Electric Kool-Aid Acid Test*, helped to popularize the spirit of the Beats in the 1960's. Ginsberg's advocacy of peace, homosexual liberation, drug experiences, and environmental awareness fit well with the decade's spirit of life. As a result of the victories of the Beats in court cases involving literary censorship, new freedom of expression became possible in the 1960's, and advocates of free speech pressed for further gains.

Subsequent Events Ginsberg died in New York City on April 5, 1997, and Burroughs died in Lawrence, Kansas, on August 2, 1997.

Additional Information Anthologies of Beat literature include *The New American Poetry* (1960), edited by Donald Allen; *The Portable Beat Reader* (1992), edited by Ann Charters; and *The Beat Book* (1996), edited by Anne Waldman. See John Tytell's *Naked Angels: The Lives and Literature of the Beat Generation* (1976) for biographical background and interpretation of the works of Burroughs, Ginsberg, and Kerouac. For a broader view of the members of the Beat generation, see *The Beats: Literary Bohemians in Postwar America* (1983), a two-volume encyclopedia edited by Charters that offers background on dozens of authors and includes many photos and illustrations.

William T. Lawlor

See also Be-ins and Love-ins; Drug Culture; *Electric Kool-Aid Acid Test, The*; Ferlinghetti, Lawrence; Free Love; Gay Liberation Movement; Ginsberg, Allen; Greenwich Village; Hippies; Leary, Timothy; Literature; LSD; Poetry; San Francisco as Cultural Mecca.

■ Beatles, The

Pop music quartet from Liverpool, England. The Beatles were the most successful and influential band of the decade, leading the British invasion of American music and revolutionizing rock in the 1960's.

After John Lennon and Paul McCartney met as high school students in Liverpool, England, Lennon invited McCartney to join his band, the Quarrymen. At McCartney's request, George Harrison was brought into the group, then Lennon convinced Stuart Sutcliffe, who had just sold a painting for a large sum of money, to buy a bass guitar and join them. Drummer Pete Best became part of the group in 1960, just before the band first played clubs in Hamburg, Germany. In 1961, when Sutcliffe left to pursue art, McCartney switched to bass guitar. In

1962, Best was fired in favor of Ringo Starr, shortly before the Beatles recorded their first single, "Love Me Do."

From their first major single in the United States, "I Want to Hold Your Hand," in 1964, through the album *Let It Be* in 1970, the Beatles evolved through several styles and caused significant changes in pop music. With producer George Martin, the Beatles expanded the bounds of popular music, adding orchestras, reversed tapes, hooks, gimmicks, and new instruments to rock.

In February, 1964, the Beatles came to the United States, appearing first on *The Ed Sullivan Show* before a screaming crowd carried away by "Beatlemania." Early songs, including hits such as "Can't Buy Me Love," "She Loves You," and "Yesterday," were mostly about romantic love, although the song-writing team of Lennon and McCartney began to experiment with changing points of view and complex chord changes. Early albums contained a mixture of self-penned songs and standards, often from Motown. The Beatles also released two popular movies, *A Hard Day's Night* in 1964 and *Help!* in 1965. Hints of a maturing musical style emerged on *Rubber Soul* (1965), *Yesterday . . . and Today* (1966), and *Revolver* (1966).

The strains of touring and the increasing complexity of their music led the Beatles to abandon touring in 1966 and become purely a studio band. This decision bore fruit on *Sgt. Pepper's Lonely Hearts Club Band* (1967), which would provide the perfect backdrop for the Summer of Love. By this time, illicit drugs had become an increasing influence in the Beatles' lives and music, as reflected in this album's psychedelic music. Later that year, the Beatles experimented with Indian mysticism, spending time with the Maharishi Mahesh Yogi in early 1968. They later became disillusioned with the Maharishi, but Indian philosophy and music continued to influence the band, mostly through Harrison, who usually contributed a song to each album side. The group released another film, *The Magical Mystery Tour*, in 1967. The animated *Yellow Submarine* (1968) featured Beatles songs and voice-overs by actors imitating the Beatles.

Under the Apple Record label, in 1968, they released the double album *The Beatles* (often known as the "White Album" for its white cover), a work that by its divergent styles showed how their interests and lives were beginning to separate. Lennon became

The Beatles' appearance on The Ed Sullivan Show *in 1964 drew a television audience of more than seventy million.* (Popper-foto/Archive Photos)

inseparable from Japanese avant-garde artist Yoko Ono, whom he married in 1969, and McCartney married Linda Eastman, an American photographer, who died in 1998. The demise of the band was inadvertently chronicled in the film *Let It Be* (1970), which was recorded before *Abbey Road* (1969) although its soundtrack was released as the Beatles' final album of new material.

Impact The Beatles ended the reign of surfing bands and teen idols on American pop radio and led the way for countless other British bands. Their music and appearance influenced many later musicians. Young Americans adopted the music, hairstyles, clothing, and later, the facial hair and drug use of the Beatles. The group's feature films and the short promotional films released concurrent with singles after their retirement from touring sowed the seeds of the music video revolution a generation later.

Subsequent Events The Beatles broke up in 1970 amid a torrent of lawsuits and countersuits. Each

former Beatle embarked on a solo career that occasionally produced excellent and commercial music but never matched the artistic achievement or originality of the Beatles. A much-hoped-for reunion of the band never materialized. Lennon, who had briefly retired from public life in the 1970's, was killed by a fan, Mark David Chapman, outside his New York City apartment on December 8, 1980, as he was returning from a recording studio.

In the mid-1990's, the surviving Beatles began working on a three-part television documentary on the band, entitled *Anthology*. The project included the release of three albums containing alternate takes and demos of previously released material and songs recorded but not released during the 1960's. The albums contained two new songs, "Free as a Bird" (1996) and "Real Love" (1996), which the remaining Beatles completed using tracks Lennon had been working on at the time of his death. McCartney, Harrison, and Starr have dismissed any speculation that they might reform for performances.

Additional Information *Shout!* (1981), by Philip Norman, provides an in-depth look at the Beatles in the 1960's. Roy Carr and Tony Tyler's *The Beatles: An Illustrated Record* (1975) focuses on the recorded output of the band, and the *Ultimate Beatles Encyclopedia* (1992), by Bill Harry, details every person, place, or thing ever connected with the band.

Barry M. Stentiford

See also British Invasion; Music; Ono, Yoko; Rolling Stones.

■ Bell Jar, The

Published 1963 (England), 1971 (United States)
Author Sylvia Plath (1932-1963)

An influential novel about gender-role conflicts facing women in the 1960's. The story, in part autobiographical, follows the promise, frustration, and decline of a talented young writer from her arrival in New York to her hospitalization for mental illness following an attempted suicide.

The Work In *The Bell Jar*, Esther Greenwood, a nineteen-year-old girl from a small eastern town, was an excellent student who won many awards including a college scholarship. As a contest winner, she received a one-month appointment as a college representative to the editorial board of a well-known New York fashion magazine. Her month in New York provided many maturing experiences, but emotionally, she still felt very insecure. Esther did not believe that she had the skills necessary to fulfill a traditional woman's role. She was bothered by society's double standard and different social expectations for men and women. She was drawn to the life of change and excitement enjoyed by men, the life she associated with a writing career. She felt, however, pressure to settle down, marry, and have children. Her self-doubt coupled with the awareness of differing role expectations laid the foundation for an internal conflict that resulted in depression. Because she could not eat or sleep, she was referred to a psychiatrist, who suggested shock treatments. These treatments did not relieve her condition, and she began to contemplate and later attempt suicide. With the help of a benefactor, Esther was treated at a private asylum with insulin and electric shock treatments. As her condition improved, Esther moved to less restrictive environments and was accorded more privileges. She described her relief as the "bell jar lifted." Upon her release, she returned to college.

Impact Plath originally published *The Bell Jar* under the pseudonym "Victoria Lucas." Until Plath's suicide, the book received only minor attention. In the first reviews, critics were struck by her imagery and ruthless, pessimistic style. They described her writing as intelligent, precise, and passionate. A work dealing with mental illness posed some tricky problems for the reviewers. The book was more than just literature; it was the author's life, her experience. They found it difficult to critique the types of internal conflict that could lead to suicide. However, Plath's own mental illness did not diminish the truth of her story. Reviewers were impressed with her brilliance and the depth of her personal pain.

Plath lived and wrote at the beginning of a period of great social change in the United States. The 1960's ushered in the growth of the Civil Rights movement and the emergence of the women's movement. People began to question traditional values, resulting in considerable experimentation in forms of family life, religion, sexual mores, and drug usage. *The Bell Jar* and Plath's life highlight a number of these issues. For example, Esther felt that marriage was a form of brainwashing in which women were conditioned to believe that they should serve men. Plath questioned the personal value of religion, which she saw as cold and stressing sin. She was for most of her life a Unitarian, although she thought about becoming a Catholic to counter her suicidal thoughts and inclinations. Through Esther's struggles, *The Bell Jar* also addresses Plath's attempt to come to terms with her sexuality. Plath did marry, but her loneliness, depression, and the demands of their small children led her to separate from her husband, Ted Hughes, who later became poet laureate of England. She was a single mother when she committed suicide. In many ways, her life and her work became archetypes for the turbulent, value-testing, social experimentation of the 1960's.

Because *The Bell Jar* was first published in England, it did not have a strong influence on U.S. society until its reissue in 1971. By this time, the social forces of the 1960's had had time to mature. Gender roles were changing, various groups had gained their civil rights, and people were experimenting with various lifestyles. *The Bell Jar* portrayed a young woman struggling against many constricting forces, including her own personal demons. These struggles reflect the conflicts faced by many young middle-class women in the 1960's. The book stands as a criticism of 1960's American society. Although the negative forces in Plath's life eventually won, she left behind a legacy of intense, passionate, and honest life pictures.

Related Works Plath's two poetry collections, *The Colossus* (1962) and *Ariel* (1965), express many of the same sentiments evident in *The Bell Jar*. A film version of *The Bell Jar* was released in 1979.

Additional Information For articles placing Plath's novel and poetry in an intellectual and cultural perspective, including biographical information and other examples of her writing, see *The Art of Sylvia Plath* (1970), by Charles Newman.

Janice Rienerth and Mike Wise

See also Civil Rights Movement; *Feminine Mystique, The*; Literature; Poetry; Women's Identity.

■ Berlin Wall

Date August 12-13, 1961

International crisis surrounding the city of Berlin during the Cold War era.

Origins and History Following Germany's defeat in World War II, the capital city Berlin was occupied—as was the entire country—by the four victorious powers: the United States, the Soviet Union, Britain, and France. Berlin, located deep within the Soviet zone of occupation, however, was to be administered jointly by the four powers. In 1948, when the ideological rift between the East and West increased, the Soviets denied the Western powers access to Berlin. The Western allies had sponsored the establishment of the Federal Republic of Germany, made up of the Western zones of occupation. The Soviets' main purpose for the blockade was to drive the West out

President John F. Kennedy (on platform, center front) looks at and over the Berlin Wall erected in 1961. During his visit, he reaffirmed the United States' support for West Berliners. (John F. Kennedy Library)

of Berlin to gain a free hand in converting their zone into a communist dictatorship. The Soviets rightly feared that a continued Western presence in the middle of their planned state would prevent the consolidation of the communist political and economic system.

The answer of the Western allies to the challenge of closed land routes to Berlin was an eleven-month-long airlift that brought food, fuel, and other supplies to the more than two million inhabitants of the three Western sectors of the city. The Berlin Air Lift, a logistical masterpiece, proved a propaganda nightmare for the Soviets, who lifted the blockade in May, 1949.

The Wall By tacit agreement, the Western sectors of Berlin were allowed to participate in the political and economic system of the Federal Republic, and East Berlin became the capital of the newly founded German Democratic Republic, a Communist satellite state modeled after the Soviet Union. Fortified border defenses cordoned off the Communist bloc from Western Europe. Berlin remained the only loophole in the Iron Curtain because people from the communist world could escape to the free world. In this divided city, escaping was as easy as crossing the street from an Eastern to a Western district. Between 1945 and 1961, an estimated six million people (three million since 1953) fled from communist domination. The people fleeing to the West were some of the most skilled and productive in society, and their leaving threatened the stability of a strong communist regime in East Germany.

In 1958, the new Soviet leader, Nikita Khrushchev, delivered an ultimatum that he would turn control of the city and its approaches over to the East Germans. The threat of closing off Berlin led to an increase in the number of refugees. In 1960, more than 230,000 people left East Germany, three-fourths of them under forty-five years of age. At the Vienna Summit, where Khrushchev and the newly inaugurated U.S. president John F. Kennedy met, the Soviets repeated threats for a unilateral change of the status of Berlin. Despite efforts by the East German police to restrict citizens' access to Berlin and aggressive patrolling of the boundaries of the Soviet sector of the city, the rate of refugees rose to more than 20,000 per month. The hemorrhaging of East Germany was widely publicized by the Western media.

On Sunday, August 13, 1961, at 2:00 A.M., East German troops closed the checkpoints between East and West and sealed off the entire Soviet sector with barbed wire in accordance with a decree passed the previous day. The temporary barrier was soon replaced by a crude cement block wall running thirty miles through the center of Berlin, as well as surrounding all of West Berlin. The West had been completely taken by surprise but could intervene only at the risk of war. The coarse makeshift wall was soon replaced by a twelve-foot-high wall of prefabricated cement slabs. The Wall effectively stopped the flow of refugees and started a period of consolidation and economic growth for the East German state.

This gain was not without costs. After the Wall was built, the United States dispatched high-profile politicians to Berlin, including Vice President Lyndon B. Johnson and the former U.S. high commissioner Lucius D. Clay, who represented the United States during the Berlin blockade. President Kennedy personally came to see the Wall and made his famous *"Ich bin ein Berliner"* ("I am a Berliner") speech to reassure the population of West Berlin of continued U.S. support. The West German government took every important visitor and world leader to inspect the horrendous structure, thus keeping media attention focused on the division of Germany.

Impact The West accepted the Berlin Wall as an alternative to continual international crisis verging on the brink of war and benefited from the negative publicity it generated for those who built it. The structure vividly demonstrated the failure and inhumanity of a system that needed to wall in its people to keep them from running away.

Subsequent Events In the fall of 1989, popular demonstrations for more democracy by East Germans led to a replacement of the leading Communist politicians. At an international news conference in East Berlin on the evening of November 9, 1989, as the result of continuous popular unrest, the new Communist leadership announced a policy of free travel. Thousands of East Berliners spontaneously went to the border crossings to test the new policy, demanding passage to West Berlin. This demand caught the border guards by surprise. In panic, they telephoned the Communist Party chiefs to confirm the new policy, adding that they did not have enough forces to contain the growing and angry crowd. They received word to let the people pass without formalities. The news of the open Wall reached others via Western radio and television. The number of East Berliners who crossed into West Berlin that night reached several hundred thousand. An unprecedented fiesta of celebration and fraternization commenced. The impromptu festivity lasted until dawn when most Easterners returned home. The very next day, as a prelude to the formal unification of Germany on October 3, 1990, Berliners from East and West dismantled the Wall with hammers and chisels.

Additional Information In *The Crisis Years: Kennedy and Khrushchev, 1960-1963* (1991), Michael A. Beschloss details the encounters between President Kennedy and the Soviet leader. Norman Gelb, in *The Berlin Wall* (1986), describes the building of the Wall

Composer and conductor Leonard Bernstein leads the New York Philharmonic during a rehearsal. (AP/Wide World Photos)

and its role in the Cold War. William Atwood's *The Twilight Struggle* (1987) provides anecdotal information on the Cold War.

Herbert Luft

See also Cold War; Kennedy, John F.; Khrushchev's UN Visit.

■ Bernstein, Leonard

Born August 25, 1918, Lawrence, Massachusetts
Died October 14, 1990, New York, New York

One of the most important musicians of the latter half of the twentieth century. As a composer and conductor, Bernstein enjoyed unparalleled success in and influence on the cultural life of the United States during the 1960's.

Early Life Leonard Bernstein started playing piano as a child and studied music at Harvard and the Curtis Institute of Music in Philadelphia. In 1943, he became assistant conductor of the New York Philharmonic. During the 1940's and 1950's, he worked as a composer, pianist, and conductor. His 1957 musical, *West Side Story*, was acclaimed as a classic. In 1959, he became music director of the New York Philharmonic, a post he would hold through 1969.

The 1960's During the decade, Bernstein greatly influenced cultural life in the United States. In September, 1962, he inaugurated the country's premier performing arts center, New York's Lincoln Center for the Performing Arts, and in November, 1963, he conducted the New York Philharmonic in a televised concert commemorating slain President John F. Kennedy. Capitalizing on the renown that came with national television exposure, by the mid-1960's Bernstein was the most popular classical musician in the United States, a media star. His name was mentioned in Hollywood films such as *Breakfast at Tiffany's*, and popular magazines such as *Look* and *Time* published profiles of him and his family. He wrote several popular books: *The Joy of Music* (1963), *The Infinite Variety of Music* (1966), and *Leonard Bernstein's Young People's Concerts for Reading and Listening* (1961).

During the 1960's, Bernstein's musical career focused on conducting the New York Philharmonic and the great orchestras of the world and promoting the music of Gustav Mahler. In 1966, he conducted the Vienna Philharmonic in a performance of Mahler's *Das Lied von der Erde*. The event marked the first time that the orchestra had performed this monumental work because Mahler's music had fallen out of favor with the Viennese. At first, anti-Jewish and anti-American sentiment presented obstacles for Bernstein, but by the time of the performance, he had won the unfailing loyalty of musicians and audiences alike.

Bernstein became a political activist in the 1960's. He lent his support to liberal causes such as the Black Panthers, the peace movement, and the political struggles of Israel, conducting an outdoor concert at Jerusalem's Mount Scopus following the Six-Day War of 1967.

Later Life In 1969, Bernstein was appointed conductor laureate of the New York Philharmonic. In his later years, he returned to composing and continued to conduct the great orchestras of the world. He also gave lectures on music at Harvard and elsewhere.

Impact Bernstein took advantage of the high profile afforded by his tenure as music director of the New York Philharmonic with a seemingly endless energy for self-promotion. He was keenly aware of the power of television and the long-play recording to reach large audiences. He conducted a series of nationally televised Young People's Concerts, an educational introduction to classical music viewed by millions, and beginning in the late 1960's, he recorded nearly all of his performances in audio and video formats. These recordings were marketed worldwide, increasing Bernstein's fame and enormous success even more.

His very animated style of conducting, which involved wild gestures and even leaping from the podium, as well as intensely inward turnings, was ideally suited to highlighting the emotional nuances of Mahler's music, resulting in performances that spawned renewed interest in Mahler virtually worldwide.

Additional Information The details of Bernstein's life are covered in numerous biographies and in Bernstein's memoirs, *Findings*, published in 1982.

Richard Allen Roe

See also Music; Rubinstein, Arthur; Thomson, Virgil.

■ Berrigan, Daniel

Born May 9, 1921, Virginia, Minnesota

■ Berrigan, Philip

Born October 5, 1923, Two Harbors, Minnesota

Two of the most important American Catholic antiwar activists during the Vietnam War. The Berrigan brothers, Roman Catholic priests, were sentenced to federal prison for conducting nonviolent but attention-getting protests.

Early Life The fifth and sixth sons of an Irish and German family, Daniel Joseph and Philip Francis Berrigan grew up in a pious, poor Catholic household in rural Minnesota and upstate New York. Daniel, the older of the two, entered the Jesuit order in 1939 and was ordained a priest in 1952. His training included a year in France, where he encountered the Priest Workers, progressive clerics seeking to recast the role of the church to increase its support of the disenfranchised. During Daniel's religious training, he also developed as a poet. In 1957, his first book of poetry received the Lamont Prize and a nomination for the National Book Award. While working at LeMoyne College, he initiated several projects for students to promote justice in housing and employment.

Philip was drafted and served as an artillery officer in Europe during World War II. In 1950 he entered the Josephites, a religious order dedicated to working with African Americans. Following ordination in 1955, he served in several parishes and in a New Orleans high school, where he helped integrate the previously segregated church.

In correspondence from 1953, they both agreed that the measure of their priesthood would be how they confronted U.S. social issues, such as racism, with Catholic principles.

The 1960's Two of the defining issues of the 1960's, racism and U.S. involvement in the Vietnam War, became the focus of the Berrigans' activity. Philip, who disliked the gradual, genteel, sometimes patronizing approach his liberal religious superiors took against racism, served in his order's ministries while continuing his activism.

By 1965, Daniel, working in New York City, had become one of the most vocal Catholic opponents to the Vietnam War. The New York archbishop, Francis Cardinal Spellman, openly encouraged the

Daniel Berrigan (right) and his brother, Philip Berrigan (center), both Roman Catholic priests, throw matches on burning draft records taken from a Baltimore, Maryland, facility in 1968. That same year, the pacifist brothers were arrested and later tried for throwing napalm on draft files in Catonsville, Maryland. (AP/Wide World Photos)

United States' participation in the war and used his influence to force Daniel's Jesuit superiors to exile him. The Jesuits sent Daniel to South America, ostensibly to fulfill an editorial job in the order. Once news of Daniel's whereabouts leaked to the press, his exile became a rallying point for many U.S. Catholics. The backlash was immediate and more severe than the cardinal had expected. While in South America, Daniel became acquainted with the most progressive figures in the Catholic Church as well as with some of the world's most appalling poverty. After a four-month absence, he returned to a hero's welcome and immediately took up unfettered antiwar activities in his new post as chaplain at Cornell University.

As the war escalated, so did the resistance to it. On October 22, 1967, thousands of protesters marched on the Pentagon. A small group, including Daniel, committed civil disobedience and were arrested and jailed. Five days later, Philip was arrested after he and three others entered the Baltimore, Maryland, Customs House and poured blood over several drawers of draft files that they had scattered on the floor. On May 17, 1968, the Berrigan brothers and seven other Catholic activists made a raid on the Selective Service office in Catonsville, Maryland. Using homemade napalm, they destroyed hundreds of draft files. Their trial—the transcript of which Daniel later fashioned into a play, *The Trial of the Catonsville Nine*—led to their conviction and imprisonment. Before the date set for his surrender to the authorities, Daniel went underground for four months, surfacing playfully now and then, frustrating an angry J. Edgar Hoover, director of the Federal Bureau of Investigation. The actions of the Berrigans inspired fifty other raids on government property before the end of the Vietnam War.

During their imprisonment, Philip began a correspondence with Elizabeth McAlister, a nun whom he married not long after his release from prison in 1972. The FBI intercepted that correspondence and concluded that Philip, Elizabeth, and five others were conspiring to blow up government buildings in Washington, D.C., and to kidnap Henry Kissinger, foreign policy adviser to President Richard M. Nixon. They were indicted in 1971, and the trial was held in Harrisburg, Pennsylvania. Although the indicted conspirators declined to put on a defense, the prosecution was able only to convict Philip of smuggling letters to Elizabeth.

Later Life After their marriage, Philip and Elizabeth had three children. The couple founded Jonah House in inner-city Baltimore, a community center for neighborhood organizing and peace-making activities. In the 1980's and 1990's, they continued to be involved in various antiwar efforts, including antinuclear demonstrations that resulted in arrests and jail sentences.

Daniel remained in the Jesuit order, continued to write (thirty-five books), lecture, and demonstrate widely in favor of peace. In 1979, he became a regular volunteer with dying cancer patients and, five years later, with AIDS patients as well.

Impact The Berrigan brothers, who in 1965 were the only clerics to advocate total "noncooperation" with the Vietnam War effort, were responsible for involving many clerics in antiwar efforts. Their efforts helped the clergy feel it was acceptable to voice their opposition to the war for moral and religious reasons. Pacifism became highly visible in U.S. Catholicism, and groups made up of clerics from various religious organizations and religious laypeople became involved in civil disobedience and demonstrating for peace. After the Vietnam War ended, many religious groups continued to work for peace, turning to antinuclear protests and to promoting peace in war-torn nations around the world.

Additional Information For additional information on the Berrigan brothers, see *Disarmed and Dangerous: The Radical Lives and Times of Daniel and Philip Berrigan* (1997), by Murray Polner and Jim O'Grady.

Daniel A. Brown

See also Civil Rights Movement; Draft Resisters; Vietnam War.

■ Biafran War

Unsuccessful war of secession in Nigeria. The war highlighted the tensions in U.S. foreign policy between stability of sovereign countries and the rights of peoples to self-determination against dictatorial governments.

The Biafran war was a civil war in which Biafra, a southeastern state dominated by Ibos, attempted to separate from Nigeria. The first incident in the war was a January 15, 1966, coup attempt. The civilian government had traditionally been controlled by the mostly Islamic Hausa and Fulani of northern Nigeria. Although the conspirators failed, the new military leadership took steps to change Nigeria from a regional federal system to a more unitary government. Northerners perceived this as a plot against them and launched a counter-coup in July, 1966. This coup succeeded, except in the Ibo-dominated Eastern Region.

A series of ethnic massacres later in 1966, mostly by northerners against the Ibo, foreclosed the possibility of reunification between the southeast, led by Lieutenant Colonel Emeka Odumegwu Ojukwo, and the rest of Nigeria, led by General Jakubo Gowon. Over one million Ibos fled other parts of Nigeria for the Eastern Region, and media throughout Nigeria fanned ethnic resentments. In May, 1967, Gowon announced the reorganization of Nigeria from four large geographic regions to twelve ethnic states: The Ibo section of the east would be in a different state from the oil-rich eastern coast. Having already appropriated most of the region's revenue and begun arming a regional army, Ojukwo declared independence for Biafra on June 1. After some brief success in taking the war toward Lagos, the Nigerian capital, the Ibo regions of Biafra were surrounded by federal troops and besieged. Biafra mostly failed in achieving international recognition: The official position of the Organization of African Unity was to support the retention of the original colonial boundaries and to not intervene in members' internal conflicts. The British and Soviets supplied the central government with arms; France provided less-open aid to Biafra. This, and a stream of humanitarian aid, helped maintain a yearlong stalemate beginning in late 1968. Nigeria, fearing further secession, would not concede national unity, especially in the light of its military advantage. Biafra, fearing genocide, refused to surrender. Biafran resistance collapsed in January, 1970. Estimates of Biafran casualties range between five hundred thousand and two million, mostly as a result of the siege. The feared postwar genocide did not materialize.

Impact The humanitarian aspect of the crisis in Biafra, with thousands of people dying daily from 1968 on, held the greatest attention in the United States. Media reports and photographs of ill and starving children and adults filled American newspapers and television screens. Groups such as the American Committee to Keep Biafra sent funds and supplies to Biafra, although the U.S. government maintained an arms embargo on both sides of the

conflict. President Lyndon B. Johnson was pressed by opponents, including Eugene McCarthy and Richard M. Nixon, to do more for Biafra; Nixon's policy as president was not markedly different from Johnson's. In the radical atmosphere of the late 1960's, the United States policy of nonintervention was vulnerable to criticism. The sentiments and dilemmas presented by the Biafran crisis have since been revisited in other countries such as Bangladesh, Somalia, and Bosnia-Herzegovina.

Additional Information John de St. Jorre, a war correspondent with the London *Observer*, has written a detailed account of the war and its broader significance in *The Brothers' War: Biafra and Nigeria* (1972).

Thomas S. Mowle

See also Johnson, Lyndon B.; McCarthy, Eugene.

■ Bilingual Education Act

Initially introduced to address the high dropout rate among Spanish-speaking Americans. The Bilingual Education Act of 1968 sought to prevent economic and social discrimination against students with limited English proficiency by increasing the students' English-language skills while maintaining their native cultural heritage.

Historically, immigrants to the United States tried to learn English as quickly as possible in an attempt to assimilate into their adopted country. Immigrant children were plunged into schools where all the instruction was in English and forced to "sink or swim," an approach that was viewed as speeding their adaptation to American ways. Any loss of cultural heritage was not viewed as important.

On January 17, 1967, Ralph Yarborough, Democratic senator from Texas, introduced the Bilingual Education Act, which amended the 1965 Elementary and Secondary Education Act by supplying federal funds to local educational agencies for the development and implementation of bilingual U.S. education programs. Emphasizing the history of Texas, Yarborough sought to address the high dropout rate among Spanish-speaking peoples of the Southwest, who made up 12 percent of the population. However, the bill's limitation to Spanish-speaking peoples drew sharp criticism for neglecting the well-being of other ethnic groups and undermining continued attempts to promote mutual respect and ethnic tolerance. Some feared that "ethnic divisiveness" would result if Spanish were taught as the native language and English as a second language. Later, language in the act was amended to address the needs of "children who come from environments where the dominant language is other than English." On January 2, 1968, President Lyndon B. Johnson signed the Bilingual Education Act into law.

Impact The Bilingual Education Act, an alternative to sink-or-swim public education, authorized $320 million to be dispersed between 1968 and 1973. However, a discrepancy emerged between fund authorization and actual allocation. Although $15 million was authorized in 1968, no funds were allocated; in 1969, $30 million was authorized but only $7.5 million was allocated. Three general standards determined the dispersal of funds: the geographic distribution of children between three and eighteen years of age with limited English proficiency, the capacity of local education agencies to advance bilingual programs, and the number of persons in low-income families (earning less than three thousand dollars per year or receiving payments from Aid to Families with Dependent Children) who would benefit. The act limited bilingual education to children from low-income families and failed to consider the participation of the English-speaking students. In addition, no systematic method for monitoring and assessing the success of bilingual education programs existed. Dependent on federal funding, these programs usually failed to garner fiscal commitment from state and local agencies.

Subsequent Events In 1974, the U.S. Supreme Court ruled unanimously in *Lau v. Nichols* that schools may violate the Civil Rights Act of 1964 if they deny special instruction to students with limited English proficiency. In 1975, Congress extended the Voting Rights Act of 1965, requiring bilingual voting assistance and placing a permanent ban on literacy tests for voting. In 1984, Congress extended the Bilingual Education Act through 1988, funding programs that help students maintain their mother tongue after learning English. In 1994, Congress passed the Improving America's Schools Act, altering federal grant provisions for the Bilingual Education Act.

Additional Information For further information on the act and the issues surrounding it, see Arnold Leibowitz's *The Bilingual Education Act: A Legislative Analysis* (1980) and James Crawford's *Language Loy-*

alties: A Source Book on the Official English Controversy (1992).

Sue Hum

See also Civil Rights Act of 1964; Education; Voting Rights Legislation.

■ Birmingham March

Date April 4-May 7, 1963

Protest march against segregation. A series of demonstrations in Birmingham, Alabama, sponsored by the Southern Christian Leadership Conference (SCLC), were designed to draw attention to the violent racism that underlay white southerners' defense of segregation.

Origins and History A disappointing campaign in Albany, Georgia, in 1962, prompted the Southern Christian Leadership Conference (SCLC) to select Birmingham, Alabama, as its subsequent target for nonviolent demonstrations. Protests against segregation had failed in Albany because the city's chief of police, Laurie Pritchett, had held white mobs at bay and prevented the violent confrontations between police and protesters that would produce media coverage. Martin Luther King, Jr., and other SCLC leaders met in Savannah, Georgia, at the end of 1962 to plan a series of demonstrations in Birmingham, a city noted for its racial violence and uncompromising stand against the Civil Rights movement. The strategists hoped to gain national attention by provoking Birmingham officials into explicit displays of racial antagonism, thereby revealing the true face of southern segregation.

The March Project C, the SCLC's code name for its assault on segregation in Birmingham, proceeded in three stages. First, on the morning of April 4, 1963, an economic boycott of downtown businesses went into effect, and small groups began staging sit-ins at downtown lunch counters. After Chief of Police Eugene "Bull" Conner ordered arrests, the protest caught the attention of the media and the administration of John F. Kennedy. Stage two began on April 6 with daily marches on city hall. As the protest leaders had expected, the Birmingham police arrested all of the demonstrators while flashbulbs popped and television cameras whirred. King himself was arrested and during his incarceration penned his "Letter from Birmingham Jail," an eloquent statement of the motivations that guided the

In April-May, 1963, a series of protests against segregation in Birmingham, Alabama, caught the attention of the media when police began to beat demonstrators and turn fire hoses and dogs on them. (AP/Wide World Photos)

Civil Rights movement. Police began to respond to the daily marches with less and less restraint, and African Americans began turning out for the marches in ever-larger numbers and tightened the economic boycott. The sit-ins, protest marches, and police violence had riveted a national audience to their television sets by the time the third stage began on May 2. That morning, more than one thousand African American children exited the Sixteenth Avenue Baptist Church as adult spectators cheered them on. The "children's crusade" sang and danced its way into the paddywagons waiting to take them to jail. Extensive criticism of the decision to use children rained down from both sides of the struggle, but King and the other leaders had little choice. Adults had become reluctant to march and serve jail time. More important, the protest leaders recognized that the sight of children being arrested would stir the heart of the nation. The police's actions—beating and turning fire hoses on protesters—and their continued brutality were captured by the media as the marches and arrests continued until May 7.

The Senior Citizen's Committee, which had been organized by the Birmingham Chamber of Commerce to handle racial matters, feared that continued racial violence would drive away business and permanently damage the city's reputation. On the afternoon of May 7, they met in secret session and ordered their negotiators to open talks with the SCLC. After three days of negotiations, the two sides reached an agreement that called for the desegregation of public accommodations, nondiscrimination in the hiring and promoting of African American workers in Birmingham industries, and the formation of a biracial committee. Even though the SCLC compromised and allowed gradual rather than immediate implementation of these measures, the demonstrations in Birmingham were considered a significant victory for the movement.

Impact Public reaction to the events in Birmingham, along with the easing of Cold War tensions, convinced President Kennedy that the time had come for federal action in defense of civil rights, and he asked Congress for civil rights legislation. The Civil Rights Act of 1964 was signed into law on July 2 by President Lyndon B. Johnson, Kennedy's successor. The act prohibited segregation of public accommodations, made discrimination by employers and unions illegal, and created the Equal Employment

Opportunity Commission. The broader impact of the march was to change the tone of the Civil Rights movement from gradualism to immediacy; the African American community was no longer willing to wait for decent jobs, adequate housing, and a quality education. The march also marked the entry of poor and unemployed African Americans into the struggle.

Additional Information Accounts of the Birmingham march can be found in Harvard Sitcoff's *The Struggle for Black Equality* (1993) and Taylor Branch's *Parting the Waters: America in the King Years, 1954-1963* (1988).

Robert E. McFarland

See also Civil Rights Act of 1964; Civil Rights Movement; King, Martin Luther, Jr.; Southern Christian Leadership Conference (SCLC).

■ Birth Control

A revolution in methods of contraception and patterns of human reproduction. The birth control pill became the most widely used contraceptive at a time when the United States was undergoing the most rapid, sustained decline in the birthrate it had ever experienced.

Various forms of birth control have been used since ancient times. However, the forms commonly used in the 1950's—rhythm, sterilization, and barrier methods—were simply improvements on old techniques rather than new methods. In the 1960's, a new form of contraceptive, a pill that manipulated women's hormone levels to prevent pregnancy, began to be sold in the United States. The birth control pill was touted as a "magic bullet" because it was easy to use and very effective.

Family Planning At the start of the decade, contraception was illegal in several states, and many women—married or single—had no access to any form of birth control. In Louisiana, for example, birth control devices and information were virtually unavailable, except to the rich. Also, until late in the 1960's, most birth control clinics would not counsel unmarried women.

A turning point in the constitutional struggle for reproductive rights was the U.S. Supreme Court ruling in *Griswold v. Connecticut* (1965). The Court struck down a Connecticut law that had led to the arrest of the executive director and medical director of the Connecticut Planned Parenthood birth control clinic for violation of the nineteenth century state law banning the distribution of contraceptive devices or information. The Court ruled that married persons have a constitutionally protected right to privacy that allowed for the use of contraceptives. It also determined that although the right of privacy was not explicitly mentioned in the Constitution, the right itself was older than the Bill of Rights. The Court extended the right to privacy to unmarried persons in 1972. The right to privacy paved the way for the Supreme Court's ruling in *Roe v. Wade* (1973), which recognized the constitutional right to abortion.

By the middle of the 1960's, excessive population growth began to be considered one of the most pressing problems of the modern age. U.S. government experts began to support population control, viewing it as the best hope for economic development in the Third World and impoverished areas within the United States. Population control became such a priority that foreign nations wishing to receive aid had to establish family-planning programs. In addition, contraceptives were removed from the list of materials that could not be purchased with Agency for International Development funds. Domestically, federal antipoverty grants were used to establish family-planning clinics in minority and low-income neighborhoods in the late 1960's and early 1970's. The Social Security amendments of 1967 specified that at least 6 percent of maternal and child health care funds must be spent on family planning. These changes clearly demonstrated the federal government's support of family planning, which was greatly aided by two technological advances in contraceptives that were first marketed during the 1960's.

The Pill and IUDs The birth control pill was developed in the mid-1950's by Gregory Pincus of the Worcester Foundation for Experimental Biology and Harvard gynecologist Howard Rock. Pincus is widely credited with being the "father of the pill." In 1960, the Food and Drug Administration (FDA) approved commercial distribution of an oral contraceptive, the G. D. Searle Company's Enovid, a combination of the hormones progesterone and estrogen. Manufacturers marketed the pill as the perfect, ultimate birth control method. By 1966, nearly six million women—one-fifth of all women of child-bearing age—were taking oral contraceptives. A year later, pill use began to decline because some women suffered side effects such as headaches, weight gain, nausea, or menstrual abnormalities. By 1969, the problems and health risks associated with the high-dosage pills became evident, and safer, lower-dosage pills were introduced.

A major change in birth control methods used by couples occurred between 1960 and 1965, when the pill supplanted the condom as the most popular means of contraception. Even among Catholics, who predominantly used the rhythm method, the pill had become the second most popular method of birth control. Among younger women, however, the pill was the overwhelming favorite, even among Catholics. As a result, the use of the diaphragm, condom, and rhythm declined significantly.

The intrauterine device (IUD) was reinvented during the 1960's. IUDs had been in existence for centuries, but two post-1945 innovations—antibiotics for uterine infections and malleable, inert plastic—made the device much safer. The new IUDs were extremely promising when introduced in the early 1960's. The most popular IUD used in the 1970's, the Dalkon Shield, was designed in 1968 by gynecologist Hugh Davis and electrical engineer Irwin Lerner. This particular IUD, manufactured by the A. H. Robins Company, was eventually shown to have caused at least twenty deaths in the United States. In addition, it probably contributed to hundreds of thousands of severe infections and injuries, which led to sterility and other permanent damage and long-lasting pain.

Women's Rights During the 1960's, many women strove to claim control over their own reproductive health, which they felt was being controlled by men and male physicians. Female midwifery, the home-birth movement, feminist health collectives, and health centers operated by and for women became increasingly popular.

The feminist movement that emerged in the late 1960's focused not only on women's right to select and use contraceptives but also on their right to choose whether to have abortions and sterilizations. The movement saw itself as a force for "reproductive rights." Feminists endorsed the view common among young people that unmarried women have the right to have sex, and they sought to empower women to control their own bodies by providing access to contraceptives and making abortion legal. The Civil Rights, student, and antiwar movements of the late 1950's and the 1960's helped revive and strengthen the feminist movement. The women's movement emerged during a period of expanding opportunity, especially for white, prosperous, and educated women, and was influenced by the assertiveness of the New Left and its critique of conformist culture.

A Changing Society By 1965, most Catholic couples in the United States were using birth control methods prohibited by the Roman Catholic Church, and many hoped that the Church would liberalize its teachings. However, the Catholic hierarchy was alarmed by the familial and sexual liberalization taking place in the 1960's and upset by its failure to prevent divorce and contraceptive use. With the publication on July 29, 1968, of the encyclical *Humanae Vitae*, Pope Paul VI ended nearly a decade of controversy and speculation about the possible revision of the official Church position. The Pope did not deviate from the traditional teachings of the Church, which banned any use of "artificial" birth control.

Popular awareness of abortion for eugenic or medical reasons grew in 1962 during an epidemic of rubella that caused deformities in fetuses. The pro-abortion rights cause received considerable favorable publicity as a result of the plight of Sherrie Finkbine. She was forced to fly to Sweden to have an abortion when she learned the thalidomide she had taken would probably result in a deformed infant.

The sexual revolution of the 1960's further reinforced the already commonplace practices of contraception and sterilization for birth control purposes. The number of sterilizations performed increased after the American College of Obstetricians and Gynecologists recommended a liberalization of the indications for sterilization in 1969-1970. During the decade, abortions continued to be performed frequently, with women obtaining illegal abortions or traveling to other nations where abortion was legal. In 1969, radical feminists began a campaign to repeal abortion laws. Many activists demanded an unconditional right to abortion.

Groups opposed to abortion were also active in the period. The phrase "right to life" was used as early as 1963. In 1966, the National Conference of Catholic Bishops began monitoring abortion law reform across the United States and would later widen the fight against abortion. In the 1960's, the movement to legalize abortion was not backed by a single large formal organization but by organizations such as the National Association for Repeal of Abortion Laws and the National Organization for Women, which lobbied for repeal of abortion laws in 1967.

By the end of the decade, fertility control had become virtually universal in the United States. Sex and birth control were topics that had previously been taboo, but social scientists writing at the end of the decade stated that a veritable revolution in attitudes about and practices in birth control and reproduction was under way.

Impact The demand for birth control, spurred partly by a concern for the worldwide population explosion, helped drive technological development and legal change during the 1960's. Contraception became more accessible and dependable, thereby freeing many women from unplanned pregnancies and increasing the individual's ability to decide when and how often to become a parent. Birth control became a tool for individual self-determination and sexual freedom. In addition, the introduction of forms of contraceptive that could be controlled by the woman (the birth control pill and the IUD), gave a boost to the burgeoning women's movement by providing women with greater control over their reproductive function.

Subsequent Events Problems with high-technology contraceptive methods, including the birth control pill and IUDs, prompted many men and women to turn to sterilization, which has been the most common form of birth control for U.S. women since the 1970's. Further technological innovations, including implants and improved birth control pills, have improved women's contraceptive choices.

Additional Information For a classic history, see *Woman's Body, Woman's Right: Birth Control in America* (1990) by Linda Gordon. Other major sources include *The Politics of Abortion and Birth Control in Historical Perspective* (1996), an anthology edited by Donald T. Critchlow; *Reproduction in the United States—1965* (1971), an exhaustive study of attitudes by Norman B. Ryder and Charles F. Westoff; and *Controlling Reproduction: An American History* (1997), an anthology of essays and selected documents edited by Andrea Tone.

Fred Buchstein

See also Abortion; Demographics of the United States; Feminist Movement; Free Love; Marriage; Pill, The; Sexual Revolution; Women's Identity.

■ Black Christian Nationalist Movement

A religious movement emphasizing the ethnic characteristics of African Americans. It correlated black Protestantism in the United States with African American heritage, culture, and political values.

African American Protestants have often had a sense of separation from other Christians in the United States, mostly because of slavery, segregation, and the formation of African American churches and denominations within the black community. This separation led to belief systems that stressed the history of oppression among African Americans and often likened them to the ancient Israelites living in slavery. This biblical analogy allowed African American Christians to interpret themselves as a religious people who were distinct, a people with their own national characteristics. The interpretation was supported in the 1960's and later by nationalistic political movements among African Americans who were secular but dependent on the support of churches and religious organizations.

The movement termed Black Christian Nationalism is not one event but a series of occurrences including the establishment of congregations based on Black Christian Nationalist ideology, the publication of writings by major African American theologians, and the dissemination of the movement's ideas, which found varying levels of receptivity among religious African Americans. The most institutionalized example of Black Christian Nationalism was the formation during the 1960's of churches called The Shrine of the Black Madonna in Detroit, Michigan, and some southern cities by the Reverend Albert Cleage. The foremost African American theologian promoting these ideas was Professor James Cone of Union Theological Seminary in New York City, author of *Black Theology and Black Power* (1969) and *Black Theology of Liberation* (1970). These explicit examples, however, do not capture the much broader dissemination of Black Christian Nationalist ideas.

Younger, more formally educated pastors of African American Protestant congregations—denominations such as Methodists, Presbyterians, and Baptists—had been influenced both by biblical analogies and current events of the 1960's. These pastors preached sermons relating the plight of African Americans to the Israelites, stressing that African Americans in the United States were a separate nation that had been conquered by the larger surrounding white nation. They called for obedience to a God who was on the side of oppressed people, a Jesus who was dark skinned and non-European, and for identification with the nation of African Americans. The less-educated, more evangelical holiness and Pentecostal ministers were less influenced by the ideas of Black Christian Nationalism. Some black Catholic priests interpreted Black Christians as a religious group for a separate "nation" of African Americans within the United States.

Impact The somewhat disassociated congregations, writings, and dissemination of ideas by young educated pastors that make up Black Christian Nationalism drew on two resources: an interpretation of the Bible associating African Americans with the enslaved people of God, the Israelites, and the Civil Rights and Black Power movements of 1960's that clarified what constituted an oppressed nation within a nation. As Black Christian Nationalist views began to influence pastors and congregations, churches often abandoned the idea of the separation of church and state, and politics were considered a part of religious commitment. Being African American was identified as distinct from being any other sort of American, and religious organizations were perceived as the appropriate place to announce the religious-political ideology of Black Christian Nationalism.

Additional Information For Professor Cone's major ideas, see *God of the Oppressed* (1975). For a history of the subject see Gayroud Wilmore's *Black Religion and Black Radicalism* (1973). For a discussion of the relation between traditional Christianity and black nationalist feeling, see Major Jones's *Christian Ethics for Black Theology* (1974).

William Osborne and Max C. E. Orezzoli

See also Black Power; Church Bombings; Nation of Islam.

■ Black Liberation Front

A relatively small black power organization. It embraced militant, guerrilla tactics in order to bring about a civil rights revolution in the United States.

The origin of the Black Liberation Front is obscure, but the group can be traced back to late 1964 and the Civil Rights movement. The organization, like other groups associated with the Black Power movement that emerged in the mid-1960's, adopted a more militant posture than more mainstream civil rights organizations.

In 1965, according to police sources, the Black Liberation Front was allegedly planning terrorist attacks on several national landmarks, including the Statue of Liberty, the Washington Monument, and the Liberty Bell. Attacks were also planned on the White House and several police stations. The alleged plot was foiled by police and agents from the Federal Bureau of Investigation, who were able to infiltrate the Black Liberation Front.

Impact The Black Liberation Front itself had almost no discernible impact on American society in the 1960's. However, in the context of the larger, militant Black Power movement, the organization helped contribute to the fears harbored by many suburban whites that a black revolution was imminent.

Additional Information *New Day in Babylon: The Black Power Movement and American Culture, 1965-1975* (1992), by William L. Van Deburg, provides the best overview of the Black Power movement.

Phillip A. Cantrell II
See also Black Panthers; Black Power; Civil Rights Movement; Malcolm X.

■ *Black Like Me*

Published 1961
Author John Howard Griffin (1920-1980)

A unique social document of the 1960's. This book provided a generation of white Americans with poignant insights into what it meant to be black in the Deep South by revealing the region through the eyes of a white man posing as an African American.

The Work In 1959, Texas journalist John Howard Griffin began studying the conditions in which African Americans were living in the South. As a white southerner, however, he felt he could not appreciate what it meant to be black and wondered what it would take fully to understand the realities of racial discrimination. "How else," he eventually concluded, "except by becoming a Negro could a white man hope to learn the truth?" *Black Like Me* is the story of his subsequent experiment in masquerading as an African American to answer the questions his study posed.

Assisted by a dermatologist, he used dyes, oral medications, and sun lamps to darken his skin, shaving his head to complete his physical transformation. He then slipped into a November New Orleans night to begin life as an African American. He kept a journal over the next month and a half, during which he visited cities in Louisiana, Mississippi, and Alabama. His journal entries form the narrative of his book. In simple, stark descriptions of each day, they reveal the powerful lesson that Griffin learned during his brief odyssey: that being black, especially in a strange town, could make even the most trivial aspects of day-to-day life—such as finding a "colored" bathroom or getting a drink of water—a perilous adventure. Many of his experiences were so ordinary as to seem banal, especially in contrast to the horrendous violence that many African Americans then faced. Griffin's narrative meant little or nothing to black southerners; to his white readers, however, they were revealing and even startling.

Impact The idea that a white man could actually pass for a black man seems improbable (as a later film adaptation of Griffin's book demonstrated), but that scarcely mattered to those who read *Black Like Me*. The book transcended that problem, making white readers see African American life in ways that narratives written by African Americans could not. By looking at the injustices African Americans suffered through the eyes of a white person, white readers could imagine themselves in his place. They instantly became more sensitive to the inconveniences, indignities, and perils that millions of fellow Americans who happened to be black experienced daily—particularly in the South. Many readers found Griffin's simple story shocking.

Black Like Me first appeared in 1961, just as the Civil Rights movement was about to crest and the entire nation was to witness—through the spectacle of live television—the full brutality of racial discrimination in 1960's America. The book's publication

James Whitmore played journalist John Griffin in the 1964 film adaptation of Black Like Me *(1961). The book chronicles the white Griffin's experiences after he transformed himself into a black man in order to experience racial discrimination firsthand.* (Museum of Modern Art/Film Stills Archive)

instantly raised a storm of controversy—one that lasted through the 1960's and never fully abated. The book made the best-seller lists and was adopted for classroom use in many high schools and colleges. The general sensation it caused made it one of the most influential American books of the decade.

The conditions that Griffin described as an eyewitness in his book were mild compared with the vivid displays of racial injustice exposed on television and in newspapers and magazines during the mid-1960's. Nevertheless, many white southerners charged that he portrayed the South unfairly. This charge stuck to the book, which became one of the most-banned books in U.S. schools and libraries throughout the last third of the twentieth century.

Related Work Jules Tannebaum directed a film adaptation, *Black Like Me* (1964), in which James Whitmore portrayed the character based on Griffin. Among the film's failings was a makeup job on Whitmore so unconvincing that it spoiled the credibility of the story's premise: that a white man could pass as a black man.

Additional Information In 1959—the same year that Griffin undertook his masquerade—Stetson Kennedy, another southern journalist, published *Jim Crow Guide to the USA: The Laws, Customs, and Etiquette Governing the Conduct of Nonwhites and Other Minorities as Second-Class Citizens*. This book (available in reprint editions) catalogs all the discriminatory laws that the Civil Rights movement worked to overcome during the 1960's.

R. Kent Rasmussen

See also Civil Rights Movement; *Confessions of Nat Turner, The*; Literature.

■ "Black Manifesto"

Published 1969
Author Introduction by James Forman (1928-), body of document unknown

A call by militant black leadership for white Christian churches and Jewish synagogues to pay reparations to American blacks for the hardships of slavery.

The Work The "Black Manifesto" was presented by

Student Nonviolent Coordinating Committee (SNCC) member James Forman to the National Black Economic Development Conference in Detroit, Michigan, and was adopted on April 26, 1969. The manifesto was a call to arms for blacks in the United States to overthrow the current government, which it characterized as capitalist, racist, and imperialist, and to set up a black-led socialist government. The "Black Manifesto" demanded the payment of $500,000,000 in reparations to African Americans by white churches and Jewish synagogues in payment for the hardships of slavery. Churches were specifically targeted because they were seen as agents of U.S. imperialism. The monies that were demanded in the manifesto were to be used to establish land banks, television studios, universities, and black presses. To pressure churches to pay the reparations, the manifesto advocated the disruption of church services and the seizure of church property.

Impact The initial reaction to the demands of the "Black Manifesto" was positive with promises of support coming from several denominations and groups, but soon the religious press across the spectrum attacked the manifesto and its strategies, which echoed Malcolm X's "by any means necessary" revolutionary strategies. The manifesto particularly alienated Jewish groups.

Additional Information For more information about the manifesto and its impact, see *Black Manifesto: Religion, Racism, and Reparations* (1969), edited by Robert S. Lecky and H. Elliott Wright.

C. A. Wolski

See also Black Liberation Front; Black Power; Malcolm X; Nation of Islam; Religion and Spirituality; Student Nonviolent Coordinating Committee (SNCC).

■ Black Panthers

An African American revolutionary organization often seen as the "vanguard" of the radical movement in the late 1960's. The Black Panthers captured the imagination of both disaffected youth and the media by combining an urban paramilitary style with a program dedicated to "serving the people."

Origins and History Founded in early October, 1966, at an antipoverty community center in North Oakland, California, the Black Panther Party for

Self-Defense was the brainchild of Huey P. Newton, community organizer, law student, and street tough. Newton and the party's cofounder, Bobby G. Seale, an army veteran, sheetmetal worker, and aspiring comedian who also worked at the community center, had been active in black nationalist circles while they were students at Oakland's Merritt College during the early 1960's. Born in the South, they came of age in the urban ghetto, and although they were inspired by the Civil Rights movement, it was Malcolm X, not Martin Luther King, Jr., who fired their imaginations. After years of frustration with college-based African American militants who paid insufficient attention to Newton's "brothers on the block" and especially in the wake of the massive Watts riot in Los Angeles, which Newton and Seale saw as the beginning of a new era, the two formed their own organization dedicated to armed self-defense among the African American masses.

The idea for the name of the organization came from a Student Nonviolent Coordinating Committee (SNCC) project in Alabama that was spearheaded by Stokely Carmichael. This project, the Lowndes County Freedom Organization, used a black panther as its symbol. "The panther is a fierce animal," Newton explained later, "but he will not attack until he is backed into a corner; then he will strike out." Other groups also took the name, in Harlem and San Francisco in 1966 and in Los Angeles the following year, but only the Oakland group survived. Black Panther membership, at the height of the group's activity in the late 1960's, is disputed; estimates range from the high hundreds to the low thousands. By 1969, the group had chapters in most major northern cities and an international division.

Part of the reason for the party's success in the late 1960's—and for its failure in the 1970's—may have been the nature and evolution of its ideology, which quickly proved to be class-conscious rather than race conscious. Newton and Seale drew eclectically from foreign revolutionaries and domestic militants in fashioning a program of black liberation predicated on the legitimacy of violence: They had read Mao Zedong, Frantz Fanon, and Che Guevara, who endorsed armed revolution; they were also familiar with the writings and activities of Robert F. Williams in North Carolina, the Deacons for Defense and Justice in Louisiana, and Malcolm X, all of whom advocated armed self-defense. However, as Newton explained in 1970, the Panthers became

Marxist-Leninists who embraced dialectical materialism, which in four short years took them from black nationalism (liberation of the black "colony" in the United States), to revolutionary nationalism (nationalism plus socialism), to internationalism (solidarity with the oppressed peoples of the world), and finally to "intercommunalism" (world revolution pitting oppressed communities against the U.S. "empire"). Newton later claimed to have undergone a slow transformation from black nationalism to socialism while he was in college in the early 1960's, based on his "life plus independent reading." Therefore, the party's original program called for full employment ("if the white American businessman will not give full employment, then the means of production should be taken from the businessmen and placed in the community"), decent housing ("if the white landlord will not give decent housing to our black community, then the housing and the land should be made into cooperatives"), an end to police brutality, exemption from military service, and release of all African Americans from prison.

Activities Though one of their first campaigns was to force the city of Oakland to erect a traffic light at a dangerous intersection, initially the Panthers' political work consisted mainly of confronting law enforcement officials (whom they called an "occupying army"), especially while "patrolling the police." The activity involved groups of armed Panthers observing interactions between local residents and the police, advising the residents of their rights and, as a result, often engaging in tense confrontations with the officers. This direct attempt to confront white authority in the black community, which Newton later claimed was a way of exhausting all legal means to protect African Americans' rights in anticipation of revolutionary activity, was an enormous leap in

Members of the Black Panther Party stand outside the Oakland, California, courthouse where Huey P. Newton, one of the founders of the black paramilitary organization, is being tried in 1968. Newton's conviction was overturned in 1970. (AP/Wide World Photos)

the history of African American resistance in the United States. However, in the summer of 1967 when the California assembly passed legislation curbing the carrying of firearms, a bill aimed at the Panthers, the group stopped the patrols and dropped "for Self-Defense" from its name. As Black Panther chapters multiplied throughout the country, however, physical confrontations grew, with deaths on both sides. At the same time, the Panthers established what they called "survival programs," beginning with free breakfasts for school children and expanding into areas such as medical care, clothing, and education.

Before the California gun-control law was passed, Newton sent some thirty armed Panthers to protest at the state capitol in Sacramento. This dramatic demonstration generated some national publicity, but what set the stage for the Panthers' dramatic growth occurred early one morning in October, 1967, when the Oakland police stopped Newton after he had spent the night celebrating the end of his probation for assault. Gunfire followed, and the Panther leader was wounded, as was one policeman; another patrolman, Officer John Frey, died. Newton was charged with Frey's murder and faced possible execution. Charismatic ex-convict and writer Eldridge Cleaver, who edited the party newspaper, *The Black Panther*, and became its minister of information in 1967, orchestrated a national "Free Huey" campaign that made Newton a virtual icon.

Newton's celebrated 1968 trial ended in a manslaughter conviction, and the campaign to free him succeeded in 1970 when the conviction was overturned on appeal. Although these events earned for the Panthers national recognition, they also brought the attention of the authorities. The ensuing raids, prosecutions, and the promotion of internal dissension by the Federal Bureau of Investigation (FBI) decimated the Black Panther Party. By 1970, much of the national and even regional leadership had gone underground or was awaiting trial, in jail, or in exile.

Impact FBI director J. Edgar Hoover called the Black Panther Party the "greatest threat to the internal security of the country," and the U.S. government viewed them as a serious danger; however, the Panthers were more often ridiculed. According to Allen J. Matusow in his 1984 book, *The Unraveling of America: A History of Liberalism in the 1960's*, in one

influential survey of the 1960's, the Panthers are described as a "handful of blacks with a mimeograph machine" who "existed mainly in the demented minds of white leftists." The group did attract the support of the leading militant African Americans, SNCC leaders Carmichael, H. Rap Brown, and James Forman, and even managed a short-lived alliance of sorts (the Panthers called it a "merger") with SNCC in 1968. In early 1969, the Students for a Democratic Society (SDS)—at its height but soon to be destroyed by internal factionalism—endorsed the Panthers as the vanguard of the revolution in the United States. The Panthers also provided the model for other groups such as the Brown Berets, the Young Lords, the White Panther Party, the Red Guards, and the Gray Panthers; the group's ten-point platform and program (What We Want, What We Believe) became the blueprint for other 1960's groups. Finally, the Panthers changed the popular lexicon; for example, they introduced the epithet "pig," in reference primarily to police officers but also to government officials, the rich, and sometimes evildoers.

Subsequent Events Especially damaging was the public and bloody falling-out between Newton and Cleaver in early 1971, the climax of two years of internal splits and purges. The rift with Cleaver was a product of Newton's attempt to direct the group away from militant confrontation and to community organizing through the survival programs it had developed. Newton's continued run-ins with the law, however, resulted in his fleeing to Cuba, where he stayed from 1973 to 1977. The Black Panthers lived on in his absence and, after his return, remained a viable organization into the early 1980's, but it never regained its role as a leading revolutionary group.

Additional Information *Off the Pigs!* (1976), edited by G. Louis Heath, provides a long historical introduction (based mostly on government sources and FBI informants), a sampling of primary documents, and an extensive bibliography. *The Black Panthers Speak* (1970), edited by Philip S. Foner, offers a good collection of writings and speeches. Important Panther autobiographies and memoirs include Seale's *Seize the Time* (1970) and Newton's *Revolutionary Suicide* (1973). A sympathetic journalistic account can be found in Michael Newton's *Bitter Grain* (1980); a particularly negative treatment is presented in Hugh Pearson's *The Shadow of the Panther* (1994).

Jama Lazerow

See also Brown, H. Rap; Carmichael, Stokely; Cleaver, Eldridge; Hampton-Clark Deaths; Student Nonviolent Coordinating Committee (SNCC); White Panthers.

■ Black Power

An ideological shift away from integrationism and nonviolence and toward a radical black nationalism. This new way of thinking strongly influenced a wide range of movements and organizations in the 1960's.

Black nationalism as a tool for social, economic, and psychological empowerment has a long history, as seen, for instance, in the writings of Marcus Garvey (social activist and civil rights leader in the 1920's and 1930's) and Malcolm X (spokesperson for the Nation of Islam). After the February, 1965, assassination of Malcolm X, some civil rights activists turned toward a revolutionary nationalist philoso-

The raised fist symbolized black power, a movement away from integration and nonviolence and toward black nationalism. (Library of Congress)

phy that urged aggressive tactics and separatism and the abandonment of civil disobedience, legal cases, and other more reformist strategies.

The first use of "black power" as a slogan was during a 1966 march to Jackson, Mississippi, following the shooting of James H. Meredith, the first African American student to attend the University of Mississippi. Some in the Student Nonviolent Coordinating Committee (SNCC) felt nonviolent interracial action was ineffective and that SNCC should become an all-black organization. On June 16, several marchers were arrested and jailed in Greenwood, Mississippi, including SNCC chair Stokely Carmichael, who told supporters after he was released: "I ain't going to jail no more. What we gonna start saying now is 'black power.' " At the urging of SNCC activist Willie Ricks, who yelled, "What do you want? Black power!", the crowd of supporters picked up the chant. After national news coverage of Carmichael's release, the slogan rapidly spread across the nation.

The actual concept of black power remained contested and imprecise, although it divided the Civil Rights movement. Less radical organizations such as the National Association for the Advancement of Colored People and Martin Luther King, Jr.'s Southern Christian Leadership Conference opposed black power, while SNCC and the Congress of Racial Equality backed it. By the late 1960's, black power advocates were a diverse group that included businesspeople who used black power to push black capitalism, the paramilitary revolutionaries of the Black Panther Party who sought an end to capitalism, and the cultural nationalists of Ron Karenga's US organization. The advent of black power paralleled a geographic shift for the Civil Rights movement: In contrast to the nonviolent church-based southern civil rights struggle of the 1950's and early 1960's, African American "rebellions" had exploded in dozens of northern and western cities in 1964-1965, areas where civil rights organizing would continue through the late 1960's and 1970's.

Impact Black power resulted in greater racial pride and self-esteem for some African Americans. It also brought the interracialism of the early Civil Rights movement to a close, leading some white activists to shift their work to white communities and other causes. Others viewed black power as merely defiant symbolism that did not achieve real structural change. Nevertheless, its influence was widespread, spurring the creation of black studies programs in universities, the founding of the League of Revolutionary Black Workers within the labor movement, and the growth in the numbers of African Americans elected as representatives. Puerto Ricans, Chicanos, and Native American activists (who coined the phrase "red power" during the Alcatraz Island occupation), often stated that they were inspired by black power.

Subsequent Events The extensive Federal Bureau of Investigation infiltration of black nationalist groups and subsequent state repression directed at these groups along with internal divisions (often along the lines of cultural versus revolutionary nationalism) led to the decline of many black power organizations by the mid-1970's. Black nationalism continued in various forms, including the popularity of Afrocentrism in the 1990's.

Additional Information Manning Marable's *Race, Reform, and Rebellion: The Second Reconstruction in Black America* (1991) chronicles the complex political transformations during the black power period. Clayborne Carson's *In Struggle: SNCC and the Black Awakening of the 1960's* (1981) examines how black power shaped a key civil rights organization. A documentary history of black power from 1791 to the late 1960's can be found in *The Black Power Revolt: A Collection of Essays* (1968), edited by Floyd Barbour.

Vanessa Tait

See also Black Panthers; Carmichael, Stokely; Civil Rights Movement; Congress of Racial Equality (CORE); King, Martin Luther, Jr.; League of Revolutionary Black Workers; Malcolm X; Meredith, James H.; Nation of Islam; Southern Christian Leadership Conference (SCLC); Student Nonviolent Coordinating Committee (SNCC).

■ Black United Students

A militant group of African American college students. These students, spurred by the Black Power movement, worked toward establishing black studies departments in colleges and universities.

Origins and History In the latter half of the 1960's, African American college students, inspired by the Black Power movement, formed collectives in colleges and universities throughout the United States in order to improve the lives of African American students and institute black studies departments. The first record of students organizing as the Black United Students was at San Francisco State University in 1968. The group was organized by Professor Nathan Hare, who later denied his part in the student strike, and supported by the Third World Liberation Front, a coalition of minority groups.

Activities In November, 1968, the Black United Students, with the encouragement of the Black Panther Party, called for a student strike at San Francisco State University. The group presented the campus administration with fifteen nonnegotiable demands relating to the creation of a black studies department and the improvement of black student life. In response to the students' protest, San Francisco State University created the first integrated black studies program in 1969. Previously, Meritt Junior College in nearby Oakland, California, had begun offering a few courses in black studies, primarily to appease some members of the Black Panther Party, such as Huey P. Newton, who were attending the junior college, but it did not create a complete black studies department.

In addition to their efforts toward establishing black studies departments, the Black United Students actively joined with other campus groups in antiwar, antiestablishment protests in the late 1960's and early 1970's. The most noteworthy of these protests occurred in 1970, when the Students for a Democratic Society (SDS) and the Black United Students cosponsored a demonstration at Kent State University in Ohio, where four young people were killed by the Ohio National Guard.

Impact The efforts of the Black United Students and similar African American groups helped establish black studies departments in numerous colleges and universities in the late 1960's and the following decades. By the 1990's, approximately two hundred black studies programs had been created across the nation. These programs have evolved from the original 1960's programs, which were sometimes cursory and not very well thought out, into degree-granting, three-tiered programs. At the first level, these programs provide an introduction to African history and to the African experience in the Americas and in other parts of the world. At the second level, they begin to include more specific courses and examine current issues and research, delving into issues such as the place of African Americans in American society. At the third level, the programs offer an integrated look at African influences on and experiences of psychology, economics, political science, sociology, history, and literature.

In the late 1990's, a number of organizations calling themselves the Black United Students were located on campuses across the United States. These organizations act to further the interests of African American students.

Additional Information *Turmoil on the Campus* (1970), edited by Edward J. Barder, discusses various issues raised by African American students in the 1960's.

Annita Marie Ward

See also Black Panthers; Black Power; Civil Rights Movement; Student Rights Movement.

■ *Blow-up*

Released 1966
Director Michelangelo Antonioni (1912-   )

A film that embodied for American audiences the allure of swinging London in the early 1960's. In the film, director Antonioni uses the pop culture figure of the fashion photographer to explore the particular combination of glamour and emptiness in London at the start of the Beatles era.

The Work The film *Blow-up* explores the contradictions of 1960's London by showing fragments of the daily life of a trendy photographer named Thomas (David Hemmings). Thomas is shown leaving a homeless shelter after a night of surreptitious shooting for an art book, engaging model Verushka in a steamy glamour shoot, and barking orders to both studio staff and models for a fashion spread. He seems totally in control of his life, but this changes

Trendy London photographer Thomas examines the pictures he shot of a couple in a public park in the 1966 film Blow-up. *His glamorous and empty life is used to demonstrate the city's cultural decadence. (Museum of Modern Art/Film Stills Archive)*

when he photographs a couple he has followed into a secluded park. Before this sequence is over, the man has disappeared from sight and the woman (Mary, played by Vanessa Redgrave) is desperately trying to get the photographer's film. Later, at Thomas's studio, Mary again tries to get the film. In this scene, the decade's spirit of liberated sexuality is prominent. In the end, the photographer keeps the film and, intrigued, begins to print and enlarge (blow up) the negatives. In the grainy images, he finds a man aiming a pistol and then the corpse of Mary's companion. Beneath the placid surface of the park, Thomas has found murder. However, two would-be models and a posh drug party distract him from the mystery, and the theft of his photographs leaves him with nothing. At the end, Thomas is lured into a fantasy tennis game by some clowning mimes. A long, high-angle shot traps him in the realization of his own futility.

Impact *Blow-up* treated a variety of 1960's themes in a manner that mirrored and communicated the cultural decadence of London in the 1960's. In the London of the film, social problems are subordinate to trendy aestheticism. Therefore, for Thomas, the homeless men he photographs are merely pretexts for art. Likewise, the nuclear-arms protesters are presented as listless and ineffective. The apoliticism director Michelangelo Antonioni sees in London contrasts with the politically charged atmosphere of American culture during the era.

The sexual liberation of the 1960's is also very much in display in *Blow-up*. Virtually all the women wear the revealing fashions of the era. Antonioni includes a long scene in which Redgrave is partially nude and an orgy sequence in which Thomas has sex with two teenage fashion groupies. Intermingled with sexual scenes are two extended drug-taking sequences, a further elaboration on the hedonism of swinging London.

Ultimately, London in the 1960's is presented as a self-indulgent society whose citizens skate across the surface of a life of flattering glamour, ignoring the harsh realities that lurk below the surface. Thomas's predicament with his photographs is a critique of his shallow use of his art and the myopic narcissism of 1960's mod culture.

Related Work The 1981 film *Blow Out*, directed by Brian De Palma and starring John Travolta and Nancy Allen, follows a similar story line.

Additional Information Seymour Chatman's *Antonioni or the Surface of the World* (1985) contains an excellent study of *Blow-up*.

Roger J. Stilling

See also Film; Media; Photography.

■ Bond, Julian

Born January 14, 1940, Nashville, Tennessee

Prominent civil rights activist. Bond's major accomplishments during the 1960's were his cofounding of the Student Nonviolent Coordinating Committee and his controversial election to the Georgia legislature.

Early Life Horace Julian Bond, the son of Horace Mann Bond, a distinguished black educator who became president of Lincoln University, grew up in relative comfort in Bucks County, Pennsylvania, in a family that valued education and Christian morality.

Julian Bond, civil rights activist and cofounder of the Student Nonviolent Coordinating Committee, won election to the Georgia House of Representative in 1965 but was denied his seat because of his antiwar stance. He regained his seat through a Supreme Court ruling in 1966. (National Archives)

Bond attended a private Quaker school, excelling in sports and journalism. After his father accepted a post as a dean at Atlanta University, Bond enrolled at Morehouse College, part of the Atlanta University complex.

The 1960's Four days after the first sit-in took place in Greensboro, North Carolina, in 1960, Bond and classmate Lonnie King organized a student movement at Atlanta University to protest against segregation. Subsequently, Bond helped form the Committee on Appeal for Human Rights, a citywide civil rights group. One sit-in that Bond organized led to the arrest of the Reverend Martin Luther King, Jr., which in turn prompted John F. Kennedy, the Democratic nominee for president, to intercede on King's behalf. Many political scientists contend that this gesture helped Kennedy win the lion's share of the African American vote and the presidency.

In April, 1960, Bond traveled to Raleigh, North Carolina, where he helped found the Student Nonviolent Coordinating Committee (SNCC). Upon his return to Atlanta, which served as SNCC's headquarters, Bond launched an alternative newspaper, the Atlanta *Inquirer*. Not long afterward, he became the director of public relations for SNCC. In an organization that valued action, Bond spent much of his time in an office drafting press releases, editing the SNCC newspaper, the *Student Voice*, and effectively cultivating support for the movement.

In 1965, Bond ran for the Georgia House of Representatives in a predominantly African American district in Atlanta. Winning 82 percent of the vote, he became one of the first African Americans in the South to be elected to office. However, because of his opposition to the Vietnam War, the Georgia state legislature denied him his seat. After the Georgia House refused to seat him a second time, Bond filed suit. In *Bond v. Floyd* (1966), the Supreme Court ruled in Bond's favor, stating that the Georgia House could not deny Bond his seat because of his political views. In 1968, Bond again made headlines when insurgent delegates nominated him to be the Democratic Party's vice presidential candidate.

Later Life In 1986, Bond ran unsuccessfully for the U.S. Congress against John Lewis, a SNCC cofounder. Bond remained active as an educator, writer, speaker, and board member of the National Association for the Advancement of Colored People in the 1990's.

Impact Bond played a seminal role in building SNCC into one of the most significant protest organizations in modern history. His precedent-setting suit to be granted his seat in the Georgia House not only paved the road for greater political power for African Americans in the South but also expanded the First Amendment rights for all candidates for public office.

Additional Information Bond's *A Time to Speak, A Time to Act* (1972) and Julian Neary's *Julian Bond: Black Rebel* (1971) are good starting points for understanding Bond's beliefs.

Peter B. Levy

See also Carmichael, Stokely; Civil Rights Movement; Democratic National Convention of 1968; Student Nonviolent Coordinating Committee (SNCC).

■ *Bonnie and Clyde*

Released 1967
Director Arthur Penn (1922-   )

The decade's most controversial film because of its graphic use of violence. It was one of the first American films to reflect a distinctive European influence.

The Work Loosely inspired by the crimes of 1930's bank robbers Clyde Barrow and Bonnie Parker, *Bonnie and Clyde* depicts their unusual meeting in West Dallas, Texas, when Bonnie (Faye Dunaway) stops Clyde (Warren Beatty) from stealing her mother's automobile. Bored and restless, Bonnie flings herself into Clyde's life of crime. The pair are joined by Clyde's brother, Buck (Gene Hackman), and sister-in-law, Blanche (Estelle Parsons), as well as C. W. Moss (Michael J. Pollard), a young mechanic. The Barrow gang storms through the Southwest and Midwest, dramatically robbing banks and eluding police. Because a spate of foreclosures on farms had left banks in the region with a tarnished image, the outlaws become celebrated for their exploits. Finally, Texas Ranger Frank Hamer (Denver Pyle) traps Bonnie and Clyde in an ambush, and they are riddled with bullets.

Impact Director Arthur Penn, working with the first screenplay by Robert Benton and David Newman, created an elegiac ode to nonconformity punctuated by bursts of violence. *Bonnie and Clyde*'s antiestablishment stance struck a chord with young view-

Warren Beatty and Faye Dunaway play 1930's outlaws in the 1967 film Bonnie and Clyde. *The film's violence provoked controversy.* (Museum of Modern Art/Film Stills Archive)

ers. This audience identified with the young protagonists' dissatisfaction with the dullness of daily life and their disdain for authority figures. The film depicts the outlaws as victims of social forces over which they have no control and against which they must fight. The film appealed to those who felt misunderstood by the older generation and persecuted for their social and political views. The film's sense of impending doom, including Clyde's unease when he discovers that a man they have kidnapped is an undertaker, was felt by those facing the possibility of combat during the Vietnam War. Many newspaper and magazine articles and editorials about the film, however, condemned its graphic violence. Even some of the film's proponents accused Penn of romanticizing criminal behavior, but he clearly shows the consequences of crime. When a bank employee foolishly pursues the robbers and Clyde shoots him in the face in close-up, the audience is meant to be appalled. The use of slow motion, soft-focus photography and the sudden shifts from comedy to violence

reflect the influence of French New Wave films such as Jean-Luc Godard's *A bout de souffle* (*Breathless*, 1960) and Francois Truffaut's *Jules et Jim* (*Jules and Jim*, 1961). Most of these thematic and cinematic elements were ignored by many reviewers who condemned *Bonnie and Clyde* as a crude gangster film. After Pauline Kael's passionate, insightful assessment appeared in *The New Yorker*, many gave the film another look, and it became one of the first that young people saw again and again. Its popularity helped initiate what came to be called "the film generation."

Related Work *The Wild Bunch*, 1969, directed by Sam Peckinpah, is an even more stylized and graphically violent look at outlaws.

Additional Information *Focus on Bonnie and Clyde* (1973), edited by John G. Cawelti, includes reviews, essays, and interviews related to the film.

Michael Adams

See also Film, *Wild Bunch, The*.

■ Boston Five Trial

Date May 20, 1968-June 14, 1968

Perhaps the most famous of the more than fifteen hundred draft resistance cases prosecuted by the federal government during the Vietnam War. On January 5, 1968, the United States indicted five prominent citizens for conspiracy to "willfully counsel, aid, and abet" draft resisters.

Origins and History By the end of 1967, the United States had five hundred thousand troops fighting in Vietnam, despite the growth of a large antiwar movement. Believing the government to be unresponsive to their concerns, many antiwar activists sought to force the war's end by both traditional political means and by draft resistance. Some thought the sight of young men burning or turning in their draft cards would move the nation's conscience, and others hoped that if enough people resisted, the armed forces would lack the manpower to continue the war.

Among the thousands who advocated draft resistance were the five individuals who came to be known as the "Boston Five": Benjamin Spock, the respected pediatrician whose *The Common Sense Book of Baby and Child Care* (1946) guided a generation of mothers; the Reverend William Sloane Coffin, Jr., the well-known chaplain at Yale University; Marcus Raskin, cofounder of the Institute for Policy Studies, a liberal think tank in Washington, D.C.; Mitchell Goodman, a novelist; and Michael Ferber, a graduate student at Harvard University.

It is difficult to ascertain why the government indicted these five activists. Although they were all involved in the antiwar movement, they did not know each other well, in some cases not at all, before they were indicted—an oddity, considering that they were charged with conspiring to urge draft resistance. The government based this indictment on four separate instances in which they claimed the defendants encouraged young men to resist the

Four of the five activists arrested for conspiracy to aid draft resisters meet with the press after being convicted in 1968. From left to right are novelist Mitchell Goodman, pediatrician Benjamin Spock, Harvard graduate student Michael Ferber, and Yale University chaplain William Sloan Coffin, Jr. The fifth defendant, Marcus Raskin, was found not guilty, and all four convictions were subsequently overturned. (AP/Wide World Photos)

draft. No single instance involved all five individuals, though at least two were involved in each.

The first "overt act" of aiding draft resistance cited by the government was a petition circulated in August, 1967, called "A Call to Resist Illegitimate Authority." The petition was written largely by Raskin and signed by all the defendants except Ferber as well as by more than two hundred other people. The government's indictment cited only Coffin and Spock for "causing [the petition] to be distributed."

The second act upon which the indictment was based took place on October 2, 1967. All the defendants except Ferber held a press conference in New York City as part of an effort to publicize Stop the Draft Week, a national protest planned by draft resistance groups across the country.

One of the actions of Stop the Draft Week formed the third point cited in the indictment. On October 16, at the Arlington Street Church in Boston, a religious service was held at which Coffin delivered a sermon and Ferber a speech entitled "A Time to Say No," in opposition to the Vietnam War. During the service, a number of draft cards were collected and burned in protest.

The fourth and final basis for the government's indictment took place on October 20, when Coffin, Raskin, Spock, Goodman, and others met with a Justice Department official. At that meeting, held at the Department of Justice in Washington, D.C., the activists stated their opposition to the war on the grounds that it was undeclared and therefore illegal. To further demonstrate their opposition, they gave the official a briefcase containing a number of draft cards turned in by resisters, including the ashes of draft cards burned at the Arlington Street Church on October 16.

The Trial The trial of the Boston Five began on May 20, 1968, at the Federal District Court in Boston. The five defendants wanted to use the indictment to put the war on trial—to argue that it was unconstitutional because Congress had never declared war; that it was unjust because armed U.S. involvement violated the Geneva Accords of 1954; and that it was immoral because the conflict was a civil war between the North and South Vietnamese, who ought to be able to choose their own government without foreign interference. Therefore, they reasoned, citizens had a right, even a moral duty, to

resist the war even if it violated the selective service laws.

The trial judge, eighty-five-year-old Francis Ford, ruled all arguments regarding the morality or constitutionality of the war irrelevant. He refused to hear any evidence other than whether the defendants had conspired to resist the draft. Therefore, the larger questions the defendants wanted to present for public scrutiny were ignored, and the trial turned on whether the defendants' admitted words and actions acted to "counsel, aid, and abet" draft resistance and whether their individual actions toward these ends constituted a criminal conspiracy.

On June 14, the all-male jury (the prosecution actively worked to prevent women from serving on the jury, fearing they would be sympathetic toward Spock) convicted all defendants except Raskin. Each was sentenced to two years in jail and fines of five thousand dollars, except for Ferber, whose fine was set at one thousand dollars. The defense appealed the convictions of the remaining four defendants to the U.S. Court of Appeals. The following July, the three-judge panel that had reviewed the trial determined that Judge Ford had made a serious error in instructions he gave to the jury during the Boston Five trial and overturned the convictions. The panel further ruled that there was not enough evidence against Spock and Goodman for the government to try them again. Coffin and Ferber were eligible to be retried, but the government never filed a new indictment.

Impact The trial of the Boston Five yielded no important victory for either the antiwar movement or the federal government. The fact that the convictions were reversed by the court of appeals can be viewed as a victory for civil liberties, but Judge Ford's rulings prevented the defendants from using the trial as a forum for publicizing questions of the war's morality and legality. If the government's desire was to muzzle opposition to the war by prosecuting some of its best-known leaders, it did not succeed because opposition to the war grew unabated.

Additional Information Journalist Jessica Mitford attended the trial in Boston; *The Trial of Dr. Spock* (1969), highly sympathetic to the defendants, was the result. Coffin and Spock both wrote memoirs that devote chapters to the trial. Lynn Z. Bloom's biography, *Doctor Spock: Biography of a Conservative Radical* (1972), explains the legal aspects of the conspiracy charge. For the trial's broader historical context, see Tom Wells's *The War Within: America's Battle over Vietnam* (1994).

Christopher Berkeley

See also Draft Resisters; Spock, Benjamin; Vietnam War; War Resisters League.

■ Boston Strangler

Mass media epithet given to Albert DeSalvo following his dubious confession to the gruesome murders of eleven Massachusetts women that made him one of the United States' most feared killers in the mid-1960's.

From June, 1962, through January, 1964, eleven women were murdered in eastern Massachusetts. Although not all the victims were strangled or killed in Boston, local and national media assumed a single perpetrator for these heinous crimes and invented the epithets the "Phantom Fiend" and the "Boston Strangler," which they used in their sensational and emotionally charged stories. Fed by a constant barrage of increasingly graphic and sensationalist newspaper and television stories, women in the greater Boston area lived in virtual terror of the killer, and the Massachusetts public demanded an intensified investigation by national, state, and local law enforcement agencies.

In 1964, in the face of the mounting pressure, Massachusetts attorney general Edward Brooke formed a strangler task force to coordinate the investigation of these murders that had occurred in five separate cities and three counties. The Commonwealth of Massachusetts offered a ten-thousand-

In 1965, Albert DeSalvo, on trial for unrelated charges of armed robbery and rape, confessed to being the Boston Strangler, a serial killer believed responsible for the deaths of eleven women in the Boston area from June, 1962, through January, 1964. (AP/Wide World Photos)

dollar reward for information leading to the arrest and conviction of the murderer and, over a period of several months, received thousands of letters and telephone calls from all over the world.

In 1965, Albert DeSalvo, a married thirty-three-year-old laborer arrested for armed robbery and rape, confessed to being the Boston Strangler through his attorney, the flamboyant F. Lee Bailey, in an apparent legal strategy to avoid a life sentence in a maximum security prison. Bailey's strategy backfired, and after a ten-day trial in January, 1967, DeSalvo was convicted of the armed robbery and rape charges and sentenced to life imprisonment in a state penitentiary at Walpole, Massachusetts. He was never charged with the Boston Strangler murders. In February, 1967, DeSalvo sent one last wave of panic through Massachusetts when he escaped from prison, but he was recaptured within forty-eight hours. His repeated appeals for a new trial were denied by the Massachusetts appellate and supreme courts.

Subsequent Events DeSalvo had served six years of his life sentence when he was stabbed to death in prison in 1973. His murder remains unsolved, and no one has ever been charged with the murders attributed to the Boston Strangler.

Impact From 1964 through 1967, the case of the Boston Strangler was the predominant crime story across the nation. It marked the first case involving a serial killer in which the mass media, state and national law enforcement officials, media-savvy and flamboyant attorneys, a terrified community, and a captivated national audience had all played a part. Subsequent research indicates that DeSalvo probably was not the murderer but rather the unknowing victim of a rush to judgment that served the interests of Massachusetts politicians, law enforcement officials, attorneys, and the mass media.

Additional Information Susan Kelly's provocative *The Boston Stranglers* (1995) makes a strong case against DeSalvo's murdering all eleven women, while Gerold Frank's *The Boston Strangler* (1966) contends that, though never convicted, DeSalvo was the serial killer.

Ronald Lettieri

See also Crimes and Scandals; Genovese Murder; *In Cold Blood.*

■ *Boys in the Band, The*

Produced 1968
Author Mart Crowley (1935-   )

The first play to focus exclusively on homosexual characters and the gay experience. The drama heralded the gay liberation movement and was followed by many similarly themed works.

The Work In *The Boys in the Band*, an affluent, thirty-year-old gay man named Michael has invited a number of his homosexual friends to his stylish New York City apartment for a birthday party honoring their gay Jewish friend, Harold. The group includes Donald; Michael's present lover; Emory, a portrait of the effeminate gay stereotype; Hank, once married and the father of two children but now living with Larry; Bernard, a gay black man; and a male prostitute who is Emory's birthday gift to Harold. Michael's former college friend, Alan, who is married and hostile toward homosexuals, crashes this party. Alan soon recognizes the stereotypical Emory as a homosexual, is offended by his behavior, and punches him; however, Alan is later surprised to discover that the others also are gay, especially Hank, who Alan thinks is heterosexual. The action of the play culminates in a party game that Michael designs; each guest must telephone the one person he truly believes he has loved and confess his deepest feelings. Michael intends for this game to reveal Alan's latent homosexuality, but Alan's telephone call goes to his wife. The play ends with Harold characterizing Michael as a gay man consumed by self-loathing.

Impact Crowley's play, radically new in 1968, was extremely popular in its original New York City production and enjoyed another successful run in London before being released as a feature film in 1970. The play was enjoying commercial success as the Stonewall Inn riots launched the gay liberation movement in the summer of 1969 in Greenwich Village, New York City, and for many years the play was performed in regional, community, and college theaters around the United States as the gay rights movement gained momentum. With its significant popular success, *The Boys in the Band* set a precedent for stage and film honesty in succeeding decades, paving the way for sympathetic portrayals and increasing tolerance of homosexual characters and the homosexual lifestyle. For example, Terrence

McNally's widely popular 1994 award-winning Broadway play, *Love! Valor! Compassion!*, certainly has its roots in Crowley's groundbreaking comedy. *The Boys in the Band* became somewhat dated in subsequent decades because of its politically incorrect caricature of Emory and its pre-AIDS tolerance of sexual promiscuity.

Related Work *Midnight Cowboy* (1969), a feature film directed by John Schlesinger and starring Dustin Hoffman and Jon Voight, achieved significant popularity in spite of its homoerotic implications and frank portrayal of male hustling.

Additional Information For a thorough and interesting history of the portrayal of homosexuals on stage, see *Not in Front of the Audience: Homosexuality on Stage* (1992), by Nicholas de Jongh.

Terry Nienhuis

See also *City of Night*; Gay Liberation Movement; *Midnight Cowboy*; Stonewall Inn Riots.

■ Branch Banks

Extensions of existing banks. Changing demographics, particularly in the southwestern states, helped spur an increase in the number of branch banks.

The rapid expansion of auto ownership, the rise of suburbs, and the expanding consumer economy of the 1950's placed new demands on the banking systems of the most rapidly growing states of the Southwest and South. Some of those states, including California, Arizona, Nevada, and Florida, had permitted branch banks to operate for many years.

A branch bank differed from a unit, or single, bank in that it was an extension of an existing bank and did not require a new charter or separate capitalization. More important, the funds of branch banks—assets and liabilities alike—could be comingled, meaning that each branch bank did not have to show a profit all the time and could ride out unprofitable cycles. This feature provided branch banks with a substantial advantage over unit banks in that branch systems could diversify their investments and risks by making loans in different parts of the state and to different industries. Even more important, as the branch systems in Arizona and California found during the 1920's and the Great Depression, the information mechanisms available to branch banks vastly surpassed those available to unit banks (which

might be competitors of each other), and thus bank runs could be dealt with more successfully.

Branch banks proved particularly suited to the new suburban culture of the 1960's in that they were cheaper, on average, to establish than a unit bank and could draw support from the home bank until they established a customer base. They allowed the mobile population of the decade to, in essence, take their bank with them by offering a familiar name with which to do business in a new setting.

In 1960, there were 2,523 banks (905 national banks) operating 10,702 branches. By 1970, that number had increased to 4,294 banks (1,684 national) operating 22,508 branches. California led the nation in branch banking, with the Bank of Italy (later Bank of America) and Security Pacific Bank establishing branches early in the century. Likewise, Arizona, with a population of just more than one million in 1960, had a flourishing branch banking network through Valley National Bank.

Impact Branch banking fit perfectly with the mobile, suburban society of the most rapidly growing sections of the nation in the Southwest. Branching not only provided banking services for new and expanding communities but also generated new pools of capital that those areas could tap for further growth. It is entirely likely—although not completely proven—that branching helped smooth out the growing economies in California, Arizona, and many states in the South.

Although branch banking had many benefits, unit bankers (people who owned single banks) in states where branch banking was not permitted, fiercely resisted changes in legislation that would allow this type of banking. They feared that large, often out-of-state, corporations would control a state's banking industry. States such as Colorado and Nebraska had powerful unit bank lobbies that kept branch banks out, and many states had antibranch clauses in their constitutions. However, the trend was clear, and the competitive pressure to give banks the flexibility they needed remained strong even in unit bank states. By the end of the 1960's, many states were reviewing their legislation to permit branch banking, and some had even started to reconsider interstate branch banking. Its benefits were impressive enough that by the 1980's, many states had changed or amended antibranching provisions in their laws.

Additional Information *The Encyclopedia of American Business History and Biography: Banking and Finance, 1913-1989* (1990), edited by Larry Schweikart, includes sections on branch banking, legislation related to branching, and an editor's introduction that summarizes the history and trends of banking in the United States.

Larry Schweikart

See also Business and the Economy; Demographics of the United States.

■ Brautigan, Richard

Born January 30, 1935, Tacoma, Washington
Died September, 1984, Bolinas, California

American poet and novelist. Brautigan's quirky, often humorous countercultural writing embodied both the Beat and the hippie movements, establishing him as one of the most prominent West Coast writers of the 1960's.

Early Life Relatively little is known of Richard Gary Brautigan's life before his move to San Francisco in 1958 because of his infamously shy and reclusive personality. Born in Tacoma, Washington, he spent his childhood there and in Oregon and Montana. His writing reveals a troubled and poverty-stricken upbringing and a familiarity with fishing, hunting, and the outdoors, which would ultimately play an invaluable role in his work. *Lay the Marble Tea: Twenty-four Poems*, published in 1959, is believed to be Brautigan's first book.

The 1960's The publication of the book of poetry *The Pill Versus the Springhill Mine Disaster* (1968) and the novels/prose pieces *A Confederate General from Big Sur* (1964), *Trout Fishing in America* (1967), and *In Watermelon Sugar* (1968) established Brautigan as one of the representative writers who captured the revolutionary spirit and cultural freedom of the late 1960's.

Although never regarded as a major or serious poet by critics, Brautigan was nevertheless hugely successful and viewed as a cult hero both nationally and abroad. His poems were often short bursts of freewriting that revealed on various levels his moods, observations, views of society, and playful sense of humor. His novels all depicted young men on searches for the peculiarities of their identities as Americans. Written almost consciously in the vein of Jack Kerouac's *On the Road* (1957), they were ex-

tremely popular among hippies and those living in communes. They also topped best-seller lists on college campuses.

Later Life Brautigan continued to write and publish poetry and fiction throughout the 1970's and in the early 1980's, dividing his time between San Francisco and a ranch in Montana. He died of a self-inflicted gunshot wound in Bolinas, California, in September, 1984. Owing, perhaps, to Brautigan's penchant for reclusiveness and privacy, his body was not discovered until October 25 of that year.

Impact It could be argued that Brautigan's largely first-person narrative poetry, which was written during a period of deep imagism, helped bring about the personal narrative poetry that emerged in the 1980's. In addition, Brautigan's technique of compiling short prose pieces as chapters of novels can be seen as an influence in the works of novelists such as Kurt Vonnegut, Jr., Tom Robbins, and John Irving.

Additional Information A critical study of Brautigan's writing before 1972 can be found in Terence

Richard Brautigan's poetry and prose captured the irreverent, free spirit of the counterculture that emerged in the 1960's. (Erik Weber)

Malley's *Richard Brautigan: Writers for the Seventies* (1972). A biography of Brautigan by his friend Keith Abbott can be found in *Downstream from Trout Fishing in America: A Memoir of Richard Brautigan* (1989).

Gary Juliano

See also Beat Generation; Hippies; Literature; Poetry; San Francisco as Cultural Mecca.

■ British Invasion

A fascination that British culture held for American teenagers in the mid-1960's. The phenomenon began with music but eventually encompassed magazines, fashion, theater, film, and travel.

After World War II, most American teenagers developed their interests and values without any reference to cultural events outside the borders of their nation. They listened to American music and created their own teenage culture. In the latter half of 1963, they were first exposed to a new, unusual singing group: a British rock group called the Beatles, which had combined rhythm and blues and Latin beats to create a new sound. As teenagers became caught up in "Beatlemania," they began to crave the culture of the nation that had spawned this group.

The Music When the Beatles debuted in the United States, teenagers went crazy. They not only bought the records, but they also read everything they could find on the group. Not satisfied with the information available in domestic publications, teenagers began subscribing to British fan magazines such as *Beatles Monthly* and *The Mersey Beat*, both of which highlighted groups from Liverpool, England. As the teenagers grew increasingly enamored of the Beatles, they wanted more. Dozens of other British groups began touring the United States.

The early British groups were relatively clean-cut; their longish hair was neatly groomed and their concert attire consisted of Eton-collared suits and Cuban-heeled boots. They looked and played to a formula successfully established by the Beatles. The Rolling Stones brought the United States back to its musical roots by playing a heavily blues-influenced rhythm and blues, and its members' scruffy appearance began to alter the image of the British rock star.

The Clothes Before long, American teenagers, who had read in the fan magazines about the burgeoning British fashion industry on Carnaby Street and King's Road, began to imitate the new styles. Girls shortened their skirts and dresses and wore doll-like makeup; both sexes wore the British flag on clothing and let their hair grow longer. British teenagers fell into two camps, the Rockers and the Mods, but it was the Mods rather than the rough-looking Rockers that American teenagers chose to imitate. British models such as Patti Boyd, Jean Shrimpton, and—most famous of all—Twiggy demonstrated the British look in American and British teen magazines. Twiggy's extremely slender, boyishly angular figure became the ideal. Frosted lipstick, false eyelashes, heavy eyeliner, and cartoon-like lower lashes were extremely popular.

Youthful fashions began to be rendered in bright colors and bold patterns. The most popular designer was Mary Quant, a young British woman who used natural fabrics and focused on clothing textures in addition to style. Teenage girls wore short shirts called miniskirts accompanied by wide belts, poor-boy tops, and clunky wooden jewelry. They also began to wear hip-hugger pants.

The Carnaby Street look meant change for teenage boys as well. Teenage boys, who had previously faded into the fashion background, suddenly blossomed. They wore textured vests and bright colors similar to those teenage girls wore, giving rise to unisex clothing. Their ties (when they wore them) were wide and bright. So revolutionary was this interest in fashion on the part of teenage boys that several songs celebrated it, including the Kinks' "Dedicated Follower of Fashion." The teenagers' long hair and brightly colored clothes drew taunts from many adults, including "Are you a boy, or are you a girl?" which became the title of a song by the Barbarians. These comments only served to heighten the teenagers' spirit of rebellion, and gradually, even conservative businessmen began wearing paisley prints and colored shirts.

Theater and Film British drama, including John Osborne's *Look Back in Anger* (first performed in 1956), had begun to capture the sense of rebellion felt by many of that nation's youth. Plays about these young people and British life in general began to be performed in the United States. Peter Brook, director of the Royal Shakespeare Company, had the company performing new drama from Europe, and his 1970 production of Shakespeare's *A Midsummer*

Night's Dream presented New York audiences with a vibrant, acrobatic theatrical event quite unlike a traditional staging of the revered playwright's work.

When *The Knack* (1965) was filmed in Britain, it was done in black and white and featured actors unknown to screen audiences, including Rita Tushingham and Michael Crawford. The popular *Tom Jones* (1963) introduced actor Albert Finney to Americans, and *Alfie* (1966) introduced Michael Caine. *Blow-up* (1966), which questioned the meaning of reality, was probably among the strangest films of the decade. Many of the films poked fun at the conservative British society or questioned its values and assumptions. The Beatles, well aware of the cinematic scene in England, filmed their first film, *A Hard Day's Night* (1964), on location in England. They wanted their film to be artistically sound and not merely a video catalog of songs, so they contracted with noted director Richard Lester and used cutting-edge techniques (black-and-white film, long stretches without dialogue, and Marx Brothers-like antics), which netted the film critical acclaim.

As the Vietnam War heated up and the teenagers who had caught Beatlemania turned into young adults, their attention focused on events affecting them much more directly; the hunger for British culture had generally disappeared from the American scene by 1967.

Impact When *The World Book* encyclopedia's 1964 year book mentioned the Beatles, teenagers knew they had influenced mainstream America. Although the British invasion lasted less than five years, it affected the United States for years to come. Americans were no longer focused on only their own continent. British music, theater, films, styles, and publications regularly appeared in the United States. More men began to enjoy dressing stylishly in a variety of colors and patterns, and the men's fashion industry developed to meet their demands. Long hair on men slowly became commonplace, first showing up on businessmen, then on truck drivers and construction workers, the very men who had most vociferously criticized the style. Even bed sheets, which had mostly been white, blossomed with stripes, flowers, and bold patterns in bright colors.

Additional Information Jane and Michael Stern, teenagers during the 1960's, wrote *Sixties People* (1990), which looks at the decade's styles and trends through its people. Todd Gitlin, a former campus

activist, puts the decade in its political and historical perspective in *The Sixties: Years of Hope, Days of Rage* (1987). *The Sixties* (1995), edited by Gerald Howard, discusses the arts and culture of the time.

Tracy E. Miller

See also Baby Boomers; Beatles, The; *Blow-up;* Fashions and Clothing; Film; Mod; Music; Rolling Stones; Theater; Twiggy.

■ Brooks, Gwendolyn

Born June 7, 1917, Topeka, Kansas

The first African American writer to win a Pulitzer Prize. Brooks's poetry is based on her strong identification with the lives of ordinary African Americans. She is dedicated to public readings, support of black-owned publishing houses, and the teaching and encouragement of young people.

Early Life. The parents of Gwendolyn Elizabeth Brooks, a janitor and schoolteacher, encouraged the young girl's literary gifts and provided a loving home and an excellent education for her and her younger brother. As a high school student, Brooks received advice from African American poets James Weldon Johnson and Langston Hughes. After attending Wilson Junior College, she studied poetic technique in the Southside Community Art Center, where she read modern British and American poetry and began seriously to consider a career as a writer. She married Henry Blakely in 1939 and is the mother of two children. Her early poetry, which centered on African American life in Chicago, was written in conventional style in the European American tradition. Brooks was awarded the Pulitzer Prize in 1950 for her second collection of poetry, *Annie Allen* (1949).

The 1960's The year 1967 was a turning point in Brooks's creative work. Although themes of black consciousness appeared in her 1960 collection, *The Bean Eaters*, Brooks's awakening came at the Black Writers Conference at Fisk University in 1967, where she met younger African American writers committed to the Black Power movement. From that time, she directed her poetry to an audience of African Americans. *In the Mecca* (1968), an experimental work, departed from her previous expression in fixed forms and described with compassion, often bitter humor laced with irony, the desperate lives of poor African Americans in Chicago. *Riot* (1969) was a response to the death of the Reverend Martin Luther King, Jr. Some critics found these works darkly pessimistic, but Brooks believed they reflected her new vision of herself as a black woman writer whose audience was African Americans.

Although Brooks never considered herself a political writer, critics agree that her work in the 1960's and beyond reflected not only a growing sophistication in her craft but also an increasingly revolutionary stance. Brooks has described her creative vision as a positive celebration of blackness. After 1967, she published exclusively with African American presses. As a result of her worldwide travel, including visits to Africa, her poetry expresses international themes and a special concern with the lives of children. Brooks became the poet laureate of Illinois in 1968, succeeding Carl Sandburg.

Later Life Brooks was elected to the National Women's Hall of Fame in 1988 and has received numerous honorary degrees from colleges and universities.

Impact Critics consider Brooks one of the foremost American poets and praise her superb poetic technique that transcends ideology. Although her creative impulse is firmly rooted in her experience as an African American woman, her uncompromising vision goes beyond race to speak to the human condition. She is noted for her generosity, both her financial support to young people and her involvement in workshops and readings.

Additional Information Brooks has written two autobiographies, *Report from Part One* (1972) and *Report from Part Two* (1996). Jacquelyn Y. McLendon's critical analysis of her work appears in *African American Writers* (1991), edited by Valerie Smith.

Marjorie Podolsky

See also Black Power; Literature; Poetry.

■ Brown, H. Rap

Born October 4, 1943, Baton Rouge, Louisiana

Militant black power advocate. Brown, a militant spokesperson for radical African American ideas, was active in the Student Nonviolent Coordinating Committee (SNCC).

Early Life Born in Baton Rouge, Louisiana, Hubert Geroid "Rap" Brown attended an all-African American grade school operated by white missionaries. It

Militant black power advocate H. Rap Brown was known for giving inflammatory speeches in which he urged African Americans to use violence to achieve their goals. (Archive Photos)

was here that he was nicknamed "Rap" because of his ability to rap, or converse in rhyme, with poor, street-smart African Americans. He attended public high school in Baton Rouge for a time and then, at the insistence of his mother, enrolled in an inexpensive all-African American private high school affiliated with Southern University, also in Baton Rouge.

The 1960's Brown attended Southern University for three years, dropping out to devote himself full-time to the struggle for civil rights. In 1965, he joined Stokely Carmichael and the Student Nonviolent Coordinating Committee (SNCC) in Lowndes County, Alabama, and quickly developed a national reputation for militant speeches. In 1967, he replaced Carmichael as SNCC chairman. This position put him in the spotlight as the new spokesperson and national symbol of African American militancy.

Brown never accepted nonviolence as a tactic and often carried a gun, believing that whites respected firepower. He believed armed self-defense was necessary and racial violence inevitable. His fiery orations generated a great deal of fear in white America. In Dayton, Ohio; East St. Louis, Illinois; and Cambridge, Maryland, riots erupted after Brown made inflammatory speeches. He repeatedly urged African Americans to take up weapons, wage war, burn, loot, and kill. In 1968 in New Orleans, Brown was convicted of transporting a gun across state lines, a federal charge.

Later Life In large part because of his violent rhetoric, Brown was pursued by authorities in several states and arrested several times on various charges. In 1970, he went into hiding just before he was to be tried on charges of inciting a riot in Cambridge. The Federal Bureau of Investigation placed him on its ten most-wanted list. In 1971, he was wounded in a shootout with New York City police while holding up a tavern. He was convicted and sentenced to five to fifteen years for his role in the hold-up and shootout. While in prison, Brown adopted the Muslim faith and a new name, Jamil Abdullah Al-Amin. In 1973, he was paroled and moved to Atlanta, Georgia, where he opened a grocery store and is active in the local mosque.

Impact Brown's outspoken militancy and encouragement of violence earned him the fear and animosity of most of white America and played into the hands of pro-segregation presidential candidate George Wallace and Republican nominee Richard M. Nixon in the election of 1968. The fear Brown helped generate fueled anti-civil rights sentiment and conservative law and order rhetoric, helping to elect Nixon to the presidency.

Additional Information Published in 1969, Brown's book, *Die Nigger Die!* is an autobiographical and ideological account of his life and beliefs.

Lisa Langenbach

See also Black Power; Carmichael, Stokely; Civil Rights Movement; Student Nonviolent Coordinating Committee (SNCC).

■ Brown, James

Born May 3, 1933, Barnwell, South Carolina

Known as the "Godfather of Soul." Brown became a legend in the music business during the 1960's and early 1970's.

Early Life Raised by his father and aunt from age four, James Joe Brown, Jr., grew up in a roadhouse

James Brown, the "Godfather of Soul" known for his energetic live shows, was criticized by black militants for embracing somewhat conservative political views in the late 1960's. (Frank Driggs Collection/Archive Photos)

where he learned how to play musical instruments, sing, and dance. In his youth, he picked cotton and peanuts, shined shoes, and resorted to criminal activity in order to survive. From 1949 to 1952, he served time in a juvenile correction facility for breaking into automobiles. While incarcerated, Brown formed a gospel quartet that earned him the nickname "Music Box." After being paroled, he joined a local rhythm-and-blues singing group called the Flames. The group's hit song, "Please, Please, Please," released in 1956 by King Records, launched Brown's career and eventually became his first million seller. Brown went on tour with the Flames, wearing a purple cape during the lively, dance-filled stage show. In 1958, King Records released his second hit, "Try Me," which soared to number one on the rhythm-and-blues charts. The group made very little money from their first hits, however, and continued to play in nightclubs and anywhere else that paid. Brown worked almost every night of the year, a practice that earned him the title of the "Hardest-Working Man in Show Business."

The 1960's On October 14, 1962, Brown recorded what many critics have called the greatest live album in history, *The James Brown Show Live at the Apollo*. He produced the album at his own expense, convinced that a live recording would capture the essence of his music. Peaking at number two on *Billboard*'s pop album chart, the 1963 release spent more than a year on the charts. Brown later recorded more than one hundred hits, including "Papa's Got a Brand New Bag" (1965), "Don't Be a Dropout" (1966), "Cold Sweat" (1967), and "Say It Loud, I'm Black and I'm Proud" (1968). Brown's political activism during the 1960's led to much criticism. Active in stay-in-school campaigns, he also promoted African American businesses, denounced racial violence, and performed for U.S. troops in Vietnam. Black militants criticized him for many of his political positions, especially his endorsement of presidential candidates Hubert Humphrey in 1968 and Richard M. Nixon in 1972. In 1969, he was voted best male pop vocalist by *Cash Box* magazine. By that time, however, his financial situation had become grim. In 1968, the Internal Revenue Service (IRS) demanded almost two million dollars in back taxes and his wife initiated divorce proceedings.

Later Life Brown managed to revive his career in the 1980's with such hits as "Living in America" (1985). From 1988 to 1991, he served time in a South Carolina prison for assault and continued to be dogged by charges from the IRS for an outstanding tax debt of eleven million dollars. In the late 1990's, Brown filed a lawsuit against the U.S. Customs Service for the return of $260,743 that he claimed was seized by a "government overreaching and abusing its power."

Impact Brown's unique style of music and stage performance has had a tremendous impact on music from the 1960's to the present. Many popular award-winning contemporary artists have credited Brown's influence on their music. As a result, he was one of the first individuals inducted into the Rock and Roll Hall of Fame in 1986.

Additional Information In 1986, Brown published an autobiography entitled *James Brown: Godfather of Soul*.

Donald C. Simmons, Jr.

See also Motown; Music; Presidential Election of 1968.

■ Brown, Jim

Born February 17, 1936, St. Simons Island, Georgia

One of professional football's greatest players. Brown also achieved recognition for his outspoken nature and his social activism.

A native of Georgia, James Nathaniel "Jim" Brown moved north to Long Island, New York, when he was nine years old. He played several sports at Manhasset High School, including basketball, track, and football. At the age of twenty, he became an All-American in football at Syracuse University.

Following a successful college football career, Brown was drafted by the Cleveland Browns of the National Football League, for whom he played for nine seasons. In 1963, Brown ran for 1,863 yards, at that time the most yardage gained by a player in a single season. He was named the league's rookie of the year in 1958 and its player of the year in 1958, 1963, and 1965.

Upon his retirement from professional football, Brown began an acting career. He appeared in such

Jim Brown of the Cleveland Browns scores his hundred and sixth career touchdown in this 1965 game against the Philadelphia Eagles. (AP/Wide World Photos)

Hollywood films as *The Dirty Dozen* (1967), *Ice Station Zebra* (1968), *Three the Hard Way* (1975), and *I'm Gonna Get You Sucka* (1988). He was elected to the Pro Football Hall of Fame in Canton, Ohio, in 1971.

Impact Still prominent into the late 1990's, Brown encouraged African Americans to take active roles in community service and business, and he remained an outspoken advocate for the black community.

Additional Information Brown's autobiography *Out of Bounds*, written with Steve Delsohn, was published in 1989.

Joseph R. Paretta

See also Football; Namath, Joe; Sports.

■ Brown Berets

A paramilitary organization formed by Mexican Americans in Southern California. The group sought to improve conditions in the Mexican American community and end discrimination.

Origins and History A group of young Mexican American students living in the barrios of East Los Angeles, California, founded the Brown Berets, a paramilitary organization resembling the Black Panthers, in November, 1967. The group's symbol was a brown beret emblazoned with the words "La Causa" (the cause) and crossed rifles superimposed on a cross. The group, led by college student David Sánchez, identified with the broader Mexican American movement, La Raza (the Mexican American, or Chicano, nation), and stressed the movement's cultural roots in precolonial Indian societies such as the Aztec nation. The Brown Berets opposed discrimination against Mexican Americans and aggressively and actively pursued social change. Its members included street youths as well as high school and college students. The militaristic Brown Berets expanded to include chapters in more than twelve states, but the group was unable to create a national base and disbanded in 1972.

Activities The Brown Berets worked to enrich Mexican American communities by improving school and health care facilities and housing and also sought to end police harassment of community members. The group established a free medical clinic in East Los Angeles and printed a newspaper called *La Causa*. In 1968, the Brown Berets sup-

ported numerous student walkouts in Los Angeles and other cities in the Southwest. In these walkouts, the students demanded better education, including courses in Mexican American history, and more Latino teachers and staff members. In 1969, the Brown Berets, along with other Mexican American organizations, participated in the National Chicano Moratorium on Vietnam.

Impact The Brown Berets were successful in making many people aware of discrimination against Mexican Americans and in initiating some changes in their communities. However, the group's rigid military stance threatened law enforcement and led to police infiltration of and raids on the organization that, along with internal struggles, led to the group's disbanding.

Subsequent Events In 1972, the Brown Berets seized Santa Catalina Island off the coast of Southern California and renamed it "Aztlán Libre." They charged that the United States had unfairly taken the island from Mexico before the Treaty of Guadalupe Hidalgo in 1848.

Additional Information The Brown Berets and the Chicano movement are described in Stan Steiner's *La Raza: The Mexican Americans* (1970).

Carl Henry Marcoux

See also *Chicano: Twenty-five Pieces of a Chicano Mind*; Chicano Movement; Young Lords.

■ Bruce, Lenny

Born October 13, 1925, Mineola, New York
Died August 3, 1966, Los Angeles, California

One of the most controversial entertainers of the early 1960's. Bruce satirized political, sexual, religious, and moral attitudes.

Early Life Following his discharge from the U.S. Navy at the end of World War II, Lenny Bruce (born Leonard Alfred Schneider) worked as a stand-up comic in insignificant burlesque theaters and small clubs in New York City. By the late 1950's, he had developed a national reputation among the "in crowd" with an act primarily targeting show business and built upon improvisational delivery.

The 1960's When Bruce changed from comedian to critic and satirist of the political, sexual, religious, and moral attitudes of society, his legal problems began. Within a few years, he was arrested nineteen times, mostly on the charge that his acts were obscene. (On occasion, he was also charged with use and possession of narcotics.) Although Bruce was acquitted of obscenity charges and never imprisoned, the controversies surrounding his legal problems resulted in a sharp reduction in his professional engagements.

Three cases illustrate different aspects of the obscenity charges brought against him. In March, 1962, Bruce was tried in San Francisco for obscenity in a performance the previous October. The arresting officer cited a few words from the act, ignoring the context of the presentation. The defense countered that Bruce was presenting social criticism within the tradition of satire common in English literature and language. Bruce was acquitted.

In December, 1962, Bruce was arrested in Chicago. This time, the police objected to whole segments of his act. Fortunately, the act had been taped, and Bruce was able to present the entire theme and context to the court. The major objection in this case seemed to be Bruce's unrelenting criticism of the Roman Catholic Church and incongruities between

Lenny Bruce's comedic attacks on the political, sexual, religious, and moral views of mainstream America resulted in numerous arrests for obscenity and other charges. (Library of Congress)

teachings and practices he observed in organized religions. Bruce was found guilty of obscenity, but the judgment was reversed by the Illinois Supreme Court, which ruled that materials having any social importance are constitutionally protected.

The major trial among Bruce's legal battles began in New York City in June, 1964. Arrested by the Public Morals Squad under an archaic statute in the city code that outlawed "indecent, immoral, impure" performances, conviction would bar Bruce from performing in New York City. This six-week trial was the longest, costliest, most vigorously contested and publicized obscenity trial that had taken place in the United States. Bruce was represented by the best censorship and obscenity lawyer in the country and was supported by a petition published in major New York newspapers and signed by eighty prominent members of the cultural community who maintained that the arrest constituted a violation of Bruce's civil liberties and that the obscenity law was being used to harass this controversial social satirist, working "in the tradition of Swift, Rabelais, and Twain."

The New York district attorney and his chief prosecutor opposed what they perceived as a decline of morality in contemporary art, especially in theater and film, and took it upon themselves to determine whether performances were in accord with "contemporary community standards" and redeemed by "social importance."

Because the alleged crime was only a misdemeanor, the case was heard by a panel of three judges. Because of the pretrial publicity, the courtroom filled with members of the national media and representatives from the artistic and educational community. Expert witnesses were heard, and Bruce unsuccessfully attempted to testify on his own behalf. In November, 1964, the verdict was read to a packed courthouse. Bruce was found guilty by a two-to-one decision, and six weeks later was sentenced to four months in jail.

The verdict was followed by a series of legal maneuvers, restraining orders, and injunctions that consumed Bruce, who was now acting as his own lawyer, for the remainder of his life. Had he followed proper legal procedure in his appeals, as friends and lawyers advised, he most likely could have had this verdict overturned, especially because at that time the U.S. Supreme Court was ruling favorably on such matters.

In 1966, Bruce, died of a morphine overdose at the age of forty.

Impact In 1967, afraid that the country was becoming increasingly permissive, Congress identified obscenity and pornography as "a matter of national concern" and established a special commission. However, when the *Report of the Commission on Obscenity and Pornography* was finally published in 1970, it concluded that all censorship on the grounds that materials were obscene or pornographic (and should therefore be withheld from the adult public) was contrary to the First and Fourteenth Amendments to the Constitution. The commission recommended that all obscenity and pornography legislation—federal, state, and local—should be repealed.

Many comedians who came after Bruce have acknowledged their debt to him for paving the way and enabling them to joke about sex and politics without fearing arrest on obscenity charges.

Additional Information Bruce's autobiography *How to Talk Dirty and Influence People* (1965) presents his side of the story; a biography by Albert Goldman entitled *Ladies and Gentlemen—Lenny Bruce!* (1974) is a sympathetic treatment.

Thomas H. Falk

See also Censorship; Free Speech Movement; Social Satires; Supreme Court Decisions.

■ Buckley, William F., Jr.

Born November 24, 1925, New York, New York

A major spokesman for conservative political viewpoints as author, magazine editor, columnist, speaker, and television host. Buckley's efforts helped focus, vocalize, and popularize conservatism as a political, social, and cultural force.

Early Life William Frank Buckley, Jr., was born into a wealthy, large Roman Catholic family. As a student at Yale, he was an outspokenly conservative debater and editor of the school paper. In 1951, he published *God and Man at Yale: The Superstitions of "Academic Freedom,"* an indictment of what he saw as Yale's anti-Christian, anticapitalistic academic atmosphere. He married Patricia Taylor in 1950; they had one son, Christopher. He worked briefly for the Central Intelligence Agency in Mexico and as associate editor of *American Mercury* magazine. Buckley and brother-in-law Brent Bozell wrote *McCarthy and His Enemies* (1954) in defense of the early stages of

Outspoken and articulate William F. Buckley, Jr., responds to a Chicago Tribune *article about him. His talk show,* Firing Line, *popularized conservatism in the United States.* (AP/Wide World Photos)

Senator Joseph McCarthy's attack on communists in the U.S. government. In November, 1955, Buckley and associates founded *National Review*, a weekly (later biweekly) journal that reflected the tenets of cultural conservatism, libertarianism, and anticommunism. The publication's purpose was to "stand athwart history, yelling 'Stop,' at a time when no one is inclined to do so." Buckley served as editor in chief until 1990. Circulation rose from 18,000 in 1957 to 54,000 in 1961 and 110,000 in 1969.

The 1960's In the early 1960's, the U.S. conservative movement lacked leadership and organization, and *National Review* attempted to unify it without alienating mainstream Republicans, whose political support they needed. *National Review* refused to endorse either Dwight D. Eisenhower or Richard M. Nixon for president because of their political moderation but attacked what the magazine termed far-right "crackpottery" such as that of the John Birch Society and followers of author Ayn Rand's atheistic self-autonomy. *National Review* supported southern resistance to federally mandated desegregation on the grounds of states' rights, but it decried southern racists and uncompromising segregationists.

In September, 1960, Buckley helped found Young Americans for Freedom, a conservative student group. In 1962, he began a nationally syndicated newspaper editorial column (published in 250 papers in 1969) and began to emerge as a national celebrity. *Playboy* magazine published Buckley's debate with liberal novelist Norman Mailer in 1962, and *The New York Times Magazine* published his debate with African American author and activist James Baldwin in 1965.

Buckley and *National Review* supported conservative Republican senator Barry Goldwater's presidential campaign in 1964. Both Goldwater's popularity and his defeat convinced Buckley that conservatism could go on the offensive but only in a prudent and constructive manner. Buckley ran as Conservative Party candidate for New York City mayor in 1965, attempting to block election of liberal Republican John Lindsay. Buckley quickly became known among New Yorkers for his suave and insouciant personal style, formidable debating skills, and ready wit. When asked what he would do if elected, Buckley quipped, "Demand a recount." Although he did not win, he received 13.4 percent of the vote. Several of his positions were controversial, especially those that decried what he saw as a lack of leadership in the African American community. He based his views on *Beyond the Melting Pot* (1963), by Nathan Glazer and Daniel P. Moynihan, whose conclusions pointed to the need for self-help rather than government handouts to improve the conditions of poor urban minorities. He chronicled his experiences in *The Unmaking of a Mayor* (1966).

This exposure spurred Buckley to create a local (soon national) television talk show, *Firing Line*, in April, 1966. Rather than feature interviews with his guests, the talk show presented what were termed "polemical exchanges of opinions" in the form of "bare-knuckled intellectual brawls" that highlighted Buckley's stances against communism, the welfare state, campus unrest, civil rights-related violence, and changes in Roman Catholic liturgy. His dogmatism softened, however, as he directly engaged his ideological opponents, and his national celebrity grew. Buckley's rising popularity coincided with many Americans' growing anxiety about the radical and sometimes violent Left, a fear that helped lead to the nomination and election of Nixon, a Republican, to the presidency in 1968. At the 1968 national party conventions, ABC television paired a reluctant Buckley with liberal novelist Gore Vidal to provide commentary, resulting in a verbal spat and additional fame for Buckley.

Buckley served Nixon's administration as a member of the U.S. Information Agency Advisory Commission from 1969 to 1972.

Later Life Buckley went on to edit or write more than thirty books and to continue his columns, television programs, and role as editor at large of *National Review*.

Impact Buckley was instrumental in moving conservative politics into the mainstream by serving as a joyful, attractive, and articulate spokesperson and by defining and popularizing the issues that late twentieth century conservatism embraced. As such, he was influential in conservative political victories in the 1980's and 1990's.

Additional Information Detailed information on Buckley's life and views can be found in *William F. Buckley, Jr.: Patron Saint of the Conservative* (1988), by John Judis, and Buckley's own book, *On the Firing Line: The Public Life of Our Public Figures*, published in 1989.

Joseph P. Byrne

See also Conservatism in Politics; Goldwater, Barry; John Birch Society; Nixon, Richard M.; Young Americans for Freedom.

■ Burger, Warren

Born September 17, 1907, St. Paul, Minnesota
Died June 25, 1995, Washington, D.C.

A conservative judge on the United States Court of Appeals, District of Columbia, for most of the 1960's. Burger's 1969 appointment as chief justice of the United States Supreme Court marked a surprising move toward the center on social issues.

Early Life Born in Minnesota in modest circumstances, Warren Earl Burger attended the University of Minnesota and St. Paul College of Law (which later became the William Mitchell College of Law). Burger practiced law in Minnesota until 1953 and taught part-time at the William Mitchell College of Law, 1931-1948. A lifelong Republican, Burger entered national politics in 1948. At the 1952 Republican National Convention in Philadelphia, he threw Minnesota's support behind Dwight D. Eisenhower; consequently, Eisenhower appointed Burger assistant attorney general of the United States, chief of the civil division of the Department of Justice. In 1955, Eisenhower nominated him for the United States Court of Appeals for the District of Columbia. Known as a conservative, Burger advocated reforms in judicial decisions. In 1933, he married Elvera Stromberg; they had one son and one daughter.

The 1960's Throughout the 1960's, Burger attracted national attention as circuit judge in the District of Columbia. He led the court contingent that supported leeway for police, prosecution lawyers, and trial judges while opposing the extension of criminal defendant rights and modifications of the insanity defense.

In 1961, Burger argued that the Durham rule (1954), which broadened the definitions of the criminally insane, "ignored the moral basis of criminal law." In 1966, Burger attacked a significant Supreme Court decision, the Miranda rights ruling (1966), which required police officers to warn suspects of their rights before interrogation.

Burger continued to advocate judicial system reforms. In 1966, he delivered a landmark civil rights decision ordering the Federal Communications Commission to hear complaints from minority groups regarding the allegedly biased programming of a Jackson, Mississippi, television station. While giving a speech in Wisconsin in 1967, he called for an emphasis on rehabilitation within the prison system. During another speech in September, 1968, at Columbus, Ohio, Burger stated that United States had "the most complicated system of criminal justice and the most difficult system to administer of any country in the world." Burger also stated that the Supreme Court "should have used the mechanism provided by Congress . . . [rather] than changing the criminal procedure and rules of evidence on a case by case [basis]."

On May 21, 1969, President Richard M. Nixon appointed Burger chief justice of the Supreme Court.

Later Life Burger served as chief justice until September 26, 1986. In his position, Burger served as chair of the judicial conference of the United States

and chair of the Federal Judicial Center. Appointed chair of the Commission on the Bicentennial of the United States Constitution by President Ronald Reagan in 1985, Burger was active in fund-raising until 1992, promoting celebrations and seminars on the Constitution. In 1987, he wrote the foreword of *Constitutional Journal.* Burger wrote *It Is So Ordered,* a book that detailed fourteen landmark constitutional law cases, in 1995. He died in Washington, D.C.

Impact Burger, expected to be conservative, left a court close to the center on social issues. Some of his more significant decisions resulted in the validation of busing as a means of school integration, a legal definition of obscenity, increased protection against sexual discrimination, affirmation of First Amendment guarantees of free speech and free press, and protection of constitutional rights to abortion on the basis of privacy. Burger wrote the opinion for a unanimous court that forced President Nixon to surrender tapes and papers related to the Watergate scandal. Burger's influence led Congress to approve measures that streamlined and modernized the operations of the federal judiciary.

Additional Information Two books that look at the life and work of Burger are *The Burger Court: The Counter Revolution That Wasn't* (1983), edited by Vincent Blasi, and Bernard Schwartz's *The Ascent of Pragmatism: The Burger Court in Action* (1990).

Karan A. Berryman

See also Busing; *Miranda v. Arizona*; Nixon, Richard M.; School Desegregation; Supreme Court Rulings; Warren Report.

■ Business and the Economy

A period of transition from an industrial to a postindustrial business and economic order. The economic expansion that began after World War II continued, producing a broad range of consumer goods and services during the 1960's.

When President John F. Kennedy promised in 1960 to get the economy moving again, he optimized the use of federal fiscal policies to stimulate higher rates of growth. Economic growth had averaged about 3 percent per year from 1953 to 1960, but the averages masked eccentric yearly swings, from declines of 2 percent in certain years to growth of 5 percent in others. As it shaped the macroeconomic environment, the federal government played a key role in

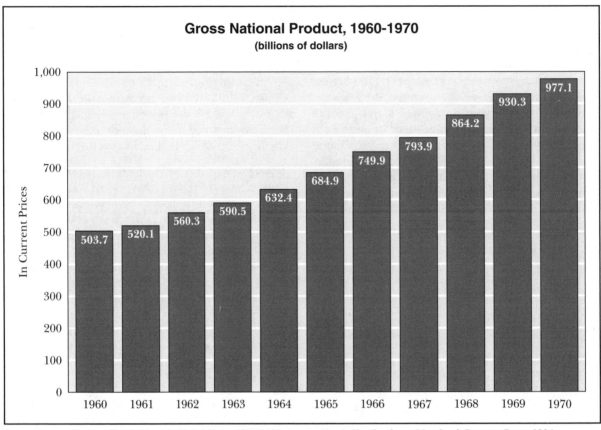

Gross National Product, 1960-1970
(billions of dollars)

In Current Prices

Year	Value
1960	503.7
1961	520.1
1962	560.3
1963	590.5
1964	632.4
1965	684.9
1966	749.9
1967	793.9
1968	864.2
1969	930.3
1970	977.1

Source: Kurian, George, *Datapedia of the United States, 1790-2000, America Year by Year.* Lanham, Maryland: Bernam Press, 1994.

fine-tuning the balance of unemployment against inflation. Walter Heller, a University of Minnesota economist appointed by Kennedy to chair the Council of Economic Advisers, was in charge of the economic agenda. Heller advocated the Keynsian model of full employment through prosperity, corporate-led growth, controlled deficit spending, and the use of targeted tax cuts as incentives.

Rather than stimulate the economy directly through government expenditures, the Kennedy administration pursued tax adjustments and cuts that encouraged private capitalization and investment. In April, 1961, Kennedy sent Congress a message urging elimination of a number of complicated tax deductions, or loopholes, that had arisen since 1945. In addition, he believed that business would invest more capital if Congress enacted investment tax credits. These incentives would encourage businesses to modernize their plants and equipment. His detailed proposal reduced federal tax revenues by $11 billion from individuals and $2.6 billion from

corporations. Although Congress preserved most of the loopholes, a revised tax bill that passed in 1964 during the early months of the Lyndon B. Johnson administration lowered the top tax rate for individuals and provided targeted cuts for corporations.

President Johnson, who began his term during a time of national prosperity, decided to pursue broad social goals through increases in federal government spending. Congress passed the Economic Opportunity Act of 1964 authorizing, among other things, the spending of $947.5 million over three years for a Job Corps that would train youths and for housing and urban development. Johnson's goals received some help from the private sector in 1968, when a group of responsible business leaders formed the National Alliance of Businessmen, which focused on employment, training, and educational programs to help the disadvantaged improve their business and economic opportunities. For example, Aetna and other insurance firms helped initiate and finance the rebuilding of downtown Hartford, Connecticut. By 1966, the number of U.S. families with annual incomes of $7,000 or more had reached 55 percent, compared with only 22 percent in 1950. By 1968, the average annual income of a family in the United States was $8,000, or double the level only a decade earlier. White families experienced a 69 percent growth in income, and black families saw their income rise 109 percent. However, African Americans still averaged only 61 percent of what white Americans earned.

Alliances and Conflicts Business and the economy reflected the growing alliance among Pentagon officials, corporate contractors, and funded university research—what former president Dwight D. Eisenhower had labeled the "military-industrial complex." During the early 1960's, a bitter battle ensued between Boeing and General Dynamics over a $7 billion contract to build a new Air Force plane. Spending for the military and for space exploration continued to flow to the states in the South, Southwest, and the West. By the end of the 1960's, federal payrolls accounted for $10 billion per year in the Sunbelt states, double the amount in all the other states combined. This kind of "warfare" state linked national defense with domestic prosperity.

The apparent shift in power from the Northeast to the Sunbelt was caused by developments in a number of industries and firms. In particular, the oil industry, long headquartered in the Northeast, relocated to Texas, Oklahoma, and California. In 1964, T. Boone Pickens, a Texas oil man, established Mesa Petroleum. Getty, Union, Occidental, and Signal Oil Companies, all based in Los Angeles, grew to prominence during the decade. Phillips Petroleum of Bartlesville, Oklahoma, and Tenneco in Houston, Texas, challenged New York-based companies such as Mobil and Texaco.

The close relationship between the federal government and big business nearly unraveled when Roger Blough, chairman of the board of the U.S. Steel Corporation, offended President Kennedy in April, 1962, by an apparent violation of an agreement negotiated by Secretary of Labor Arthur Goldberg. To forestall demands for a large wage increase, Goldberg had convinced the Steelworkers Union to accept a modest 3 percent wage hike and agree not to strike. In return, the administration expected U.S. Steel to hold the line on prices, thereby demonstrating "industrial statesmanship." However, Blough an-

nounced that his company would charge an additional six dollars per ton, approximately 8 percent more than the previous rate. Outraged, Kennedy decided to force Blough to rescind the price increase. The Defense Department began purchasing from Inland Steel Company rather than U.S. Steel. The Federal Trade Commission launched an inquiry into the possibility of collusive price-fixing, and the Treasury Department spoke of a tax investigation. The Department of Justice announced that it would explore whether antitrust laws had been violated. U.S. Steel surrendered, rolling back its prices, although steel prices were permitted to rise quickly the subsequent year.

In the mid-1960's, a series of new regulations increased the federal government's power over industry. In 1965, consumer advocate Ralph Nader published *Unsafe at Any Speed: The Designed-in Dangers of the American Automobile*, which pointed out dangerous design defects in the Chevrolet Corvair and other automobiles; his book eventually caused General Motors to abandon production of the Corvair. After congressional investigations into General Motors operations, the National Highway Traffic Safety Administration was created in 1966 to govern the design of automobiles sold in the United States. Consumers increasingly turned to the federal government for protection. The legal barriers protecting manufacturers had begun to crumble as early as 1960, when the New Jersey Supreme Court ruled that the driver of a new Chrysler automobile in which the steering mechanism had suddenly failed, causing accident and injury, did not have to prove that the manufacturer was negligent. In 1963, more than 250,000 product liability cases appeared before U.S. courts; in 1970, the number climbed to 500,000. The courts abandoned the legal doctrine of *caveat emptor*, or let the buyer beware, during the 1960's.

Banking Money and banking underwent significant transformations in the 1960's. North Carolina National Bank grew the fastest and earned the most money of any bank in the nation. New entities, among them the United Bank of Los Angeles, Valley National Bank of Phoenix, and Columbia Savings and Loan of Los Angeles, each built assets of more than one billion dollars. San Francisco's Bank of America became the largest bank in the nation, with hundreds of branches serving retail customers. Alert to consumer trends, it promoted its credit card,

Bankamericard, among the middle class. In 1965, four big Chicago banks started MasterCard; two years later, four California banks created Master Charge. Card issuers made money in three ways: charging interest to purchasers who did not repay their balances within a grace period; collecting a fee from merchants who accepted the cards; and franchising the Bankamericards, MasterCards, and Master Charge cards so that other banks could issue them. Eventually, Bank of America sold shares of its credit card business to a consortium of other banks and changed the name of the card to VISA, and Master Charge merged with MasterCard, retaining the latter name. Soon, customers used their credit cards to purchase gasoline, clothing, meals, and virtually everything else.

The Stock Market From 1963 to 1966, the stock market enjoyed its greatest growth since the 1920's, with stock prices more than doubling. Gerald Tsai, Jr., working for the Boston-based Fidelity Fund, led the way with a dazzling series of investment strategies and maneuvers. He continuously reassessed the relative strengths of the companies inside and outside his fund's portfolio. One profitable tactic was to buy glamour stocks just as they hit the market and sell them when other bidders pushed their prices sky-high. Other managers soon copied this strategy, and a number of funds experienced complete turnovers in their holdings during a single year. These funds appeared to be outperforming composite indicators such as the Dow Jones industrial average. By 1965, the funds were conducting one-fourth of all the transactions on the New York Stock Exchange. Institutional investors, primarily pension funds and insurance companies, increasingly represented a democratizing force in capital markets.

The Power of Size One effect of the bull market of the 1960's was the development of industrial conglomerates, an extreme embodiment of a broad movement toward diversification. Audacious deal makers, often from the Sunbelt, arranged for one firm to buy another in an unrelated product area in order to create a conglomerate. The parts of the resulting merged enterprise had little to do with one another economically, but the balance sheets showed increased profits, which pleased shareholders. From 1961 to 1968, International Telephone and Telegraph (ITT) acquired fifty-two companies with combined assets of $1.5 billion, including such

established names as Avis, Continental Baking, William Levitt and Sons, and Sheraton Corporation. American Tobacco became American Brands, Ling Temco Vought became LTV, a defense contractor that then bought the Wilson meat-packing corporation. Litton Shipyards, renamed Litton Industries, acquired the Stouffer food company.

Large firms continued to dominate an economy of national scale and scope in the 1960's. In 1965, IBM introduced its first third-generation mainframe computer, the 360, in response to moves by several of its competitors to substitute integrated circuitry for transistors. That year, with gross revenues of nearly $2.5 billion and a net income of $333 million, IBM commanded 65 percent of the market share for computers in the United States. IBM World Trade became one of the United States' major multinationals. Even though the Department of Justice filed an antitrust suit against IBM and urged the courts to break it up in 1969, the company set the standard among computers for a generation. In 1963, the revenues of General Motors were eight times those of New York state and nearly one-fifth those of the federal government. In 1965, three industrial giants—General Motors, Standard Oil of New Jersey, and Ford—earned more gross income than all of the farms in the United States. In 1968, the Pennsylvania and New York Central Railroads merged into the Penn-Central. Two years later, the merged entity collapsed in a spectacular bankruptcy.

A mass consumer market helped engender a retailing revolution during the 1960's. One innovative form of retailing called "discount merchandising" produced a new kind of store, one that used self-service techniques to sell products on very low margins. Discounters undersold conventional retailers because they obtained their merchandise directly from manufacturers and kept costs low, using high volume turnover, computerized inventory systems, and marketing gimmicks. The year 1962 was a watershed in the evolution of discount merchandising. In addition to Wal-Mart, three other significant discount chains—Kmart, Woolco, and Target—were opened. During the 1960's, the sales of the discount industry exceeded those of the department stores, rising from $15 billion in 1966 to $22.2 billion in 1970. At the end of the decade, there were 4,635 discount outlets nationwide.

Whatever the power of corporate America, innovative ways of doing business were critical factors in the success of companies in a number of industries. Fast food restaurants such as McDonald's and Kentucky Fried Chicken and motels such as Holiday Inn expanded by selling franchises across the nation. By 1967, sales by franchised businesses accounted for about 10 percent of the gross national product (GNP). Professional sports became big business when television dramatically increased the size of viewing audiences and made advertising at sports events more attractive.

Other companies succeeded by concentrating their efforts on a specific group of consumers. For example, Pepsi pursued a strategy of market segmentation when it employed advertisements specifically targeting young people. New market segments, such as ecologically minded consumers, were soon the focus of small startup companies selling products such as wind- and solar-powered devices. In 1968, the Whole Earth Catalog, which described thousands of ecological products for this market, became a national best-seller. The stay-at-home market had for years been successfully targeted by Tupperware and Avon Cosmetics. In 1963, Mary Kay Ash decided to market her own line of personal care products in a similar manner. She formed a company specializing in a limited number of items, which grew into a nationwide marketing organization that provided an income to seventy thousand self-employed salespeople. As a means to spur competition and expansion, Mary Kay Cosmetics held inspirational meetings and conventions at which it awarded prizes to its most energetic workers—usually women. The prizes included cars painted in the company's distinctive pink color.

International Trade International trade underscored much of domestic economic development in the 1960's. The Development Loan Fund, created by Congress in 1961, provided capital for underdeveloped countries in order to stimulate their purchases of goods made in the United States. That same year, the Senate ratified a treaty making the United States a member of the newly created Organization for Economic Cooperation and Development. Furthermore, the Trade Expansion Act in 1962 was designed to establish closer ties with the European Common Market through reciprocal concessions. Another feature of the act was a system of trade adjustment assistance that helped U.S. firms and workers adversely affected by lower tariffs. A number of executive actions sustained a strong dollar, and the balance-of-trade deficit gradually decreased. In fact, U.S. exports rose sharply during the early years of the decade.

The domestic and international policies worked to uplift a listless economy but only within the context of a supportive monetary policy and high consumer confidence. By the first quarter of 1966, more than seven million new jobs had been created. From 1960 to 1966, the realized growth rate of the economy reached 4.5 percent. Corporate profits after taxes also doubled, and the total real compensation of all employees was about 30 percent higher. In 1961 and 1962, inflation as measured by the consumer price index fell to nearly 1 percent per year. By the end of 1963, automobile sales were up 10 percent, and profits after taxes were up 60 percent. The GNP increased 7 percent in 1964, 8 percent in 1965, and 9 percent in 1966. As growth held to a steady 3 percent per year, unemployment declined from 6 percent to less than 5 percent, achieving the equivalent of full employment.

Impact By the end of the decade, the U.S. national economy had weakened. By 1966, the inflation rate began to fluctuate between 2.5 percent and 4 percent per year, and interest rates soared. Banks began paying more than 5.5 percent for passbook accounts, more than savings and loan associations were legally permitted to offer. Rates on government securities, consistently below 3 percent in previous years, rose to 6 percent. From 1966 to 1967, prices increased by more than 4 percent per year; by 1968, inflation rose to 6 percent. Higher wages reduced profits, which fell from 10.6 percent of the nation's income in 1966 to 7.2 percent in 1970. The Vietnam War and the heightened demand for goods and services it caused overstimulated the economy and engendered slow but steady increases in prices. In addition, the dollar—the standard currency of international trade—faltered as European holders of U.S. paper currency began to redeem it for gold when prices rose in the United States. By 1968, the $20 billion gold reserves of the United States represented less than one-third of the dollars held by foreigners. In effect, the overexpansion by the end of the decade discouraged savings, made long-term investment difficult, and undermined the public will to support the costly antipoverty programs initiated by Johnson.

The administration of Richard M. Nixon, however, did not curtail federal spending but instead increased a number of federal expenditures. Social Security benefits were increased and liberalized in 1969, and production of federally subsidized housing proceeded at a steady pace. In addition, a family assistance plan designed to provide a minimum income for all families with dependent children was proposed, though it failed in Congress.

In 1969, the trading volume of securities dramatically dropped, thereby reducing the commissions brokers earned and heightening the alarm on Wall Street. The 7.7 percent growth in GNP that year was accounted for entirely by price increases rather than productivity gains in real output. Therefore, the average worker's real disposable earnings actually declined. Meanwhile, unemployment rose from 3.5 percent in December, 1969, to 6.2 percent a year later—the highest level in nearly a decade. In a bizarre development that economists would later call "stagflation," businesses and the economy experienced the onset of stagnant recession simultaneously with continued inflation. Ostensibly, stagflation undermined the inverse relation between inflation and unemployment.

Inflation continued to accelerate far beyond the expectations of economists. In an anti-inflationary move, the government in 1969 and 1970 raised certain taxes and effected large cutbacks in defense spending and space projects. However, due to monetary constriction, interest rates shot up to the highest point in a century, thereby depressing the housing and automobile industries. By 1970, U.S. firms also encountered increased competition from overseas firms. The industrial economies of Western Europe and Japan, rebuilt from scratch after World War II, began to outproduce the older, less modernized factories in the United States. Merchandise exports from the United States fell to 18 percent of the world market share, as cheaper, more efficiently produced products from abroad penetrated the U.S. market. During the 1960's, foreign automobiles increased their share of the U.S. market from 4 percent to 17 percent. In the expanding field of consumer electronics, imported products moved from 4 percent to 31 percent of U.S. purchases.

Subsequent Events The restructuring of business and the economy that followed the 1960's produced slower rates of growth, loss of market share to for-

eign competitors, and corporate downsizing. In the emerging postindustrial society of the United States, the service sector accounted for two-thirds of the nation's GNP by 1970. The stage was set for the triumph of monetarism over fiscal activism in subsequent decades.

Additional Information For surveys of U.S. business and economic history, see *Business Enterprise in American History* (1994), by Mansel G. Blackford and K. Austin Kerr; *The Unfinished Journey: America Since World War II* (1986), by William Chafe; and Robert Sobel's *The Last Bull Market: Wall Street in the 1960's* (1980).

Brad Lookingbill

See also Credit and Debt; Gross National Product (GNP); Inflation; International Trade; Japanese Imports; Nader, Ralph.

■ Busing

The use of buses to alter a school's racial balance to achieve integration. Controversies raised by busing were more pronounced than those brought about by changes in housing, transportation, and voting.

In May, 1954, in response to a lawsuit by the National Association for the Advancement of Colored People (NAACP), the U.S. Supreme Court declared that legally segregated schools—then prevalent in the southern states, and in Topeka, Kansas—were contrary to the Fourteenth Amendment to the U.S. Constitution, guaranteeing every citizen equal protection under the law. A second decision (1955), ordering that desegregation take place "with all deliberate speed"—kept the pace of southern school desegregation glacially slow until the Supreme Court, in *Green v. New Kent County* (1968), outlawed the merely token integration of the South's freedom-of-choice plans.

The 1954 decision was riddled with ambiguity; it did not make clear whether the injustice of segregation lay in the fact that African American students were set apart by law or that they were not able to mingle with white schoolchildren. Many, if not most, African Americans supported the decision, believing, on the basis of bitter experience, that all-black public schools would inevitably be starved of public funds by school boards beholden to majority-white electorates.

In areas of the rural South where blacks and

whites lived side by side, the end of legal segregation could mean the true integration of the public schools, barring a massive flight of white children to private schools. In metropolitan areas of the North and in some urban areas of the South, however, blacks and whites tended to live in separate neighborhoods; large-scale white migration to the suburbs in the 1950's exacerbated this tendency. As the 1960's began, more and more school boards in northern cities came under pressure from black civil rights groups and their liberal white allies to try to reduce or eliminate de facto public school segregation.

Early Attempts The first experiments in busing for integration, on a small scale, were carried out in New York City. In 1961, pupil transfers were arranged between white Yorkville and black and Latino East Harlem in Manhattan. Just before the 1964-1965 school year, Superintendent of Schools Calvin Gross announced a plan of exchange of pupils between predominantly black schools and predominantly white schools in certain parts of Brooklyn and Queens; only a few of the city's 850 public schools were affected by this plan. Because some, but not all, of the pupil exchanges between black and white schools involved transportation by bus, the process came to be known as "busing."

Throughout the country, other communities acted in a similar fashion. In 1965, the California community of Riverside instituted a program of busing for integration; between 1964 and 1968, Berkeley, California, under the direction of school chief Neil Sullivan, used busing to integrate its ele-

Black students in Boston board a bus headed for schools in the city's predominantly white suburbs. This 1965 pilot program was designed to integrate the area's schools. (National Archives)

mentary and junior high schools (the senior high school was already integrated). In 1967, Evanston, Illinois, began a program of busing for integration. In Massachusetts, in 1965, the state legislature passed the Racial Imbalance Act to penalize local school boards that had too many all-black schools. In the same state, a voluntary busing program was created in 1965, in which some schools in the white suburbs accepted token numbers of black pupils from inner-city neighborhoods. In 1966, a similar program, Project Concern, linked Connecticut suburbs with nearby Connecticut inner-city neighborhoods (in both Massachusetts and Connecticut, participation by suburban school boards was purely voluntary). Proposals to bus children for purposes of integration were also made in other parts of the country; where local authorities were resistant to the idea, civil rights activists sued them in court.

The Civil Rights Act of 1964 mandated denial of federal education aid to school districts practicing segregation; yet from 1964 to 1969, the Department of Health, Education, and Welfare used enforcement powers more vigorously in the South than in the North. In the early and mid-1960's, the courts neither encouraged nor discouraged busing for integration. In 1964, a federal judge rejected a lawsuit demanding that the Gary, Indiana, schools do something to end de facto segregation derived from residential patterns. When white parents challenged a Long Island school board's attempt to reduce segregation through busing, however, a New York state court decided, in 1965, that the board's action was constitutional. It was not until late 1969 that a federal judge (James McMillen) actually ordered a school district (Charlotte-Mecklenburg, in North Carolina) to use busing to create racially integrated schools. The Supreme Court would confirm that lower court decision in April, 1971, in *Swann v. Charlotte-Mecklenburg Board of Education.*

The Controversy Begins By the end of 1969, busing had already aroused much controversy. In many communities where busing for school integration was introduced or even seriously discussed, it encountered vehement resistance from white parents of school-age children. Some white parents simply disliked the inconvenience caused by their children being required to attend school farther from home; others feared for their children's safety in strange schools and strange neighborhoods; and others opposed the mixing of black and white schoolchildren for racist reasons, fearing that their children's attending the same school with black children might eventually lead to interracial marriage. Even when white children were not bused, the busing of black children into previously all-white schools aroused antagonism when white homeowners feared that integration of the school might lead to the neighborhood becoming black. In the autumn of 1964, parents in Brooklyn and Queens (New York) organized in the Parents and Taxpayers association (PAT), illegally withdrew their children from school in a one-day boycott to protest a plan that involved busing their children into previously all-black schools. The furor led to Superintendent Gross's resignation in August, 1965. In 1969, in Richmond, California, and in Denver, Colorado, school board members who had voted for busing for racial integration were voted out of office. In Chicago, in the 1967-1968 school year, school superintendent James Redmond announced a plan that would transport black children into underutilized schools in white neighborhoods; howls of outrage from white parents and the absence of any support from Mayor Richard Daley led to the busing plan's first being scaled back drastically and then abandoned completely. Despite the 1965 Massachusetts law mandating racial balance, the members of the Boston School Board fought so tenaciously against busing for integration that it was not carried out until the middle of the following decade. Faced with a 1963 lawsuit demanding action for integration, the school board of Los Angeles, California, was able to stave off the introduction of busing until 1978. In 1966, amendments to education legislation forbidding forced busing began to be introduced in the U.S. Congress; in 1969, an unsuccessful motion to ban busing was raised in the New York state legislature, and in the same year, a *Newsweek* poll revealed overwhelming opposition to compulsory busing for integration among middle-income white Americans.

Impact A short-term consequence of busing for integration was, sometimes, the inflammation of conflict between white and black students. Black students who attended previously all-white schools often gained the benefit of newer textbooks and better school buildings. Busing for integration sometimes hindered the participation of parents in the life of the school and of students in afterschool activities. There is evidence that, in some localities at least, the integration of black children achieved through busing raised their level of academic performance; whether this was true of all black children who were bused is difficult to determine.

What is easier to assess is the political impact of busing. Antagonism toward busing for integration, combined with other conflicts with African Americans over jobs and housing, helped drive working-class ethnic white voters in the metropolitan areas of the North away from their traditional allegiance to the Democratic Party, whose liberal wing had become strongly identified with the black struggle for civil rights. Republicans, badly beaten at the polls in 1964, began to gain seats in the congressional off-year election of 1966; in 1968, the Republican Richard M. Nixon was elected president.

Subsequent Events Throughout the 1970's, plans to carry out racial integration of the schools through busing were carried out in numerous communities across the United States. In almost all cases (except that of Seattle, Washington, in 1977), busing resulted not from local initiative but from the orders of federal courts that found school boards guilty of deliberate segregation. Presidents Nixon and Gerald Ford both openly denounced busing; President Jimmy Carter was slightly more favorable to busing as a tool for integration. The U.S. Supreme Court, having approved busing in the *Swann* case and in *Keyes v. School District Number One of Denver* (1973), suddenly changed course in its 1974 *Milliken v. Bradley* decision, in which, by a five-to-four margin, it rejected a metropolitan area (suburb-city) busing plan ordered for the Detroit area by a lower federal court. (It did not nullify all plans for suburb-city busing, however.) Turmoil sometimes resulted from court-ordered busing; the worst violence took place in Boston in 1974-1975.

No new busing orders were implemented under Republican President Ronald Reagan, an outspoken foe of busing. In the early 1980's, brief experiments at busing in Chicago and Los Angeles, both undertaken in the 1970's under outside pressure, were ended. In the 1990's, the U.S. Supreme Court allowed some localities to abandon busing. Busing produced long-term racial integration when (as in Charlotte, North Carolina), it was applied to an entire metropolitan area, not merely within the political boundaries of a city; otherwise, white flight to

the suburbs produced resegregation. In some places (for example, California), heavy immigration in the 1980's ensured that many urban schools would be multicultural, even if they contained few children of native-born non-Hispanic whites.

Additional Information Diane Ravitch's *The Great School Wars: New York City, 1805-1987* (1974) is a mine of information on attempts in 1964 at busing for integration in New York City. W. J. Rorabaugh's *Berkeley at War: The Sixties* (1989), a historian's study of that California university town, has a good chapter on race relations and the origins of the area's busing plan. For a look at the conservative-liberal struggle over busing in Richmond, California, in the late 1960's, sociologist Lillian Rubin's *Busing and Backlash: White Against White in a California School District* (1972), based on firsthand observation and interviewing of participants, is useful. For the origins of busing in Charlotte, North Carolina, one can consult Davison M. Douglas's *Reading, Writing, and Race: The Desegregation of the Charlotte Public Schools* (1995). The historian Ronald Formisano's *Boston Against Busing* (1991), although it concentrates mainly on the crisis of 1974-1975, has good background material on the 1960's.

Paul D. Mageli

See also Civil Rights Act of 1964; Civil Rights Movement; Education; School Desegregation.

■ Butch Cassidy and the Sundance Kid

Released 1969
Director George Roy Hill (1922-   )

A motion picture with witty outlaws as heroes. It shows the influence of the antiestablishment attitude and sexual revolution of the 1960's on the American Western.

The Work As Butch Cassidy (Paul Newman) and his Hole in the Wall gang are robbing the Union Pacific a second time, horsemen charge from a freight car on another train and chase Butch and the Sundance Kid (Robert Redford) for countless miles over immense, rugged country. Astonished at the tracking skill of this elite posse hired by E. H. Harriman to protect his railroad, the desperate outlaws plunge into a mountain river, which sweeps them to temporary safety. They debate enlisting to fight Spain but decide against it as they would risk arrest. Seeing no

Paul Newman (left) and Robert Redford starred in the 1969 western Butch Cassidy and the Sundance Kid. *The outlaws' antiauthoritarian stance struck a chord with 1960's viewers.* (Museum of Modern Art/Film Stills Archive)

future in the outlaw business in the American West where an era is ending, Butch and Sundance, along with Sundance's lover, Etta Place (Katharine Ross), travel to Bolivia; here Etta tries to teach her companions enough Spanish for them to rob Bolivian banks. In an attempt to trick an American detective who may be following them, Butch and Sundance take legitimate jobs as payroll guards; however, in this work, for the first time, Butch is forced to shoot someone. Finally, after Etta has left for the United States, the loyal friends Butch and Sundance, having returned to banditry, die together in a plaza, gunned down by dozens of Bolivian soldiers.

Impact Based loosely on historical thieves who started their careers in the Rocky Mountain states at the end of the nineteenth century, *Butch Cassidy and*

the Sundance Kid presents two handsome, amiable robbers struggling to make a living despite the supposedly foolish patriotism of the underpaid Union Pacific expressman Woodcock (George Furth) and the unsportsmanlike conduct of establishment figures such as bank presidents and railroad tycoons. In this Western made in the late 1960's, the townspeople remain unmoved by the appeal of the marshal (Kenneth Mars) to form a posse; it is the antagonist, a faceless detective, who wears a white hat; it is implicitly ironic that the United States Army would not let criminals fight in a war; and it is explicitly ironic that Butch and Sundance kill when they go straight. Furthermore, Etta and Sundance are clearly unmarried, and Butch's woman Agnes (Cloris Leachman) is obviously a prostitute working in a brothel. This popular, award-winning film distinctly shows and reinforces the abandonment by some Americans of traditional rules governing sexuality.

Related Work *Butch Cassidy and the Sundance Kid* was followed by another huge, box-office success in 1970, Charles M. Warren's *Little Big Man*, another Western that poked fun at establishment figures.

Additional Information In his book *In Search of Butch Cassidy* (1977), Larry Pointer points out that al-though the historical Sundance Kid died in Bolivia, Butch, whose real name was Robert LeRoy Parker, returned to the United States, where, as William Thadeus Phillips, he operated a business in Spokane and died of cancer in 1937, nearly three decades after his death as depicted in the motion picture.

Victor Lindsey

See also Counterculture; Film; Sexual Revolution; Vietnam War; *Wild Bunch, The.*

C

■ Camelot

The presidency of John F. Kennedy. Camelot, the name of King Arthur's legendary city, seemed an appropriate appellation for the glamorous and appealing Kennedy administration.

Shortly after the assassination of President John F. Kennedy, his widow, Jacqueline, was interviewed by Theodore White, who was writing an article on the fallen president's impact on history for *Life* magazine. In the interview, the president's widow likened the White House during her husband's tenure to King Arthur's legendary city, Camelot, and in his article, White describes the Kennedy administration as "one brief shining moment that was known as Camelot."

The election of 1960 resulted in one of the most charismatic and glamorous presidencies in U.S. history. Kennedy, who served only about a thousand days, forced Soviet premier Nikita Khrushchev to remove nuclear missiles and bomber planes from Cuba in October, 1962. The president began the process that led to détente by establishing a hot line with Khrushchev and initiating a nuclear test ban treaty in 1963. Furthermore, Kennedy created the Peace Corps and introduced significant civil rights legislation.

President Kennedy inspired millions of Americans, especially young people, to ask not what their country could do for them but what they could do for their country. The television industry further expanded the impact of Kennedy and his beautiful wife. It almost seemed as if the United States had its first "royal" couple.

Impact Despite later criticism of the young president, the Camelot myth continued to dominate the public's opinion of Kennedy, who remained one of the nation's most popular presidents. Kennedy's legend moved his successors in the White House to alter their styles to suit the public's longing for another American Camelot.

Additional Information The Kennedy administration is revealed in detail in *A Thousand Days* (1965), by Arthur M. Schlesinger, Jr., and Paul R. Henggeler's *The Kennedy Persuasion* (1995).

J. Christopher Schnell

See also Assassinations of John and Robert Kennedy and Martin Luther King, Jr.; Kennedy, Jacqueline; Kennedy, John F.

■ Cancer

A disease characterized by rapid proliferation of cells within the body, often starting with a tumor. In the 1960's, the battle against the disease became better organized as research institutes began to take a statistical approach to analyzing cancer occurrence, possible causes, and treatment results.

The term "cancer" is used to describe a number of diseases that all are characterized by rapid, uncontrolled cell growth in the body. As the disease progresses, cancerous cells spread to other parts of the body. Although the cause of cancer is not fully understood, various chemicals and substances in the environment, dietary factors, and viruses are known to produce cancer.

Cancer was a widely feared and poorly understood disease in the early part of the twentieth century. In 1945, the American Society for the Control of Cancer reorganized as the American Cancer Society with the aim of educating laypeople and medical workers and raising money for cancer education, treatment, and research. In 1959, the American Joint Commission for Cancer brought together the six major organizations concerned with cancer into one integrated group. This enabled regular forecasts of the national incidence, distribution, and survival rates of site-specific cancers to be published in *CA—A Cancer Journal for Clinicians*, the journal of the American Cancer Society, starting in the early 1960's.

Occurrence At the beginning of the twentieth century, most of the people who contracted cancer died within a few years. By the 1960's, detection and treatment had improved to the point that one out of three cancer patients survived five or more years after treatment. Despite higher survival rates, cancer, which had been the eighth highest cause of death in the United States in 1900, had become the second leading cause of death by 1960, killing more than 250,000 Americans each year. During that decade, the leading cause of cancer death in men was lung cancer, followed by colorectal and prostate cancer, respectively. In women, the most deaths resulted from breast cancer, followed by colorectal and lung cancer, respectively.

Smoking and Cancer In the 1960's, lung cancer became the focus of attention because it had gone from a rare disease in 1940 (fewer than ten deaths per 100,000 population) to the leading cause of cancer deaths in men (more than twenty deaths per 100,000 population), a rate of increase not seen in any other form of cancer.

In 1962, Surgeon General Luther L. Terry, at the request of President John F. Kennedy, put together a committee of ten scientists to examine the possible link between cancer and cigarette smoking. Over a two-year period, the committee examined and compiled data from previously existing research. They concluded, in a 387-page report, that cigarette smoking was the "principal etiological factor in the increase of lung cancer." The committee also found a connection between cigarette smoking and heart disease and emphysema. The tobacco industry, however, disputed the surgeon general's findings, saying that finding a correlation between smoking and lung cancer was not the same as proving that smoking caused cancer.

Diagnosis Early diagnosis of cancer had been identified as an important factor in its successful treatment. During the 1960's, scientists developed a number of ways to detect cancers more effectively and earlier. Researchers found that most colorectal cancers could be detected by the thirty-centimeter rigid sigmoidoscope (a long tubular instrument used to view the crooked part of the colon above the rectum). This discovery led to the recommendation that men over age forty, the group most likely to develop this form of cancer, receive routine annual checks.

Physicians had been using endoscopes (an instrument used to view the insides of hollow organs) to detect and examine cancerous tissue in the body, but the rigidity of these devices prevented them from viewing certain critical areas. The development of flexible fiberoptic endoscopes during the 1960's permitted easy examination and biopsy of the larynx, trachea, bronchial tubes, esophagus, stomach, and colorectal area.

The death rate for uterine cancer (which included cancers of the cervix and endometrium), which had been slightly more than thirty per 100,000 population in 1930, began to decline in the mid-1930's and continued this trend through the 1960's, declining to slightly more than ten deaths per 100,000 population by 1970. Part of this decline is attributable to the use of the Pap smear, a simple test for cervical and some types of uterine cancer in which a sample of cervical cells is examined for the presence of cancerous or precancerous cells. This test allowed physicians to detect the disease at an early stage, when it is most treatable. In addition, it was discovered that some patients with genital herpes simplex tended to develop cervical cancer. Doctors used this knowledge to advise patients with the herpesvirus and monitor them for signs of cancer.

Scientists were beginning to find links between certain substances and specific cancers. Some were carcinogens (cancer-causing agents) and others indicated that a patient probably had or would develop a specific form of cancer. For example, alpha-fetoprotein (a type of fetal protein) was determined to be a marker for some primary cancers of the liver. Some of these links later suggested possible ways to prevent certain cancers or enabled physicians to better diagnose cancers.

Treatment The goal of treatment was to remove the cancer from the body and prevent its recurrence. In the 1960's, radical surgery was the main form of treatment of most cancers although chemotherapy (the use of drugs to kill cancerous cells) and radiation (the use of X rays to destroy cancerous cells) were also used. Lung cancer, the most common cancer in men, was treated by removal of the entire affected lung, along with, if possible, the associated lymph nodes. Breast cancer, the most common cancer in women, was generally treated by radical mastectomy—removal of the entire breast, overlying skin, and the muscles and glands in the underarm area. Some surgeons advocated removing part of the chest wall in selected cases. This extremely radical operation was performed to remove involved lymph

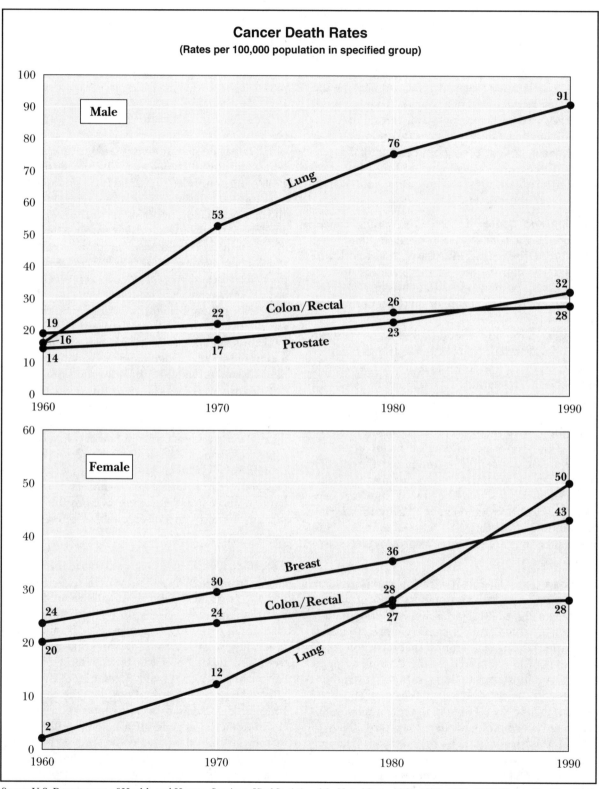

Cancer Death Rates

(Rates per 100,000 population in specified group)

Male

Lung

Colon/Rectal

Prostate

91
76
53
32
28
26
23
22
19
17
16
14

Female

Breast

Colon/Rectal

Lung

50
43
36
30
28
28
27
24
24
20
12
2

Source: U.S. Department of Health and Human Services. *Vital Statistics of the United States 1960, 1970, 1980, 1990.* Hyattsville, Maryland: 1964, 1974, 1984, 1994.

nodes along the chest wall to ensure that the cancer did not come back.

In 1958, the National Surgical Adjuvant Breast Project (NSABP), a cooperative group of physicians, nurses, and medical professionals performing clinical trials in breast cancer, was formed. (It has since expanded to include colorectal cancer research.) Its clinical trials had a great impact upon the treatment of breast cancer in the 1960's. Among its first discoveries was that radiation therapy following a radical mastectomy did not increase the mastectomy's effectiveness and that surgical removal of the ovaries as a preventative measure (in the absence of any sign of disease) was not beneficial. The project was later to find that a lumpectomy (removal of the cancerous lump and some surrounding tissue) followed by radiation therapy was as effective as a radical mastectomy.

Melanomas, uncommon but sometimes deadly skin cancers, were treated by excising the diseased area and unaffected tissue five centimeters on all sides of the cancerous area. The lymph glands draining the site were also removed if possible.

Many cancer researchers began to study lasers, which had been developed in 1960, in hopes that they could replace some surgical techniques or otherwise aid in the treatment of cancer. This early research resulted in lasers routinely being used in treatment of some early-stage cervical and larynx cancers in the following decades.

Radiation, however, was commonly used during the 1960's to destroy cancerous cells in the body. Most radiotherapy machines were low-voltage models although high-voltage machines, which were less injurious and more effective, were slowly becoming available. By the end of the decade, almost seven hundred high-voltage machines were in use.

Chemotherapy was still almost an experimental model of treatment although researchers were reporting promising results when chemotherapy was used alone or in combination with another form of treatment. Preoperative radiation therapy and chemotherapy had been shown to have beneficial results in certain cancers such as Wilms's tumors (kidney), choriocarcinomas (skin cancer), Burkitt's lymphoma (large abdominal masses with central nervous system involvement), and some testicular tumors.

Researchers also devised methods of parenteral nutrition (intravenous or other feeding of patients who could not ingest food) and determined appropriate nutrients that could be administered by vein. This became an important therapeutic tool in the treatment of cancer patients.

Impact Cooperative studies performed in the 1960's, such as those done by the NSABP, provided statistical evaluation of the effectiveness of various treatment methods. This ability to better assess the results of various treatments, combined with technological improvements in radiation therapy and new discoveries in chemotherapy, improved the effectiveness of cancer treatment and minimized the impact upon patients. The radical and extremely radical surgical procedures used for the treatment of lung and breast cancer for most of the 1960's began to be used less frequently.

Trials conducted by the NSABP demonstrated that a lumpectomy (removal of the cancerous lump and a minimum of surrounding tissue) followed by radiation therapy was as effective as mastectomy.

Studies during this decade also provided a better understanding of the role of radiation therapy and chemotherapy in conjunction with surgery, which led to more efficient use of combination therapies. Combination therapies have proved particularly effective with certain soft-tissue tumors, and new chemotherapeutic agents have revolutionized the treatment and prognosis for many cancers, especially some of the lymphomas and leukemias.

The surgeon general's 1964 report on the link between smoking and cancer led Congress to take action; however, the attempt to force cigarette manufacturers to place clear, strongly worded warnings on each pack was diluted by legislators from the tobacco-growing states. On January 1, 1966, each pack had to bear the following statement: "Caution: Cigarette smoking may be hazardous to your health."

The percentage of smokers in the population did decline, falling from 50.2 percent of men in 1965 to 30.9 percent in 1988 and from 31.9 percent of women in 1965 to 25.3 percent of women in 1988. However, by the late 1980's, lung cancer, a distant third in the 1960's, had replaced breast cancer as the leading cause of cancer death among women.

Additional Information *The History of Cancer: An Annotated Bibliography* (1989), by James S. Olson, is an organized list of other sources and studies through its date of publication. For a study of the effects of the disease on American society, see James T. Patterson's *The Dread Disease: Cancer and Modern American Culture* (1987).

Ranès C. Chakravorty

See also Cyclamates; Medicine; Smoking and Tobacco.

■ Career Girl Murders

Date August 28, 1963

One of the most sensationalized crimes in New York City during the 1960's. The brutal murders of two young working women exemplified the legal controversies brewing over defendant's rights, police effectiveness, and the death penalty.

Origins and History On the morning of August 28, 1963, Janice Wylie, a *Newsweek* magazine employee, and Emily Hoffert, an elementary school teacher, were found brutally murdered in their third-floor Manhattan apartment. The New York press dubbed the sensational crime the "career girl murders." The women had been tied together and stabbed to death, and Wylie had been sexually assaulted. A third roommate had already left for work at the time of the murders.

The Investigation In April, 1964, eight months after the murders, police arrested and indicted George Whitmore, Jr., a nineteen-year-old African American man with no previous record who had been picked up for questioning regarding an attempted rape. After twenty-six hours in detention, during which time he was intensively questioned, Whitmore confessed to the attempted rape, to a murder that had occurred ten days earlier, and to the Wylie and Hoffert murders. When he was arraigned, he recanted his confession, saying that it had been coerced. The judge ruled that the confession was voluntary and admitted it as evidence. However, some members of the district attorney's office, whose job it was to prosecute the case, became convinced that Whitmore was innocent. One assistant district attorney, Melvin Glass, upon carefully reading all of the police records, realized that Whitmore's confession did not contain a single fact that the police did not know about before his arrest. Further investigation revealed it was virtually impossible for Whitmore to have been in Manhattan at the time of the killings.

About the time that the case against Whitmore was crumbling, the police received information about Richard Robles, who lived only nine blocks from the slain women's apartment. Nathan Delaney, a friend of Robles and fellow heroin addict, told police that Robles had admitted to the slayings. A month after Delaney told the police about Robles eavesdropping devices were placed in three locations. In January, 1965, on the basis of the information gained by the tapes, Robles was arrested and charged with the murders of Wylie and Hoffert. In December of that year, he was found guilty of two counts of felony murder. During the trial it was revealed that Robles had chosen the apartment to burglarize by chance and entered by climbing from the outer ledge of a hall window into an open kitchen window. He picked up a knife in the kitchen, then sexually assaulted Wylie. When Hoffert unexpectedly entered the room, he tied the women together on the bed and stabbed them to death.

Impact Whitmore's indictment for the murders of Wylie and Hoffert was based on a confession that violated standards set by the U.S. Supreme Court's ruling in *Mallory v. United States* regarding reasonable interrogation before arraignment. This violation of Whitmore's civil rights came just shortly after the Supreme Court's decision in *Escobedo v. Illinois*, which involved a similar situation. In that decision, Justice Arthur Goldberg, writing for the majority, stated that a law enforcement system that relies on confessions instead of corroborating evidence and investigation is "less reliable and more subject to abuse." Goldberg also wrote that a good legal system has nothing to fear from letting accused people contact their lawyers and exercise their constitutional rights.

The Whitmore case provoked fresh thought about the validity of capital punishment. If the career girl murders had not received such a tremendous amount of publicity, Whitmore might have been executed for a crime he did not commit.

Additional Information A May 16, 1965, *New York Times Magazine* article, "The Suspect Confesses—But Who Believes Him?" by Sidney E. Zion, highlights the impact the Whitmore confession had on the legal community.

Cheri Vail Fisk

See also Crimes and Scandals; *Miranda v. Arizona*; Speck Murders; Supreme Court Decisions.

■ Carmichael, Stokely

Born June 29, 1941, Port of Spain, Trinidad
Died November 15, 1995, Conakry, Guinea

Civil rights activist and leading spokesperson for black power. Carmichael's leadership of the Student Nonviolent Coordinating Committee (SNCC) helped transform the civil rights group into a militant, racially separatist organization.

Early Life Born in the Caribbean nation of Trinidad, Stokely Carmichael immigrated to the United States with his parents as a young child. He attended the prestigious Bronx High School of Science in New York City and associated with young white leftists and Communist Party members while there. Toward the end of his high school years, Carmichael met southern African Americans working in the Civil Rights movement and joined them in several demonstrations.

The 1960's In the fall of 1960, he enrolled at Howard University in Washington, D.C. While a stu-

dent, he assumed the leadership of the Nonviolent Action Group (NAG), a civil rights group that was affiliated with the Student Nonviolent Coordinating Committee (SNCC). As a student and shortly thereafter, he participated in many civil rights demonstrations, including Freedom Rides, lunch counter sit-ins, marches for voter registration in Mississippi, and Martin Luther King, Jr.'s march in Selma, Alabama, to secure voting rights. He was arrested many times. Carmichael graduated with a degree in philosophy in 1964 and went to work full-time for the SNCC in Mississippi.

During the years Carmichael spent in Mississippi working for SNCC, he became increasingly angry at and frustrated by white resistance to civil rights demands. He began to speak in increasingly radical tones, drawing on his earlier associations with leftist ideology.

In 1966, Carmichael became chair of SNCC and pushed the organization further away from nonviolence by bringing the ideas of black power to it.

Civil rights activist Stokely Carmichael raises his fists to express his support of the Black Power movement. Head of the Student Nonviolent Coordinating Committee and prime minister for the Black Panthers, Carmichael was a vocal spokesperson for the movement. (Archive Photos)

Black power was a philosophy of African American self-determination and separatism that spoke of confrontation with a racist white society. In 1967, Carmichael, in conjunction with African American university professor Charles V. Hamilton, published *Black Power: The Politics of Liberation in America*, the definitive treatise on black power.

While touring Africa for four months in 1967, Carmichael developed a close relationship with exiled Ghanaian leader Kwame Nkrumah and Guinean president Sekou Toure (whom he honored by changing his own name to Kwame Toure). His association with African leaders strengthened his reputation among increasingly militant African Americans as one of the nation's most respected African American leaders.

Shortly after returning from Africa, his term of office at SNCC over, Carmichael met with two leaders of the Black Panther Party and agreed to become the party's prime minister. Although Carmichael's Pan-African ideology differed from the more Marxist ideology of the Black Panthers, he still proved useful to them. Carmichael's oratorical skills and reputation, surpassed only by those of Martin Luther King, Jr., were a great draw as he traveled around the United States giving speeches denouncing what he termed white racist society and advocating revolutionary violence. By the spring of 1968, differences in ideology and personality disputes between SNCC and the Black Panther Party led to the rupture of relations between the two groups. Carmichael was expelled from SNCC but continued to work for the Black Panthers. However, in July, 1969, he resigned, citing disagreement with the Panther's association with white radicals.

Later Life Carmichael, who had earlier married African singer Marian Makeba, moved to the African nation of Guinea in 1968. After his resignation from the Black Panthers in 1969, he largely faded into obscurity.

Impact Carmichael's activities in the first half of the 1960's helped win civil rights for African Americans. However, it was his organizational and oratorical skills that won him the most praise. As head of SNCC and later as prime minister of the Black Panthers, Carmichael can be credited with setting the tone and tenor of a militant Black Power movement, one which was to have significant impact on the 1968 presidential election. In this election, independent candidate George Wallace and Republican nominee Richard M. Nixon played off white America's fears of black power, the Black Panthers, and African American militancy in general. One of the main spokespersons for these ideas was, of course, Carmichael. White Americans, alarmed by the major urban race riots in 1967 and the violent inflammatory rhetoric of Carmichael and other black power and Black Panther spokespersons, found Wallace appealing, and ultimately elected Nixon.

Additional Information The best exposition of black power ideology can be found in Carmichael and Hamilton's *Black Power: The Politics of Liberation in America* (1967) and in John T. McCartney's *Black Power Ideologies: An Essay in African American Political Thought*.

Lisa Langenbach

See also Black Panthers; Brown, H. Rap; Student Nonviolent Coordinating Committee (SNCC).

■ Carson, Rachel

Born May 27, 1907, Springdale, Pennsylvania
Died April 14, 1964, Silver Spring, Maryland

Marine biologist, naturalist, and author of a seminal book documenting the dangers of synthetic insecticides. Carson exploded the public's blind faith in scientific advancement and stimulated the emergence of the environmental movement.

Early Life As a small child, Rachel Louise Carson connected to the natural world. Educated in part by her mother, who employed a popular naturalist curriculum, Carson learned to respect and preserve life. She wanted to be a writer but switched from English to zoology in her junior year at Pennsylvania College for Women (later Catham College). Her research on the sea began during a summer at the Woods Hole Massachusetts Marine Biology Laboratory. She received her masters degree in marine biology from Johns Hopkins University. Carson taught briefly but needed more income to support her parents. She eventually became an aquatic biologist for the U.S. Bureau of Fisheries, where she wrote and later edited public information. She also wrote on her own, combining scientific findings with poetic prose. An essay, "Undersea," published in *The New Yorker*, led to *The Sea Around Us* (1951), a best-seller that gave her the income to write full time.

The 1960's When the decade of change arrived, Carson was already hard at work compiling data to educate Americans about pesticides. She recognized the impending devastation from government programs, such as the frequent sprayings of large areas with fuel oil and DDT (dichloro-diphenyl-trichloroethane), killing not only pests but also beneficial insects and songbirds. She worried about increasing evidence that insects developed immunity to pesticides while residues built up in eggs, milk, and higher life-forms in the food chain. Feeling personally inadequate to stimulate society toward regulation, Carson tried to persuade other scientists to publicize their findings. She valued her privacy and was certain of resistance and attack from irresponsible chemical companies and government agencies. By 1958, Carson committed to writing first an essay, then a short book. In the end, it required four years of painstaking research and volumes of correspondence to substantiate her claims.

In her book, *Silent Spring*, published in 1962, Carson aimed to report on the effects of the annual production and dispersal of six hundred million tons of DDT, along with a large number (five hundred or more in the early 1960's) of other chemicals introduced to the market each year. To persuade the public, she had to produce a book that argued like a legal brief, educated the layperson to the methods of science, and taught the interdependence of all life-forms. Her research had to be solid enough to withstand libel suits.

Carson's success as a naturalist and science writer uniquely prepared her for the task and readily established credibility with readers. She argued for biological control of pests rather than chemical campaigns based on the misbegotten belief that human control of nature was not only right but also inevitable. She compared the residues of spraying to nuclear fallout in the introductory vignette, a portrait of a "silent" spring, one in which no birds sang—having all been poisoned. Her case studies included failed spraying programs for gypsy moths and fire ants. She warned of the risks posed by the cumulative effects of pesticides and of human health problems, including cancer, that could emerge many years later.

Despite threats of lawsuits and accusations that Carson was only a hysterical woman (based on pre-releases), a condensed version of *Silent Spring* appeared in *The New Yorker* before the book's September, 1962, publication. *Silent Spring* became the October Book-of-the-Month Club choice with advance sales of forty thousand. The attacks on the work continued, but Carson's scholarship withstood criticism, igniting government action. During this time, Carson had concealed her own battle with breast cancer, fearing that publicity about her illness would weaken the impact of her efforts. Carson testified in the congressional hearings on the environment and received great recognition, including the National Wildlife Federation Conservationist of the Year Award.

Impact Carson was seen as a brave leader. *Silent Spring* compelled belief in the need for ecological balance. Administrators and legislators became convinced that chemical companies had to be regulated in the public interest. By the end of the 1960's, DDT had been banned by several states and was the subject of a two-year phase-out program conducted by the federal government. In 1969, Congress passed the National Environmental Policy Act, which required environmental impact reports from federal agencies. In addition, the U.S. Environmental Protection Agency was created to enforce compliance.

Subsequent Events Environmental regulation enacted in the 1970's and later years often failed to stop abuses; however, activists continued to fight for ecological balance.

Additional Information *Rachel Carson: Witness for Nature* (1997), by Linda Lear, provides a closer look at the woman and her work.

Margaret A. Dodson

See also Air Pollution; Environmental Movement; Water Pollution.

■ Castro, Fidel

Born August 13, 1926 or 1927, near Birán, Cuba

Leader of the Cuban Revolution and prime minister of Cuba after 1959. His alliance with the Soviet Union, forged after the U.S.-sponsored Bay of Pigs invasion of 1961, brought the world to the brink of nuclear war during the Cuban Missile Crisis of 1962.

Early Life The son of a prosperous Spanish-born landowner and his Cuban wife, Fidel Castro Ruz first became active in politics as a student at the University of Havana in the 1940's, where he imbibed

Cuban leader Fidel Castro addresses the general assembly of the United Nations in 1960. His climb to power just before the start of the decade and his strengthening alliance with the Soviet Union created fears among Americans of a growing communist presence in Latin America. (United Nations)

equally from the nationalist rhetoric of nineteenth century Cuban patriot José Martí and the doctrines of socialist thinker Karl Marx. The *coup d'etat* of army general Fulgencio Batista in 1952, which resulted in economic ruin for much of the peasant and working classes, convinced Castro that only Marxist revolution could improve social conditions in Cuba and simultaneously make Martí's vision of independence from the economic might of the United States come true. In July, 1953, Castro and a small band of followers mounted a surprise attack on an army camp in the city of Santiago de Cuba, hoping to spark a national uprising against Batista. The plot failed and Castro was jailed but later pardoned. After fleeing to Mexico, he returned secretly to Cuba in 1956 to launch an insurrection that lasted three years and culminated in the ouster of Batista on January 1, 1959.

The 1960's Assuming the premiership of the Cuban government in 1959, Castro decreed a radical land-reform program, nationalization of foreign property, and the elimination of all political parties except the Cuban Communists. Opposed to the left-wing tilt of the revolution, the United States broke off diplomatic relations and banned trade with Cuba after 1960. In 1961, President John F. Kennedy launched an ill-fated plan designed to reverse the revolution, whereby anti-Castro exiles invaded Cuba at the Bay of Pigs. The Cuban leader used the occasion to proclaim his revolution officially socialist and sought assistance from the Soviet Union to forestall future U.S. assaults by placing nuclear missiles on the island. Kennedy ordered a naval blockade of Cuba in October, 1962, to be kept in place until the weapons were withdrawn. Castro lost much political prestige when Soviet premier Nikita Khrushchev (1958-1964) agreed to Kennedy's terms, but he found a useful diplomatic bargaining chip in promoting anti-U.S. guerrilla movements throughout Latin America. The death in combat of longtime Castro aide Ernesto "Che" Guevara in Bolivia in 1967 at the hands of U.S.-trained troops marked the failure of this enterprise. The administration of President Richard M. Nixon (1969-1974) tried to isolate Cuba further by fostering friendlier relations with Castro's Soviet patrons. Rather than being the vanguard of the Latin American revolution, Cuba remained an exception—a socialist republic ninety miles from the shores of the United States. Accepting this, Castro devoted the rest of the 1960's to the institutionalization of his regime, the reorganization of the Cuban Communist Party with himself as first secretary, and the full integration of the Cuban economy with that of the Soviets through barter agreements.

Later Life Castro regained some diplomatic influence in the 1970's when pro-Cuban revolutionary factions came to power in Nicaragua and the Caribbean nation of Grenada. The inauguration of Ronald Reagan as president of the United States in 1981, however, signaled the beginning of a series of setbacks for Castro. A U.S. invasion toppled the government of Grenada in 1983, and his Nicaraguan allies were defeated at the polls in 1990. The extinction of the Soviet Union in 1991 resulted in a severe economic crisis for Cuba. Deemed a mortal threat to the security of the United States in the 1960's, by the end of the century, Castro was merely an irritating problem.

Impact Few international leaders had such an important influence on U.S. foreign policy during the 1960's as Castro did. The fear that his revolution might spread to the rest of the hemisphere figured significantly in the establishment of programs such as the Alliance for Progress and the decision to instruct Latin American armies in counterinsurgency warfare. Castro's revolution also resulted in a flood of immigrants arriving in Miami after 1959, altering the demographic and political makeup of Florida and contributing to a further rift in relations between Cuba and the United States.

Additional Information Robert E. Quirk's biography *Fidel Castro*, published in 1993, is particularly perceptive on his subject's lifelong antipathy for the United States.

Julio César Pino

See also Bay of Pigs Invasion; Cold War; Cuban Missile Crisis; Immigration.

■ *Catch-22*

Published 1961
Author Joseph Heller (1923-1999)

The ultimate pacifist tract for counterculture antiwar rebels. This Kafkaesque satire on the institutionalized illogic of the military mind provided readers with the perfect reason to turn their backs on the Vietnam War and the establishment behind it.

The Work *Catch-22* is set on the imaginary island of Pianosa during World War II and focuses on Captain John Yossarian and his attempts to survive the fanatical lunacy of his bomber squadron's commanders long enough to get home. As the death toll rises, the quota of bombing missions required for home leave is repeatedly increased. By pleading insanity, Yossarian hopes to find a way out. However, his doctor quotes the infamous Catch-22: To get out of flying missions, a bombardier must plead insanity, but wanting to get out of flying missions is proof of sanity, so the minute a bombardier says he does not want to fly, he must. Yossarian is slow to realize the full implications of his predicament, but when he does, he has the courage to take the only definitive action still open to him: He heads for neutral Sweden.

Orr, a combat pilot and Yossarian's tent-mate and alter ego, also functions as the "alter hero" of the book. In Orr there is something of the real "prophet," for it is he who prepares the way for Yossarian. From the beginning, he is Yossarian's double, acting in many ways like the ego to Yossarian's id. Orr reacts objectively and rationally to their common predicament, while Yossarian behaves subjectively, whining, protesting, and acting moody. Orr is resourceful and cunning, living among his enemies in the guise of a shallow-minded joker while plotting his revenge; Yossarian has trouble getting beyond his own moods and emotions. The archvillain of the piece is Colonel Cathcart, model of robotlike conformity, always trying to adjust to the dictates of the bureaucracy and to avoid confrontations with officialdom. At the other extreme is the anonymous Soldier in White, the "archvictim," bandaged from head to foot and kept alive by an endless recycling of body fluids. What begins as a grim joke—fluids excreted at one end are injected at the other—becomes a grotesque symbol of the mechanical regulation of human life: facelessness, self-containment, and the withdrawal and isolation of the patient thoroughly dehumanized yet kept alive. In the case of the Soldier in White, it is unclear whether there actually is a man beneath the bandages. If there is, can that person hear what is going on around him? Or even worse, can he still think and feel? These are horrible questions that carry the madness of war beyond the battlefield.

Impact As disenchantment with U.S. policy in Vietnam and government "oppression" at home mounted in the 1960's, Catch-22 became the rationale for opposition, desertion, draft dodging, dropping out, or whatever it took to lodge a protest against what many considered an unjust war. Yossarian, like his 1960's readers, finds it impossible to live within the establishment, even in order to reform it, because he feels its dehumanization is pandemic and irreversible. It is a system that tends to use war more to regulate its own people than to fight a national enemy. (The book contains almost nothing about an actual enemy.) The system also fosters power struggles that victimize the fighting man in wartime and the creative person in peacetime. On every level, the system needs scapegoats and always finds them. Corruption runs rampant in all professions and institutions because private greed is sanctified.

Bombardier John Yossarian takes a bite out of his companion's shoulder in the 1970 film version of Joseph Heller's 1961 book, Catch-22. *Antiwar protesters and members of the counterculture identified with Yossarian's predicament when faced with the paradoxical catch-22.* (Museum of Modern Art/Film Stills Archive)

Yossarian's principles reflect those of the counterculture. For example, Yossarian values individuality and freedom more than status or official recognition, and he thinks of money and machinery as means rather than ends. He is also more interested in humanity than in organizations, and when the organization turns against human values, Yossarian has the courage to remember that there is a higher law than the state.

Related Work *Closing Time*, the sequel to *Catch-22*, published in 1994, never achieved the popularity of the original work.

Additional Information For further commentary on the place of *Catch-22* in the cultural climate of the 1960's and its reflection of counterculture attitudes, see *From Here to Obscurity: The Moral Battlefield of Joseph Heller* (1982), by Stephen W. Potts.

Thomas Whissen

See also Counterculture; Draft Resisters; Literature; Metafiction; *Slaughterhouse-Five*; Vietnam War.

■ *Cat's Cradle*

Published 1963
Author Kurt Vonnegut, Jr. (1922-   )

The sardonic end-of-the-world novel that introduced the fictional religion of Bokononism and marked Vonnegut's transition from cult figure to popular author. It satirized religion, science, and politics as it described the world's destruction by a new form of ice.

The Work The narrator of *Cat's Cradle*, John, who calls himself Jonah, sets out to write a book called *The Day the World Ended*, a fictional account of what various people were doing on the day the atomic bomb was dropped on Hiroshima, Japan. In the course of researching this book, he becomes involved with the peculiar offspring of the late Dr. Felix Hoenikker, a brilliant but emotionally detached physicist whose crowning achievement was the discovery of ice-nine, a form of ice that has a melting point of 114.4 degrees and freezes anything it touches. Hoenikker's children, Angela, Franklin, and Newt, have divided the only existing sample of ice-nine among themselves. As Angela and Newt barter their portions for the love of, respectively, a handsome industrialist and a Russian midget, Franklin trades his for a post on the cabinet of "Papa" Monzano, military dictator of the island of San Lorenzo, a stereotypical banana republic.

Jonah goes to San Lorenzo to write an article about Julian Castle, a philanthropist who has founded a hospital on the island. There the narrator learns of the ongoing conflict between Monzano and Bokonon, the island's outlawed religious leader. Bokononism is a sham religion that admits it is based on *foma*, or "harmless untruths." Monzano's opposition to Bokononism is also a sham. Conveniently for the dictator, the continuing struggle between church and state provides the impoverished people of San Lorenzo with a grand spectacle to distract them from their own misery. All of this comes to an end, however, when Monzano kills himself with the ice-nine provided by Franklin. The dictator's body accidentally falls into the sea and instantly freezes all the oceans of the world, ultimately destroying all life on earth.

Impact *Cat's Cradle* combined the wild playfulness of *The Sirens of Titan* (1959), Vonnegut's second novel, and the darkness of *Mother Night* (1961), his third, to launch Vonnegut into the mainstream of popular culture and set the stage for the later success of *Slaughterhouse-Five* (1969). In *Cat's Cradle*, Vonnegut took aim at all the major institutions of American life: religion, politics, and especially science. Ice-nine symbolizes the destructive potential of scientific discovery, and Dr. Hoenikker represents the apparent indifference of many scientists to the ways their discoveries are used.

Related Work Robert Heinlein's *Stranger in a Strange Land* (1961) uses a fictional religion comparable to Bokononism to create its own form of social criticism.

Additional Information For a study of Vonnegut's early novels, including *Cat's Cradle*, see *Kurt Vonnegut: Fantasist of Fire and Ice* (1972), by David H. Goldsmith.

Ed McKnight

See also Literature; *Slaughterhouse-Five*.

■ Censorship

Any attempt to suppress information or entertainment presented live or through the mass media. In the 1960's, free speech advocates won many important legal battles, and censorship of political speech and entertainment media declined.

Attempts by authorities to control the thoughts of citizens are as old as recorded history. Government censorship, the prior restraint or punishment of speech by the state, is the most obvious form. The First Amendment to the U.S. Constitution says "Congress shall make no law . . . abridging the freedom of speech, or of the press." However, U.S. courts have restricted freedom of speech to prevent other harm. More subtle forms of censorship are corporate censorship, where those who control the mass media suppress information, and self-censorship, where people withhold information for fear of negative consequences.

Government Censorship The Supreme Court originally believed that only political speech was protected by the First Amendment. In the late 1940's, the Court extended First Amendment protection to art, literature, and entertainment. U.S. films, however, remained politically and socially conservative because of industry self-regulation and a network of state and local censorship boards.

The Court, however, consistently maintained that obscenity is unprotected speech. In *Roth v. United States* (1957), Justice William Brennan defined obscenity as "whether to the average person, applying contemporary community standards, the dominant theme of the material taken as a whole appeals to the prurient interest." The words "prurient interest" referred to a shameful, unhealthy, or morbid interest in sex.

In a series of early 1960's cases, the Supreme Court clarified the *Roth v. United States* definition of obscenity. In *Memoirs v. Massachusetts* (1966), the Court overturned the conviction of the publisher of John Cleland's *Memoirs of a Woman of Pleasure* (1749, also known as *Fanny Hill*). Justice Brennan summarized several cases by stating that, to be considered obscene, the dominant theme of the work had to appeal to the prurient interest, and the work must be patently offensive by contemporary community standards and utterly without redeeming social value. It was almost impossible to prove that a work had no social value.

Freedom of the press was also expanded during the 1960's. In a landmark libel case, *New York Times Company v. Sullivan* (1964), the court ruled that public figures could not collect damages unless the press either knowingly published false information or acted in reckless disregard of the truth of the

information. In addition, President Lyndon B. Johnson signed the Freedom of Information Act in 1966, establishing the public's right of access to nonclassified government documents.

However, the 1960's also produced some restrictions on mass media. In *Sheppard v. Maxwell* (1966), the Court reversed the murder conviction of physician Sam Sheppard because the press had deprived him of a fair trial through inflammatory pretrial publicity. It outlined the steps judges must take to avoid prejudicial publicity, including shifting the trial to another location, prohibiting comments by attorneys and witnesses, and sequestering the jury. In 1967, the Federal Communications Commission ruled that the Fairness Doctrine required television stations to run antismoking messages to balance cigarette advertisements. In 1969, Congress banned cigarette advertising on television, effective 1971.

During the 1960's, civil rights and antiwar activists staged public protests to dramatize their concerns. In Columbia, S.C., 187 demonstrators were convicted of disturbing the peace for gathering at the state capitol to protest racial discrimination. The Court overturned their conviction in *Edwards v. South Carolina* (1963), thus upholding the right of protesters to assemble peacefully in public places.

Nonverbal forms of protest were sometimes interpreted as symbolic speech. In *United States v. O'Brien* (1968), the defendant was convicted of burning his draft card to protest the Vietnam War. In a defeat for free speech advocates, the Court upheld the verdict of the lower court, holding that the law forbidding destruction of draft cards furthered an important government interest. However, the Court did hold that flag burning

The Supreme Court ruled that flag burnings, such as the one that took place during the March Against Death in 1969, were a protected form of protest. (Terry Atlas/Archive Photos)

is a protected form of protest in *Street v. New York* (1969).

In the 1960's, the Supreme Court gradually narrowed the category of speech that could be prohibited on the grounds that it presented a "clear and present danger" of illegal actions. In *Brandenburg v. Ohio* (1969), the Court overturned the conviction of a speaker at a Ku Klux Klan rally, ruling that a speaker's words can be interpreted as an incitement to crime only if the defendant explicitly advocates an imminent illegal act and believes that the audience will actually carry it out.

Self-Censorship and Corporate Censorship As government censorship lessened, media owners continued to engage in self-censorship, either at the urging of government or on their own. In November, 1960, an article in *The Nation* magazine charged that the United States planned to invade Cuba. President John F. Kennedy persuaded *The New York Times* to withhold evidence of the impending Bay of Pigs invasion, and the other news media followed its lead. Kennedy later acknowledged that, had the press published the story, the nation would have been saved from making "a colossal mistake." As a result of the media's uncritical acceptance of the 1964 Warren Report on the Kennedy assassination, critics had difficulty getting their opinions heard. Bystander Abraham Zapruder's home movie of the assassination was not shown on national television until 1975. In March, 1968, 570 Vietnamese civilians were murdered in My Lai. Both the military and the media ignored the story for several months, until the *Dispatch News Service* published Seymour Hersh's investigative report in November, 1968. *The Smothers Brothers Comedy Hour*, a weekly television program that featured political satire, was heavily censored by the Columbia Broadcasting System. The show was canceled in 1969.

Impact The 1960's was part of a gradual trend toward the relaxation of political censorship that began in the early twentieth century. By the end of the decade, Americans were more informed about current news and public affairs, investigative reporting flourished, and it was difficult to conceal political scandals.

The move toward greater freedom of expression was more abrupt in the entertainment media, but not soon enough to prevent one tragedy. The brilliant but controversial comedian Lenny Bruce was driven to despair by a series of obscenity trials in the early part of the decade and died of a drug overdose in 1966. By the mid-1960's, the motion picture industry was effectively free of government censorship. According to adult film producer David Friedman, in 1960, only twenty theaters in the country showed adult films exclusively, but by 1970, this number had grown to seven hundred and fifty. *I Am Curious— Yellow* (1967), a Swedish political film featuring male and female frontal nudity, was the subject of several censorship battles, most of which it won. By the end of the decade, documentaries such as *Censorship in Denmark* (1970) included explicit sex scenes, and Hollywood had increased the amount of nudity, graphic violence, and profanity in mainstream productions.

By the late 1960's, there were signs of a backlash from those who saw unrestricted free expression as a symptom of cultural decline. President Johnson appointed a Commission on Obscenity and Pornography in 1967 in the expectation that it would find pornography harmful and recommend legal strategies to control its spread. However, in the commission's final report, published in 1970, it found no evidence that pornography caused criminal behavior. Violence also came under fire when in 1968, the National Commission on the Causes and Prevention of Violence concluded that violence on television encouraged violent behavior in viewers. The Motion Picture Association of America, the regulatory agency for the film industry, responded to public criticism of sex and violence in mainstream films by establishing a voluntary rating system in November, 1968.

In 1969, Vice President Spiro T. Agnew launched a series of attacks on the news media, accusing them of favoring liberal causes. Many people hoped President Richard M. Nixon's 1969 appointment of conservative Chief Justice Warren Burger would bring about greater government control of expression.

Subsequent Events The expansion of the rights of free speech, free press, and assembly continued in the following decades with only occasional setbacks. However, although the public was undoubtedly better informed, the large volume of news increased public cynicism about politics and government.

In *Miller v. California* (1973), Chief Justice Burger delivered a new definition of obscenity that made it slightly easier to convict defendants. The decision had little impact on the spread of sexually explicit materials, however, and by 1975, hard-core pornography was readily available at adult theaters and bookstores.

In the long term, the greatest threat to freedom of information may be corporate censorship produced by the concentration of the control of news and entertainment in the hands of a small number of large corporations.

Additional Information The most complete account of the decline of censorship in the arts and literature is *Girls Lean Back Everywhere* (1992), by Edward de Grazia. Other accounts include Rodney Smolla's *Free Speech in an Open Society* (1992) and Joel Spring's *Images of American Life* (1992).

Lloyd Stires

See also Bay of Pigs Invasion; Bruce, Lenny; Burger, Warren; Film; *I Am Curious—Yellow; Memoirs v. Massachusetts*; Motion Picture Academy of America Rating System; My Lai Incident; National Commission on the Causes and Prevention of Violence; *New York Times Company v. Sullivan*; Sheppard, Sam; *Smothers Brothers Comedy Hour, The.*

■ Central Intelligence Agency (CIA)

An agency of the federal government that gathers information on foreign military, economic, and political activities. It also conducts covert political operations against governments to promote national security.

Origins and History Throughout most of the history of the United States, gathering intelligence was viewed as an unsavory activity to be conducted only in wartime. It was not until the outbreak of World War II that the United States moved to establish a distinct intelligence-gathering body. In the immediate aftermath of Japan's attack on Pearl Harbor, President Franklin D. Roosevelt approved existing plans for the creation of a centralized intelligence apparatus. The Office of Strategic Services coordinated numerous espionage, sabotage, and psychological warfare operations until the war ended in 1945. President Harry S Truman moved to strengthen peacetime intelligence-gathering capabilities by sponsoring the 1947 National Security Act. A section of this act called for the creation of an executive agency, the Central Intelligence Agency (CIA), designed to conduct covert actions abroad and coordinate intelligence gathering and analysis for the president and the newly created National Security Council. As the Cold War with the Soviet Union escalated during the 1940's and 1950's, the CIA became increasingly involved in secret operations around the globe designed to counter Soviet influence. In addition to using agents, the CIA sponsored research on technology that would enable U.S. policymakers to monitor military and political activities around the world.

Activities In the 1960's, as tensions with the Soviet Union increased and the Vietnam War escalated, U.S. leaders became increasingly dependent on covert actions—attempts to influence governments though bribery, propaganda, military intervention, and other clandestine means—to avoid embarrassing and divisive debates on the conduct of foreign affairs. In the 1950's, by means of covert actions, the CIA had successfully subverted and weakened regimes considered hostile to U.S. interests in Iran and Guatemala, and these actions became increasingly central to the operations of the CIA. Subsequent congressional investigations of CIA activities revealed that between 1962 and 1970, funding for clandestine activities accounted for approximately 52 percent of the CIA's entire budget.

The CIA suffered several high-profile intelligence failures during the 1960's. In May, 1960, U.S. officials were embarrassed when a U-2 spy plane was shot down over the Soviet Union during a summit meeting between President Dwight D. Eisenhower and Soviet premier Nikita Khrushchev. Eisenhower, a strong proponent of covert action, was forced to publicly acknowledge that the United States was flying over the Soviet Union for espionage purposes. Additional failures during the Bay of Pigs invasion in 1961 and the Cuban Missile Crisis in 1962 did little to bolster the reputation of the CIA among policymakers.

President John F. Kennedy, embarrassed by the nation's failure to overthrow the Cuban government during the Bay of Pigs invasion, approved another CIA operation, a plot to assassinate Cuba's leader, Fidel Castro, called Operation Mongoose. The various methods, from hiring Mafia assassins to poisoning Castro's cigars, were unsuccessful. Detailed examinations of CIA activities during this period indicate that although the CIA never directly killed a head of state, it did fail to stop and in some cases signaled tacit approval for assassinations in the Congo, the Dominican Republic, and Vietnam.

Perhaps the most controversial activity of the CIA during the 1960's involved the Vietnam War. CIA analysts, at the direction of Eisenhower, had expended enormous resources on providing decision makers with intelligence about Vietnam. During the early 1960's, CIA analysts were largely pessimistic about the outcome of a U.S. land war designed to provide support for the South Vietnamese government. As the *Pentagon Papers* (1971) would later reveal, both Presidents Kennedy and Lyndon B. Johnson rejected CIA recommendations and became increasingly involved in Vietnam. As the United States became more deeply committed, U.S. policymakers used various covert actions to strike at the North Vietnamese leadership. The most notable CIA operation in Vietnam was the Phoenix Program, which was supposed to identify and eliminate North Vietnamese agents working in South Vietnam. Although the exact number is unknown, it is estimated that more than twenty thousand suspected North Vietnamese agents were killed in combat or assassinated by U.S. and South Vietnamese agents over a three-year period.

Impact In the latter part of the 1960's, the failure of the United States to bring the war in Vietnam to an end fueled public cynicism about intelligence operations. Covert actions, the mainstay of CIA activities of the early 1960's, were increasingly viewed as an abuse of power. The CIA also hurt itself by allowing its mission to be subverted for political ends. In the 1970's, as the administration of President Richard M. Nixon became increasingly embroiled in the Watergate scandal, the CIA was forced to explain domestic surveillance of political figures conducted during the previous decade in clear violation of the CIA's 1947 charter.

Subsequent Events Public cynicism about alleged abuses of civil liberties by the CIA led to both executive and congressional investigations in the 1970's. Vice President Nelson Rockefeller led a commission that recommended a reevaluation of the CIA's charter and functions. Senator Frank Church conducted high-profile hearings concentrating on covert actions undertaken by the CIA. The Church Committee recommended increased oversight of covert operations by the legislative branch and a renewed emphasis on "traditional notions of fair play" in U.S. intelligence operations.

Additional Information A comprehensive and readable history of the CIA can be found in *The Agency: The Rise and Decline of the CIA* (1986), by John Ranelagh. A thoughtful analysis of intelligence gathering in the United States is presented in *America's Secret Power: The CIA in a Democratic Society* (1989), by Loch K. Johnson. An account of the Church Committee's findings can be found in *The Central Intelligence Agency: History and Documents* (1984), edited by William M. Leary.

Lawrence Clark

See also Bay of Pigs Invasion; Cold War; Cuban Missile Crisis; U-2 Spy Plane Incident; Vietnam War.

■ Chamberlain, Wilt

Born August 21, 1936, Philadelphia, Pennsylvania
Died October 12, 1999, Los Angeles, California

The greatest single-season scorer in the history of the National Basketball Association. Chamberlain's accomplishments in basketball represent an unsurpassed career in the sport.

Early Life Wilton Norman Chamberlain began his basketball career in junior high school, where his height reached six feet eleven inches. In high school, Chamberlain electrified crowds and attracted large numbers of college recruiters and sports reporters, who gave him the nickname "Wilt the Stilt." Chamberlain decided to play college basketball at the University of Kansas, where he set a record by scoring 52 points in his first varsity game and became a consensus All-American in 1957 and 1958.

The 1960's During Chamberlain's first season (1959-1960) in the National Basketball Association, he easily broke the league scoring record with an average of 37.6 points per game. However, Chamberlain was much more than a tall man who could dunk a basketball. He also led the league in rebounds (averaging 27.0 per game) and displayed a deadly fall-away jump shot. He broke salary records when he signed a contract to play for sixty-five thousand dollars a year, more than any player had received in the history of professional basketball. By the end of the 1960's, his salary had risen to two hundred thousand dollars per year—more than that of any other professional athlete.

Wilt Chamberlain of the Philadelphia 76ers just barely loses control of the rebound to Bill Russell of the Boston Celtics in this January, 1967, game. (AP/Wide World Photos)

Chamberlain dominated the decade in professional basketball. Playing for the Philadelphia (later San Francisco) Warriors, the Philadelphia 76ers, and the Los Angeles Lakers, he led the NBA in scoring seven years in a row, including a sensational 50.4 per game average in the 1961-1962 season. On March 2, 1962, Chamberlain scored 100 points against the New York Knicks, a record that was unmatched more than thirty years later.

Later Life Chamberlain modified his style in the 1970's, scoring less and passing more. In 1972, the year he led the Los Angeles Lakers to the NBA championship, his scoring average dipped to 14.8 points per game, but he finished second on the team in assists. To many observers, this transition proved that Chamberlain was not the selfish player his critics

claimed he was. Following his retirement in 1973, Chamberlain briefly became the coach of the San Diego Conquistadors of the American Basketball Association and made celebrity appearances.

Impact Chamberlain revolutionized the game of professional basketball. By the time he retired, he had led the NBA in rebounding eleven times, made the all-star first team seven times, and received the most valuable player award four times. Two of the teams he led, the Philadelphia 76ers (1967) and the Los Angeles Lakers (1972), won NBA championships.

Additional Information The best sources for detailed information on Chamberlain are *The Sports Encyclopedia: Pro Basketball* (1989) by David S. Neft and Richard M. Cohen, Kenneth Rudeen's *Wilt Chamberlain* (1970), and "NBA's Fabulous Fifty: You Can Start with Russell and Chamberlain," an article by Michael Wilbon in the October 30, 1996, *Washington Post.*

J. Christopher Schnell

See also Basketball; Russell, Bill; Sports.

■ Chappaquiddick Scandal

Date July 18-19, 1969

The most infamous traffic fatality of the 1960's. When Senator Edward "Ted" Kennedy's car plunged off the Dike Bridge on Chappaquiddick Island, killing Mary Jo Kopechne, Kennedy's unsatisfactory explanations of the event effectively ruined his chances to be elected president of the United States.

Origins and History After the assassinations of his brothers, President John F. Kennedy and Robert Kennedy, Senator Edward "Ted" Kennedy became the final hope for the continuation of a Kennedy family "dynasty." The Kennedy mystique remained so strong in 1969 that the presidency was widely thought to be the senator's to lose. On the weekend of July 18-19, a group of workers from Robert Kennedy's 1968 presidential campaign held a reunion barbecue at a small rented cottage on Chappaquiddick Island in conjunction with the Edgartown Regatta. The party was attended by Senator Kennedy; his cousin, Joe Gargan; lawyer Paul Markham; Kennedy's part-time chauffeur, John Crimmins; and two other Kennedy campaign aides. Joining them were six young women, referred to as the "boiler room girls," who had worked on Robert Kennedy's 1968 campaign.

The Accident On the afternoon of July 18, Senator Kennedy arrived in Edgartown to take part in the regatta and to attend the party on Chappaquiddick Island, accessible from Edgartown by ferry. At some point, probably between 11:00 P.M. and midnight, Kennedy left the party with Mary Jo Kopechne, one of the "boiler room girls." By his own account, Kennedy had several alcoholic drinks during the course of his day, but he claimed not to be impaired in any way. What happened between the time the couple left the party and the next morning at 9:45 when Kennedy reported the accident and made a statement to the local police has been subject to much speculation.

Sometime during that night, the 1967 Oldsmobile in which Kennedy and Kopechne left the party plunged off Dike Bridge on Chappaquiddick Island. Senator Kennedy managed to escape from the submerged car, but Kopechne did not. According to Kennedy, he took a wrong turn on his way back to the ferry to Edgartown and drove off the Dike Bridge. He somehow managed to free himself from the car (although he claims not to remember how this happened) and then dove back into the water several times in an unsuccessful attempt to save Kopechne. When his efforts failed, he returned to the party to enlist the help of Gargan and Markham, but they were equally unsuccessful. After failing at these efforts, Kennedy, who claims to have been in a state of shock, dove into the water and swam back to Edgartown and returned to his hotel room. In the morning, he first called a family legal adviser and then reported the accident to local police, who had already found the car and Kopechne's body.

Kopechne was buried three days later without an autopsy, and on July 25, Kennedy pled guilty to leaving the scene of an accident and was given a suspended sentence. On the same day, he gave a poorly received nationally televised speech in which he admitted that his behavior in not immediately reporting the accident was indefensible, although

Edward "Ted" Kennedy, accompanied by his wife, Joan, leaves the courthouse after pleading guilty to leaving the scene of an accident. His companion, Mary Jo Kopechne, was killed when Kennedy drove off the Dike Bridge. (AP/Wide World Photos)

he did not adequately explain his actions on that night. On July 31, he returned to his duties in the United States Senate, and on the same day, District Attorney Edmund S. Dinis requested a formal inquest into Kopechne's death. The inquest was closed to both the press and the public, no indictment was returned, and the case was closed.

Many unanswered questions lingered long after the accident, effectively extinguishing Kennedy's presidential aspirations. Kennedy's inability to convincingly explain his reason for waiting ten hours to report the accident to the local authorities opened the door to the suspicion that he was more concerned with covering up his involvement in the accident than in saving a young woman's life. Speculation also centered on rumors that Kennedy asked his cousin, Gargan, to shoulder the blame for the accident or that Kennedy wanted to claim that Kopechne was driving the car. His failure to stop at a nearby cottage to seek help or telephone the authorities also was never adequately explained. Because Kennedy provided so few believable details of that evening's events, the incident has been fertile territory for "conspiracy" theorists and amateur sleuths.

Impact The impact of the Chappaquiddick incident on Kennedy's political career was enormous. The most immediate consequence was his defeat as Senate majority whip in January of 1971, but a more lasting consequence was his failure to gain his party's nomination for president. The accident was still too fresh in the minds of the voting public for Kennedy to run for the nomination in 1972, but his advisers felt that by 1976, all would be forgotten. In fact, as time went on, the public seemed only to have more questions regarding Kennedy's role in Kopechne's death and his behavior after the accident.

Kennedy challenged President Jimmy Carter for the Democratic presidential nomination in 1980, but even after a decade, the legacy of Chappaquiddick haunted him, and he was defeated. Finally, in 1985, he and his advisers came to the conclusion that they could never escape the unanswered questions of Chappaquiddick, and Kennedy announced that he would not run for the presidency in 1988.

Additional Information The *Bridge at Chappaquiddick* (1969), by Jack Olson, was the first book written about the accident and is a thorough report of events with no particular bias. *The Last Kennedy* (1975), by

Robert Sherrill, is a very hard-hitting investigation of the events of that night in 1969, tracking down, for instance, the rumor that Gargan was supposed to have taken the blame for Kennedy. In Leo Damore's *Senatorial Privilege: The Chappaquiddick Cover-up*, published in 1988, twenty years after the accident, several participants in the events, including Gargan, speak up for the first time. In Damore's account, Gargan claims that Kennedy tried to get him to take the blame for the accident.

Mary Virginia Davis

See also Assassinations of John and Robert Kennedy and Martin Luther King, Jr.; Camelot; Kennedy, Edward "Ted"; Kennedy, John F.; Kennedy, Robert F.

■ Charlie Brown

Published 1950
Author Charles M. Schulz (1922-2000)

The central character in a comic strip populated by children wrestling with the worldly problems of adults. Out of the mouths of these babes come lighthearted discussions of religion, psychiatry, education, alienation, loneliness, and loss.

The Work Charlie Brown is the main character in *Peanuts*, a comic strip that uses children, overwhelmed by the world, to mirror the concerns and insecurities of adults. There is no single, overruling plot; the pint-sized characters find themselves in a variety of situations. Charlie Brown is the perpetual underdog, lovable but hopelessly inept in all his pursuits, whether playing baseball, kicking a football, flying a kite, or expressing his unrequited love for the little red-haired girl. Lucy is loud, brash, domineering, opinionated, and crabby. She dispenses psychiatric advice for a nickel from her lemonade stand/sidewalk booth and is the self-appointed tormentor of Linus, her younger brother. Linus is extremely intelligent, as insecure as Charlie Brown, and an astute commentator on the Bible. He is usually depicted sucking the thumb of his right hand while clutching his security blanket in his left. Schroeder is totally absorbed in his music as he plays his tiny toy piano, which sports a bust of his idol, Ludwig van Beethoven, and is completely oblivious to the fawning adoration of Lucy. Snoopy is Charlie Brown's beagle, an ordinary dog with an extraordinary imagination that transforms his doghouse into a World War I airplane, an art gallery, or a pool room as the beagle assumes the identities of pilot, mystery writer, attorney, college student, and astronaut in his various flights of fancy.

Impact Although a product of the 1950's, *Peanuts* became a pop culture phenomenon in the 1960's. Published in thousands of newspapers worldwide, the strip spawned books, television specials, a feature film, an off-Broadway musical, record albums, stuffed animals, and an enormous array of licensed merchandise. *Peanuts* images appeared on everything from lunch boxes to lunar landing vehicles, and the strip was popular with everyone from college students to U.S. military pilots fighting the Vietnam War. The strip was also influenced by the 1960's: Late in the decade, a new character appeared in the strip, a small hippie bird named Woodstock after the 1969 New York rock festival. *Peanuts* characters appeared on the covers of the magazines *Time, Life, Newsweek,* and *Saturday Review;* the term "security blanket" became part of the nation's vocabulary; and a line from the strip, "Happiness is a warm puppy," was enshrined in *Bartlett's Familiar Quotations.* The strip displayed a touch of naïve innocence in a not-so-innocent decade by using youngsters in a safe, protected childhood environment to play out familiar human weaknesses, providing a small preview of the rough edges of life that adults faced.

Related Work *You're a Good Man, Charlie Brown* (1967), a musical play by John Gordon and Clark Gesner, contains episodes from the lives of the *Peanuts* characters.

Additional Information *Good Grief: The Story of Charles M. Schulz* (1989), an authorized biography by Rheta Grimsley Johnson, covers the history and themes of Schulz's work.

Peggy Waltzer Rosefeldt

See also Pop Psychology; Religion and Spirituality; Woodstock Festival.

■ Chávez, César

Born March 31, 1927, near Yuma, Arizona
Died April 23, 1993, San Luis, Arizona

One of the nation's leaders in the struggle to gain social justice through nonviolence. Chávez devoted his life to bringing recognition, respect, and improved working conditions to farm laborers in the United States.

Early Life César Estrada Chávez was born on an Arizona farm that his grandfather first cultivated during the 1880's. Hit hard by the economic chaos created by the Great Depression, the Chávez family lost the farm and a small grocery store by 1937. The young Chávez and his family joined the ranks of migrant farmworkers, traveling throughout the southwestern United States in search of work. From 1944 to 1946, Chávez served in the U.S. Navy, returning to work in the agricultural fields around Delano, California, upon his discharge. He married Helen Fabela in 1948. Chávez's direction in life changed dramatically after he met Fred Ross in 1952. Ross, an organizer for the Community Service Organization (CSO), was affiliated with Saul Alinsky, founder of the Chicago-based Industrial Areas Foundation, and successfully recruited Chávez to work with his organization. Chávez's involvement with the CSO during the 1950's laid the groundwork for his founding of the United Farm Workers union.

The 1960's Driven by his desire to improve conditions for farmworkers, Chávez left the CSO in 1962. He devoted all of his efforts to organizing farm laborers, founding the Farm Workers Association. Chávez recruited CSO colleague Delores Huerta to his fledgling organization. By 1964, the National Farm Workers Association (NFWA) had one thousand members in fifty areas, mostly in California. A black eagle on a red background and the words "Viva la causa" (long live the cause) became the emblem and motto of the union. Chávez embraced the concept of nonviolence, incorporating the philosophies of Martin Luther King, Jr., and Mohandas Gandhi into his work.

Chávez, who had been organizing farmworkers to protest low wages and rent increases in the migrant labor camps, joined with other organizations in 1965 to support a strike against grape growers in Delano. Organized by the Filipino workers of the Agricultural Workers Organizing Committee (AWOC), the strike was also supported by the Student Nonviolent Coordinating Committee (SNCC) and the Congress of Racial Equality (CORE). This action led to a successful five-year effort that combined the strike with a boycott of table grapes and lettuce that eventually won international support.

The grape strike helped focus national attention on the conditions endured by migrant farm laborers. In 1966, Senator Robert F. Kennedy of New York

César Chávez, head of the United Farm Workers, helped organize a grape workers' strike and national boycott of grapes in order to improve conditions for the workers. (Library of Congress)

conducted Senate hearings in Delano about the agricultural industry's treatment of farmworkers. Chávez assembled a coalition of supporters that included labor unions, religious and minority groups, students, and consumers. The NFWA merged with AWOC to become the United Farm Workers (UFW), affiliated with the AFL-CIO (American Federation of Labor-Congress of Industrial Organizations). The UFW membership pledged to adhere to the principles of nonviolence, seeking peaceful methods of protest and social action such as marches, rallies, and demonstrations. In 1968, Chávez demonstrated his personal commitment to nonviolence by fasting for nearly a month when fights broke out on UFW picket lines. By 1970, most table grape growers, tired of the successful boycott, had signed contracts with the UFW.

Later Life Although Chávez gained enormous respect for his commitment to social justice and nonviolence, the agricultural industry quickly turned to the Teamsters Union in the early 1970's to negotiate more favorable contracts. Chávez called for a worldwide grape boycott. Public opinion polls indicated that by 1975, seventeen million Americans supported this effort. California, under the leadership of Governor Jerry Brown, enacted the first law governing farm labor organizing, which established the Agricultural Labor Relations Board.

In the early 1980's, UFW health clinics began to see a rise in the number of pesticide poisonings among farmworkers. Calling attention to the harmful effects of pesticide residue on produce, Chávez and the UFW embarked on a new grape boycott in 1984. In addition to marches and demonstrations, the UFW produced a film entitled *The Wrath of Grapes*, which graphically depicted the effects of pesticide poisoning. Chávez also held another hunger fast protesting the use of pesticides by the agricultural industry.

Chávez, still serving as president of the UFW, died of natural causes in 1993 at the age of sixty-six.

Impact Chávez was a charismatic leader whose quiet dignity inspired the social activists of the 1960's and beyond. He is credited by many as being one of the most influential Latino leaders in this country's history. Working conditions for farm laborers improved greatly because of his efforts, and he successfully engineered the passage of the nation's first farm labor law in the late 1970's.

Additional Information Although many works have been published about Chávez and the UFW, one that stands out is Richard Griswold del Castillo and Richard A. Garcia's *César Chávez: A Triumph of Spirit* (1995).

Cecilia M. Garcia

See also Chicano Movement; Civil Rights Movement; Grape Workers' Strike; Teatro Campesino, El; Unions and Collective Bargaining.

■ Cheever, John

Born May 27, 1912, Quincy, Massachusetts
Died June 18, 1982, Ossining, New York

Award-winning novelist and short-story writer. Cheever's vision of the foibles and weaknesses of American society mixes irony, compassion, and whimsy in a prose shot through with symbolism.

Expelled from Thayer Academy because of poor conduct and application, John Cheever used the experience in his first story, "Expelled," published by the *New Republic* in 1929. In the 1930's, he lived mostly in New York City, publishing stories in *New Republic, Collier's, Story, Atlantic*, and the *New Yorker* (for which he became a regular contributor). He worked at odd jobs and taught advanced composition at Barnard College. In 1941, he married Mary Winternitz and fathered three children. After two years of wartime service, he won a Guggenheim Fellowship (1951) and wrote television scripts. His first book, *The Enormous Radio and Other Stories* (1953), included some of his most anthologized stories. He earned an O'Henry Award, a National Institute of Arts and Letters Award, and the National Book Award (for *The Wapshot Chronicle*, published in 1957), establishing himself as a master chronicler of the upper middle class.

The *Wapshot Scandal* (1964), a sequel to *The Wapshot Chronicle*, is an incisive portrayal of the horrors of suburbia and of a world of missiles and computers. Written with detached understatement, the novel ends with faint hope, making it seem a shadowy, flawed pastoral. *Bullet Park* (1969), an allegorical novel of chaos and irrationality, is a baroque black comedy, rich but confusing in its time shifts and points of view and uneasy in its mixture of realism and bizarre fantasy. Cheever won most of his plaudits for his short stories, particularly the sixteen in *The Brigadier and the Golf Widow* (1964), where several pieces deal with expatriate life and others, such as "The Swimmer," are clearly experimental. All reprints from the *New Yorker*, the stories show wit, charm, and deceptive simplicity in their treatment of the ambiguity of human experience. A recurring theme is nostalgia, with characters' yearnings growing out of loneliness and moral disarray.

Untouched by history or politics, Cheever continued to mix whimsy with seriousness. *Falconer* (1977), a symbolic fable about a paranoid man incarcerated (despite his protestations of innocence) for his brother's murder, includes terrible scenes of cruelty, lust, and degradation. The novel's meditation on confinement and liberation is undercut by whimsy.

The collection *The World of Apples* (1973) has a complex, Chekhovian beauty as it depicts misunderstandings and a lack of love through seemingly inconsequential events. The sixty-one pieces in *The Stories of John Cheever* (1978)—three of which were adapted for the Public Broadcasting Service—show Cheever's fictive voice progressing from a cynically

tough, unforgiving certitude to a growing humaneness and honest confusion about a mean-spirited world.

Impact Cheever's reputation rests not on his characters but on his chronicling of mid-century manners in generally elegant prose. His fiction, like J. D. Salinger's and John Updike's, shows that it is possible to identify with the young while writing satirically about ethical concerns and failures.

Subsequent Events After his death from cancer, his daughter, Susan Cheever, published *Home Before Dark* (1984), a moving memoir of her father as man and artist tortured by alcoholism, paternal inadequacies, aristocratic pretensions, and bisexuality.

Additional Information *The Letters of John Cheever* (1988) were edited by his son, Benjamin Cheever.

Keith Garebian

See also Literature; Metafiction; Updike, John.

■ Chessman, Caryl

Born May 27, 1921, St. Joseph, Michigan
Died May 2, 1960, San Quentin, California

A San Quentin inmate executed in May, 1960. Chessman, with his many public appeals for the repeal of the death penalty, made capital punishment the subject of national and worldwide scrutiny.

Early Life Carol Whittier Chessman was born in St. Joseph, Michigan, but spent most of his life in Southern California. His father was a shiftless laborer, unable to find regular and satisfying work, and his mother was an attentive and intelligent woman who suffered many years of paralysis after a car wreck. Chessman (who later changed the spelling of his name to Caryl) was apparently raised in a difficult childhood environment and was often ill. Though relatively friendless as a schoolboy, occasionally, he did quite well in school and was known to be an excellent debater when necessary, a skill that later would be an immense asset to him.

Chessman got in trouble with the law even in his youth. He committed petty theft and took cars for joyrides and twice was incarcerated in the Preston State Industrial School for youth offenders. At eighteen, after another conviction for auto theft, he began his manipulation of the criminal justice system and wrote a penitent treatise that convinced a judge to release him on probation. Two years later, he was convicted for several burglaries and assaults and was sent to San Quentin. His marriage to a teenage bride ended in divorce while he was in San Quentin. After two years of good behavior, Chessman was transferred to an open prison at Chino, California, from which he promptly escaped, by his own assertion to assassinate Adolf Hitler. He was recaptured and sent back to San Quentin, from which he was paroled in 1947.

In January, 1948, Chessman made his mark as a criminal. Just a month after parole, he stole a gray Ford and equipped it with a spotlight to which he affixed red cellophane. He used this to impersonate a police officer and stopped lovers in their cars in outlying areas of Los Angeles. Chessman, dubbed the "Red Light Bandit," robbed these individuals at gunpoint. On at least two occasions, he forced the women to get into his car and perform "unnatural sex acts." He was caught after an armed robbery and went to trial on fifteen counts of robbery and assault and two counts of kidnapping, which were the basis on which the death penalty was sought and won, even though the farthest Chessman had taken either of the women was twenty-two feet to his car. The jury quickly convicted him in July, 1948, and Judge Charles W. Fricke sentenced Chessman to death. However, this was just the beginning of Chessman's notoriety. On death row, Chessman's skill for argument was to become his greatest weapon to gain time. Over the next twelve years, he won eight stays

of execution and wrote numerous writs and motions. He educated himself in prison, became a skilled lawyer, and learned four foreign languages.

The 1960's Although more than one hundred and fifty prisoners were on death row at the time, Chessman ignited public and worldwide outrage against capital punishment with his first of four books *Cell 2455: Death Row* (1954), which won acclaim from reviewers and the public alike. California governor Edmund G. "Pat" Brown, who was deeply opposed to capital punishment, refused to grant Chessman clemency, partly because of Chessman's arrogant refusal to seek it directly and the case's political notoriety. Brown even used the Chessman affair to attack capital punishment in the California legislature but failed to win the legislature's sympathy. In spite of the public outcry, however, after Chessman's last appeal ran out, he was executed in the gas chamber at San Quentin on May 2, 1960.

Impact The Chessman case brought the issue of capital punishment into sharp focus in the very beginning of the decade of protests and causes. From the 1930's to the 1960's, the Supreme Court had been struggling with the application of the death penalty, and many groups had pointed out apparent discriminatory sentencing patterns across the United States, especially in the South. By the time of the Chessman controversy, attention had begun to turn to racial issues, and soon the burgeoning war in Vietnam would create waves of social unrest. People began to examine the old order of things and attack the social and racial assumptions behind concepts such as the death penalty. The protesters who picketed California's capitol and marched outside of the walls of San Quentin on Chessman's behalf were only the beginning in this decade of turmoil. Later, of course, Chessman's argument against the injudicious application and cruelty of the death penalty would gain greater acknowledgment.

The 1972 moratorium on the death penalty following *Furman v. Georgia* gave the Supreme Court time to oversee a revision of sentencing procedures, and numerous states complied with significant guidelines to control arbitrary and unjust sentencing practices. By 1976, following *Gregg v. Georgia*, the moratorium was lifted, and more than thirty states resumed capital punishment, Texas and Florida carrying out the greatest number of executions.

Caryl Chessman, convicted of robbery, assault, and kidnapping, appealed his sentence and wrote books about his experiences on death row in San Quentin prison. His execution in 1960 sparked questions about capital punishment. (Archive Photos)

Additional Information Chessman's own books, *Cell 2455: Death Row* (1954) and *Trial by Ordeal* (1955), are fascinating reading. Chessman made the cover of the March 21, 1960, *Time* magazine, and the cover story is comprehensive and includes a contemporary discussion of the death penalty issue. Adam Hugo's *The Death Penalty in America* (1982) is a comprehensive work on the subject.

Marc E. Waddell

See also Crimes and Scandals.

■ Chicago Riots

Date July 25-September 24, 1967

A series of riots that occurred in Chicago during the summer of 1967. Combined with more extensive riots in more than thirty other U.S. cities during the summer, the Chicago riots indicated serious race relations problems in the nation.

Origins and History Many African Americans from the southern United States began migrating to Chicago in the early 1900's. Racism and mostly unsuccessful competition with whites over jobs and housing persisted for decades. As the summer of 1967 began, about eight hundred thousand African Americans, many feeling frustrated and hopeless, lived in the city's crowded black ghettos.

The Riots On Tuesday night, July 25, African American youths began looting, smashing car windows, and throwing firebombs on Chicago's West Side. During the next week, vandalism, looting, and arson occurred on the South Side and the West Side. Police attributed the riots to reports of racial conflicts in other cities, and Mayor Richard Daley announced that live ammunition would be used against rioters. Police exchanged gunfire with youths firing from a building, and five Molotov cocktails were thrown into a store. About a hundred people were arrested. On August 1, an African American man was shot by a white man, and a firebomb was thrown. Fifty-two African Americans were arrested after they did not disperse, and more firebombs were thrown.

On August 3, the Reverend Jesse Jackson requested that Chicago be declared a disaster area. The situation calmed down, but on August 26, shots were fired while a blaze was being fought in the South Side, and nine African American youths were arrested. On September 14, an African American power rally sponsored by the Student Nonviolent Coordinating Committee (SNCC) charged police with brutality and fascism, and window smashing, rock throwing at cars, and scattered sniper fire was reported. Police, aided by leaders of African American street gangs, calmed the area. The next day, African American students boycotted classes to protest inadequate school conditions.

On September 22, in the suburb of Maywood, five hundred people pelted police cars with bottles because no African American students had been nominated for homecoming queen. Thirty people were arrested. The following day, after police shot and critically wounded a burglary suspect, about three hundred African Americans threw bricks and bottles through store windows, and police used tear gas. On September 24, ten African Americans and eleven whites were arrested in Maywood by police in an attempt to prevent a third night of violence. The Chicago riots were over for the summer of 1967.

Impact The riots of 1967 were largely responsible for President Lyndon B. Johnson appointing a Commission on Civil Disorders on July 27, 1967. The commission issued a report referred to as the Kerner Commission Report after its chairman, Governor Otto Kerner of Illinois. Although the commission did not select Chicago for one of its in-depth investigations, the conditions described in the report were also found in Chicago, and the Chicago riots were part of the unrest that led to the report.

Additional Information The *Report of the National Advisory Commission on Civil Disorders*, published by Government Printing Office in 1968, gives the best understanding of the Chicago riot; Bantam Book's 1968 reprint of the report, entitled *The Kerner Report*, gives a good background.

Abraham D. Lavender

See also Detroit Riot; Jackson, Jesse; Kerner Commission Report; New York Riots; Newark Riot; Student Nonviolent Coordinating Committee (SNCC); Watts Riot.

■ Chicago Seven Trial

Date September, 1969-February, 1970

The quintessential trial of 1960's radicals. The flamboyance of the defendants and their ability to capture the media turned the event into a battleground between the antiwar movement and the government.

The defendants in the Chicago Seven trial address the media in February, 1970. From left to right, they are Lee Weiner, Rennie Davis, David Dellinger (holding his granddaughter), Abbie Hoffman, Tom Hayden (behind Hoffman), Jerry Rubin, and John Froines. (AP/Wide World Photos)

Origins and History In the fall of 1968, the Walker Study Team, the investigative arm of the National Commission on the Causes and Prevention of Violence, issued a report on the riots in Chicago during the Democratic National Convention. The antiwar protesters behaved provocatively, the report concluded, but it was the police who rioted. However, Chicago mayor Richard Daley and President Lyndon B. Johnson rejected the idea of putting the police on trial. A federal grand jury under the direction of Judge William Campbell, Daley's protégé, focused on the role of the protesters. In October, 1968, Federal Bureau of Investigation (FBI) chief J. Edgar Hoover announced that twenty protesters would be indicted. In agency memos, he noted that a successful prosecution would defuse the New Left and restore the tarnished image of the FBI. Attorney General Ramsey Clark opposed White House plans for a big, showy trial of antiwar activists, and he delayed the grand jury proceedings for six months, much to President Johnson's annoyance.

After Richard M. Nixon became president and John Mitchell became attorney general, indictments were handed down swiftly. In March, 1969, eight protesters, most of them highly visible leaders, were charged with conspiracy and crossing state lines with the intent of creating a riot during the 1968 Democratic National Convention. Three of the defendants, Abbie Hoffman, Jerry Rubin, and Lee Weiner, were Yippies. Four of the defendants, Tom Hayden, Rennie Davis, John Froines, and David Dellinger, were conspicuous antiwar activists. The eighth defendant, Bobby Seale, was chairman of the Black Panther Party.

The Courtroom Drama Seale played an insignificant role at the protests in 1968, but he dominated the courtroom during the initial phase of the trial, which began in Chicago in September, 1969, and received intensive media attention, much to the delight of the Yippies. When Black Panther lawyer Charles Garry was unable to represent his client, Seale repeatedly requested the right to serve as his own counsel. He was denied that right by Judge Julius Hoffman, a seventy-three-year-old former corporate attorney and member of Chicago's elite Jewish community, who showed signs of being biased against the defendants. On October 29, the confrontation between Judge Hoffman and Seale came to a head. Bailiffs gagged the Black Panther leader, taped his mouth shut, and shackled his hands and feet. When he struggled to free himself, he was assaulted, then forcefully removed from the courtroom. Judge Hoffman severed his case; the Chicago Eight became the Chicago Seven.

Thomas Foran and Richard Schultz, the prosecuting U.S. attorneys, argued that the defendants were part of a conspiracy intent on fomenting violent revolution. Witnesses for the government, including undercover police agents, testified that the defendants taunted law enforcement officials and urged their followers to engage in criminal activity. At the start of the trial, the defendants and their lawyers, William Kunstler and Leonard Weinglass, had no coherent strategy. Yippies Hoffman and Rubin seized the initiative and brought guerrilla theater to the courtroom. Insisting that the government ought to be on trial, they disrupted the proceedings, conducted daily briefings for the media, and made their case a popular cause on college campuses.

Initially, Kunstler, a veteran civil rights lawyer and a moderate, took a traditional legal approach and argued the case on First Amendment grounds. He gradually adopted the freewheeling Yippie strategy and eventually insisted that the case was about cultural revolution and that the defendants were indicted because they were long-haired, marijuana-smoking hippies of the sort who had gathered at the August, 1969, Woodstock Music and Art Fair. Throughout the trial, Kunstler and Weinglass traded verbal barbs with Judge Hoffman, who, in his own way, was as theatrical as the Yippies were. The courtroom atmosphere became increasingly tense after two Black Panthers, Fred Hampton and Mark Clark, were killed by the Chicago police in a raid on December 4. Both the defendants and the prosecution dropped all pretense of civility.

Witnesses for the Chicago Seven included folksinger Pete Seeger and poet Allen Ginsberg, who performed for the conservative jury and for the partisan courtroom spectators. Novelist Norman Mailer and historian Staughton Lynd described the moral fervor of the defendants. Abbie Hoffman's testimony in December, 1969, illuminated the generation gap that existed in the nation. Insisting that he was an "orphan of America" and lived in the Woodstock Nation, which he defined as a country of "alienated young people," he claimed that at the 1968 Democratic National Convention, the government conspired to deprive the youthful protesters of their constitutional rights to freedom of speech and assembly.

After nearly two hundred witnesses testified and two million dollars in taxpayers' money had been spent, the trial reached a resounding crescendo. In Yiddish, Yippie Hoffman denounced Judge Hoffman for betraying his Jewish origins and collaborating with the enemy. Not surprisingly, he and his codefendants and their lawyers were sentenced to prison for contempt of court. On February 14, the case went to the jury. After four days of bitter dispute, the jury reached a compromise verdict. Froines and Weiner were found not guilty on all counts. Hoffman, Rubin, Hayden, Dellinger, and Davis were found not guilty of conspiracy but guilty of crossing state lines with the intent to create a riot. Judge Hoffman sentenced them to the maximum penalty: five years in prison and five thousand dollars in fines. Kunstler and Weinglass immediately appealed the conviction, and after a brief incarceration in Cook County Jail, the defendants were released on bail. The Chicago Seven case was finally resolved in November, 1972, when the U.S. Court of Appeals for the Seventh Circuit reversed the convictions and rebuked Judge Hoffman for depriving the defendants of their right to a fair trial.

Impact The trial contributed to the polarization of the nation. After the trial, President Nixon feted Judge Hoffman at a White House reception, and the verdict was hailed as a triumph for law and order at Republican Party rallies. Supporters of the Chicago Seven rioted in the streets and protested at courthouses around the country.

Additional Information Defendant Tom Hayden's *Trial* (1970) and John Schultz's *Motion Will Be Denied* (1972) capture the courtroom drama.

Jonah Raskin

See also Black Panthers; Counterculture; Democratic National Convention of 1968; Hampton-Clark Deaths; Hippies; Media; Yippies.

■ Chicano Movement

A social movement spawned by Mexican Americans. Its goals were to increase Chicanos' pride in their ethnic heritage, improve their social and economic standing, and gain civil rights.

Before the Chicano (or Mexican American) movement's birth, most Mexican Americans sought assimilation and took a nonconfrontational approach to obtaining their rights. This led several writers to call them the "invisible Americans" and the "sleeping giant." However, when Mexican American veterans returned from World War II, they expected to receive the same rights and freedom for which they had fought overseas. Many used the G.I. Bill (1944) to obtain college degrees and consequently had higher qualifications and bigger aspirations. The early civil rights protests of the late 1950's and early 1960's acted as catalysts, providing models of action and making it acceptable to question government policies and the fairness of American society. The movement's birth cannot be traced to a particular event but can be found in a series of events, each with its own leaders, objectives, and tactics. Most of these activities occurred in the Southwest—California, Texas, New Mexico, Colorado, and Arizona—where about three-fourths of all Mexican Americans lived.

Early Activism In the early 1960's, Mexican Americans began to become more involved politically, and a few were elected to political offices. One of the most notable was Henry B. González, a Texan who won election to the U.S. House of Representatives in 1961. Three years later, fellow Texan Eligio "Kika" de la Garza also won a seat in the House, and Joseph Montoya of New Mexico won a seat in the Senate. Although these early steps were within the system, Mexican American activists had begun to pursue other means of obtaining their civil rights and increasing ethnic pride.

César Chávez, a migrant farmworker, organized farm laborers into a union, the Farm Workers Association, in 1962. Chávez led a series of strikes under the banners of the Aztec eagle, serpent, and cactus, symbolizing Mexican nationalism, and the Virgin of Guadalupe, symbolizing Mexican Catholicism. He is remembered most for helping organize a grape workers' strike in Delano, California, which involved a nationwide boycott of grapes that began in September, 1965. In July, 1970, the grape growers accepted Chávez's union, renamed the United Farm Workers of America, as the bargaining agent for workers.

In May, 1966, fifty Chicanos walked out in protest at a meeting of the Equal Employment Opportunity Commission in Albuquerque, New Mexico, which had been convened to hear complaints of racial discrimination against minorities, particularly Native Americans, in the Southwest. The protesters, asking that the commission hear the problems of Mexican Americans, demanded more federal jobs and greater voice in programs affecting them. Although President Lyndon B. Johnson scheduled a meeting in El Paso, Texas, three prominent Chicano leaders, Chávez, Rodolfo "Corky" González, and Bert N. Corona, boycotted the meeting and instead held the La Raza Unida Conference in a poverty-stricken Mexican American area of the city.

Student Activism In the mid-1960's, students at the high school and college levels began to become politically active. In 1966, a conference at Loyola University in Los Angeles, attended mostly by middle-class Mexican American students, examined the philosophy of Chicanismo, a new ideology that emphasized Chicano nationalism and self-determination.

A number of Mexican American student organizations were formed, each with specific constituencies or objectives. They included United Mexican American Students (formed in Albuquerque, New Mexico), Mexican American Student Association, and Mexican American Youth Organization (founded in Texas by José Ángel Gutiérrez). In 1967, a number of student organizations came together in a confederation called El Movimiento Estudiantil Chicano de Aztlán, or Chicano Student Movement of Aztlan (MEChA).

In March, 1968, Chicano high school students in Los Angeles and other Southwest cities participated in a boycott of classes. More than ten thousand students in Los Angeles walked out, demanding bilingual education, more Latino teachers, improved education, and greater awareness on the part of the school system of Chicano students' needs. The class boycott, led by teacher Salvador Castro, lasted several days. Castro and numerous students were arrested; however, administrators did agree to some of the students' demands.

In 1969, activist Rodolfo "Corky" Gonzáles, a former boxer, organized the inaugural Chicano Youth

Liberation Conference in Denver, bringing together young representatives from many Chicano organizations. In 1965, Gonzáles had founded the Crusade for Justice in Denver, Colorado, to improve education, job opportunities, and police relations for Chicanos. At the first youth conference, the delegates adopted *El Plan Espiritual de Aztlán,* a manifesto of political and cultural nationalism. The plan called for a revival of Aztlán, the legendary homeland of the Aztecs, which was often identified as the Southwest and held a strong appeal for many youthful leaders.

A More Radical Approach In 1963, Reies López Tijerina formed the Alianza Federal de Mercedes (Federal Alliance of Land Grants) in New Mexico for the purpose of reclaiming land that he felt had been stolen from Mexicans in the 1848 Treaty of Guadalupe Hidalgo, which ended the Mexican American War. In 1967, Tijerina led a raid on the courthouse in Tierra Amarilla, New Mexico, to make a citizen's arrest of the district attorney whom he felt had been harassing his organization by arresting its members. Shots were fired, Alianza members were freed from jail, and Tijerina and his accomplices fled. Tijerina was later arrested and sent to prison for his protest activities

In 1967, David Sánchez, Carlos Montez, and Ralph Ramírez formed a paramilitary organization called the Brown Berets in Los Angeles. The group, which consisted largely of former gang members, had the stated purpose of aiding and protecting the Chicano community. In 1968, the Brown Berets were involved in demonstrations and protests in an attempt to motivate and unite the Chicano community to take action for better education and social conditions. They were subsequently accused of inciting a riot, using narcotics, and being communists, and some members were brought to trial. In 1972, twenty-six members of the Brown Berets invaded Santa Catalina Island off the coast of California. They renamed the island "Aztlán Libre" and occupied it until forced to leave twenty-four hours later. That same year, Sánchez disbanded the organization.

Gaining Power The 1967 La Raza Unida Conference held in a poverty-stricken area of El Paso led to the establishment of a political party called La Raza Unida. José Ángel Gutiérrez and others in Texas created the militant party in 1970 so that Chicanos would have an alternative political voice. The party enjoyed some limited success in electing its members to political office but ultimately failed because it was so closely identified with the Latino community that it was unable to attract large numbers of non-Latino voters.

Other organizations with political objectives included the Mexican American Political Association, the National Association of Latino Elected and Appointed Officials, and the Political Association of Spanish-Speaking Organizations. Catholic priests and nuns also formed activist groups, including the Padres Asociados por Derechos Religiosos, Educativos, y Sociales and Las Hermanas. Other organizations include the Mexican American Legal Defense and Education Fund and the National Council of La Raza.

Another way that the Chicano movement empowered its members was to heighten their ethnic pride through cultural and artistic elements. During the 1960's, Mexican Americans produced literature, paintings, plays, and films that portrayed their culture, experiences, aspirations, and visions for the future. Some of the better-known writers are Rodolfo "Corky" Gonzáles, whose "Yo Soy Joaquín" (1967), an epic poem describing Chicano history, was widely circulated, and Raymond Barrio, whose book, *The Plum Plum Pickers* (1969) described the lives of prune pickers in Santa Clara County. These works presented and encouraged a Chicano view of the world and defined who and what Chicanos were.

Impact The term Chicano was selected by some Mexican Americans to refer to their people and the movement because the term connected them to their Mexican and Indian roots. It was important that an ethnic designation be self-selected and not imposed upon them because the movement was about self-determination and the creation of a new identity. Many Mexican Americans, however, did not accept the term because earlier in the twentieth century it had carried a negative connotation and because it was identified with the more activist elements of the movement.

Not only did other Americans become more aware of Mexican Americans and their concerns because of the movement, but also Mexican Americans became more aware of themselves as a group and their potential power. As a result, more attention, political and economic, has been paid to them.

For example, some state universities initiated Chicano studies programs. This in turn led to an awareness among all Latinos that it is to their advantage to unite.

Subsequent Events Since the 1960's, the number of Latino politicians elected to office has increased at the local, state, and national level. This accomplishment is partly due to the efforts of Willie Velasquez, who helped form the Southwest Voter Registration Education Project in 1974.

Latinos have also made progress in the Catholic Church. Aided by the Chicano movement, Patrick Flores became the first Mexican American bishop in the United States in 1970. In 1983, the U.S. bishop's pastoral letter, *The Hispanic Presence: Challenge and Commitment*, instructed pastors to help accommodate Latinos in the Church.

Additional Information Insight into Mexican American culture and leaders of the 1960's is provided by Stan Steiner's *La Raza: The Mexican Americans* (1970). A Chicano perspective on the movement is presented by Armando Rendon in *Chicano Manifesto* (1971). Carlos Muñoz, Jr., one of the Chicano movement's leaders, wrote a history of the movement entitled *Youth, Identity, Power: The Chicano Movement* (1989).

Philip E. Lampe

See also *Chicano: Twenty-five Pieces of a Chicano Mind*; Grape Workers' Strike; *Plum Plum Pickers, The*.

■ Chicano: Twenty-five Pieces of a Chicano Mind

Published 1969
Author Abelardo B. Delgado (1931-   )

A collection of twenty-five poems that address the concerns of Mexican Americans in the revolutionary spirit of the 1960's. The works, all of a page or less in length, celebrate important figures and themes while challenging the exploitation of Mexican workers.

The Work In *Chicano: Twenty-five Pieces of a Chicano Mind*, Delgado (who published this collection under just his first name, Abelardo) seeks an artistic voice for Chicano (Mexican American) workers and their families, who during the 1960's were often hired at extremely low wages to perform the exhausting, difficult work that other Americans no longer wanted to do. The plight of farmworkers, who joined in strikes organized by César Chávez, is the most dramatic example. The poems, some in Spanish, some in English, and some in both languages, speak of land, people, and hopes for the future in voices that are sometimes angry and sometimes sentimentally hopeful. One poem calls the Rio Grande "*la puerta mas cruel y mas dura*," or "the cruelest door," while in another the land is "the patient mother who will listen/ to the sunbaked lament of one who toils."

The people celebrated range from almost stereotypical figures such as La Hembra, a Mexican earth mother, to Mama Lupe, the apparition of the Virgin Mary at Tepayac Hill in 1531, who as our Lady of Guadalupe is praised in one poem as mother of La Raza, (literally, "the race"). Two of these poems became especially well-known and praised: "El Imigrante" (literally, "the immigrant") depicts migrant workers as "*bumerangas que la mano de dios/ por este mundo tiro*" ("boomerangs that the hand of God shoots through this world"); "stupid america," the only free-verse poem in this collection, invokes the *santero*, an ancient woodcarving tradition native to New Mexico and dating from the earliest Spanish settlements, ("that chicano/ with a big knife/ . . . doesn't want to knife you/ he wants to sit on a bench/ and carve christ figures") and Pablo Picasso, the twentieth century Spanish painter who began the cubist movement. Delgado says the United States is destroying the Chicano artist, who "is the Picasso/ of your western states/ but he will die/ with one thousand masterpieces/ hanging only from his mind."

Impact Delgado is most admired for his role in fathering (along with poets Rodolfo "Corky" Gonzáles and Ricardo Sánchez) the artistic side of the Chicano movement. He befriended other poets and encouraged younger colleagues in their work; he read his poetry widely in public and was known as a powerful performer. His poetry itself received mixed reviews. "El Imigrante" is often cited for its boomerang metaphor and another in which the migrants are "*golondrinas*" or "migrating swallows"; "stupid america" to some appears prophetic in warning that "that chicano/ shouting curses on the street/ . . . is a poet/ without paper and pencil/ and since he cannot write/ he will explode." Elsewhere, however, it is noted that Delgado's insistence on using conventional meter leads to some distortions ("how soon do you stop being a muchacho?/ why do you wear as heart a ripe pistachio?") and that his poetry often needs editing, a criticism with which Delgado has agreed. During the 1960's, his work was not published by a major publisher—he often mimeographed his poems or paid to have them printed himself—and his reputation remained largely confined to the Latino community.

Additional Information For a critical assessment of the contributions of Delgado as well as other Chicano poets, see *Chicano Poetry: A Critical Introduction* (1986) by Cordelia Candelaria.

Tim Frazer

See also Chávez, César; Chicano Movement; Grape Workers' Strike; Poetry; Teatro Campesino, El.

■ Chisholm, Shirley

Born November 30, 1924, Brooklyn, New York

A prominent outspoken African American politician, teacher, and author. In 1968, Chisholm, elected to the United States House of Representatives from New York, became the first African American congresswoman.

Shirley Anita (St. Hill) Chisholm, born the first daughter of West Indian immigrants, received her early education in Barbados. In 1934, she returned to Brooklyn and enrolled in the public schools. She received a bachelor's degree from Brooklyn College in 1946 and a master's degree from Columbia University in 1951. She began her teaching career in 1946 at Mount Calvary Day Care Center.

In 1960, Chisholm cofounded the Unity Democratic Club, which aimed to provide candidates for the Seventeenth Assembly District. In 1964, Chisholm became a candidate and was elected to the New York State Assembly, where she served until 1968. After she was elected the first African American United States congresswoman in 1968, she was in office for seven terms.

In 1969, Chisholm received national attention when she proposed a bill in support of minimum wages for domestic workers. Also, in 1972, Chisholm became the first African American and the first woman to campaign for the Democratic presidential nomination.

Impact Chisholm was responsible for several pieces of legislation that helped the disadvantaged, especially minority students and minority female domestic employees.

Subsequent Events In 1982, Chisholm retired from Congress and returned to her first love, teaching. In 1983, she was named Purington Professor at Mount Holyoke College in South Hadley, Massachusetts.

Additional Information Chisholm published two autobiographical books entitled *Unbought and Unbossed* (1970) and *The Good Fight* (1973).

Nila M. Bowden

See also Abzug, Bella; Civil Rights Movement.

■ Church Bombings

The bombings of African American churches in the South generated international interest. White segregationists in the 1960's expressed their rage at civil rights groups by destroying the churches that served as a focal point for African American activities.

In the 1950's, the slow desegregation of public facilities began in the United States. The era was symbolized by the Montgomery, Alabama, bus boycott led by ministers of African American churches including Martin Luther King, Jr. Activists, often initially African American college students, challenged public places that required separate facilities such as transportation agencies, retail outlets, and medical centers. As the Civil Rights movement developed, a broader spectrum of the African American populace and some whites participated. As more African Americans demonstrated resistance to segregation, the reaction to that resistance increased. Although the protesters were largely peaceful, the reaction to them was often violent.

Bombings of African American buildings— churches, private homes, businesses, and schools— was fairly widespread by the early 1960's. By 1963, racially motivated bombings had been reported in Alabama, Arkansas, Florida, Georgia, Louisiana, Mississippi, South Carolina, and Virginia. However, some incidents went unreported because some victims were too afraid; other incidents were not publicized by local law-enforcement personnel who were often suspected of having condoned or having taken part in the bombings. The exact numbers of bombings of African American structures in the 1960's cannot be calculated, but it certainly far exceeds the few widely publicized incidents that eventually drew national and international attention.

Homes and Churches Besides churches, the homes of civil rights activists were a prime target. In Birmingham, Alabama, the home of the brother of Martin Luther King, Jr., was nearly demolished by a bomb. A firebomb was used to partially destroy the home of an African American congressman in Clarksdale, Mississippi, and in Jackson, Mississippi, a bomb exploded in the carport of Medgar Evers, the state's leader of the National Association for the Advancement of Colored People, who was later murdered. Bombs exploded at the University of Alabama at Tuscaloosa, where an African American woman was enrolled, and at the integrated University of Mississippi at Oxford. Black-owned businesses in Birmingham, the Mississippi towns of Greenwood and Gulfport, and Charleston, South Carolina, were also targeted. In many cases, the homeowners or business employees and clientele inside the structures were injured. In most cases, the targeted people and institutions were somehow associated with desegregation events. Often, the bombings were not

fully investigated, no one was charged, and perpetrators, if identified, were unrestrained. In cases where indictments were sought, penalties were sometimes modest.

African American churches became a focal point of the bombings. White segregationists correctly understood how significant the churches were in the 1960's struggles for civil rights. First, the church was the most important community organization among African American people. A majority of African Americans were either members of a church or viewed it as a center of black life in the towns and cities in which they resided; no other institution was as widespread or as symbolic of African American values. Second, the churches had historically produced communal leadership. Ministers were not only spiritual leaders, they helped educate people, provided social services to the needy, and became important political leaders. Third, civil rights activists held their major meetings as well as strategy sessions in African American churches. Often, the

Hundreds of mourners gather around the front of St. John's African Methodist Church in Birmingham, Alabama, as pallbearers carry out the casket bearing fourteen-year-old Carol Robertson, one of four girls killed September 15, 1963, when a bomb ripped through the nearby Sixteenth Street Baptist Church. (Library of Congress)

churches were the only sites where African Americans could gather under black leadership without interruption by whites. The churches encouraged the development of leadership that was not dependent on the larger community, and this group of ministerial and lay leaders was interpreted as a threat by whites attempting to preserve segregation.

African American churches in the South had been vandalized and terrorized before the 1960's, sometimes by individual whites and sometimes by groups of whites expressing racist feelings. The bombings of the 1960's differed in that far more organization was behind the acts. Often the major white supremacist organizations, such as the Ku Klux Klan and the White Citizens Councils, planned and executed these events. Giving covert support to these organizations were white community leaders who would explicitly state their segregationist views but would not personally commit any violent acts, preferring to let the members of the supremacist organizations act on their behalf. These community leaders included governors and congressmen.

Arkansas and Birmingham The most-publicized African American church bombings that took place in the 1960's occurred in Pine Bluff and Gillet, Arkansas, and in Birmingham. In Gillet, no reason was ever given for the dynamiting of a rural African American church. In Pine Bluff, the bomb that set an African Methodist Episcopal church on fire was perceived to be a reaction to the pastor's activities: He had been an adviser to African American students who were attempting to desegregate lunch counters in the city.

The bombings of churches in Birmingham were part of forthright resistance to segregation in the 1950's and 1960's that included the use of fire hoses and police dogs against unarmed, peaceful civil rights protesters. By 1963, Bethal Baptist Church, an African American congregation, had been bombed twice, with devices strong enough to damage homes in the area. In the latter part of 1963, the Sixteenth Street Baptist Church was shattered by a bomb, and that event became an international symbol of the danger for African Americans struggling to desegregate the South. The church, a centrally located, large, and prestigious edifice, was the main meeting place for activists, until September 15, 1963, when a bomb not only injured worshipers but also killed four young girls aged ten to fourteen. They died in their Sunday school classrooms, and their small bodies were mutilated by the force of the blast. Photos of the destruction accompanied by pictures of the victims when they were alive appeared in newspapers and on television screens around the world. For many, Birmingham symbolized the depth of racism in the United States, and the four dead girls and twenty-three wounded parishioners were martyrs in a struggle for social justice. The Sixteenth Street Baptist Church was no longer safe to use for further rallies; the bombers had accomplished their immediate goal in destroying the facility. King wired Alabama governor George Wallace that the blood of the victims was on Wallace's hands. The governor disclaimed any association with the bombers and any responsibility for establishing a social climate that would lead to such acts.

Impact The response to the church bombings varied. White southern politicians who favored segregation did not admit any responsibility for the bombings, and very few clearly stated their opposition to the violence and the groups believed responsible for it. Some politicians made no comment, and others claimed that civil rights activists associated with the churches had indirectly encouraged the violence. Northern and western politicians and the international press evidenced concern and some alarm, especially following the bombing of the Sixteenth Street Baptist Church in Birmingham. This concern, along with other factors, later resulted in some national policy changes: The passage of the Civil Rights Act of 1964 was clearly influenced by the overt violence against religious organizations and especially by the deaths of the four young children attending Sunday school in Birmingham. The image of innocent girls dying in a house of worship evoked both an emotional response and a practical one on a national and international level. However, although northern and western politicians decried the bombings, they did not relate these events to the more subtle racism that existed in their own districts.

The impact of the church bombings on the African American community was quite different from the intimidation that the bombers had intended. Some researchers think that the bombings and the resulting injuries and deaths were a major factor in causing many African Americans to turn away from nonviolent protest and become more attracted to organizations that emphasized self-defense and separation of the races. Integration became less attractive; black power became more inviting. Nonviolent protest organizations such as King's Southern Christian Leadership Conference (SCLC) were considered by some to be ineffectual in such circumstances, while the relatively militant Black Panther Party and the Nation of Islam, with its spokesperson Malcolm X, grew increasingly influential. The bombers of African American churches may have achieved their immediate goals, but they did not prevent desegregation or the empowering of African Americans. Rather, they further discredited the segregationist cause and encouraged many African Americans to move toward a more militant ideology.

Additional Information The bombings of churches and other buildings in the South is examined in Francis M. Wilhoit's *The Politics of Massive Resistance* (1973) and *Racial Violence in the United States* (1969), edited by Allen Grimshaw.

William Osborne and Max C. E. Orezzoli

See also Black Christian Nationalist Movement; Black Panthers; Black Power; Civil Rights Movement; Evers, Medgar; King, Martin Luther, Jr.; Ku Klux Klan (KKK); Malcolm X; Nation of Islam; Southern Christian Leadership Conference (SCLC); Wallace, George.

■ City of Night

Published 1963
Author John Rechy (1934-   )

A best-selling book that explored the sexual underworld of big cities. The novel revealed the frenetic lives of the outwardly hardened but inwardly desperate outcasts of American society.

The Work The unnamed narrator of *City of Night* flees from his stifling home and community in El Paso, Texas, to the sexual skid rows of New York, Los Angeles, and other cities. The book alternates chapters entitled "City of Night"—sociological sketches of the world of gay prostitutes, young drug addicts, old winos—with vignettes of individuals who populate that world.

The narrator becomes a male prostitute. He maintains his sense of heterosexual masculinity by allowing gay men to perform sexual acts on him only in return for money, while he never reciprocates or shows any emotional response to their offers of friendship or love. The narrator is addicted to the anarchy of street life, to the seething shadowy world of New York's Times Square and similar sex and drug supermarkets.

His vignettes offer portraits of Pete, who teaches the narrator the rules of sexual hustling; Miss Destiny, a beautiful, well-educated drag queen who lives in a fragile world of illusion and shows the narrator that, underneath the exciting aura of anarchic freedom offered by the city of night, its inhabitants are all trapped by their desires and fears; and Jeremy, who offers the narrator love, from which he flees in fear.

The narrator learns hard lessons about himself, about his loneliness, and about his need for the love that he fears acknowledging. He understands that the city of night is partly a product of the darkness of his own soul.

Impact Larry McMurtry, James Baldwin, and other major writers recognized Rechy as an important new voice in American literature, and Rechy's best-selling book was translated into many other languages and would later be taught in many literature courses. However, the novel, written before the advent of the gay liberation movement, deeply offended many critics. Even friendly critics hurt Rechy's literary career by labeling him as a gay writer, focusing attention on his subject matter rather than on the quality of the writing itself.

City of Night contributed to the growth of the counterculture in the 1960's and to the gay liberation movement. Rechy's narrator felt that his innocence had been destroyed by a flawed and uncaring nation. He expressed the restlessness, alienation, and existential despair that became a major theme in the artistic and political life of the 1960's. The narrator and many other young people shared a need to escape the confines of family and community by entering the anarchy and anonymity of the big cities.

Related Work In 1983, Rechy published *Bodies and Souls*, a novel that takes up many of the same concerns and problems of the characters in the earlier work.

Additional Information For a sketch that reveals the autobiographical nature of *City of Night*, see "John Rechy," in *Contemporary Authors: Autobiography Series*, 1986, edited by Adele Sarkissian.

William E. Pemberton

See also Baldwin, James; *Boys in the Band, The*; Counterculture; Gay Liberation Movement; Literature; *Midnight Cowboy*; Stonewall Inn Riots.

■ Civil Rights Act of 1960

A federal law passed to ensure African Americans equality in requirements for voting. The Civil Rights Act of 1960 quickly proved ineffective.

The Fourteenth and Fifteenth Amendments to the Constitution, ratified in 1868 and 1870 respectively, made illegal all attempts to prevent individuals from exercising their voting rights on the basis of race. However, these amendments were in practice ineffective because the white people who controlled the political system and social institutions created impediments such as literacy tests, residency requirements, and poll taxes to block black citizens' access to political participation. Additionally, white supremacist groups such as the Ku Klux Klan employed terrorism to intimidate those African Americans who wanted to exercise their voting rights.

In the 1950's, the emerging Civil Rights movement created a backlash in the South. Opponents of the movement responded with violence, firebombing homes, churches, and other buildings associated with civil rights activities. The implicit threat of violence intimidated African Americans and prevented many from registering to vote.

The Civil Rights Act of 1957, designed to protect a person's right to exercise the right to vote, authorized the attorney general of the United States to intervene through court action whenever citizens were illegally excluded from voter registration. However, the case-by-case suits proved to be time-consuming and hard to resolve.

In 1959, the U.S. Commission on Civil Rights presented a report documenting numerous incidents in which African Americans had been denied the right to vote in southern states. The commission recommended that voter registration be handled by the federal government, but Attorney General William P. Rogers proposed instead that referees handle citizen complaints filed with federal courts. A bill based on the attorney general's referee plan passed in the House and gained passage in the Senate with the aid of Majority Leader Lyndon B. Johnson and Minority Leader Everett Dirksen. The Civil Rights Act of 1960 became law on May 6, 1960, and was later known as the Voting Rights Act of 1960. The act sought to protect every citizen's right to vote by empowering the attorney general to appoint voting referees to investigate and act, using federal courts, on complaints that state officials denied people the right to exercise their right to vote on the basis of their race or color. The referees would examine the complaints, and if they found that an applicant met the voting requirements, the person would be granted a voting certificate. Election officials who refused to honor the certificate could be found in contempt of court.

To prevent destruction of voting records, the act also required election officials to preserve all records of federal elections for twenty-two months. In addition, to prevent violence against and intimidation of civil rights activists and voters, the act provided for the prosecution of those who fled to other states after damaging or destroying any building or other real or personal property.

Impact The 1960 act did not address impediments to voting such as literacy tests but simply mandated that the requirements be applied equally to voters, regardless of their race. Although the act represented an advance over previous civil rights legislation, it proved to be ineffective because in every case of alleged discrimination, the attorney general, in concert with federal courts, had to establish that an individual was denied the right to vote solely on the basis of the person's race or color.

Additional Information *Civil Rights and the American Negro* (1968), edited by P. Albert Blaustein and Robert L. Zangrando, places the Civil Rights Act of 1960 in the context of the long historical struggle that led African Americans from slavery to freedom.

Mathew J. Kanjirathinkal

See also Church Bombings; Civil Rights Act of 1964; Civil Rights Act of 1968; Civil Rights Movement; Ku Klux Klan (KKK); Voting Rights Legislation.

■ Civil Rights Act of 1964

Landmark federal legislation that ended the practice of racial segregation in public facilities. The act also included a ban on gender discrimination, a provision that provided women with a legal foundation in their struggle for equal rights.

President Lyndon B. Johnson signs the Civil Rights Act of 1964 on July 2, 1964, surrounded by those who helped it pass. Standing at the corner of the table are minority leader Everett Dirksen (left) and Vice President Hubert Humphrey (right). (AP/Wide World Photos)

The 1896 U.S. Supreme Court ruling in *Plessy v. Ferguson* affirmed the constitutionality of "separate but equal" racial segregation. The Court's 1954 ruling in *Brown v. Board of Education of Topeka, Kansas* prohibited segregation in public schools, but in the early 1960's, segregation still remained the law and the custom in most southern states. Civil rights activists hoped for federal legislation to end segregation, but President Dwight D. Eisenhower proved unwilling and President John F. Kennedy was reluctant to battle a Congress dominated by powerful southern senators.

Introducing the Bill Seeking to force the federal government to act, Martin Luther King, Jr., and other prominent leaders in the Civil Rights movement provoked a confrontation with law enforcement officials in Birmingham, Alabama, in April and May, 1963. News broadcasts featuring police and mob violence against civil rights protesters shocked the nation and led to international condemnation of American racism. Shocked by the violence and

concerned with the United States' prestige abroad, President Kennedy announced on national television on June 11, 1963, that he would introduce a civil rights bill to Congress.

Kennedy's bill, which he sent to Congress on June 18, included provisions banning racial discrimination in public accommodations such as restaurants, hotels, parks, and swimming pools. Southern Democrats and conservative Republicans immediately made clear their opposition to the civil rights legislation. King hoped that the August, 1963, March on Washington would pressure Congress into working on the bill, but the protest had no effect on congressional opinion, and the bill continued its slow progress through various committees in the House of Representatives. However, Kennedy's assassination on November 22, 1963, led to renewed activity as the new president, Lyndon B. Johnson, made passage of the legislation a top priority.

Passing the Bill Johnson, a former Senate majority leader, possessed considerable skills as a legislator.

Committed to the civil rights cause and dedicated to securing the enactment of a strong civil rights bill, Johnson began building congressional and popular support for the legislation. He shrewdly played on the nation's sense of loss, declaring before a joint session of Congress that "no memorial oration or eulogy could more eloquently honor President Kennedy's memory than the earliest passage of the civil rights bill for which he fought so long." He later met with several civil rights leaders to coordinate efforts to obtain passage of the stalled legislation. Opponents vigorously fought the bill in the House of Representatives, even adding a provision barring sex discrimination in the hope that it would increase opposition. Despite these efforts, the House approved the measure by a vote of 290 to 130 on February 10, 1964. However, the bill's passage was not assured. Senate passage of the act would prove far more difficult.

Using a technique called the filibuster, senators could bring the business of the Senate to a halt. A senator who opposed any bill could take the floor and make extended speeches, thus preventing the Senate from debating the bill. The Senate could end a filibuster by voting to invoke cloture, a rule that limited the length of time that a senator could speak. In order to stop a southern filibuster, the bill's proponents needed two-thirds of the Senate to vote for cloture. However, many senators cherished the tradition of unlimited debate and were reluctant to vote for cloture, and southerners opposed to the bill filibustered through the months of March, April, and May, preventing the Senate from considering the civil rights legislation. However, the bill's proponents secured the assistance of Everett Dirksen, leader of the Republicans in the Senate. After long negotiations with the White House, Dirksen and other Republicans agreed to vote for cloture, and on June 10, the filibuster, which had lasted for 534 hours and consisted of more than four million words, came to an end. Nine days later, the Senate passed the bill by a vote of 73 to 27. On July 2, 1964, President Johnson signed the Civil Rights Act of 1964 into law in a public ceremony attended by civil rights leaders and congressmen who had supported the bill.

Impact The Civil Rights Act of 1964 ended legal segregation. Throughout the southern United States, signs that banned African Americans from entering public facilities or required the use of separate water fountains and bathrooms were removed. The act also provided the framework for the passage of voting rights legislation in 1965. Passage of the bill also marked the decline of the Democratic Party in the South, as conservative southerners switched to the Republican Party.

Subsequent Events Provisions requiring equal employment opportunities caused controversy during the 1970's and 1980's. Proponents argued that the 1964 act demanded affirmative action, while critics argued that this interpretation went beyond the boundaries defined in the act. During the 1960's, the federal government was slow to enforce the section in the law that banned gender discrimination. However, during the 1970's, amendments to that section provided feminists with powerful legal tools to combat discrimination against women.

Additional Information Charles and Barbara Whalen detail the legislative battles surrounding passage of the act in *The Longest Debate: A Legislative History of the 1964 Civil Rights Act* (1985), as does Robert D. Loevy in his *To End All Segregation: The Politics of the Passage of the Civil Rights Act of 1964* (1990). Loevy also edited *The Civil Rights Act of 1964: The Passage of the Law That Ended Racial Segregation* (1997). Hugh Davis Graham provides an overview of federal civil rights activities in *The Civil Rights Era: Origins and Development of National Policy, 1960-1972* (1990). Denton L. Watson profiles an important behind-the-scenes lobbyist in *Lion in the Lobby: Clarence Mitchell, Jr.'s Struggle for the Passage of Civil Rights Legislation* (1990).

Thomas Clarkin

See also Birmingham March; Civil Rights Act of 1968; Civil Rights Movement; Dirksen, Everett; King, Martin Luther, Jr.; March on Washington; Voting Rights Legislation.

■ Civil Rights Act of 1968

Sometimes called the Fair Housing Act or "Indian Bill of Rights." This federal legislation, somewhat of an omnibus bill, includes provisions dealing with riots, rights of American Indians, fair housing, and civil disorders.

Following the passage of civil rights legislation in 1960, 1964, and 1965, the Reverend Martin Luther King, Jr., leader of the Southern Christian Leadership Conference, led demonstrations in Chicago in 1966 pushing for a federal law to prohibit discrimination in housing—a practice that knew no regional or geographic boundaries in the United States. Banks, real estate agents, sales agents, and landlords had routinely discriminated against minorities in the sale and rental of housing units and the granting of home loans for many years. Throughout the nation, certain neighborhoods were designated as minority housing areas in a practice known as "redlining," making it difficult for minorities to obtain housing outside these specified districts.

Proponents of national fair housing standards included King, President Lyndon B. Johnson, the National Association for the Advancement of Colored People (NAACP), liberal Democrats in the Senate, and civil rights activists. Opposition to such legislation was widespread and included many southern Republicans, private citizens, real estate agents, bankers, and landlords. They believed that because houses and apartments were privately owned, the owners were entitled to determine who rented or purchased housing and in what neighborhoods. To appease this considerable opposition, certain types of houses and apartments were exempted; however, the law still covered about 80 percent of the nation's housing units.

To secure passage of the fair housing provision, supporters accepted the inclusion of a section that made it a crime to cross state lines in order to incite a "riot." This antiriot section was designed to control political activists, particularly those associated with the Black Power movement, which some people held responsible for the race riots in many cities across the country in the late 1960's.

When legislators realized that Native Americans were not specifically covered by any of the previously passed civil rights legislation, they decided to include them in this law. The 1968 Civil Rights Act extended the federal Bill of Rights and previously passed civil rights legislation to Native Americans who lived on reservations. Non-Indians enthusiastically supported these provisions, but many Native Americans viewed the Indian Bill of Rights with suspicion because they feared that additional federal legislation could interfere with traditional tribal customs and even undermine claims of tribal sovereignty.

In the Senate, Minority Leader Everett Dirksen, in exchange for some minor modifications of the bill, helped prevent a filibuster by southern senators and enabled the bill to pass the Senate on March 11, 1968. King's assassination on April 4 created support for the bill, which passed the House of Representatives and was signed into law on April 11.

Impact The Civil Rights Act of 1968 outlawed discrimination on the basis of race, religion, or national origin in the sale, rental, advertising, and financing of housing. Although hard to enforce, the act led to the passage of more specific and stricter federal housing legislation in the 1970's. The provisions regarding Native Americans did not harm their claims of tribal sovereignty and led to more legislation for Indians during the presidency of Richard M. Nixon. The antiriot section initially calmed many Americans' fears of additional race riots, although it seemed unnecessary as the nation's attention turned to concerns about the Vietnam War.

Additional Information *Federal Civil Rights Acts* (1994), by Rodney A. Smolla and Chester James Antieau, discusses the politics of passing the bill and sets the law within its historical context.

Maureen K. Mulligan

See also American Indian Civil Rights Act of 1968; Civil Rights Act of 1960, Civil Rights Act of 1964; Civil Rights Movement; Housing Laws, Federal.

■ Civil Rights Movement

The quest by African Americans to achieve legal equality and fair treatment from the mainstream American society. The Civil Rights movement achieved landmark success, even inspiring political action on the part of other minorities, before fragmenting in the late 1960's.

African Americans have a long history of oppression, dating from when they were first brought to the United States. Through churches, community organizations, and the National Association for the Advancement of Colored People (NAACP), established in 1910, they had waged formal and informal struggles against racism and legal discrimination. By 1940, lawsuits supported by the NAACP had begun to overturn racial discrimination in higher education, and in 1954, the Supreme Court ruled against segregation in public schools in *Brown v. Board of Education of Topeka, Kansas*. A successful boycott in Montgomery, Alabama, from 1955 to 1956 curbed discrimination by bus companies in southern communities. In the face of massive and violent resistance from many southern whites, organizations such as the Southern Christian Leadership Conference (SCLC), the Congress of Racial Equality (CORE), and the NAACP increasingly called for help from the federal government in combating private and state-sponsored discrimination.

At the beginning of the 1960's, civil rights activists focused on getting the federal government to help remove legal obstacles to African Americans' full participation in society. Signs of their success were soon evident. At the start of the decade, Congress passed the Civil Rights Act of 1960, which strengthened the ability of the Department of Justice to investigate and act on cases involving the denial of voting rights. In the fall of that year, voters elected Democrat John F. Kennedy to the presidency. Kennedy was generally viewed as supportive of the Civil Rights movement and often met with civil rights leaders to find solutions to the problems of racial discrimination.

Desegregation Despite some political support for the movement, it was civil rights activists, not politicians, who propelled the movement forward. African American college students, many of whom had affiliated themselves with the Student Nonviolent Coordinating Committee (SNCC), began a series of protests that highlighted racial discrimination and forced authorities to remedy the situation. On February 1, 1960, students from North Carolina Agricultural and Technical College, a historically African American institution, sat down at a lunch counter in Greensboro, North Carolina, and demanded to be served, although seating by law and custom was reserved for whites. These peaceful sit-ins were in keeping with the philosophy of nonviolent confrontation behind much of the Civil Rights movement. Sit-ins proliferated across the Deep South, and many participants were arrested for disorderly conduct and trespassing. A few were beaten. The sit-ins

Thirty African Americans protesting racial segregation kneel and pray on the sidewalk on their way to the city hall in Birmingham, Alabama, in April, 1963. The demonstrators were arrested minutes later. Nonviolent protests such as this prayer march were typical of the early civil rights movement. (Library of Congress)

proved successful in achieving desegregation because white southerners could offer no compelling reason for denying African Americans the right to eat at a lunch counter or use a public library.

In 1961, an interracial group of students led by James Farmer, director of CORE, rode buses from Washington, D.C., toward New Orleans to test whether the federal government would enforce existing laws forbidding racial discrimination against passengers in interstate transport. After the buses entered Alabama, Freedom Riders endured beatings and the torching of one of their buses by the Ku Klux Klan (aided by local law enforcement) near Anniston and in Birmingham. The federal government sent four hundred federal marshals to protect the Freedom Riders upon their arrival in Montgomery. Many of the civil rights protests, though nonviolent in nature, precipitated an excessive response on the part of southern whites or the local or state government. These violent responses, often televised, brought the problems of discrimination to the attention of Americans throughout the nation and created widespread support for change.

In response to the violence in Alabama and several other episodes, Congress passed the Civil Rights Act of 1964, which made racial discrimination in businesses engaged in interstate commerce—which included nearly all lunch counters—illegal. The act also forbade discrimination because of race or gender in hiring and limited the ability of states to interfere with voting rights.

Voting Rights With support from the federal government, the University of Mississippi and the University of Alabama were desegregated, in 1962 and 1963 respectively, despite the opposition of state authorities. Further backlash against the Civil Rights movement, including police brutality toward protesters in the Birmingham march in 1963, demonstrated that the federal government had to find ways to ensure that state and local governments complied with federal law. It, therefore, had to find ways to compel southern states to permit duly qualified African Americans to vote.

During the early 1960's, CORE and the NAACP had conducted voter registration drives with mixed results. Freedom Summer (1964), an attempt to register African American voters in Mississippi, led directly to the murder of three civil rights workers—Michael Schwerner and Andrew Goodman, both

white, and African American James Chaney—in Neshoba County by a group of white men, including members of the Ku Klux Klan. At the 1964 Democratic National Convention, Fannie Lou Hamer challenged the party's seating of an all-white Mississippi delegation, and her riveting testimony offered clear proof that African Americans could not achieve meaningful civil rights if the vote was systematically denied them by southern states. In Mississippi, 64 percent of the voting-age population was African American, but African Americans made up only 9 percent of the registered voters. In 1965, the Reverend Martin Luther King, Jr., led a protest march from Selma to Montgomery, Alabama. State troopers beat and teargassed marchers, but after several starts, the march was completed. The march, which was widely televised, led to the passing of the Voting Rights Act of 1965, which empowered the federal government to register African American voters where their attempts to register were thwarted by whites and outlawed various voter tests designed to disqualify African Americans. Armed with this legislation, African Americans began voting in greater numbers, slowly gaining a voice in government.

The Birth of Black Power Until 1965, the Civil Rights movement was led by African Americans but enjoyed much white support. It concentrated on improving conditions in the former Confederate states and followed a policy of nonviolence in achieving the goals of desegregation and equality before the law. The zenith of this phase of the movement was the 1963 March on Washington, which ended with a speech delivered by King to a multiracial audience. King described his dream for a racially integrated society in which people's worth was based on their character and not the color of their skin.

By 1965, the Civil Rights movement had spread from the South into the cities of the North and West, where racial prejudice expressed itself in custom rather than in law. In the Watts section of Los Angeles in August of that year, young African Americans rioted in response to the economic destitution and pervasive discrimination they faced, burning down buildings, especially those belonging to white absentee landlords.

Although African Americans who lived outside the Deep South had long battled discrimination, their task in the 1960's was especially difficult. Attitudes that compel discriminatory behavior are less susceptible to legal remedy than racist practices prescribed by law. The coming-of-age of the baby boomers compounded the difficulty. Young African Americans seemed less willing to endure low wages, discriminatory hiring practices, and substandard housing; they demanded immediate change. Many of them rejected the nonviolent philosophy of King and the SCLC. Their cry was "black power," and it assumed a variety of intellectual and institutional forms. Led by Stokely Carmichael, SNCC embraced black power and encouraged African Americans to topple the white power structure rather than integrate it. Organizations such as the Black Panthers patrolled the streets of Oakland, California, protecting African Americans from police brutality while offering courses in African American history, operating antidrug campaigns, and offering free food for the poor. The concept of black power was heavily influenced by the ideas of Marcus Garvey, a Jamaican Black Nationalist who early in the twentieth century encouraged African Americans to start businesses and become independent of whites, and those of Nation of Islam leaders Elijah Muhammad and Malcolm X, who encouraged spiritual liberation and autonomy from white culture. The Black Power movement fostered feelings of cultural pride in many African Americans, who expressed preference for African names, religions, and fashions, rejecting many white norms outright. However, black power cost the Civil Rights movement the support of middle-class whites, who associated black power with riots, violence, and rejection of common values. They based their feelings in part on the rhetoric of the movement. Black power advocate Carmichael had said, "When you talk about black power, you talk of building a movement that will smash everything Western civilization has created." Many whites associated Carmichael's statement with racial violence such as the riot that took place in Detroit, Michigan, in the summer of 1967, which left forty-three people dead, two thousand wounded, and five thousand homeless.

The Civil Rights movement also collided with the reality of the Vietnam War, which created in its own way a debate about the values and mission of the United States. African American leaders became alarmed at the high percentage of blacks being killed in Vietnam; they challenged the assumption that African Americans should support what they viewed as an imperialist war while African Americans

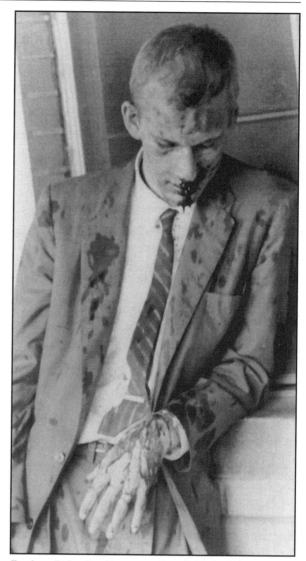

Freedom Rider Jim Zwerg was beaten at the bus station in Montgomery, Alabama, on May 20, 1961. Many sympathetic white Americans participated in the early Civil Rights movement. (AP/Wide World Photos)

were being victimized by white imperialism in their own country.

A Year of Change The white backlash expressed itself in the presidential election of 1968, which Richard M. Nixon won with promises of law and order and a curbing of federal involvement in civil rights. In reality, though, federal laws and court decisions continued to remove obstacles to African American participation in American society. In March, 1968, Congress had passed the Civil Rights

Act of 1968, which outlawed racial discrimination in rental housing. In 1969, the Supreme Court compelled the immediate desegregation of many school districts in the Deep South that had managed through legal maneuvering to avoid complying with earlier rulings to integrate. Congressional legislation, Title VII of the Civil Rights Act of 1964, had created the concept of affirmative action (moves designed to redress the effects of past discrimination), and by the end of the decade, many states and private employers were experimenting with implementation programs.

Just as the rise of black power in 1965 marked a critical time for the Civil Rights movement, the year 1968 was also crucial. In April, King was murdered by James Earl Ray in Memphis, Tennessee, an episode that led to further rioting throughout the United States and deprived African Americans of a powerful leader with a hopeful vision. In June, Robert F. Kennedy, a candidate for the Democratic Party presidential nomination, was assassinated. Many people viewed Kennedy as the last politician of national stature in his generation who could speak successfully across the abyss of race in the United States. His attitude contrasted sharply with that of George Wallace, an Independent Party candidate who rallied many working-class voters to his thinly veiled platform of white supremacy in an unsuccessful bid for the presidency in 1968.

By the end of the 1960's, African Americans had become divided along intellectual and economic lines concerning civil rights. As jobs fled the inner city, many African Americans became mired in poverty and contemptuous of behaviors associated with capitalism. Some of these people joined blacks who were calling for radical reorganization of society and revolution. Others, mostly African American professionals who had achieved some level of success within the system, followed the mainstream of the Civil Rights movement and sought redress through the political process. By 1976, more than eighteen hundred African Americans had been elected to public office.

Impact The Civil Rights movement profoundly changed the United States. It ended legal segregation by race, broke the monopoly on political power enjoyed by southern whites, and forced the federal government to become the guardian of the civil rights of its citizens. The movement initiated a sig-nificant dialogue on race within the United States and discussion about the mission and meaning of the nation. Its inability to bring about total racial equality, however, highlighted the limitations of legislating change. The power of the Civil Rights movement diminished in the late 1960's after the multiracial coalition supporting the movement dissolved and it became apparent that the movement's achievements had failed to halt the economic decline of the inner city.

Subsequent Events Inspired by the Civil Rights movement, Native Americans, women, Mexican Americans, and other minority groups launched their own movements for liberation, reform, and equality, often following the example of either King's nonviolence or Carmichael's black power. During the 1970's, the Civil Rights movement pursued its aims through voting and educational rights suits and through plans for affirmative action in hiring and promotion. In 1980, many white voters who had recoiled at the black power demonstrations in the mid-1960's voted for Ronald Reagan for president.

Additional Information The best study of the Civil Rights movement in context is *From Slavery to Freedom* (1994), by John Hope Franklin and Alfred A. Moss. David Garrow's *Bearing the Cross* (1986) is a thorough and readable volume on King and the SCLC. *The Black Panthers Speak* (1970), edited by Philip S. Foner, provides essays by the members of this group. John White's *Black Leadership in America* (1990) traces the competing strategies for achieving African American equality from slavery to the 1990's. J. Harvie Wilkinson's *From "Brown" to "Bakke"* (1979) offers a good summary and discussion of affirmative action.

Edward R. Crowther

See also Assassinations of John and Robert Kennedy and Martin Luther King, Jr.; "Black Manifesto"; Black Power; Carmichael, Stokely; Chicago Riots; Civil Rights Act of 1960; Civil Rights Act of 1964; Civil Rights Act of 1968; Congress of Racial Equality (CORE); Detroit Riot; Freedom Rides; Freedom Summer; Kennedy, John F.; King, Martin Luther, Jr.; March on Selma; March on Washington; New York Riots; Newark Riots; Presidential Election of 1968; Schwerner, Goodman, and Chaney Deaths; Sit-ins; Southern Christian Leadership Conference (SCLC); Student Nonviolent Coordinating Committee (SNCC); Voting Rights Legislation; Washington, D.C., Riots; Watts Riot.

*Eldridge Cleaver, minister of information for the Black Panther Party, helped make millions of Americans aware of the Black Panthers'
cause and of the Black Power movement.* (AP/Wide World Photos)

■ Cleaver, Eldridge

Born August 31, 1935, Wabbaseka, Arkansas
Died May 1, 1998, Pomona, California

*A famous proponent of black power and a leader of the Black
Panther Party. Cleaver was an outspoken critic of American
society and one of the most visible African American radicals of the 1960's.*

Early Life A native of Arkansas, Leroy Eldridge
Cleaver and his family joined the exodus of African
Americans from the South during World War II. In
the 1940's, thousands of migrants moved to California in search of lucrative industrial jobs in the shipyards and aircraft factories. Like many other young
African Americans who left the South for the West,
Cleaver found that the promise of upward mobility
was a myth, and he joined the swelling ranks of
alienated youths in the inner-city ghettos of San
Francisco, Oakland, and Los Angeles.

The 1960's Cleaver spent much of the early 1960's
in the California state prison system for assault and
attempted rape of a white nurse. He briefly joined
the Nation of Islam and became an adherent of Malcolm X while he was in prison, and he began to develop his own radical, black nationalist ideology, expressing himself in essays that were published as *Soul
on Ice* in 1968, two years after his parole. The book, a
central document in the black power era, quickly became a best-seller and launched his career as a writer.
Cleaver, a San Francisco resident, also became a
leading figure in that city's growing Black Arts movement. With the assistance of white radicals, he established the city's Black House, which became a center
for radical plays and performances and attracted
such African American literary stars as the revolutionary playwright LeRoi Jones (Amiri Baraka).

In 1967, Cleaver joined the Black Panther Party,
became its minister of information, and began to
edit its weekly paper, *The Black Panther*. He helped

publicize the Black Panthers' activities, and while Huey P. Newton was in prison for allegedly killing a police officer, Cleaver assumed control of the group. He engineered a coalition with the radical Peace and Freedom Party and ran for president as the party's candidate in 1968. To avoid imprisonment after an April, 1968, shoot-out with police, in 1969, Cleaver fled to Algeria, where he established the international office of the Black Panther Party.

Later Life In the 1970's, Cleaver and Newton disagreed over the future of the Black Panthers, and their conflict split the party. Cleaver advocated preparing for more violent confrontations with the police and denounced the Black Panthers' efforts to create its Community Survival Programs and its forays into electoral politics in Oakland. He returned to the United States in November, 1975, to face parole violations and became a born-again Christian while in prison. He was released in August, 1976, and renounced his former radicalism. During the 1980's, he supported conservative Republican politicians, including his former foe, Ronald Reagan, and environmentalist causes.

Impact Cleaver helped bring the Black Panthers into the nation's spotlight and personified the collective rage of many young African Americans in the late 1960's. As the voice of the most militant strain of the Black Power movement, Cleaver demonstrated the power and danger of radical black nationalist thought.

Additional Information Cleaver published an autobiography, *Soul on Fire*, in 1978. In 1989, Kathleen Rout published a biography of Cleaver entitled *Eldridge Cleaver*.

Daniel E. Crowe

See also Black Panthers; Black Power; Malcolm X; Nation of Islam.

■ Cold War

The Cold War was an extended period of tension between two world powers, the United States and the Soviet Union, that threatened to erupt into a worldwide nuclear catastrophe.

The Cold War, which began as early as 1917 and intensified after 1945, reached a peak in the early 1960's. Its causes were multiple and controversial. Some historians place the blame on U.S. expansion

after 1945, others on Marxist ideology and the Soviet Union's traditional insecurity. By 1960, the Soviet Union and the United States were nuclear powers and leaders of alliances that represented conflicting worldviews.

Berlin In May, 1960, U.S. president Dwight D. Eisenhower attended a summit meeting with Soviet premier Nikita Khrushchev, who renewed pressure on the Western powers to leave West Berlin. However, the discussions collapsed at the outset when a U.S. U-2 reconnaissance plane piloted by Gary Powers was shot down over Soviet territory and Eisenhower refused to apologize. At the next summit in Vienna in June, 1961, Khrushchev tried to bully the newly elected President John F. Kennedy, whom he believed to be weak. Once again, the meetings failed to settle the Berlin issue, and in August, the East Germans erected the Berlin Wall to stem the flow of emigrants to the West.

Bay of Pigs While Eisenhower was still in office, a crisis developed in Cuba. After the 1959 revolution, Cuban leader Fidel Castro announced that he was a Marxist-Leninist and would align his country with the Soviet Union. Increasing difficulties between the United States and Castro's revolutionary state persuaded Eisenhower to break off diplomatic relations with Cuba in January, 1961. The Central Intelligence Agency began training antirevolutionary Cuban exiles for a possible invasion of the island, and the invasion was approved by Eisenhower's successor, Kennedy.

On April 17, 1961, an exile force of about thirteen hundred, armed with U.S. weapons, landed at the Bay of Pigs on the southern coast of Cuba. The popular support that the invaders believed would greet their efforts did not materialize; they were unable to cross the island to Havana and were overwhelmed by the Cuban army. President Kennedy chose not to deploy the U.S. Air Force against the Cubans, and two days later, the episode was over. Ninety exiles had been killed and a great many taken prisoner. Private groups in the United States later ransomed the prisoners. Castro naturally became wary of the United States and was certain that another attempt to overthrow him was being planned, this time with direct governmental involvement. This fear of a U.S. invasion prompted the next major crisis eighteen months later when Soviet missiles were installed in Cuba.

In May, 1960, a U-2 spy plane like this one at the Strategic Air Command Museum in Nebraska crash-landed during a reconnaissance mission over the Soviet Union. (McCrea Adams)

Cuban Missile Crisis The Soviet decision to deploy the missiles stemmed in part from the Kremlin's insecurities. Khrushchev, aware that the United States had missiles in Turkey just 150 miles from the Soviet border, feared a nuclear first strike by the United States. The Soviet premier was looking for a way to counter the United States' lead in the arms race, and Cuba was only 90 miles off the coast of Florida. In late April, 1962, Soviet premier Khrushchev conceived the idea of placing intermediate-range missiles in Cuba. A deployment in Cuba would double the Soviet strategic arsenal and deter any U.S. plans to attack either the Soviet Union or Cuba. Castro approved of Khrushchev's plan, and in summer, 1962, Soviet military technicians worked furiously but secretly to erect the missile installations in Cuba.

For the United States, the crisis began on October 15, 1962, when reconnaissance photographs revealed Soviet missiles under construction in Cuba. President Kennedy immediately organized an emer-

gency committee of twelve of his closest advisers to handle the crisis. Following seven days of intense debate within this committee, Kennedy gave the order to impose a naval quarantine around Cuba to prevent the arrival of more Soviet offensive weapons on the island. On October 22, Kennedy informed the nation about the missile installations and the quarantine. He also proclaimed that any nuclear missile launched from Cuba would be regarded as a Soviet attack on the United States and demanded that the Soviets remove all of their offensive weapons from Cuba.

Tensions rose dramatically on both sides. Kennedy ordered low-level reconnaissance missions once every two hours over the coastal waters. On October 25, Kennedy raised military readiness. The next day, the emergency committee received a letter from Khrushchev, who proposed removing Soviet missiles and personnel if the United States would guarantee not to invade Cuba. A U.S. U-2 spy plane was shot down over Cuba on October 27, and the United States received a second letter from Khrushchev demanding the removal of U.S. missiles in Turkey in exchange for the removal of Soviet missiles in Cuba. The United States decided to ignore the second letter and notified Soviet ambassador Anatoly Dobrynin of the president's assent to the first letter.

The worst of the crisis was over when, on October 28, Khrushchev announced that he would dismantle the installations and return the missiles to the Soviet Union, expressing his trust that the United States would cancel plans to invade Cuba. Further negotiations were held to implement the October 28 agreement, which included a U.S. demand that Soviet light bombers be removed from Cuba and the exact form and conditions of United States' assurances not to invade Cuba.

Officials of the superpowers were still working out the difficult terms of a formal agreement when Cas-

tro, feeling betrayed by Khrushchev, tried to halt the removal and inspection of the missile sites. Pressure from the United Nations (UN) compelled the Cuban leader to acquiesce and allow a UN inspection team to monitor removal of the missiles and demolition of the missile bases. The Soviet navy shipped the missiles back to the Soviet Union under the watchful eye of U.S. reconnaissance planes whose pilots counted the missiles to make sure that all had been removed. By November 20, the Soviet light bombers had been dismantled and returned to the Soviet Union. On November 21, Kennedy formally ended the quarantine and lowered the status of military readiness.

Many people felt that the world had been one step away from nuclear war. If war had broken out, casualties on both sides would have been high. The military analysts had grossly underestimated Soviet

At the White House in October, 1962, President John F. Kennedy (right) and his brother, Attorney General Robert F. Kennedy, discuss developments in the Cuban Missile Crisis, a pivotal point in Soviet-U.S. relations. (AP/Wide World Photos)

and Cuban forces. Military intelligence calculated 10,000 Soviet troops on the island plus an additional 100,000 Cubans. The actual numbers were 43,000 and 270,000, respectively. Plans for the U.S. invasion had called for an amphibious landing of only 180,000 troops. Kennedy's emergency committee also knew nothing about the Soviet tactical nuclear weapons positioned along Cuba's shore. Had they been deployed, the United States would have had no choice but to retaliate, probably against Soviet territory.

Partial Détente The Cuban Missile Crisis was complicated by the lack of a reliable form of communication between the United States and the Soviet Union. Both governments realized that the time it took to transmit a message between Washington, D.C., and Moscow—up to seven hours—could create misunderstandings. They created a "hot line" between the Kremlin and the White House, allowing the two world leaders to communicate immediately.

Nine months after the crisis ended, in summer, 1963, Kennedy and Khrushchev signed an agreement to ban nuclear testing in the atmosphere, the Nuclear Test Ban Treaty. This marked the beginning of what seemed to be a new willingness to cooperate and communicate. However, on November 22, 1963, President Kennedy was assassinated in Dallas, Texas. Eleven months later, Premier Khrushchev was removed from office by Communist opponents in the party's central committee. Numerous talks through the remainder of the decade between their successors, Lyndon B. Johnson and Leonid Brezhnev, failed to result in agreements to limit nuclear warheads.

The Superpowers and the Third World The Cold War extended to the colonial world as the Soviet Union and China argued persuasively to the Third World that Marxism was the only true road to independence. In the early 1960's, the United States, heir to French administrators in former Indochina after 1954, began to have difficulties preserving South Vietnam from northern insurgents and communist nationalists in the South. Kennedy accepted Eisenhower's fear that the loss of South Vietnam would act as the domino that would fall on the other states of Southeast Asia; hence he upped his military support to Ngo Dinh Diem, president of South Vietnam. When his generals thought that Diem was looking to find a compromise with Hanoi, they sought U.S. support for a *coup d'état* that toppled

Diem from power on November 1, 1963. Soon, Moscow became apprehensive after the United States launched strikes against North Vietnamese forces on August 5, 1964, in retaliation for the alleged North Vietnamese attacks on U.S. destroyers in the Gulf of Tonkin. However, the Soviet Union refrained from direct involvement in the war in Southeast Asia although the United States became an active participant there. The Soviet Union sent military supplies to the communist forces in that theater and used its presence in the United Nations to forcefully denounce U.S. actions in Southeast Asia but fell short of sending troops to that region. Harsh rhetoric, combined with this measured response, was condemned by the Chinese as insufficient, and the Chinese continued to promote wars of national liberation, partly to embarrass the Soviets. Chairman Alexei Kosygin of the Soviet Union continued to seek a diplomatic solution to the Vietnam crisis, even if it would allow the United States to save face, much to the consternation of Beijing. Although China hoped to direct the foreign policies of North Vietnam, Soviet influence would predominate.

In another triangular Cold War crisis in the Third World, China came out on the losing side. President Akhmed Sukarno of Indonesia had been courted by both Moscow and Peking for many years, playing off overtures from Washington, D.C. In the early 1960's, U.S. Information Agency offices in Djakarta were burned on a number of occasions, and Sukarno even went to Moscow to receive the coveted Lenin Prize. However, Moscow was disappointed at the failure of the Indonesian leader to invest Soviet money in industries, as he had promised, and bad relations ensued. China urged Sukarno to oust his noncommunist generals, and when he took that advice, it backfired. In the autumn of 1965, Sukarno was reduced to the status of a figurehead in Djakarta. Both Washington and Moscow were relieved, and Peking was angry.

In another part of the world, Moscow's policy of clientage failed. For many years, the Soviets had courted the Arab states in the Middle East against the U.S.-backed state of Israel. They offered symbolic aid by sending the Soviet fleet to the Mediterranean Sea to offset the intimidation of the U.S. Sixth Fleet. However, that simply emboldened Egypt to attempt riskier undertakings; it refused to heed Moscow's warnings not to blockade the Gulf of Aqaba. When Israel easily won the Six-Day War in

1967, it was an embarrassment to Moscow as well as an expense.

However, the more diplomatic position of Moscow in Vietnam and elsewhere in the Third World was enhancing the Kremlin's image as a normal, peaceful society in contrast to the irrationality of China and the irresponsibility of the United States. This would change in 1968.

Eastern Europe By the end of the decade, the Soviet Union had achieved nuclear parity with the United States, but the economic success of the West was beginning to erode the commitment of Eastern European nations to the restrictive policies of the Council for Mutual Economic Assistance, the Soviet economic plan for Eastern Europe. Czechoslovakia was a case in point. The Czechoslovak communist government showed genuine signs of increasing economic cooperation with its Western neighbors and, more dangerous to Moscow, was strictly limiting the activities of the Soviet secret police in its country. Alexander Dubcek was appointed first secretary of the Czechoslovak Communist Party but showed no inclination to stem the tide of economic and political reforms. Moscow began to fear that the Czechoslovaks might leave the Warsaw Pact when it became clear that Soviet nuclear installations there could not be protected by the Red armies. Soviet troops were based in East Germany, Poland, and Hungary but were as yet unwelcome in Czechoslovakia. Using a letter from several members of the Czech Communist Party's central committee requesting that Premier Brezhnev intervene on their behalf as an excuse, the Soviets sent troops into Prague on August 21, 1968, to restore a more conventional communist regime there, one much more agreeable to Soviet interests. Although the casualties were light (about one hundred deaths), the reforms ended, and the Red armies were allowed to stay. Western powers denounced this invasion as old-style imperialism but felt that the threat of nuclear confrontation made more direct responses inappropriate.

Earlier, in February, 1963, the Romanian government had partly separated itself from Soviet economic goals. The nation remained economically independent throughout the decade and startled Moscow when it allowed state exchanges with the U.S. government in 1969 and 1970. Nevertheless, Premier Nicolai Ceaucescu fully supported Soviet foreign policies (except for the invasion of Prague)

and maintained strict Communist controls over his own society.

Impact Despite the crises in Vietnam and Czechoslovakia, the decade ended with the Cold War somewhat less "cold" than when Kennedy and Khrushchev confronted each other in 1961 and 1962. In 1968, most of the world states subscribed to the nonproliferation treaty, a restriction of nuclear powers that helped ease fears regarding the likelihood of nuclear war. The Berlin issue was moribund because the new German chancellor, Willi Brandt, was initiating his own détente with the Soviet Union. The immediate threat to the Soviet Union was a series of border skirmishes along its borders with China. The Vietnam War was still a source of much aggravation in Moscow but was a much bigger problem for the United States as the war spread into Laos and the stepped-up firepower of U.S. aircraft failed to achieve the results expected by President Richard M. Nixon. Meanwhile the Soviet Union had spent considerable money to support Arab states in the Middle East against their technically superior rival, Israel, backed by the United States.

Subsequent Events President Nixon ended the military involvement of the United States in Vietnam by 1973 and made an historic trip to Moscow to promote détente. However, the Soviets invaded Afghanistan in December, 1979, reviving the arms race and Cold War until the advent of the government of Mikhail Gorbachev in 1985. Gorbachev's liberal policies brought an end to the Soviet Union by 1992.

Additional Information *Anglo-American Defense Relations 1939-1980: The Special Relationship* (1984) is a study of the Cold War by John Baylis, one of the top scholars on the topic. Notable books about the Cold War include Michael L. Dockrill's *The Cold War, 1945-1963* (1988); John Lewis Gaddis's *Strategies of Containment: A Critical Appraisal of Post War American Security Policy* (1982); Walter La Feber's *America, Russia, and the Cold War, 1945-1980* (1991); and Adam B. Ulam's *Expansion and Coexistence: Soviet Foreign Policy Since World War II* (1935).

John D. Windhausen

See also Bay of Pigs Invasion; Berlin Wall; Castro, Fidel; Cuban Missile Crisis; Czechoslovakia, Soviet Invasion of; Kennedy, John F.; Khrushchev's UN Visit; Nixon, Richard M.; Nuclear Test Ban Treaties; U-2 Spy Plane Incident; Vietnam War.

■ Communes

Intentional communities formed by groups of people who collectively use and own property and share similar interests and objectives. Many people of all ages, ethnicities, and segments of society joined or started communes during the 1960's.

During the nineteenth century, a number of communes, partly inspired by works such as Henry David Thoreau's *Walden* (1854) and Samuel Butler's *Erewhon* (1872), arose in the United States. These included the inspirationists of Amana, the Transcendentalists of Brook Farm, the Rappites of Harmony, the Shakers, and the perfectionists of Oneida. Most of these communes disappeared, though the Shakers linger and the Oneida imprint on silverware bears witness to the success of that group's experiment.

Communes continued to flourish unobtrusively in the twentieth century, but during the 1960's, their numbers and types underwent rapid growth. Communes, which represented a radical break with the existing system and a fairly intense search for something better, began to appeal to many Americans. The search for alternative lifestyles was fueled by the general discontent with the war in Vietnam, the increasing awareness of the failure or shortcomings of existing institutions precipitated by the Civil Rights movement, a rising feminism, and a certain yearning for a simpler life, closer to nature and the land. Between 1965 and 1970, more than two thousand communes came into existence. Some of the better-known communes are Drop City (a rural artist and hippie community established in 1965 near Trinidad, Colorado, whose members lived in geodesic domes incorporating auto parts), The Hog Farm (a hippie commune in New York City), New Buffalo (a hippie commune in Taos, New Mexico), Lama Foundation (a religious community set up by guru Ram Dass in 1967 near Red River, New Mexico), Fort Hill (created by Mel Lyman in Boston in 1966), Twin Oaks (a Skinnerian community founded in 1967 in Virginia), and Harrad West (a group marriage community in California). Some of these communes were more or less inspired by the works of Aldous Huxley, George Orwell, Yevgeny Zamyatin, and B. F. Skinner as well as by the very successful communitarian experiment of Israel's kibbutzim. Generally, these communes enshrined a strong, though loosely articulated, anti-institutional ideology as well as a fervid belief in the possibility of true human solidarity. They also provided opportunities for experiments with different social and familial arrangements.

One such experiment was Harrad West, a six-member community in California that practiced group marriage. Inspiration came in part from Robert H. Rimmer's novel, *The Harrad Experiment* (1966), which held that people can be taught to love more than one person at a time. In this commune, as a concession to the practical needs of three sexually active couples, one chart, revised every two weeks, determined who would sleep with whom on any given night, while another apportioned chores.

One of the most successful larger communes was Twin Oaks, which was based on ideas presented in Skinner's *Walden Two* (1948). It was founded in the summer of 1967 by eight Skinner admirers who leased land in Louisa County, Virginia. By the early 1970's, the commune had forty members, and several buildings had been added to the original house and barns. During the first few years, membership was unstable. Many people came looking simply for a place to live and left unhappy with the group's structure and the rules forbidding drugs and alcohol. Later members, who came because they believed in the value of communitarian life, tended to stay. Income came initially from crops of hay and tobacco, but the commune soon developed a rope hammock industry and a printing press to support itself. Additionally, members worked in Richmond, barely an hour away, and at the University of Virginia at Charlottesville.

Based on Skinner's model, work in this commune was credited according to its difficulty and the degree of interest it held, with credit assignment changing from week to week. Members had to earn a certain number of credits per week and were allowed to accumulate additional credits to be used toward taking a longer vacation than the two weeks given all members. For a long time, the presence of small children created difficulties because it was not clear who bore responsibility for them, the parents or the community at large. Eventually a policy was established modeled on the Israeli kibbutzim. A nursery was built, and a new job of care provider was introduced and appropriately credited.

During the 1960's, interest increased in older, more established communes such as the Bruderhof (a Hutterite offshoot founded in Germany in 1920 and brought to the United States in the 1950's) and the Koinonia Farm (an interracial rural community founded in Georgia in 1942 by Southern Baptist preacher Clarence Jordan). In addition, many people seeking alternative lifestyles turned toward communal religious organizations such as the Hare Krishnas (International Society for Krishna Consciousness), who proselytized actively and inspired strong opposition from the general public.

Most communes founded during the 1960's lasted only a few months or, at most, a couple of years. However, some, such as Twin Oaks, still thrive. The communes that were successful and endured had members who shared strong and firmly held beliefs and deliberately developed a structure that supported and ensured the continuation of those beliefs. While many of the people joining communes during the 1960's shared similar beliefs, the majority of the structures they created failed to support their beliefs in direct and clear ways. This failure is understandable because most of them sought to reform or do away with existing institutions rather than create new ones. In too many cases, this led to the elimination of all structure. Without appropriate structure, beliefs could not be sustained.

Impact The overall impact of the communes of the 1960's on the United States is difficult to assess. The alternative lifestyles practiced in the various communes made them the subject of much criticism. Although the idea of a utopian community appealed to many people, the forms that the communes took were difficult for many to accept.

Many commune members no doubt experienced difficulty in integrating the dream of brotherhood and love with the reality of communal life and became disillusioned with the idea of establishing a paradise on Earth. However, the proliferation of communes during the 1960's kept alive the dream of human solidarity and maintained the consciousness of its possibility.

Subsequent Events In the 1990's, more than 250 communes were known to exist in the United States. Communes remain controversial, and well-publicized incidents involving some religious communes—the legal troubles of Bhagwan Shree Rajneesh and his commune in Oregon in the 1980's and the 1993 deaths of the Branch Davidians in Waco, Texas—indicate the sometimes precarious nature of communal life.

Additional Information The communes of the 1960's are described in detail in *The New Communes* (1971), by Ron E. Roberts.

Ignacio L. Götz

See also Cults; Hippies; Religion and Spirituality.

■ Communications

The collection and distribution of information by the media. The 1960's was a period of marked advances and changes in new coverage, which became instant and massive and affected the nation's values and culture.

The launch by the Soviet Union in October, 1957, of Sputnik, a tiny Earth satellite, also inspired plans to conduct military battles in space and led to the race to the Moon, which was for millions of years the only significant satellite of Earth. In the summer of 1969, Neil A. Armstrong's first steps on the Moon were recorded by a small video camera placed on the steps of the landing craft. An estimated 600 million people on six continents viewed this event on their television sets.

Communications satellites revolutionized telecommunication systems, and despite the great investment required, they cut costs and greatly sped up the transmission of data. Before satellites, it cost $2,000 to transmit half an hour of live television programming from coast to coast in the United States by a terrestrial microwave system. With a satellite, it cost $400. Communication satellites, along with computers, have brought Americans from the wireless age (1900-1970) to the present integrated grid age. The 1960's was the last decade of the era of wireless communication and brought major developments in technology and the dissemination of information.

By the end of 1958, the United States had launched three satellites and broadcast a prerecorded Christmas message from President Dwight D. Eisenhower. In 1962, Bell Laboratories launched Telstar, which provided the first instantaneous retransmission of telephone messages and live television pictures between the United States and Europe. The first geosynchronous satellite, Syncom, launched some twenty-two thousand miles above the equator by the National Aeronautics and Space Administration (NASA) in 1963, permitted the relay of television programs and telephone conversations twenty-four hours a day. In 1962, the Communica-

Number of Newspapers and Radio and Television Stations, 1950-1970

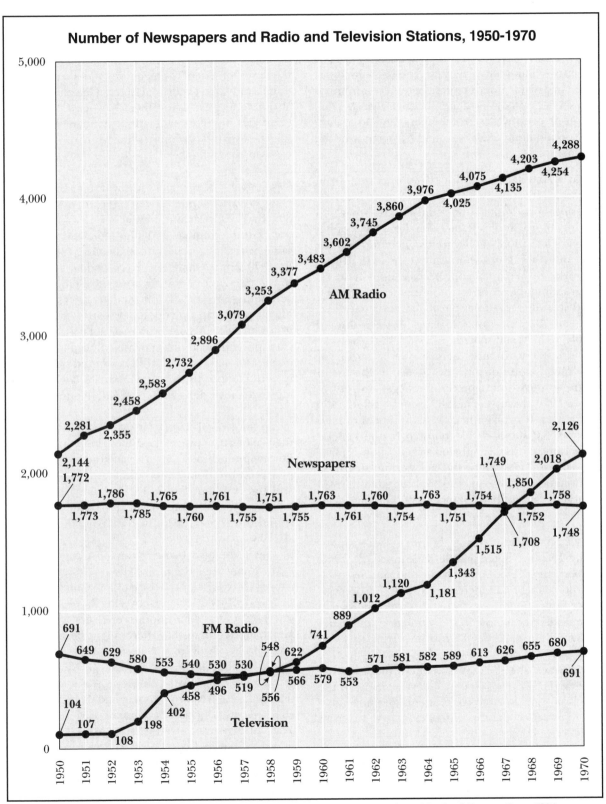

Source: Kurian, George, *Datapedia of the United States, 1790-2000, America Year by Year.* Lanham, Maryland: Bernam Press, 1994.

tions Satellite Corporation (COMSAT) was set up by Congress as a joint venture between the private and public sectors. Early Bird was put into orbit in 1965 by an international cooperative, Intelsat, which was set up to provide international satellite communication services at cost to all member nations. By 1969, sixty-four countries were members, and to ensure U.S. domination, COMSAT held 61 percent of the ownership.

Radio Radio faced continued competition from television. It saved itself by securing more local advertising, abandoning drama and variety shows, and playing more music. Radio also left the evening hours to television and began to concentrate on the early morning hours when Americans were driving to work. Format radio or specialization in music programming such as jazz continued to be developed in order to attract particular audiences. Announcers became disk jockies, who were offered payola, money, and sometimes drugs, by the recording industry to induce them to play a particular recording. Sound quality improved with the use of magnetic recording tape. Profits began to return, and by 1970, there were nearly seven thousand radio stations, up from slightly more than four thousand in 1960. FM stations were boosted by the Federal Communications Commission's (FCC) nonduplication rule in 1965, which did not permit owners of combination AM-FM stations to duplicate their AM content for more than 50 percent of their broadcast day.

Television Cable television did not grow as rapidly in the 1960's as some people had hoped. By 1960, 1.4 percent of U.S. homes had cable, and by 1970, that percentage had increased to only 7.6 percent. Cable flourished in areas where over-the-air signals were weak or nonexistent. It did not move into cities because of the expense of laying underground cable and the FCC's prohibition in 1966 of cable in large markets to foster the development of ultrahigh frequency (UHF) television. The development in the 1960's of transistorized components and new cable materials raised the capacity of cable systems from three to twelve channels.

Telephones Push-button and touch-tone telephone service introduced in 1961 set the stage for a new age in electronic communications. Before the Carter-phone ruling by the FCC in 1968, the American

Telephone and Telegraph Company (AT&T) had not permitted "foreign attachments" to its monopoly of telephone lines. This ruling paved the way for the development of fax machines, mobile telephone units, and answering machines. Consumers were also able to purchase rather than lease telephone hand sets in colors other than standard black and select designer telephones made in the shape of cartoon characters.

Newspapers Newspapers in the 1960's tried to cut rising costs by mergers and adoption of new technology. By 1970, circulation had risen to about 62 million, but the number of dailies remained about the same, with 1,763 dailies in 1960 and 1,748 in 1970. By 1970, approximately 157 chains had 60 percent of the circulation, and 89 percent of cities had no competing newspapers. In the late 1960's, competing morning and afternoon newspapers that desired to lower costs by combining some facilities sought exemption from antitrust prosecution. The Newspaper Preservation Act (1970) permitted newspapers to combine production and circulation while keeping their news departments separate and competitive.

Technological changes in printing brought about the use of offset presses and the demise of hot type. Linotype machines were replaced by cold type, or photocomposition. Fewer employees were needed, and the resultant layoffs led to labor unrest. The nation's longest strike in late 1967 and early 1968 closed the *Detroit News* and the *Detroit Free Press* for 267 days.

The press also turned from just reporting on government and politics to also examining social issues. Since 1900, professional journalists had emphasized objectivity and covering both sides of a story, but in the 1960's, some reporters agreed with Marshall McLuhan that there might be more than two, perhaps even forty, sides to a story. A group of journalists began to experiment with New Journalism, a more subjective writing style. At the same time, much of the reading public had become disenchanted with and critical of established institutions. The underground or alternative press, which published politically liberal news and opinions on cultural topics such as art, music and film, arose to meet their needs. The underground press was irreverent, occasionally outrageous, and not afraid to present a point of view. Dozens of papers flourished; the best known are the *Los Angeles Free Press*, *Village Voice*, *Berkeley Barb*, and the *Rolling Stone*. Some of these papers, such as the *Village Voice*, went above ground, but their major impact was the inclusion of more soft, feature stories in the mainstream newspapers. Even wire services such as the Associated Press and United Press International began to run more stories that gave both facts and an interpretation of those facts.

Impact Despite the efforts of newspapers to adjust to their audience, the 1960's marked a shift by the public from newspapers to television for news. Roper's polls found that by 1961, television had eclipsed newspapers as a source of news. By 1968, television had a two-to-one lead over newspapers. The public seemed to be hungry for news, and in September, 1963, Columbia Broadcasting System (CBS) expanded its evening news on television from fifteen minutes to half an hour. Within days, National Broadcasting Company (NBC) also expanded

its evening news. Several years later, American Broadcasting Company (ABC) went to a half-hour format. The 1960's saw the rise of the anchorman as an air personality. Television news anchors Chet Huntley, David Brinkley, and Walter Cronkite became household names.

The use of videotape rather than film permitted stories to be fed live over telephone lines or satellite rather than being taped and then rebroadcast. News gained in immediacy. In November, 1963, President John F. Kennedy was assassinated. Millions saw Jack Ruby kill Lee Harvey Oswald, the accused assassin, and watched Kennedy's funeral cortege make its way to Arlington Cemetery.

Soon Americans watched the events of the United States' involvement in a distant war in Southeast Asia unfold on their television screens. Popular accounts credit television with bringing the war into living rooms throughout the United States and suggest that viewers then became a catalyst for protest against the Vietnam War. Historians Stanley Karnow

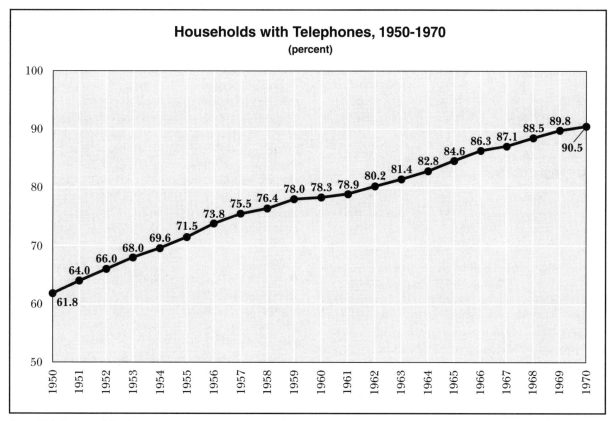

Source: U.S. Bureau of the Census. *Historical Statistics of the United States, Colonial Times to 1970.* New York: Basic Books, 1976.

and David Hallin submit that the role of the press has been exaggerated because the press tended to follow rather than lead public opinion. In the early years of the war, both the press and the public supported U.S. involvement. As criticism of the war mounted at home, the press took a more active role in covering the war.

Subsequent Events Technical developments in rocketry and solid-state electronics during the 1960's led to new communications technologies that enhanced old technologies such as telephones, radio, and television. The 1970's and 1980's made new communication technology available to the consumer. Personal computers, the videocassette recorder, the handheld video camera, and the satellite-receiving dish gave consumers a greater number of choices for information and entertainment. This technology also gave them more control over the production of messages and the scheduling of those messages.

Additional Information *The "Uncensored War": The Media and Vietnam* (1986), by Daniel C. Hallin, discusses the news coverage of this war. *New Media Technology: Cultural and Commercial Perspectives* (1996), by John V. Pavlik, examines the corporate, governmental, and institutional forces that own, operate, and regulate developments in communications.

Fran Hassencahl

See also Computers; Cronkite, Walter; Media; Science and Technology; Telecommunications Satellites; Television; Weather Satellites.

■ Computers

Electronic, programmable devices for storing, retrieving, and processing data. In the 1960's, computers ventured out of research laboratories to fulfill functions in the business world and the daily lives of Americans.

Modern electronic computers emerged in the late 1940's when the Electric Numerical Integrator and Computer (ENIAC) was created and vacuum tubes and internally stored computer programs were developed. The 1950's brought advances such as the transistor and magnetic core memory, both of which made computers smaller and faster, and the debut of the Universal Automatic Computer (UNIVAC).

Hardware and Software The 1960's spans both the second generation of computers, based upon the transistor, and third generation, based upon the integrated circuit (IC). ICs greatly reduced the size and price of computers while immensely increasing their speed and ability. By 1969, computers were thousands of times faster and smaller than they were at the beginning of the decade, and they cost a tenth of their 1960 price.

Computers are operated using programs, which must be written in some sort of computer language. The COmmon Business Oriented Language (COBOL), a high-level, file-oriented language, was the most significant programming language during the decade for several reasons. COBOL was developed by major computer manufacturers and users in an attempt to standardize software, and it supported the needs of business users as opposed to scientists. In addition, it was based on English rather than arithmetic, making it easier to learn and use. In 1965, researchers at Dartmouth College developed Beginner's All-purpose Symbolic Instruction Code (BASIC), a simple, easily learned language that allowed users to interact directly with the computer. In the 1970's, users of personal computers often worked in BASIC.

The many computing inventions in the 1960's included hardware and technological advances such as disk drives, the graphical user interface, the mouse, cache and virtual memory, editing of magnetically stored data, and time sharing (simultaneous use of a mainframe computer by multiple users). Software advances included aircraft navigation systems, computer games, and database programs. Some "personifying" innovations included voice activation and recognition; optical recognition of shapes, handwriting, and typed characters; and a lip-reading device patented by International Business Machines (IBM). Computers were used to generate music and art, translate Chinese and Russian, and convert library card catalogs to electronic form.

Automation As early as the 1950's, many people, concerned about losing their jobs, came to fear computers and automation. In 1961, Bank of America began replacing thousands of bookkeepers with the Electronic Recording Method of Accounting (ERMA). This computer system processed transactions at the rate of 550 checking accounts per minute; a bookkeeper's rate was only 250 accounts per hour. Although the bookkeeping staff was reduced, the total number of employees actually rose as a result of ERMA. Other industries also automated

Computer Milestones

1962	International Business Machines introduces a computer-data storage system that uses disks.
	American Airlines introduces first computerized system for airline reservations.
1963	Digital Equipment Corporation introduces its minicomputer, the PDP-8.
1964	Sara Lee foods opens the first fully automated factory in Deerfield, Illinois.
	Dartmouth College's John Kemeny and Thomas Kurtz develop the first easy-to-use computer programming language, Beginner's All-purpose Symbolic Instruction Code (BASIC).
1965	International Business Machines introduces its System/360 family of business computers, which use integrated circuits.
1969	American engineer Marcian E. Hoff invents the first microprocessor (set of integrated circuits on a single chip).
	Bell Laboratories' Andrew H. Bobeck develops bubble memory, an electronic equivalent of magnetic tape storage.

parts of their systems. By the mid-1960's, newspapers in New York, California, Oklahoma, and Florida had begun to set type by computer, and in San Francisco, planning began for the Bay Area Rapid Transit (BART) system, a passenger train system that was to be operated by computer. In 1964, the Sara Lee foods company created a completely automated factory in which computers controlled product manufacture, storage, retrieval, and preparation for shipping. Although many workers were eliminated because of automation, the process also created jobs, albeit often requiring different skills.

Space and Defense Applications The space race did much to legitimize computers and to fuel the growth of the computer industry. The IC, although developed in the 1950's, was largely unused until the National Aeronautics and Space Administration (NASA) needed small and lightweight computers. In 1964, IBM helped create a small, nearly 100 percent reliable onboard computer guidance system for the Apollo spacecraft, without which a lunar landing would have been impossible. NASA's greatest contribution to computer science was in developing fail-safe software.

The Department of Defense, under the urging of Secretary Robert McNamara, advanced computer technology by investing in research and commissioning computer-enhanced weapons and defense systems including aircraft, communications and intelligence systems, and guided missiles, all for use in the Vietnam War. Although computers strengthened the armed forces, some historians and military personnel blame the loss of the war on the overdependence upon computer technology on the battlefield. Computers also played a large role in the development and use of the Naval Tactical Data System (NTDS), North American Aerospace Defense Command (NORAD), and the Semi-Automatic Ground Environment (SAGE), all of which were expressly developed for fighting the Cold War and winning the arms race.

The computing industry had a major effect on the U.S. economy. Computer sales rose from approximately five hundred million dollars in 1960 to five billion dollars in 1969. The integration of the computer into the economy as a whole steadily increased: The number of computers in use rose from ten thousand in 1960 to one hundred thousand in 1969. U.S. manufacturers dominated the world market, leading several European countries and Japan to intervene to protect their fledgling national industries. The United States, to avoid helping its Cold War adversaries, placed export restrictions on computer technology.

The first patent for a computer, ENIAC, was issued in 1964; however, after legal battles, it was invalidated in 1973. The first computer program was patented in 1968, and the first computer crime, software piracy, was prosecuted that same year. Furthermore, IBM, having settled many antitrust claims and facing more lawsuits, unbundled its systems (separated sales of its software from its hardware), thus allowing other manufacturers to produce products for IBM equipment.

At the beginning of the 1960's, a number of companies were producing computers, many of which had an impact on society. Digital Equipment Corporation (DEC) introduced the first computer with a monitor and keyboard, the PDP-1, and, in 1963, the first minicomputer, the PDP-8, both of which were relatively inexpensive and able to be purchased by many secondary schools and colleges. Secondary schools began teaching computer programming, and colleges established computer science departments. Computer research and higher education soon became inseparable partners. In addition to scientists, scholars and students in fields such as biblical studies, history, folklore, literature, and psychology began using computers in research, and universities began automating their record-keeping systems.

IBM's System/360 series, introduced in 1965, solidified the place of the computer in the business world and IBM's status as the world's leading computer company. At the time, the development of the System/360, which cost more than a billion dollars, was the most expensive research project that had been privately funded. Sales of the System/360 were recordbreaking, tripling IBM's already vast revenue in just a few months. As a result, several large corporations exited the computer manufacturing business, including General Electric and Radio Corporation of America (RCA). The major manufacturer of supercomputers (large-scale scientific computers used primarily by the U.S. government) Control Data Corporation (CDC), created the 6600 and 7600 models in 1966 and 1969 respectively. Designed in part by Seymour Cray, one of the most well-known U.S. computer engineers, these supercomputers were the highest performers and set the standard for such systems.

Impact During the 1960's, developments in hardware and software enabled computers to be used in a wide variety of applications and made them a productive business tool. However, many Americans, some quite correctly, felt that computers would replace them in the workplace. Computers did displace workers and create localized unemployment, but they also created jobs. Other Americans feared that humans were too reliant on computers, and this dependence would result in a diminishment of human initiative, harmful psychological and sociological consequences, decreased personal privacy, and misuse of collected data. In fact, in 1965, the Credit Data Corporation began to track consumers' credit information. In 1966, the federal government proposed the creation of a citizens' personal information data bank; but because of the public outcry, the project never materialized. Stanley Kubrick's film *2001: A Space Odyssey* (1968) contains a well-known segment in which a problem arises because of overreliance on computers. A real life example of overreliance on computers' supposed infallibility was the 1962 failure of the Mariner 1 rocket soon after launch because of the omission of a single hyphen from the computer program.

Subsequent Events A number of important computer technologies were invented in the 1960's but would not become commercially available until later, including the modulator-demodulator (modem), the UNIX mainframe (which would later become the industry standard and form the basis of the Internet), and the use of lasers to encode computer data, which led to the development of the compact disc and CD-ROM.

Additional Information Donald D. Spencer's *Computers in Society* (1974) discusses the impact of computers, and his *Timetable of Computers* (1997) provides a chronology of computer history. Robert Slater's *Portraits in Silicon* (1987) contains biographies of the leading figures in computing history. The magazine *Computer* devoted its October, 1996, issue to computing history.

Beau David Case

See also Apollo Space Program; Arms Race; Cold War; Communications; Lasers; McNamara, Robert; Mariner Space Program; Space Race; *2001: A Space Odyssey*; Vietnam War.

■ Conant Report

Published 1963
Author James Bryant Conant (1893-1978)

A sweeping recommendation for overhauling teacher education. The Conant Report blamed the inadequacies of the prevailing system of teacher education for the many failings of public schools in the United States.

The Work Conant, former Harvard president and professor of chemistry and former ambassador to West Germany, carried out an extensive investigation of U.S. public schools, especially high schools, in the late 1950's and 1960's. He viewed the public school system as the vehicle for producing a meritocracy, a system in which talented people would lead and govern the nation. His preferred structure was the comprehensive high school, which would bring together students from different social backgrounds to participate in a general-education core program. Gifted students would still be permitted to take more heavily academic programs, but vocational programs would be included in the comprehensive high school curriculum rather than offered in separate vocational high schools.

As Conant delved more deeply into conditions in the public schools, primarily the high schools, he became increasingly convinced that the schools' inability to stimulate, encourage, and select the ablest students had its roots in the failings of the prevailing system of teacher education. Conant therefore turned his attention to teacher training.

Armed with a generous grant from the Carnegie Corporation, in 1961, Conant assembled a staff of professional academicians and visited seventy-seven teacher-training institutions in twenty-two states, including church-affiliated colleges, private colleges, state universities, state colleges, and county or municipal colleges. On the basis of these observations, he recommended a sweeping overhaul of the system of teacher education by changing the system in five major ways: certifying teachers; funding student teachers; hiring, paying, and promoting teachers; strengthening requirements for graduating teachers and those who train them; and altering the method of accrediting teacher-training programs. His recommendations were published in 1963 as *The Education of American Teachers*, known informally as the Conant Report.

Impact Conant's proposals were immediately seen as an attack on the state education bureaucracies and on the National Education Association, a reaction he had predicted. However, his report, *The Education of American Teachers*, rapidly became a bestseller and was widely commented on in the press. More than fifty thousand copies were sold within three months, and an additional five thousand complimentary copies were distributed. The report's impact was heightened by public alarm at the seeming inadequacies of U.S. education revealed by the Soviets' ability to place a satellite, Sputnik 1, in orbit in 1957.

Conant's emphasis on general education for teachers of all subjects and on solid academic performance were perceived by progressives in the educational establishment as an attack on their "child-centered" approach. His recommendation of special programs for the academically gifted made him vulnerable to the charge of elitism, though he had long expressed a preference for public over private, especially parochial, schools.

The study provoked much controversy in the educational establishment, but its actual effects appear to have been modest. Those students seeking teacher certification continued to be required to take certain courses, and teacher remuneration continued to be based largely on seniority. Conant's belief in the importance of practical classroom experience did result in more emphasis on practice teaching while future teachers were still in college. Many colleges and universities offering teacher-training programs reevaluated their programs in light of Conant's criticism, but the system of accreditation devised by the National Council for the Accreditation of Teacher Education still dominated, though the group was broadened to include a few more representatives of academic groups.

Education continued to provoke widespread controversy. Almost every decade since the 1960's, some researcher or group has brought to light the poor performance of many products of the U.S. educational system. The poor performance of U.S. students, especially in comparison with Japanese students, in many international tests conducted in the decades that followed the Conant Report's publication indicated that public schools in the United States did not measure up to Conant's ideal. The controversy that arose in the 1990's over school standards suggested that Americans were deeply divided over what public schools should be and do.

Studies showing that African American students in predominantly black schools generally do not perform as well as students in predominantly white suburban schools do, suggest that neither improved teaching training nor additional funds will suffice to bring about fundamental change. The U.S. educational system continues to suffer from the chasm between the ideal, as outlined by Conant, and the reality.

Additional Information A. Harry Passow's *American Secondary Education: The Conant Influence* (1977) summarizes all of Conant's studies of the U.S. educational system. Robert M. Weiss provides a collection of commentaries on the Conant Report, including his own, in *The Conant Controversy in Teacher Education* (1969). Conant's own memoirs, *My Several Lives* (1970), contains one short chapter on his studies of American education as does James Hershberg's biography, *James B. Conant: Harvard to Hiroshima and the Making of the Nuclear Age* (1993).

Nancy M. Gordon

See also Education; School Desegregation; Teacher Strikes.

■ Condon Report

Published 1969
Author Edward U. Condon (1902-1974)

An official United States government report on the existence of unidentified flying objects (UFOs). The investigation concluded that such objects did not exist.

The Work Hundreds of sightings of unidentified flying objects (UFOs) have been reported since the 1940's. One of the first reports was made by a pilot in 1947 who claimed to have seen a formation of "saucerlike" disks over Mount Rainier in the state of Washington. Newspapers coined the term "flying saucer" based on his observations. After several more reported sightings, the United States Air Force began keeping records of the alleged observations; its investigations became known as Project Blue Book. The Air Force compiled information on several hundred UFO incidents from 1952 to 1969. In 1969, however, the secretary of the Air Force terminated the project and no more records were collected. The main reason for ending this project was publication of the Condon Report, formally titled *Scientific Study of Unidentified Flying Objects*. The report

was known by the name of its principal author, Edward U. Condon, a highly regarded physicist at the University of Colorado.

In 1966, Condon and a group of thirty-five other scientists were hired to investigate the sightings collected by Project Blue Book. The Air Force acted after several Congressmen began demanding investigations into strange reports of unusual sightings made by their constituents. The most widely reported sighting came from a sheriff in Ohio who said he had chased a UFO for more than eighty miles across rural roads during the early morning of April 17, 1966. Five other policemen reported witnessing the same object, but the Air Force rejected all their eyewitness accounts.

After much criticism from members of Congress, the Air Force decided to hire a highly regarded group of experts to conduct an unbiased examination of the evidence. Condon was a highly regarded physicist who had taught at Princeton and the University of Minnesota. During World War II, he had worked on the development of radar and the atomic bomb. The committee Condon established included many experts in the fields of astronomy and space travel; however, it met with much criticism and frequent controversy. Condon made very skeptical comments about UFOs that were criticized by people who believed in the existence of UFOs and others who found the chief investigator highly biased. The day after his appointment, Condon told a reporter there was no scientific "evidence that there is advanced life on other planets." After three months of investigations, he told his staff, "It is my inclination right now to recommend that the government get out of this business. My attitude right now is that there's nothing to it, but I'm not supposed to reach a conclusion for another year." These comments convinced many people interested in the investigation that the final report would not be impartial and unbiased.

Despite the criticisms, the Condon committee issued a 1,465-page report on UFOs on schedule in 1969. It was filled with photographs, charts, and diagrams and concluded that no evidence gathered by or submitted to the Air Force had demonstrated conclusively the existence of any extraterrestrial vehicles. The National Academy of Sciences reviewed the evidence in the report and totally agreed with Condon's findings. "Our general conclusion," Condon wrote, "is that nothing has come from the study of UFOs in the past twenty-one years that has added to scientific knowledge. Careful consideration of the record leads us to conclude that further extensive study of UFOs probably cannot be justified in expectation that science will be advanced thereby." The committee said that what people perceived as UFOs were weather balloons reflecting sunlight from high above the earth, strangely shaped and experimental aircraft, or just delusions of people with extremely vivid imaginations.

Some scientists questioned the findings of the report. The investigators acknowledged that about one-third of the ninety cases they studied in detail could not be explained. This high rate of failure piqued the interest of other scientists, including James McDonald, a physicist at the University of Arizona. McDonald reasoned that because one-third of the cases remained unexplained, the committee was wrong in concluding that further study was not needed. The public also had its doubts about the report. A survey of adult Americans done shortly after its appearance showed that 51 percent believed that UFOs were real, not just delusions. And 11 percent said they had actually seen a UFO.

Impact The Air Force agreed with Condon's recommendation and closed Project Blue Book in December, 1969. All documentation regarding the investigations made by the Condon committee was transferred to the National Archives and Records Service in Washington, D.C. The material was made available to the public to help reduce doubts concerning the findings of the investigators. Reports of UFOs continued to be received by the Air Force, but it no longer investigates such sightings. No agency of the U.S. government is presently engaged in such activity.

Subsequent Events In 1997, the Air Force issued a report in response to criticisms that previous reports on UFOs had been biased and had rejected important evidence. In particular, the Air Force dealt with the reported crash of an extraterrestrial aircraft in

The Condon committee investigated numerous sightings of "flying saucers" such as the one shown in this still from a film made in 1959; however, it failed to find evidence of extraterrestrial vehicles. (Archive Photos)

Roswell, New Mexico, in 1947, a well-known episode rejected out of hand in the Condon report. Many people believed that the Air Force had allegedly found debris and dead bodies from the craft and was hiding them in a secret facility. The 1997 report presented undeniable evidence that the debris was the wreckage of a balloon that had been launched by scientists at a nearby military base. The "bodies" picked up by Air Force personnel were actually test dummies from unrelated Air Force crash tests conducted. However, not even this direct evidence swayed some believers in UFOs.

Additional Information J. Allen Hynek's *The UFO Experience* (1972) attempts to understand the view of the believers, and Philip Klass's *UFOs Explained* (1974) is highly critical of the believer's view. The great scientist Carl Sagan provides his appraisal of the evidence in *UFOs: A Scientific Debate* (1974).

Leslie V. Tischauser

See also Unidentified Flying Objects (UFOs).

■ Concorde

The world's first successful supersonic transport aircraft. The Concorde is capable of cruising at twice the speed of sound (approximately 1,350 miles per hour).

Military aircraft had flown at supersonic speeds since the end of World War II, but in the 1960's, France, Britain, the United States, and the Soviet Union were racing to build the first civilian supersonic transport (SST), primarily for purposes of national prestige and commercial advantage.

Believing in the need to share the cost of building such an expensive aircraft, Britain and France signed a treaty on November 29, 1962, for joint development and manufacture of the airplane. The mounting costs of the project, which eventually exceeded $1.5 billion, created constant concern. In 1969, Concorde prototypes flew for the first time, reaching the speed of sound in subsequent tests that year.

Impact The development of the Concorde resulted in a dramatic increase in aeronautical technology, especially in regard to engine development and wing design. It also made possible comfortable, swift flights between North America and Europe. In addition, because of its attendant noise, pollution, and excessive fuel consumption, the aircraft increased environmental awareness in the United States and Britain.

Subsequent Events Regularly scheduled commercial service was inaugurated by British Airways and Air France in 1976. The American version of the SST

Prototypes of the Concorde, the first civilian supersonic transport aircraft, flew in 1969. (AP/Wide World Photos)

was abandoned in 1971, chiefly because Congress, led by Senator William Proxmire of Wisconsin, cut off funds for development, mainly on the grounds of the project's excessive costliness and the aircraft's potentially adverse environmental impact.

Additional Information For an introduction to the complex technology of the Concorde and a brief history of the project, see Brian Calvert's *Flying Concorde* (1982).

David C. Lukowitz

See also Supersonic Jets; Travel.

■ *Confessions of Nat Turner, The*

Published 1967
Author William Styron (1925-   )

A highly controversial novel. This 1960's best-seller furthered a growing split between black and white Americans.

The Work *The Confessions of Nat Turner* begins with Nat Turner, a black preacher, lodged in a jail cell in Jerusalem, Virginia, in 1831. Nat listens as the "confession" he has dictated to Thomas R. Gray, his court-appointed attorney, is read back to him and begins to reflect on his life experience. While he was Samuel Turner's slave, he learned to read and studied the Bible. At age twenty-one, he went to work in Richmond, Virginia, as a carpenter to prepare for the emancipation his master had promised. Unfortunately for Nat, Samuel Turner went bankrupt, selling Nat to the Reverend Mr. Eppes, who agreed to carry out the promised emancipation but instead overworked Nat and then sold him to slave traders. Nat eventually became the property of Thomas Moore and found his disappointment had turned to hate. At the same time, a homosexual encounter with a younger slave resulted in guilt that sparked a religious conversion. Increasingly identifying with the Old Testament prophets, Nat accepted what he believed was a divine commission to kill the whites of Southampton County. Recruiting followers through his Bible class, Turner launched an insurrection in August, 1831, in which fifty-five whites were killed. Nat, himself, however, killed only Margaret Whitehead, a girl who had treated him kindly but unknowingly exerted a strong sexual attraction on the slave. After three days of rebellion, Nat was captured. Awaiting his execution, he is sure that he would revolt again but is unsure what God wills.

Impact Published by Random House, *The Confessions of Nat Turner* became a Book-of-the-Month Club main selection, received largely favorable reviews, and in 1968 won the Pulitzer Prize. However, that same year, Beacon Press published a collection of essays, edited by John Henrik Clark, under the title *William Styron's Nat Turner: Ten Black Writers Respond*, in which the book is criticized for being historically inaccurate and racist. According to essayist Alvin Poussant, in the novel, which was loosely based on a historical slave revolt, Styron projected a racial stereotype that emasculated and degraded African Americans. Styron defended his book in some public appearances, but the strongest defense of the book was a piece in *The New York Review of Books* (1968) written by Marxist historian Eugene Genovese. Genovese rebutted the essayists strongly, beginning a debate in that publication that continued for several weeks. Of the many articles published on Styron's book during subsequent years, the most significant was Seymour L. Gross and Eileen Bender's "History, Politics and Literature: The Myth of Nat Turner," published in the *American Quarterly* (1971), which placed Styron in a long tradition of writers who used Turner for their own purposes. Nonetheless, most white and black intellectuals continued to hold strongly differing opinions regarding the value of Styron's novel.

Related Work Styron's "Nat Turner Revisited," in the October, 1992, issue of *American Heritage*, gives the author's account of the genesis of the novel and the controversy surrounding it.

Additional Information Albert E. Stone examines the entire Styron-Nat Turner controversy in *Return of Nat Turner: History, Literature, and Cultural Politics in Sixties America*, 1992.

Gary Land

See also *Black Like Me*; Civil Rights Movement; *Guess Who's Coming to Dinner*.

■ Congress of Racial Equality (CORE)

A leading civil rights organization throughout the 1960's. CORE gained national attention by sponsoring the Freedom Rides, which integrated buses across the South and thereby forced desegregation.

Origins and History The Congress of Racial Equality (CORE) was founded in 1942 by students at the

Members of the Congress of Racial Equality chain themselves together in front of New York City Hall in this nonviolent protest. (Archive Photos)

University of Chicago led by James Farmer. Their first major action involved sit-in demonstrations against discrimination at a Chicago restaurant. Farmer, who was influenced by Mohandas Gandhi's ideas of nonviolence and direct action, envisioned the organization as an interracial force for the promotion of civil rights. He advocated "relentless non-cooperation, economic boycotts, and civil disobedience." After attempting unsuccessfully to deter CORE from pursuing a more radical focus in the mid-1960's, Farmer resigned. Beginning in 1966 under the leadership of Floyd B. McKissick, a former civil rights lawyer, the organization embraced black consciousness and the ideal of self-government by African Americans. In 1968, Roy Innis began his longtime leadership of CORE, but after 1968, the organization's power waned.

CORE was involved in direct-action civil rights activism before the 1960's. In 1947, the organization sent its first Freedom Riders into the South. In 1958, CORE led one of the first successful African American boycotts when it challenged a St. Louis, Missouri, bread manufacturer. However, the organization did not gain national attention until the 1960's. At the outset of the decade, CORE participated in lunch counter sit-ins, including the famous one at Greensboro, North Carolina, in 1960. The organization was instrumental in training activists in nonviolent, direct-action techniques. CORE was also among the participants in the 1960 meeting at Atlanta University where civil rights leaders, including Martin Luther King, Jr., coordinated what would become part of the decade's civil rights strategy. By 1964, CORE had emerged as a leader in the movement and a sponsor of the Freedom Schools and Mississippi's Freedom Summer.

CORE has been considered one of the nation's "big four" civil rights groups, along with the National Association for the Advancement of Colored People, Student Nonviolent Coordinating Committee, and Southern Christian Leadership Conference. CORE's objective was and remains "to establish in practice the inalienable right for all people to determine their own destiny." Headquartered in New York City, CORE has numerous local affiliates and chapters throughout the United States and parts of Africa, the Caribbean, and Central America.

Activities CORE is best known for the Freedom Rides designed to test Supreme Court desegregation rulings. In 1961, Farmer organized a bus ride that would send both black and white volunteers through the segregated South in an effort to force desegregation of the interstate busing system and public facilities. The Freedom Rides began on May 4, 1961, when riders—seven blacks and six whites—boarded two buses in Washington, D.C. They rode through North Carolina, South Carolina, Georgia, Alabama, Mississippi, and Louisiana. The ride started peacefully but was soon met by white mob violence in Rock Hill, South Carolina, and later with a string of incidents in Alabama. A bus on which the Freedom Riders were traveling was firebombed, and riders were attacked and beaten by angry white mobs.

These incidents drew national attention when public officials in Alabama failed to ensure the safety of the riders. King and other civil rights leaders came to Montgomery, Alabama, in a show of support for the riders. However, the First Baptist Church, where the civil rights activists were meeting, and the federal marshals who were assigned to "guard" the building were attacked. Still, the riders persisted. After arriving in Jackson, Mississippi, in May, many riders and peaceful activists were jailed. The event brought further attention to the cause, ultimately helping the Freedom Rides achieve their objectives.

Throughout the 1960's, CORE was involved in a host of civil rights activities: sponsoring black candidates for public office (including Annie Devine, who ran for a seat in the U.S. House of Representatives from Mississippi), organizing voter registration drives and voter education projects, and planning and participating in civil rights demonstrations in the South. The organization also established Freedom Schools in the South and supported African Americans in the urban ghettos of the North. CORE worked in cooperation with other prominent civil rights groups and leaders and participated in some of the most famous and important events of the Civil Rights movement, including sit-ins at Woolworth restaurants, King's 1962 campaign in Albany, Georgia, and the 1963 March on Washington. CORE volunteers worked alongside other civil rights activists during Freedom Summer, 1964, in Mississippi, attempting to register African American voters.

Impact The direct-action strategy was successful when Freedom Riders encountered violence in the South. The incidents invited media attention, bringing the glare of national scrutiny on the South's institutionalized racism and segregation. Ultimately, the Interstate Commerce Commission issued rulings banning all segregation in public transportation. Although the Freedom Riders were beaten, arrested, and jailed, they persisted. Considering themselves to be the "shock troops" of the Civil Rights movement, CORE's activists and Freedom Riders played a pivotal role in the United States' struggle for equality and civil rights.

Subsequent Events After the 1960's, CORE's power and prestige declined dramatically. CORE itself underwent changes. By the late 1960's, many civil rights activists had become frustrated with the slow pace of change and had become interested in exploring alternative or more militant courses of action. An ideological battle over the direction and nature of the movement resulted in a black power orientation and agenda within CORE. The organization, which had at one time been two-thirds white, gradually became less multiracial. Voters at the organization's national convention in 1967 removed the word "multiracial" from CORE's language on membership. CORE's political power and financial support deteriorated by the close of the decade, and its membership declined from a peak of seventy thousand members with offices in thirty-three states during the 1960's.

In the late 1990's, CORE remained an active force in civil rights. The organization sponsored Martin Luther King, Jr., national holiday celebrations and engaged in such initiatives as supporting a legal defense fund, providing immigration assistance, monitoring racism on the Internet, training civil rights workers, and administering job training programs such as Project Independence, designed to train and find employment for inner-city young adults and young, single mothers reliant on public assistance.

Additional Information For a comprehensive history, see *CORE: A Study in the Civil Rights Movement, 1942-1968* (1973), by August Meier and Elliott Rudwich. Robert E. Jakoubek's 1994 book, *James Farmer and the Freedom Rides* details the organization's famous bus rides. CORE founder Farmer offers his perspective in *Freedom, When?* (1966). For documentary footage and interviews with Freedom Riders, see the Public Broadcasting System videotape "Ain't Scared of Your Jails" (1993) from the *Eyes on the Prize* series on the Civil Rights movement.

Robert P. Watson

See also Civil Rights Movement; Freedom Rides; Freedom Summer; Sit-ins.

■ Conservatism in Politics

A loosely organized political movement or collection of political tendencies responding to the effects of New Deal liberalism on the American mainstream. In the 1960's, conservatives moved from the margin to the center of political life, taking over the Republican Party and laying the groundwork for their subsequent political successes and intellectual influence.

In the 1940's and 1950's, small groups of libertarians, traditionalists, and Cold War anticommunists began to develop networks organized around journals and magazines such as *Modern Age, American Mercury,* and *National Review* and organizations such as the Foundation for Economic Education, Young Americans for Freedom, and the Intercollegiate Society of Individualists. Inspired and heartened by the successes of such works as Friedrich Hayek's *The Road to Serfdom* (1944) and Russell Kirk's *The Conservative Mind* (1953), they sought to develop and sustain a critique of liberalism, which had been the dominant political philosophy since Franklin D. Roosevelt's New Deal. Some of the conservatives were concerned principally with the global competition between the Soviet Union and the United States. Some of these conservatives, such as the prolific writer James Burnham, focused on geopolitics and international strategy, and others, such as Joseph McCarthy, Republican U.S. Senator from Wisconsin, and the John Birch Society, sought to discover communist penetration of the United

States government. It is, however, safe to say that in the 1940's and 1950's, conservatives were relatively isolated and did not control the Republican Party.

In the 1960's, conservatives entered the mainstream of American politics. In 1964, they wrested control of the Republican Party from Northeastern liberals such as Nelson A. Rockefeller, governor of New York, and in 1968, the support of conservatives enabled Richard M. Nixon to win the presidential election. These two pivotal events can be explained by a change in the nature of the Republican Party and by a series of developments in U.S. society at large.

Goldwater In 1964, Barry Goldwater, U.S. Senator from Arizona, won the Republican nomination for the U.S. presidency. Although he was crushed in the general election by Lyndon B. Johnson, the incumbent Democrat who as vice president had succeeded to the presidency after John F. Kennedy's assassination in 1963, Goldwater did manage to establish conservatives as a force to be reckoned with in Republican politics. Hitherto dismissed or underestimated by the centrists and liberals who had controlled the party, Goldwater and his allies represented the growing power of two new regions—the South and the West—in Republican politics. Activists in these regions tended to view the exercise of federal power much less favorably than their counterparts in the Northeast.

Although they ran a very ineffective campaign that permitted the Democrats to emphasize Goldwater's apparent extremism, especially with respect to such issues as nuclear war and Social Security, conservative activists gained a great deal of valuable political experience in 1964. Most important, they learned how to conduct successful organizing efforts at the political grass roots. In addition, they brought to the forefront a new generation of political stars, chief among them Ronald Reagan, who was elected governor of California in 1966 and was already a serious contender for the Republican nomination for the presidency in 1968.

Nixon That year, however, belonged to Nixon, who had been Dwight D. Eisenhower's vice president from 1953 to 1960 and the Republican nominee in 1960. Nixon, who has stated that his own political tendencies were centrist rather than conservative, had been careful in 1964 not to burn his bridges with the pro-Goldwater forces. Having won the nomination in 1968, he capitalized on the disarray in the Democratic Party, born in large part of the unpopularity of the Vietnam War and the growing concern among important parts of the New Deal coalition—especially southerners and labor unionists—that the liberals in the party were at best insufficiently firm in their disapproval of the excesses of the New Left and at worst actually sympathetic. In the face of race riots in the cities and increasingly disorderly protests on prominent college campuses, the Nixon campaign's emphasis on domestic law and order and "peace with honor" in Vietnam seemed solid, sober, and reassuring to a substantial portion of the electorate. Despite significant support in the Deep South for George Wallace, a populist former Democrat from Alabama who ran as an independent, Nixon managed handily to defeat Hubert Humphrey, the Democratic nominee, who was Johnson's vice president and had been a longtime and well-loved liberal activist in the party.

Coming just four years after Goldwater's defeat, Nixon's presidential victory was in some ways a significant reversal of fortunes for conservatives. At the same time, however, Nixon did not pursue a consistently conservative policy, instituting wage and price controls (anathema for supporters of the free market), inaugurating the earliest forms of affirmative action, and pursuing rapprochement with both the Soviet Union and the People's Republic of China.

Still, conservatives had joined the political mainstream. They had outlived the excesses of the McCarthy era anticommunist "witch-hunts." They had essentially repudiated the conspiracy mongering of the John Birch Society, which had its heyday in the late 1950's and early 1960's. They had elected candidates to office and knew how to do so again. They knew how to reach outside the ranks of ordinary party activists to recruit support at the grass roots. Also, their intellectual organizations and journals had survived the lean years of the 1950's to experience the comparative prosperity of the 1960's.

The Evolution of Conservatism In addition to these political developments, the philosophical or theoretical evolution of U.S. conservatism should be noted. There were three principal strands of conservative thought: libertarian, traditionalist, and anticommunist. Although all conservatives opposed communism, which means that those whose energies were devoted to that cause did not engage in

controversies with the other camps, libertarians and traditionalists were at odds with one another. Inspired by the classical liberalism of the eighteenth and nineteenth centuries, libertarianism emphasized the centrality of human freedom in any social order, arguing that individual freedom is best protected where markets are as open as possible and state intervention and regulation are kept to a bare minimum. On the other hand, traditionalists tended to favor an orderly and hierarchical community devoted to the cultivation of virtue and built around the common acceptance of absolute moral truths, usually grounded in religion. Although both sides might agree in opposing New Deal liberalism, with its egalitarianism and heavy reliance on "social engineering" or the state regulation of markets, they often disagreed when it came to defining a positive political program.

In the early 1960's, Frank Meyer, a leading conservative intellectual, attempted to articulate a "fusion" of the traditionalist and libertarian positions. He argued, in essence, that what was most important for the individual cultivation of virtue was the protection of human freedom. Libertarians and traditionalists could or ought to agree that virtue should be the end; they ultimately disagreed, he argued, only on the appropriate means. As long as libertarians did not devote themselves to freedom as an end in itself and traditionalists did not embrace authoritarianism in the name of virtue, they could find substantial common ground. By the mid-1960's, this position had prevailed among many conservative intellectuals, becoming, for example, the editorial line taken by *National Review*.

Impact Through the early part of the 1960's, New Deal liberalism encountered no significant challenge from the right. There were conservative voices in the wilderness, but they lacked the resources, the organization, and the political acumen to mount a substantial challenge to the liberals. By the end of the decade, all this had changed. Conservatives had seized control of the Republican Party and its organizational resources. Political operatives who had cut their teeth on the Goldwater campaign were actually winning elections. Liberals could no longer afford to overlook their conservative opponents, whether in the political or in the intellectual arena.

Subsequent Events Had it not been for the 1972 break-in at the Watergate Hotel offices of the Democratic National Committee and the cover-up, which ultimately brought down the Nixon administration, Republicans might well have controlled the White House throughout the 1970's. In any event, Reagan, who entered the national political scene as a supporter of Goldwater in 1964, was elected president in 1980 and gave his name to an era. Other former Goldwater supporters, such as author Richard Viguerie, rose to prominence by taking advantage of a network and deploying the techniques—in Viguerie's case, direct-mail fund-raising—first developed in the 1964 campaign.

Additional Information A useful study of Republican Party politics in the 1960's is Mary C. Brennan's *Turning Right in the Sixties: The Conservative Capture of the GOP* (1995). Helpful accounts of the intellectual underpinnings of U.S. conservatism can be found in Jerome L. Himmelstein's *To the Right: The Transformation of American Conservatism* (1990) and George

H. Nash's *The Conservative Intellectual Movement in America Since 1945* (1979).

Joseph M. Knippenberg

See also Buckley, William F., Jr.; Cold War; Goldwater, Barry; John Birch Society; Liberalism in Politics; Nixon, Richard M.; Presidential Election of 1964; Presidential Election of 1968; Rockefeller, Nelson A.; Young Americans for Freedom.

■ *Cool Hand Luke*

Released 1967
Director Stuart Rosenberg (1927-　　)

A film encapsulating the attitudes and conflicts of 1960's youth. The film used classic conventions: prison as microcosm and defiant existential prisoner.

The Work In *Cool Hand Luke*, war hero Luke Jackson (Paul Newman) is on a 1940's southern prison road gang for drunkenly decapitating parking meters. His

The defiance of prisoner Luke in the 1967 film Cool Hand Luke *captured the feelings and conflicts experienced by many young people during the 1960's.* (Museum of Modern Art/Film Stills Archive)

dying mother's visit reveals Luke's lifelong clashes with authority. Luke adjusts to the brutal constrictions of prison, asking permission for every daily action. The warden (Strother Martin) looks askance at Luke, who particularly provokes "No-Eyes," the silent guard in reflective sunglasses who is anxious to shoot an escaping prisoner. Luke's refusal to stay down when he has clearly lost a fistfight charms prison boss Dragline (George Kennedy) as does his working double time while paving a road simply to irritate his keepers. On a bet, he eats fifty boiled eggs in one hour to show he can. However, Luke's real rebellion comes after solitary confinement in "The Box" when his mother dies: The warden, in violation of his professed code of reacting only to prisoner behavior, had placed him there simply because he might escape. Luke subsequently escapes twice, making fools of his captors and sending the prisoners a picture of himself with two showgirls. Furious at the challenge, the guards make the recaptured Luke dig and fill ditches and endure beatings and solitary confinement. When Luke finally begs for mercy, they warn that another escape will be fatal. Yet Luke, accompanied by Dragline, steals a prison truck, only to be trapped in a church. After a one-way conversation with God, Luke surrenders but is shot down by "No-Eyes." The last scene shows Dragline telling stories about Luke to the assembled prisoners: The myth of the unbreakable prisoner lives on, despite Luke's admission of defeat.

Impact While in the tradition of prison films highlighting the indomitable human spirit, *Cool Hand Luke* has larger ambitions. The religious theme is inescapable in Luke's frequent challenges to the ultimate authority, God, daring him to show his power; in the repeated visual allusions to crosses and crucifixions; in Luke as reluctant savior of the prisoners' spirits; and in Dragline's enthusiastic performance as Luke's apostle. These thematic threads comment on the human condition—life is a prison camp, and just when we have mastered the rules, they are changed, and we are punished for no apparent reason. Yet Luke's reluctant antiheroic leadership is entirely secular: How are free spirits compromised by even minimal roles of social responsibility? This prototypical 1960's question was asked in communes, antiwar organizations, and counterculture groups as leadership pressures transformed individualistic rebels into their opposites. Though Luke

never formalizes rebellion, Dragline clearly wants to. Finally, like the Steinbeck/Kazan film *Viva Zapata!* (1964), the film explores mythmaking. The skinny, directionless Luke, though he refutes Dragline's claim that he tricked the bosses, is transformed into a heroic figure, cunning and undefeatable. This exploration reveals another of the decade's concerns—how we distinguish reality from illusion and truth from reality.

Related Works *Cool Hand Luke* echoes Ken Kesey's *One Flew over the Cuckoo's Nest* (1962). Luke, like Kesey's central character, Randle P. McMurphy, is a Christ figure slaughtered by authority but inspiring a mythology of rebellion.

Additional Information For a discussion of Luke as existentialist antihero, see Charles Champlin's *The Movies Grow Up (1940-1980)*, published in 1981.

    Andrew F. Macdonald and Gina Macdonald

See also Counterculture; Film; *One Flew over the Cuckoo's Nest*; Religion and Spirituality.

■ Corporate Liberalism

A concept assigned by the New Left to describe Cold War liberal attitudes and ideology. Corporate liberalism became a derogative term used to explain liberal acquiescence to corporate imperialism.

Beginning as early as the Progressive era and accelerating after World War II, corporate business leaders eschewed full-blown competition and worked with big government to establish regulation to ensure a strong, progressive, imperialistic economy. After World War II, the containment of communism was added as a powerful component to the corporate liberal ideology. Anticommunist liberals such as Arthur Schlesinger, Jr., and Daniel Bell best epitomized the belief that only through a strong cooperative relationship with corporate leaders based on strong economic development, a powerful military, and some degree of political progressivism could the United States maintain its hegemony. These tenets continued through the 1950's and found their greatest expression in the John F. Kennedy and Lyndon B. Johnson administrations.

    The term "corporate liberalism" was first used by Martin Sklar in a 1960 article to explain Wilsonian liberalism. Originally, New Left activists placed some faith in the Kennedy administration and liberals in

Congress to create a society based more on equal rights, social justice, and peace. The Bay of Pigs invasion, the Cuban Missile Crisis, the Vietnam buildup, and failure to support the Civil Rights movement (such as the refusal to seat the Mississippi Freedom Democratic Party) convinced activists that liberals were more willing to compromise with southern conservatives than to build a new society. Richard Flacks enunciated these critiques in two 1960's pieces, and Carl Ogelsby used the term in a 1965 speech to attack deepening commitment in Vietnam, especially the willingness of congressional liberals to support greater funding of the war at the expense of social programs. Gradually, corporate liberalism became a byword to explain refusal of liberals within the Democratic Party to take a strong stand against imperialistic adventures and for social justice. By 1966, corporate liberalism was a widely used concept that convinced activists that working within the two-party system was not a viable alternative.

Impact Corporate liberalism was a key 1960's concept that provided the underpinning to push the New Left toward a more militant and radical direction. It helped provide an understanding of Cold War liberalism's dedication to corporate advancement and anticommunist imperialism. This realization led the way to a more outspoken and activist attack on the U.S. free enterprise mentality and provided an intellectual foundation for revolutionary activities by such groups as the Weathermen and the Black Panthers.

Subsequent Events Corporate liberalism led to New Left attacks on the Kennedy wing of the Democratic Party. These attacks reached their highest pitch at the 1968 Democratic National Convention in Chicago and contributed to the demise of corporate liberals in the Richard M. Nixon and later Jimmy Carter administrations. The concept continues to be a viable method of explaining post-World War II U.S. capitalist ideology.

Additional Information The concept is explained in Flack's "SDS and the New Era" and "Is the Great Society Just a Barbecue?" in *The New Left: A Documentary History* (1969), edited by Massimo Teodorit, and "Reaganism as Corporate Liberalism," in *Policy Studies Review*, 10:1. The term was first used in Sklar's "Woodrow Wilson and the Political Economy of

Modern United States Liberalism," in *Studies on the Left* (1960).

R. David Myers

See also Cold War; Democratic National Convention of 1968; Liberalism in Politics; Students for a Democratic Society (SDS); Weathermen.

■ Counterculture

A loosely organized movement of hippies, antiwar activists, and many young people whose values, behaviors, and beliefs were in contrast to those held by mainstream Americans. Their search for the "Good Society" involved experiments with drug use and alternative lifestyles.

Throughout history, there have been people who through choice or circumstance find themselves on the periphery of society. Some antecedents of the counterculture include nineteenth century American Transcendentalists such as Henry David Thoreau, Ralph Waldo Emerson, and Margaret Fuller and poets such as Walt Whitman. These philosophers and poets stressed the spiritual capacity of people and the importance of contact with nature and political involvement in progressive causes. After World War II, the Beat generation (which included writers such as Allen Ginsberg, Jack Kerouac, and Gary Snyder) professed world-weariness in a post-nuclear environment, endorsed the use of marijuana and amphetamines, and admired people on the fringes of American society, including African Americans and Mexican Americans. Norman Mailer's *The White Negro* (1957) defined the philosophy of these new "psychic outlaws," stating that anticipation of apocalypse and existential anxiety are key elements of "hipness," with its high regard for feeling and veneration of the present. A revival in the late 1950's of folk and blues music, which often expresses the indomitable spirit of long-suffering people, further prepared the way for the birth of the counterculture.

Although the term was not yet used, the counterculture became a significant social phenomenon about 1964, when Bob Dylan's song, "The Times They Are a-Changin' " was released. Young people gathered, often near universities, to listen to folk music in coffeehouses, smoke marijuana, and discuss such topics as the atomic bomb and other political and philosophical issues. They shared a view of society as increasingly mechanistic and conformist as well as willing to risk the dangers of nuclear holocaust. They objected to the nation's racism and materialism and rejected the clean-cut appearances favored by their more conservative peers. Although on the surface America appeared to be politically and economically strong, some people believed that the country was spiritually impoverished and acting counter to its national commitment to freedom of thought and expression. At the University of California, Berkeley, in 1964, Mario Savio, leader of the Free Speech movement, spoke for many people: "There is a time when the operation of the machine becomes so odious, makes you so sick at heart, that you can't take part; . . . and you've got to indicate to the people who run it . . . that unless you're free, the machine will be prevented from working at all."

Searching for the Good Society Agreeing with Black Panther leader Eldridge Cleaver that "You're either part of the problem or part of the solution," the counterculture sought to form the nucleus of a new, reformed society, perhaps even a utopia. They reacted to the malaise of American society with political protests and a search for higher values. Some members of the counterculture studied Eastern religious philosophies such as Zen Buddhism or Taoism, which they found appealing because of their lack of dogma and their goal of spiritual enlightenment. Others experimented with drugs, initially marijuana, later LSD (lysergic acid diethylamide), and amphetamines. LSD became a feature of countercultural communities in the Haight-Ashbury section of San Francisco, Greenwich Village in New York City, and the University District in Seattle. By the summer of 1967, the Summer of Love, thousands of young people had moved to Haight-Ashbury, where they enjoyed a lifestyle that revolved around psychedelic drugs, free love, rock music, colorful clothes, and long hair. These young people, called hippies, promoted communal living and were fascinated with Native Americans (including the peyote cults that used drugs in their religious ceremonies). Ken Kesey and the Merry Pranksters (whose story is told in *The Electric Kool-Aid Acid Test*, 1968) developed the acid tests, multimedia spectacles with dancing, rock music (initially supplied by the Grateful Dead), and light shows, intended to celebrate (and simulate) the use of LSD.

The fundamental principles of the hippies included individual freedom ("do your own thing as long as you don't hurt anybody else"), peace and love, uninhibited sexuality, mind expansion, and elevation of the human spirit. Underground newspapers (such as *The Helix* in Seattle, *The Great Speckled Bird* in Atlanta, the *San Francisco Oracle*, and the *Berkeley Barb*) articulated the hippie philosophy, shared information about drug use, and provided news about countercultural activities as well as editorial opinion about the war in Vietnam and civil rights. Many hippies adopted the adage of Timothy Leary to "turn on, tune in, and drop out" by forming communes (ideally outside cities) and seeking closer contact with nature. Citing R. Buckminster Fuller's dictum that "There is no such thing as genius; some children are less damaged than others," some hippies started "free schools" stressing student autonomy, curricular experimentation, and a Romantic view of children.

Many members of the counterculture, such as this couple at the 1969 Woodstock Festival, favored long hair, blue jeans, and Volkswagen Buses painted in vivid, expressive designs or decorated with brightly colored stickers. (AP/Wide World Photos)

Politics and the Counterculture Although many hippies ridiculed political protest as a demeaning social "game," others saw no contradiction between spiritual enlightenment and political involvement. Beat poet Snyder felt that both were essential for a meaningful life: People should aid those who suffer. The Yippies, led by Abbie Hoffman and Jerry Rubin at the Democratic National Convention in Chicago in 1968, combined political protest and a playful, mocking attitude toward authority; they protested the Vietnam War and the upcoming election by nominating a pig for president and staging protests that led to what a government report later called a "police riot."

At the height of the Vietnam War, the antiwar movement brought together a significant cross section of the U.S. population, including many students who participated in large rallies such as the Vietnam Moratorium on November 15, 1969. (After the U.S. invasion of Cambodia in 1970, more than a million students identified themselves as "revolutionaries.") By this time, frustrated with the seeming futility of peaceful protest, a minority of antiwar activists concluded that violent revolution was the only way to stop the war and change society. Some members of Students for a Democratic Society established the Weather Underground (Weathermen), dropped out from society, and engaged in terrorist activities such as the Days of Rage in October, 1969. Most people in the antiwar movement remained committed to nonviolence.

Subsequent Events Although the counterculture still exists, many of the overt characteristics and espoused causes of the hippies have disappeared or become part of the greater society. By the end of the decade, long hair and colorful clothes had become part of mainstream fashion. Casual drug use had led to addictions and other problems for many people, including many Vietnam veterans, giving rise to an antidrug faction that would gain strength in the late 1970's and early 1980's. Most of the free schools and rural communes the hippies had established did not last much beyond the 1960's. Antiwar protests continued into the 1970's. In May, 1970, for example, strikes and protests against the U.S. invasion of Cambodia were held on more than five hundred campuses and involved about half of the nation's students.

Impact The counterculture did not create the Good Society. Its members made numerous mistakes (some attributable to youth). Blaming social problems on the "establishment," many countercultural youths fell prey to us-versus-them thinking. Many others moved successfully into conventional jobs, suggesting to cynics that alternative values were not deeply held. However, the counterculture left a significant heritage. Significantly, the counterculture helped in forcing the withdrawal of U.S. troops from Vietnam in the early 1970's and in realizing civil rights in American society. Perhaps its greatest contribution was an "abundance" philosophy, the idea that there is enough to go around, which provided compensatory hope in apocalyptic times. This hope sustains many still seeking to create the Good Society. The human potential movement, which had its roots in the 1960's, shared the counterculture's positive view of human nature, although sometimes its adherents failed to see the accompanying need to work to improve society. A skeptical view of authority and truth and a cautiously optimistic view of human beings have influenced schools and the larger society. The exploration of alternative views of history (for example, the debunking of Columbus's "discovery" of America) and a multicultural emphasis in curricula are part of the legacy of the counterculture. After the 1960's, there was less emphasis on "absolute" truth and a greater propensity toward process in solving problems. Another inheritance from the counterculture is recreational drug use. Some states have periodically (and heatedly) debated the decriminalization of marijuana.

Additional Information For primary documents from the counterculture, see *The Sixties Papers: Documents of a Rebellious Decade* (1984), edited by Judith and Stewart Albert; Jerry Rubin's *Do It! Scenarios of the Revolution* (1970), and Abbie Hoffman's *Revolution for the Hell of It* (1968). Secondary sources include Charles Perry's *The Haight-Ashbury: A History* (1984), Todd Gitlin's *The Sixties: Years of Hope, Days of Rage* (1987), William L. O'Neill's *Coming Apart: An Informal History of America in the 1960's* (1971), and Irwin and Debi Unger's *America in the 1960's* (1988).

Richard A. Hill

See also Beat Generation; Be-ins and Love-ins; Communes; Drug Culture; *Electric Kool-Aid Acid Test, The*; Flower Children; Free Speech Movement; Ginsberg, Allen; Haight-Ashbury; Hippies; Leary,

Timothy; Love-ins; LSD; Marijuana; Sexual Revolution; Summer of Love; Underground Newspapers; Yippies; Youth Culture and the Generation Gap.

■ Credit and Debt

Household borrowing, chiefly home mortgages and installment borrowing. During the 1960's, households in the

United States more than doubled their indebtedness, mostly to purchase houses, automobiles, and other durable products.

The 1960's was an exceptionally prosperous period in the United States. The National Bureau of Economic Research classifies the period from February, 1961, to December, 1969, as a single, uninterrupted

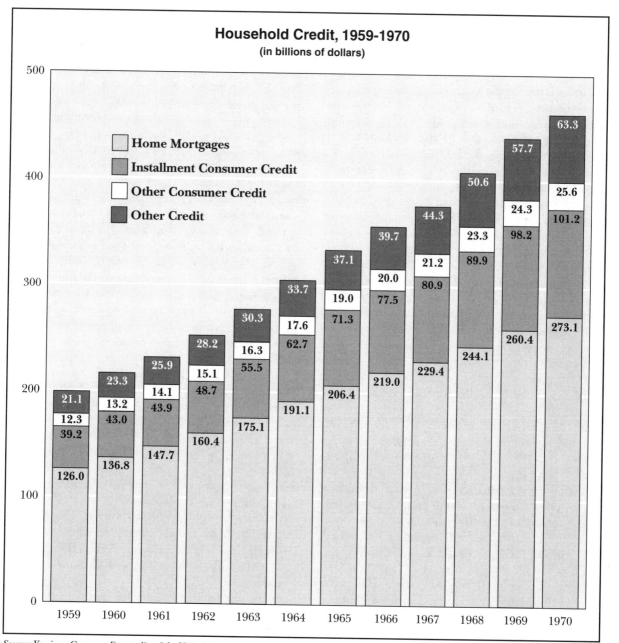

Household Credit, 1959-1970
(in billions of dollars)

Legend:
- Home Mortgages
- Installment Consumer Credit
- Other Consumer Credit
- Other Credit

Year	Home Mortgages	Installment Consumer Credit	Other Consumer Credit	Other Credit
1959	126.0	39.2	12.3	21.1
1960	136.8	43.0	13.2	23.3
1961	147.7	43.9	14.1	25.9
1962	160.4	48.7	15.1	28.2
1963	175.1	55.5	16.3	30.3
1964	191.1	62.7	17.6	33.7
1965	206.4	71.3	19.0	37.1
1966	219.0	77.5	20.0	39.7
1967	229.4	80.9	21.2	44.3
1968	244.1	89.9	23.3	50.6
1969	260.4	98.2	24.3	57.7
1970	273.1	101.2	25.6	63.3

Source: Kurian, George, *Datapedia of the United States, 1790-2000, America Year by Year.* Lanham, Maryland: Bernam Press, 1994.

business-cycle expansion—the longest on record to that time. Unemployment averaged only 4.8 percent of the labor force. Per capita income and consumption spending, adjusted to remove the effects of the 2.3 percent annual inflation, rose by a healthy 3 percent per year.

During the decade, U.S. households increased their indebtedness more quickly than their incomes were rising. The Federal Reserve estimated the total debt of the household sector at $208 billion in 1959 and $462 billion in 1969. The 1959 debt was 54 percent of personal income for that year, and 1969 debt was 62 percent of income for that year.

Mortgage Debt Home loans, or mortgages, were the most common form of household debt. About three-fifths of U.S. families lived in houses that they owned, a percentage that remained virtually constant during the 1960's. Most of these families took out a mortgage to finance their purchase. A typical mortgage used the property as collateral and initially covered 80 percent or more of the purchase price. Loans were often scheduled for repayment over twenty years or more by monthly installments, or payments, for principal (the amount borrowed) and interest.

Home-mortgage debt on residential units designed for one to four families increased from $126 billion at the end of 1959 to $260 billion at the end of 1969. Borrowing increased to accommodate the growing population and the increase in median house price from about $16,000 in 1960 to $23,000 in 1970. Increases in the market value of existing houses made many people view them as good investments.

In 1959, about 40 percent of mortgage debt was federally insured under either Federal Housing Administration (FHA) guarantee or Veterans Administration (VA) insurance. By the end of 1969, this percentage had fallen to 34 percent, mainly because the VA program had ceased to grow. These federal programs reduced the risk to lenders and permitted lower down payments and longer payoff periods than conventional mortgages. However, they set limits on the interest lenders could charge. As market interest rates increased, some mortgage holders preferred to lend without federal guarantee so that they could charge higher rates. In the early 1960's, mortgage interest rates were relatively stable, around 6 percent per year, but inflationary pressure in the latter half of the decade drove rates up to 7.8 percent in 1969.

Prospective home buyers often obtained mortgages from commercial banks or from savings and loan associations. In addition, many mortgages were originated with specialized mortgage companies, which would then resell them to institutional investors such as insurance companies.

Installment Debt Household installment debt increased from $39 billion at the end of 1959 to $98 billion ten years later. Automobile loans rose from $16 billion to $36 billion during this period. The share of households owning a car increased slightly, from 74 percent to 79 percent, but the percentage owning more than one car rose from 15 percent to 27 percent. About two-thirds of new-car purchases were financed. Credit was also frequently used to purchase other durable goods, such as furniture and appliances, and the proportion of households owning color television sets, air conditioners, dishwashers, and clothes dryers increased substantially. The rise in the rate of inflation in the late 1960's motivated consumers to "buy now and beat the price increase." Personal installment loans showed large proportional growth, going from $9 billion to $29 billion during the decade. Some of these were associated with expenditures for medical care or education. Loans to finance college educations became more widespread under the influence of the subsidy and guarantee provisions of the National Defense Education Act of 1958.

Most installment loans were repayable over two to four years. Many were initially arranged through the seller of goods—the automobile dealer or appliance store. However, consumers could also obtain installment loans in cash from commercial banks, credit unions, and personal finance (small-loan) companies. Interest rates (expressed as annual percentage rates, or APR) were often quite high—personal loan companies in many areas could charge as much as 40 percent. Often the most favorable terms were offered by credit unions, organized on the cooperative principle. Credit unions, aided by favorable tax and regulatory treatment, tripled their assets during the decade.

Survey research data revealed significant patterns of use of installment credit. In 1967, about 48 percent of families had installment debt. However, about 70 percent of families headed by people age eighteen to twenty-four had installment debt, compared with only 12 percent in households headed by people over sixty-five. Credit use was widest among middle-income families. Low-income families often could not quality for credit—only 24 percent of families with income under three thousand dollars reported installment debts, half of them with debts of two hundred dollars or less. The highest percentage of indebted families was the middle-income group, but higher income groups also had relatively high credit use and were most likely to have large installment debts. Low-income families, however, had the highest ratio of installment payments to income.

Long-standing concern about confusing and misleading credit terms led to adoption of the federal Consumer Credit Protection Act in 1968. The major provisions of the law, phased in over three years, dealt with truth in lending. Lenders and sellers using credit options were required to disclose the full cost of their finance charges both in dollars and in APR terms. Consumers were also given a three-day grace period to withdraw from credit contracts if they had second thoughts.

The 1960's witnessed an explosive growth in the use of credit cards. Bank of America led the banks' entry into credit card activity. In 1961, about a million customers held this bank's credit card, the Bankamericard. The market mushroomed after Bank of America began nationwide licensing of its card in 1966. By the end of the 1960's, more than 50 million bank credit cards were in circulation, compared with only five million in 1965. However, bank credit card debt was only about $3 billion, a relatively small proportion of household debt.

Impact   Poor Richard's maxim, "He that goes a borrowing goes a sorrowing," was true for some Americans. In the 1960's, personal bankruptcies continued the rapid rise they had shown since 1946. The number of personal bankruptcies rose from 98,000 in 1960 to 192,000 in 1967, then declined slightly to 178,000 in 1970. These represented only a tiny fraction of the total population; however, many more households experienced emotional stress over debts. Fortunately, delinquency and foreclosure rates on home mortgages showed no significant increase during the decade.

For most families, however, going into debt was, paradoxically, a way of becoming wealthier. Most

borrowing was associated with the acquisition of real assets, such as houses and automobiles. By borrowing, families were able to obtain these assets earlier in life and to pay for them as they enjoyed them. The typical repayment provisions for an installment loan imposed financial discipline, a kind of "forced saving." Because buyers were usually required to make a down payment in cash, the value of their assets increased by more than their liabilities. Between 1959 and 1968, the value of residential structures increased from $415 billion to $683 billion, and the value of the stock of consumer durables rose from $136 billion to $234 billion. Moreover, households added immensely to their ownership of financial assets such as bank deposits, stocks and bonds, insurance, and pension reserves. Federal Reserve estimates showed an increase in household financial assets from $935 billion in 1959 to $1,840 billion in 1969. A more conservative estimate showed personal net wealth rising from $643 billion in 1959 to $1,206 billion in 1969. This increase in wealth was, however, divided very unequally among U.S. households.

From a macroeconomic viewpoint, the expansion of household debt helped generate an abundant flow of expenditures for housing and durable goods, stimulating those sectors of the economy to expand production and employment and helping the economy achieve a remarkably low level of unemployment.

Additional Information   Throughout the 1960's, the Survey Research Center, University of Michigan, published the *Survey of Consumer Finances*, an annual loaded with valuable data and discussion. *The Consumer in American Society* (1970), by Arch W. Troelstrup, adds a human dimension to the topic. Housing issues are reviewed in *The Revolution in Real Estate Finance* (1985), by Anthony Downs. Other useful publications include *Personal Finance* (1966,) by Elvin F. Donaldson and John K. Pfahl; *The National Wealth of the United States* (1976), by John W. Kendrick; and *Consumer Durables and Installment Debt: A Study of American Households* (1976), by Gary Hendricks and Kenwood C. Youmans.

Paul B. Trescott

See also   Branch Banks; Business and the Economy; Gross National Product (GNP); Prosperity and Poverty; Unemployment.

■ Crimes and Scandals

Violence, government misconduct, revelations about the American Mafia, corporate misdeeds, and scandals touching prominent politicians. A large number of shocking incidents combined to create an uneasy feeling in the minds of many Americans during the 1960's.

The pervasive increase in crime in the United States that began in the mid-1960's was primarily caused by the baby boomers reaching the maximum crime-committing ages of fifteen to twenty-four. The baby boomers, born during a post-World War II increase in the birthrate beginning in 1946 and lasting until 1964, raised enormously the proportion of potential and actual delinquents and criminals in the society. Although critics blamed pediatrician Benjamin Spock's baby care books, the atomic bomb, and even rock and roll for this increase in crime and delinquency, its primary cause was this demographic bulge.

Personal Crimes Personal crimes are crimes against people, such as murder, robbery, and rape, that are perceived as directly threatening by the public. An event that underscored the public's feeling that crime was out of control was the murder of Kitty Genovese. At 3 a.m. on March 13, 1964, she was brutally attacked and murdered outside her apartment building in New York City. Even though she screamed for help for more than thirty-five minutes and was heard by at least thirty-eight of her neighbors, no one came to her assistance or even called the police. The public perception of her neighbors' lack of action was that the growing impersonality of modern urban life was depersonalizing people and turning them into apathetic, isolated individuals lacking any sense of community.

Such senseless violence was best exemplified by the multiple murders that occurred during the 1960's, such as those committed by serial killer Albert DeSalvo, the "Boston Strangler," who murdered thirteen women, most of whom he first raped, from 1962 through 1964, or by mass murderers such as Charles Whitman, Richard Speck, and the Charles Manson "family." Serial murder involves killing several victims in three or more separate incidents, and mass murder involves killing several victims at once. In 1966, former Eagle Scout leader and engineering honor student Whitman murdered his wife, Kathy, and mother, Margaret. He then climbed to the top

of a tower at the University of Texas in Austin and randomly shot sixteen people and wounded thirty before being killed by police. Speck's murder in 1968 of eight Chicago student nurses was followed in 1969 by two multiple murders by a cult headed by Manson.

Political Crimes Although personal crimes escalated the public's fear, political crimes punctuated the 1960's. African Americans in the South as well as civil rights workers were subject to systematic acts of terrorism and murder, particularly at the hands of the Ku Klux Klan. The decade witnessed the assassinations of some popular leaders, including President John F. Kennedy in 1963, his brother Senator Robert F. Kennedy in 1968, civil rights leader Martin Luther King, Jr., in 1968, and African American leader Malcolm X in 1965. The murders of President Kennedy and King have been the subject of numerous conspiracy theories. Although it is clear that Lee Harvey Oswald pulled the trigger, the leading, and unproven, theory about the president's death points to the involvement of organized crime. In the King murder, many believe racist forces were behind the actual trigger man, James Earl Ray.

Urban racial disorders in the nation's cities began in 1963 and peaked in April, 1968, in the aftermath of the assassination of civil rights leader King. In 1967, more than one hundred riots erupted in U.S. cities. The Kerner Commission (formally the National Advisory Commission on Civil Disorders), which had conducted an investigation into urban unrest, issued a report on February 29, 1968, calling for a major national commitment to social programs to undo growing racial divisions.

By the late 1960's, the United States was mired in the longest and perhaps most unpopular military engagement in its history, an undeclared war in Vietnam. A particularly inglorious incident that occurred during this war was the 1968 My Lai massacre. A platoon from Charlie Company, led by Lieutenant William Calley, Jr., while conducting a search-and-destroy mission, slaughtered three hundred and fifty Vietnamese villagers, including one hundred unarmed civilian men, women, and children. Although many believed Calley was a scapegoat for higher-ups who had issued the orders, he was convicted of murder in 1971. Charges were later reduced, and Calley was released on parole in 1974.

The Vietnam conflict produced massive antiwar

protests and demonstrations that reached their peak in the events and riots surrounding the 1968 Democratic National Convention in Chicago. Before the Democratic Party reformed its primary system, party-appointed delegates chose its presidential candidate irrespective of the results of state primaries. When it became apparent that Eugene McCarthy, the peace candidate and winner of the majority of primaries, was not to be chosen but that Vice President Hubert Humphrey was to become the candidate, numerous organizations and antiwar groups organized protests. When Mayor Richard Daley refused to issue parading and camping permits and ordered the police and National Guard to clear the parks, a major riot broke out between demonstrators and overly zealous police. The harsh police response

to the mass protest had the effect of escalating rather than ending the conflict. Some of the demonstration organizers, such as Abbie Hoffman, Jerry Rubin, and Tom Hayden, were later prosecuted in what became known as the trial of the Chicago Seven; however, the federal government was unsuccessful in making conspiracy charges stick.

Government Misconduct In the mid-1970's, Congress conducted investigations into alleged major misconduct by the Central Intelligence Agency (CIA), Federal Bureau of Investigation (FBI), and military intelligence agencies during the 1960's. Much of this misconduct stemmed from the government's Cold War fears and its reaction to social movements such as those supporting civil rights,

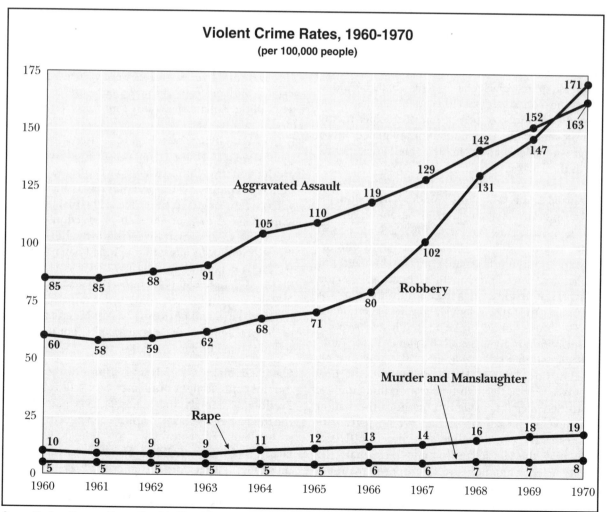

Source: Kurian, George, *Datapedia of the United States, 1790-2000, America Year by Year.* Lanham, Maryland: Bernam Press, 1994.

student rights, and an end to the war in Vietnam. Government agencies were found to have participated in illegal surveillance, disruption, and harmful experiments in the name of protecting the state or fighting communism.

In 1967, President Lyndon B. Johnson directed the CIA to investigate foreign, probably communist, influences in domestic protest activity. Operation Chaos, as it was called, violated the CIA's charter, which prohibited domestic involvement. Agents infiltrated radical groups and collected thirteen thousand files on their members, over half of whom were U.S. citizens. As part of the Counterintelligence Program (COINTELPRO) launched against numerous radical groups and their members, the FBI committed more than two hundred break-ins and later attempted to destroy records of such activities. Civil rights groups, including King's Southern Christian Leadership Conference, were disrupted, harassed, and made the subject of disinformation campaigns designed to discredit them. It was even charged that the FBI attempted to blackmail King with the threat of release of materials related to his sexual behavior unless he committed suicide. Such activities and related revelations of secret, harmful experiments on innocent civilians by military intelligence led to congressional curtailing of covert intelligence activities in the 1970's.

Organized Crime The sinister underworld of organized crime attracted its share of attention in the 1960's. In September-October, 1963, a Senate committee held a widely televised investigation into organized crime that fascinated and mesmerized the public. The star witness in these hearings was Joe Valachi, the first informer from within the ranks of the American Mafia. Valachi, a low-level member of the Genovese family, broke the code of *omerta*, a pledge of honor, silence, and obedience to the mob, and claimed that the real name of the organization was the "Cosa Nostra." He described in detail how the Cosa Nostra, through twenty-six crime families, controlled illegal activities throughout the nation and how the organization had set up legitimate businesses and compromised government officials.

In 1957, the McClellan Committee (formally the Senate Select Committee on Improper Activities in the Labor or Management Field) launched a three-year investigation of Teamster Union president Jimmy Hoffa, whom they suspected of abusing his

position. The committee uncovered evidence of numerous irregularities and apparent links to the underworld. However, attempts to prosecute him were largely unsuccessful until 1964, when evidence of jury bribing led to his eventual imprisonment in 1967. Hoffa was paroled in the early 1970's and disappeared in 1975.

Corporate Crime Although crime in the streets and involving the government had the public's attention, corporate crime had caught the eye of the prosecutors. Crime in the business world had long been ignored because of the power and influence of giant corporations, but signs of change took place beginning in February, 1961, with the electrical industry conspiracy, involving price fixing of Tennessee Valley Authority equipment by major electrical equipment manufacturers. Seven executives from firms such as General Electric and Westinghouse were given jail sentences of thirty days, a strong warning to price fixers that such behavior would be regarded more seriously. In all, twenty-nine companies and forty-five executives were convicted of bid rigging and price fixing and fined approximately two billion dollars. Not all white-collar crime was bloodless, however.

The Ford Pinto case began in the early 1960's when the Ford Motor Company decided to rush to production the Pinto, a compact automobile designed to compete with foreign imports such as the Volkswagen "bug." To save time and costs, the company decided to proceed with production despite the results of its own crash tests, which showed that the rear-mounted gas tank exploded when the car was hit from behind. By the early 1970's, roughly five hundred people had been burned to death because of Ford's decision. According to a company memorandum, Ford had performed a cost-benefit analysis of the problem and decided it was cheaper to ignore the problem and face the lawsuits.

Scandals Many scandals and crimes of the 1960's did not come to light until later. Scandals related to President Kennedy, for example, took place when the media largely chose to ignore personal or private scandals that were unrelated to public policy. Similarly, FBI Director J. Edgar Hoover was reportedly unwilling to attack organized crime because crime-family members had provided gambling favors and were using information abut his private sexual life to blackmail him.

Perhaps the most noteworthy scandal of the 1960's was the Chappaquiddick incident, which took place on July 18, 1969, on Chappaquiddick Island, Massachusetts, and involved Senator Edward "Ted" Kennedy, the younger brother of assassinated John and Robert Kennedy and heir apparent to the presidency. On that summer evening, Kennedy drove his car off a bridge to the mainland. His only passenger, twenty-eight-year-old aide Mary Jo Kopechne, drowned. Kennedy was convicted of leaving the scene of an accident and gave the impression of trying to cover up the incident. His presidential hopes were dashed; however, Kennedy was reelected to the Senate although he lost a later primary bid to James "Jimmy" Carter for the Democratic presidential nomination in 1980.

Another scandal involved the suicide of actress Marilyn Monroe in 1962. Monroe was the blonde beauty of her era and a major box-office attraction. She had been married to New York Yankee baseball hero Joe DiMaggio as well as playwright Arthur Miller. At the time, her early, unexpected suicide was believed to have been caused by the pressures of Hollywood stardom; however, later investigators allege that her death may have been related to secret affairs with both President Kennedy and his brother Robert, who was then attorney general. Although none of the allegations have been proved, one of the charges holds that Monroe became depressed when it became apparent that President Kennedy was not about to divorce his wife in order to marry her.

Another scandal touching the president involved a close friend of President Lyndon B. Johnson, Billie Sol Estes, who was convicted in 1965 of swindling finance companies out of twenty-two million dollars. Estes secured loans on the basis of false collateral: nonexistent fertilizer tanks that he claimed to own in Texas. Estes had farmers purchase the storage tanks on installment payments and lease them back to him at the same price. He then sold the installment notes to finance companies, although less than two thousand of the thirty thousand tanks actually existed. He served six years of a fifteen-year sentence.

Impact The 1960's was a tumultuous decade in U.S. history. The upheavals associated with the war in Vietnam, civil rights and antipoverty campaigns, sexual revolution, and drug culture all combined with violent crimes and scandalous incidents to make other decades appear calm by comparison.

The rising crime rates of the 1960's had a lasting effect on the public, politics, government, and the criminal justice system in the United States. Increasing fear of crime made voters far more willing to support law-and-order candidates and legislation that promised to curb crime. Increasingly, public opinion came to favor incarceration rather than rehabilitation of criminals. Crime, particularly violent crime, continued to occur in the United States at a far higher rate than in other developed countries and had a profound impact on the deterioration of the inner city as the middle class fled to what it regarded as safer suburban enclaves. Continuing wars on drugs swelled the prison population and particularly affected young minority males. Passage of the Organized Crime Control Act of 1970 provided invaluable legal tools against organized crime, which when implemented in the 1980's crippled the leadership of the Cosa Nostra, opening the way for other organized crime groups to gain strength. Congressional hearings in the 1970's attempted to place greater oversight and control over intelligence-agency operations.

Additional Information Accounts of crime during the 1960's can be found in Frank Hagan's *Introduction to Criminology* (1998). Other sources of information include the Kerner Commission Report (1968) and the Warren Report (1964).

Frank E. Hagan

See also Civil Rights Movement; Kerner Commission Report; Organized Crime; Warren Report.

■ Cronkite, Walter

Born November 4, 1916, St. Joseph, Missouri

One of the nation's most prominent, respected, and trusted broadcast journalists. Cronkite was a leader in bringing television news into the mainstream of American life.

Early Life Walter Leland Cronkite, Jr.'s career in journalism started with newspapers in Texas. In 1937, he took a position with the news service, United Press (UP), which led to foreign correspondent assignments. Cronkite covered World War II from 1942 to 1945 and the Nuremberg Trials that followed in Germany. He then served as UP's chief correspondent in Moscow from 1946 to 1948. Cronkite turned down a UP job in London for a

Walter Cronkite, news anchor of The CBS Evening News *from April, 1962, to 1981, was a trusted face in an influential medium.* (Library of Congress)

position as the Washington, D.C., bureau head for a group of Midwestern radio stations, arriving in time to cover Harry S Truman's presidential inauguration in 1949. He joined the Columbia Broadcasting System (CBS) as a television news correspondent for the network's newly purchased WTOP-TV in Washington, D.C., in 1950 when television was in its infancy. His significant journalism experiences later led to a position in television news that made him a major national influence.

The 1960's Television became the dominant medium in this decade of great social and political upheaval. Cronkite rose to superstar status as a broadcast journalist and became one of the most trusted individuals in the United States. On April 16, 1962, he became news anchor of *The CBS Evening News.* The power and influence of television news increased significantly when CBS lengthened the evening newscast from fifteen to thirty minutes on

September 2, 1963. The initial half-hour program featured Cronkite's interview with President John F. Kennedy. Television news was increasingly making national and world affairs more accessible to Americans.

As a television news anchor, Cronkite became a trusted voice reporting on significant events such as elections, space flights, civil rights protests, assassinations, and the Vietnam War. He, like much of the American establishment, was an early supporter of the country's military involvement in Southeast Asia. However, as a result of his reporting trips to Vietnam, he became disenchanted with the war. After the Tet Offensive in early 1968, Cronkite broadcast a special CBS news report critical of U.S. involvement. The influence of his report, along with growing public criticism of the war, contributed to President Lyndon B. Johnson's decision not to seek a second term as president.

Later Life Cronkite's influence as a highly trusted CBS news anchor continued through the 1970's. In 1981, he gave up the position to become a CBS special correspondent. He also hosted cultural and public affairs programs and produced television documentaries for syndication.

Impact Cronkite set the standards by which others in television news were judged. He was a dominant figure in a medium that grew to have major influence on public opinion and the course of events. During the 1960's, public figures and political leaders were evaluated by how well they measured up to him.

Additional Information In 1996, Cronkite published an autobiography, *A Reporter's Life*, reflecting on his life and career in journalism.

R. Brooks Garner

See also Media; Television; Tet Offensive; Vietnam War.

■ Cuban Missile Crisis

Date October 22-28, 1962

A major watershed in nuclear-age international politics. The crisis brought the world sufficiently close to a nuclear war to cause the United States and the Soviet Union to pursue nonconfrontational paths of competition throughout the remainder of the Cold War.

Origins and History The employment of the atomic bomb against Japan in 1945 abruptly ended World War II and ushered in the age of nuclear weapons. Within a decade, the United States and the Soviet Union had become the primary competitors in a world dominated by these two superpowers, each armed with vastly destructive thermonuclear weap-

ons (hydrogen bombs). In October, 1962, Soviet and U.S. diplomats were forced to align their policies with this immensely dangerous combination of geopolitics and the technology of mass destruction.

The Missile Crisis During the summer of 1962, several considerations tempted Soviet premier Nikita

Newspaper headlines during the October, 1962, Cuban Missile Crisis reveal how strained Soviet-U.S. relations became. The threat of nuclear war caused the two superpowers to find ways to lessen the likelihood of future confrontations. (AP/Wide World Photos)

Khrushchev to take the dangerous step of deploying in Cuba twenty-four strategic nuclear weapons, each with twenty times the destructive capacity of the bombs dropped on Japan. These included Khrushchev's mistaken belief that President John F. Kennedy was a weak leader who would back down in a confrontation and Khrushchev's desire to neutralize U.S. missiles aimed at the Soviet Union from Italy and Turkey and to discourage a U.S. attack on the Soviet Union's Cuban client. Whatever his reasoning, Khrushchev grossly underestimated Cuba's importance to the United States. His action not only threatened to reorder unacceptably the nuclear balance between Washington, D.C., and Moscow but also challenged the oldest of U.S. foreign policies, the 1823 Monroe Doctrine that had declared the Western Hemisphere off-limits to noncontinental actors.

The U.S. response to the situation was swift, forceful, and laden with danger. Aerial photographs taken by a U-2 spy plane on October 14 indicated two dozen nearly operational medium-range Soviet ballistic missiles in Cuba. On October 16, President Kennedy convened a top-level advisory Executive Committee (Ex-Comm) to respond to the threat. For a week thereafter, Kennedy kept the missiles a secret from the public while the military prepared for air strikes against military targets in Cuba or even an invasion of the island. On October 22, the president went on television to declare a quarantine on Cuba. The U.S. Navy would turn back any ships carrying offensive weapons. More important, he demanded that Khrushchev quickly dismantle the missiles already there.

Kennedy's speech inaugurated a six-day period during which the world hovered on the brink of nuclear war. Both sides exchanged threats, U.S. forces were placed on the highest military readiness short of war, Soviet cargo and naval vessels pursued a collision course toward the U.S. forces blockading Cuba, and powerful voices in the U.S. military and Congress lobbied for an invasion, especially after a U.S. military officer was killed on October 27 when his reconnaissance plane was shot down over Cuba. Then, though publicly embarrassed but better aware than Kennedy of how close the world was to catastrophe, Khrushchev accepted the diplomatic olive branch extended to him on October 28. In return for a U.S. pledge not to invade Cuba, he agreed to remove the missiles. A secret part of the agreement

was that, after several months and without Soviet comment, the United States would remove its missiles from Turkey.

Impact The lasting significance of the Cuban Missile Crisis was its effect on U.S.-Soviet relations. U.S. think tanks calculated that the risk of all-out nuclear war over Cuba was one in three. The Soviet Union knew that it had been much higher. Unknown to Washington, Soviet field commanders possessed six tactical nuclear missiles they were prepared to use in the event of an invasion. Sobered by the dangers they had just escaped, the leaders of both countries sought to avoid future confrontations. A hot line was installed between Moscow and Washington to minimize the possibility of accidental wars. The superpowers also began to work toward the creation and signing of nuclear test ban treaties and agreements to limit arms sales to Third World countries whose rivalries might draw the superpowers into a conflict. Most important, a tacit understanding involving proxy wars was reached. It was understood that in any future conflict directly involving either U.S. or Soviet troops, the other superpower would use only local forces to fight them by proxy. The policy, followed in both Vietnam and Afghanistan, outlived both the Kennedy and Khrushchev administrations.

Additional Information The best book on the Cuban Missile Crisis is *Thirteen Days: A Memoir of the Cuban Missile Crisis* (1968), by Robert F. Kennedy, the president's brother and an important member of Ex-Comm.

Joseph R. Rudolph, Jr.

See also Arms Race; Bay of Pigs Invasion; Kennedy, John F.; Kennedy, Robert F.; Nuclear Test Ban Treaties; Vietnam War.

■ Cults

Small religious groups that have structures, beliefs, and practices very different from those of mainstream religious groups in the United States. Cults in the 1960's could be seen as integral to the widespread countercultural movement.

Numerous alternative religions had emerged in the United States as early as the nineteenth century; however, the number of cults grew significantly in the 1950's and continued to expand in the 1960's, gaining membership from individuals seeking an alternative, countercultural lifestyle. The cults were small, new religious groups that held beliefs and followed practices markedly different from those of the established, dominant religious groups in the United States. They were often communal in structure and led by a powerful, charismatic figure. Some religious groups that were actually sects (groups that broke off from an existing religious organization) were perceived as cults because their beliefs were radically changed from the parent religion or non-Western in origin and thus unfamiliar to most Americans. The new religions formed in the 1950's and 1960's fall into three broadly defined categories: faiths based on Asian or mystical religions, Christian-based religions, and those arising from spiritual and human potential movements.

Eastern Influences The Asian-based "cults" that flourished in the 1960's were usually based on Buddhism, Hinduism, or lesser-known Indian beliefs and sometimes were actually branches of established Asian religions or sects rather than cults. In the 1950's and early 1960's, Zen Buddhism, an old established religion, enjoyed popularity in the United States, largely because of Alan Watts and other Beat generation members' interest in the religion, and centers sprang up on both coasts of the United States. In 1960, Nichiren Shoshu of America, a U.S. branch of a Japanese Buddhist organization, was set up in San Francisco and enjoyed remarkable success in recruiting members in the following years, reaching a membership of about seventy thousand in 1970. Although this group was a sect and not a cult, its powerful, charismatic leaders, aggressive recruiting style, and distinctive Buddhist practices gave it the aura of a cult.

In 1957, Maharishi Mahesh Yogi, an Indian, introduced transcendental meditation (TM) in the United States. The practice, based on Hinduism, is a form of meditation designed to produce a higher state of consciousness. The emphasis on meditation rather than religious teachings made it possible for people to practice TM without abandoning their former religious beliefs. That doctrinal flexibility and its practice by members of the Beatles in the late 1960's gave it enduring popularity, leading to the establishment of a TM university in Iowa. A more popular but controversial Hindu sect, the International Society for Krishna Consciousness (ISKCON, also known as Hare Krishnas), was founded by A. C.

Bhaktivedanta Swami Prabhupada in New York City in 1965. ISKCON's spiritual sources were India's Vedic culture. Despite its other-worldly ascetic practices, it appealed largely to white, middle-class youth.

Also in 1965, a former member of the Church of Scientology, Paul Twitchell, founded ECKANKAR, based on the Sant Mat tradition of India, in Las Vegas. This group introduced "bilocation," which it described as the ancient science of soul travel. In 1968, a former ECKANKAR member, John-Roger Hinkins, left the group and founded a group with similar beliefs and practices, the Movement of Spiritual Inner Awareness. In 1969, Yogi Bhajan set up the Healthy-Happy-Holy Organization (3HO), which promoted kundalini yoga and meditation, in California. Its religious ideas derived primarily from Sikhism but incorporated other traditions as well. Other alternative religions based on Asian traditions included the Integral Yoga Institute, Satya Sai Baba, Ananda Marga Yoga, and the Tibetan Nyingma Meditation Center.

Christian Influences A number of Christian-derived religious groups sprang up in the 1960's. Their religious beliefs and practices were varied, often based largely on the beliefs of a central figure. In 1964, psychologist Arthur Kleps organized the Neo-American Church, which used psychedelic drugs as its sacraments and employed irreverence and satire. Two years later, Anton LaVey founded one of the most controversial cults, the Church of Satan, in San Francisco. The church followed a hedonistic philosophy of physical and mental gratification, self-assertion, and antiestablishment attitudes. Also in 1966, Hobart Freeman established Faith Assembly to promote abstinence from all medication and medical means of health care.

Toward the end of the 1960's, a Christian derivative of the hippies, the Jesus people movement, emerged in California. Of all the major groups that sprang from the Jesus people, the Children of God (later known as the Family of Love or the Family) was considered the most radical. Founder David Berg (later known as Moses Berg) began his coffee-house ministry in California in 1968. The Children of God denounced capitalism, endeavored to develop Christian socialism, and experimented with a number of proselytization techniques and living arrangements. Another controversial group that emerged from the Jesus people movement was the

The Beatles' visits to the Maharishi Mahesh Yogi in 1967 popularized this Indian guru and the practice of transcendental meditation. (Popperfoto/Archive Photos)

Christian Foundation (also known as the Music Square Church or the Alamo Foundation). Susan Alamo and Tony Alamo started the foundation as a street ministry in Hollywood, California, in 1969. The foundation was a conservative, evangelical anti-Catholic Protestant group whose members had to observe strict behavioral rules. Two other 1969 Jesus people movement splinter groups, the Church of Armageddon (also known as Love Israel) and Shiloh, took the form of Christian communes.

Other alternative religious groups that appeared in the late 1960's included the Metropolitan Community Church, a Pentecostal church affirming the dignity of homosexuals, and the Holy Order of Mans, a Rosicrucian-style church synthesizing traditional Christian monasticism, New Thought philosophy, the Western esoteric tradition, and Tantrism.

Growth also occurred in groups that had come into existence in the 1950's. The two most prominent of these groups, the Peoples Temple, led by Jim Jones, and the Holy Spirit Association for the Unification of World Christianity (Unification Church or Moonies), led by the Reverend Sun Myung Moon, grew rapidly in the 1960's. The Peoples Temple,

although termed a cult after its members committed mass suicide in 1979, was actually affiliated with the National Council of Churches of Christ in the USA, a mainstream Christian group. The Unification Church expanded rapidly after its leader moved to the United States in 1973.

New Interpretations The spiritual and human potential movements of the 1950's and 1960's created a number of new faiths and quasi-religious groups. One such movement was neopaganism, which started in 1961 with a group that called itself the Church of All Worlds. The movement stressed feminine principle in divinity and believed in "instant karma" and magic. The majority of the neopagans came from the white, urban middle class.

In 1963, spiritualism was revitalized when Jane Roberts claimed to have received messages from the entity Seth. Other people began to report hearing internal voices that urged them to speak or write. The thoughts expressed were said to have originated with a person from the past (usually a wise person) who was "channeling" thoughts through the speaker. Channelers sometimes wrote books or summoned these entities to speak to assembled groups.

The human potential movement resulted in the establishment of the Esalen Institute, a New Age educational institution, in 1962 near Carmel, California. The institute promotes human potentials and values through seminars and workshops that deal with therapeutic techniques based on spirituality and science. Dreams, meditation, art, and dance are part of the institute's teachings.

Impact Although the cults and alternative religions of the 1960's were especially attractive to youth, marginalized persons, idealists, and dissidents in the mainstream churches, they also appealed to a wide spectrum of the U.S. population, including educated professionals and the middle class. These religions offered an alternative way of relating to the physical and spiritual world and generated a new culture that was in opposition to the empirical, rationalistic dominant American culture. In the late 1960's, many Americans became neoromanticists, learning to value the role of imagination and ecstasy in knowledge. The dreamlike altars and vigorous dancing of ISKCON, the monotonous sutra chanting of Nichiren Shoshu of America, and the colorfulness and conspicuousness of the charismatic cult leaders all embodied neoromantic ideas.

During the 1967 Summer of Love, thousands of college students flocked to San Francisco, Berkeley, and Hollywood to be part of the hippie movement. As the hippie scene began to fade, many of these young people became involved in youth-oriented cults and alternative religions such as ISKCON, Children of God, the Christian Foundation, and the Unification Church. They had come in search of the new and unusual, ready to pursue countercultural values in an alternative lifestyle, and the cults offered this break with tradition. Many of the young people who joined communal cults simply dropped out of college and broke contact with their families.

Subsequent Events Many of the cults flourished and experienced real growth in the 1970's. Children of God, ECKANKAR, ISKCON, Nichiren Shoshu of America, Peoples Temple, the Unification Church, the Church of Satan, and the Holy Order of Mans, all reached their peak membership and influence in that decade. Many cults actively sought new members, often recruiting on university campuses. Inspired by the Church of Satan, satanic churches multiplied in the 1970's.

Cults also increasingly drew criticism from the parents of the young converts. When their children dropped out of school, refused to pursue careers, and began believing in unusual ideas and adopting austere lifestyles, their parents became upset and alarmed. One group of parents formed the Parents Committee to Free Our Children from the Children of God in 1972, giving rise to the anticult movement. The anticult movement attacked other controversial new religions, charging that the groups used improper recruiting methods and brainwashed their followers. It developed "deprogramming" techniques and sophisticated forms of psychological and physical coercion to separate followers from their chosen cults. Although the deprogramming process provoked controversy and its success rate was only about 50 percent, the anticult movement succeeded in discrediting many of the new religions, dramatically reducing the number of converts.

Additional Information An exhaustive treatment of cults can be found in Gordon Melton's *The Encyclopedia of American Religions* (1993). Melton's *Encyclopedic Handbook of Cults in America* (1992) provides detailed information about the prominent cults of the nineteenth and twentieth centuries. Another source of information on specific cults is Timothy Miller's *America's Alternative Religions* (1995), which analyzes and categorizes many new religions. *The Anti-Cult Movement in America* (1984) by Anson Shupe, et al., presents a comprehensive picture of the movement and its impact.

Cheris Shun-ching Chan

See also Counterculture; Hare Krishnas; Hippies; Religion and Spirituality.

■ Cyclamates

Artificial sweetener used as a sugar substitute. Possible links between cyclamates and cancer led to a ban on cyclamates in many countries, including the United States.

Cyclamates were first synthesized in 1937. They are about fifty times sweeter than sugar and contain no calories. In 1950, products containing cyclamates became available in the United States.

In the early 1960's, recognition of the adverse health effects of obesity led to widespread use of cyclamates as sugar substitutes. Although the evidence was minimal that the modest decrease in calorie consumption obtained by using such substitutes would result in weight loss in most individuals, large numbers of soft drinks, tabletop sweeteners, and diet foods containing cyclamates soon appeared on the market.

In 1966, researchers found that cyclamates can break down in the body. A short time later, two studies appeared indicating increased levels of bladder cancer in mice or rats fed high doses of cyclamates. Although other researchers found no link between cyclamates and cancer, concerns about possible health effects led the Food and Drug Administration to place a total ban on cyclamates in food products in 1969.

Subsequent Events Additional laboratory studies have failed to show a strong link between cyclamates and cancer. The development of alternative low-calorie sweeteners (such as aspartame) in the 1980's has removed the need for cyclamate.

Additional Information A discussion of cyclamates can be found in *Sweet Talk: Media Coverage of Artificial Sweeteners* (1986), by Philip Lawler.

Jeffrey A. Joens

See also Cancer; Medicine; Thalidomide.

■ Czechoslovakia, Soviet Invasion of

Date August 20, 1968

The abrupt end to the Prague Spring. The invasion of military forces of the Warsaw Treaty Organization (WTO) led to the dismantling of reform communism in Czechoslovakia and to a repressive regime that ruled until the Velvet Revolution of 1989.

Origins and History In the mid-1960's, reformers in the Czechoslovak Communist Party called for political change in the neo-Stalinist party and new economic policies in place of the disastrous emphasis on heavy industry. The 1967 Writers Congress also featured demands for political reforms. Writers, filmmakers, and many people active in the theater were simultaneously concentrating on artistic experimentation and innovation.

The Invasion The events that led to Prague Spring and the Soviet invasion that ended that experiment in reform communism began in January, 1968, when Alexander Dubček replaced Antonín Novotný as first secretary of the Communist Party. Dubček rep-

resented a moderate approach to economic and political reform and also the Slovak interests in the party in their protest against the neglect of Slovakia by the Czechoslovak Communist Party in the past.

Reforms began cautiously. Censorship ended in March, and in April, the government announced an Action Program that concentrated on production of consumer goods and the expansion of political freedom. Plans for more radical political reform, drawn up for presentation at the Fourteenth Party Congress, envisioned a transition to a more pluralistic but nevertheless one-party system.

Events quickly outstripped the intentions of the reformers within the party. Quasi-political clubs appeared, and the Social Democratic Party was revived. A radical declaration, "Two Thousand Words," written by Ludvík Vaculík and signed by a large number of intellectuals and cultural leaders, appeared in June. By this time, reform had solid support from students, intellectuals, and also the working class, but the conservative elements within the party were growing increasingly nervous about maintaining the party's dominant position. Also, the Warsaw Treaty Organization (WTO) issued an ultimatum in June, calling for an end to reforms. In addition to the Soviet Union, the German Democratic Republic and Poland wanted the Czech experiments to end. Two meetings between Czech party leaders and WTO leaders followed, one at Čierná nad Tisou in July and the second at Bratislava in August. In each case, Dubček worked hard to convince WTO leaders that Czechoslovakia would remain in the WTO.

On the night of August 20, 165,000 WTO troops and 4,600 tanks crossed into Czechoslovakia in Operation Danube. Within a week, the invasion force numbered about 500,000 men and more than 6,000 tanks. The Czechs followed a policy of nonviolent protest, which slowed but did not stop the invasion. Dubček and other leaders were arrested and taken to Moscow but later returned when other Czech leaders refused to cooperate. The "normalization" of Czechoslovakia was a slow but steady process. Dubček was replaced by Gustáv Husák in April, 1969. In the next few years, about half a million members of the Communist Party were thrown out of the party and in most cases lost their jobs. Nearly two decades of moral and economic decay followed. Charter Seventy-seven, a response to the Helsinki Final Act of 1975, was the major challenge to the repressive government of this period. Václav Havel, later presi-

A Czechoslovak student waves his nation's flag while standing atop a tank belonging to the Soviets, who invaded his country in August, 1968. (AP/Wide World Photos)

dent of the Republic of Czechoslovakia and then of the Czech Republic, was the most prominent member of this challenge.

Impact Soviet leader Leonid Brezhnev announced the Brezhnev Doctrine in defense of the invasion. The doctrine stated that one socialist country may intervene in the affairs of another socialist country if the continued existence of socialism was in danger. This was the end of attempts at national reform in eastern and central Europe until Mikhail Gorbachev and *perestroika*. It was also the last use of force by the Soviet Union in this area. For some people in the United States in 1968, the Soviet invasion and the end of the Prague Spring seemed one more example of counterrevolution destroying the hopes of re-

formers and revolutionaries in a year filled with shocks and disappointments. The Soviet invasion, although much criticized in the United States, did not prevent the continued development of détente in Soviet and American relations over the next few years.

Additional Information *The Prague Spring and Its Aftermath: Czechoslovak Politics, 1968-1970* (1997), by Kieran Williams, analyzes the reform movement and its suppression by the Soviet Union using archival sources available since the events of 1989. H. Gordon Skilling's *Czechoslovakia's Interrupted Revolution* (1976) is a classic study of the reform.

Michael Richards

See also Cold War.

D

■ Dances, Popular

Dances that reflected the style and lyrics of popular music. Couples gyrated as partners—but with little or no physical contact.

The popular dances of the 1960's were rooted in the rock and roll of the 1950's. In 1959, young African Americans created a dance for the hit record "The Twist" by Hank Ballard. Singer Chubby Checker recorded Ballard's song, and when he performed it and the dance in 1960 on Dick Clark's television show, *American Bandstand*, the song, along with the twist, became an instant hit.

The twist, popularized by Checker, embodied the era with its "anything goes" informal attitude. It was the first rock-and-roll dance to cross the generation gap; its combination of rock music and free, percussive movements—which made dance classes unnecessary—appealed to everyone. Its popularity lasted for several years.

Dances of the 1960's became as diverse as the music styles introduced. Some dances, including the fish, the hitchhiker, and Popeye, lasted as long as a record was a hit. The Batman appeared briefly as a dance following the introduction of the television show featuring the comic book hero *Batman*. Another short-lived dance was the Freddie, named after Freddie Garrity of Freddie and the Dreamers. The dance imitated the wild, up-and-down hopping he did on stage. La Bostella came to the United States from Paris, France, where, at a discotheque, French photographer Jacques Bostel accidentally tripped and fell to the floor. Other dancers imitated his fall, and a new dance was created.

Imported from Paris, the discotheque (a nightclub that features recorded rather than live music for dancing) soon flourished throughout the United States. Beginning with the Peppermint Lounge, where the twist was popularized with the song, "Peppermint Twist," New York City soon overflowed with discos. The more famous included Sybil, Arthur, Ondine, the Dom, and Hippopotamus. Clubs hired professional "go-go dancers" to perform the latest dances, often on pedestals above the dance floor. Patrons could take time out from their gyrations to rest, watch these dancers, and pick up new moves.

Amid the popularity of the twist, dances such as the alligator, the bug, the dog, the pony, the frug, the watusi, the hitchhiker, the hully-gully, the jerk, and the boogaloo found their way onto the dance floor. Many of these were performed with pantomimic hand and arm motions appropriate to the dance's name. To do the swim, dancers moved their arms as if swimming the crawl as they twisted. Variations included holding the nose with one hand while sinking to the floor as though going underwater. Other swim strokes added to the dancer's repertoire. For the mashed potato, the dancer moved the feet as if mashing something with them, and the slop called for sloppy walking in place. When little body or foot action was part of the dance, dancers desiring more action added their own special movements.

Some dances had roots in earlier dance forms. The frug contained elements of the shimmy, and the heebie-jeebies was the basis for the bug and the monkey. Components of the slow drag reemerged as the pony. As the dances multiplied, the quality diminished. Many dances remained unnamed.

By the mid-1960's, the twist's popularity had waned. Replacements included the frug and the jerk, which continued to be danced into the late 1960's. A spot dance, the frug began at Syracuse University in New York. Frug dancers swiveled their hips side to side and moved their arms in the frug swing, in which dancers alternately curved their left and right arms to mid-chest from hip level. Other gestures included a scolding motion with a pointing index finger and a hand extended palm up, as if asking for a handout. The jerk debuted in 1964 with a song by the Larks. A dancer held one arm high in front of the body, then jerked the body downward, bringing the arm down as well. The dancer then lifted the other arm while jerking the body upward.

Impact Seeking to capitalize on the dance craze, advertisers created dances to sell products. The mule, which included a kick in keeping with its name, was invented to sell a brand of vodka and a soft drink. However, in the late 1960's, popular music moved in a more lyrical direction, and people stopped frequenting discotheques. Those still interested in dancing turned to soul music, which provided dances such as the funky chicken, in which dancers flapped their arms and mimed the laying of eggs. By the end of the decade, old style rock had been largely replaced by acid rock. This new type of rock was meant to be heard at rock concerts, which encouraged listening and swaying to the music rather than formalized dancing.

Additional Information A brief overview of popular dances of the 1960's may be found in *Let's Dance* (1996), by Frances Fyfield.

Mary Pat Balkus

See also *American Bandstand*; Counterculture; Music; Twist.

■ Davis, Angela

Born January 26, 1944, Birmingham, Alabama

An African American professor who espoused radical causes. Davis became the Communist Party's best-known member during the 1960's and 1970's.

Early Life Born in Birmingham, one of the centers of the Civil Rights movement, Angela Yvonne Davis became a participant in political struggles at an early age. She lived with her parents, B. Frank and Sallye E. Davis, in a segregated neighborhood and attended segregated public schools. She took part in civil rights demonstrations with her mother, and homes in her neighborhood were bombed by white supremacists. After her second year of high school, Davis won a scholarship to attend a private school in New York, and in 1961, she won a scholarship to attend Brandeis University.

The 1960's At Brandeis, Davis came into contact with Herbert Marcuse, a renowned Marxist philosophy professor, who convinced her that communism held the solution to African American oppression. After graduation in 1965, she studied in Germany and then earned a master's degree at the University of California, San Diego. In San Diego, she became involved with several activist groups, including the Student Nonviolent Coordinating Committee and the Black Panthers. She joined the Communist Party in 1968 and became active in a black communist

University professor and Communist Party member Angela Davis supported radical causes during the 1960's. Her activities led to her arrest on charges of which she was later acquitted. (Library of Congress)

group, the Che-Lumumba club. In 1969, Davis took a job as assistant professor at the University of California at Los Angeles. Her involvement in demonstrations and protests in Los Angeles drew attention to her Communist Party membership, and the university's board of regents fired her. Davis won her job back after a court order but was denied tenure in 1970.

Davis received national publicity in 1969 and 1970 when she took up the cause of the Soledad Brothers, a group of African American prisoners in Soledad Prison who had tried to organize a radical group. After one of the Soledad Brothers was shot by a guard, Davis purchased weapons. Some of these weapons were used in an attempt to rescue members of the Soledad Brothers and take hostages during a trial at the Marin County Courthouse. Charged with kidnapping, conspiracy, and murder, Davis became a fugitive and was placed on the Ten Most Wanted List of the Federal Bureau of Investigation. She went to jail for sixteen months but was acquitted of involvement in the Marin County Courthouse incident in 1972.

Later Life After her acquittal, Davis gave lectures around the United States and made a trip to the Soviet Union. She also returned to university teaching and served as a professor at San Francisco State University and the University of California, San Diego. She continued her efforts on behalf of the Communist Party of the United States, sitting on the party's central committee. In 1980 and in 1984, she was the Communist Party's candidate for vice president of the United States.

Impact Davis was an outspoken advocate of radical causes and helped to draw national attention to African American and leftist issues. She also helped publicize the Communist Party of the United States, an organization that historically enjoyed little popular support in the United States.

Additional Information In 1988, Davis published *Angela Davis: An Autobiography*.

Carl L. Bankston III

See also Black Panthers; Civil Rights Movement; Student Nonviolent Coordinating Committee (SNCC).

■ Days of Rage

Date October 8-11, 1969

Four days of intense anti-Vietnam War protest in Chicago's Lincoln Park. The event was never intended to be peaceful.

The Students for a Democratic Society (SDS) and the Weathermen planned a massive demonstration, four Days of Rage, to coincide with the trial of the Chicago Seven, antiwar activists who had been arrested and charged with conspiracy for their part in protests surrounding the 1968 Democratic National Convention in Chicago. The demonstration was designed to be a political statement against the Vietnam War and start the next American revolution.

On October 8, 1969, eighty Weathermen gathered in Chicago's Lincoln Park to force U.S. troops to withdraw from Vietnam and to start a revolution that would end imperialism worldwide. Approximately five hundred demonstrators, flying the Viet Cong flag, listened to speakers in the park. The mob became angry the evening of October 8, and vandalism of businesses and cars escalated as the demonstrators marched the streets. When the protesters reached Lake Shore Drive, the police contained and arrested them. The National Guard was alerted the

next day. The violence subsided, only to flare one more time on the weekend. Richard Elrod, a Chicago city attorney, was severely injured during this second march. The citizens of Chicago were outraged at the riots; most of the demonstrators left town after the attorney was injured.

Impact The SDS, already fractionalized, died a natural death after the riots. The Weathermen, although suffering from a lack of faith from many former supporters, continued their resistance by going underground and eluding law enforcement officials.

Additional Information Allen J. Matusow describes the encounter and the resultant loss of power of the Students for a Democratic Society and the Weathermen in *The Unraveling of America: A History of Liberalism in the 1960's* (1984).

Karan A. Berryman

See also Chicago Seven Trial; Democratic National Convention of 1968; Students for a Democratic Society (SDS); Weathermen.

■ *Death of a President, The*

Published 1967
Author William Manchester (1922-   )

A study of the events surrounding the assassination of President John F. Kennedy. The book became the center of a public storm just before it was published.

The Work *The Death of a President* was written by reporter William Manchester, author of *Portrait of a President: John F. Kennedy in Profile* (1962), at the request of Jacqueline Kennedy, John F. Kennedy's widow. Jacqueline Kennedy hoped that the authorized account of the assassination that took place in Dallas in November, 1963, would preempt other books on the subject. Manchester, a passionate admirer of President Kennedy, wrote a long narrative that often placed Vice President Lyndon B. Johnson, who had become president after Kennedy's death, in an unflattering light, presenting him as a power-hungry boor. Johnson told aides "it makes me look like a son of a bitch."

Impact The book, released when political tension between Johnson and Senator Robert F. Kennedy, the dead president's brother and attorney general, was increasing, seemed likely to worsen the already bad relations between the two men. In an ill-considered move, Jacqueline Kennedy sued Manchester to compel him to delete negative language about Johnson and personal matters of which she disapproved. During the resulting public furor, the reputations of all involved suffered. Kennedy was seen as trying to censor an author whose work she disliked. Finally, lawyers for Manchester and Kennedy reached an out-of-court settlement. *The Death of a President* became a best-seller. It is remembered as a significant episode in the bitter animosity between Johnson and Robert F. Kennedy. It was also the moment when Jacqueline Kennedy's public image suffered its first serious reverse since the murder of her husband.

Related Works Hundreds of books have since been written about the assassination; one of the better accounts is *The Assassination of John F. Kennedy: A Complete Book of Facts* (1992), by historians James P. Duffy and Vincent L. Ricci.

Lewis L. Gould

See also Assassinations of John and Robert Kennedy and Martin Luther King, Jr.; Johnson, Lyndon B.; Kennedy, Jacqueline; Kennedy, John F.; Kennedy, Robert F.

■ Death of Hippie

Date October 6, 1967

An event staged to formally signal the end of the Summer of Love in San Francisco. It was a melange of ritual, street theater, and publicity stunt intended paradoxically to ward off further mainstream news coverage of the Haight-Ashbury counterculture.

Haight-Ashbury community activists organized the Death of Hippie event in hopes of symbolically re-

Members of the counterculture held a mock funeral in October, 1967, to mark the end of the Summer of Love and to attempt to stop excessive media coverage of hippies. (Popperfoto/Archive Photos)

versing their neighborhood's precipitous decline. Its central act involved an entourage of hippies bearing a coffin down Haight Street. Mourners were encouraged to cast into it such offerings as love beads, incense sticks, and copies of local newspapers. These last items signified that the now deceased "hippie" was, in the end, "the son of mass media." According to the organizers, the procession was construed as a rite of exorcism that would reportedly "free the boundaries of the Haight-Ashbury district" and "destroy the 'we/they' concept inherent in the idea of a 'hip.'" Participants were encouraged to move out of the district and henceforth refer to themselves as "free men" instead of hippies.

Impact Through this event, members of the counterculture attempted to gain narrative control over the direction of their movement. By changing their collective name and dispersing, they signaled that they had assumed a new form that would not be subject to easy distortion by the mass media. Although the counterculture did diffuse geographically in the Summer of Love's aftermath, the term "hippie" was too well established in popular parlance to be so easily dislodged.

Additional Information Charles Perry's *The Haight-Ashbury: A History* (1984) examines the hippies and their lifestyle.

Michael Wm. Doyle

See also Counterculture; Flower Children; Haight-Ashbury; Hippies; San Francisco as a Cultural Mecca; Summer of Love.

■ Decency Rallies

Patriotic rallies of the radical right largely against liberal social trends. Many families assembled in God-and-country rallies to protest sex education in public schools and the ban on school prayer.

The Cold War heightened the belief that American values and institutions were under assault. Some fundamentalist preachers built national followings by exploiting the real and imagined dangers facing the United States.

In the 1960's, religious and secular forces on the far right found enemies behind every tree, attacking communism, court-ordered integration of schools, and what they perceive as permissiveness and lawlessness. In 1963, a Supreme Court ruling had effectively banned prayer and Bible readings from public classrooms. The far right saw the Court decision as an example of godless infiltration in public schools. Fundamentalist leaders such as the Reverend Carl McIntire of Collingswood, New Jersey, and the Reverend Billy James Hargis of Tulsa, Oklahoma, portrayed themselves as defenders of a Christian nation battling atheistic communism. These men trained their troops through sermons, books, radio addresses, and God-and-country rallies. *The New York Times* reported that by 1966, fully 13 percent of the nation's public schools still held Bible readings.

The primary catalyst for a nationwide decency crusade was the introduction of sex education in public schools. In 1965, a school district in Anaheim, California, began teaching a sex education class, which generated angry reactions from some parents. Gordon V. Drake, director of education of B. J. Hargis's Christian Crusade, joined the assault on sex education in the public schools. Drake claimed that the Sex Information and Education Council of the United States (SIECUS), which assisted school districts that wished to form a sex education curriculum, and the National Education Association (NEA) were linked to communist sympathizers. Drake's 1968 book, *Blackboard Power: NEA Threat to America*, and his radio broadcasts resonated throughout the nation. Drake and the Christian Crusade spread their message through Family, School, and Morality rallies, where delegates were taught about the supposed dangers of sex education, sensitivity training, and the communist subversion of American youth through rock and roll.

Impact The fact that professional associations such as the American Medical Association, the National Council of Churches, and the NEA endorsed sex education curricula provided additional fodder for far-right groups, which believed these associations promoted what they termed "one-world government." In January of 1969, Robert Welch, founder of the John Birch Society, joined the crusade against sex education when he said he had discovered in these programs a "communist plan to destroy the moral character of a generation." The society formed national and local chapters of the Movement to Restore Decency (MOTOREDE). It also spawned dozens of similar local groups designed to promote public decency.

Subsequent Events *Look* magazine reported that the fight against sex education spread to thirty-four states and split many communities. Article author Mary Breasted wrote, "It seemed that every right-wing pamphleteer, radio preacher, . . . and freelance Commie-hater . . . had taken up the standard of all-American decency." In the fall of 1969, *Redbook, Reader's Digest, Life,* and *Look* magazines corrected the misinformation spread by opponents of sex education.

Additional Information Information about these protests and similar ones that occurred later can be found in *No Longer Exiles: The Religious New Right in American Politics* (1993), edited by Michael Cromar-

tie. Of particular interest is George Marsden's essay, "The Religious Right: A Historical Overview."

Dale W. Johnson

See also Conservatism in Politics; Education; *Engel v. Vitale*; John Birch Society; O'Hair, Madalyn Murray; Prayer in Schools.

■ Democratic National Convention of 1968

Date August 26-29, 1968

A national political meeting of the Democratic Party that seriously divided the party and weakened it for years. The widespread violence and political conflict that occurred in

A Chicago police officer chases an antiwar protester during the Democratic National Convention of 1968. The violence that erupted between protesters and police outside the convention was widely televised. (AP/Wide World Photos)

Chicago during this convention symbolized generational and cultural differences and policy conflicts over the Vietnam War.

Origins and History From 1932 through 1968, six Democratic national conventions were held in Chicago. Democratic Party leaders favored Chicago because of its geographically central location and the ability of the local Democratic machine to maintain security within and outside the convention halls. For example, during the 1940 Democratic National Convention, Chicago mayor Edward Kelly ordered convention officials to promote the controversial third-term candidacy of President Franklin D. Roosevelt and discourage delegates who opposed a third term. In 1968, Chicago mayor Richard Daley was faced with the more complex, contentious issues of the unpopularity of the Vietnam War and the presumed selection of Vice President Hubert Humphrey, who was vigorously opposed by antiwar demonstrators and some delegates, as the Democratic nominee for president.

The Convention After 1964, the expanding U.S. military role in Vietnam became more controversial among Americans, particularly college students, some leading media figures, and certain members of Congress, including liberal Democrats such as Senator Eugene McCarthy of Minnesota and Senator Robert F. Kennedy of New York. McCarthy, promising a prompt end to the Vietnam War through diplomacy, declared his presidential candidacy on November 30, 1967. With the help of thousands of college students and other antiwar activists, McCarthy almost defeated President Lyndon B. Johnson, who was a write-in candidate, in the March 11 New Hampshire Democratic presidential primary. Shortly thereafter, Kennedy, also emphasizing an antiwar theme, announced his candidacy. On March 31, 1968, Johnson announced that he would not seek his party's nomination for another term as president.

McCarthy and Kennedy competed for the support of antiwar activists and organizations and college students in several major presidential primaries. Kennedy had better name recognition, more campaign funds, a charismatic speaking style and personality, and a broader, more diverse coalition of supporters. In addition to attracting antiwar activists and college students, Kennedy appealed to African Americans, Latinos, and white blue-collar workers.

Kennedy defeated McCarthy in most of the primaries that both entered. On June 4, in California's presidential primary, he defeated the senator from Minnesota by a margin of 4 percent and appeared to be on the verge of becoming the Democratic presidential nominee. However, he was shot shortly after giving his victory speech at the Ambassador Hotel in Los Angeles and died on June 6.

Much of the anger, division, protest, and chaos that occurred within and near the Democratic National Convention that year can be attributed to the uncertainty, disillusionment, and frustration that many of the more moderate antiwar activists and convention delegates experienced after Kennedy's assassination. Despite the absence of his toughest competitor, McCarthy's campaign stagnated. Moderate former Kennedy supporters began to commit delegates to Humphrey rather than to McCarthy. In addition, militant antiwar organizations and leaders planned to conduct demonstrations in Chicago shortly before and during the August 26-29 convention.

The most prominent of these militant antiwar activists were the Yippies (short for the Youth International Party), led by Abbie Hoffman and Jerry Rubin. They demanded an immediate U.S. military withdrawal from Vietnam. The Yippies were part of the counterculture, sharing its appearance and beliefs and practices, which included sexual freedom, recreational drug use, and alienation from the establishment. For the Yippies and other members of the counterculture, the establishment included corporations, the media, and political traditions such as the two major parties and their nomination and platform-making processes at national conventions. The Yippies were joined in Chicago by other youth-oriented antiwar organizations, particularly the National Mobilization Committee to End the War in Vietnam (MOBE), Students for a Democratic Society (SDS), and the Black Panthers.

The violent, antagonistic relationship between antiwar demonstrators and the Chicago police and other security forces resulted in a major incident in Lincoln Park on August 26. After the Yippies conducted a mock convention in which they nominated a live pig, Pigasus, for president, they refused to obey an 11 P.M. curfew and did not leave the park. The police physically ejected them from the park.

The police, National Guard, and other security forces surrounded the International Amphitheater and hotels used by the Democratic National Convention in order to protect participants. Outside the convention, violent clashes continued to take place between security forces and demonstrators, many of whom were college students. On August 28, a large group of protesters who were marching toward the convention site were met by Chicago police officers wielding billy clubs. The officers attacked protesters, bystanders, and reporters alike, and their actions were televised throughout the nation. The officers were widely criticized for using excessive and indiscriminate physical force. During a dramatic, tense moment of the convention, Senator Abraham Ribicoff of Connecticut addressed the convention to nominate Senator George McGovern of South Dakota as an antiwar candidate for president. In his speech, he accused the Chicago police of "Gestapo tactics." Television cameras showed Mayor Daley and several Illinois delegates angrily jeering Ribicoff.

Although McCarthy did not have enough delegate support to be nominated for president at the convention, he and his delegates challenged Humphrey and his more numerous supporters on several issues. For example, the McCarthy forces were more likely than the pro-Humphrey delegates to challenge the credentials of delegations from southern states, citing racial imbalance in the makeup of these delegations as evidence of probable racial discrimination in the selection of delegates.

Despite the disorder and conflict that occurred outside of and, to a lesser extent, within the convention, Humphrey received the Democratic nomination for president by a wide margin on the first ballot. Humphrey chose Senator Edmund Muskie of Maine for his running mate. The delegates nominated Muskie for vice president by an even wider margin.

In contrast to the relative ease with which Humphrey and Muskie were nominated, the wording and adoption of a foreign policy plank on the Vietnam War for the party's platform was a highly divisive, contentious issue for the delegates and convention officials. Heavily influenced by the pro-Humphrey convention officials, the party's plank on the Vietnam War was moderate and vaguely worded, generally supported the Johnson administration's policy, and did not include unconditional support of an end to U.S. bombing. For the most part, antiwar delegates who had previously supported Kennedy, McCarthy, or McGovern were dissatisfied with this plank and felt alienated from Humphrey.

Impact The heckling and other forms of vocal opposition that Humphrey first experienced during the Democratic National Convention continued throughout his fall presidential campaign. Unlike McCarthy or McGovern, Humphrey held a position on the Vietnam War that resembled that of Richard M. Nixon, the Republican nominee for president. Both candidates basically promised to combine diplomatic negotiations with reduced military force to end the war. Neither promised an unconditional end to U.S. bombing or an immediate, complete U.S. military withdrawal from Vietnam.

The televised violence and chaos that occurred in Chicago helped both Nixon and Alabama governor George Wallace, presidential nominee of the American Independent Party, attract the support of socially conservative white voters by emphasizing law and order. Wallace drew some votes away from Nixon, making Humphrey more competitive against the Republican candidate. In the 1968 presidential election, Nixon defeated Humphrey by a popular vote margin of less than 1 percent.

Antiwar activists Hoffman, Rubin, David Dellinger, Rennie Davis, Tom Hayden, Lee Weiner, John Froines, and Bobby Seale were prosecuted for their roles in the Chicago protests. They were known as the Chicago Eight, then as the Chicago Seven when Seale's case was tried separately. Their theatrical trial further polarized the nation, deepening the rift between conservatives and liberals.

After the 1968 election, the Democratic Party significantly changed its rules for choosing delegates to national conventions in order to promote a more participatory process. The commission that oversaw these reforms was cochaired by McGovern and Representative Donald Fraser of Minnesota. McGovern's prominence as an antiwar presidential candidate at the 1968 Democratic National Convention and his role in reforming his party's presidential nomination and convention processes helped him win the Democratic presidential nomination in 1972.

Additional Information For further reading on the convention, see *Chicago '68* (1988), by David Farber; *Countdown to Chaos: Chicago, 1968, Turning Point in American Politics* (1969), by Jeffrey St. John; and Theodore White's *The Making of the President 1968*, published in 1969.

Sean J. Savage

See also Black Panthers; Chicago Seven Trial; Humphrey, Hubert; Kennedy, Robert F.; Liberalism in Politics; Muskie, Edmund; National Mobilization Committee to End the War in Vietnam (MOBE); Nixon, Richard M.; Students for a Democratic Society (SDS); Vietnam War; Wallace, George; Yippies.

■ Demographics of the United States

Population changes in a decade of crises. Changes in residence and occupations, alterations in the status of major ethnic groups, shifts in the birthrate from baby boom to baby bust, added longevity, and new roles for women were among the more important demographic trends of the 1960's.

Although the population of the United States grew from 181 million in 1960 to 205 million in 1970, continuing "flight from the farm" was depopulating the countryside. Farm employment declined from 7 million in 1960 to 4.4 million in 1970, and total U.S. farm population dropped from 15.6 million to 9.7 million. Expensive mechanization, chemical techniques, and federal subsidies geared to acreage helped larger agribusiness-type operations replace the 160-acre family farm of the plains states. In the South, mechanical cotton pickers were a factor in displacing many African American tenant farmers and sharecroppers. Agriculture prospered, but farmers became almost marginal as a population group and social force.

At the same time, the total urban population increased from 125.3 million in 1960 to 149.3 million in 1970. Most of the growth took place in metropolitan areas, which grew from 95.8 million people to 118.4 million. Total population of central cities rose slightly, from 57.9 million to 63.9 million, largely because of southern and southwestern urban increases, but the population living in suburbs grew enormously, from 37.8 million to 54.5 million people.

Housing The postwar suburban housing boom was largely financed by the federal G.I. Bill, which provided veterans with home loans and business credits in addition to funds for education, thus greatly increasing the size and proportion of the nation's middle-class population. Also, by the 1960's, the interstate highway system, with its urban bypasses, was reshaping the outer metropolis into a ring of suburbs linked by automobiles. Zoning codes and real estate "steering" practices, which enjoyed explicit or tacit government support until 1968, effectively excluded working-class elements and racial minorities in order to "protect property values." The attractions of the relatively affluent suburbs included ample space for raising children and modern high schools whose students advanced to the more selective and expensive private colleges. Grandparents, although not necessarily excluded from these youth-centered neighborhoods, tended to remain in small towns or to move to suburbs designed for retirees.

Industry In the 1960's, industry was migrating from its base in the Northeast to the South and Southwest. Shorter winters, cheap land and housing, air-conditioning, nonunion labor, and well-advertised tax incentives combined to persuade industry to locate or relocate in the South. Workers from the Rust Belt moved to jobs in the Sun Belt and West Coast locations as far north as Seattle, Washington. California attracted so many people that by 1970, some of its nearly 20 million inhabitants were emigrating to the less crowded Western states.

A major factor in industrial relocation was the relative decline in the importance of heavy industries and the increasing importance of plastics and microelectronics. Broadly speaking, fewer people were required in production, and more jobs developed in service and office categories. In 1959, 45.5 percent of white men in the United States worked in blue-collar jobs, and 39.7 percent were white-collar workers. By 1971, the balance had shifted: 43.7 percent in blue-collar and 44.6 percent in white-collar jobs. For white women, the 1959 figures were 17.2 percent blue-collar and 61.1 percent white-collar workers, and in 1970, 15.3 percent blue-collar and 64.9 percent white-collar workers. The blue-collar working class was beginning to shrink as a proportion of the United States' population.

Minorities Residential migration had special significance for some minority groups. For many African Americans, the 1960's brought a new societal status. In 1960, 60 percent of African Americans lived in the South. By 1970, about 53 percent remained in the South, about 40 percent lived in the North, and about 8 percent in the West. This migration away from the racial mores of the South combined with the Civil Rights movement opened the way for tangible progress. The median income of nonwhites (90 percent of whom were African Americans) rose from $3,233 in 1960 to $6,510 in 1970, measured in 1967 dollars. In the 1960's, the numbers of African Americans employed increased by 22 percent and doubled in professional, technical, and clerical fields. Meanwhile, nonwhite unemployment declined from 12.4 percent in 1960 to 6.5 percent in 1970, although it jumped to 8.2 percent later in 1970. Educationally, 38 percent of African Americans were high school graduates in 1960 and 56 percent by 1970. Also, in 1970, African Americans represented 7 percent of all college enrollments. By the standards of an earlier generation, the progress of some African Americans during the 1960's was revolutionary.

On the other hand, by the end of the decade, although only 11.5 percent of the population was African American, 30 percent of those in poverty and 40 percent of poverty-level children were African American. Nonwhite median income in 1970 still lagged far behind the white median income of $10,236. The unemployment problem remained acute, approaching 40 percent for young African American men in the inner city. Although 40 percent of African Americans (and two-thirds of whites) were home owners in 1970, home-loan frauds perpetrated against the urban poor particularly affected African Americans. Many livable African American neighborhoods were practically destroyed by the riot in the Watts area of Los Angeles in 1965, the Detroit riot of 1967, and the widespread violence following Martin Luther King, Jr.'s assassination in 1968. Leaving the South did not benefit all African Americans equally.

According to the 1970 census, the other large minority consisted of the 9 million Americans classified as "Spanish." This group included more than 4.5 million Mexican Americans, 1.4 million Puerto Rican Americans, some 800,000 Americans with Central and South American roots, and more than 500,000 from Cuba, many of these anti-Fidel Castro refugees. Latinos became increasingly dispersed, although the most noticeable concentrations were still in the Southwest, Southern California, New York City, and Florida. This rapidly growing and diverse part of the population was generally reported in somewhat inconsistent terms. "Spanish surname," "Spanish-speaking," or of "Spanish heritage" were obviously inexact classifications, whether "observer defined" or "self-described." The same problem is naturally inherent in classifying any Americans of mixed ancestry.

The Census Bureau included American Indians among "other races," a category that rose from 1.5 million in 1960 to 2.9 million in 1970. The largest contribution to this category was made by Asian immigrants, whose numbers rose dramatically after the 1965 Immigration Act took effect in 1968.

From Boom to Bust Among the major demographic trends of the 1960's were the last years of the baby boom and the beginnings of the baby bust, each involving major economic and social consequences. The baby boom can be seen as a wave, climbing from a trough of 2.3 million births and a live birthrate of 18.4 per thousand women aged fifteen to forty-four in 1936 to a peak of 4.3 million births and a rate of 25.3 in 1957, then subsiding to another trough of 3.1 million births and a rate of 14.8 in 1975. Most baby boomers, however, tend to define their generation as those individuals born in 1946 through 1964. Demographers had expected a brief postwar spike in births followed by a return to a normal birthrate of less than zero population growth, estimated at 21.1, and a U.S. population plateau or decline before the year 2000. Instead, the postwar spike became a nineteen-year "generation" of 76 million people, a bulge of population pressure on maternity wards, schools, clothing manufacturers, cars, homes, resthomes, and cemetery lots that would take a journey through society that sometimes would be compared with the progress of a pig through a python. The extent to which the rest of the population was forced to adjust to the baby boomers demonstrated the extent of this group's powers.

Some demographers believe that economic opportunity influenced the parents of baby boomers, many of whom were born into families with one or two children in the 1920's and 1930's, to decide to have three or four children. The Depression and World War II postponed many marriages, and wartime private savings and postwar antirecession policies provided the economic opportunities. The G.I. Bill, housing programs, industry reconversion credits, the Marshall Plan, the North Atlantic Treaty Organization, defense budgets for the Korean War and the Cold War, highway construction, a greater need for automobiles, new products, and the baby

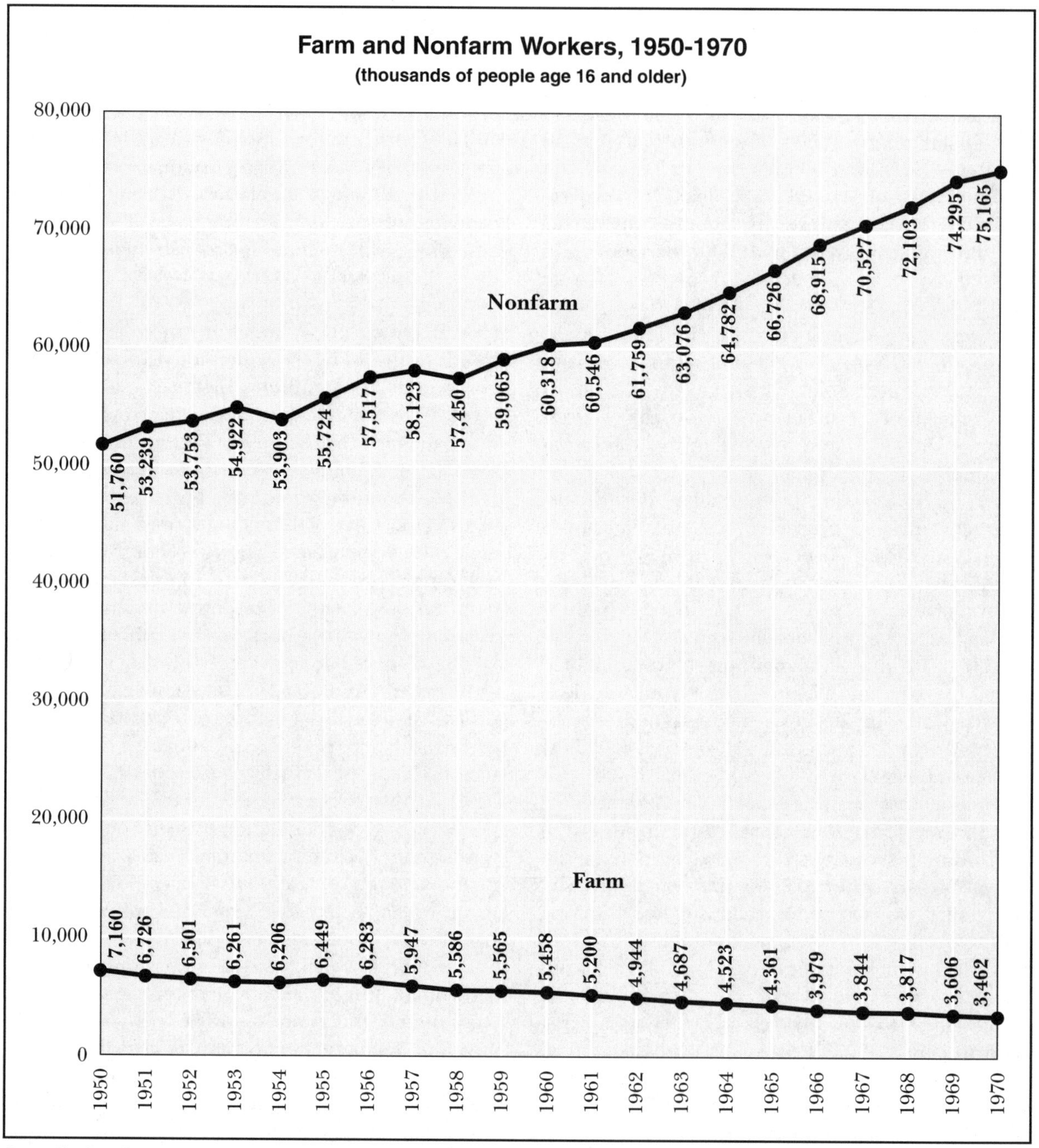

Farm and Nonfarm Workers, 1950-1970
(thousands of people age 16 and older)
80,000
70,000
60,000
50,000
40,000
30,000
20,000
10,000
0
Nonfarm
51,760
53,239
53,753
54,922
53,903
55,724
57,517
58,123
57,450
59,065
60,318
60,546
61,759
63,076
64,782
66,726
68,915
70,527
72,103
74,295
75,165
Farm
7,160
6,726
6,501
6,261
6,206
6,449
6,283
5,947
5,586
5,565
5,458
5,200
4,944
4,687
4,523
4,361
3,979
3,844
3,817
3,606
3,462
1950
1951
1952
1953
1954
1955
1956
1957
1958
1959
1960
1961
1962
1963
1964
1965
1966
1967
1968
1969
1970

Source: Kurian, George, *Datapedia of the United States, 1790-2000, America Year by Year.* Lanham, Maryland: Bernam Press, 1994.

boom itself all stimulated the economy, providing fathers with jobs at salaries that could support stay-at-home wives who raised three to four children in relative material comfort.

Economics may also be behind the decline in the birthrate after 1957 and the sharper drop in the rate in 1965. In the mid-1960's, the economy was slowing down as inflation was being fed by the costs of the space program and budgets for the Vietnam War and the Great Society program. At the same time, baby-boom parents were feeling less affluent as they began to bear the burden of paying for college educations for several offspring at once. The late baby boomers are sometimes called the "lost generation" because they faced shrinking economic opportunities. These same economic problems along with societal factors discouraged the early baby boomers from having children of their own. The Vietnam War draft posed a threat to normal marriage and parenthood, and many young people were too involved in civil rights demonstrations and antiwar protests to be interested in starting families.

Longevity As the numbers of young people grew, increasing longevity began to create problems in financing the retirement and care of the elderly. The reduction in infant deaths and those from childhood diseases such as measles, scarlet fever, and whooping cough had been followed by a virtual conquest of tuberculosis, diphtheria, polio, and typhoid and the introduction of sulfa drugs and antibiotics that ended pneumonia's role as a killer of the elderly. The extension of female life expectancy in the 1940's and 1950's was followed by a comparable extension of male life expectancy in the 1970's. In 1966, the government enacted Medicare, followed by a more generous Social Security payments schedule with cost-of-living adjustments. The elderly poor of the early 1960's became less needy but a greater tax burden by the 1970's.

Women The role of women in American society began to change in the 1960's. From 1947 through 1958, the typical suburban wife stayed home and stayed married. However, in the mid-1960's, as the economy slowed and families tried to support several college students and sometimes ailing grandparents, married women increasingly took jobs to help pay the bills. Women's wages in the 1960's slipped to slightly less than 60 percent of men's wages for similar work, and the concentration of women in clerical and similar occupations tended to reduce wages in these fields and limited women's power to force higher wages by strikes. However, the tendency that developed in the 1950's for wives to outlive their husbands by about a decade provided another argument for women to have some marketable skills.

As married women went to work, they gained an independent income, more social contacts, and increased mobility. Fertility rates declined, and the number of divorces increased from a postwar low of 393,000 in 1960 to 708,000 in 1970. The higher likelihood of divorce in turn increased the need for

women to have some earning capacity. A feminist movement for greater legal rights, independence, and opportunity began in the late 1960's, drawing some of its members from the ranks of civil rights and antiwar activists. Though the feminist movement had some failures and some of the goals it sought had unexpected consequences, 1960's feminism did lead to economic progress for women.

The declining rate of live births to married women in the late 1960's was also affected by a number of other societal factors. Abortion was becoming increasingly common, although the Supreme Court would not define the practice as a constitutional right until its 1973 decision in *Roe v. Wade.* In addition, the birth control pill, introduced in 1960, enabled women to have greater control over when they would have children. The birth control pill also allowed women to have sexual intercourse without much fear of pregnancy, previously a major deterrent to premarital sex. Cohabitation and sex without marriage became more and more common in the latter part of the 1960's. The number of babies born to unwed mothers increased from 224,000 in 1960 to 399,000 in 1970. The rate of births to single mothers continued to be higher among African Americans, but the rate of increase was more marked among whites. The traditionally structured family of the 1950's lost ground, but most 1960's young people still opted for marriage.

Additional Information *Historical Statistics of the United States, Colonial Times to 1970* (1975), a publication of the Bureau of the Census, and *The American People: The Findings of the 1970 Census* (1973), by E. J. Kahm, provide an overall look at the demographics of the 1960's. *Black Migration in America* (1981), by Daniel M. Johnson and Rex R. Campbell, and *The Suburbs* (1995), by J. John Palen, describe two migratory trends during the decade. Society's role is examined in *Feminism, Children, and the New Families* (1988), edited by Sanford M. Dornbusch and Myra H. Strober, and Richard A. Easterlin's *Birth and Fortune* (1987).

K. Fred Gillum

See also Agriculture; Baby Boomers; Birth Control; Business and the Economy; Civil Rights Movement; Feminist Movement; Immigration; Interstate Highway System; Medicine; Prosperity and Poverty; Sexual Revolution; Women in the Workforce.

■ Detroit Riot

Date July 23-28, 1967

The costliest riot in U.S. history. Forty-one people died, nearly two thousand were injured, and damage estimates ranged from a quarter to a half billion dollars.

Origins and History Urban race riots, which had taken place in Harlem in New York City in 1964 and 1967 and Watts in Los Angeles in 1965, had become part of the social upheaval of the decade. The urban unrest peaked during the summer of 1967. From Omaha, Nebraska, to Washington, D.C., riots took place in nearly 150 U.S. cities. In a July 12-16 riot in Newark, New Jersey, twenty-seven people died, more than eleven hundred were injured, and property damage reached fifteen million dollars.

The Riot Detroit, Michigan, was a curious place for violence to erupt. Many African Americans commanded high wages in the automobile factories and high positions in the liberal United Automobile Workers union. About 40 percent of Detroit's 550,000 African Americans owned or were buying their own homes. Community leaders, both black and white, had made a civics lesson of the city's bloody race riot of 1943, which had left thirty-four dead and moved President Franklin D. Roosevelt to send in federal troops. Detroit's mayor, Jerome Cavanagh, had been elected with the support of the African American community.

However, a minor police incident on July 23 provided the spark that ignited the Detroit ghetto. An early-morning raid of a speakeasy on a rundown street resulted in knots of African American onlookers taunting the police. A brick crashed through the window of a police cruiser. At this point, the police could have either pulled out or used force to break up the crowd. They did neither. They dispatched cruisers but did nothing else; consequently, mobs gathered and started fires, then looting began. As the fires spread, so did the looting, creating a carnival atmosphere in the ghetto. Children joined adults in racing from stores with their arms full of groceries, liquor, or jewelry. Cars pulled up to businesses and their occupants filled them with appliances and other goods.

Both the mayor and the governor were paralyzed. To alleviate the summer heat and thereby calm inner-city residents, Mayor Cavanagh ordered more swimming pools opened, and Governor George Romney suggested seeding rain clouds above the ghetto. Neither police nor peacemakers could stop the riot.

In order to quell the riot, Governor Romney deployed the National Guard, and President Lyndon B. Johnson sent in U.S. Army paratroopers. Although the Army troops were able to secure their sector of the ghetto, events went badly elsewhere. The National Guard and the police seemed to assume a license to kill. A subsequent investigation by the *Detroit Free Press* found that most of the official reports about the forty-three riot-related deaths (all but eight of them African Americans) had been pure fabrications. Three African Americans were shot as they sat in a car. A deaf man was killed because he couldn't hear a warning. A child holding a broom was gunned down. Finally, on the sixth day, July 28, the riot just burned itself out.

Impact President Johnson moved quickly to appoint a commission to study the roots of urban racial unrest. The Kerner Commission, named for its chairman, Governor Otto Kerner of Illinois, operated on the twin premises that the nation must ensure the safety of its people and that the nation must get at the root causes of racial strife.

The commission, which released its report in 1968, determined that the riots were not directed at white Americans but instead at their property and authority. It described a causal chain of "discrimination, prejudice, disadvantaged conditions, . . . all culminating in the eruption of disorder at the hands of youthful, politically aware activists." The frustration experienced by African Americans living in the ghetto was found to have deep historical roots. The commission noted that the historical pattern of black-white relations had been "pervasive discrimination and segregation," which had resulted in whites leaving the inner cities and thus creating black ghettos. Young African Americans, alienated by the conditions produced by discrimination and segregation, had flocked to the banner of black power.

The commission concluded that the United States was moving toward separate and unequal societies, white and black. It called for increased national communication among races in order to end stereotypes and hostility.

Additional Information Richard N. Goodwin, a former speech writer for President Johnson, fits the

The urban race riot that erupted in July, 1967, in Detroit, Michigan, was one of the worst of the more than one hundred riots that took place in cities across the nation that summer. (Archive Photos)

Detroit riot into the context of the times in *Remembering America: A Voice from the Sixties.* Journalist William Serrin's article, "The Crucible," in the January/February, 1991, issue of the *Columbia Journalism Review,* is a firsthand account of the riot.

Brian G. Tobin

See also Chicago Riots; Kerner Commission Report; New York Riots; Newark Riot; Washington, D.C., Riots; Watts Riot.

■ Didion, Joan

Born December 5, 1934, Sacramento, California

One of the nation's leading novelists and journalists, Didion is also an accomplished screenwriter, hailed for her impressive command of American culture on both the East and West Coasts.

Early Life Joan Didion, an only child, grew up in an old California family and steeped herself in the history of the West. She attended high school in California and was graduated from the University of California, Berkeley, majoring in English. In 1956, she won *Vogue* magazine's Prix de Paris prize for young writers and moved to New York to work as a journalist, becoming a novelist in the early 1960's. The city, she has said, represented to her the whole gamut of experiences a young writer should encounter. She wrote feature pieces for *National Review* and *Mademoiselle.*

The 1960's *Run River* (1963), Didion's California novel (covering the years 1938-1959), received mixed reviews and relatively little attention. Beginning in the mid-1960's, however, her pieces in *The Saturday Evening Post* distinguished her as one of the

United States' foremost essayists—one of the first to provide incisive and novelistic commentary on the hippies in the Haight-Ashbury section of San Francisco and on related episodes in what she deemed the "California dream." An acute observer with a good ear for 1960's speech rhythms, Didion captured both the joy of American iconoclasts and the apocalyptic mood that resulted from the assassinations of this decade. *Slouching Towards Bethlehem* (1968) is her classic volume of reportage and commentary on the American scene. The collection's title evokes a line from William Butler Yeats's great poem, *The Second Coming*, which is the quintessential expression of dread over the violence of the twentieth century.

Later Life Didion's stature as a novelist was enhanced with the publication of *Play It as It Lays* (1970), *A Book of Common Prayer* (1977), and *The Last Thing He Wanted* (1996). She also continued her fine reportage in *The White Album* (1979) and other book-length works while collaborating with her husband, John Gregory Dunne, on numerous screenplays. Didion and Dunne have owned homes in California and New York and have written on the contrasts between the two coasts.

Impact To a large extent, Didion's essay writing helped define the cultural and political mood of the 1960's. She is regularly cited in histories of the decade, along with Norman Mailer, Susan Sontag, and Gore Vidal. She is distinguished from them, however, in her firm grasp not only of contemporary life but also of California history. Less philosophical than Sontag, less cynical than Vidal, and less focused on her personality than Mailer, she offers a more empirical view of 1960's events and sensibilities.

Additional Information *Joan Didion: Essays and Conversations* (1984), edited by Ellen G. Friedman, includes key interviews with Didion as well as important discussions of her major work, and Katherine Usher Henderson's *Joan Didion* (1981) provides a succinct introduction to Didion's work, with a chronology, notes, and bibliography.

Carl Rollyson

See also Counterculture; Drug Culture; Flower Children; Haight-Ashbury; Literature; Mailer, Norman; San Francisco as Cultural Mecca; Sontag, Susan.

■ DiMaggio, Joe

Born November 25, 1914, Martinez, California
Died March 8, 1999, Hollywood, Florida

One of the best players in baseball history. DiMaggio played in ten World Series and was named the American League's most valuable player in 1939, 1941, and 1947.

Early Life A native San Franciscan, Joseph Paul DiMaggio began his fifteen-year tenure with the New York Yankees in 1936. He married Dorothy Arnold in 1939; the couple had one child and were divorced in 1944. In 1941, DiMaggio hit in a record-breaking fifty-six consecutive games and acquired the nickname "Joltin' Joe." Later, he also became known as the "Yankee Clipper" for being one of the best outfielders. He spent several of his prime years in the Army during World War II and retired after the 1951 baseball season. His uniform number was retired in 1952, and he was inducted into the Hall of Fame in 1955. In 1954, DiMaggio married the actress Marilyn Monroe, but they were divorced less than nine months later.

The 1960's Although divorced, DiMaggio and Monroe remained good friends until her death on August 5, 1962. When he was informed of Monroe's death, DiMaggio personally took charge of all the funeral arrangements.

DiMaggio was active in newspaper, radio, and television advertising campaigns for a savings bank and a coffee-maker company. He was also involved in numerous public relations activities. In 1968, DiMaggio became vice president of the Oakland Athletics and was helpful in identifying future successful ballplayers for the organization.

In 1968, the singer and composer Paul Simon referred to DiMaggio in his song "Mrs. Robinson," recorded by Simon and singing partner Art Garfunkel for use in the film *The Graduate*. The famous line "Where have you gone, Joe DiMaggio? Our nation turns its lonely eyes to you" became a part of the national idiom, expressing the country's yearning for simpler times and untarnished heroes.

Later Life In a 1969 poll conducted in celebration of baseball's centennial, DiMaggio was designated "the greatest living ballplayer." In 1977, President Gerald Ford presented the Medal of Freedom, the highest civilian decoration, to DiMaggio. Early in January, 1980, DiMaggio became a member of the board of directors of the Baltimore Orioles. In 1986, he received the Ellis Island Medal of Honor for his achievements on the baseball field and for serving as a role model for the nation's youth.

Impact In his playing years, DiMaggio provided young people with a visible example of a seemingly ideal professional athlete. After his retirement from baseball, he remained in the public spotlight as a result of his involvement with Monroe and the use of his name and image to symbolize a vanished past.

Additional Information For biographical background, see Maury Allen's *Where Have You Gone, Joe DiMaggio? The Story of America's Last Hero* (1975) and George De Gregorio's *Joe DiMaggio: An Informal Biography* (1981).

James E. Lawlor

See also Baseball; *Graduate, The*; Koufax, Sandy; Mantle, Mickey; Maris, Roger; Mays, Willie; Monroe, Marilyn; Simon and Garfunkel.

■ Dirksen, Everett

Born January 4, 1896, Pekin, Illinois
Died September 7, 1969, Washington, D.C.

Republican minority leader in the United States Senate. Dirksen played a crucial role in drafting and passing the civil rights legislation of the 1960's.

Everett McKinley Dirksen, one of twins, was born to German immigrants. He attended the University of Minnesota until 1917 when he joined the U.S. Army and fought in World War I. Dirksen returned a war hero and was elected to the House of Representatives in 1932. He unsuccessfully sought his party's nomination for the presidency in 1944 and became an ardent anticommunist. Dirksen won a stunning upset election to the Senate in 1950 and rose through the leadership to be elected minority leader in 1959.

As minority leader, Dirksen strongly supported civil rights legislation throughout the 1960's. He worked closely with his congressional colleagues and Presidents Dwight D. Eisenhower, John F. Kennedy, and Lyndon B. Johnson, earning both their respect and admiration. For example, in 1963, his support of the Nuclear Test Ban Treaty ensured its passage, and a year later, his efforts on behalf of the Civil Rights Act of 1964 enabled it to pass despite a filibuster in the Senate.

Dirksen became a widely recognized and popular figure because of his television program, in which he appeared with his Republican counterparts in the House. He died of complications following lung surgery in 1969.

Impact Dirksen's numerous contributions during his tenure in Congress were wide ranging and varied. Apart from his efforts toward civil rights, the moderate senator greatly influenced other legislation and policies, with his most significant achievements coming during the 1960's.

Additional Information *Dirksen: Portrait of a Public Man* (1970), by Neil MacNeil, is a political biography of the senator from Illinois.

Brett Eric Smithson

See also Civil Rights Act of 1964; Civil Rights Movement; Conservatism in Politics; Nuclear Test Ban Treaties.

■ *Do It! Scenarios of the Revolution*

Published 1970
Author Jerry Rubin (1938-1994)

The book that captured the revolutionary generation gap embodied by the Youth International Party (the Yippies). The book is both an autobiography of Yippie cofounder Jerry Rubin and a statement of Yippie philosophy.

The Work Jerry Rubin's *Do It! Scenarios of the Revolution* (1970) is a series of forty-three vignettes describing Rubin's personal evolution and his involvement in events such as the Berkeley Free Speech movement of 1964, the National Mobilization Committee to End the War in Vietnam antiwar demonstration at the Pentagon in 1967, and the 1968 Democratic National Convention in Chicago. A key theme of *Do It!* is that revolutionary change is accomplished in the theater of everyday life rather than through abstract theorizing. The book embodies some of the tactics it advocates: spectacle as subversion, myth as politics, and parody as critique.

Impact Journalists for the mainstream and alternative press described *Do It!* as a collection of vulgar and childish exclamations of a clownish pseudorevolutionary. With total sales of more than 250,000, however, even the most scathing reviews conceded that *Do It!* tapped into the pulse of American youth and contained some valid critiques of middle-class life. In *Do It!*, Rubin voiced the sentiments of many disaffected white, middle-class youths who felt alienated by both the right and the left.

Related Work Rubin's *We Are Everywhere!* (1971) is the sequel to *Do It!*

Additional Information For a more complete discussion of the Yippie movement of the 1960's, see *The Underground Revolution: Hippies, Yippies, and Others* (1970), by Naomi Feigelson.

Kim Heikkila

See also Chicago Seven Trial; Democratic National Convention of 1968; Free Speech Movement; National Mobilization Committee to End the War in Vietnam (MOBE); Pentagon, Levitating of the; Yippies; Youth Culture and the Generation Gap.

■ *Dr. Strangelove*

Released 1964
Director Stanley Kubrick (1928-1999)

The motion picture that best encapsulates the Cold War atmosphere of the 1960's. This cinematic amalgam expresses societal angst about nuclear war, Soviet relations, communism, and military intelligence.

The Work In *Dr. Strangelove: Or, How I Learned to Stop Worrying and Love the Bomb*, the rabidly anticommunist, insane General Jack D. Ripper (Sterling Hayden) initiates World War III for the good of his country by isolating his Air Force base and launching bombers against targets in the Soviet Union. A polite visiting British officer, Group Captain Lionel

Peter Sellers (rising from the wheelchair) starred in the 1964 film Dr. Strangelove, *which humorously dealt with the nation's most horrifying Cold War fears.* (Museum of Modern Art/Film Stills Archive)

Mandrake (Peter Sellers), attempts to reason with Ripper, while the base is under attack by other U.S. military units. Meanwhile in Washington, D.C., the ineffectual, liberal president (also played by Sellers) invites the Soviet ambassador into the War Room to avoid global nuclear war. Opposing the president are General Buck Turgidson (George C. Scott), who fears and distrusts Soviets because they are not Americans, and the cracked genius Dr. Strangelove (again, Sellers), whose interest lies entirely in the efficiency and power of military weaponry, and who becomes so excited by the prospect of nuclear war that he launches himself from his wheelchair shouting: "Mein Führer, I can walk!" The only other truly successful people are the crew of one bomber who evade Soviet interception and accurately deposit their payload.

Impact *Dr. Strangelove*, at once humorous and horrifying, presented the viewer with a parody that twisted every convention apparent in Hollywood war films. That generals are not heroic, just venal; that government officials are not statesmen but self-absorbed politicians; that diplomacy is a matter of wading through the buffet table on the way to the bar—all reinforced the commonly held fear that the welfare of the average citizen was not foremost in the minds of those in charge. The singular force of public-spirited reason, a British officer unable to make a dent in the idiocy around him, paralleled the average person's alienation in the face of a tremendous depersonalized bureaucracy. The biting satire and black comedy created a nightmare vision of military efficiency gone haywire. The fear of global annihilation and the growing pessimism about nuclear weapons in the hands of unelected, and in most cases unknown, military hierarchy were reflected by this version of private dementia becoming military, and by extension, public policy. The character Dr. Strangelove, with his self-willed arm and quirky manner, became synonymous with the untrustworthy and dangerous manipulators of public policy and opinion, an embodiment of the unholy marriage of science and the military. The film was a critical and commercial success, confirming Kubrick's filmmaking genius and his personal (and society's) pessimism.

Related Work *Fail-Safe*, 1964, directed by Sydney Lumet, provides a suspenseful Hollywood version of the same fear of "accidental" nuclear war.

Additional Information For an interpretation of *Dr. Strangelove* that focuses on Kubrick as filmmaker, see *Stanley Kubrick: A Film Odyssey* (1975), by Gene D. Phillips.

Sharon Randolph

See also Film.

■ Dominican Republic, Invasion of

Date April-May, 1965

An event that aroused international controversy interconnected with the Vietnam War and the Cold War. In April, 1965, President Lyndon B. Johnson ordered U.S. troops to land in Santo Domingo.

Origins and History From 1930 to 1961, Rafael Leónidas Trujillo Molina tyrannically ruled the Dominican Republic. After Trujillo's assassination, leftist Juan Bosch, promising democratic and social reforms, was elected president in December, 1962. Bosch's reforms enraged the military, Dominican conservatives, and U.S. policymakers and businessmen. Bosch was overthrown in September, 1963. In the midst of corruption, terrorism, and oppression, a right-wing civilian triumvirate, led by J. Donald Reid Cabral, ruled the country for nineteen months. Meanwhile, pro-Bosch groups, known as the Constitutionalists, organized a movement to restore Bosch to power. The anti-Bosch forces, or loyalists, viewed the movement as a communist threat. Violent confrontations ensued.

The Intervention On April 25, 1965, rebel military and civilian leaders succeeded in overthrowing the triumvirate. The ouster of the triumvirate, however, split the military. Junior officers, led by Colonel Francisco Caamaño Deñó, who supported the Constitutionalists, clashed with the loyalist forces under the command of Colonel Elías Wessin y Wessin. The fighting intensified. The Constitutionalists were well entrenched in downtown Santo Domingo, where they had the support of thousands of civilians armed with rifles, machine guns, and other weapons that had been taken from the military arsenals. The loyalists controlled the rest of the city and most of the provinces. By April 26, it appeared as if the pro-Bosch forces were on the road to victory; the leaders of the military junta established by the loyalists and U.S. officials in Santo Domingo claimed

Dominican Americans in New York City protest against U.S. intervention in a civil war in their motherland. (National Archives)

that communists were leading the revolution.

On April 27, President Lyndon B. Johnson announced that four hundred Marines had landed in Santo Domingo to protect American lives. By April 30, in an attempt to avoid repeating the United States' experience in the Bay of Pigs or Vietnam, Johnson authorized the deployment of the Eighty-Second Airborne Division. Gradually, U.S. military units landed at San Isidro airbase. Johnson justified the massive military intervention by declaring a need to prevent a communist takeover. On May 17, U.S. troops in Santo Domingo totaled 22,289. They combined operations with the military junta, separating the Constitutionalists from the rest of the country. Once this mission was accomplished, U.S. troops assumed additional nonmilitary and humanitarian duties and adopted a more "nearly neutral stance" in the conflict.

The U.S. intervention violated the charter of the Organization of American States (OAS) and the objectives of the United Nations. To deflect criticism, the United States persuaded the OAS to establish an Inter-American Peace Force (IAPF). Under Brazilian command, the U.S. forces were integrated into the IAPF along with troops from Brazil, Costa Rica, Honduras, Nicaragua, and Paraguay. The main mission of the IAPF was to create conditions for a negotiated settlement.

On August 31, after four months of bloody battles, about three thousand deaths, and intense negotiations, the Act of Dominican Reconciliation ended the civil war. Neither Constitutionalists nor loyalists wound up in charge. Héctor García-Godoy, a career diplomat and businessman, was sworn in as president of a provisional government. To facilitate upcoming elections, the U.S.-backed García-Godoy forced rival military leaders to accept overseas positions. In June, 1966, Joaquín Balaguer was elected president. The gradual withdrawal of the IAPF began after the election, and on September 31, 1966, the last U.S. forces left the Dominican Republic.

Impact U.S. involvement changed the course of the conflict in the Dominican Republic from a civil war to an international imbroglio. It was the first military intervention undertaken by the United States in Latin America in thirty years. The intervention generated strong anti-American sentiment in Latin America and mild to severe criticism around the world. Domestic protests against the United States' "arrogance of power" strongly condemned the intervention. On the other hand, the intervention allowed the United States to reorganize the Dominican armed forces through a program of economic military aid and gradual military reform. Nevertheless, for about twelve years after the armed conflict ended, military and police forces continued jailing, torturing, or murdering thousands of Dominicans, many of whom were accused of being communists.

Additional Information Two opposing interpretations of this event are presented in *Overtaken by Events* (1966), by John Bartlow Martin, former U.S. ambassador and presidential envoy in 1965 to the Dominican Republic, and Juan Bosch's *Pentagonism: A Substitute for Imperialism* (1968).

Valentina Peguero

See also Bay of Pigs Invasion; Castro, Fidel; Johnson, Lyndon B.; Vietnam War.

■ Doors

A popular rock-and-roll band of the late 1960's. The Doors introduced a dark style of drug-influenced rock music, enhanced by the controversial performances of lead singer Jim Morrison.

Jim Morrison was the founder and artistic soul of the Doors. Born shortly before his father, a high-ranking naval officer, departed for the Pacific War, Morrison led a gypsy childhood, following his father's military assignments. Gifted and gregarious, Morrison nevertheless rejected his family's solid Republican, middle-class values and, in 1964, enrolled at the University of California at Los Angeles, to study film.

Morrison met keyboard player Ray Manzarek in the summer of 1965, and they recruited Manzarek's fellow meditation classmates, drummer John Densmore and guitarist Robby Kreiger. In their first year, the Doors played local shows and small clubs, developing a blues-rock style heavily influenced by the emerging California drug culture. The band's first break came when they were offered a contract

The controversial stage performances of Jim Morrison, the Door's lead singer and group founder, kept the group in the spotlight. (Archive Photos)

by the prestigious Whiskey-A-Go-Go club on the Sunset Strip, venue for the biggest names in the Los Angeles psychedelic scene. After three months of shocking audiences with loud music and sexually taboo language, they were fired.

In 1966, the Doors signed with Elektra and recorded their first album, *The Doors* (1967). Their debut album rose steadily on the charts, kept from the top spot only by the remarkable fifteen-week run by the Beatles' *Sgt. Pepper's Lonely Hearts Club Band*. The Doors' first single, "Light My Fire," spent two weeks at number one. Both *The Doors* and the group's next album, *Strange Days* (1967), sold more than one million copies and brought Morrison's sexually suggestive performance style to the attention of a worldwide audience. An international reputation boosted record sales but also drove Morrison into heavier drug and alcohol use. The band's third album, *Waiting for the Sun* (1968), was less successful, but a series of spectacular concerts around the country kept the Doors in the spotlight. During these concerts, Morrison often invited angry audience response, and fans soon began to expect outrageous events.

The Doors were booked to play a concert in

Miami, Florida, on March 1, 1969. Morrison arrived late and intoxicated to meet an overcrowded hall of edgy fans. After several poorly performed songs, Morrison began to berate the screaming audience, demanding that they "love my ass." Dancing around the stage, he removed his shirt and began unbuttoning his pants. It is unclear what then happened, though some observers claimed that Morrison revealed his genitals and feigned masturbation. He was eventually pushed into the crowd, and the concert ended after only forty-five minutes.

The media exaggerated the story, and thirty concerts on the tour were canceled. Morrison was charged with lewd and lascivious behavior, drunkenness, and indecent exposure. Eventually he was released on five thousand dollars bail pending a trial. In the meantime, the general public was outraged. The Doors' songs received less radio airtime, and booking agents began requiring a five-thousand-dollar deposit to ensure trouble-free performances. In August, 1970, Morrison was convicted on counts of profanity and indecent exposure and received the maximum sentence of a five-hundred-dollar fine and six months of hard labor in a Florida jail, though an appeal was immediately filed and Morrison remained free on a fifty-thousand-dollar bond.

Subsequent Events After the Miami concert, the Doors recorded their final albums. *The Soft Parade* (1969) was harshly reviewed, but the album's hit single, "Touch Me," rose to number three on the charts. *Morrison Hotel* (1970) was a minor success along with two compilation albums. *L.A. Woman* (1971), the Doors' last major album, was widely praised, but Morrison's controversial style had already begun to destroy the band's cohesiveness. Morrison, more interested in poetry than music, moved to Paris, where he died in 1971 of heart failure.

Impact In only four years, the Doors evolved from a Los Angeles house band to philosopher prophets of a modern hedonism. Though the Doors distanced themselves from the San Francisco dropout culture, middle-class America feared their brooding and calculated sexuality. Morrison was the first widely popular musician of the 1960's to use theatrical techniques, in addition to music, to psychologically manipulate audiences into rejecting social norms. In doing so, he shocked middle-class Americans who remained critical of the connection between rock music, sexuality, and the counterculture.

Additional Information A brief account of the Doors' lifestyle and musical career, including a discography, can be found in *The Doors* (1984), by John Tabler and Andrew Doe. A film based on the group's story, *The Doors*, directed by Oliver Stone, was released in 1991; Val Kilmer played the part of Morrison.

John Powell

See also Decency Rallies; Drug Culture; Music; Sexual Revolution.

■ Draft Resisters

Participants in the most significant movement against conscription in U.S. history. Those opposed to the military draft included religious and secular conscientious objectors as well as draft dodgers who fled the country to escape military service.

Conscription, or the drafting of American men into the armed forces, has always been controversial. Although enforcement varied, conscription in North America was first imposed in the Virginia colony in 1629. With the exception of Quaker-dominated Pennsylvania, each of the American colonies required every able-bodied white male between sixteen and sixty years of age to perform military service when and if necessary. Conscription at the national level was first imposed by both the Union and the Confederacy during the Civil War. It was subsequently employed during World Wars I and II and during the Korean and Vietnam Wars. Although resentment of the draft was commonplace, resistance was sporadic until the late 1960's during the Vietnam War. The most dramatic early example was the New York City draft riots of July, 1863, when during a five-day period more than one hundred rioters, bystanders, soldiers, and police were killed. Draft resistance during the 1960's was never that violent, although it took place over a longer period of time, the number of participants was much larger, and unlike the New York riots, it was in large part successful.

Conscientious Objectors The strongest resistance to the Vietnam War draft occurred during the late 1960's and the early 1970's when the war was at its peak. The conscription policy was based on the Selective Service Acts of 1940 and 1948 and a 1951 amendment. It authorized exemption from the armed services for conscientious objectors whose religious beliefs forbade them taking the life of another person in any and all armed conflict between nations, not just in one conflict alone, such as the Vietnam War. Alternative service as determined by the conscientious objectors' local draft board was also required. Usually, the requirement could be satisfied by serving in a health-related occupation for two years, the same length of time a draftee must serve in the Army, and at the same level of pay.

From 1948 to 1969, General Lewis B. Hershey was head of the Selective Service System, which included more than four thousand local draft boards scattered throughout the United States. Hershey believed that conscription could be used as a social tool providing opportunities for minorities and lower-class whites, while at the same time protecting middle-class whites so that they could continue their education or remain employed in their current professions, such as medicine or engineering. The assumption was that certain individuals could contribute most to their country by serving in the armed forces, while the contributions of others could best be maximized through deferment from the military. One result during the late 1960's was that African Americans, who made up 11 percent of the eligible draft population, accounted for 31 percent of the combat troops in Vietnam and 24 percent of the combat deaths.

Earlier in 1965, the Supreme Court in *United States v. Seeger*, declared that conscientious objectors no longer had to belong to one of the so-called peace churches, such as the Quakers or Mennonites, to fulfill the conditions required for belief in a supreme being. Those with "a sincere and meaningful belief which occupies in the life of its possessor a place parallel to that filled by the God of those admittedly qualifying for the exemption" were now exempt themselves. Also, as a result of increased U.S. military participation in the Vietnam War, the monthly draft quotas tripled in 1966 from ten thousand to thirty thousand and later climbed to fifty thousand. The result was a growing increase in antidraft sentiment among young American men, until finally in 1970, the Supreme Court in *Welsh v. United States* declared that even an atheist could be a conscientious objector if his beliefs were "ethical and moral." However, the Court did remain firm in refusing to allow those petitioning for conscientious objector status to selectively choose to object to only the Vietnam War. The objection had to include all wars past, present, and future. More than 170,000 men

eligible for the draft were classified as conscientious objectors between 1965 and 1970.

Draft Evasion Most draft resisters, however, were not conscientious objectors. They found other means of evading their obligation to serve in the military. The quality and quantity of draft counseling aimed at resisting the draft increased. Antidraft rallies and draft-card burnings became more frequent along with increased attendance. The twist given to the 1968 Tet Offensive by the media, depicting it as a U.S. defeat, helped stiffen resistance. Postponement of graduation from college to prolong deferment, legal machinations to thwart or delay induction, and the outright flight of more than thirty thousand draft-eligible men to Canada, Sweden, and other nations were other ways to evade the draft. Many people even sought entry into the Reserves or

A young University of Washington student burns his draft card during a demonstration against Dow Chemical Company, a napalm manufacturer recruiting seniors at the college. (AP/Wide World Photos)

Draftees and U.S. Forces during the Vietnam War, August, 1964-January, 1973
(thousands)

U.S. Military Forces Total	8,744
Draftees	
Classified	75,717
Examined	8,611
Rejected	3,880
Inducted	1,759

Source: U.S. Bureau of the Census. *Statistical Abstract of the United States: 1996* (116th edition). Washington, D.C.: Government Printing Office, 1996.

National Guard (neither of which was activated during the war) to avoid serving. Although Curtis Tarr, who replaced Hershey in 1969, instituted a lottery system for the draft, it did little to quiet the opposition. Slightly more than six exemptions per one hundred draft inductees in 1965 grew to more than twenty-five in 1970, and by 1972, there were 30 percent more draft-eligible men deferred from the draft than were actually drafted.

Impact By 1969, draftees made up only 16 percent of U.S. armed forces, but they made up 88 percent of the infantry riflemen in Vietnam and more than 50 percent of the battlefield deaths. Resistance to the draft was both cause and effect of a serious weakening of the U.S. will to win the war in Vietnam.

Subsequent Events Eventually, 8,750 draft evaders were convicted, and 4,000 served prison sentences. Student deferments were abolished in 1971. The draft ended in 1973 and was replaced by the all-volunteer force. Although there were intermittent compulsory draft registrations during the following years, the draft was not renewed during the Persian Gulf War, 1990-1991.

Additional Information Although much has been written about opposition to the Vietnam War, readings about opposition to the draft have been less abundant. A useful article by John Whiteclay Chambers II, "Conscientious Objectors and the American State from Colonial Times to the Present," appears in *The New Conscientious Objection: From Sacred to Secu-*

lar Resistance (1993), edited by Charles C. Moskos and Chambers. Other sources include Charles De Benedetti's *An American Ordeal: The Antiwar Movement of the Vietnam Era* (1990); Margaret Levi's *Consent, Dissent, and Patriotism* (1997); and Stephan M. Kohn's *Jailed for Peace: The History of American Draft Law Violators* (1986).

John Quinn Imholte

See also Tet Offensive; Vietnam War; War Resisters League.

■ Drug Culture

A segment of the counterculture characterized by widespread experimentation with drugs to achieve heightened pleasure and insight. Traditional restraints on behavior declined as the baby boomers came of age and questioned the norms of their parents, including the idea that drug usage is morally and physically destructive.

Drug usage in the United States has usually waxed and waned according to the political climate. Therefore, before the passage of the first major antidrug legislation, the Harrison Act of 1914, a cross section of Americans consumed liberal amounts of opium and its derivatives, cocaine, and other narcotics for medical and recreational purposes.

When reformers mustered the political strength, as they did between World War I and the 1950's, the government launched campaigns against drug use. During these years, nonmedical consumption of drugs tended to be confined largely to the artistic and minority communities. By mid-century, however, Beatnik behavior, the emergence of the baby boomers, and leisure generated by affluence sired a new culture, a counterculture that attacked the traditional norms. In the words of a 1960's song, "There's a whole generation with a new explanation," one that not only boldly denied the notion that drug taking was bad but also defiantly proclaimed that it was a positive activity. The banner of cultural revolt flew proudly in artistic circles, on university campuses, and at youthful gatherings such as be-ins and happenings. By the late 1960's, these assaults on tradition succeeded in generating mass acceptance of what had been taboo only a decade earlier, including the widespread recreational consumption of drugs.

Not until 1963 did the cluster of thought and behavior patterns spawn a counterculture of which drug consumption was a prominent part. Young people wanted to rebel against rationalism, religion, and nature—rationalism because it favored the cold, calculating mind over the sympathetic, humane spirit; religion because it embodied the assumptions of the outer, materialistic world at the expense of the inner, spiritual individual; and nature because it was viewed as a resource to be manipulated instead of an environment to be treasured. For increasing numbers of young people, drugs promised deliverance from the narrow confines of rationalism to the vast expanse of introspection and from the corruption of the objective realm to the integrity of the subjective domain.

Music, Art, and Drugs In the United States, musicians and artists led the assault against convention. Musicians fearlessly injected drug references into lyrics. For example, Bob Dylan's "Subterranean Homesick Blues" (1965) begins with "Johnny's in the basement mixing up the medicine" (that is, drugs); the Fifth Dimension's "Aquarius/Let the Sunshine In" (1969) speaks of "mystic crystal revelations" (an allusion to LSD, lysergic acid diethylamide or acid); Jefferson Airplane's "White Rabbit" (1967) makes reference to drug taking; and the Doors' "Break on Through (to the Other Side)" (1967) alludes to the new insights gained from chemical stimulation of the brain. Rock bands such as the Rolling Stones, the Grateful Dead, and the Who not only sang of drugs but also became avowed users, frequently celebrating the creative consequences of some elixir. Acid rock, a San Francisco-rooted genre inspired by LSD, took music a step further with instruments that produced Asian sounds, strobe lights, shocking costumes and makeup, and bizarre on-stage exhibitions, such as Jimi Hendrix smashing his guitar (quite unremarkable by the late twentieth century). An acid trip (the experience of taking LSD), when

While members of the counterculture advocated marijuana use, law enforcement agents, including these narcotics agents posing with marijuana seized in a 1963 drug bust, took a dim view of the practice. (Library of Congress)

accompanied by appropriate music, was reputed to lead to an ecstasy of sensations and perceptions. The Woodstock Music and Art Fair, an August, 1969, weekend music festival that turned into a large-scale party featuring sound, sex, and drugs in Sullivan County, New York, has been aptly labeled the "counterculture's biggest bash."

In the theater, musicals such as *Hair* (1967) treated drug ingestion quite matter of factly, depicting it as both natural and safe. Films such as *Alice's Restaurant* (1969) included scenes in which the characters smoke marijuana or use other drugs. Bestselling books often highlighted the excitement associated with drugs. New Journalism writer Tom Wolfe's *The Electric Kool-Aid Acid Test* (1968) chronicled the antics of Ken Kesey and his Merry Pranksters as they traveled across the country in their psychedelic-colored school bus, which always contained ample quantities of orange juice laced with LSD. Psychedelic art employed a kaleidoscopic display of color in painting, sculpture, or stage lighting that emotionally enveloped the viewer. It often took the form of posters that announced upcoming rock concerts.

LSD and the Summer of Love In the early part of the 1960's, Harvard psychology professor Timothy Leary, who was studying the effects of hallucinogenic drugs, ingested LSD to get a firsthand account of its effects and ultimately encouraged its use as an agent to release what he regarded as the truth that resided in each individual. Leary urged people to "turn on, tune in, drop out," by which he meant take drugs, open the mind, and abandon the conventions of society for the pleasures of truth. His International Foundation for Internal Freedom and its journal, *Psychedelic Review*, promoted the free use of drugs, as did his later League for Spiritual Discovery. Leary and other like-minded scholars communicated a scholarly challenge to the idea that drugs were inherently bad, and baby boomers in college or in the military began to experiment with various drugs. James Kunen's *The Strawberry Statement* (1969) suggests that heroin was the only drug not used by students and that marijuana was "a little less common than cigarettes."

Rock concerts, student demonstrations, protest marches, be-ins, happenings, or any event where great numbers of young people came together also effectively promoted drug use. The most notable—

although vaguely delineated—event was San Francisco's Summer of Love. This massive event began around October 6, 1966, when LSD became illegal; gathered momentum at the January, 1967, Human Be-in at the city's Golden Gate Park, where Leary exhorted the crowd to turn on to drugs; and gained intensity at the Monterey International Pop Festival in June. Most of the Summer of Love participants did their loving, singing, dancing, and drug taking in the Haight-Ashbury section of the city, where those at this "wild hippie party" obtained free food, medical care, entertainment, and communal living. At the thirty-year Summer of Love reunion, Mayor Willie Brown, along with singer Country Joe McDonald, Starship (previously Jefferson Airplane), and other groups, gathered on Columbus Day to remember the summer and pay tribute to the city's residents who had lost their lives in Vietnam.

Impact The consequences of the unbridled use of drugs, which remained pervasive into the 1970's, cannot be measured precisely. One reaction to the drug culture was a growing opposition. Even as the assault on the older generation's values peaked between the Summer of Love and the United States' withdrawal from Vietnam in 1973, the "silent majority"—people in the mainstream culture who had quietly gone about their business in the 1960's—mounted an attack against counterculture thought and behavior. This reaction is reflected in the popular music of the time. The revival of Elvis Presley's career in the late 1960's is largely due to his attractiveness to those who held mainstream values. Presley, a religious, anticommunist performer, did not align himself with liberals or members of the counterculture. His drug of choice was not mind-expanding mushrooms or LSD, and his music was not designed to be listened to while on an "acid trip" (taking LSD). Merle Haggard's "Okie from Muskogee" ridiculed "the hippies up in San Francisco" for doing drugs and bragged that people from his town drank "white lightning," or moonshine, instead.

As the 1960's progressed, some hippies began to reduce or curtail their drug usage. The members of the Morningstar commune, founded in 1966 by musician Lou Gottlieb, north of San Francisco, valued hard work and eschewed LSD. As one inhabitant declared, "I'd rather have beautiful children than beautiful visions," a reference to the genetic damage that ingestion of some drugs was believed to cause.

From the outset, drug usage had produced unwanted consequences, including "bad trips," or unpleasant LSD-taking experiences. Drugs began to play a part in the deaths of many young people and famous stars, including Jimi Hendrix, Janis Joplin, Jim Morrison of the Doors, and Alan "Blind Owl" Wilson of Canned Heat. In countless cases, drugs caused other serious problems for their users. These deaths and drug-related problems provided sobering pictures for the American people. Public admissions about the ravages caused by drug abuse frequently ended up on the news or in documentaries. In later decades, singer and songwriter Elton John, Keith Richards of the Rolling Stones, and John Phillips of the Mamas and the Papas openly recounted the downside of drugs. Moreover, numerous antidrug programs initiated by the U.S. government made trafficking and consumption of drugs both more risky and less socially acceptable. LSD and to a lesser extent marijuana were replaced by cocaine and crack, and drugs were taken for escape and reasons other than mind expansion. By the 1980's, drug use was on the decline.

Subsequent Events As the baby boomers reached maturity, got regular jobs, began families, and moved into suburbs, most of the outward signs of drug usage and tolerance disappeared. However, elements of the drug culture lingered on into the 1990's. The theme song of the early 1990's hit television show *The Wonder Years,* Joe Cocker's "A Little Help from My Friends" (1969), played weekly to an audience largely unaware that its original message involved a person's reliance on drugs. Public acceptance, if not society's embrace, of narcotic symbols can be seen in its sanction of a perfume called Opium, 1990's rock bands called Morphine and Jane's Addiction, T-shirts and bumper stickers bearing the number 420 (the California Penal Code prohibiting marijuana), and emaciated models that look like heroin users in clothing advertisements. In addition, a one-time marijuana user who did not inhale, Bill Clinton, was elected and re-elected president of the United States.

By the 1980's, most of the members of the counterculture had become part of the American establishment. In his last act of civil disobedience, Yippee radical turned Yuppie entrepreneur Jerry Rubin was struck by a vehicle and killed as he jaywalked across a Los Angeles street to his condominium. In

1997, folksinger Bob Dylan, whose 1964 song "The Times They Are a-Changin' " challenged the older generation, performed for Pope John Paul II, paying tribute to an institution that most of Dylan's fans considered a bastion of backwardness three decades earlier. The establishment, though temporarily battered by drug experimentation and other convention-defying acts, survived and flourished.

Additional Information James J. Farrell's *The Spirit of the Sixties* (1997), William L. O'Neill's *Coming Apart: An Informal History of America in the 1960's* (1976), and Nora Sayre's *Sixties Going on Seventies* (1996) all portray the counterculture during the 1960's, including drug use. The historical context is exhaustively discussed by physician David F. Musto in *The American Disease* (1987), and the recreational side of drug experimentation is thoroughly examined by psychiatrist Thomas Szasz in *Ceremonial Chemistry* (1974).

Thomas Reins

See also Baby Boomers; Beat Generation; Communes; Counterculture; Doors; Dylan, Bob; *Electric Kool-Aid Acid Test, The;* Fitzpatrick Drug Death; Grateful Dead; *Hair;* Hendrix, Jimi; Hippies; Jefferson Airplane; Joplin, Janis; Leary, Timothy; LSD; Marijuana; Monterey Pop Festival; Presley, Elvis; Rolling Stones; *Strawberry Statement, The;* Summer of Love; Woodstock Festival; Yippies; Youth Culture and the Generation Gap.

■ Dylan, Bob

Born May 24, 1941, Duluth, Minnesota

A singer and songwriter whose works changed the face of American music. Dylan's songs greatly influenced folk and rock music and also the nation's political and social attitudes.

Early Life Bob Dylan, born as Robert Allen Zimmerman in Duluth, Minnesota, the son of a middle-class Jewish couple, moved to the small town of Hibbing when he was six years old. His earliest musical interests were in the country-western songs then popular in northern Minnesota. He discovered rock music about 1955, when he saw the film *Rebel Without a Cause,* and began to emulate James Dean, its star. He formed a band, the Golden Chords, while in high school, and in 1957, they performed "Big Black Train," a blues song that is his first known composition.

Bob Dylan started the 1960's singing folk songs in Greenwich Village coffeehouses and ended the decade a musical legend. (AP/Wide World Photos)

The 1960's In 1959, he entered the University of Minnesota in Minneapolis, where he discovered folk music and bought an acoustic guitar. He began to perform in coffeehouses as Bob Dylan, and after he came across the music of folk legend Woody Guthrie, he began to model his life on that of his new hero. He set off for New York in December, 1960, saying he wanted to meet Guthrie, who was dying of Huntington's chorea, a debilitating nerve disease, in a hospital in New Jersey.

After Dylan arrived in New York in January, 1961, he began to regularly visit Guthrie and to perform in Greenwich Village coffeehouses, the center of the folk music revival. Later that year, Dylan signed with Columbia Records. His first album, *Bob Dylan*, released in March, 1962, contained traditional folk songs performed in Dylan's rough, pared-down style and two original compositions, "Song to Woody," a tribute to Guthrie, and "Talking New York," rendered in an energized version of Guthrie's talking blues format.

Dylan's second recording, *The Freewheelin' Bob Dylan* (1963), contained Dylan's first protest songs: "Blowin' in the Wind" (later a hit for Peter, Paul, and Mary), "A Hard Rain's a-Gonna Fall," and "Masters of War." Singer Joan Baez recorded some of Dylan's songs and took him on tour with her for part of the summer of 1963. Dylan's fame grew as young people began to identify with the sentiments expressed in his songs. In 1964, he released *The Times They Are a-Changin'*, which contained both protest songs, such as "With God on Our Side" and the title track, and songs with more personal lyrics. For many young listeners, the title track precisely described the atmosphere of the mid-1960's.

In *Bringing It All Back Home* (1965), Dylan began the switch from an all-acoustical traditional folk music style to a fusion of folk and rock that would become known as folk rock. On about half of the album's songs, Dylan was backed by a rock-and-roll band. On July 25, 1965, at the Newport Folk Festival, Dylan appeared on stage with an electric guitar and backed by the Paul Butterfield Blues Band, an electrified band. He was loudly booed by the stunned, then angry, folk purists in the audience. Aficionados of traditional folk music objected because his songs sounded like rock and roll and the lyrics—though complex and somewhat enigmatic—were not about social injustice or other traditional folk themes. However, Dylan's electrified sound only increased his popularity, and the 1965 single "Like a Rolling Stone" reached number two on the charts. In August, Dylan released a fully electric album, *Highway 61 Revisited*, and followed it with *Blonde on Blonde* in 1966.

In July, 1966, Dylan was in a motorcycle accident and disappeared from public view for a year and a half. During his isolation, he and the Band, his backup group, recorded a number of songs that were bootlegged then released in 1975 as *The Basement Tapes*. In 1968, he reemerged with the country-tinged *John Wesley Harding* and wrote "All Along the Watchtower," which rock artist Jimi Hendrix recorded, and in 1969, Dylan released the overtly country *Nashville Skyline*, which produced the hit "Lay, Lady, Lay" and included a duet with well-known country singer Johnny Cash.

Later Life Dylan continued to perform and produce albums throughout the next three decades. In the mid-1970's, he toured and recorded with a new rock band, the Rolling Thunder Revue. In 1979, Dylan became a born-again Christian and recorded songs with a religious theme, a phase that appeared to end by about 1982. In the 1980's, Dylan toured with Tom Petty and the Heartbreakers and the Grateful Dead and appeared with Petty, George Harrison, and Jeff Lynn as one of the Traveling Wilburys in addition to releasing nine albums. He was inducted into the Rock and Roll Hall of Fame in 1988. In the 1990's, he did a number of live concerts, appeared on *MTV Unplugged*, and continued to release albums. In 1998, he won a Grammy for best album for *Time Out of Mind*.

Impact Dylan's music—in each of its incarnations—had a profound effect on the 1960's music scene. During the first half of the decade, Dylan's work was instrumental in popularizing the use of traditional folk music styles to address contemporary political and social issues. In mid-decade, his adoption of an electrified, rock-style sound ushered in the new musical format called folk rock, a format that many

other musicians adopted. His late 1960's country-tinged rock helped lead the way for the country rock that emerged in the 1970's. Many subsequent musicians have been compared to Dylan, and he influenced the sound of many artists, including rock artist Bruce Springsteen.

Dylan's early 1960's protest songs were enthusiastically adopted by a young generation in rebellion against traditional values. Songs such as "Blowin' in the Wind" and "The Times They Are a-Changin' " became anthems for members of the Civil Rights movement, and other songs, such as "Masters of War," were favored by those opposed to nuclear arms proliferation and later the Vietnam War.

Additional Information Bob Spitz's *Dylan, A Biography* (1989) provides an excellent outline of the singer's life and works through the end of the 1980's.

Marc Goldstein

See also Baez, Joan; Folk Music; Music; Newport Folk Festivals; Protest Songs; Youth Culture and the Generation Gap.

E

■ East Village

Neighborhood adjacent to Greenwich Village in lower Manhattan. It became a major center for the counterculture in the Northeast.

The East Village was originally part of the lower East Side, populated by Eastern European and Jewish immigrants. It was reinvented in the 1960's as a haven for artists and rebels. African Americans and Latinos helped create a lively ethnic mix in the East Village, but it was the youth culture that dominated, creating an atmosphere of radicalism in art and politics. Hippies, Yippies, and hangers-on gathered at St. Marks Place and in Tompkins Square Park to demonstrate, panhandle, and socialize. They developed their own underground newspapers, the *East Village Other* and the *Rat*. The influx of this youthful and adventurous counterculture also led to the creation of theaters, cafés, bookshops, head shops (stores selling drug paraphernalia), discos such as the Electric Circus, and inexpensive restaurants, especially vegetarian eateries such as The Cauldron. Of particular note is Bill Graham's Fillmore East auditorium, which hosted rock performers such as the Grateful Dead and Jimi Hendrix.

Impact The East Village was a tumultuous mecca for the counterculture, sending a message of social tolerance that encouraged self-expression and experimentation with politics, lifestyles, and drugs.

Subsequent Events In the 1970's, the prevalence of drugs led to social instability, and many of the hippies in the East Village dispersed. Some important figures in the arts, such as Allen Ginsberg, continued to live in the area, however, and in the 1980's, the East Village became a center for art galleries and for support of gay rights and the homeless.

Additional Information Yuri Kapralov's *Once There Was a Village* (1974) is an illustrated history of the East Village.

Margaret Boe Birns

See also Counterculture, Drug Culture; Youth Culture and the Generation Gap.

■ *Easy Rider*

Released 1969
Director Dennis Hopper (1936-   )

A trendsetter in American filmmaking. It used the social context of the period to express the dissatisfaction of youth with the status quo.

The Work *Easy Rider* is the story of Wyatt (or "Captain America," played by Peter Fonda) and Billy (Dennis Hopper), two freewheeling, long-haired, social dropouts/hippies. After making the drug deal of their lives with a dealer in Mexico (Antonio Mendoza) and their U.S. connection (Phil Spector, the famous rock-and-roll producer in a cameo role), the two men decide to ride their motorcycles from California to New Orleans, the promised land of the Mardi Gras. On the way, they meet a number of unusual characters: a rancher and his family, a hitchhiker who lives in a hippie commune, hookers, rednecks, and most notably alcoholic southern lawyer George Hanson (Jack Nicholson, in a role that propelled him to stardom). Wyatt and Billy meet George in a southern jail, where George assures them that they can get out of jail with his connections if they "haven't killed anybody. Least nobody white." George, intrigued by their apparent freedom, decides to join them on their trip. After being harassed by locals at a Louisiana café, George is murdered in his sleep. When Wyatt and Billy reach New Orleans, to honor George, they visit a brothel, which the lawyer had wanted to do. They and two prostitutes take LSD (lysergic acid diethylamide, or acid) in a cemetery, but the acid trip is a bad one (the drug-taking experience is unpleasant). Although Billy feels they have been successful in their quest for freedom, Wyatt tells him, "We blew it." Outside of town, the two men are shot to death by a tobacco-chewing hillbilly.

Impact *Easy Rider*, basically a road film, captured the spirit of the 1960's with its tale of a search for freedom in a conformist society, despite paranoia, bigotry, and violence. The film commented on the prejudices of a nation that was supposed to provide

Billy (Dennis Hopper) looks over at Captain America (Peter Fonda) and his passenger George Hanson (Jack Nicholson) as they roll on down the road in the 1969 film Easy Rider. *(Museum of Modern Art/Film Stills Archive)*

freedom for everyone and exposed the underside of a southern society that was seething with hatred for anyone who was different. The extremely successful, low-budget, countercultural film illustrated the discontent and alienation of 1960's youth and featured sex, drugs, and a pulsating rock-and-roll soundtrack reinforcing or commenting on the film's themes. A ritualistic experience, the film was viewed repeatedly by youthful audiences who were intrigued by the film's central tenet: the question of whether people have really achieved freedom or are simply living an illusion. The film was followed by a series of youth-oriented films in the 1970's such as *The Strawberry Statement* (1970), and its use of music to capture an era can be seen in films such as *American Graffiti* (1973).

Related Work The film *Electra Glide in Blue* (1973), directed by James W. Guerico, covers many of the same issues as does *Easy Rider* and has been called "*Easy Rider* with cops."

Additional Information A more complete discussion of *Easy Rider* can be found in *Movies of the Sixties* (1983), edited by Ann Lloyd. Complete information about the film's casting is also provided.

Ronald Nelson

See also Counterculture; Drug Culture; Film; LSD; *Strawberry Statement, The.*

■ *Eat a Bowl of Tea*

Published 1961
Author Louis H. Chu (1915-1970)

A fictional work that reflected social change in the New York Chinatown community during the 1950's and 1960's. The novel showed a second-generation Chinese American man carving a new future for himself out of the stagnant lifestyle of his father.

The Work In *Eat a Bowl of Tea*, both Wang Wah Gay, owner of a mahjong club, and Lee Gong, a retiree, are old "bachelors" in New York City's Chinatown.

They decide to marry their children, Wang Ben Loy, a local waiter, and Lee Mei Oi, who lives in China. Their separation from their wives in China for more than twenty-five years prompts the two old men to agree that Ben Loy should bring Mei Oi to the United States after their marriage. Mei Oi, as a newcomer, has difficulty adjusting to the male-oriented communal life in Chinatown, and Ben Loy, pressured by work and his father's expectation that he will produce a son to continue the family line, fails to comfort her with love. The young wife, coveted by other "bachelors," finally falls victim to the predatory Ah Song, who impregnates her. When the affair is discovered, Ben Loy shuns the community for fear that his impotency has been disclosed. Mei Oi cannot confide in her father, a total stranger. Wah Gay, shamed by the incident, resorts to violence, cutting off Ah Song's ear. Both Wah Gay and Ah Song are forced to leave Chinatown. Ben Loy, after drinking this bitter bowl of tea, resolves the problem by moving with Mei Oi to San Francisco's Chinatown, where they can make a fresh start.

Impact This novel portrays a major social change in the Chinese community during the 1950's and the 1960's. Before 1949, the Chinese Exclusion Act prohibited Chinese laborers from bringing their families to the United States. These so-called "bachelors" usually had wives in China, with whom they reunited only occasionally to have children. The lack of family life caused these men to live dissipated lives, gambling and visiting prostitutes. After 1949, new brides crossed the Pacific Ocean and started to change the communal scene in Chinatown. The impact of their arrival reached its climax in the 1960's when the "bachelor" lifestyle became moribund. Author Louis Chu did not achieve fame or financial success with this book because his unexotic, realistic depiction of early Chinese Americans was not attractive to American readers. With this novel, however, Chu succeeded in bringing the issue of Chinese American communal life to public attention.

Additional Information For a literary analysis of the novel, see "Portraits of Chinatown" in Elaine Kim's *Asian American Literature: An Introduction to the Writings and Their Social Context* (1982). Another novel on the same topic is Lin Yutang's *Chinatown Family*, published in 1948.

Fatima Wu

See also Literature; *Lucky Come Hawaii.*

■ Economic Opportunity Act of 1964

Legislative initiative to combat poverty in the United States. This act was part of President Lyndon B. Johnson's War on Poverty, which sought to mobilize human and financial resources in order to give all citizens a chance to share in the nation's promise.

The Economic Opportunity Act (EOA) of 1964 was the result of various proposals and ideas that dated back to the social welfare initiatives of the New Deal in the 1930's. The EOA established the Office of Economic Opportunity (OEO) in the executive office of the president, which launched several programs in the War on Poverty, a domestic "war" that was necessary, according to President Lyndon B. Johnson, "so as to eliminate the paradox of poverty in the midst of plenty." The various programs had, as their feature value, a focus on opportunity. The EOA's declaration of purpose, in part, is to provide "the opportunity for education and training, the opportunity to work, and the opportunity to live in decency and dignity." The EOA provided the funds for vocational training, created a Job Corps to train youths in conservation camps and urban centers and the Head Start program to help preschoolers from low-income families, encouraged Community Action Programs, extended loans to small-business owners willing to hire the unemployed, gave grants to farmers, set up a work-study program for college students, and established Volunteers in Service to America (VISTA), the domestic counterpart of the popular Peace Corps created by President John F. Kennedy.

President Johnson's dream of the Great Society and his attitude that government should use its powers for great accomplishments came, in part, from his political mentor, President Franklin D. Roosevelt. Like Roosevelt's New Deal legislation and Kennedy's New Frontier plans and policies, Johnson's vision included the hope of socially and politically engineering a better country for everyone. The concept and rationale of the many programs created by the EOA were quite controversial during their formative stages. Eventually, as with almost any piece of legislation, what finally got enacted reflected compromises and trade-offs among the various lobbies, administrative agencies, and congressional power blocs. Possibly the most controversial program established by the EOA was the Job Corps. It was one of the first government efforts directed at the problem of hard-core, unemployable youth.

The EOA was supported by New Deal Democrats (including Senator Hubert Humphrey, who later became Johnson's vice president) who envisioned a transformation of poverty-stricken individuals into well-adjusted, motivated, and upwardly mobile people. The act was opposed primarily by conservative Republicans who were against government intervention in domestic affairs, especially where it concerned social welfare legislation, and were concerned about the high costs of running these programs. Johnson was successful in passing the EOA partly because of the favorable pro-Democrat atmosphere created after Kennedy's assassination.

Impact The programs enacted by the EOA under the auspices of the OEO ranged from well-known programs such as Head Start and the Job Corps to lesser-known projects such as Senior Opportunities and Services, Legal Services, and Community Economic Development. All had the goal of helping the poor break the cycle of poverty and advance to live a better, fuller, more productive life. Some of the programs, such as Head Start, are generally regarded as successful; others remain controversial or have vanished. However, between 1964 and 1969, poverty rates decreased from 19 percent to 12 percent of the population.

Subsequent Events The OEO was abolished by the Head Start, Economic Opportunity, and Community Partnership Act of 1975, which created the Community Services Administration. The EOA was repealed except for titles VIII and X by the Omnibus Budget Reconciliation Act of 1981.

Additional Information Further information on the EOA and its place in Johnson's War on Poverty can be found in *The Vantage Point* (1971), President Johnson's memoirs. Another source is the *Public Papers of the Presidents of the United States: Lyndon B. Johnson*, 10 volumes (1965-1970) in the National Archives.

Joseph E. Bauer

See also Goldwater, Barry; Great Society Programs; Head Start; Humphrey, Hubert; Job Corps; Kennedy, John F.; Peace Corps; War on Poverty; Welfare State.

■ *Economy of Cities, The*

Published 1969
Author Jane Jacobs (1916-   )

A work of social criticism that asserts that city inefficiencies and creative local economies are vital elements contributing to healthy urban development. It contains a vision of why cities either grow or decay and articulates a scenario for city economic development based on wide-ranging examples from historical and contemporary cities.

The Work A central theme in *The Economy of Cities* is that development is a process by which a group of cities engaged in trade with each other create "new work" to add to the work already being done. This process depends on having a large number of diversified economic organizations whose interactions lead to "economically creative breakaways." Therefore, in describing development in Birmingham, England, Jane Jacobs states that "fragmented and inefficient little industries" were responsible for adding new work and creating new organizations. In her opinion, "valuable inefficiencies," not efficiency in producing existing goods and services, results in new work. Jacobs believes that cities grow by gradually diversifying and differentiating their economies, and that this process starts with exports and their suppliers. However, she attributes "explosive" city growth to the effects of import replacement. Import replacement brings rapid expansion of total economic activity, expanding markets for rural goods as the composition of city imports shifts, and rapid growth in jobs. This leads to a further expansion and diversification of exports.

Impact When she wrote *The Economy of Cities*, Jacobs already had a reputation as a defender of cities against planners and architects who promoted urban renewal in the form of sterile housing projects. In her earlier work, *The Death and Life of Great American Cities* (1961), she contemptuously cast aside contemporary urban planning and promoted the dynamic qualities of city neighborhoods. Writing in 1968, her most prominent critic, Lewis Mumford, applauded her "fresh insights and pertinent ideas" but decried her "series of amateurish planning proposals that will not stand up under the most forbearing examination."

In *The Economy of Cities*, Jacobs drew parallels between cities that were centuries and continents apart and peremptorily rejected the ideas of economists when they conflicted with her unusual and original thesis. Urban planners attacked her approach because she disregarded scientific studies of cities and regions. However, the general public and the academic community agreed with Charles Abrams, a Harvard University professor who noted the book's timeliness and hoped that the book would focus public attention on neglected issues and theories.

Related Work *The Urban Prospect* (1968), by Lewis Mumford, is a collection of essays on urban development that contains Mumford's critique of Jacobs's *The Death and Life of Great American Cities*.

Additional Information For a further examination of cities and why they are decaying, see *Cities and the Wealth of Nations: Principles of Economic Life* (1984), by Jane Jacobs.

Jerome Picard

See also Demographics of the United States; Great Society Programs; Housing Laws, Federal, Prosperity and Poverty; Urban Renewal.

■ *Ed Sullivan Show, The*

Produced 1948-1971
Producer Ed Sullivan

A weekly hourlong prime-time live television variety show hosted for more than two decades by former newspaper columnist Ed Sullivan. The popular program featured a wide range of new talent and established performers who appealed to a large national television audience.

The Work Premiering on the Columbia Broadcasting System (CBS) in 1948 as *Toast of the Town*, the program became known as *The Ed Sullivan Show* in 1955. Sullivan and the program, which ended in 1971, received numerous awards and honors from the media industry. Sunday night television during the 1950's and 1960's was largely dominated by *The Ed Sullivan Show*. Although tremendously successful, Sullivan's on-camera presence was always visibly awkward. Critics and friends referred to him as "Stone Face" because he seldom smiled or expressed much emotion. Comedians Jack Carter and John Byner's on-air parodies of Sullivan became audience favorites.

Sullivan lacked stage presence and any performing talent, but he possessed one significant attribute that contributed to his lasting success—he was an adept producer. He always understood what the audience liked, and because he controlled the show, he delivered quality entertainment that consistently attracted American viewers. As producer, Sullivan selected the acts, beginning with the first *Toast of the Town* show featuring, among others, Dean Martin, Jerry Lewis, Richard Rodgers, and Oscar Hammerstein. He organized the show around well-known artists and personalities such as Maurice Chevalier, Carl Sandburg, Bing Crosby, Victor Borge, Gloria Swanson, Fred Astaire, Marilyn Monroe, and Elvis Presley and also invited lesser-known acts.

The 1960's included some changes and challenges for *The Ed Sullivan Show*. The program experienced a viewership decline beginning with the 1960-1961 season. Suddenly, a show accustomed to winning its time period each week was dropping behind in its ratings. The program tallied a 38.4 seasonal average rating in 1956-1957, then tumbled to a 25 rating by 1960-1961 and only 23.5 the following season. Low ratings prompted Sullivan to replace his longtime coproducer, Marlo Lewis, in 1960. To provide new direction and a ratings increase, Sullivan selected his son-in-law, Bob Precht, as coproducer. Amid controversy, Precht immediately changed the 1950's on-air appearance of the program by introducing innovative set design and improved production techniques.

Precht's vision of change encompassed an additional refinement involving the delicate transition of authority between himself and Sullivan. Precht became the show's producer and gained responsibility for choosing who appeared on *The Ed Sullivan Show*. A change in talent booking was necessary to avoid talent overexposure, introduce new talent, and compete with other variety shows in an attempt to revive sagging audience ratings. Audience measurements improved for the 1962-1963 season. Among the top twenty-five shows, Sullivan's show ranked fourteenth and had a seasonal average rating of 25.3. Although the program reached eighth place and a 27.5 average rating during the 1963-1964 season, it never attained better placement or higher seasonal ratings. By the end of the decade, the show had fallen out of the top twenty-five.

The United States' obsession with race relations in the 1960's contributed to the loss of Sullivan's program sponsor. Numerous African American artists, including Louis Armstrong, Pearl Bailey, Duke Ellington, Ella Fitzgerald, and Diana Ross, appeared regularly on Sullivan's show. The 1960-1961 season opened without longtime sponsor Lincoln-Mercury. The automaker withdrew advertising support in part because of escalating costs and growing dealership concern about Sullivan's embracing of African American entertainers.

British rock musicians, including the Rolling Stones and the Dave Clark Five, appeared on the Sullivan show to gain American exposure. In 1964, *The Ed Sullivan Show* made television history by posting a phenomenal 44.6 rating, making it among the top-rated programs of all time. The Beatles' appearance on February 9 reached a viewing audience of recordbreaking size.

Impact The concept of a prime-time network television show that was part circus and part vaudeville and featured a shy, bumbling host seems incredible, especially in terms of audience receptivity and on-air longevity. That such a program could attract thirty to forty million viewers each week for more than twenty years demonstrates that *The Ed Sullivan Show* truly gave Americans what they wanted to see.

This successful program exposed Americans to a galaxy of talent and culture not readily available in the 1960's. A typical telecast might have featured opera, dance, comedy, music, dramatic readings, puppets, animals, heroes, and celebrities. Entertainers from throughout the world made their debut on *The Ed Sullivan Show.* Prominent stars appeared to promote their latest efforts and lesser-known talents sought national exposure that might launch their careers.

Additional Information An excellent book about the Sullivan program is *A Thousand Sundays: The Story of The Ed Sullivan Show* (1980), by Jerry Bowles.

Dennis A. Harp

See also Beatles, The; Rolling Stones; Supremes; Television; *Tonight Show, The.*

■ Education

A dramatic decade marked by educational expansion, experimentation, and reform, as well as campus unrest. Developments include federal financial support for improving education and equalizing educational opportunity; innovative schools, colleges, and programs; and new fields of study and perspectives that incorporated previously excluded groups.

The 1960's was a particularly volatile time in education, marked by significant reform efforts in lower and higher education. A number of concerns and trends of the late 1950's, such as the quest for academic excellence and anxiety over the Cold War continued in the early 1960's until other issues, such as the pursuit of equity and equality and ameliorating social injustice, gained ascendency.

In Search of Academic Excellence In the 1950's, discussions of education focused on academic quality and the role of educational institutions. The Soviet launch of Sputnik in 1957 made Americans reexamine how science and technology were taught in U.S. classrooms, and reformers such as James B. Conant, author of *The American High School Today* (1959), pushed for a large comprehensive high school where all students would be educated, but special attention would be given to college-bound youth, particularly talented boys and young men. Groups of specialists aided by National Science Foundation (NSF) funds made major curriculum revisions that stressed the inquiry method and the concepts in particular academic disciplines rather than rote memorization. Their work resulted in the new science, new math, and new social studies curricula of the early 1960's. These efforts to improve the content of education influenced elementary and secondary schools in urban and suburban settings.

In the late 1950's and early 1960's, higher education was viewed as increasingly important to national security interests, and NSF funds propelled basic research in universities, particularly in the sciences. Federal and private funds for university research continued to grow throughout the 1960's. In his 1963 study, *The Uses of the University*, Clark Kerr, president of the University of California, coined the term, "multiversity," to describe these massive university enterprises with their large bureaucratic structures, competing interest groups, and significant links to the larger society. By the mid- and late 1960's, the multiversity had become the subject of criticisms leveled by both students and education reformers.

An Opportunity to Learn As the universities developed, they grew, but not fast enough to keep up with the baby boomers (born 1946-1964). A growing number of students were graduating from high school and competing for admission to elite and increasingly selective colleges. In recognition of this

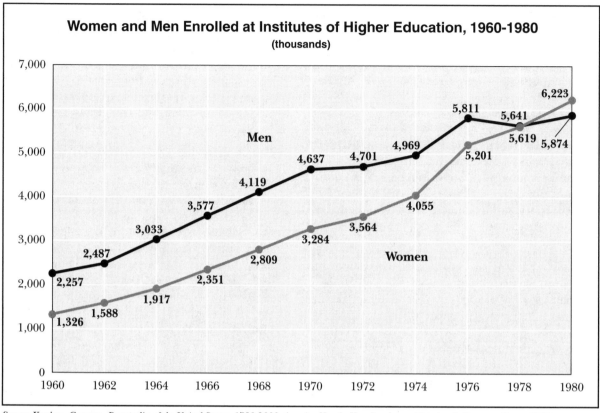

Women and Men Enrolled at Institutes of Higher Education, 1960-1980
(thousands)

Source: Kurian, George, *Datapedia of the United States, 1790-2000, America Year by Year.* Lanham, Maryland: Bernam Press, 1994.

expansion and also to support greater access to higher education—an issue that would grow in importance in the late 1960's—President John F. Kennedy drew attention to the need for federal funding for higher education. In 1963, Congress passed the Higher Education Facilities Act, which provided funds for building construction to meet the needs of the expanding higher education sector.

Many states, the federal government, and educational institutions attempted to extend educational opportunity during the 1960's. For example, efforts were made to remove financial barriers to a college education and to recruit minority students to attend predominately white institutions. The federal government, through the Higher Education Act of 1965, committed itself to equalizing educational opportunity for needy students by providing financial support. Colleges and universities developed policies of "open admissions" in the late 1960's and the 1970's, and the growing number of community colleges were urged to open their door to all high school graduates.

Desegregation Toward the end of the 1950's and the early part of the 1960's, efforts to desegregate public schools were being made in accordance with the Supreme Court's 1954 decision in *Brown v. Board of Education of Topeka, Kansas.* The Court overturned the 1896 *Plessy v. Ferguson* "separate but equal" doctrine as it applied to public schools, declaring that "separate but equal" was "inherently unequal." A year later, the Court ordered the desegregation of schools with "all deliberate speed." Several southern and border states failed to comply, and on occasion, federal troops had to be deployed to ensure the safe desegregation of educational institutions. In 1962, for example, Kennedy sent federal troops to secure the admission of James H. Meredith to the University of Mississippi.

As the 1960's progressed, the focus would shift from the rural South to the large urban cities of the North and from desegregation of schools segregated by law to integration of northern schools where de facto segregation existed because of housing and residential patterns. During this period, the Office of Education warned urban school systems that they would lose funds if they did not eliminate racial imbalances. The use of busing in the North to secure racial balance would develop into a contentious issue in the 1970's and beyond.

Relevance and Education In the mid-1960's, the quest for equity and equality took center stage in many school reform efforts. Issues and problems inside and outside of schools—civil rights and racial and gender discrimination, poverty amid affluence (particularly visible in the inner cities with large minority populations), assassinations of political and civil rights leaders, urban riots, youth alienation, attacks on authority, student protests, and an increasingly unpopular war in Vietnam—had a significant impact on educational reform. Some political leaders, including President Lyndon B. Johnson, viewed the schools as vehicles for ameliorating social problems, most notably for educating the children of the poor and breaking the poverty cycle.

One important effort in this direction was compensatory education, which emphasized equalizing educational opportunity. The federal government, elementary and secondary schools, and colleges embarked upon programs aimed at providing enrichment and services for low-income children from preschool through high school. Research on learning from the 1950's and 1960's pointed to the importance of education during a child's early years and its subsequent influence on later achievement. In 1965, the Office of Economic Opportunity, part of Johnson's War on Poverty, created Head Start, a preschool program designed to prepare disadvantaged children for success in school through intellectual stimulation and special services. The Elementary and Secondary Education Act of 1965 provided an infusion of funds into the education sector, and Title I of that act concentrated on compensatory programs that targeted young children and those in higher grades. These programs included efforts aimed at identifying talented disadvantaged students and encouraging them to go to college.

Educational reformers, students, and community leaders also targeted school programs and curricula, teacher recruitment, and issues of community control. They felt that the contributions of women and minority groups were largely invisible in the predominately male, Eurocentric portrayal of a homogeneous American society taught in most schools.

They insisted that courses and instructional materials used in elementary and secondary schools include the history and literature of African Americans, other minority groups, and women and that classes taught in the inner city be relevant to children of the urban poor. These developments coincided with the emergence of new historical scholarship. Reformers demanded that schools recruit minority teachers who would be more understanding of and responsive to minority students' needs. In colleges and universities, requests for the creation of black studies departments and for classes in history and literature to include the contributions of African Americans were followed by similar demands from other disenfranchised groups. This quest for relevance paralleled the emergence of the Black Power movement, which emphasized black identity, culture, power, separatism, and confrontation. In some schools, tension arose over charges of racism and demands for more minority teachers, more relevant courses, and special programs. As schools grappled with these problems, efforts were made to move toward a portrayal of American society that emphasized ethnic identity and multiculturalism in courses and instructional materials.

Students' Rights Other important developments in the mid- and late 1960's included the move toward a more student-centered, humanistic teaching approach that allowed students to have a greater choice and provided them with more services in a variety of areas. Numerous books published in the 1960's, ranging from A. S. Neill's *Summerhill* (1960) to Jonathan Kozol's *Death at an Early Age* (1967) advocated different notions of child rearing, targeted urban education, and critiqued the impersonal bureaucratic structures and learning environment as heartless, stifling, and alienating to children and youth. This trend resulted in the open classroom movement and in challenges to authority and the hierarchical relationships between teachers and students. Schools experimented with team teaching, experiential learning, electives, independent study, and special learning departments and services such as bilingual education, which would get federal support in 1967.

By the mid-1960's, higher education had begun experiencing tumultuous change. The decade saw developments such as campus unrest and activism, innovation and experimentation in undergraduate education, the growth and expansion of higher education, the infusion of state and federal funds, and attempts to equalize educational opportunity. Campus protest (which sometimes included faculty as well as students and was prevalent in a number of the elite universities) involved a wide range of issues. Student lifestyle and education demands included a broadening of curricula choice, a loosening of course requirements, an end to parietal rules, and admission of more minority students. Students also protested the schools' hierarchical authority, the impersonality and massiveness of universities and their bureaucratic structures, and their links to the military-industrial complex and corporate capitalism. The quest for student rights paralleled the development of the Civil Rights, Black Power, and feminist movements and the rise of the New Left and the counterculture. Students at many campuses were also involved in activities and demonstrations focusing on the inequities in American society, including racism, sexism, and poverty, and an increasingly unpopular war in Vietnam.

Propelled by educational reformers and students, undergraduate education became a prime focus of reform efforts. Some of the reforms that occurred were widespread and touched the majority of colleges and universities, others were more individualized and focused, relating to the particular college. Colleges experimented with more choice in student majors; abolition of fixed requirements; new courses and programs such as black studies, Native American studies, women's studies, and environmental stud-

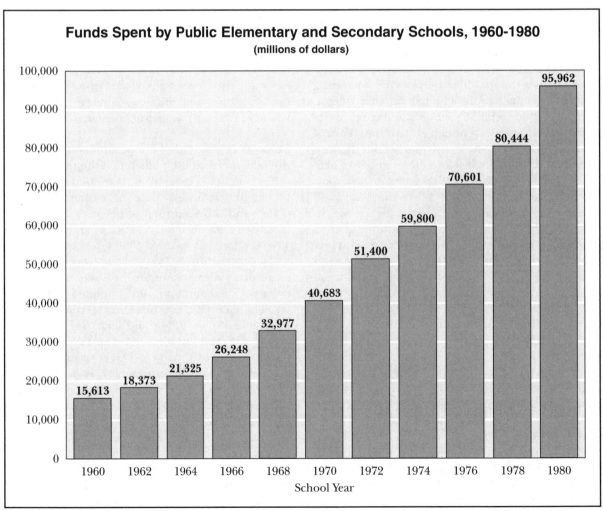

Funds Spent by Public Elementary and Secondary Schools, 1960-1980
(millions of dollars)

Source: Kurian, George, *Datapedia of the United States, 1790-2000, America Year by Year.* Lanham, Maryland: Bernam Press, 1994.

ies; credit for experiential and off-campus learning; seminars; and student participation in policymaking. Some eschewed departmental structure and focused on interdisciplinary study. Some colleges rejected the research-university model with its emphasis on graduate education and sought alternate academic environments. For example, the University of California, Santa Cruz, which opened in 1965, featured distinctive cluster colleges with learning communities that rejected hierarchical authority and ranking, utilized a pass/fail system instead of grades, blurred the distinction between the curricular and extracurricular, and emphasized the affective as well as the intellectual. Santa Cruz's Kresge College, which opened in 1970, featured small "kin groups" of faculty and students that produced an alternate and innovative collegiate community. The college of Human Services in New York (which opened in 1965 as the Women's Talent Corps and later became Audrey Cohen College) aimed to produce students who would act as client advocates and agents for change in the helping professions.

Impact All these developments had a multifaceted and controversial impact, influenced most educational institutions, and raised questions about the social fabric and the predominant culture of American society. Those who had been invisible in the curricula, had faced discrimination, or had not received any of the fruits of American society developed a sense of group consciousness and went in quest of educational equity. Their demands as well as new learning theories and studies and the federal government's commitment to equity led to the creation of new programs and courses and special services.

Every aspect of education, from admissions policies to curricula and academic structure and services, came under public and institutional scrutiny. Federal programs and funding provided enrichment and services for children from low-income families and helped to reduce financial barriers to attending college. Efforts at desegregation, integration, and equalization of educational opportunity aided in providing educational opportunities for African American and other minority students. Government funds improved education at all levels, with the hope that children from low-income families could use education to break the cycle of poverty and that education would solve many of the nation's social and economic problems.

Education became responsive to the needs of minorities. Colleges began offering special programs such as African American and Native American studies, and history and literature courses began to include the contributions of minorities and women. Elementary and secondary schools became more aware of the needs and sensitivities of their communities. Schools and universities started to include more minorities and women among their staff. During this decade, the portrayal of a homogeneous American society from a male, predominately Eurocentric perspective was challenged, and the multicultural approach that emerged influenced education and society in the 1960's and beyond.

Students, particularly at the college level, gained more autonomy and, with the abolition of fixed requirements in many institutions, were relatively free to chart their educational course. Students gained freedom from parietal rules, and some won power in university policy-making bodies. In lower education, a variety of courses, options, and services in response to the quest for equity came to fruition in numerous schools, in many instances with federal financial support.

The move toward the pursuit of student rights was accompanied by a search for a new sense of community and helped lead to a number of alternative academic structures in collegiate education. Student protests and the rise of the New Left on campus, the counterculture, and the Civil Rights, Black Power, and women's movements influenced the crosscurrents between the academy and the larger society. In the midst of all this, conflict over the war in Vietnam, urban riots, assassinations of major leaders, and poverty in the face of affluence dramatized the problems in American society. Some education reformers and political leaders viewed education as a panacea for society's inequities, even when some disillusionment crept in at not achieving all the results hoped for through these special efforts.

Subsequent Events The focus on equity continued in the early 1970's with measures such as the expansion of federal financial aid programs for needy college students and the prohibition of sex discrimination in federally assisted education programs under the provisions of Title IX of the Education Amendments of 1972. The educational turmoil of the 1960's and the ensuing reform efforts were debated in the 1970's, 1980's, and 1990's, with conservative critics bemoaning the state of the academy. Nevertheless, the new courses, programs, and interpretations that included the voices of previously excluded groups and new curricula that recognized cultural diversity and multiculturalism served as a continuing reminder of the legacy of the 1960's.

Additional Information For an analysis of federal education policy, see *The Uncertain Triumph: Federal Education Policy in the Kennedy and Johnson Years* (1984), by Hugh Davis Graham. Through a series of case studies, Gerald Grant and David Riesman explore reform in undergraduate education during the 1960's in *The Perpetual Dream: Reform and Experiment in the American College* (1978). For the story on graduate education, see Roger L. Geiger's *Research and Relevant Knowledge: American Research Universities Since World War II* (1993). Developments in the education of women within a larger historical framework are analyzed in Barbara Solomon's *In The Company of Educated Women: A History of Women in Higher Education in America* (1985). Reform efforts in the community colleges in the 1960's are explored in Steven Brint and Jerome Karabel's *The Diverted Dream: Community Colleges and the Promise of Educational Opportunity in America, 1900-1985* (1989). *New Perspectives on Black Educational History* (1978), edited by Vincent P. Franklin and James D. Anderson, includes essays on various institutions and the educational experience of African Americans, with material relevant to efforts in the 1960's. An analysis of educational reform in the 1960's in elementary and secondary education is included in Robert L. Church and Michael W. Sedlak's *Education in the United States: An Interpretive History* (1976). For insights into the dramatically conflicting perspectives on school reform with relevant sections on 1960's efforts, compare the interpretations of Michael B. Katz in *Class, Bureaucracy, and Schools: The Illusion of Educational Change* (1971) and his more recent *Reconstructing American Education* (1987) with those of Diane Ravitch in *The Troubled Crusade: American Education, 1915-1980* (1983).

Marilyn Tobias

See also Bilingual Education Act; Busing; Civil Rights Act of 1964; Conant Report; Great Society Programs; Head Start; Higher Education Act; Johnson, Lyndon B.; Meredith, James H.; School Desegregation; Student Rights Movement; Teachers Strikes; War on Poverty.

■ Eichmann, Adolf

Born March 19, 1906, Solingen, Germany
Died May 31, 1962, Ramle, Israel

One of Nazi Germany's bloodiest war criminals. Eichmann became the focus of media attention and international controversy when captured, tried, and executed by the newly created nation of Israel.

Early Life Adolf Eichmann was born in Germany but grew up in Austria. He became a member of the Austrian Nazi Party in 1931 and later joined the fanatical SS (*Schutzstaffel*), the party's elite military corps. During World War II, he was in charge of rounding up millions of Jews throughout Nazi-occupied Europe and transporting them to such infamous extermination camps as those at Auschwitz, Belsen, and Dachau. After Germany's defeat in 1945, Eichmann escaped from a U.S. Army prison camp and fled to the Middle East. In 1958, he settled in Buenos Aires, Argentina, where he assumed the name Ricardo Klement. He lived with his family, maintaining a low profile as a factory worker, until his capture by agents of the Israeli Security Service on May 11, 1960, ended fifteen years of flight.

The 1960's The trial of Eichmann in Jerusalem for crimes against the Jews during World War II was one of the most dramatic incidents of the 1960's. The newly invented medium of television brought vivid scenes into American living rooms every night. Eichmann had to be protected by bulletproof glass because feeling against him was so intense. The emotion-choked prosecutors presented more than one hundred witnesses and sixteen hundred documents to the three presiding judges. It was the first time the full horror of the Holocaust was presented to a judicial body and to the international news media.

Eichmann pleaded not guilty to all fifteen charges. He was represented by a team headed by a West German lawyer in a trial lasting four months. The defense arguments echoed the worldwide controversy surrounding the event. The defense team claimed their client could not get a fair trial in Israel, that the trial was illegal because Eichmann had been kidnapped, and that the offenses in the indictment had been committed outside Israel's borders and before Israel's establishment. Showing remarkable composure, Eichmann testified for twenty-five days, insisting he was only obeying orders and was only a small cog in the vast machinery of Nazi persecution of European Jews.

Eichmann was found guilty and sentenced to death on December 15, 1961. American Jews were divided in their reactions. The Central Conference of American Rabbis asked Israeli leaders to commute the sentence to life imprisonment. Eichmann's appeal for clemency was rejected by the Israeli supreme court on May 29, 1962, and he was hanged at midnight on May 31.

Impact Anti-Semitism in America declined appreciably, and antifascism increased. Many Americans felt guilty that their country, which had offered sanctuary to so many immigrants, had done so little to aid the Jews during the 1930's and 1940's. The trial inspired American educators, members of the legal profession, members of the news media, and countless others to discuss its legal, social, educational, psychological, religious, and political ramifications. Holocaust historiography in the United States became more sophisticated and intense. Stronger efforts were made to identify the German war criminals believed to be hiding in the United States. Most important, the Eichmann trial persuaded many Americans to support the dream of Zionism, the reestablishment of a Jewish national homeland.

Israel's survival as a nation was problematic because it was surrounded by heavily populated Arab nations that had publicly vowed to destroy it. These enemies were aided and abetted by the United States' great antagonist in the Cold War, the Soviet Union. Israel became an important U.S. ally in the Middle East, and public opinion tended to support the U.S. government policy of providing Israel with financial, military, and political assistance. The United States exerted heavy diplomatic and economic pressure on the Soviet Union to allow Jews within its borders to emigrate to Israel.

Subsequent Events The Eichmann trial not only demonstrated the dramatic potential of Hitler's Final Solution but also provided invaluable factual information for magazine articles, books, television shows, and motion pictures for decades afterward. *Schindler's List,* a film dramatizing the horrors of the Holocaust, won the Academy Award for Best Motion Picture of 1993. A two-hour television documentary that had a powerful effect on the nation's conscience and consciousness was *The Trial of Adolf Eich-*

Former Nazi officer Adolf Eichmann stand trial for war crimes in Israel in 1961. He was hanged in May, 1962. (AP/Wide World Photos)

mann, broadcast by the Public Broadcasting System in 1997.

Additional Information Hannah Arendt covered Eichmann's trial for *The New Yorker* and reprinted her controversial articles in *Eichmann in Jerusalem: A Report on the Banality of Evil* (1963), prompting Jacob Robinson to attack her in the equally comprehensive *And the Crooked Shall Be Made Straight: The Eichmann Trial, the Jewish Catastrophe, and Hannah Arendt's Narrative* (1965).

Bill Delaney

See also Media; Six-Day War; Television.

■ *Electric Kool-Aid Acid Test, The*

Published 1968
Author Tom Wolfe (1931-   )

The book that tells the story of Ken Kesey and the Merry Pranksters and depicts the lifestyle of the hippies. This influential nonfiction novel describes the impact of LSD on the drug culture.

The Work Tom Wolfe characterizes Ken Kesey, acclaimed author of *One Flew over the Cuckoo's Nest*(1962) and *Sometimes a Great Notion* (1964), as one of millions of post-World War II "superkids" living out the American Dream of power, possibility, and immunity from inhibiting obstacles. Portrayed as a modern pioneer exploring inner space through psychedelic drugs, Kesey first took LSD (lysergic acid diethylamide, or acid) as a volunteer for government drug experiments in 1959 while studying creative writing at Stanford University. For Kesey, LSD was a religious experience providing meaning in a society that had lost its spirit of adventure. It introduced Kesey to "Edge City," Wolfe's term for a life-risking but spiritually enlightening psychic cataclysm. Kesey felt that LSD broke down the psychological barriers between the self and others, creating a feeling of living in the "now."

In 1964, seeking a more spontaneous form of communication, Kesey quit writing and traveled with the Merry Pranksters across the United States in a reconverted 1939 International Harvester bus, ingesting LSD and capturing the experience on thousands of feet of film. On the way from San Francisco to New York and during the next few years, Kesey and the Pranksters participated in a number of antics designed to shake up conformist middle-class people. They shocked staid clergy (and delighted some young people) at a Unitarian Church conference, partied with the Hell's Angels motorcycle gang, and created the acid tests, multimedia happenings involving dancing, rock music, strobe lights, colorful swirling images projected onto a screen (light shows), and the use of LSD.

After returning from Mexico, where he fled to evade marijuana possession charges, Kesey held an acid test graduation, encouraging people to move "beyond acid" and to incorporate the insights obtained with the drug in their everyday lives. Wolfe's book concludes with the sober message that Kesey's awareness is difficult to translate into practical social applications. "We blew it," said Kesey, who served a prison sentence on the marijuana charges in 1967, went to Oregon, and resumed writing.

Impact Immediate critical response was positive, with reservations. Some reviewers felt that Wolfe lacked critical distance from his subject. Others praised Wolfe's attempt to mirror Kesey's subjective reality. Most critics judged the book to be an important example of New Journalism, blending fiction and nonfiction techniques and recognizing the implausibility of objective reporting. New Journalism influenced the development of Creative Nonfiction, whose proponents (including John McPhee, Annie Dillard, and Barry Lopez) realized that the writer is inevitably part of the story.

Thematically, Wolfe's book provides a reflection on the American Dream. The perennial debate between individual freedom versus social order was renewed in the turbulent 1960's. Although many young people were inspired by Kesey's vision of social experimentation, Wolfe suggests that his concept of freeform association, as appealing as it is, may not work for an entire society. Wolfe is cautious about any role for mind-expanding drugs in the pursuit of a new understanding of humanity's potential.

Related Works Other examples of the New Journalism include *Armies of the Night* (1968), by Norman Mailer; *In Cold Blood* (1966), by Truman Capote; and *Dispatches* (1977), by Michael Herr.

Additional Information For information on the nonfiction novel, see *The New Journalism* (1973), edited by Tom Wolfe. William McKeen has examined Wolfe's writing in *Tom Wolfe* (1995).

Richard A. Hill

See also Counterculture; Drug Culture; Flower Children; Hell's Angels; Hippies; *In Cold Blood*; Literature; Leary, Timothy; LSD; Mailer, Norman; Marijuana; *One Flew over the Cuckoo's Nest*; Thompson, Hunter S.; Trips Festival.

■ *Engel v. Vitale*

Supreme Court case that determined that prayer in public schools violates the U.S. Constitution. In 1962, the Court ruled that a state cannot require prayer in a public school setting even if the prayer is denominationally neutral and participation in the prayer is voluntary.

The New York State Board of Regents recommended to a local board of education that the following prayer be recited at the beginning of each school day: "Almighty God, we acknowledge our dependence upon Thee, and we beg Thy blessings upon us, our parents, our teachers and our Country." The parents of ten students brought legal action, claiming that this official prayer was contrary to their beliefs and religions.

The American Ethical Union and the American Jewish Committee joined the parents in arguing that the state law authorizing the school district to mandate prayer in public schools violated the First Amendment's bar to government establishment of religion. They believed that the state-composed prayer, by invoking God's blessing, declared a state preference for certain religious beliefs over others in violation of the First Amendment. They further contended that the voluntary and denominationally neutral character of the prayer did not prevent the prayer from exerting coercive pressure to follow officially approved religious beliefs.

Twenty-two states officially joined New York in the attempt to preserve school prayer. They argued that because the law allowed nonparticipation by students, there could be no violation of the free-exercise clause of the First Amendment. They claimed that the voluntary nature of the prayer demonstrated that the state was not forcing any religious beliefs on the students. They further argued that because the prayer was denominationally neutral, there could be no claim that the state was supporting one religion over another. Legislators such as Republican senators Barry Goldwater and Everett Dirksen went even further, stating that the Courts had no right or power to remove God from the public schools.

The Supreme Court ruled, seven to one, on June 25, 1962, that prayer in public schools violates the establishment clause of the First Amendment and cannot be required by the state. This case resolved the immediate issue concerning the prayer mandated by the State of New York but raised many new questions concerning how far the Supreme Court would extend its ruling to safeguard separation of church and state.

Impact In 1963, the Supreme Court extended the ruling in *Engel v. Vitale* to prohibit Bible reading and recitation of the Lord's Prayer in public schools. These decisions prompted a flood of letters to Congress in support of a constitutional amendment to allow voluntary school prayer. In 1964, the Republican Party platform was revised to include support for a voluntary school prayer amendment. However, in 1966, a vote on a voluntary school prayer amendment fell short of the required two-thirds majority by nine votes.

Subsequent Events The Supreme Court continued to limit religious activity in public schools throughout the 1970's, 1980's, and 1990's despite continued public opposition.

Additional Information Robert S. Alley has written a well-balanced book outlining the history and arguments surrounding school prayer entitled *School Prayer: The Court, the Congress, and the First Amendment* (1994).

Corey Ditslear

See also Goldwater, Barry; O'Hair, Madalyn Murray; Prayer in School; Supreme Court Decisions.

■ Environmental Movement

A social movement primarily concerned with protecting natural resources and fighting pollution. In the 1960's, the movement achieved its objectives through effective use of public education campaigns, legislative initiatives, and growth in environmental organizations.

The environmental movement in the 1960's focused on raising public awareness of the dangers of pollution and on using public policy to protect natural resources. Pollution of the environment had been escalating in the United States, and scientists, especially biologists, had campaigned against it to little or no avail. However, in the 1960's, works by three major writers and a number of widely publicized environmental crises succeeded in alerting the public and policymakers to the danger of pollution and the need for government action to protect the environment.

The publication in 1962 of Rachel Carson's *Silent Spring*, a best-seller describing the deleterious effects of pesticides on the environment, particularly birds, brought the issue of pollution to the attention of many Americans and helped lead to the passage of ecologically minded legislation, including the Pesticide Control Act of 1972. Carson's book exerted a powerful influence on the nature and development of green, or environmental, politics and led to the founding of numerous environmental organizations. Many of these organizations, such as Friends of the Earth (FOE), owe much of their success to the campaign-writing techniques so ably demonstrated by Carson.

The other two writers who brought environmental issues to the public's attention were zoologist Paul Ehrlich, who wrote *The Population Bomb* (1968),

Environmental Milestones

1960	Congress passes the Multiple Use-Sustained Yield Act, which states that forests are to be used for recreation, range, timber, watershed, and wildlife and fish purposes.
1961	Studies of the Columbia River near the Hanford Nuclear Reservation in Richland, Washington, reveal shellfish heavily contaminated with radiation; later studies link workers' death and illness to radiation exposure.
1962	The United States begins spraying the defoliant Agent Orange, which contains the toxic dioxin, on Vietnam, exposing thousands of Vietnamese and soldiers before the use of the herbicide is ended in 1971.
	Rachel Carson's best-seller *Silent Spring* warns that wildlife is being endangered by the use of insecticides such as dichloro-diphenyl-trichloroethane (DDT).
	Fallout for atmospheric nuclear tests is found to be responsible for a high concentration of Cesium-137 in the bodies of Alaskan Eskimos, who eat caribou that consume fallout-contaminated lichens.
1963	The United States, Britain, and the Soviet Union sign the Test Ban Treaty, which bans nuclear testing in the atmosphere, outer space, and under water but not underground.
	Clean Air Act of 1963, the first law to grant the federal government power to enforce air pollution regulations, is signed into law.
1964	Congress passes the Wilderness Act, the first legislation to protect wild, undeveloped land.
1965	The Motor Vehicle Air Pollution Act gives the federal government the authority to set national standards for automobile emissions.
	The federal Water Quality Act toughens regulations against pollution and gives the federal government control over water-quality management.

Continued on next page

describing the dangers of overpopulation, and biologist Barry Commoner, who wrote several publications on the hazards of nuclear wastes and chemical pollution, including *Science and Survival* (1966).

Besides the works of these writers, a number of 1960's environmental crises created awareness of serious problems. The worst event occurred in the summer of 1969, when the industrially polluted Cuyahoga River near Cleveland, Ohio, burst into flames. The sight of a burning river, televised throughout the nation, truly brought the depth of the problem home to the American public. In addition, in the summer of 1969, nearby Lake Erie was declared a dying sinkhole because of sewage and chemical pollutants.

Media's Role As the 1960's wore on, the mainstream media increased its coverage of environmental events. The media began to cover environmental issues not only as part of routine news reporting but also as featured topics in news programs and as issues in political campaigns.

In January and February, 1969, two devastating oil spills occurred off the coast of California, and the media captured the essence of the spills with images of birds soaked in gooey, black oil and pristine, white

1965 (cont.)	The Highway Beautification Act limits the use of billboard and other advertising along roadways in the United States.
	The federal government and five states—Indiana, Michigan, New York, Ohio, and Pennsylvania—agree to work together to stop the pollution of Lake Erie.
	The Solid Waste Disposal Act is the first federal law to try to improve the management of garbage.
1966	Congress passes the Endangered Species Preservation Act to protect and conserve species threatened with extinction.
1967	A group of activists organize the Environmental Defense Fund, a militant organization that brought suit against environmental offenders.
	The Air Quality Act expands the role of government in controlling air pollution and setting emissions controls for industries.
1968	Congress passes an amendment to the Federal Aviation Act of 1958 designed to reduce noise pollution caused by aircraft taking off and landing.
	The Wild and Scenic Rivers and National Trails System act is passed, allowing some areas to be protected and others to be developed for recreational use.
1969	Conservationist David Brower forms Friend of the Earth, an organization designed to preserve wilderness areas.
	An oil slick on the very polluted Cuyahoga River at Cleveland, Ohio, catches fire, dramatizing the need for cleaner water.

beaches soiled with globs of oil that washed up with each tide. The media's coverage of these events showed that President Richard M. Nixon, who had just taken office, was faced with an environmental crisis for which he was unprepared.

The Sierra Club, an environmentalist organization, created additional public exposure for the environmental movement when it sued to protect New York's Storm King Mountain from construction of a power plant in 1965 and when it took out full-page advertisements in *The New York Times* and *The Washington Post* protesting the building of a dam that would flood the Grand Canyon in 1969. These actions boosted the club's prestige and membership and helped save the canyon.

The Role of Organizations During the 1960's, the environmental movement in the United States expe-rienced an upsurge in organizations. The number of environmental groups expanded during the 1960's, and existing groups experienced tremendous growth. The Sierra Club's membership grew from seven thousand to seventy thousand from 1952 to 1969, and the Wilderness Society increased from twelve thousand members in 1960 to fifty-four thousand in 1970.

The scope of activities also broadened, although the primary function of most mainstream organizations remained lobbying for favorable environmental policies. Organizations such as the Sierra Club, the Wilderness Society, and the National Parks and Conservation Association emphasized the preservation of public lands for future generations, and groups such as the National Wildlife Federation and the Izaak Walton League, whose members include outdoor sports enthusiasts and hunters, were more involved with preserving habitats for wildlife. Other activities included preservation, litigation, scientific research, and political campaigning. Existing groups began to expand their interests. For example, the National Audubon Society enthusiastically supported campaigns against pesticides, and the National Wildlife Federation began a legal challenge to polluters. New and more confrontational organizations such as the World Wildlife Fund (1961), African Wildlife Foundation (1961), Council on Economic Priorities (1969), Environmental Defense Fund (1967), Environmental Defense League (1968), FOE (1969), Zero Population Growth (1969), Greenpeace (1969), and National Resources Defense Council (1970) were founded. The Environmental Defense Fund and later the National Resources Defense Council made litigation an art form, moving interest group strategy from the legislative to the judicial arena.

Impact A number of factors that contributed to the growth in the environmental movement in the 1960's were the activist culture of the 1960's, which encouraged mass mobilization to address society's ills; greater scientific knowledge and greater media coverage of environmental problems; a rapid increase in outdoor recreation, which heightened commitment to preservation; and post-World War II economic expansion and affluence. From the perspective of the environmental movement, the 1960's was a period of intense political activity.

Although there were several legislative precursors during the 1940's and 1950's, many hallmark pieces of pollution and environmental legislation were enacted into law during this decade. Environmental preservation legislation included the national forest Multiple Use-Sustained Act of 1960, Land and Water Conservation Fund Act of 1964, the Wilderness Act of 1964 (which created the National Wilderness Preservation System), the Endangered Species Preservation Act of 1966, the Wild and Scenic Rivers Act (1968), and the National Trails System Act (1968). Pollution-related regulation included the Clean Air Act of 1963 (amended as the Air Quality Act in 1967), the Water Quality Act of 1965, the Solid Waste Disposal Act of 1965, and the Highway Beautification Act of 1965. However, possibly the most important legislation of the 1960's was the National Environmental Policy Act (NEPA) of 1969 (signed into law on January 1, 1970, and which led to the creation of the Environmental Protection Agency in 1970) and the Endangered Species Act amendments of 1969, which served as the foundation for environmental policy in the coming decades.

The activities of the environmental movement in the 1960's brought profound changes in people's attitudes and created ecological legislation in that decade and beyond. The celebration of Earth Day in April, 1970, symbolized the growth of environmental consciousness and activism, and the Environmental Protection Agency has played an important role in subsequent decades in determining the environmental impact of proposed construction projects. These and other achievements of the movement led to the 1960's being labeled the environmental decade in the United States. Indeed, the impact of the activities of the environmental movement in that decade have made environmentalism a part of everyday life.

Subsequent Events As early as the end of the 1960's, the environmental movement began to experience a backlash. Because of the speed in which the movement accomplished its legislative agenda and raised public consciousness, many businesses felt that they were unfairly targeted. They formed organizations to fight environmental regulations that they believed were unduly restrictive and threatened their economical well-being.

Despite the growth of opposition, much existing legislation was strengthened and numerous new laws were enacted in subsequent decades. Preservation and conservation legislation included the Federal Land Policy and Management Act of 1976, the Resource Conservation and Recovery Act of 1976, and the National Forest Management Act of 1976. Water and air pollution-related legislation included the Federal Water Pollution Control Act Amendments of 1972, the Safe Drinking Water Act of 1974, the Water Quality Act of 1987, the Ocean Dumping Act of 1988, the Oil Pollution Prevention, Response, Liability, and Compensation Act of 1990, the Clean Air Act Amendments of 1990, and the Safe Drinking Water Act of 1996. Other pollution-related acts include the Comprehensive Environmental Response, Compensation, and Liability Act of 1980, the Nuclear Waste Policy Act of 1982, the Food Security Act of 1985, the Superfund Amendments and Reauthorization Act of 1986, the Pollution Prevention Act of 1990, and the Energy Policy Act of 1992.

Additional Information The environmental movement and the issues surrounding it are described in *The Green Reader: Essays Toward a Sustainable Society* (1991), edited by Andrew Dobson; *Environment and Society: Human Perspectives on Environmental Issues* (1996), by L. Charles Harper; and *Environmental Politics: Domestic and Global Dimension* (1994), by Jacqueline Vaughn Switzer.

Telemate Alioma Jackreece

See also Air Pollution; Carson, Rachel; Motor Vehicle Air Pollution Act of 1965; Water Pollution.

■ Ephron, Nora

Born May 19, 1941, New York, New York

News reporter and essayist during the women's movement. Ephron's humorous and penetrating observations about popular culture in the 1960's explored some otherwise overlooked aspects in a period of intense social change.

Early Life The oldest of four daughters, Nora Ephron was born in New York City but raised in Hollywood, California. Her parents, Henry and Phoebe Ephron, were screenwriters, and their children grew up in the rarefied atmosphere of the film industry. Influential house guests included the witty New York writer Dorothy Parker, in whose footsteps Ephron dreamed of following. The professional life led by Ephron's mother gave Ephron a will to succeed on her own talents rather than by nurturing a man's ambitions. Hollywood exposed her to fashion, cinema, and cuisine, all of which became topics in her writing.

The 1960's After graduating from Wellesley College in 1962, Ephron worked from 1963 to 1968 as a reporter for the *New York Post*, a low-prestige job with abysmal working conditions. The space limitations placed on her articles led her to adopt a dense, fact-filled style that painted lively and unusually intimate portraits of her subjects. As a newspaper reporter, Ephron had to write as an observer of, not a participant in, events, and this remove stayed in her writing style after she quit and became a freelance writer for publications such as *Good Housekeeping, Holiday, Esquire,* and *The New York Times Magazine.* Until the end of the 1960's, Ephron wrote about figures and trends in mass culture: actors, food, fashion, and publishing. A collection of these articles formed her first book, *Wallflower at the Orgy,* published in 1970.

Later Life An essayist during the 1970's, Ephron turned to fiction after her second marriage, in 1976, and the subsequent birth of two sons. In the 1980's, she became a screenwriter with a number of critical hits. She began directing films in 1992 and married a third time, to writer Nicholas Pileggi.

Impact Ephron's writing in the late 1960's tempered the anger and turmoil of the period by providing well-researched, often affectionate insights into the cultural scene. Her articles about Helen Gurley Brown, editor of *Cosmopolitan* magazine, and about popular novelist Jacqueline Susann balanced the criticism of "unliberated" women coming from more strident writers.

Subsequent Events From 1972 to 1974, Ephron wrote essays about the women's movement, mostly for *Esquire* magazine. These were published in 1975 as *Crazy Salad*; another book, *Scribble Scibble* (1978), looked at media issues. Ephron, whose marriage to writer Dan Greenberg had ended, married *Washington Post* reporter Carl Bernstein in 1976, and after a bitter divorce in 1979, she wrote a fictionalized account called *Heartburn* (1983). Ephron began writing screenplays in the 1980's (among them *Silkwood, Heartburn,* and *When Harry Met Sally . . .*), and in 1993 she directed *Sleepless in Seattle.*

Additional Information Ephron traces the development of her writing style in "Dorothy Schiff and the *New York Post*" in *Scribble Scribble.* In "The Pill and I," from *The Sixties* (1977), she examines an important social advance.

Nan K. Chase

See also Fashions and Clothing; Media; *Sex and the Single Girl*; Susann, Jacqueline; Women's Identity.

■ Equal Pay Act of 1963

Prohibits sex-based discrimination in wages. The law requires equal pay for women and men for jobs in the same establishment that require substantially similar skills, effort, and responsibility and that are performed under similar working conditions.

Women in the 1960's represented about 40 percent of the United States labor force. Historically, women in the labor force have earned a median average wage only about three-fifths that of men, and in the 1960's, lower pay for women was justified based on the belief that a man's role in society (as breadwinner) entitled him to be paid more than a woman, even if they were performing the same function. A rising social consciousness during the Civil Rights movement resulted in an awareness of the comparatively lower wages women were receiving and of the inequity of this practice.

To remedy this situation, the administration of President John F. Kennedy sponsored equal pay legislation in 1962 to give women equal pay for "comparable" work. The legislation, which ultimately became law in 1963, was revised to read equal pay for "equal" work.

The Equal Pay Act of 1963 faced little opposition in Congress, although some debate occurred in the House of Representatives. Proponents such as Congressman Charles Goodell of New York cited a number of reasons for creating the legislation. Simple justice demanded that the inequity be remedied. In addition, this practice meant that businesses that hired lower-paid women instead of higher-paid men had an unfair advantage. Trade unions and their supporters in Congress favored the act because it would protect men from competing with women who were willing to take a lower wage.

The few opponents of the act were concerned that it could be used to harass businesses and would require comparable worth. Supporters were quick to point out that the act was very narrow in scope and required equal pay only when men and women performed virtually identical jobs under the same working conditions. Congressman Paul Findlay of Illinois was concerned that equal pay for women could mean a decline in job opportunities for women if some employers viewed women as less desirable to hire than men at the same wage.

The supporters of the act prevailed, and Congress passed the Equal Pay Act on June 10, 1963, as an amendment to the Fair Labor Standards Act. The act prohibits discrimination between the sexes in wages only; it does not prohibit other forms of discrimination. It was effected one year later on June 10, 1964. Under the act, a plaintiff must prove four things. First, that the individual is doing the same tasks as an employee of the opposite sex. Second, that the work is substantially equal in terms of skills, effort, and responsibility. Third, that the work is performed under similar working conditions in the same establishment. Fourth, that the other employee is compensated at a higher rate. Small differences in duties or differences in title alone do not justify large pay differences. The employer is allowed four defenses: merit, productivity, seniority, and any factor other than sex.

Impact The Equal Pay Act did not have a measurable impact on women's earnings in the 1960's. According to the U.S. Department of Commerce, women's median annual earnings remained about three-fifths that of men throughout the 1960's. This trend continued in subsequent decades with only small percentage increases for women. Research by the National Academy of Sciences and other organizations identified some of the reasons for the earnings gap. Many women work in low-paying occupations, and many men work in higher-paying jobs. Also, more women than men work in part-time jobs, which typically pay less. The Equal Pay Act does not address other forms of wage discrimination, including discrimination based on age, race, national origin, color, religion, or disability. Sex discrimination that does not lead to a difference in wages is also not addressed by the Equal Pay Act.

Subsequent Events The most important legislation designed to eliminate sex discrimination in private employment is Title VII of the Civil Rights Act, which was passed in 1964. The Civil Rights Act is more comprehensive than the Equal Pay Act of 1963, covering other aspects of employment in addition to wages.

Additional Information The law is summarized in Claire Sherman Thomas, *Sex Discrimination in a Nutshell* (1991). An industrial relations discussion is found in Walter Fogel, *The Equal Pay Act: Implications for Comparable Worth* (1984).

David E. Paas

See also Civil Rights Act of 1964; Prosperity and Poverty; Unions and Collective Bargaining; Women in the Workforce.

■ Equal Rights Amendment

The centerpiece of legislation for women's rights. This proposed constitutional amendment, though never enacted, well served the cause of equality for women in American society.

First proposed in 1923 by the National Woman's Party, the Equal Rights Amendment (ERA) aimed to extend the protections of the Fourteenth Amendment to women. It reads: "Equality of rights under the law shall not be denied or abridged by the United States or by any State on account of sex." In 1968, the National Organization for Women (NOW) made passage of the ERA a prime objective, and it was reintroduced in Congress.

Women of every feminist stripe—from Betty Friedan, author of *The Feminine Mystique* (1963) and one of the founders of the National Organization for Women, to Robin Morgan, founder of the radically feminist Women's International Terrorist Conspiracy from Hell (WITCH), to average women—supported the amendment to ensure women's equal treatment before the law in divorce, employment, taxes, Social Security, insurance, and other matters. Supporters argued its necessity because of marked and provable disparity in the treatment of women at every level of society. They believed a constitutional amendment would be the most expedient, effective road to gender equality.

Those against the legislation claimed the ERA to be unnecessary because existing legal protections applied regardless of a person's gender. Some argued that women would actually lose special legal protections they enjoyed in alimony, child custody and support, and working conditions. Some believed that women's conscription into the armed forces would result. Others, fearing a disruption of traditional social structures, focused on such matters as unisex public restrooms. Southern congressman Howard Smith proposed including sex discrimination in the Civil Rights Act of 1964, probably to ridicule the legislation he opposed by adding what he and many others, such as Senator Jesse Helms, considered to be obvious nonsense. At the Senate Subcommittee on Constitutional Amendments, the National Council of Jewish Women, the National Council of Catholic Women, the AFL-CIO, and the International Ladies Garment Workers' Union (among others) spoke against its passage.

In October, 1971, the House of Representatives passed the ERA, followed by Senate passage in 1972. Legislatures of thirty states ratified the ERA in 1973 (eight short of the two-thirds required for ratification). During the next few years, some states rescinded their approval, while others eventually gave it. By June 30, 1982, a deadline set by Congress, only thirty-five of the necessary thirty-eight states had ratified the ERA. It never became law.

Impact The divergence of opinion led to public polarization, especially with speculation, both rational and specious, concerning the actual enforcement of such legislation. Throughout the 1960's and the following decade, attention to the issue highlighted women's problems, in legal and social matters, as problems of concern to everyone. The ERA was therefore indirectly successful, prompting legislation favorable to women at both state and federal levels.

Subsequent Events In June, 1982, the ERA was reintroduced to Congress; neither house passed the bill.

Additional Information The Equal Rights Amendment Project of the California Commission on the Status of Women has compiled an excellent set of essays entitled *Impact ERA: Limitations and Possibilities* (1976).

Sharon Randolph

See also Feminist Movement; Friedan, Betty; National Organization for Women (NOW); Women's Identity.

■ Estes, Billie Sol

Born January 10, 1925, on a farm three miles from Clyde, Texas

A prominent fraud perpetrator of the early 1960's. Estes defrauded lending institutions of millions by using nonexistent fertilizer tanks as collateral for loans.

Early Life Billie Sol Estes grew up in West Texas. He had a reputation as a shrewd businessman by the time he was sixteen and was a millionaire by his thirtieth birthday. His business ethics were questionable even at a young age. As a boy, he sold a cow to a farmer with the promise that the cow would produce four gallons of milk. When the farmer later complained that the cow was not producing the expected quantity of milk, Estes replied that he never guaranteed how long it would take the cow to produce four gallons. He was named one of the outstanding men of Texas, one of the ten most outstanding young men in the United States, and was a friend of former president Harry S Truman and then vice president Lyndon B. Johnson. His daughter, Pam Estes, later wrote that her father had occasionally supplied Johnson with "great wads" of money.

Billie Sol Estes (left), prominent Texan and friend of Lyndon B. Johnson, is led away to begin serving a fifteen-year prison sentence for fraud in 1965. (AP/Wide World Photos)

The 1960's Estes was a leading citizen of Pecos, Texas, and was an active member of the local Church of Christ. He owned two airplanes and the largest house in town, with a swimming pool and two tennis courts. He was so religious that when he invited guests to swim in his pool, the men and women were not allowed to swim together at the same time. As prescribed by the precepts of the Church of Christ, the men would swim, and then the women. In 1961, he ran for a position on the Pecos School Board promising to eliminate dancing at all school functions and to require cheerleaders to wear longer skirts. He lost the election.

Estes's scam was to use the same collateral for multiple loans. He sold anhydrous-ammonia fertilizer tanks to farmers on an installment basis, then used the notes signed by the farmers as security to obtain loans at various financial institutions. However, he used each note several times, generating many more loans than could be supported by the notes. By the time his scheme was uncovered, Estes had obtained approximately thirty thousand loans on eighteen hundred tanks of fertilizer.

The scheme was exposed by a former friend, John Dunn, a member of the John Birch Society, who had purchased a part interest in the local newspaper—a newspaper that did not support the liberal democratic beliefs of Estes and his friends. Estes tried to defame the doctor and drive the newspaper out of business. Dunn began an investigation of Estes's activities and turned the evidence over to the Federal Bureau of Investigation and the Internal Revenue Service. Those records, some of which were stolen from Estes' own office, showed fraud of more than forty million dollars.

In the spring of 1963, Estes received a fifteen-year sentence following his conviction for fraud. He was paroled and released eight years later. As to why Estes perpetrated his fraud, one friend theorized that he was a scared little boy with a large inferiority complex. His motivation early in the game was a pathological contempt for wealth or for anyone with wealth. At the end, this had reversed itself, and he appeared to glory in personal wealth and power.

He was a generous man, always ready to help out anyone who was down-and-out or sick. A doctor friend stated that Estes often supplied an airplane and pilot, at no expense, to transport sick patients to distant cities for specialized medical care. Estes made sure, however, that such benevolence was made public knowledge. Democratic politicians were also the beneficiaries of his benevolence.

Later Life Following his release from prison in 1971, Estes was unable to stay out of trouble. In 1979, he was indicted on charges that included income-tax evasion and mail fraud. During the trial, Estes claimed to have paid ten million dollars to Johnson as business expenses, but he had no proof of this transaction. He was convicted of conspiracy to defraud investors and concealment of assets and sentenced to another ten years in prison. He was paroled in November, 1983.

Impact The Estes fraud had a great impact on auditing procedures in the United States. Both auditors and lenders had been misled by Estes's shell game of switching identification plates on fertilizer tanks. The case also gave big business a bad name because many people believed that all business deals were at least somewhat shady. Politicians also suffered public relations problems because Estes claimed that he made payoffs to many prominent individuals.

Additional Information In 1983, Pam Estes wrote a biography of her father entitled *Billie Sol: King of the Texas Wheeler-Dealers.*

Dale L. Flesher

See also Agriculture; Crimes and Scandals; John Birch Society; Johnson, Lyndon B.

■ Evers, Medgar

Born July 2, 1925, Decatur, Mississippi
Died June 12, 1963, Jackson, Mississippi

One of the nation's most prominent, active, and nonviolent civil rights leaders. Evers's murder in 1963 hastened passage of civil rights legislation.

Early Life A native of Mississippi who served in the United States Army from 1943 until the end of World War II, Medgar Wylie Evers participated in the invasion of Normandy. Upon returning to Mississippi, he attended Alcorn Agricultural and Mechanical College in Lorman, but because of segregation, he was not permitted to enroll in law school at the University of Mississippi. In 1951, he married Myrlie Beasley; the couple subsequently had three children. As an adolescent, Evers saw the lynching of one of his father's friends for insulting a white woman. This event inspired his stand against racism and motivated him to work for civil rights.

The 1960's Throughout the 1950's and in the early 1960's, Evers was an active member of the National Association for the Advancement of Colored People, working primarily to organize new chapters in his home state. On several occasions, he also investigated murders of local blacks—at once attempting to help provide justice and to lessen the incidence of racially motivated killings. Although he relentlessly practiced nonviolence, he found himself in

Medgar Evers, civil rights activist and member of the National Association for the Advancement of Colored People, pictured in a 1962 television interview, was gunned down outside his home in June, 1963. (Library of Congress)

confrontations with governments and the white citizenry. In 1960, he was fined and jailed for criticizing a legal court decision. In 1961, he was beaten for applauding a defendant in court. In 1963, he helped James H. Meredith register at the University of Mississippi.

Beginning in 1962, Evers became more centrally involved in the Civil Rights movement in Jackson, where he urged the hiring of black police officers and the creation of an interracial commission to improve race relations. An effective and efficient organizer, Evers advocated the use of economic boycotts and led voter registration drives. More specifically, he helped integrate the Mississippi State Fair, Leake County schools, and the city's privately owned bus company.

For years, Evers and his family had received death threats—his house had previously been attacked and firebombed. On June 12, he was shot in front of his home as he stepped from his car. He died later that night and was buried with full military honors in Arlington National Cemetery. Shortly thereafter, Byron de la Beckwith, whose fingerprint was on the weapon dropped by the gunman, was arrested for the murder. He was released from jail in 1964, however, after two mistrials by all-white juries.

Impact By far the most visible and effective civil rights leader in Mississippi for years before his death, Evers helped bring about important changes that eventually desegregated buses, schools, businesses, and society itself. In death, the injustice of the nation's inability to convict Evers's killer kept alive and furthered the necessity for the changes for which he worked. The mistrials remained a focal point of national attention, as well as proof for all that the system of segregation was evil and corrupt.

Subsequent Events In 1990, Beckwith was arrested and tried a third time for the murder; still asserting his innocence, he was convicted in 1994.

Additional Information In 1967, Myrlie Evers published a memoir detailing the events in the life and family of Medgar Evers, entitled *For Us, the Living.*

Sharon Randolph

See also Civil Rights Movement; National Association for the Advancement of Colored People (NAACP).

F

■ Faithfull, Marianne

Born December 29, 1946, London, England

Known for her delicate singing voice and striking beauty, Faithfull became a casualty of the rock-and-roll lifestyle through her romantic involvement with the Rolling Stones' lead singer Mick Jagger.

Born Marian Evelyn Faithfull in the Hampstead borough of London, she is the only child of Glynn Faithfull and Eva von Sacher-Masoch Faithfull. Her parents met during World War II and married in Vienna, Austria, in 1945. Her mother was an Austrian baroness. Settling in England after the war, Glynn Faithfull became a university lecturer in Renaissance studies. Although given the name Marian, her mother always referred to her as Marianne. When she was about six, her parents separated. Faithfull was educated at St. Joseph's Convent School in Reading, England.

In June, 1964, her boyfriend John Dunbar took her to a party where she met a number of celebrities, including the Rolling Stones' manager Andrew Loog Oldham. Although Faithfull was introduced to Mick Jagger, Keith Richards, and Brian Jones of the Rolling Stones, it was Oldham who was most impressed with her. She told him that she would like to be a folksinger. Taken with her beauty and her ambition, Oldham decided to sign Faithfull to a recording contract. Signing with Decca Records, she recorded the Jagger/Richards ballad "As Tears Go By" in July, 1964. By September of that year, her version of "As Tears Go By" had reached number nine on the British single charts. It would reach number twenty-two on the U.S. charts in January, 1965. Faithfull and Dunbar were married on May 6, 1965, and she gave birth to a son, Nicholas, in November. In 1966, she separated from Dunbar and began a four-year relationship with Jagger. Although Faithfull had a handful of hit singles by 1966, she became famous for being Jagger's girlfriend. As part of the "swinging" 1960's, she attended wild parties and became a regular user of drugs. Her talent, charm, and beauty began to fade. By 1970, Faithfull

had divorced Dunbar, separated from Jagger, and become a heroin addict.

During the early 1970's, Faithfull struggled with her addiction. In 1979, she made a dramatic comeback with the release of the poignant album *Broken English*. No longer possessing a delicate voice, she sang with a raspy voice that seemed to add power to the blistering songs of the album. Since then, Faithfull's music was never less than interesting.

Impact Because of her beauty, talent, notoriety, and involvement with Jagger, Faithfull was at the forefront of the "swinging" 1960's.

Additional Information In 1991, Mark Hodkinson's biography, *Marianne Faithfull*, was published. Faithfull's autobiography *Faithfull* was published in 1994.

Jeffry Jensen

See also Jagger, Mick; Rolling Stones.

■ Fallout Shelters

Subterranean constructions designed to protect people from the effects of radioactive fallout. Proponents of fallout shelters believed they would serve as a deterrent to a Soviet first strike if or when World War III began.

Fallout shelters, bomb shelters designed to protect people from radioactive fallout in the event of a nuclear war, were advocated by the Federal Civil Defense Administration (FCDA) in the 1950's. The Korean War (1950-1953) and the Hungarian Revolt (1956) spurred fears of imminent war between the United States and the Soviet Union, both of which possessed nuclear weapons. The *Bulletin of the Atomic Scientists* published a steadily ticking "doomsday clock," and many popular films and works of fiction focused on the possible effects of nuclear war. Edward Teller, father of the hydrogen bomb, argued that the U.S. government should spend billions of dollars on shelters because he believed they might save 90 percent of the population. Nevertheless, only fifteen hundred shelters had been built by 1960.

John F. Kennedy had advocated civil defense when he was a congressman and senator, and his

Kenneth Gelpey emerges from his fallout shelter, dressed in protective clothing and ready to test for radiation, after his family spent a fall, 1961, weekend trying out the structure. (AP/Wide World Photos)

presidential campaign in 1960 warned of a so-called missile gap between the United States and the Soviet Union. Tensions between the superpowers had mounted in 1960 because of the shooting down of a U.S. U-2 spy plane over Soviet territory in May, Soviet General Secretary Nikita Khrushchev's blustery United Nations speech in October, and lingering questions regarding the status of Berlin. Kennedy's first year in the White House (1961) was fraught with similar crises: the failed U.S.-backed Bay of Pigs invasion of Cuba in April and Khrushchev's continuing threat of conflict over Berlin.

In a May, 1961, meeting with the president, governors from all over the United States expressed their desire that the federal government fund a national shelter construction program. On July 25, Kennedy addressed the nation on radio and television, saying that in the event of a nuclear attack, the lives of people who were not hit by the blast and fire could be saved if they sought refuge in a fallout

shelter. After the speech, the FCDA was deluged with more requests for information in a week than it normally received in a month.

Hundreds of shelter construction firms appeared, and thousands of shelters were built, mainly in the suburbs. "Survival stores" opened, selling air-filtering devices, chemical toilets, first-aid kits, dried food products, and canned water. Government agencies and large corporations in the cities took steps to create large group shelters. Many of the individual shelters did not meet FCDA standards. Some unscrupulous companies simply dug holes and then departed. That fall, fears lingered over construction of the Berlin Wall and the resumption of nuclear tests by the Soviets. In September, a *Life* magazine cover story, "How You Can Survive Fallout," depicted a man in a fallout suit and stated that "ninety-seven out of one hundred people can be saved." The boom in shelter construction, however, subsided until the Cuban Missile Crisis in October,

1962. For thirteen days, panic spread in varying degrees in several cities, and a fearful public hoarded food and shovels. After the resolution of the crisis, the desire for shelter construction subsided considerably. Relatively few shelters were built thereafter, as Americans' attitudes toward the Cold War changed.

Impact During the height of the shelter frenzy in 1961, many feared that the number of shelters was inadequate, especially in the cities. Some suburban shelter owners stated that they would kill trespassers. Economist John Galbraith, in a letter to President Kennedy, wrote that the idea of building individual shelters was a "design for saving Republicans and sacrificing Democrats." Some clergymen chastised shelter owners, warning against the sin of selfishness during a time of national crisis. Rod Serling's science-fiction television show, *The Twilight Zone*, ran an episode in 1961 entitled "Shelter," depicting a scenario of panic and selfishness during an imagined nuclear attack. When the siren sounded, signifying that it had only been a drill, the bewildered people were dumbfounded by their uncivilized behavior. By 1962, the government realized that panic might actually sweep the nation, and it began downplaying the importance of individual family fallout shelters.

Subsequent Events Few events spurred shelter construction after 1962, as détente replaced confrontation in superpower relations. A few people built shelters in the early 1980's when fear of war between the superpowers was revived by the Soviet invasion of Afghanistan (1979); the KAL 007 incident (1983), when the Soviets shot down a Korean airplane with Americans on board; and the U.S. invasion of Grenada (1983). In 1994, however, after the collapse of the Soviet Union and the end of the Cold War, the Smithsonian Institution placed a fallout shelter on exhibit as an artifact of a bygone era.

Additional Information Paul Boyer's *By the Bomb's Early Light* (1985) and Spencer Weart's *Nuclear Fear* (1988) provide good overviews of the climate in which shelters were constructed.

William E. Watson

See also Arms Race; Bay of Pigs Invasion; Berlin Wall; Cold War; Cuban Missile Crisis; Khrushchev's UN Visit; U-2 Spy Plane Incident.

■ Farm Subsidies

Government support payments for farmers. The United States had used such payments to relieve the economic distress of the nation's farmers since the 1930's.

The Agricultural Adjustment Act of 1933, part of President Franklin D. Roosevelt's New Deal Program, attempted to address the problem of depressed prices for farm commodities by restricting the production of U.S. farmers. Producers of cotton, wheat, corn, rice, tobacco, and milk received subsidy payments from the government in return for taking agricultural land out of production. Similarly, the Agricultural Adjustment Act of 1938 allowed acreage limitations to be established for certain crops and enabled farmers to receive government subsidies for conserving soil by taking some of their land out of production. The act also provided for the creation of vast storage facilities so that the government could buy surplus crops, which, if sold on the open market, would depress prices. These programs generated significant improvement in farm incomes.

In 1941, the government guaranteed farmers that crop prices would not fall below a certain percentage of parity, which was based on the prevailing agricultural prices during the golden years of farming just before World War I. In 1949, Congress determined that crop prices should be maintained at 90 percent of parity, but in 1954, President Dwight D. Eisenhower ended this support program.

In the late 1950's, scientific advances in agriculture—improved crop varieties and heavy use of fertilizers, insecticides, and herbicides—resulted in a sharp increase in output per acre. The amount of food in storage facilities soared and soon came to exceed capacity.

In November, 1960, the election of President John F. Kennedy and a Democratic Congress created new opportunities to deal with the problem of farm surpluses. In March, 1961, an emergency program was adopted to reduce stocks of feed grains (grains primarily fed to livestock). A guaranteed price was offered to farmers producing agricultural commodities if they would adopt soil conservation measures on 20 percent to 50 percent of their acreage. By 1963, this program had significantly reduced feed grain stocks. At the same time, efforts were made to use the food surpluses to help the poor through other government programs such as those involving food stamps and school lunches. Additional efforts were made to make food surpluses available to underdeveloped nations overseas.

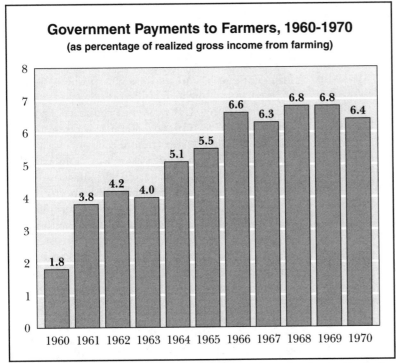

Government Payments to Farmers, 1960-1970
(as percentage of realized gross income from farming)

Year	Value
1960	1.8
1961	3.8
1962	4.2
1963	4.0
1964	5.1
1965	5.5
1966	6.6
1967	6.3
1968	6.8
1969	6.8
1970	6.4

Source: Kurian, George, *Datapedia of the United States, 1790-2000, America Year by Year.* Lanham, Maryland: Bernam Press, 1994.

In 1962, the Food and Agriculture Act created price support payments, cash payments to farmers that consisted of the difference between the old and the new support price, based on world prices. By 1963, this system of ensuring a certain level of farm income through cash payments became the dominant method of support. Farmers participating in the program also received cash payments for diverting land from production. In 1965, this system was extended through 1969.

Impact The agricultural subsidies of the 1960's raised farm income but resulted in significant costs for the U.S. government. Government payments climbed from $702 million in 1960 to $3.7 billion in 1970. The subsidies also highlighted the differences between the Republican and the Democratic approach to the farm problem. The Democrats sought to enlist the government's aid in maintaining farm incomes; the Republicans wanted to return to a free-market system, in which excess production would result in lower prices that would drive marginal producers out of agriculture.

Subsequent Events The Agricultural Act of 1970 suspended marketing quotas for individual crops and base acreages for wheat, cotton, and feed grains. Farmers of these crops who agreed to set aside a certain number of acres and not produce crops on the set-aside lands were allowed to participate in price support programs and receive cash payments. The amount that farmers could receive from the government was capped at $55,000; in 1973, this figure was lowered to $20,000.

During the late 1970's and the 1980's, under Republican administrations, the free-market approach tended to prevail; however, Democrat-controlled Congresses were unwilling to eliminate existing subsidies such as tobacco allotments. In the mid-1990's, the Republicans gained control of Congress and passed legislation to phase out virtually all subsidies by early in the twenty-first century.

Additional Information The most detailed information about agricultural subsidies in the 1960's appears in *American Farm Policy, 1948-1973* (1976), by Willard W. Cochrane and Mary E. Ryan. Gilbert C. Fite's *American Farmers: The New Minority* (1981) presents a longer-range perspective. More compact accounts can be found in two publications from the Organization for Economic Cooperation and Development, *Agricultural Policy in the United States* (1974) and *A New U.S. Farm Policy for Changing World Food Needs* (1974).

Nancy M. Gordon

See also Agriculture; Food Stamp Program.

■ Farrow, Mia

Born February 9, 1945, Los Angeles, California

Unconventional and a free spirit, Farrow gained notoriety for both her acting skills and for the men with whom she became involved.

Maria de Lourdes Villiers Farrow, the daughter of writer/director John Farrow and actress Maureen O'Sullivan, was the third of seven Farrow children. Although growing up in an idyllic environment, she was stricken with a mild case of polio when she was nine. Although she appeared to be frail, Farrow proved to be strong and overcame her illness. Educated at an English convent school, she had thoughts of becoming a nun when she was twelve. In 1959, Farrow had a very small role in her father's film *John Paul Jones*.

By the early 1960's, Farrow had decided that she would like to pursue an acting career. Although she had little acting experience, she appeared in an Off-Broadway production of Oscar Wilde's *The Importance of Being Earnest* (1895) in 1963. Tragically, her beloved father died of a heart attack earlier in the year. In 1964, Farrow was cast as Alison McKenzie in the prime-time television soap opera *Peyton Place*. Through *Peyton Place*, she became very popular with American teenagers.

Although almost thirty years his junior, Farrow married Frank Sinatra on July 19, 1966. Considered an odd match at best, the couple's every move was scrutinized by the tabloid press. The marriage would last for only about two years. In 1968, Farrow appeared in Roman Polanski's classic horror film *Rosemary's Baby*. With the completion of filming *Rosemary's Baby* and the collapse of her marriage, she went off to India to meditate under the instruction of the Maharishi Mahesh Yogi. Farrow began a relationship with the world-renowned conductor Andre Previn although he was married at the time. Once again, she found herself at the center of controversy. In 1969, she appeared in the film *John and Mary* with Dustin Hoffman and the film *Secret Ceremony* with Elizabeth Taylor. After she gave birth to twins, she and Previn were married in 1970.

In the 1970's, Farrow continued her acting career. Some of her most noteworthy appearances include *The Great Gatsby* (1974), *A Wedding* (1978), and *Death on the Nile* (1978). In 1978, she and Previn separated. During her marriage with Previn, Farrow began adopting children. In 1982, she appeared in Woody Allen's *A Midsummer Night's Comedy*. They became involved, and Farrow would appear in twelve more of Allen's films, including *Broadway Danny Rose* (1984), *The Purple Rose of Cairo* (1985), *Hannah and Her Sisters* (1986), *Crimes and Misdemeanors* (1989), and *Husbands and Wives* (1992). In 1992, Farrow

Mia Farrow gained fame through her role on the television series Peyton Place, *her 1966 marriage to singer Frank Sinatra, and her role in the 1968 film* Rosemary's Baby. *(Popperfoto/ Archive Photos)*

learned that Allen had begun an affair with her adopted daughter Soon-Yi Previn. A long and unseemly custody battle ensued. In 1993, Farrow was awarded custody of the three Allen children.

Impact As a free spirit, Farrow struck out on her own independent path during the turbulent 1960's and the strength of her personality made her popular with a generation of young women.

Additional Information In 1991, Edward Z. Epstein and Joe Morella's biography, *Mia: The Life of Mia Farrow*, was published. Farrow published her own memoir, *What Falls Away*, in 1997.

Jeffry Jensen

See also Allen, Woody; Film; *Rosemary's Baby*.

■ Fashions and Clothing

A decade of extremes in fashions and clothing. Rules and standards of dress were broken in the 1960's as the conservative look of the Kennedys gave way to the wild informality of the hippies.

In the 1950's, fashions and clothing were conservative and gender specific. For men, the gray flannel suit was the equivalent of a business uniform, and for women, the prevalent style of the decade was designer Christian Dior's New Look, introduced in 1947. The New Look, promoted by theater, television, and mass media, was an image of curvaceous femininity that was glamorous and elegant. Casual wear for both sexes was ultraconservative in cut and color.

In the early 1960's, the neat and tailored look of the 1950's remained popular with men and women of all ages. First Lady Jacqueline Kennedy popularized the Chanel suit worn with coordinated hat, gloves, purse, shoes, and jewelry, a look that was copied by many women. Men favored dark-colored two-piece suits and white shirts for work and for formal occasions. For leisure time activities, women wore either shirtwaist dresses or blouses with coordinated dirndl skirts. Younger women, when at home and for informal occasions, often replaced the skirt with trousers, which varied in length. Popular styles were ankle length with snugly fitted legs, knee-length pedal pushers, and just-above-the-knee Bermuda shorts. For relaxing, men favored loose-fitting trousers and short-sleeve, button-front shirts in white or light colors. Favorite hairstyles for females were the beehive or bouffant, puffy styles in which the hair was back-combed to add height and sprayed stiff. Men wore their hair in a modified crew cut called the flattop or short and neatly trimmed with a side part.

The Youthful Look During the early 1960's, differences in dress were related almost exclusively to gender. However, as social and political issues began to surface, these concerns found expression in people's clothing choices. One of the first changes in dress, especially for women, came about because of the British-based youth revolution, which redefined the idea of feminine beauty emphasizing youth and sex appeal. Twiggy, a British fashion model with an extremely slender childlike body, epitomized this new image of beauty. Designers followed this trend by creating fashions that left the mature woman with few selections in clothing styles. Garments that young women favored were the miniskirt popularized by designer Mary Quant, go-go boots, and body stockings. The greatest change in men's dress as a result of the youth revolution was the adoption of fabrics with bold designs and bright color. The term "peacock revolution" was used to describe this bursting forth of color, which even produced color-coordinated men's undergarments. The change in menswear fabrics was followed by experiments in the forms of garments and accessories. Brightly colored shirts were decorated with frills at the collars, cuffs, and front openings. Chain necklaces became fashionable for young men.

As the youth revolution matured, an emphasis on being single, having fun, and enjoying freedom from responsibilities emerged. Women's clothes took on a sexy, carefree look, and women began to wear less restrictive and fewer undergarments, donning garments such as bikini panties, pantyhose, and stretch, seamless bras. They wore see-through blouses with miniskirts and garments decorated with large, prominently placed zippers and buttons to create a message of easy access. Long, straight hair became popular, and women went to the extreme of ironing their locks to create an even-straighter bouncing mane. The youth revolution's emphasis on the single lifestyle began to affect the clothing of middle-aged and older women. Even Queen Elizabeth I and other prominent women in conservative positions shortened their skirts, wearing garments that fell just above the knee. Boned undergarments for women of all ages were replaced by seamless foundation garments made of Lycra spandex, a new fiber that was three times stronger than other elastomeric fibers.

New Fibers and Fashion By the mid-1960's, developments in science, technology, and art began to affect fashions and the business world. In particular, a new synthetic fiber known as polyester fashioned into double knit changed clothing styles and clothing care procedures and greatly affected the textiles industry. Polyester men's business suits, known as leisure suits, began to replace traditional fabrics and styles. Double-knit polyester—washable and wrinkle-free—was used almost exclusively in outer garments for women. The cotton market reached a low point in its history, and Cotton, Inc., a research and marketing organization, was formed to reclaim cotton's share of the textile market. The Op Art movement provided designers with fresh ideas. The futuristic designs of André Courrèges and Pierre Cardin, which incorporated plastics and metals in garments with geometrical cuts, reflected this movement. The brightly colored psychedelic patterns used in fabrics incorporated elements of the Op Art movement and the drug culture.

Clothes as a Statement By 1967, the concepts behind social and political movements had begun to be expressed in the dress of their supporters. Touched by the Civil Rights movement, the fashion industry was jarred in the late 1960's when *Harper's Bazaar* featured an African American model on the cover. Until then, most fashion-conscious black women had imitated the styles favored by white women. They straightened their hair, used skin light-eners, and wore cosmetics formulated for light skin. The slogan Black Is Beautiful began to appear in the fashion media. Both black and white men and women began to wear their hair in such traditional African styles as the Afro and corn rows. Angela Davis, an African American civil rights activist, projected and promoted this new image of black beauty.

Feminists protested women being portrayed as sex objects and in submissive and passive roles. They attempted to adopt nonsexist styles of dress, favoring baggy, nonrestrictive clothes in duller colors and shunning garments designed to increase sexual appeal, including bras. Their attempt at nongender-specific dressing gave rise to the unisex look in the fashion world.

The hippie movement of the late 1960's was accompanied by its own distinctive hair and clothing styles. Hippie men favored bell-bottom blue jeans,

The trend toward casual, colorful, and fun-to-wear clothing finds expression (left) in this upscale flower-motif cocktail outfit designed by Emanuel Ungaro in 1968 and (right) in the hippie garb—huarache sandals, beads, ankle bracelet, faded jeans, and freeform dress—favored by this couple during the Summer of Love. (AP/Wide World Photos)

kaftan-like shirts often in floral prints, and long, untrimmed hair. Hippie women wore men's fly-front blue jeans and men's shirts or long, tentlike dresses. Both sexes adorned their bodies with colorful love-bead necklaces, flowers, body paint, body piercing, peace-symbol jewelry, and garments made of all-natural fibers.

The Casual Approach By the end of the 1960's, the unisex dress initiated by feminists and adopted by hippies had reached its zenith with identical clothing and adornment for men and women. Middle-aged and older people were disturbed by the unisex look and various hippies styles, considering them representative of decadent behavior, but older people's conservative clothing styles were gradually affected by the new trends. Natural fibers, fabrics with rainbow-hued designs, and the hippies' casual approach to clothing were slowly adopted by people in mainstream society. Coordinated separates—tops and bottoms in different yet matching fabrics—became popular for business and casual wear for women and men. Women accepted slacks into their business and leisure wardrobes, and the pant suit became fashionable. Stiletto-heeled shoes were displaced by chunky-heeled shoes and sandals. Hats for business and formal occasions became a thing of the past for men and women. By the end of the 1960's, the rules of proper dress were no longer followed by those involved in the hippie movement, and other people soon followed with less formal attire.

Impact Newly developed synthetic fibers such as polyester and spandex were widely used in apparel during the 1960's. These machine-washable, quick-drying, stretchy fibers worked well in the less restrictive, easy-care apparel demanded by women. Rules of dress were relaxed, and matching separates became both popular and accepted by the masses for work and leisure activities by the end of the decade. The boundaries regarding gender differences in dress were weakened when females donned garments such as pants, especially blue jeans, which were once considered to be exclusively for men. Many issues and movements of the 1960's affected dress, and at the same time, dress was used by those involved in the movements to convey social and political messages and identities.

Subsequent Events Polyester's popularity faded in subsequent decades as people began to favor cotton

and other natural fibers. However, spandex and other synthetics continued to be popular in exercise wear and sports clothing. During the 1990's, many of the hippie styles of the 1960's enjoyed a revival among the nation's youth, and the relaxed approach to dress that began in the 1960's found expression in the weekly casual-dress days adopted by major companies such as IBM.

Additional Information An introduction to fashion and dress as social phenomena is presented by Elizabeth Rouse in *Understanding Fashion* (1989). *Esquire's Encyclopedia of Twentieth Century Men's Fashions* (1973) displays a panoramic view of men's fashion. Lynn Schnurnberger's *Let There Be Clothes* (1991) provides a historical perspective to fashion and clothing.

Sue Bailey

See also Davis, Angela; Hairstyles; Hippies; Miniskirts; Op Art; Quant, Mary; Twiggy.

■ Federal Aid to the Arts Bill

In 1965, Congress elected to support the arts by creating the National Foundation on the Arts and Humanities, a holding company for the National Endowment for the Humanities (NEH) and the National Endowment for the Arts (NEA). These endowments could provide grants to states, nonprofit organizations, and individuals to promote the arts and humanities.

In 1948, leaders of twelve national arts organizations formed the Committee on Government and Art to secure federal support for the arts. They investigated the feasibility of federal support, but legislative commitment was minimal. In 1955, Senator Nelson A. Rockefeller, a proponent of the cause, supported an arts bill that passed in the Senate but failed in the House. In 1960, Rockefeller helped form the New York State Council on the Arts, and the same year Michigan created a state arts agency.

In 1960, presidential candidate John F. Kennedy supported an advisory committee on art. He endorsed the development of an advisory council in 1962 and appointed August Heckscher consultant on the arts. Heckscher wrote a report outlining why and how the federal government should support the arts and helped increase governmental and popular support for an arts bill. In 1963, Kennedy issued an executive order creating an arts commission. Kennedy considered Michael Straight for chair of the commission, but scandal erupted when Straight admitted to knowledge of Soviet espionage activities. Kennedy selected Richard Goodwin as commission chair but was assassinated before he could announce his selection. President Lyndon B. Johnson appointed Roger Stevens adviser for the bill in 1964. The National Arts and Cultural Development Act of 1964 passed in the House and Senate and was approved by Johnson, who named Stevens chair. The bill established a national council of the arts and a national arts foundation, and in 1965, the National Foundation on the Arts and Humanities was created. Although the 1964 act authorized annual appropriations of ten million dollars and a five-million-dollar treasury fund, authorized monies did not match the appropriation and the foundation received only half that amount.

Impact Although the establishment of the National Foundation on the Arts and Humanities sent a positive message—that the federal government would support the arts—many other issues still had to be addressed. For example, the financial backing provisions were weak and the foundation's responsibilities were greater than it could conceivably accomplish. In addition, the act allowed money to be allotted to a variety of causes including the visual arts, theater, music, architecture, museums, and art education, but the foundation had the difficult task of deciding who would get how much. In 1969, President Richard M. Nixon asked Congress to double the appropriations of the endowments, which helped the foundation meet more of its goals.

Subsequent Events Throughout the 1970's, the foundation's monetary allotment increased. Improvements in the system, such as establishing a panel to judge requests for money and setting specific goals and criteria, helped the foundation function. Since the 1960's, questions have arisen regarding whether the federal government should support the arts, how anyone can determine the value of one kind of art over another, and whether welfare or the public interest should take priority.

Additional Information Gary Larson's *The Reluctant Patron: The United States Government and the Arts* (1983) examines the role of the government in supporting the arts.

Andrea Donovan

See also Art Movements; Great Society Programs.

■ *Feminine Mystique, The*

Published 1963
Author Betty Friedan (1921-   )

The book that captures the essence of women's discontent with the gender status quo of the 1950's and 1960's. It shatters the myth that a woman's only fulfilling role is as a wife and mother.

The Work In *The Feminine Mystique*, Betty Friedan, a freelance writer and 1942 Smith graduate, intertwines anecdotes and observations from her own life with facts and analysis from her research, creating a work with which the feminine reader can readily identify. Her starting point was her own personal experience. Friedan had everything a woman in the 1950's was supposed to have—a good husband, wonderful children, financial security, and a nice house—but she was not completely satisfied. Society said the truly fulfilled, feminine woman was a full-time homemaker who completely devoted herself to her husband and children. Friedan was a devoted wife and mother who loved and enjoyed her family. Still, something important seemed to be missing from her life.

Friedan began to wonder about the experiences of other homemakers and whether they were completely satisfied or if they also felt that something important was missing from their lives. In 1957, Friedan decided to find out, turning to fellow Smith College graduates for the answers. Her research revealed these highly educated, intelligent suburban housewives were discontented. Like Friedan, many women experienced uneasy feelings of incompleteness or emptiness. Others felt unexplainable fatigue. Sometimes anger and frustration welled up inside of them. They were not supposed to have these kinds of feelings—but they did. Such feelings were viewed as problematic, not only by the women themselves but also by the larger society.

In the early 1960's, concern increased over this discontent, which Friedan calls the "Problem that Has No Name." Sociologists and psychologists studied this "women's problem," looking for causes and solutions. Women's magazines presented readers with the latest information and advice. Often the discontent was attributed to a flaw within the woman, which might be remedied by psychoanalysis. Some researchers blamed less-than-perfect husbands and children. Some recommended having a baby to "fill the emptiness." A few experts even suggested that since college-educated women tended to become restless homemakers, women's education should prepare them for domesticity rather than for careers. Superficial lifestyle changes were recommended. Women were told to dye their hair blond since "blondes have more fun."

Friedan concludes that the real problem is rooted in the feminine mystique, the post-World War II American ideology that defines the ideal feminine woman exclusively in terms of traditional marriage and motherhood. According to the feminine mystique, the ideal feminine woman is passive, selfless, and completely devoted to her family. She needs and wants nothing more than to marry and have babies and her own home. Ultimate fulfillment is realized as the ideal woman cheerfully cooks, cleans, and serves her family. The unfortunate woman who wants a career is to be pitied and feared. She is unfeminine, her desires "unnatural." Perhaps, she is even neurotic.

Friedan develops the concept of the feminine mystique and examines how it colors perceptions of the women's movement of the late 1800's, how it relates to Sigmund Freud's theories on sexuality and the writings of sociologist and anthropologists such as Margaret Mead, and how the educational system fosters a belief in the concept. She also examines the reasons that the feminine mystique has existed for as long as it has, including the security or "safety" from freedom that retreating into the home provides and homemakers' economic role as consumer.

During the 1950's and 1960's, the feminine mystique was especially powerful. Women everywhere tried to live up to it. College-educated women abandoned their career prospects and intellectual pursuits to marry and have babies. Women retreated to the home, closing themselves off from the outside world because they believed this would make them truly feminine and happy. It did not. Friedan, who discusses the self-actualization theories of humanistic psychologists, argues that when women completely immerse themselves in the domestic world, they lose their self-identity. They stop growing emotionally and intellectually. Such women are not persons first; as wives and mothers, they are the objects of others. If women are to be fulfilled, they must first be persons with interests and goals of their own. Friedan asserts that, contrary to popular opinion,

abandoning the family is not necessary to the development of personhood and that women's horizons must be expanded beyond home and family. Reasoning that domestic duties need not be all-consuming as the mystique demands, Friedan concludes her book with a plan of action for women, encouraging women to channel their energy into activities that foster personal growth: pursuit of career, development of personal interests and talents, and participation in politics.

Impact *The Feminine Mystique* struck a deep chord in millions of American women who saw themselves and their experiences reflected in the experiences of Friedan and the Smith College class of 1942. This unsettling best-seller was cathartic: It raised the consciousness of women throughout the United States and spurred them to develop their own identities independent of their relationships with men. As these women discovered the various legal and cultural barriers in their way, they took up the cause of female equality and justice. The book was one of the focal points for the developing women's movement, and its author, Friedan, became president of the newly formed National Organization for Women in 1966.

Additional Information Friedan also wrote *"It Changed My Life"* (1976), a book that discusses both the development of *The Feminine Mystique* and women's reaction to the book.

Susan Green Barger

See also Feminist Movement; Friedan, Betty; National Organization for Women (NOW); *SCUM Manifesto*; Women in the Workforce; Women's Identity.

■ Feminist Movement

A movement whose first aim was to ensure female equality in a male-dominated world. It gave rise to the National Organization for Women and to various women's groups that examined all aspects of women's lives and sought liberation from things deemed to make women second-class citizens.

During World War II, American women achieved a sort of liberation and independence that they had not known before the war and lost after it. This liberation and independence were attributable to women's having to work at traditionally male jobs

Women in New York City take to the streets in their struggle for equal rights. The feminist movement grew by leaps and bounds during the 1960's. (Archive Photos)

because millions of men were fighting in the war and to their having to take total responsibility for families while the men were away.

After the war, American women retreated inside their homes to pick up their duties as wives and mothers. In the prosperous 1950's, American women were expected to remain at home, cleaning the house, cooking the meals, consuming the products offered on network television, and caring for their children. Authorities such pediatrician Benjamin Spock admonished women that going to work outside the home and leaving children behind could have a negative effect on the children's development.

The Feminine Mystique One of the housewives caught in the cultural expectations of the 1950's was Betty Friedan, a 1942 graduate of Smith College who had concentrated her energy for nearly two decades on being a homemaker and mother. Friedan found stifling the 1950's idea that women could establish their identities by vicariously living through the activities of their husbands and children. She believed that many wives would prefer the liberation that women had experienced during World War II to the 4security they were provided during the 1950's. In *The Feminine Mystique* (1963), Friedan suggested that women had been taught to accept the feminine mystique in which it almost did not matter who "the man was who became the instrument of your feminine fulfillment." Friedan described the isolated suburban home of the 1950's and 1960's as "a comfortable concentration camp," and she suggested that a woman's hiding of her independent self caused the "housewife's fatigue, ennui, and depression."

Although many people, both men and women, scorned the idea that women should find fulfillment in ways other than caring for home, husband, and children, Friedan struck a chord with some women, and she became a celebrity and best-selling author, spending the 1960's appearing on talk shows and lecturing at college campuses. Among those who could relate to Friedan's message were younger women who had gone to college in the 1950's and who were prepared to reject the idea offered by some psychologists that women could find true satisfaction only by sublimating their ambitions to those of their husbands. One of these young women was Kate Millett, who had attended the University of Minnesota in the 1950's. All during her college career, Millett questioned why women should be expected to find satisfaction solely as homemakers and mothers and why women should be assumed to be inferior to men. Her views were published in 1970 in her book *Sexual Politics*. Another young woman interested in Friedan's ideas was Gloria Steinem, who was working as a journalist in New York in the 1960's and later was one of the founders of the feminist magazine *Ms.*

The Founding of NOW In 1966, three years after publication of *The Feminine Mystique*, Friedan, along with a group of other professional, well-educated women, organized the National Organization for Women (NOW). Friedan served as the first president of this organization, and she declared that NOW was a civil rights organization whose purpose was to eliminate discrimination against women, which she termed as "evil and wasteful as any other form of discrimination." NOW originally had a board of directors composed of twenty-eight well-known professionals, about 10 percent of whom were men. Within a year, chapters of NOW had sprung up all across the United States. Millett and Steinem were early members of the group, and by the end of the 1960's, about three thousand women had joined.

NOW was organized in response to many incidents that occurred in the United States in the early 1960's. Friedan's book certainly served as a catalyst for much of the feminist activity. However, other events also served as impetus for this organization. President Kennedy's Commission on the Status of Women, chaired by Eleanor Roosevelt, had recommended the establishment of federal and state commissions to help women. These commissions, composed of influential women, gave women opportunities to meet and discuss women's issues related to employment and woman's place in society. In 1964, Congress passed the Civil Rights Act. Title VII of this act prevented sex discrimination in employment in businesses with twenty-five or more employees. However, some government officials suggested that the law could not be enforced and that its greatest effect would be to make it possible for men to become Playboy bunnies. In 1965, Mary King and Casey Hayden sent a memo to the Student Nonviolent Coordinating Committee (SNCC) complaining about women's position in the Civil Rights movement and suggesting that this movement relegated women to a caste and, at times, exploited them. Statistics showed that American women earned only a little more than half of what American men earned, only 1 percent of engineers were women, and women made up less than a quarter of college faculties. Friedan and others were convinced that it was time to organize a civil rights movement to acquire equality for women, particularly in the workplace.

Early Activism In 1966, NOW, in its first official act, petitioned the Equal Employment Opportunity Commission (EEOC) on the subject of help-wanted ads that advertised jobs as being for either men or women. According to NOW, this sort of advertisement had been made illegal by the provisions of Title VII of the Civil Rights Act of 1964 and that the effect of this advertising was to relegate women to low-paying, nonprofessional positions.

In 1966, NOW organized demonstrations against airlines because they required flight attendants (then called stewardesses) to retire if they married and when they reached the age of thirty-two. In 1967, Congress held hearings on NOW's charges against the airlines. At these hearings, Congresswoman Martha Griffith told the airline executives that if they wanted "to run a whorehouse in the sky, [they should] get a license."

In 1967, feeling that the EEOC had not been responsive to its requests, NOW members picketed commission offices across the United States. They also picketed the offices of *The New York Times* because that newspaper continued to run help-wanted ads labeled "male help wanted" and "female help wanted." In 1968, NOW brought suit against the EEOC, demanding that it enforce federal law relating to sex discrimination in employment. Finally, in 1968, the EEOC issued federal guidelines banning newspaper ads that advertised jobs as "for male only" or "for female only." In 1969, after the Supreme Court had ruled in *Rosenfeld v. Southern Pacific* (1968) that Title VII of the Civil Rights Act of 1964 superseded state law, the EEOC issued guidelines against state protective labor laws that applied only to women.

In 1967, at NOW's second annual convention, Friedan presented a bill of rights for women. This bill of rights demanded paid maternity leave, a tax deduction for child care, educational aid, job training, and access to contraception. Friedan also called for passage of the Equal Rights Amendment (ERA), which had been introduced in Congress by Alice Paul's National Women's Party in 1923, and for legalization of abortion. Friedan's demands for passage of the ERA and for legalization of abortion were stumbling blocks for unity within NOW, and some of the original members immediately withdrew from the organization.

A More Radical Approach During the latter part of the 1960's and into the 1970's, NOW preferred to keep its focus on issues relating to women's employment and status in society. However, in the late 1960's, other feminist organizations began to deal with all aspects of women's lives and to seek equality in every facet of women's existence. In 1967, the first female consciousness-raising session was held, and these sessions spread throughout the country. At every session, women got together to talk about all aspects of their lives. Women, perhaps for the first time, began to reveal to each other information about abortions, relationships, and sexual experiences—all in an effort to understand why they behaved as they did and to bring a feminist perspective to their daily lives not just to issues of employment or status. The first female consciousness-raising session was organized by the New York Radical Women, a radical feminist group formed in 1967. This group eventually split into the Redstockings and Women's International Terrorist Conspiracy from Hell (WITCH).

In 1968, the Jeanette Rankin Brigade and New York Radical Women participated in antiwar demonstrations in Washington, D.C., using the slogan Sisterhood Is Power, the first recorded use of this slogan. That same year, WITCH put a hex on the New York Stock Exchange, and some feminists, describing themselves as "radical," began using the term "sexism." In September, 1968, a group of feminists, inspired by the rhetoric of the New York Radical Women, protested against the Miss America pageant in Atlantic City, dumping symbols of women's subjugation—bras, girdles, and dishcloths—into a Freedom Trash Can. Just as the new Miss America was crowned, the protesters unveiled a banner with the words "women's liberation" written on it. With these protests, the women's movement, which up to this point had been primarily represented by the reasoned demands of NOW, became radicalized and enlarged to encompass events and political activities that related to every aspect of women's lives. One of the most passionate topics explored by groups such as the New York Radical Women was abortion. The New York group was responsible for organizing "speakouts" in which radical feminists talked about their experiences with abortion. Later speakouts would cover topics such as rape, incest, and sexual harassment. The purpose of speakouts was to expose unfair laws and unfair cultural attitudes.

In 1968, the first Women's Liberation Conference, held in Chicago, was attended by about two hundred women. During the late 1960's, more conservative members of the feminist movement, represented by NOW, joined with the more radical members of the women's liberation movement to act on issues that related to the agenda of both branches of the women's movement. In 1969, the Redstockings and NOW protested at abortion hearings of New York women. Also, in 1969, an organization called The Feminists protested at the New York City Marriage Bureau, claiming that marriage demeaned women. Earlier that year, members of NOW had invaded the Oak Room of the Plaza Hotel in New York City, claiming that it was unfair that women were not served in this room because business was conducted there.

Impact By the end of the 1960's, many Americans, men and women, were aware of the women's movement and of the inequities that movement was struggling to change. During the 1960's, some changes did take place: Sex discrimination in employment became illegal; President Lyndon B. Johnson signed an order making sex discrimination in federal employment illegal and making it possible for women to move higher than the rank of colonel in the military; and newspapers no longer could advertise jobs as "for males only" or "for females only." However, many of the goals of the women's movement were not achieved until the 1970's.

Subsequent Events By 1990, many of the demands outlined in the women's bill of rights created by NOW had been accomplished. As a result of *Roe v. Wade* (1973) abortion had become legal in the United States; women were working in almost every profession although their income had not reached parity with men's; some women did receive paid maternity leaves; tax credits for child care had been created; and contraceptives were readily available. Moreover, about twenty thousand elected officials throughout the United States were women. However, in 1982, the Equal Rights Amendment, three states short of the thirty-eight it needed, failed to be ratified.

Additional Information Marcia Cohen discusses the feminists of the 1960's and their contributions to the women's movement in *The Sisterhood: The True Story of the Women Who Changed the World* (1988). Flora Davis offers a history of the modern women's movement in *Moving the Mountain: The Woman's Movement in America Since 1960* (1991). Gloria Steinem offers her insights into the modern women's movement in *Outrageous Acts and Everyday Rebellions* (1983).

Annita Marie Ward

See also Abortion; *Bell Jar, The*; Birth Control; Civil Rights Act of 1964; Equal Pay Act of 1963; Equal Rights Amendment; *Feminine Mystique, The*; Friedan, Betty; Miss America Pageant of 1968; National Organization for Women (NOW); Pill, The; *SCUM Manifesto*; Steinem, Gloria; Women in the Workforce; Women's Identity.

■ Ferlinghetti, Lawrence

Born March 24, 1919, Yonkers, New York

The most widely read of the poets who came to prominence during the emergence of the Beat movement. Ferlinghetti's use of a kind of beat vernacular made his lyrical and political poetry very popular during the 1960's.

Early Life After graduating from the University of North Carolina at Chapel Hill with a B.A. in journalism in 1941, Lawrence Monsanto Ferlinghetti enlisted in the U.S. Navy, serving until the end of World War II and seeing action in both the Atlantic and Pacific theaters. He earned an M.A. in literature at Columbia University in 1948 and went on to get a doctoral degree from the Sorbonne in 1950. In 1953, he and Pete Martin founded the City Lights book shop in San Francisco and in 1955, he published his first collection of poetry, *Pictures of the Gone World*, as the first volume in the Pocket Poets series. Allen Ginsberg's *Howl and Other Poems*, published in 1956, was the fourth book in this series and catapulted Ferlinghetti into national prominence as a central figure in the Beat movement. When Ferlinghetti's *A Coney Island of the Mind* was issued by James Laughlin's pioneering New Directions Press in 1958, Ferlinghetti was firmly established as an important part of the alternative American literary landscape.

The 1960's By the early 1960's, Ferlinghetti had become recognized as a powerful voice for the burgeoning counterculture. His ability to combine a hip stance—knowing, skeptical, secretly idealistic—with strong political convictions and a flair for the romantic lyric gave his work an accessibility and appeal that went beyond that of both academic poets limited by their adherence to traditional conventions and other contemporaries who were pushing the boundaries of language beyond the reach of a general literate audience. In 1961, he published *Starting from San Francisco*, a volume containing fourteen poems that took as a general theme Ferlinghetti's journeys to Latin America and Cuba and across the United States. Using surreal images to emphasize the disjunction between the "America" he admired and the political currents he blamed for its decline, Ferlinghetti continued his amalgam of the personal and the political. The concluding poem, "One Thousand Fearful Words for Fidel Castro," deftly described U.S. foreign policy in mocking, ironic terms while taking the edge off the potentially (and prophetically) tragic consequences of an imperialist vision by placing the poem in the context of a man musing in a saloon "among the salami sandwiches and spittoons."

Ferlinghetti remained active as a leading publisher of some of his most prominent contemporaries (Ginsberg and Jack Kerouac) at City Lights Books during the early 1960's, writing almost no poetry himself, but his predilection for political statements led to a prose poem, "Telegram from Spain," in 1965 in which he vigorously attacked Francisco Franco, the longtime fascist dictator of Spain. His travels in Europe that year also resulted in a poem, "Kyrie Eleison Kerista or The Situation in the West, Followed by a Holy Proposal," which linked explicit sexuality with a sort of spiritual enlightenment and which he read at the Albert Hall Festival in London, and a poetic tribute to an admired old master, "Pound at Spoleto," an homage to the invention and maverick style of the controversial Ezra Pound.

During the second half of the decade, Ferlinghetti was actively involved in numerous meetings and demonstrations directed against the U.S. government's escalation of the war in Vietnam, reading the prose poem "Where Is Vietnam?" at Reed College in March, 1966, and writing two poems, "Santa Rita Blues" and "Salute" about his incarceration after an antiwar demonstration in Oakland in December. Like many other artists during the 1960's, Ferlinghetti experimented with psychedelic drugs as a means of promoting creativity, an experience he explored in "After the Cries of Birds," and he continued to record his impressions of his extensive travels in poems such as "Moscow in the Wilderness, Segovia in the Snow." The terrible violence that wracked the United States in 1968 led to "Assassination Raga," an attempt to offer a life-affirming song in the face of tragedy. That poem, along with the nine-part "The Canticle of Jack Kerouac" and other work concerned with travel, politics, visionary experience, and the use of musical phrasing (as in "Big Sur Sun Sutra") was collected in *The Secret Meaning of Things* (1968), Ferlinghetti's second major book of the decade. His last significant work in the 1960's was "Tyrannus Nix," a scathing attack against President Richard M. Nixon that Ferlinghetti described as a "populist hymn" in the spirit of poets Carl Sandburg or Vachel Lindsay.

Later Life Ferlinghetti continued as an influential poet and publisher through the last decades of the twentieth century. His later works such as *Starting from Far Rockaway* (1997) continued to find an audience.

Impact The notoriety of the Beat poets during the 1960's was instrumental in an alteration in the public's perception of the poet. Ferlinghetti's employ-

ment of an accessible vernacular both codified and created the so-called "Beat" style and voice, which was widely parodied and copied. The inclusion of a record with Ferlinghetti reading his works in the first, oversized edition of *Starting from San Francisco* (1961) helped to encourage the idea that poetry was an aural experience akin to jazz. By the end of the twentieth century, *A Coney Island of the Mind* had sold more than one million copies.

Related Work *Planet News* (1968), a book of poems by Allen Ginsberg, covers many of the same subjects as Ferlinghetti's work.

Additional Information *Ferlinghetti: The Artist in His Time* (1990), by Barry Silesky, provides an extensive discussion of Ferlinghetti's writing.

Leon Lewis

See also Beat Generation; Ginsberg, Allen; Poetry.

■ Film

An entertainment medium that experienced dramatic changes during the 1960's. The demise of censorship in the form of the Production Code permitted film directors and studios to make films that dealt with controversial political and social topics.

The Motion Picture Production Code, regulated by the Production Code Administration (PCA), was established in 1930 as an attempt by the film industry to police itself and thus avoid threats from citizen watchdog groups and government censorship. The Code specified that no films could be produced that would lower the moral standards of those who saw them. It prohibited obscenity and profanity and cautioned against the depiction of murder, crime, drug use, alcohol, costumes, religion, nationalism, and dancing. There were rules against films dealing with sex hygiene, venereal disease, and miscegenation. Bedroom scenes had to be treated with good taste and delicacy. Theaters owned by the studios that were members of the Motion Picture Association of America (MPAA) would show only films that had been given a seal of approval. The effects of the Code were felt well into the 1950's, but as more and more theaters began operating independently from the major studios, the Code had less influence on what films could be made and screened.

In the 1960's, Hollywood began to make films that were more reflective of real life with all its human imperfections, psychological problems, complex sexuality, and disturbing behavior. One film that reflected this trend was *Butterfield Eight* (1960), in which Elizabeth Taylor, in an Academy Award-winning performance, plays an expensive call girl who falls in love with one of her clients (Laurence Harvey) and tries to convince herself that he is the right man for her. Americans began to exhibit an interest in subject matter not treated by Hollywood productions and began turning to foreign films. Many of these films, such as Federico Fellini's *La Dolce Vita* (1961), depicted a kind of decadence and sensuality that had not been seen in American films since the Code was enacted. Fellini's film was banned by the Roman Catholic Church in many countries, but its underlying theme was a serious study of modern consciousness.

Gradually, U.S. films began to expose the viewing public to characters and themes that encompassed a greater breadth and depth of human experience. These films revealed a maturing process in public attitudes toward moral and sexual issues. Stanley Kubrick, an ambitious and talented director from New York, filmed an adaptation of Vladimir Nabokov's *Lolita* in 1962 that was shocking in its depiction of a middle-age man's perverse obsession with a young girl barely in her teens. This film seemed to blatantly violate the restrictions of the Code, yet *Lolita* received a seal of approval, probably because of the skill with which its theme was handled. Though *Lolita* may have represented a maturing of attitudes toward adult themes by both the studio and the public, it was still quite tame when compared with the novel. Much of the eroticism of the book was blurred or omitted. When it was released, the notice, "Approved by the Production Code Administration" appeared on the advertisements as did the warning, "Not for persons under eighteen years of age." Another 1962 film, *Days of Wine and Roses*, focused on the devastating problems of alcohol abuse by a married couple played by Jack Lemmon and Lee Remick.

Another film that led the way was *Never on Sunday* (1960) by the American director Jules Dassin. It starred the Greek actress Melina Mercouri as the warm-hearted prostitute who teaches a boorish and conventional American professor about sexual and personal freedom. In 1962, *Cleopatra*, a multimillion-dollar four-hour-long spectacle, caused quite a sensation. The film managed to get past the Code, but it raised concern that the Egyptian queen, played by a voluptuous Taylor, costumed in diaphanous silk, might reveal too much flesh. Director Joseph Mankiewicz used discreet camera angles and avoided having too many close-ups of Taylor's cleavage. That discretion may have helped to appease the censors.

Valenti and the MPAA In 1963, the head of the MPAA, Eric Johnson, died. For three years, the organization was leaderless. In 1966, a Harvard Business School graduate, Jack Valenti, became president of the MPAA. Valenti was working in advertising and public relations when he was appointed special adviser to President Lyndon B. Johnson in 1963. When Valenti became head of the MPAA, Edward Albee's powerful play *Who's Afraid of Virginia Woolf?* had already been filmed and was ready to be released. Jack Warner of Warner Bros. had bought the screen rights to the play years before and had made it into a film under the direction of Mike Nichols. It starred Taylor and Richard Burton with Sandy Dennis and George Segal in supporting roles. The story of an over-the-hill college professor and his bitter wife, the play contained rage, frustration, degrading and insulting language, expletives, and violent marital discord. The film was at first refused a seal of approval by the Code. Warner made a few hasty and minor changes in language and labeled the film "Suggested for Mature Audiences." Valenti and the MPAA accepted the compromise and the film was released to universal praise. In 1966 and 1967, a number of new releases would expand the definition of what was acceptable in a major motion picture.

Sex began to be portrayed more realistically and with more freedom in films such as *The Graduate* (1967), and *Blow-up* (1966). *The Graduate*, directed by Nichols, is a funny, touching, and unsettling story about a young man (the graduate, Ben, played by Dustin Hoffman) caught in the middle of a clash of generational values and his own desperate search for a future. In previous years, the Code enforcers would have refused to give their approval to a film that included extramarital sex between the graduate and Mrs. Robinson (Ann Bancroft), the mother of Ben's girlfriend (Katherine Ross). This hilarious film is one of Hollywood's most biting social comedies and became a popular culture milestone of the 1960's. *The Graduate* mirrors the dissatisfaction and disaffection of 1960's youth while parodying it in Hoffman's dry portrayal of the confused Ben. The film is also memorable for the popular soundtrack by Simon and Garfunkel.

Italian director Michelangelo Antonioni's *Blow-up*, starring David Hemmings and Vanessa Redgrave, is a stimulating examination of how people perceive reality. Hemming's character thinks he has taken a photograph in which a murder is being committed. Redgrave applies her charms in an attempt to steal the photograph. *Blow-up* seemed to capture that period in 1960's London when seemingly everyone was testing the limits of permissiveness. The term "swinging London" is illustrated in the film as the characters hop from nightclub to bed in fashionable style. The brief flashes of pubic hair during Hemmings's romp with several naked models brought strong objections from the Code.

Violence in the movies became more explicit in the 1960's as the effects of the Code diminished. The romanticized story of the Depression era outlaw-couple Bonnie Parker and Clyde Barrow was made into one of the finest U.S. films of the 1960's. *Bonnie and Clyde* (1967), directed by Arthur Penn, is an innovative gangster film that combined graphic violence with comedy, pathos, and social commentary. The relaxation of Code restrictions since Valenti had become president of the MPAA was apparent in the way Penn treated his outlaw characters. Though they killed in cold blood, Bonnie and Clyde's love for each other humanizes them and draws sympathy for their complex and somewhat perverse relationship. The climax of the film features an extremely violent, slow-motion, execution-like slaying of the outlaws. Caught in ambush by heavily armed law enforcement agents, Bonnie and Clyde are mercilessly riddled with bullets as they drive down a country road to pick up their mail.

Another theme taken up in 1967 was race relations. *Guess Who's Coming to Dinner* (1967), the final film pairing of Spencer Tracy and Katharine Hepburn, deals with interracial love and marriage, a theme that would have been unacceptable under the Code. The film's message of racial tolerance and acceptance was quite daring at the time of its release. Directed by Stanley Kramer, *Guess Who's Coming to Dinner* was criticized for not portraying the African American character (Sidney Poitier) as an ordinary person instead of a famous well-educated doctor. Another film that dealt frankly with racial attitudes in the United States was *In the Heat of the Night* (1967).

In this film, a rural southern sheriff (played by Rod Steiger) reluctantly joins with an African American detective from the North (portrayed by Sidney Poitier) to solve a murder. Academy Awards went to the film for Best Picture and to Steiger for Best Actor.

Voluntary Rating System With the gradual demise of the Code, prohibitions on what a filmmaker could do within the medium began to disappear. It appeared that freedom of expression might actually be possible in the making of motion pictures. The MPAA responded to the new situation by creating guidelines so that audiences could make informed decisions about film viewing. Valenti and the MPAA developed a self-regulating, voluntary rating system that could be applied to feature films. The categories were G, general audiences, all ages admitted; M, mature audiences, parental guidance suggested but all ages admitted; R, restricted, children under sixteen not admitted without accompanying parent or adult guardian; and X, no one under sixteen admitted. The new rating system primarily assisted parents in choosing films that were suitable for children or young adults. It also freed filmmakers from the threat of censorship during the creative process. Basically, anything could be considered the subject for a film. Instead of censorship, the rating system would be applied to alert the public as to the nature of the film before viewing it.

This voluntary system was accepted almost at once by filmmakers, exhibitors, and foreign-film distributors. Occasionally there were problems involving the rating given to a particular film. For example, *True Grit* (1969) was given a G rating even though it contained disturbing, violent episodes. In one scene, a man slices off another man's finger, and in another, a terror-stricken girl is attacked and molested. *True Grit* starred John Wayne as a boozing marshal who helps a strong-willed girl (Kim Darby) track down her father's killers. As Rooster Cogburn, Wayne gives one of his most memorable performances for which he won an Academy Award for Best Actor. His chief antagonist was played by Robert Duvall.

A much more graphic portrayal of violence can be found in the R-rated classic Western *The Wild Bunch* (1969), directed by Sam Peckinpah. One of the most violent films of the decade, *The Wild Bunch* depicts the desperate struggle of outlaws trying to escape pursuing law enforcement officers. The film's attractions also include interesting characters,

thoughtful dialogue, plenty of action, and a first-rate cast led by William Holden and Ernest Borgnine.

By 1969, there was little involving sex that could not be suggested or portrayed in films. Although actual hardcore pornography was still relegated to so-called triple-X theaters, other films began to push back the barriers of what was permissible to exhibit in mainstream theaters. One film that broke taboos toward the depiction of sexual situations in the cinema was *Bob and Carol and Ted and Alice* (1969). This film was about experimental 1960's lifestyles and the reevaluation of attitudes involving sexual fidelity in relationships. In it, a sophisticated couple (played by Natalie Wood and Robert Culp) try to modernize the thinking of their best friends (portrayed by Elliot Gould and Dyan Cannon) about sexual freedom. This incisive, controversial film, directed by Paul Mazursky, raised issues and questions involving the concept of monogamy. Although it did not provide answers to the questions, *Bob and Carol and Ted and Alice* at least brought to the screen a topic that was being explored in the changing attitudes and lives of many American couples.

Butterfield Eight *(starring Elizabeth Taylor, 1960), above, and* Bob and Carol and Ted and Alice *(starring left to right, Eliot Gould, Natalie Wood, Robert Culp, and Dyan Cannon, 1969) demonstrate the film industry's gradual relaxing of codes that allowed films to express more adult themes.* (Museum of Modern Art/Film Stills Archive)

Another film that dealt with certain previously taboo subjects was the 1968 thriller *Rosemary's Baby*. Directed by Polish expatriate Roman Polanski, it starred Mia Farrow, John Cassavetes, Ruth Gordon, Maurice Evans, and Ralph Bellamy. In the film, the life of young bride Rosemary (Farrow) changes drastically when her husband, Guy (Cassavetes), an aspiring actor, is tempted by greed to join a group of Satanists. The group hatches a diabolical plan to use Rosemary in fertility rituals. The scene in which she is drugged and then raped by Satan is particularly disturbing. Other graphic scenes involving birth, sex, and the occult are equally disturbing. The film was based on the 1967 novel by Ira Levin and produced by William Castle. Gordon won an Academy Award for Best Supporting Actress.

In 1969, *Midnight Cowboy* became the first X-rated film to be named Best Picture by the Motion Picture Academy. Directed by John Schlesinger, the film concerns the plight of Texas cowboy Joe Buck (Jon Voight) who comes to New York City to sell himself as a stud to rich women and ends up working as a male prostitute. Joe becomes friends with a sleazy street hustler, Ratso Rizzo (Dustin Hoffman). *Midnight Cowboy* was a watershed film because it proved high cinematic art could be achieved when a talented filmmaker was allowed to address controversial subjects in a climate of creative freedom. The issues of homosexuality, prostitution, drugs, and violence were all unabashedly dealt with in Waldo Salt's superb script. *Midnight Cowboy* also won Academy Awards for Best Director and Best Screenplay.

Politics, Space, and Popular Culture The 1960's was a decade of tremendous political and social change in the United States. The assassinations of President John F. Kennedy and Martin Luther King, Jr., the Cold War, the Vietnam conflict, the Civil Rights movement, and the rise of a youth subculture were reflected in the themes of a number of important films during the decade.

The Cold War inspired numerous films, including *Dr. Strangelove: Or, How I Learned to Stop Worrying and Love the Bomb* (1963), the story of a crazy U.S. general (Sterling Hayden) who launches a squadron of nuclear bombers on a first strike at the Soviet Union. The president (Peter Sellers) manages to call back all but one of the planes, which continues to the target and drops its bomb. The film ends with the beginning of Armageddon. This black comedy about Cold War paranoia and the madness of the military is disturbing in its grotesque depiction of the United States' fear of an international communist conspiracy. *The Manchurian Candidate* (1962) is a *film noir* thriller about political subversion at the highest levels of government. A Korean War hero, Raymond Shaw (Laurence Harvey), returns home a brainwashed assassin, programmed by the communists to kill on demand. *Fail-Safe* (1964) tells the story of a nuclear crisis created when a technical malfunction in the Pentagon's strategic control system sends a squadron of B-52's on a mission to bomb Moscow. Directed by Sidney Lumet, it starred Henry Fonda as the president, Walter Matthau, and Larry Hagman.

A film that captured the aspirations of a generation to explore new frontiers in space and consciousness was the 1968 masterpiece *2001: A Space Odyssey*, directed by Stanley Kubrick. Years ahead of its time, the film gave audiences a glimpse into a future of interplanetary space travel and alien contact using spectacular visual effects. Interestingly, it was released just before the 1969 Apollo 11 mission during which astronaut Neil A. Armstrong became the first man to walk on the moon.

Rock and the youth culture were also topics of 1960's films. *Easy Rider* (1969), a counterculture classic road movie starring Peter Fonda and Dennis Hopper, is the odyssey of Captain America (Fonda) and Billy (Hopper), two motorcycle-riding dropouts who travel across the country from Los Angeles to New Orleans in search of the real America. One of the first low-budget films to be a major box-office hit, it made a star of Jack Nicholson as the southern lawyer who joins the pair on their travels. It romanticized the drug and hippie culture of the times and was very popular with young audiences. *Easy Rider* used its rock music soundtrack innovatively to add both atmosphere and help tell the story. Rock music was the subject of the documentary *Monterey Pop* (1969), the first major rock concert film. Performances by Janis Joplin, Jefferson Airplane, Jimi Hendrix, and the Who provided a definitive look at rock music in the 1960's.

Other Notable Films Besides the films that presented controversial material that would have been unthinkable in earlier decades, a number of mainstream films stand as notable achievements in American cinema. *West Side Story* (1961), a film adaptation of the Broadway musical that was based on the William Shakespeare play *Romeo and Juliet*, became an immediate classic. Noted for its score by Leonard Bernstein and Stephen Sondheim, *West Side Story* won ten Academy Awards including Best Picture and Best Director. *My Fair Lady* (1964), a musical based on George Bernard Shaw's play *Pygmalion*, starred Rex Harrison as Professor Henry Higgins and Audrey Hepburn as Eliza Doolittle. It won eight Academy Awards including Best Picture, Best Actor, and Best Director.

Veteran filmmaker John Huston directed Marilyn Monroe, Clark Gable, and Montgomery Clift in *The Misfits* (1961), by Arthur Miller. A critically acclaimed parable about disillusionment, it was the last film for Monroe and Gable. *Breakfast at Tiffany's* (1961) is an offbeat love story by Truman Capote about a young New York writer and a very unconventional party girl. This sophisticated tale is memorable for Audrey Hepburn's unforgettable portrayal of Holly Golightly and for Henry Mancini's Academy Award-winning score. In the horror genre, Bette Davis and Joan Crawford starred in *What Ever Happened to Baby Jane?* (1962) a macabre tale of sa-

Chess player Bobby Fischer won international competitions in a sport that had been dominated by Soviets, thereby inspiring many Americans to take up the game. (Library of Congress)

dism and dementia that revived the careers of both actresses. *The Longest Day* (1963) was the epic recreation of the Allied invasion of Normandy on D day, June 6, 1944. With John Wayne and Robert Mitchum and a star-studded cast, it was a monumental feat of filmmaking.

Impact Every decade in the life of motion pictures has seen significant change in the way film depicts the human condition. During the 1960's, the maturing of American attitudes toward film as an artistic medium capable of portraying life accurately and credibly led to an era when cinema came of age as a medium that could be used to create honest and enduring works of art. The abolishment of the Code and subsequent creation of a voluntary film rating system resulted in greater artistic freedom for producers and directors. The most significant films of the 1960's reflected the changes both in the production code and in the attitudes of the film-going public toward material that contained adult themes, language, or situations. These changes allowed the film medium to continue its evolution as the major art form of the twentieth century.

Additional Information *Movies of the Sixties* (1985), edited by Ann Lloyd, provides a wealth of information about actual changes in movie content and production. Further details on many of the decade's movies can be found in David Zinman's *Fifty Grand Movies of the 1960s and 1970s* (1988).

Francis Poole

See also Beach Films; Bernstein, Leonard; *Blow-up*; *Bonnie and Clyde*; *Butch Cassidy and the Sundance Kid*; Censorship; *Dr. Strangelove*; Farrow, Mia; Gidget Films; *Graduate, The*; Hitchcock Films; *Hush . . . Hush Sweet Charlotte*; *In the Heat of the Night*; James Bond Films; Media; Motion Picture Association of America Rating System; *Midnight Cowboy*; *Rosemary's Baby*; Simon and Garfunkel; *Sound of Music, The*; Taylor, Elizabeth; *What Ever Happened to Baby Jane?*; *Wild Bunch, The*; *Who's Afraid of Virginia Woolf?*

■ Fischer, Bobby

Born March 9, 1943, Chicago, Illinois

The most renowned chess player in the United States during the 1960's. Many chess buffs—professionals and amateurs alike—identify Fischer as the strongest player in the history of the game.

Robert James "Bobby" Fischer learned chess from the instructions in a set bought by his sister Joan at a neighborhood candy store in Brooklyn, New York. A year later, at age seven, he began playing competitively. He won the U.S. Junior Championship in 1956 and the U.S. Championship in 1958. Fischer became an International Grandmaster at age fifteen.

During the 1960's, Fischer finished first or second in every tournament in which he played except one. He was U.S. Champion from 1958-1961 and from 1963-1967. In the 1964 U.S. Championship, Fischer went undefeated and untied, an unprecedented accomplishment. His first international tournament victory was in 1960 at Mar del Plata, Argentina. From 1966 through 1970, he lost only eight tournament games, finishing first at tournaments in Monaco; Skopje, Vinkovci, and Rovinj-Zagreb, Yugoslavia; Netanya, Israel; and Buenos Aires, Argentina.

In 1972, Fischer played Boris Spassky for the World Championship, winning a twenty-one-game match by four points. Thereafter, Fischer dropped out of competitive chess, forfeiting the championship to Anatoly Karpov in 1975.

Impact Fischer was the first chess player to become widely known in the United States and broke the Soviet domination of the sport. His career inspired many young Americans to take up the game, and some of them eventually rose to the top ranks of world chess.

Additional Information Frank Brady published a biography in 1965 entitled *Profile of a Prodigy: The Life and Games of Bobby Fischer*, which was revised and reissued in 1973 as *Bobby Fischer: Profile of a Prodigy*.

William B. King

See also Sports.

■ Fitzpatrick Drug Death

Date October 7-8, 1967

A violent homicide that contrasted the ideals of the flower children with the reality of urban life. The death attracted national attention and signaled an end to the innocence of the 1960's.

Linda Rae Fitzpatrick, the eighteen-year-old daughter of a Greenwich, Connecticut, spice merchant, dropped out of the exclusive Oldfields School to paint and live in lower Manhattan's East Village. After moving to a hotel on Labor Day, 1967, Fitzpa-

trick lived the life of a flower child, sampling free love and drugs. On Saturday evening, October 7, she and James Leroy Hutchinson, a twenty-one-year-old drifter known as Groovy, went to the basement of a tenement at 169 Avenue B, where both "dropped speed" (took amphetamines), unaware that three or four men were lurking in the shadows of the dark room. The men demanded to have sexual relations with Fitzpatrick. Hutchinson attempted to defend her but was struck in the face repeatedly with a brick from the boiler wall. Then Fitzpatrick was raped four times before her skull was crushed. The two nude bodies were discovered on Sunday morning, October 8. A New York City police officer described the crime as "one of the most horrible homicides we have ever seen."

Impact The violence of Fitzpatrick's death, combined with the extensive media attention it attracted, sent shock waves across the country. It showed the dark side of hippie life and the dangers that went with it.

Additional Information J. Anthony Lukas reported on Fitzpatrick's life and the contrasts of her last four months in his work, *The Two Worlds of Linda Fitzpatrick* (1967), for which he won a Pulitzer Prize.

E. A. Reed

See also Career Girl Murders; Drug Culture; East Village; Genovese Murder; Hippies; Manson Murders; Speck Murders.

■ Flast v. Cohen

Supreme Court case that established a taxpayer's right to sue the federal government. Although later limited in scope by the Supreme Court, it allowed people to challenge the constitutionality of federal spending programs that assist churches and religious schools.

In the 1960's, the U.S. government made many efforts to provide aid to private religious schools. In 1966, Florence Flast, representing Americans United for Separation of Church and State, brought suit to prevent the Department of Health Education and Welfare from spending money to assist religious schools pursuant to the Elementary and Secondary Education Act of 1965. The lower courts dismissed Flast's suit on the basis of *Frothingham v. Mellon*, a 1923 case in which the Supreme Court had ruled that federal taxpayers do not suffer a legal injury even if federal monies are spent unconstitutionally, and that consequently, taxpayers cannot sue to challenge the constitutionality of such programs. Flast appealed to the Supreme Court.

The Supreme Court ruled in favor of Flast, eight to one, on June 10, 1968. Chief Justice Earl Warren, in the majority opinion, argued that taxpayers suffer a legal injury when they can show a connection between a constitutional restriction on spending power—in this case, freedom of religion in the Bill of Rights—and their status as taxpayers. The extent of a taxpayer's interest or stake in a controversy has more to do with the issues than the amount of public money spent. Therefore, if a taxpayer claims that the government violated a specific constitutional limit on spending power, that individual can file a suit to challenge the expenditure. Warren argued that the Frothingham case was different because Harriet A. Frothingham, the plaintiff, raised a general rather than specific objection to the federal expenditures that she challenged. However, Warren's opinion carefully limited the new standing conferred on taxpayers by holding that it does not allow challenges to federal expenditures that are just incidental to the administration of laws. Taxpayers, in order for their suit to be heard, must allege that the government has violated a constitutional limit on spending power. As it turns out, the only such limit is on federal spending for religious purposes.

An elaborate dissenting opinion was submitted by Justice John Marshall Harlan. He argued that Congress should decide when taxpayers may bring suits because of the danger that numerous suits challenging federal spending might put courts in a position of dominance over Congress.

Impact The Court's 1968 decision in *Flast v. Cohen* modified *Frothingham v. Mellon*, at least to the extent of permitting taxpayers to bring suit to prevent the government from spending for religious purposes under the First Amendment. The ruling forged a powerful weapon for those opposed to government aid to religious schools and to other uses of public money that seem to aid religion. Dozens of suits have been successfully brought to prevent violation of the First Amendment prohibition that "Congress shall make no law respecting an establishment of religion."

Subsequent Events In later cases, the Court refused to broaden the scope of *Flast v. Cohen*. The taxpayers' standing exists only in freedom of religion cases.

Additional Information The Supreme Court's own discussion of standing issues in *Flast v. Cohen* is the best available for the general reader.

Robert Jacobs

See also *Engel v. Vitale*; O'Hair, Madalyn Murray; Prayer in Schools; Supreme Court Decisions.

■ Fleming, Peggy

Born July 27, 1948, San Jose, California

"America's Ballerina on Ice." Fleming won the 1968 Olympic gold medal for ladies figure skating and became television's first skating star.

Peggy Gale Fleming began skating at age nine after her family moved from California to Ohio. Fleming won her first figure skating championship in 1960, but her rise was tempered by the death of her coach and the entire U.S. skating team in a 1961 airplane crash. She captured her first of five consecutive national senior championships at age fifteen, becoming the youngest skater to win the title.

In 1966, Fleming and her family moved to Colorado Springs, Colorado, where she trained at the Broadmoor Skating Club under Carlo Fassi. With his guidance, Fleming won the 1966 world figure skating championship. The victory was bittersweet— her father died of a heart attack moments after she won.

Fleming successfully defended her national and world titles in 1967 and went to the 1968 Olympics in Grenoble, France, as the favorite. During the first live, in-color Olympic telecast, her gold medal-winning program included the first spread-eagle, double-axel, spread-eagle combination performed by a woman in international competition. After defending her world title, Fleming retired from amateur skating in 1968.

In 1970, Fleming married Greg Jenkins, with whom she had two sons. As a professional skater, she appeared in numerous television specials and ice shows and worked as a commentator for national and international skating competitions. She maintained her career as a professional skater into the 1990's.

Impact Fleming, dubbed by one columnist as "the face that launched a thousand Zambonis," was the only American to win a gold medal at the 1968 Winter Olympics. This victory, along with her other

Figure skater Peggy Fleming, shown here in Philadelphia earning her berth on the U.S. Olympic team, was the solo gold medalist among the Americans at the 1968 Winter Games. (AP/Wide World Photos)

accomplishments, returned the United States to supremacy in figure skating.

Additional Information To learn more, read *Peggy Fleming* (1974), by Charles Morse and Ann Morse.

P. S. Ramsey

See also Heiss, Carol; Olympic Games of 1968; Smith, Tommie, and John Carlos Protest; Sports.

■ *Flintstones, The*

Produced 1960-1966
Producers William Hanna (1910-   ) and Joseph Barbera (1911-   )

A prime-time animated series featuring the Stone Age character Fred Flintstone. Upon airing in 1960, the show quickly became popular, lasting almost six years in prime time and continuing to attract new viewers for many more years with syndicated reruns and spin-off television specials.

The Work *The Flintstones*, set in the Stone Age town of Bedrock, followed the misadventures of Fred Flintstone, a loud and sometimes grouchy stone-quarry worker. In the first episode, Fred (voiced by Alan Reed) and his neighbor Barney Rubble (Mel Blanc) sneak off to the bowling alley instead of going to the opera with their wives, Wilma (Jean Vander Pyl) and Betty (voiced by several different actresses). This battle of the sexes is continued in later episodes, including one in which Wilma and Betty want to join the all-male Water Buffalos lodge. The show's unique Stone Age setting provides many opportunities for visual humor—for example, the Flintstones wear caveman-style animal skins, ride in foot-powered cars with stone wheels, and employ prehistoric animals as household appliances, such as a pterodactyl that plays records with its beak and a mammoth that fills the sink with water for washing dishes. In the show's third year, a baby girl named Pebbles (Vander Pyl) is born to the Flintstones, and the Rubbles adopt a boy named Bamm-Bamm (Don Messick). Guest celebrity appearances occurred frequently, with movie stars Tony Curtis and Ann-Margret voicing their Stone Age alter-egos Stony Curtis and Ann-Margrock.

Impact *The Flintstones* was not only the first prime-time animated series, but also the first cartoon series geared toward adults as well as children. The young Hanna-Barbera production company initially had difficulty selling this unusual show to the television networks, but once it aired, *The Flintstones* quickly became a success. The show was actually very similar in tone and humor to *The Honeymooners*, a popular 1950's situation comedy starring Jackie Gleason as a loud bus driver, but the combination of familiar humor and an unfamiliar animated setting was very fresh. The audience became so involved with the Flintstones' lives that when a marketing contest invited viewers to guess Pebbles' birth weight, more than one million entries were submitted. Fred proved to be an effective advertising personality outside of the show, promoting products such as grape juice, vitamins, and even cigarettes during the commercial breaks. *The Flintstones* merchandise tie-ins, such as toys, books, lunch boxes, breakfast cereal, and children's vitamins, continue to sell widely. The show has not diminished in popularity, and a nostalgic trend in the 1990's resulted in a live-action film, *The Flintstones* (1994), starring John Goodman as Fred Flintstone, which used special effects to re-create many of the cartoon's visual pranks.

Related Works *The Jetsons*, also by Hanna-Barbera, debuted in 1962 following the success of *The Flintstones*. It depicts a family in the far future rather than in the Stone Age. In 1987, Hanna-Barbera produced a made-for-television film titled *The Jetsons Meet the Flintstones*.

Additional Information For a detailed background of *The Flintstones* and a complete episode guide, see *The Flintstones: A Modern Stone Age Phenomenon* (1994), by T. R. Adams.

Amy Sisson

See also *Jetsons, The*; Television.

■ Flower Children

A term associated with the early phase of the hippie counterculture. It connotes chiefly white youths, typically fes- *tooned with flowers, who had "dropped out" of bourgeois society to pursue a lifestyle devoted to sensuality, personal freedom, and social change.*

The identification of hippies as "flower children" may have originated with Allen Ginsberg. In fall, 1965, he encouraged organizers of Berkeley's Vietnam Day protest to deploy "masses of flowers" during their peace march as a way of pacifying hostile counter-demonstrators and the police. The idea reappeared one year later at what was perhaps the first outdoor "be-in"—San Francisco's Love Pageant Rally—which was held in the botanical splendor of Golden Gate Park. A flyer announcing the event encouraged those planning to attend to bring "flowers, feathers, beads, flags, incense, costumes." This list can be considered an inventory of the hippie accouterments for the Summer of Love in 1967.

Impact Timothy Leary, former Harvard professor and advocate of LSD (lysergic acid diethylamide), popularized the hip-floral style when he was filmed

Flower children, like these three young people at a 1967 be-in, wore vividly colored, imaginative clothing and accessories to convey their message of love and peace. (Popperfoto/Archive Photos)

at the January, 1967, Human Be-in with yellow flowers ringing his temples. Accompanied by his infamous slogan "tune in, turn on, and drop out," the image was much circulated by the news media and no doubt served as a kind of fashion plate for the nascent counterculture. A few months later, Scott McKenzie's hit song "San Francisco (Be Sure to Wear Flowers in Your Hair)" lured droves of would-be hippies and hangers-on to the Haight-Ashbury scene.

Additional Information For a closer look at the flower children and their culture, see Charles Perry's *The Haight-Ashbury: A History* (1984).

Michael Wm. Doyle

See also Be-ins and Love-ins; Counterculture; Haight-Ashbury; Hippies; Leary, Timothy; Pentagon, Levitating of the; San Francisco as a Cultural Mecca; Summer of Love.

■ Folk Music

The traditional, predominantly noncommercial music of the American people. During the folk music revival of the 1960's, many Americans embraced the country's native musical forms, favoring rural styles such as mountain ballads, blues, spirituals, and bluegrass.

At least as early as the mid-nineteenth century, Americans demonstrated an interest in printed collections of traditional music, such as slave songs, cowboy songs, and songs unique to particular geographic regions. Beginning in the 1920's, both the Library of Congress and commercial enterprises recorded a wealth of traditional American songs performed by amateur and professional artists. Many of these were field recordings made with portable equipment wherever the performers lived and worked. One of the most active such companies was New York's Folkways Records, whose exhaustive catalog of recorded traditional songs spurred tremendous interest in ethnic and rural folk music among its largely educated, northeastern clientele.

Traditional Folk Music In the 1940's, Woody Guthrie (composer of "This Land Is Your Land") and folksinger Pete Seeger traveled the nation, performing the traditional songs of America's common people, in an effort to aid a variety of left-wing political causes. In the early 1950's, Seeger's vocal group, the Weavers, had several hit records but, because of its

leftist politics, soon fell victim to the anticommunist blacklist that permeated the decade. Throughout the mid-1950's, folk music surfaced commercially on an intermittent basis. Then, in late 1958, the Kingston Trio recorded "Tom Dooley," a traditional North Carolina murder ballad. The group's rendition of the ballad, which resembled a professionally arranged pop song, sold several million copies and sparked a widespread commercial interest in American folk music that lasted well into the next decade.

The success of the Kingston Trio prompted the formation of scores of similar vocal groups, many of whom achieved commercial success. Strictly speaking, a folk song cannot be commercial. Traditionally, a song is a folk song if it is passed on orally, over the course of several generations, within a relatively insular group—such as one defined by geography or ethnicity. Group members perform the song informally and noncommercially, as an adjunct to home or community life. Typically, as a folk song travels across time and space, performers change it to address current, local circumstances. It is not a song presented in ready-made form to a mass audience for profit. Therefore, in a sense, the revival did not involve folk music but rather the commercial use of pop music derived from folk sources.

Commercialization of Folk Music For the most part, the public was unconcerned with this deviation from the traditional ideal. In the 1960's, millions of predominantly white, urban Americans purchased country ballads, blues, spirituals, and bluegrass as recorded by predominantly white, urban vocal groups such as the Limeliters, the Highwaymen, the Journeymen and, most famously, Peter, Paul and Mary. Generally, these groups perfected highly successful stage acts, complete with scripted patter, costumes, and other signs of the professional performer. Their vocals were polished and their instrumental accompaniment highly arranged, in sharp contrast to the often raw performances found on the field recordings that they used as source material. As record sales soared, the commercialization of folk music expanded. Book and magazine publishers, instrument makers, and the manufacturers of such products as liquor and cigarettes all sought to capitalize on the folk boom. By the mid-1960's, the nation's leading weekly news magazines, *Time* and *Newsweek*, had, respectively, characterized the folk phenomenon as a "frenzy" and a "craze."

Peter, Paul and Mary, one of the better-known groups, turned out highly polished, stylized versions of traditional folk songs and songs by artists such as Bob Dylan. (AP/Wide World Photos)

The movement reached its commercial pinnacle in early 1963, with the network television premiere of the weekly variety show *Hootenanny*, which regularly featured the more pop-oriented folk groups.

This commercial activity disturbed those who believed that folk music most appropriately served a community rather than a commercial function. Those critics believed that the pop groups were destroying what was unique about folk music by performing their entire repertoire in the same slick, stylized manner, without regard for the diversity in the songs' ethnic or regional origins. Guided by the example of earlier field recordings, many were interested in what they considered a "truer" rendition of American folk music and sought out artists who learned and performed the music not as professionals (though some did have professional experience) but as part of the fabric of their lives, within a community that valued traditional music for its own sake. As a result of the efforts of these often amateur folklorists, many artists who were unknown or known only regionally attained some level of na-

tional prominence. These included bluegrass pioneer Bill Monroe, North Carolina singer and guitarist Arthel "Doc" Watson, Cajun fiddler Dewey Balfa, and African American singer-guitarist Mississippi John Hurt. Folk revival activists provided professional performing and recording opportunities for these and other traditional artists.

Social Activism and Folk Music Somewhere between the commercial popularizers and the "authentic" rural artists lay a third strain of performer prominent during the revival. This group consisted of musicians who attempted to steer a middle course between outright imitation of the rural sources of their songs and the blatant show-business artifice of the successful pop groups. This group included several artists who became extremely well known, including Seeger, Bob Dylan, and Joan Baez. Having survived the blacklist of the 1950's, Seeger emerged in the 1960's as an ardent advocate of another type of performance prominent during the revival—the union of traditional folk song and social activism. Dylan built his early career around such efforts and did much to popularize the genre of folk-protest song.

Although the folk music revival can be divided into several types of performers, the actual phenomenon was more complex. Many people enjoyed both the pop folk groups as well as the more "authentic" material. The members of Peter, Paul and Mary, one of the most polished and successful of the commercial acts, were also highly active political advocates for social justice. Though some complained that commercialism destroyed the beauty of traditional song, others noted that it encouraged people to seek out and enjoy the nation's varied musical styles. The many folk music festivals held throughout the country reflected this complexity, often featuring pop, traditional, and interpretive artists, both political and apolitical, on the same stage in the course of a single weekend. In one sense, the revival merely illustrated the ability of the entertainment industry to dilute, package, and sell anything, including the cultural heritage of a people. In another sense, however, it demonstrated the extent to which Americans in the 1960's desired to understand and experience the rich and diverse heritage of their nation.

Impact The 1960's are often characterized as a time of confusion, alienation, and dissent. Although these are apt descriptions of some of the decade's traits, the folk music revival demonstrated an underlying yearning for the traditional values of simplicity and community. In that sense, it presaged, and perhaps fostered, the calls for love and community that came to prominence as part of the hippie movement toward the end of the decade. Similarly, the revival's interest in rural culture was a precursor of the late 1960's fascination with nature—a fascination exemplified by activities as diverse as environmental activism and the establishment of rural communes.

The movement's expressly political songs spread the message of the civil rights and antiwar struggles and helped unify and energize people active in those battles. More subtly, the revival's implicit message of respect for the common people, without regard to their particular heritage, underscored the decade's drive for equal rights for all humanity, from racial minorities to the young.

Subsequent Events Though the revival's most commercial manifestations faded by the mid-1960's, many people remained enthralled by the traditions that it celebrated. In the 1970's, revival activists were instrumental in founding the Folk Arts Program of the National Endowment for the Arts and the American Folklife Center, housed within the Library of Congress. Those organizations, in conjunction with many state folk arts agencies, have documented a wide range of American folk traditions, musical and otherwise, and presented them in countless exhibitions throughout the nation. In popular culture, the term "roots music" came to define a genre of popular song derived from noncommercial, uniquely American sources—the very folk music that fascinated America in the early 1960's.

Additional Information Robert Cantwell provides a comprehensive cultural history of the revival in *When We Were Good: The Folk Music Revival* (1996). Ronald D. Cohen has edited a collection of personal reminiscences of the phenomenon entitled *Wasn't That a Time: Firsthand Accounts of the Folk Music Revival* (1995). *Transforming Tradition: Folk Music Revivals Examined* (1993), edited by Neil V. Rosenberg, is a collection of scholarly pieces examining folk music revivals in general, including the American revival of the 1960's.

Michael F. Scully

See also Dylan, Bob; Greenwich Village; Newport Folk Festivals; Protest Songs; Youth Culture and the Generation Gap.

■ Fonda, Jane

Born December 21, 1937, New York, New York

One of the American screen's most famous and accomplished actresses. Fonda ran afoul of the Hollywood and Washington, D.C., establishments because of her radical political causes in the 1960's, but her best screen roles mirrored the complexity of her time and generation.

Early Life The suicide of Jane Seymour Fonda's mother and the busy career and multiple marriages of her father, actor Henry Fonda, turned Jane into a rebel who wasted two years at Vassar by partying. After brief periods in Paris, ostensibly to study painting, and in the New York office of the *Paris Review*, she appeared twice opposite her father in summer stock, terrified that she would make a fool of herself. However, her innate talent earned her entry to The Actors Studio, New York, in the fall of 1958 and led to a career on stage and screen.

Soon after appearing as an erotic space maiden in the film Barbarella *(1968), Jane Fonda became politically involved, working for liberal causes and the antiwar movement.* (AP/Wide World Photos)

The 1960's Her early career was bedeviled by weak material, although she won a Theater World Award for her Broadway debut as a young rape victim in *There Was a Little Girl* (1960) and praise as a cheerleader who tries to ensnare a college basketball player (Anthony Perkins) in the film *Tall Story* (1960). Her first major stage success was *Strange Interlude* (1963), with Geraldine Page and Franchot Tone, but Hollywood lured her into a series of inconsequential films, ranging from the sleazy, the awful, and the fluffy, to the jumbled and the ludicrously lurid. Her biggest box-office success was the satirical *Cat Ballou* (1965).

She moved to France and appeared (as a sort of American Brigette Bardot) in minor films by René Clément and Roger Vadim, earning notoriety and ridicule in Vadim's *Barbarella* (1968) as an erotic space maiden too lustful to be handled even by a sex robot. Her French period, which encompassed marriage to Vadim and motherhood, did activate her political consciousness. Cued by Parisian student

rebellion and political protest, Fonda spoke out against United States involvement in the Vietnam War before ending her marriage and returning home to do *They Shoot Horses, Don't They?* (1969). Her groundbreaking role in that film, as a cynical Depression-era marathon dancer, earned her the New York Film Critics Award and her first Oscar nomination.

Later Life In the 1970's, Fonda donated money to liberal causes (such as the Black Panthers and American Indian militants) and used her fame and finances to advance the political ambitions of her second husband, Tom Hayden. In 1972, Fonda earned the nickname "Hanoi Jane" because she traveled to North Vietnam, a trip that spawned intense criticism. Some of Fonda's detractors branded her protests a superficial form of "radical chic," while others, such as Richard M. Nixon and J. Edgar Hoover, considered her a traitor and made her a target of Federal Bureau of Investigation surveillance. Ironically, the 1970's were her most fruitful decade professionally. She shone in a wide range of roles in controversial films, winning an Oscar for *Klute* (1971) and a second for *Coming Home* (1978), a powerful antiwar story.

Impact Fonda's lifestyle in the 1980's and 1990's appeared to contradict some of the causes she had once championed. Her exercise videos, personal lines of clothing and accessories, and her marriage to corporate billionaire, Ted Turner, have made her a powerful member of the American establishment, quelling her radical politics.

Keith Garebian

See also Black Panthers; Hoover, J. Edgar; Liberalism in Politics; Nixon, Richard M.; Vietnam War.

■ Food Stamp Program

A federal program that provides low-income households with monthly vouchers for the purchase of food. Operated by the Department of Agriculture, this program essentially reduces the impact of agricultural price supports on the needy. It is the cornerstone of the nation's nutrition assistance efforts.

The food stamp program was a significant improvement over the food distribution program established by the Agriculture Act of 1949. The old program consisted of a commodity distribution effort designed primarily to promote the interests of farmers by removing excess supply from the market.

The food stamp program was established in 1964 with passage of the Food Stamp Act and was part of the Great Society programs developed under the administration of President Lyndon B. Johnson and designed to eliminate poverty. It is operated by the U.S. Department of Agriculture, which also manages the distribution of surplus commodities. The explicit objective of the program is to "permit low-income households to obtain a more nutritious diet."

People apply for food stamps not as individuals but as households. Eligibility is based on several factors, including household size, whether or not a person in the home is disabled or elderly, total assets, and monthly household income and expenses, including medical expenses. In-kind resources, such as noncash gifts from family members and friends, are not considered income under the food stamp program. A home and adjoining property are not countable resources. A vehicle is excluded if it is used primarily for employment, as a home, or to transport a physically disabled household member. The food stamp program is somewhat less restrictive than Supplemental Security Income and Aid to Families with Dependent Children.

Food stamp funding and participation expanded dramatically during the 1960's and early 1970's. With this expansion, the program exerted its most significant impact, the provision of nutrition to children and adults in low-income households. Although starvation is rare in the United States, malnutrition is common among households with incomes below the poverty level. During the 1960's, food stamps successfully reduced malnutrition among vulnerable Americans.

Impact In 1964, President Johnson declared an unconditional War on Poverty, and committed the nation to a campaign against economic deprivation. By 1973, poverty levels had fallen to historic lows that have not been duplicated since. To a limited extent, these declines in poverty are attributable to the Great Society programs established during the 1960's, including the food stamp program. Food stamps and other noncash programs such as Medicaid and subsidized housing tend to be more popular politically than those that directly provide cash to low-income families because voters prefer to ensure

proper nutrition rather than provide public monies that people could spend on less essential items.

One recurring concern related to food stamps and other means-tested programs has been their impact on the recipients' work incentive. The argument holds that availability of food stamps, welfare, and other supports reduces individuals' desire to work because benefits are reduced with increased income. Careful examination of data from demonstration programs suggests that the availability of food stamps has no measurable impact on work incentive.

Other concerns center around the program's relatively generous eligibility criteria. During the 1960's, some young people living in communal households used food stamps to support their counterculture lifestyle. In later decades, some middle-income individuals obtained food stamps fraudulently. However, the reported fraud rate in the program is estimated at under 2 percent. The most common fraudulent use of food stamps involves retail distributors who buy food stamps from recipients at a discounted value. Criticism of eligibility guidelines led President Ronald Reagan to revise these guidelines in the 1980's.

Additional Information *The Food Stamp Program: Design Tradeoffs, Policy, and Impacts: A Mathematica Policy Research Study* (1993), by James C. Ohls and Harold Beebout, describes the food stamp program and discusses the inevitable trade-offs in its design. *Confronting Poverty: Prescriptions for Change* (1994), edited by Sheldon Danziger, Gary Sandefur, and Daniel Weinberg, presents papers from a conference convened to assess and debate three decades of governmental efforts to reduce poverty in the United States. A compelling testimonial, *Starving in the Shadow of Plenty* (1981), by Loretta Schwartz-Nobel, uses case studies to illustrate the failure of the U.S. food production and distribution system to reach those in need.

Amanda Smith Barusch

See also Aid to Families with Dependent Children (AFDC); Farm Subsidies; Great Society Programs; Prosperity and Poverty; War on Poverty.

■ **Football**

One of the United States' favorite spectator sports at both the college and professional levels. Football enjoyed an increase in attendance and television audience every year throughout the 1960's.

Football evolved out of rugby on college campuses in the late nineteenth century, starting with the first intercollegiate football contest between Princeton and Rutgers in 1869, a game that resembled rugby more than the modern-day game of football. As the collegiate game grew in popularity and came to have nationally recognized teams and players, corporations such as the Indian Packing Company in Green Bay, Wisconsin, began sponsoring semiprofessional teams that played regionally, either independently or in loosely affiliated leagues. In 1920, the National Football League (NFL) was formed. It assembled several teams from the Midwest and Northeast into a nationally recognized professional league. The next forty years saw tremendous growth in interest in both the collegiate and professional games.

The collegiate game in the 1960's was dominated by traditional powerhouses such as the University of Texas, which won two national championships, and the University of Alabama, which won two national championships and shared a third. The decade also saw the re-emergence of a dormant power, the University of Southern California, which won two national championships and produced two Heisman Trophy winners. Traditionally, the biggest game every year was the Army-Navy game. Navy, with their Heisman trophy winners Joe Bellino and Roger Staubach, dominated Army in the early 1960's, and ended the decade with a 5-4-1 record against Army.

Several off-the-field stories also made headlines in college football. In 1963, the *Saturday Evening Post* reported that Wally Butts, the athletic director at the University of Georgia, had given confidential information to Paul "Bear" Bryant, the head football coach at the University of Alabama, before a win by Alabama. Both men successfully sued the magazine. In 1965, the Associated Press, one of the two major wire services that produced polls ranking the nation's top college football teams, changed its pick for national champion from Michigan State to Alabama when Michigan State lost to the University of California at Los Angeles in the Cotton Bowl. This was unprecedented as traditionally the media voted on the championship at the end of the regular season. United Press International, the other leading wire service voting on the national championship, kept with tradition and named Michigan State champion, making for a split collegiate championship. On the field, the collegiate game moved away from big passing offenses, with teams increasingly relying on defense and running games as the decade progressed.

The professional game in the 1960's was marked by expansion, the emergence of a new league, and a merger between the old and new leagues. The NFL began the decade with thirteen teams but ended with twenty-six, ten of which came from a merger with the American Football League (AFL), a league that was founded in 1960 with eight teams. At first, the NFL waited for the new league to fold, but the general rise in interest in football throughout the decade gave the AFL enough success to start competing with the NFL for star-caliber players. The competition started a salary war that neither league wanted. Finally, both leagues agreed to a merger that would take place over the course of four years. In 1966, the two leagues shared one draft, teams from each league met in preseason exhibition games, and their respective champions met in a single championship that became known as the Super Bowl. In the first years after the merger, the NFL still enjoyed superior talent, and its teams routinely defeated the AFL in exhibition games and in the first two Super Bowls. In 1969, however, in the third Super Bowl, an apparently overmatched New York Jets team beat the NFL champion Baltimore Colts. The upset signified the coming of age of the AFL and enabled it to press for the final and complete merger. By 1970, both leagues merged into an expanded NFL split into two conferences, the National Football Conference and the American Football Conference. Teams from both conferences met throughout the regular season, and all teams in the league shared the same revenue for television rights, which by the end of the decade had become quite lucrative.

The other major off-field story was the indefinite suspension in 1963 of Green Bay Packers star Paul Hornung and Detroit Lions star Alex Karras for gambling; both were accused of having placed bets on their own teams. The suspensions were lifted by NFL commissioner Pete Rozelle after eleven months, with both men allowed to return to their teams. On the field, the play was dominated by teams with strong defenses and powerful running attacks, including Green Bay, Chicago, and New York; however, offensively innovative teams such as Dallas and Baltimore in the NFL and New York, Kansas City, and

Oakland in the AFL came to prominence in the latter half of the decade.

Impact The rising ticket sales, increased television audiences, and emergence and expansion of leagues throughout the decade speak for the growing influence football had over the American population in the 1960's. By the end of the decade, football rivaled baseball, the traditional American pastime, as the nation's most popular spectator sport.

Subsequent Events The collegiate game continued its trend toward strong defensive and powerful running games throughout the 1970's, but in the 1980's, high-powered passing attacks became the formula for success, a development that continued through the 1990's. The NFL added two teams in 1976 and two more in 1995, weathered two years of competition with the United States Football League, and spawned a new league, the World League of American Football, initially with teams in the United States and Europe but later with teams exclusively based in Europe, demonstrating the growth in the popularity of American football outside the United States.

Additional Information Further information on football in the 1960's can be found in John Eisenberg's *Cotton Bowl Days: Growing up with Dallas and the Cowboys in the 1960's* (1997); Robert W. Wells's *Vince Lombardi: His Life and Times* (1997); Dave Anderson's *The Story of Football* (1997); *Total Football: The Official Encyclopedia of the National Football League* (1997), edited by Bob Carroll; and Ed Gruver's *The American Football League: A Year-by-Year History, 1960-1969* (1997).

Richard L. Mallery

See also Brown, Jim; Namath, Joe; Sports.

■ Fortas, Abe

Born June 19, 1910, Memphis, Tennessee
Died April 5, 1982, Washington, D.C.

A champion of social justice. Fortas left a partnership at a powerful law firm to become an associate justice of the Supreme Court, from which he later resigned under threat of impeachment.

Early Life Born into poverty in Memphis, Tennessee, Abe Fortas was the youngest of five children. While in high school, he helped his family financially by working in a shoe store and as a jazz violinist. He

Liberal Abe Fortas resigned from the Supreme Court after receiving an improper honorarium. (Library of Congress)

attended Southwestern College, graduating in 1930, then advanced to Yale Law School. While at Yale, he became an apprentice to William Douglas, who was later a colleague on the Supreme Court, and received his degree in 1933. In 1948, Fortas was approached by Lyndon B. Johnson because Johnson felt that his name had been illegally removed from the Texas Democratic senatorial primary ballot. Fortas agreed and was able to convince Justice Hugo Black to order Johnson's name to be reinstated. Johnson won the general election, and this was the beginning of a friendship between the two men. When Johnson was elected president, Fortas became one of his closest advisers. This role of adviser continued even after Fortas was appointed to the Court in 1965.

The 1960's On May 15, 1969, Fortas resigned from the U.S. Supreme Court under threat of impeachment. On May 4, 1969, *Life* magazine reported that Fortas had received, and then later returned, a twenty thousand dollar fee from the family foundation of Louis E. Wolfson, a multimillionaire who was later imprisoned for stock manipulation. Investigation revealed that this fee was the first in a series of annual payments that were to continue as long as either Fortas or his wife was alive. The purpose of these payments was, in Fortas's words, "to participate in and help shape the foundation's program and activities."

Fortas was first approached by Wolfson to participate in the foundation, which was created to improve community relations and racial and religious cooperation, in the spring or summer of 1965, months before Fortas was nominated to the Supreme Court. After being confirmed, Fortas was again approached by Wolfson to participate in the foundation. Believing that his Court duties would not conflict with his foundation responsibilities, Fortas became a member in January, 1966. In June, 1966, however, Fortas realized that he had greatly underestimated how much time his Court duties would entail and resigned from the foundation, terminating any further payments to either himself or his wife.

In September and October of 1966, Wolfson was indicted for stock manipulation. Following this indictment, Fortas attempted to distance himself from Wolfson and returned the twenty thousand dollars he had been paid. In so doing, Fortas sent a letter to the foundation stating that the services he had ren-

Boxer Joe Frazier won Olympic gold in 1964 and the heavyweight title in 1968. (Archive Photos)

dered for the foundation should be treated as a donation. However, the fact that the money had been returned was insufficient for many conservative members of Congress. Still angered that Fortas was serving as a presidential adviser, even after his appointment to the Court, conservative senators called for impeachment proceedings to commence. In addition, conservative members of Congress saw an opportunity to change the liberal makeup of the Court if Fortas resigned. Instead of putting himself and the Court through further public spectacle, Fortas opted to resign.

Impact As a lawyer, Fortas argued and won important constitutional cases before the Supreme Court. As an associate justice, Fortas continued his fight for civil and constitutional liberties by writing majority decisions and arguing for these issues on the Court. President Johnson nominated him to replace Earl Warren as chief justice in 1968, but in the face of considerable conservative opposition, Johnson was forced to withdraw Fortas's nomination. After Fortas resigned from the Supreme Court, Congress ended its investigation into his activities, and Fortas returned to private practice. However, his resignation resulted in closer scrutiny of the activities and investments of justices. In 1970, Fortas's seat on the Supreme Court was filled by a conservative, Harry A. Blackmun.

Additional Information *Abe Fortas: A Biography* (1990), by Laura Kalman, and *Fortas: The Rise and Ruin of a Supreme Court Justice* (1988), by Bruce Allen Murphy, take a closer look at the life of this controversial figure.

Mark L. Higgins

See also Johnson, Lyndon B.; Liberalism in Politics; Nixon, Richard M.; Supreme Court Decisions.

■ Frazier, Joe

Born January 17, 1944, Beaufort, South Carolina

An Olympic gold medalist and world heavyweight champion boxer. Frazier is best remembered for his three classic fights with Muhammad Ali.

Early Life A native of South Carolina, where he worked long days in the tobacco fields, Joseph "Joe" Frazier attended a segregated school whose administrators devoted most of their time and money to educating white children. Frazier was not interested in school, but he soon developed an affinity for boxing, which he watched on television for the first time in the 1950's. There were no boxing gyms in Frazier's hometown, so he trained using a punching bag he constructed from an old flour sack. At the age of seventeen, Frazier moved to Philadelphia, where he worked as a butcher while honing his boxing skills. A year after his move, he was discovered in a Philadelphia gym by a trainer named Yank Durham.

The 1960's Frazier improved his skills in the ring, and he won Philadelphia's Golden Gloves novice title as a heavyweight in 1962. From 1962 through 1964, Frazier lost only one amateur match. In the summer of 1964, he was chosen to represent the United States as a heavyweight at the Olympics in Tokyo. He won all four of his matches in Tokyo to become the first African American Olympic heavyweight gold medalist.

Frazier began his professional boxing career in August of 1965. He won his first professional fight by knocking out his opponent in one round. In 1967, heavyweight champion Muhammad Ali was stripped of his title by both the World Boxing Commission and the New York State Athletic Commission for failing to submit to military conscription. In 1968, Frazier won the vacant New York heavyweight title by knocking out Buster Mathis, the only boxer to whom Frazier lost as an amateur. Two years later, Frazier won the vacant world heavyweight title with a knockout of opponent Jimmy Ellis.

Later Life Frazier successfully defended his title four times from 1970 through 1972. Among these matches was a classic fifteen-round match against Ali on March 8, 1971, at New York's Madison Square Garden. Frazier lost the title to George Foreman in January, 1973. Before this loss, Frazier had won twenty-seven consecutive professional fights, twenty-four by knockout. In his final attempt at regaining the heavyweight title, Frazier was defeated in Manila, the Philippines, by newly crowned champion Ali on October 1, 1975. Frazier retired in 1976 following another loss to Foreman. Frazier was elected to the Boxing Hall of Fame in 1980.

Subsequent Events In the 1980's, Joe Frazier trained his son, Marvis, through the professional ranks. In the 1990's, Frazier worked with both amateur and professional boxers at Smokin' Joe Frazier's Gym in the Philadelphia area. He also ran Frazier's Golden Gloves youth development program.

Additional Information In 1996, Frazier wrote a book entitled *Smokin' Joe: An Autobiography*, which details the events of both his personal life and boxing career.

Joseph R. Paretta

See also Ali, Muhammad (Cassius Clay); Griffith-Paret Fight; Liston, Sonny; Olympic Games of 1964.

■ Free Love

A phrase promoting sex apart from the context of reproduction and marriage. Sexuality became a battleground over gender equality and freedom from repression.

American libertarian and anarchists writings of the eighteenth and nineteenth centuries advocated free love, arguing that love rather than marital status should be the guiding principle in sexual relationships.

The sexual revolution gave free love a more physical than romantic rationale, one rooted in pure personal pleasure. This view gained momentum from the rise of single working women and a glamorized singles lifestyle. Singles bars and apartment complexes, personal advertisements, and computer dating services proliferated. The government's approval in 1960 of Enovid brought birth control pills to the market.

The search for social justice complemented these developments, as seen in the rise of the women's and gay liberation movements. Nationwide, sexual freedom leagues rose on campuses alongside antiwar organizations. Dormitory visiting hours, coeducational living, and the right to receive oral contraceptives from student health services became issues.

Impact The debate over sexuality expanded limits in the country, affecting everything from television content to law. The liberating effect on female sexuality in particular has forever altered American social and political life.

Subsequent Events The appeal of uncommitted sex has been tempered because of AIDS, religious and political backlash, and the recognition that women's new sexual freedom had been turned into a duty—as in the 1970's antidraft slogan Girls Say Yes to Guys Who Say No. However, by the 1990's a return to pre-1960's sexual values seemed unlikely.

Additional Information Taylor Stoehr's *Free Love in America: A Documentary History* (1979) provides a historical examination of the concept.

Gary A. Olson

See also Birth Control; Feminist Movement; Hippies; Marriage; Pill, The; Sexual Revolution.

■ Free Speech Movement

The first major student protest movement in the post-World War II era. It occurred at the University of California, Berkeley, in October, 1964, and marked the beginning of the student movement's use of direct-action techniques on college campuses.

Although there had been five years of student protests at the University of California, Berkeley, no one predicted the activism that occurred in the fall of 1964. The catalyst was the Civil Rights movement and the participation of students in the movement, especially during the summer of 1964. Students who had participated in the Mississippi Freedom Sum-

mer project, including Jack Weinberg and Free Speech movement leader Mario Savio, brought back to college campuses a knowledge of civil disobedience and a dislike of bureaucratic highhandedness.

The action that led to the Free Speech movement occurred in September, 1964. The Dean of Students at the University of California, Berkeley, banned student tables on a small strip of land that had been used by the Congress of Racial Equality (CORE) and the Student Nonviolent Coordinating Committee (SNCC) to raise money and to recruit personnel. A coalition of student groups ranging from the Young Republicans to the youth group of the Communist Party protested what they saw as a denial of freedom of speech. In October, 1964, campus police arrested Weinberg for soliciting funds for CORE without university authorization; however, students blocked the police car for more than thirty hours until Weinberg was released. Free Speech movement leaders led by Savio then used rallies, marches, and sit-ins to protest the administration's actions. In December, 1964, students occupied Sproul Hall, the main ad-

Free Speech movement leader Mario Savio begins to speak to the crowd at the University of California, Berkeley. (AP/Wide World Photos)

ministration building. Following the arrest of more than eight hundred students, a student strike occurred. The faculty senate then voted to support the Free Speech movement's demands. In January, the university relented to the students' demands, and new rules were established that allowed student groups to set up tables, solicit money, and recruit on the campus.

Colleges and universities experienced large increases in enrollment during the 1960's as the first baby boomers (born 1946-1964) entered college. In 1964, college enrollment increased by more than 35 percent. Earlier generations of college students were conservative and apathetic, however, many of the students in the 1960's were more radical and activist oriented. They perceived the rapidly growing university as having become dehumanized. Professors and administrators were isolated from undergraduates, and the university was characterized as a factory turning out products needed by government and industry. Therefore, although the immediate issue was free speech, the more radical students began to see the university as a symbol of the oppressive corporate state and representative of the corrupt society.

Impact The Free Speech movement marked the beginning of the student movement's use of direct-action techniques on college campuses. Many members of the New Left, including Berkeley students Weinberg and Savio, had learned these techniques while working in the Civil Rights movement in the South during the summer of 1964. Studies showed that the movement received its greatest support from liberal and radical students and the bulk of these activists had previously been involved in civil rights or political protests. The Free Speech movement marks the climax of the developmental stage of the New Left and served as a link between the Civil Rights movement in the first half of the decade and the antiwar movement in the second half.

In 1965, U.S. involvement in the Vietnam War escalated, and many students became involved in the antiwar movement using the tactics and methods of the Free Speech movement. The Students for a Democratic Society (SDS) became a major organization on college campuses and began to focus its activities on Vietnam. During the 1967-1968 academic year, an estimated 75 percent of U.S. universities experienced major demonstrations. A con-

frontation led by SDS members at Columbia University in New York City in 1968, increased the national profile of SDS and resulted in even more campus demonstrations. In the first half of 1969, the National Student Association reported 221 major demonstrations at more than one hundred colleges and universities, and when U.S. troops entered Cambodia in May, 1970, four million students took part in antiwar protests. The convergence of the student movement and the antiwar movement was complete.

Additional Information See Hal Draper's *Berkeley: The New Student Revolt* (1965) for information on the Free Speech movement. For a broader overview of the context of the era, see Lawrence Lader's *Power on the Left: American Radical Movements Since 1946* (1979).

William V. Moore

See also Congress of Racial Equality (CORE); Freedom Summer; Student Nonviolent Coordinating Committee (SNCC); Student Rights Movement; Students for a Democratic Society (SDS).

■ Freedom Rides

Date May 4-August, 1961

One of the most significant protests of the Civil Rights movement. The Freedom Rides, which highlighted the continued segregation of interstate bus terminals throughout the South, were met with violence that caused much of the nation to support the riders' cause.

Origins and History James Farmer, the national director of the Congress of Racial Equality (CORE), an interracial, northern-based civil rights group, conceived the idea for the Freedom Rides. Modeled on the Journey for Reconciliation, the 1947 project sponsored by the pacifist Fellowship of Reconciliation, Farmer's plan called for an integrated group of civil rights activists to travel by bus from Washington, D.C., to New Orleans, Louisiana, as a means of testing southern compliance with *Boynton v. Virginia* (1960), the Supreme Court's ruling prohibiting segregation in interstate transportation facilities. Farmer believed that by demonstrating that bus terminal waiting rooms, bathrooms, and restaurants remained segregated throughout the South, the rides would highlight southern defiance of federal law and prompt federal authorities to remedy the situation.

A Freedom Rider bus burns after someone in an angry crowd near Anniston, Alabama, threw a firebomb through its window. Passengers escaped uninjured from the fire, but some were beaten. (AP/Wide World Photos)

The Rides On May 4, 1961, seven blacks and six whites divided into two interracial groups and boarded a Greyhound and a Trailways bus in Washington to begin their southern journey. The trip through Virginia and North Carolina was uneventful, but in South Carolina, white toughs attacked the riders in Rock Hill, and police arrested two of them in Winnsboro. Though they made it safely to Atlanta, Georgia, the situation worsened dramatically when they entered Alabama. Near Anniston, angry whites firebombed the Greyhound bus and beat the riders as they escaped from the burning vehicle. In Birmingham, a mob attacked those on the Trailways bus when it arrived at the terminal. Several riders were seriously injured, so CORE called off the rest of the journey.

Other civil rights activists, however, rushed to resume the rides, lest segregationists think that violence could derail the movement. Led by the Student Nonviolent Coordinating Committee (SNCC), the leading student civil rights organization, an integrated group of student activists converged on Birmingham. From Birmingham, the new riders traveled to Montgomery, where they were brutally assaulted by a mob awaiting them at the bus station. In the ensuing melee, John Lewis of SNCC suffered a concussion, James Zwerg, a white student from the University of Wisconsin, sustained spinal cord injuries, and John Seigenthaler, the administrative assistant to Attorney General Robert Kennedy, was attacked as he tried to protect several riders.

The violence in Montgomery forced the John F. Kennedy administration to act. As the riders prepared to travel into Mississippi on May 24, the administration arranged for National Guardsmen to ensure their safe passage into the state. Determined to prevent another violent disturbance, Robert Kennedy consented to the riders' arrest for violating segregationist ordinances in Jackson in exchange for assurances that state and local authorities would stop a white mob from forming at the terminal. As a result, the only white people on hand when the bus pulled into the station were National Guardsmen, state troopers, and city police officers. Local officials promptly arrested the twenty-seven Freedom Riders as they entered the whites-only areas of the terminal.

Rather than paying fines, the activists chose to stay in jail to dramatize their opposition to segregationist laws. Subsequently, Farmer called for others to travel to Jackson to be arrested for trying to exercise their constitutional rights, and by the end of the summer of 1961, more than three hundred people, most of them African American southern students, had heeded his call and had spent time in Mississippi's jails and prisons.

Impact The threat of renewed violence and continued arrests in Jackson inspired the Kennedy administration to pressure the Interstate Commerce Commission to issue explicit rules outlawing segregation in interstate travel facilities, a step the commission took in September, 1961. For civil rights activists, the Freedom Rides revealed that the federal government was an unreliable partner in the struggle for African American equality. Although the rides made it clear that violent confrontations and national media attention would impel the federal government to act, they also showed that in the absence of such conditions, federal authorities would permit others to trample on African American rights. The Freedom Rides helped deepen the participants' commitment to the Civil Rights movement and to each other. Beatings, arrests, and jailings strengthened the bonds between the activists and encouraged them to see themselves as the vanguard of the militant, direct-action wing of the movement.

Additional Information Original CORE Freedom Rider James Peck published an account of his experience in *Freedom Ride* (1962), and Taylor Branch offered a lengthy discussion of the Freedom Rides in his magisterial *Parting the Waters: America in the King Years, 1954-1963* (1988).

Gregg L. Michel

See also Civil Rights Movement; Congress of Racial Equality (CORE); Kennedy, John F.; Kennedy, Robert F.; Student Nonviolent Coordinating Committee (SNCC).

■ Freedom Summer

Date 1964

An organized challenge to racism in the heart of the South. Mississippi African Americans with the help of one thousand volunteers from all over the country succeeded, at the expense of many jailings and some deaths, in breaking some

barriers and alerting the nation to the reality of a social system maintained by terror.

Origins and History In the early 1960's, Mississippi's elected officials were determined to preserve white supremacy and segregation. Several African Americans who attempted to register to vote or to challenge the status quo were murdered. In 1961, leaders of the National Association for the Advancement of Colored People (NAACP), Student Nonviolent Coordinating Committee (SNCC), Congress of Racial Equality (CORE), and the Southern Christian Leadership Conference (SCLC) formed the Council of Federated Organizations (COFO) to further the cause of civil rights in Mississippi. The COFO planned to register voters; set up freedom schools to teach African Americans job skills, African American history, and the rights of citizens under the U.S. Constitution; form community centers from which to launch challenges to segregation under the Civil Rights Act of 1964, and canvass for the newly established Mississippi Freedom Democratic Party (MFDP), which had no standing under Mississippi law. Organizing began in especially difficult towns such as McComb in southwest Mississippi. Stokely Carmichael moved SNCC headquarters to Greenwood in the Delta area of the state, where local businessperson Amzie Moore and SNCC organizer Robert P. Moses began planning for a massive effort for the summer of 1964, which would follow the violent resistance to the enrollment of James H. Meredith at the University of Mississippi in 1962 and the murder of NAACP leader Medgar Evers in 1963. Recruitment of volunteers of all races took place, mostly on college campuses, and civil rights workers began arriving long before the summer began. Many underwent orientation in Oxford, Ohio.

The Summer Three COFO volunteers—James Chaney, Michael Schwerner, and Andrew Goodman—were murdered in Neshoba County by a mob led by Sheriff Lawrence Ramey and containing Ku Klux Klan members on June 21, 1964. However, the violence did not stop the COFO from carrying out its plans for community centers, freedom schools, and voter registration drives. White volunteers got most of the publicity, and their presence protected local African Americans to some extent, but permanent change was achieved by local people working in their own behalf, using the volunteers as a catalyst. Volunteers averaged slightly more than one arrest each by local authorities during the summer, and many were beaten or otherwise harassed. Publicity for the project had a major national impact. A reluctant Federal Bureau of Investigation and other agencies were forced into action to protect volunteers and local people, a role that has been much exaggerated in films such as *Mississippi Burning* (1988).

The MFDP challenge to regular Mississippi Democrats at the 1964 Democratic National Convention provided a showcase for local leaders such as Fannie Lou Hamer of Ruleville. Some disputes arose between Moses, who believed that local people should lead the movement for their own freedom, and Allard Lowenstein, who believed the COFO should form a close alliance with the liberal wing of the Democratic Party; however, COFO remained united until the summer project was over. Many volunteers stayed on to work with SNCC and other organizations that flourished in the wake of the pioneering 1964 effort.

Impact Freedom Summer was successful in opening the eyes of the American public to the inequities suffered by Mississippi blacks; however, the public's concern with the state of affairs in Mississippi itself did not last much longer than the summer. The white volunteers gained considerable experience during the summer, and many of them continued to be active in other organizations. Within the COFO, the divisions between black and white activists and local and outsiders grew, causing it to disband in 1965.

The MFDP gained considerable publicity when it challenged the seating of the "regular" Democratic Party delegates from Mississippi at the party's national convention in 1964. Although the MFDP was unable to replace the official delegates with any of its own, it had a lasting effect: The 1968 Democratic National Convention featured a racially integrated Mississippi delegation.

Although Freedom Summer ended without any marked improvements in the state, by the 1990's, Mississippi had more elected African American officials than any other state, social relations among the races did not differ greatly from those in other parts of the country, and educational opportunities for African Americans had greatly improved. However, tensions between whites and blacks remained and the poverty of the majority of the African American community was largely unabated.

Additional Information John Dittmer's *Local People: The Struggle for Civil Rights in Mississippi* (1994) is an analytical history of Freedom Summer. Doug McAdam's *Freedom Summer* (1988) gives the background and subsequent activities of the volunteers.

J. Quinn Brisben

See also Carmichael, Stokely; Civil Rights Act of 1964; Congress of Racial Equality (CORE); Evers, Medgar; Ku Klux Klan; Meredith, James H.; Mississippi Freedom Democratic Party (MFDP); National Association for the Advancement of Colored People (NAACP); Schwerner, Goodman, and Chaney Deaths; Southern Christian Leadership Conference (SCLC); Student Nonviolent Coordinating Committee (SNCC).

■ Friedan, Betty

Born February 4, 1921, Peoria, Illinois

One of the world's leading advocates for women's rights. Her 1963 publication on the feminine mystique reignited the women's movement in the United States.

Early Life Betty Naomi Goldstein was born into a middle-class Jewish family in Peoria, Illinois. A sickly child, considered by some to be unattractive, she was a highly gifted young woman. Graduating first in her high school class, Goldstein traveled east to Smith College to major in psychology. During her college years, she distinguished herself as a journalist by serving as editor of the school paper. After graduating summa cum laude, she spent a year as a research fellow at the University of California, Berkeley, then secured work as a reporter in New York City. At age twenty-six, she married Carl Friedan and, a year later, had her first child. After giving birth, Friedan briefly returned to work but was fired when she again became pregnant. During the early 1950's, Friedan was a suburban housewife and mother. Magazines of the era assured women that housework brought great fulfillment. Friedan, however, never experienced this promised satisfaction.

The 1960's In 1957, Friedan began research on *The Feminine Mystique*, the book that would reignite the women's movement in the 1960's. Friedan sent questionnaires to members of her 1942 graduating class at Smith, asking her former classmates to describe their lives since college. Their responses echoed her own experiences. American women were not as content as the popular literature alleged.

In 1963, Friedan published *The Feminine Mystique,* a passionate volume that articulated the frustrations of women trapped in the domestic sphere. To Friedan, women were dissatisfied not because they lacked housekeeping skills but because marriage and homemaking were not sufficient outlets for many women. Her message that women should not feel guilty about seeking self-actualization and pursuits outside the home struck a popular chord and helped spur a new spirit of feminism.

Friedan quickly emerged as the leading spokesperson of the new feminist movement. In 1966, she co-founded and served as first president of the National Organization for Women (NOW), an organization devoted to the achievement of full equality between the sexes. In 1969, Friedan helped establish the National Abortion Rights League and came up with the idea of celebrating the fiftieth anniversary of the woman suffrage amendment with a nationwide event, Women's Strike for Equality. This August 26, 1970, event received unprecedented media coverage and significantly enlarged the base of the revitalized women's movement.

Later Life In 1971, Friedan helped establish the National Women's Political Caucus (NWPC), a multipartisan feminist group dedicated to increasing the number of women in elected and appointed government offices. Later in the 1970's, Friedan became critical of NOW and NWPC for focusing on lesbian and minority rights issues, which drove many mainstream women out of the movement. She expressed her views in *The Second Stage* (1982). More recently, Friedan has written and lectured widely on the problems of aging.

Impact By articulating sentiments felt by millions of women but expressed by none, Friedan provided the catalyst that launched the modern women's move-

Betty Friedan wrote The Feminine Mystique *(1963), the book that helped give birth to a new feminist movement in the United States.* (AP/Wide World Photos)

ment. Through her insightful writings and social activism, Friedan has played a major role in reshaping American attitudes about the role of women in society.

Additional Information An excellent work that contains many personal insights into the life and thought of Friedan is her own *The Fountain of Age* (1993).

Terry D. Bilhartz

See also *Feminine Mystique, The*; Feminist Movement; National Organization for Women (NOW).

G

■ Gay Liberation Movement

A movement designed to secure basic rights for homosexuals. The activism of the 1960's encouraged homosexuals to pursue gay and lesbian visibility and become politically active.

Throughout history, people have variously viewed homosexuality as a terrible sin, a gift from the gods that bestows great wisdom and powers of healing, a mental illness, and a natural human variation. In the late 1990's, Americans increasingly began to take the fourth position, seeing homosexuality not as a chosen lifestyle but as a natural human variation.

Three milestones led to this view of gay life as a healthy human variation. Two of them involved the classification of homosexuality by the medical and scientific communities. Physician Alfred Kinsey published reports on the sexual behavior of American men in 1948 and women in 1953, reports that contained the first objective statistics on homosexuality in the United States. His research showed that 37 percent of men and 13 percent of women engaged in homosexual behavior. This information was particularly revealing in a society where homosexuals were believed to be rare. A second important milestone that changed public perception of homosexuality was the police raid on the Stonewall Inn in New York City's Greenwich Village in June of 1969. Finally, after a long and bitter internal debate, the American Psychiatric Association removed homosexuality from its official list of mental disorders in 1976. This decision came about as a result of political action on the part of gay liberation activists and new research findings by academics and scientists.

Although many believe the gay liberation movement began in 1969 with the Stonewall Inn riots, homosexuals in the United States had been seeking greater acceptance since the 1800's. In 1950, the Mattachine Society, a left-leaning homosexual society that held the view that gays were a legitimate minority living within a hostile mainstream culture,

formed in Los Angeles. The society shed its radicalism in 1953, after more conservative members joined and took control of the organization. The newcomers were primarily interested in winning acceptance on the mainstream's terms. They regarded themselves as patriots and good Americans and preferred to rely on "medical experts" rather than on political organizations to plead their cause.

Although the society turned away from political activism, in the mid-1960's, other groups and individuals stepped in to take its place. In 1964, police harassment of patrons at San Francisco's gay bars led to the formation of the Society for Individual Rights. This group, in its willingness to meet the social as well as political needs of gay men, enrolled a thousand members by 1966, becoming the largest homophile organization in the country. In 1967, Craig Rodwell opened up the Oscar Wilde Memorial Bookshop, the first gay bookstore with no pornography, which he regarded as exploitative. Rodwell used the shop as a vehicle for promoting a more positive view of homosexuality. Along with books and pamphlets, the shop carried buttons and cards relating to the homophile movement and had a community bulletin board that listed announcements of interest.

At 1:20 A.M. on the night of June 28, 1969, eight officers from the Public Morals Section of the First Division of the New York City Police Department raided the Stonewall Inn, a bar frequented by homosexual men. As the police made arrests, an angry crowd gathered, and soon the confrontation between the protesters and police developed into a riot. During the next few days, more rioting occurred. The Stonewall Inn riots changed the nature of gay and lesbian protests and caused young gay leaders to challenge the old leaders who they felt were bankrupt. Homosexuals would no longer adhere to a dress code at demonstrations, and if they felt like it, they would hold hands. These young activists were the first to believe that homosexuals were entitled to do whatever heterosexuals did in public.

Following the Stonewall Inn riots, on July 4, the conservative New York branch of the Mattachine Society, fearing a backlash from the establishment, called a public meeting to derail further demonstrations against police brutality. A shouting match began; the meeting broke up and the thirty-five to forty people who left eventually organized and founded the Gay Liberation Front (GLF). The GLF was strongly involved with other minority groups and what some gays felt were their "alien issues." It was in sympathy with the Black Panthers and the liberation struggles in Algeria and Vietnam.

On December 21, 1969, a group of nineteen people gathered to draw up a constitution for a new organization, the Gay Activists Alliance. This organization was dedicated solely to securing basic rights for homosexuals and would not protest oppression of other minorities. The alliance was willing to take to the streets and employ militant, confrontational tactics but would do so only to win acceptance for gays within the country's institutional structure. In 1969, approximately fifty gay and lesbian organizations existed in the United States.

Impact The gay and lesbian movement introduced four ideas into the existing homophile movement: that coming out and pursuing gay and lesbian visibility held the key to gay freedom; that gay freedom would change gender roles, sexism, and institutions such as the family; that gay, lesbian, and bisexual people are a part of the broad demand for social change and they need a political philosophy in order to bring greater race, gender, and economic equality; and that publicizing the gay and lesbian counterculture is an essential part of establishing lesbian and gay identity. These ideas were controversial in the late 1960's, and some of them remained unpopular in the 1990's.

Subsequent Events The aftermath of the Stonewall Inn riots raised three problems for gay political activists: how to motivate masses of people into political activism, how to define a coherent political theory and practice for a diverse group of people, and how to coordinate and organize the activities of a decentralized and personally oriented movement. Throughout the last three decades of the twentieth century, the gay movement has had to address these challenges with different strategies. The National Gay and Lesbian Task Force, founded in 1973, is the oldest national gay and lesbian civil rights advocacy

group. In 1993, it had approximately thirty-two thousand members, twenty-three full-time staff members, and a $3.3 million budget.

Beginning in the 1970's, the pace of gay emancipation in the United States accelerated. Civil rights statutes were broadened to include "sexual orientation" as a protected status in several cities and then in several states. By 1973, eight hundred gay and lesbian organizations existed in the United States.

Hundreds of thousands of gay, lesbian, bisexual, and transgendered people marched in front of the White House in 1993 to call attention to inequalities still suffered by sexual minorities. Change, however, was slowly taking place: On August 1, 1994, Vermont was the first of the fifty states to offer domestic partnership benefits to all state employees.

Additional Information The history of the gay liberation movement is examined in Eric Marcus's *Making History: The Struggle for Gay and Lesbian Equal Rights, 1945-1990, An Oral History* (1992) and Neil Miller's *Out of the Past: Gay and Lesbian History from 1869 to the Present* (1995). Urvashi Vaid's *Virtual Equality: The Mainstreaming of Gay and Lesbian Liberation* (1995) examines many of the issues involved, and Robert H. Hopcke's *Jung, Jungians, and Homosexuality* (1991) looks at the psychological aspects of being gay.

Paul T. Lockman, Jr.

See also Stonewall Inn Riots.

■ Gemini Space Program

One of the most significant and necessary programs run by the United States in the space race with the Soviet Union. Experience and information gained from the Gemini program made possible a manned lunar landing.

An outgrowth of the Mercury program of the National Aeronautics and Space Administration (NASA), Gemini was a transitional program that was designed to allow scientists to test the systems and maneuvers that would be needed in future space programs. Initially, the program was identified as Mercury Mark 2.

The two-man Gemini spacecraft were designed so that astronauts could fly precise orbital maneuvers. The spacecraft were constructed in a modular fashion that minimized weight, made efficient use of space, and reduced the time needed to install and repair crucial systems during prelaunch preparations. The vessels could maintain life support for up

Astronaut Edward H. White's tether unreels from the Gemini 4 capsule during the first spacewalk. (AP/Wide World Photos)

to two weeks, permitted astronauts to exit their cabin, and could physically join with unmanned target vehicles. NASA selected the U.S. Air Force's Titan 2 intercontinental ballistic missile as Gemini's launch vehicle.

The First Flights The first two Gemini flights were unmanned. Gemini 1, launched April 8, 1964, tested the Titan's ability to deliver the spacecraft into orbit and determined the compatibility of booster and spacecraft systems. No attempt was made to separate spacecraft and booster, so the combined vehicle suffered an eventual orbital decay. Gemini 2, launched January 19, 1965, on a suborbital trajectory, was designed to generate maximum heat upon reentry to test the heat shield.

Having qualified Gemini's spacecraft and booster, NASA prepared to launch its first manned Gemini flight. Gemini 3 was launched on March 23, 1965, bearing Virgil I. "Gus" Grissom and John W. Young. Although the spacecraft made only three orbits, this mission featured the first manually controlled maneuvers performed by astronauts or cosmonauts. On three occasions, Gemini 3's thrusters altered the spacecraft's orbital parameters.

Spacewalks Gemini 4 was launched on June 3, 1965, with James A. McDivitt and Edward H. White on board. After the spacecraft was in orbit, McDivitt attempted to approach the second stage of the Titan 2, which was in a nearly identical orbit. However, because the spacecraft was consuming too much fuel, McDivitt discontinued the rendezvous attempt. On the third orbit, White opened the spacecraft hatch, and secured by a short umbilical tether and holding a gas-thruster maneuvering gun in his hand, he attempted NASA's first extravehicular activity (EVA), or spacewalk. White's gun quickly ran out of gas, so he was forced to maneuver by tugging on his tether. White closed the hatch after spending twenty-three minutes outside. The remainder of Gemini 4's flight provided scientists with physiological data concerning prolonged exposure to weightlessness. Gemini 4 splashed down after four days, doubling NASA's cumulative man-in-space experience.

Gemini 5 had three major objectives: to demonstrate a new electrical power generation system called fuel cells, to complete an eight-day flight, and to evaluate rendezvous techniques. Fuel cells combine liquid hydrogen and oxygen, providing electrical power and drinkable water as reaction by-products and saving precious weight over storage batteries used on longer flights. Eight days was the minimum required for Apollo's lunar landing mission. Gemini 5 data would medically clear astronauts to attempt Apollo's challenge. Gemini 5 was launched August 21, 1965, with L. Gordon Cooper and Charles "Pete" Conrad on board. Fuel cell pressurization problems forced Cooper and Conrad to power down their spacecraft and drift in orbit, spending much of the mission in that condition. Rendezvous evaluations were canceled. Cooper and Conrad endured their ordeal inside bulky pressure suits, yet they returned to Earth in good shape.

Docking and Rendezvousing Gemini 6 was to attempt the first docking to an unmanned Agena vehicle launched by an Atlas booster. Unfortunately, Agena 6 failed to achieve orbit on October 25, 1965, and the flight of Gemini 6 was canceled. Instead, scientists proposed a joint flight involving two manned Gemini spacecraft. Gemini 7 would serve as a target with which Gemini 6 could rendezvous.

Gemini 7 was launched December 4, 1965, with Frank Borman and James A. Lovell on board. The fourteen-day mission was designed to be sufficiently long for technicians to prepare Gemini 6A for launch from the very same pad from which Gemini 7 had departed and for NASA to gather valuable medical data.

Gemini 6A's first launch attempt ended with a suspenseful engine shutdown on the pad. Astronauts Walter M. Schirra and Thomas P. Stafford remained calm, not ejecting from the spacecraft. On December 18, 1965, Gemini 6A was launched and began its orbital chase to locate Gemini 7, ultimately closing within a foot of that spacecraft. Gemini 6A and 7 flew in formation for several hours before completing their separate missions. Gemini 6A splashed down after 17 orbits; Gemini 7 after 206.

After a dual Atlas-Agena and Gemini-Titan launch sequence on March 16, 1966, Neil A. Armstrong and David R. Scott flew a series of rendezvous maneuvers and docked Gemini 8 to their Agena. Shortly thereafter, a spacecraft thruster fired uncontrollably, dangerously spinning the mated vehicles. The astronauts separated Gemini 8 from the Agena, located the faulty thruster, and regained attitude control, but because they had activated the reentry system to stabilize the craft, they were committed to an early return. The Gemini 8 splashed down in the Pacific Ocean, near a contingency landing zone. Scott had expected to attempt a spacewalk lasting one full orbit, but the early return made that maneuver impossible.

Gemini 9's Agena vehicle also failed to achieve orbit. However, an alternate, less-capable target called the augmented target docking adapter (ATDA) was available. The ATDA achieved orbit, but astronauts Stafford and Eugene A. Cernan could not lift off on the first attempt. Gemini 9A was launched on June 3, 1966, and successfully rendezvoused with the ATDA. Unfortunately, the ATDA's payload shroud failed to separate during ascent, leaving its docking cone covered. The ATDA resembled an angry alligator with partially opened jaws. Gemini 9A rendezvoused several times with the ATDA but could not dock. Cernan attempted a spacewalk with a special thruster backpack that was housed in the adapter section, at the outside rear of Gemini 9A. Unfortunately, the visor on his pressure suit fogged up, and he was forced to return prematurely to the spacecraft.

Perfecting Their Craft Gemini 10 was launched on July 18, 1966, after its Agena vehicle achieved stable orbit. This mission, flown by astronauts Young and Michael Collins, included a dual rendezvous with Agena 10, to which Gemini 10 docked, and the older Agena 8. Collins performed both a stand-up EVA to make ultraviolet stellar observations and a tethered spacewalk to retrieve a scientific package from Agena 8. Young and Collins returned to Earth after three days.

Gemini 11 was launched on September 10, 1966. Conrad and Richard F. Gordon accomplished rendezvous and docking with their Agena after just one orbit. Agena 11's engine boosted their spacecraft to a record 850-mile-high altitude. Gordon attempted a work-intensive EVA but overloaded his life-support system and had to come back inside the cabin after attaching a tether to the two vehicles. That tether was used for an artificial-gravity exercise involving joined rotating spacecraft, an attitude-control test that did not require thruster firings.

Gemini 12 was launched on November 11, 1966, with Lovell and Edwin E. "Buzz" Aldrin on board. After the spacecraft docked with its Agena, Aldrin performed two stand-up EVAs and one lengthy tethered spacewalk, finally demonstrating a successful way to work in space using body restraints, periodic rest breaks, and short tethers. Previous spacewalkers had expended far too much energy simply maintaining body position while weightless. After four days, Lovell and Aldrin concluded the Gemini program with a splashdown close to recovery forces.

Impact NASA's Mercury program ended after Cooper's daylong flight, and NASA seemed likely to assume leadership in the space race with its ambitious Gemini missions. However, the Soviet Union, having demonstrated a propensity for dangerous space spectaculars for Cold War propaganda purposes, scored two big victories that stole Gemini's initial thunder: The Soviets flew the first multiperson mission and accomplished the first spacewalk. In October, 1964, Voskhod 1, a modified Vostok spacecraft, carried three cosmonauts into orbit for a daylong mission. Then, less than a week before the Gemini 3 mission, Alexei Leonov exited his Voskhod 2 spacecraft for a brief jaunt in open space attached to his inflatable airlock by a short tether. Specters of another surprise space achievement by the Soviets would loom in the background throughout the remaining Gemini missions, but not a single Soviet flew in space as Gemini astronauts forged a clearly leading position in space.

The Gemini program provided a technological and operational bridge from the fledgling voyages of Mercury astronauts to the lunar missions of the Apollo program. All the program goals—long-duration flight, maneuvers during orbit, rendezvous and docking exercises, and spacewalks—were thoroughly investigated, providing the data and experience necessary for lunar landing missions. Gemini astronauts, in just twenty months, flew ten missions of varying complexity and success, providing the framework whereby Apollo had a reasonable chance of accomplishing the ambitious goal, set by President John F. Kennedy, of landing a man on the Moon during the 1960's.

Subsequent Events Two months after the Gemini program concluded, a fire on the Apollo 1 spacecraft claimed the lives of three astronauts, postponing the push toward landing a man on the Moon until the Apollo spacecraft could be thoroughly redesigned. NASA marshaled its forces and, after four evolutionary missions, was ready to attempt landing Apollo 11 in the Sea of Tranquility in July, 1969.

Many Gemini astronauts played prominent roles in the Apollo program. Six of them landed and walked on the Moon's surface, and some flew to the Moon twice.

Additional Information *Liftoff* (1988), by Michael Collins, provides descriptions of the astronaut's experience on Gemini 10 as well as of his historic Apollo 11 flight. *On the Shoulders of Titans: A History of Project Gemini* (1977), by Barton C. Hacker and James M. Grimwood, is a NASA History Series text that provides detailed information about program management, development, and flight operations. *Schirra's Space* (1988), by Walter M. Schirra with Richard N. Billings, describes the astronaut's experience on the joint Gemini 6A and 7 rendezvous mission as well as the rest of Schirra's career with NASA. *USA in Space* (1996), edited by Russell R. Tobias, includes essays written by a variety of authors about each of the manned Gemini missions. *We Reach the Moon* (1969), by John Noble Wilford, provides a look at the space program from NASA's inception to the Apollo 11 lunar landing and discusses contributions made by the Gemini program.

David G. Fisher

See also Apollo Space Program; Cold War; Computers; Johnson, Lyndon B.; Kennedy, John F.; Mariner Space Program; Mercury Space Program; Space Race; Telecommunications Satellites; Weather Satellites.

■ Genetics

The science of inheritance. The 1960's brought the cracking of the genetic code in DNA, the establishment of the mechanism of gene action, and the application of genetic technologies to evolution theory, cancer research, and the prenatal diagnosis of genetic diseases.

In 1865, Austrian monk Gregor Mendel demonstrated that the characteristics of organisms pass from parent to offspring in precise, mathematical patterns. In the 1880's, German August Weismann suggested that the controlling factors of heredity might pass from parent to offspring in the chromosomes (darkly stained bodies found in the nucleus of most cells). In 1902, American Walter Sutton and German Theodor Boveri discovered independently that the behavior of chromosomes during cell division matched the patterns Mendel had described. The nature of the genetic material was still unknown, but in 1909, Danish botanist Wilhelm Johannsen coined the term "gene," and the science of genetics was born.

In 1905, Nettie Stevens and Edmund Wilson at Columbia discovered the chromosomes that determine sex (XX in women, XY in men.) In 1911, Thomas Hunt Morgan suggested that genes might be located on or in chromosomes. He showed, furthermore, that genes closer together on a chromosome, where the chance for crossing over (exchange between chromosomes) was greater, were more likely to be inherited together than those farther apart. The first indication of a genetic causality for cancer came in 1910. Peyton Rous found that viruses isolated from tumors in chickens caused tumors when injected into other chickens.

DNA (deoxyribonucleic acid) was first isolated in 1868. The chemical compositions of DNA and a similar compound, RNA (ribonucleic acid), were detailed in 1909 and 1929 respectively by Russian American Phoebus Levene. In the 1940's, Americans George Beadle and Edward Tatum hypothesized how genes might control the production of enzymes. In 1944, Oswald Avery, a Canadian physician, asserted that DNA might be the molecule of inheritance, the gene. Alfred Hershey and Martha Chase, working at Cold Spring Harbor Laboratory, substantiated that idea in 1952. In 1953, James Watson of the United States and Francis Crick of Great Britain proposed the double helical structure of DNA, explaining—as Crick put it—"the basic mechanism by which life comes from life." In 1956, Arthur Kornberg synthesized DNA, partially confirming the Watson-Crick model.

In 1956, Joe Hin Tijo and Albert Levan devised a technique for separating and examining microscopically the forty-six chromosomes in human cells. In 1959, Jerome Lejeune discovered an extra chromosome 21 in the nuclei of cells obtained from children with Down syndrome.

As the study of heredity approached its centennial, the basic patterns of inheritance and the relationship between genes and chromosomes were becoming better understood, but the mechanism of gene action remained a mystery. At the heart of that mystery lay the puzzle of the genetic code.

Some Early Clues Significant progress came in 1961 from the work of British geneticist Mary Lyon. For many years, scientists had puzzled over the problem of the "double dose" of genes received by a woman on her two X chromosomes. When a disease-causing gene was carried on both X chromosomes, a woman seemed to be no more severely afflicted than a man who got only one such gene. Lyon showed that one of the two X chromosomes is inactivated early in the development of a female embryo. The inactivation is random—that is, different from cell to cell—but in each case only one X remains functional.

Between 1959 and 1961, three additional breakthroughs paved the way for cracking the genetic code. First, scientists discovered that the structure of the RNA molecule depended on the DNA from which it was derived. Second, they were able to isolate enzymes that use the DNA molecule as a template for the synthesis of RNA. Third, U.S. scientist Robert Holley analyzed transfer RNA, a kind of

RNA that transports amino acids into their proper places in the protein chain.

In 1961, Robert Perry demonstrated that RNA is synthesized on chromosomes. That same year, French scientists François Jacob and Jacques Monod confirmed the existence of that molecule. They called it messenger RNA because it appeared to ferry the instructions for protein synthesis from DNA in the cell's nucleus to the protein factory of the ribosomes in the cytoplasm. Soon, the assembly of proteins on the ribosome was well elaborated, but the code itself—the language of DNA—remained elusive.

The Jacob and Monod Model Nevertheless, Jacob and Monod pressed on. That same year, they found that bacteria grown in a lactose-rich medium make enzymes that break down lactose, while those grown in a solution free of that sugar do not. Those bacteria that fail to break down lactose were found to have mutations (changes) in one of three genes controlling enzyme production. This finding led Jacob and Monod to suggest that certain genes produce repressor molecules that can bind to sites on DNA called operators. Operators lie near groups of functional genes responsible for sequential steps of a metabolic pathway. Operators initiate gene action. Repressors, it seemed, could act as "switches" capable of "turning off" or inactivating operators. For their pioneering work, Jacob and Monod received the Nobel Prize for Physiology or Medicine in 1965. In 1966, Walter Gilbert and Benno Müller-Hill succeeded in isolating a repressor of the lactose-breakdown sequence. The following year, they determined that the repressor binds directly to DNA, thus providing substantial confirmation for the Jacob-Monod model.

Confirmation came also from the work of Mark Ptashne and Walter Gilbert at Harvard. They demonstrated the action of two operators in the lactose sequence. They also isolated genetic repressors and demonstrated them to be proteins. They found that repressors are more than "off switches." Some repressors turn off other repressors, in effect working as "on switches." Repressors enable the cell to control not only which proteins are made but also the duration of synthesis and the amount produced. This meant that scientists had identified two kinds of genes: structural genes that govern the amino acid sequence of a particular protein and regulatory genes that control the action of structural genes. In the years that followed, work in many laboratories elaborated the architecture and functioning of many such genes in a variety of metabolic pathways in bacteria and fungi.

Cracking the Code As work on gene action continued, few doubted that DNA's helical structure explained the structure and function of genes, but no one knew how a mere four bases in DNA (adenine, guanine, cytosine, and thymine) could direct the cell to string twenty different kinds of amino acids into long, protein chains. Two teams working independently between 1962 and 1965 cracked the code.

Watson's former collaborator Crick and Sydney Brenner (both at Cambridge in England) offered evidence from mutation studies hinting that the code was read in three letter "words"—or triplets of three adjacent bases—and read from a fixed point, much as type on a page must be read from left to right. They also argued that the twenty amino acids might each have more than one triplet code and that the code words must never overlap.

At the same time, U.S. National Institutes of Health scientists Marshall Nirenberg and Heinrich Johann Matthaei were working with a "soup" of bacterial cell parts: RNAs, energy-providing compounds, and radioactive amino acids. They experimented with an artificial RNA created in the laboratory of Severo Ochoa at New York University. The molecule contained a single base, uracil, repeated hundreds of times in a long chain. They found that this single-base RNA prompted the production of a protein containing a single amino acid, phenylalanine. This result deciphered the first DNA code word: U-U-U in RNA (corresponding to A-A-A in DNA) had to be the triplet code for phenylalanine.

By 1966, all the remaining triplets were deciphered and added to the DNA "dictionary," with much of the credit going to Ochoa at New York University and Har Gobind Khorana at the University of Wisconsin. Further experiments validated the code, as specific changes in DNA (mutations) were shown to effect predictable changes in the protein thus produced.

Other Research At the same time, evidence mounted that the genetic code was the same for all species and that work with microbes could be extrapolated to higher organisms, including human beings. In the late 1960's, a large number of scientists abandoned research on bacteria and viruses and went to work on the far more complex question of tumor-induction (cancer) in the cells of higher animals. After more than a half-century, the significance of Rous's studies of a tumor-inducing virus became apparent. Researchers found that cancer-causing genes (oncogenes) occur not only in viruses but also in normal body cells. Only under certain circumstances does the machinery of the gene go haywire, inducing the accelerated rate of cell division that defines cancer. In 1966, Rous, at age 85, received a long-overdue Nobel Prize.

In the late 1960's, scientists began experimenting with the free-floating rings of DNA called plasmids found in certain bacteria. Hamilton Smith discovered a class of proteins, called restriction enzymes, which cut DNA apart at specific sites. Daniel Nathans and Werner Arber used these enzymes to analyze the genetic material of a virus.

Impact As the 1960's began, geneticists could not answer two of their discipline's most fundamental questions: how genes control cellular structure and functioning and why certain genes are actively expressed in some cells yet dormant in others. Both questions were central to the problem of differentiation—that different cells in the same organism vary in their structure and function although they carry identical genetic information. For example, skin cells differ greatly from muscle cells, which have little in common with blood cells. Although each contains the same DNA, they do different jobs using different proteins. By the end of the decade, theoretical and experimental work had suggested the means of cellular differentiation. The deciphering of the genetic code and the description of the cellular machinery for protein synthesis linked the genetic material (DNA in the nucleus) to structural proteins and enzymes manufactured in the cytoplasm. The Jacob and Monod theory of operators and repressors explained how cells containing the same genes could make different proteins and perform different functions.

Progress in genetics also supported the refinement of the theory of evolution. In 1964, Bill Hoyer, Brian McCarthy and Ellis Bolton pointed out that similarities and differences in protein sequences constitute a biochemical measure of kinship. The greater the similarity, the more recently the evolutionary lines diverged; that is, the more nearly alike

the proteins, the more closely related the organisms. In 1967, Walter Fitch and Emanuel Margoliash calculated the relationship of twenty organisms, ranging from fungi to mammals, by comparing the arrangement of amino acids in their cytochrome C molecules.

The Watson-Crick model offered an explanation for how the gene can duplicate itself, but the extensive work of the 1960's went further to detail the mechanisms by which genes determine both the architecture of cells and the chemical reactions carried out within them. The deciphering of the genetic code explained how mutations occur. A single base change can change the protein sequence. Mutation—as a means of individual and species variability—did much to advance scientists' understanding of the natural selection of adaptive characteristics and the evolution of species.

In the research area, the DNA-RNA experiments of the 1960's carried the biological sciences closer to a union with chemistry and physics, as researchers sought explanations for the activities of whole organisms in the interactions of their constituent parts at the cellular, molecular, and even atomic levels. The biological sciences became increasingly reductionist, quantitative, and statistical.

In the applied sciences—especially medicine—the elucidation of gene mechanics and the cracking of the genetic code created opportunities for a host of practical applications, especially in medical research and treatment. The first successful prenatal diagnosis was reported in 1968. Using the technique amniocentesis—in which fetal cells floating in amniotic fluid are withdrawn from the uterus and the fetal chromosomes analyzed—doctors were able to detect an inherited disorder at an early stage in pregnancy. Amniocentesis made it possible for those who receive positive diagnosis of a genetic disease to abort the fetus and therefore raised numerous ethical issues linked to the abortion controversy.

Subsequent Events In 1973, Stanley Cohen and Herbert Boyer used restriction enzymes to snip apart segments of DNA and recombine them in novel ways. This technique, called recombinant DNA technology, spawned the biotechnology industry of the late twentieth century. In the 1980's, the Supreme Court upheld the world's first patent on a genetically engineered organism, an oil-digesting bacterium, and Harvard Medical School patented a strain of mice genetically designed for cancer research. The Food and Drug Administration approved the first genetically engineered pharmaceutical, recombinant insulin for treating diabetics. Genetic engineering techniques have become important to the prenatal diagnosis of inherited disorders such as Duchenne's muscular dystrophy and Huntington disease. Applications of recombinant technologies to agriculture include the Flavr-Savr tomato, genetically engineered for slower ripening and longer shelf life.

Yet another leap forward came with the improvement of techniques for prenatal diagnosis and the proliferation of genetic counseling centers. In 1981, sickle cell anemia became the first genetic disease to be diagnosed at the genetic level, using direct analysis of DNA. Individuals who suspect a heritable disease in their family now have access to trained health professionals who can assess family histories, interpret various laboratory tests, and advise their clients both about their own health situation and their reproductive status. Ultrasonography is routinely used to check fetal development in pregnancy, and chorionic villus sampling (using cells from one of the membranes that surrounds the fetus) provides a safe and effective alternative to amniocentesis. In certain instances, scientists have succeeded in treating and correcting genetic defects in the fetus. New blood tests have made possible the screening of large populations of adults for genes that may cause disease in their children.

Cancer studies also built on the foundation of genetic research of the 1960's. In 1979, DNA was used to transform cultured mouse cells, permitting cancer genes to be studied in cell culture. In 1982, a human oncogene was copied and propagated in bacteria.

By the mid-1980's, rapid advances in chromosome mapping and other DNA techniques led scientists to undertake the mapping of all forty-six human chromosomes. The Human Genome Project, formally initiated as an international cooperative project in 1990, set out to decode and map all one hundred thousand human genes. In 1992, a generalized map of the entire human chromosomal complement was published.

Additional Information Robert Snedden provides a simple and attractive introduction to the topic in *The History of Genetics* (1995). Caroline Arnold's overview in *Genetics: From Mendel to Gene Splicing* (1986) covers the territory in simple language. For greater detail, see *The Gene: A Critical History* (1966), by E. A. Carlson; *Towards an Understanding of the Mechanism of Heredity* (1973), by H. L. K. Whitehouse; and *Human and Mammalian Cytogenetics: An Historical Perspective* (1979), by Tao-Chiuh Hsu. For additional material on DNA, see *Discovery: The Search for DNA's Secrets* (1981), by Mahlon Hoagland; *A Century of DNA: A History of the Discovery of the Structure and Function of the Genetic Substance* (1977), by Franklin H. Portugal and Jack S. Cohen; *What Mad Pursuit* (1989), by Francis Crick; *The Path to the Double Helix: The Discovery of DNA*, (1994), by Richard Olby; and *DNA Pioneer: James Watson and the Double Helix* (1994), by Joyce Y. Baldwin.

Faith Hickman Brynie

See also Cancer; Medicine; Nobel Prizes; Science and Technology.

■ Genovese Murder

Date March 13, 1964

The fatal stabbing of Kitty Genovese as neighbors watched. This incident made Americans aware of an emerging norm of noninvolvement and diffusion of responsibility as the nation became increasingly urbanized in the 1960's.

Origins and History Catherine "Kitty" Genovese, a single twenty-eight-year-old woman, was the manager of a local tavern. She had moved to a second-story apartment in the Kew Garden neighborhood, a quiet, middle-class area in Queens, New York City, from Connecticut in 1963.

The Murder Genovese was returning home from work early in the morning on March 13, 1964. At 3:20 A.M., she parked her car in the Kew Gardens railroad station lot and started to walk the one hundred feet to her apartment. She noticed a man in the lot, so she headed for a nearby police call box, but the man grabbed her and stabbed her in front of a bookstore. She screamed, "Oh my God, he stabbed me! Please help me! Please help me!" and windows opened and lights went on in the ten-story apartment building across the street. The assailant walked away, but after the apartment lights went out, the man returned to attack Genovese, who was trying to reach her apartment. As he stabbed her again, she screamed, and again, lights went on in apartments

The numbers mark Kitty Genovese's path as she parked her car then was attacked three times before dying in March, 1964. The failure of her thirty-seven neighbors—who witnessed the crime—to come to the woman's aid shocked the nation. (AP/Wide World Photos)

and people looked out. The attacker got in his car and began to drive away, but returned a third time, this time stabbing her fatally. Not one person tried to stop the assault or telephoned the police during the assault, which lasted about thirty minutes; the first call, from a male neighbor, reached police at 3:50 A.M.

Only three people, including the caller, were on the street when the police arrived two minutes later. The caller explained his delayed call by saying, "I didn't want to get involved." When the police interviewed other neighbors in the following days and asked why they did not call the police, one woman said, "We thought it was a lovers' quarrel." Another witness simply said, "I don't know." Others said they were too frightened or afraid of becoming involved in the violence. The witnesses' failure to act shocked people throughout the country. Americans interpreted this event as a sign that people could no longer trust one another and that the city was a cold, forbidding place.

The reports of the thirty-eight witnesses enabled police to arrest Winston Moseley, a twenty-nine-year-old business-machine operator, about a week later and charge him with murder. He admitted to killing her, and although his lawyer argued that Moseley was not guilty because of temporary insanity, Moseley was found guilty and sentenced on June 16, 1964, to death in the electric chair. His sentence was later commuted to life in prison.

Impact The failure of the witnesses to act during the Genovese murder shocked Americans. A series of articles, editorials, and letters on the murder and the bystanders' apparent apathy appeared in *The New York Times*. The New York City mayor appealed to revive feelings of neighborly spirit. Other editorials decrying the inaction appeared in *Life* and *Nation* magazines. After Genovese's death, sociologists and psychologists conducted research to determine why the witnesses failed to do anything during the murder and if urbanization was responsible.

In explaining the witnesses' inaction, sociologist Louis Wirth argued that urban dwellers—like Genovese and her neighbors—live in anonymity. Their lives are marked by segmented and superficial encounters, which causes them to grow aloof from one another and indifferent to other people's problems. In short, the very sense of personal freedom

that the city provides comes at the cost of alienation. His explanation found ready acceptance among those living in small towns.

However, further research indicated that the bystanders at Genovese's death were not uncaring, alienated people. They did care that a woman was being attacked but were simply abiding by an emerging urban norm of noninvolvement. Whether male or female, urban dwellers are careful to protect themselves from unwanted intrusions from strangers by not involving themselves in these strangers' affairs. Although this attitude was very helpful in getting them through everyday city life, it was, unfortunately, dysfunctional in this situation.

Research on bystander apathy has revealed that the presence of many other people tends to diffuse the sense of responsibility. People are less likely to take action if they have reason to believe that someone else will do so. However, this does not mean that city dwellers are alienated from one another when they are among people they know or that when alone they would not help someone in trouble. This diffused sense of responsibility may be a condition of city life, but it is hardly evidence for the thesis that urban life leads to the decline of community.

Additional Information Abraham M. Rosenthal, who wrote a May, 1964, article on the slaying and public apathy for *The New York Times*, published *Thirty-eight Witnesses* (1964), an account of the Genovese murder. A full, scientific study of bystander apathy and human interaction is found in Bibb Latane and John Darley's *The Unresponsive Bystander: Why Doesn't He Help?* (1970).

Robert D. Bryant

See also Career Girl Murders; Crime and Scandals; Speck Murders.

■ Geodesic Domes

Enclosures formed by a framework of triangulated struts or polygonal facets approximating a hemisphere. Requiring no internal supports or columns, geodesic domes are light in weight and easy to construct.

R. Buckminster Fuller invented the geodesic dome in 1947 and patented the design in 1954. The domes were designed to provide maximum strength with minimum structure. The strength of the domes increases logarithmically in relation to their size. In

1958, the huge Union Tank Car Company dome in Baton Rouge, Louisiana, 384 feet in diameter and 116 feet high, was constructed, surpassing in size the largest conventional dome of Saint Peter's Cathedral in Rome.

Other large projects followed, including sports arenas, theaters, greenhouses, and exhibition halls. The United States pavillion at Expo 67 in Montreal was a seven-tenths geodesic sphere, twenty stories tall. Built from a complicated set of mathematical tables, its framework consisted of stainless-steel-alloy parts with a skin of fiberglass panels.

Smaller projects also made use of geodesic domes. By 1960, the Pease Woodwork Company of Ohio was producing a wood-framed, standardized geodesic dome house, 40 feet in diameter. By the next year, more than one hundred companies manufactured more than two thousand geodesic domes.

Impact Geodesic domes are very economical to build and transport and are able to withstand strong natural forces. Because their strength increases with their size, they have no limiting dimensions. These qualities made them ideal for use overseas by the U.S. Army and Peace Corps and in the Arctic and Antarctic, where they provide economic climate control. As homes, geodesic domes appealed to hippies, who appreciated their economic use of materials and did not mind their unconventional appearance.

Additional Information For an examination of the history of the geodesic dome, see *Buckminster Fuller's Universe: An Appreciation* (1989), by Lloyd Steven Sieden.

Kristen L. Zacharias

See also Architecture.

■ *Gideon v. Wainwright*

Established the right to free legal representation for indigent defendants in criminal cases. This case ensured that no one can be sent to prison without having had the benefit of legal assistance.

A 1942 Supreme Court case—*Betts v. Brady*—held that poor defendants were entitled to free legal representation only in death penalty cases and particular cases in which "special circumstances" produced unfairness. In 1961, Clarence Earl Gideon was con-

victed of breaking into a poolroom in Florida. He had asked the trial court to appoint an attorney for him because he had no money. The judge refused, citing the *Betts v. Brady* rule. After an unsuccessful appeal to the Florida Supreme Court, Gideon asked the U.S. Supreme Court to hear his case.

On March 18, 1963, the Supreme Court unanimously agreed to establish a flat requirement of counsel in all felony cases, thus ensuring that indigent defendants are always defended by an attorney. Associate Justice Hugo Black wrote the decision. He reasoned that even an educated and intelligent layperson "has small and sometimes no skill in the science of law," is unable to determine whether an indictment is valid, is unfamiliar with the rules of evidence, and lacks the skill and knowledge necessary to prepare a defense. Without those skills at their disposal, defendants cannot receive a fair trial, particularly since prosecutors in criminal cases are backed by the power and resources of the government. Black's opinion establishes the right to assigned counsel for indigent defendants as one of the fundamental guarantees protected against state as well as federal violation. In consequence, Gideon's conviction was reversed.

Bruce Jacob of the Florida attorney general's office argued the other side. Florida's position was that the *Betts v. Brady* rule should be preserved. Under the existing standards, Gideon had received a fair trial—and for the Supreme Court to decree a universal rule requiring the states to provide representation for indigent defendants would establish an unwarranted and expensive procedure. Jacob's position was undercut somewhat by the fact that twenty-two of the forty-eight states had already established rules requiring the provision of counsel, either through legislative action or by decision of their own supreme courts.

The Court overruled *Betts v. Brady*, which meant that every state in the nation was required to provide legal assistance to all felony defendants. Gideon had the assistance of counsel at his second trial and was acquitted by the jury.

Impact By the end of the 1960's, criminal defense work for poor defendants was paid for by the state or county government. In most states, members of the local bar are assigned such cases in rotation. The number of such cases (almost all defendants are indigent, at least for legal defense purposes) has

Sandra Dee starred in the 1959 film Gidget, *which sparked the creation of two more films about the perky, wholesome Gidget and a series of beach and surfing films.* (Museum of Modern Art/Film Stills Archive)

provided powerful impetus for extension of the plea bargaining system because the expense and time required to go to trial is too great for most cases.

Subsequent Events In 1972, in *Argersinger v. Hamlin,* the Supreme Court extended the right to assigned counsel to misdemeanor cases when there is a possibility that the defendant could be sent to jail.

Additional Information *Gideon's Trumpet* (1964), by Anthony Lewis, is an excellent book that describes the Supreme Court's procedure and workings as well as the facts and issues of the case.

Robert Jacobs

See also Supreme Court Decisions.

■ Gidget Films

Three formulaic tales of surfing and romance featuring spirited, pint-sized heroine Gidget. These films, the first mainstream productions to bring together teenagers and beaches, launched a host of 1960's beach films.

Gidget, Frederick Kohner's 1957 novel about his daughter, gave rise to a three-film series directed by Paul Wendkos. "Gidget" (a conflation of "girl" and "midget") was Francie Lawrence, a perky, diminutive California girl who loved surfing, beaches, and boys (in that order). Each Gidget film followed a simple formula: Though Gidget really loves surfer Jeff "Moondoggie" Matthews, she inevitably attracts the attention of other men, leading to perceived romantic triangles, multiple misunderstandings, and finally romantic reconciliations. James Darren played Moondoggie throughout the series, but Gidget was portrayed by three actresses, Sandra Dee, Deborah Walley, and Cindy Carol, respectively. In *Gidget* (1959), Gidget schemes to attract Moondoggie and becomes the mascot of a group of college boys who surf at Malibu. The leader, "Kahoona" (Cliff Robertson), an "older man," takes a special interest in her, piquing Moondoggie's jealousy; however, all is resolved in the film's climactic luau scene. In the sequel, *Gidget Goes Hawaiian* (1961), the Lawrence family vacations in Hawaii. Gidget, now Moondoggie's girlfriend, is drawn to nightclub singer Eddie Homer (Michael Callan). She becomes the target of a vicious rumor, temporarily leading to estrangement from her parents. In *Gidget Goes to Rome* (1963), Gidget vacations without her parents, so her father asks a friend (Cesare Danova) to keep an eye on her. Gidget misinterprets the friend's kindly intentions as romantic overtures and complications ensue. The first Gidget film is the most successful: The appeal of Dee is lost in the sequel, and the films get worse the farther Gidget wanders from the West Coast.

Impact The first Gidget film caught the public's fancy, spawning two sequels, two television series (*Gidget*, 1965-1966, starring Sally Field, and *The New Gidget*, 1986-1988), and three made-for-television films. Teenage girls wanted to be Gidget, the spunky tomboy who was popular with boys and got to spend all her time on the beach. Parents approved, seeing Gidget as a wholesome, all-American ideal. However, Gidget was also an early model of assertiveness, under the guise of "perkiness." Gidget taught herself how to surf, despite resistance from the boys she was trying to befriend. She refused to join her girlfriends on a "manhunt," risking their disapproval, and, through sheer determination, became part of the boys' gang in the one role open to her, "mascot." Gidget offered a role model for teenage girls who wanted to be an initiator rather than a follower and have some fun, yet still be thought of as appealing to boys.

The Gidget series popularized a new motion-picture genre: the beach film. The film *Beach Party* (1963), directed by William Asher, was the first in the long-running beach party series starring Frankie Avalon and Annette Funicello.

Additional Information Gidget's status as one of popular culture's first feminist role models is explored in Susan J. Douglas's *Where the Girls Are: Growing Up Female with the Mass Media* (1994).

Jennifer Davis-Kay

See also Beach Films; Film.

■ Ginsberg, Allen

Born June 3, 1926, Newark, New Jersey
Died April 5, 1997, New York, New York

One of America's best-known poets. Ginsberg was a leader of the hippie and antiwar movements during the 1960's.

Early Life Allen Ginsberg's father, Louis, was a modestly successful lyric poet and his mother, Naomi, was a communist who suffered a mental breakdown during Ginsberg's childhood. This background, combined with his sexual attraction to other men, helped to make Ginsberg a literary rebel and a nonconformist. While attending Columbia University in New York City, from 1943 to 1948, he formed a circle of friends that included William S. Burroughs and Jack Kerouac. This group became the nucleus of the literary movement known as the Beat generation in the 1950's. In 1956, Ginsberg published the poem "Howl," which brought the poet national renown after a widely publicized obscenity trial in San Francisco.

The 1960's In 1960, Ginsberg met Harvard psychology professor Timothy Leary and began taking part in Leary's experiments with the psychedelic drug LSD (lysergic acid diethylamide). During a trip to India in 1962 and 1963, Ginsberg became deeply interested in the Hindu and Buddhist religions. He let his hair and beard grow long in the style of an Indian holy man so that by the time he returned to North America in late summer of 1963, he had adopted the shaggy appearance that became his trademark for the rest of the decade. In October of that year, he took part in his first demonstration against the Vietnam War. As the decade continued, his opposition to the war became a dominant theme in his poetry. In poems such as his 1966 "Wichita Vortex Sutra," he combined Hindu and Buddhist mysticism with protests against the war.

Ginsberg had been internationally known as a countercultural figure since the publication of "Howl" and subsequent trial. His celebrity status as

Crowds gather around Allen Ginsberg as he reads his poetry in Washington Square Park in New York in 1966, following a Supreme Court ruling that allowed uncensored readings in public parks. (AP/Wide World Photos)

one of the chief representatives of the hippie movement was established in January, 1967, when he appeared on stage with Leary and others at the Human Be-in at Golden Gate Park in San Francisco, which was attended by about thirty thousand people.

Later Life Ginsberg's literary reputation continued to grow after the 1960's. He was elected to the National Institute of Arts and Letters in 1973, and in 1979, the National Arts Club awarded him its Gold Medal for lifetime achievement in poetry. He wrote and published poetry steadily until his death. He was also active as a teacher and founded the Jack Kerouac School of Disembodied Poetics at Naropa Institute in Boulder, Colorado. His political activities included participating in protests against U.S. involvement in Central America and against nuclear power.

Impact The prophetic style of Ginsberg's free verse was a major influence on American poetry during the 1960's and beyond. His mysticism, psychedelic drug use, advocacy of free love, and antiwar activities made him a symbol of the 1960's counterculture. His openness about his homosexuality made him one of the pioneers of the gay liberation movement.

Additional Information Michael Schumacher's 1992 biography of Allen Ginsberg, *Dharma Lion*, provides a detailed narrative of the poet's life.

Carl L. Bankston III

See also Be-ins and Love-ins; Beat Generation; Counterculture; Ferlinghetti, Lawrence; Flower Children; Leary, Timothy; Literature; LSD; Summer of Love; Vietnam War.

The Sixties in America

■ List of Entries by Category

Subject Headings Used in List

Arts
Asian Americans
Business and the Economy
Civil Rights
Crimes and Scandals
Drug Culture
Environment and Demographics
Film
Gender Issues
Government and Politics
Health and Medicine

Hippies and the Counterculture
International Affairs
Latinos
Laws and Acts
Literature
Media
Music
Native Americans
Organizations and Institutions
Science and Technology
Sexual Revolution

Social Revolution
Social Welfare
Space
Sports
Supreme Court Cases
Theater
Vietnam War
Visual Arts
Women's Issues

Arts

Albee, Edward
Arbus, Diane
Architecture
Art Movements
Baldwin, James
Brautigan, Richard
Brooks, Gwendolyn
Catch-22
Cat's Cradle
Cheever, John
Chicano: Twenty-five Pieces of a Chicano Mind
City of Night
Confessions of Nat Turner, The
Dances, Popular
Death of a President, The
Didion, Joan
Eat a Bowl of Tea
Federal Aid to the Arts Bill
Ferlinghetti, Lawrence
Ginsberg, Allen
Giovanni, Nikki
Hansberry, Lorraine
Hesse, Eva
House Made of Dawn
Indians
Lichtenstein, Roy
Literature
Lucky Come Hawaii
McKuen, Rod
Max, Peter

Merriam, Eve
Metafiction
Midnight Cowboy
Mountain of Gold
Oates, Joyce Carol
Oh, Calcutta!
One Flew over the Cuckoo's Nest
Op Art
Photography
Piercy, Marge
Poetry
Pop Art
Roth, Phillip
Sanchez, Sonia
Silko, Leslie Marmon
Simon, Neil
Slaughterhouse-Five
Social Satires
Stranger in a Strange Land
Susann, Jacqueline
Teachings of Don Juan, The
Teatro Campesino, El
Terry, Megan
Theater
Theater of the Absurd
To Kill a Mockingbird
2001: A Space Odyssey
Tyler, Anne
Updike, John
Warhol, Andy
Way to Rainy Mountain, The
Who's Afraid of Virginia Woolf?

Asian Americans

Eat a Bowl of Tea
Immigration
Lucky Come Hawaii
Mountain of Gold

Business and the Economy

Agriculture
Automobiles and Auto Manufacturing
Branch Banks
Business and the Economy
Corporate Liberalism
Credit and Debt
Economic Oppportunity Act of 1964
Economy of Cities, The
Gross National Product (GNP)
Inflation
International Trade
Japanese Imports
Motor Vehicle Air Pollution Act of 1965
Office of Minority Business Enterprise (OMBE)
Prosperity and Poverty
Unemployment
Unions and Collective Bargaining
Urban Renewal
War on Poverty